Arthurian Figures
of History and Legend
A Biographical Dictionary

Arthurian Figures of History and Legend

A Biographical Dictionary

FRANK D. RENO

McFarland & Company, Inc., Publishers
Jefferson, North Carolina, and London

LIBRARY OF CONGRESS CATALOGUING-IN-PUBLICATION DATA

Reno, Frank D., 1937–
Arthurian figures of history and legend :
a biographical dictionary / Frank D. Reno.
p.   cm.
Includes bibliographical references and index.

ISBN 978-0-7864-4420-5
softcover : 50# alkaline paper ∞

1. Arthur, King — Contemporaries — Dictionaries.
2. Great Britain — History — To 1066 — Biography — Dictionaries.
3. Arthurian romances — Dictionaries.   4. Great Britain —
Antiquities, Celtic — Dictionaries.   5. Great Britain — History —
To 1066 — Legends — Dictionaries.   6. Britons — Biography —
Dictionaries.   7. Malory, Thomas, Sir, 15th cent.
Morte d'Arthur — Characters.   I. Title.
DA152.5.A7R458 2011   942.01'4 — dc22   2010029787

British Library cataloguing data are available

On the cover: John Pettie, *The Vigil*, oil on canvas 60½" × 82", 1884;
sword and background image © 2011 Shutterstock

Manufactured in the United States of America

*McFarland & Company, Inc., Publishers
Box 611, Jefferson, North Carolina 28640
www.mcfarlandpub.com*

Once again, I am deeply grateful to my wife Lavinia for her continuous support, patience, contributions, and editing of this book, many times setting aside her novel to encourage me.

TABLE OF CONTENTS

Acknowledgment
viii

Preface
1

Biographical Dictionary
9

*Appendix A: A Character Index
of Malory's* Le Morte D'Arthur
243

Appendix B: Harleian MS 3859
252

Bibliography
253

Index
259

ACKNOWLEDGMENT

My deep appreciation is extended to Dr. Linda A. Malcor for writing the entry about Lucius Artorius Castus, in addition to the many enlightening conversations about a historic Arthur. Her meticulous scholarship leaves no doubt — historically and archaeologically — that the "Briton" Arthur was a second-century *dux bellorum* whose command was the protection of Hadrian's Wall. Dr. Malcor's evidence leads to assertions and affirmation which cannot be denied. No contradictory substantiation of a historic Briton King Arthur of the fifth century has come to light which refutes Dr. Malcor's stance.

PREFACE

There has never been a formalized poll to determine how many people are familiar with King Arthur, but surely, especially in English-speaking nations, a large majority — perhaps in remembrances from adolescence — know of Arthur, his court in Camelot, damsels, knights, Merlin, and Excalibur. With degrees in English language and literature, and a particular interest in writing and exposition, throughout my career in teaching I never considered Arthur more than a legendary figure. But after researching Arthuriana for more than two decades, I now realize that misinformation has distorted British history of the fifth century by ignoring a bona fide Arthur of the second century and not crediting a great king of the fifth century who was conflated with Arthur.

This reference work has multiple purposes. A major issue is to differentiate legendary figures from historic ones, and when needed, emending chronological calibrations if scribes and authors have miscalculated dates or if recent evidence points elsewhere. A primary example is Sir Thomas Malory's tome. John Lawlor, who wrote an Introduction to *Le Morte D'Arthur,* began by asserting, "Fact and fiction, romantic impossibility and historical likelihood, are intertwined at many stages of the Arthurian story." The evolution of Malory's manuscript is so complex and intricate that a resolution of what is fact and what is fiction "shows no ending," according to Lawlor. Malory's Arthurian material was extracted mainly from Geoffrey of Monmouth's *History of the Kings of Britain*, and additionally from a number of French Arthurian enthusiasts whose material appears in the entries of this biographical dictionary. Lawlor suggests that Malory was probably in southwestern France at one period, and states, "It is possible that some of his book was written while he was held captive by Jacques d'Armagnac." All of the French Arthurian sources are viewed by historians and scholars as likely legendary figures, and although Monmouth listed Arthur as a bona fide British king, not a shred of evidence has been revealed so far.

Lawlor examines two other details, one which suggests that Malory's characters are legendary, not historical. William Caxton, Malory's printer, inserted a preface which was not Malory's belief or intent: Caxton claimed the book "factitious" (Lawlor's term), and it was Caxton who titled the book *Le Morte D'Arthur,* rather than Malory's original which was *The Byrth, Lyf, and Actes of Kyng Arthur and of His Noble Knyghts of the Rounde Table*. The second interesting occurrence was the discovery in 1947 of the Winchester Manuscript, which raised the question, in Lawlor's words, "Could Malory be said to have written a 'hoole book' or instead eight separate romances?" which might have been why Vinaver titled the discovered manuscript *The Works of Sir Thomas Malory.*

Based upon this information, we can infer that Sir Thomas Malory's manuscript contains only the fictitious characters. The most well-known figures merit an entry in this text; the others are included and divided into segments which Malory (i.e., Caxton) has labeled as Book (I through XXI) and Chapter. The appendix to the present work gives each character's name and lists the book and chapter number for each one, so that the reader can easily determine how frequently the character is named and where it appears.

In August of 1988, four years prior to my retirement, I was fortunate to be one of fifteen individuals selected by the National Endowment for the Humanities to participate in an institute titled "Arthurian Literature of the Middle Ages" at the University of Puget Sound, Tacoma, Washington. The mentor, Professor Michael Curley, structured a general curriculum which allowed independent research on a topic of individual appeal. By the end of that summer, I had developed an intense interest in the probability that behind the facade of a legendary Arthur was a historic figure who had been metamorphosed.

By a fortuitous fluke, in October of 1991 (five years prior to the publication of my first book), Geoffrey Ashe, a notable Arthurian writer, had been invited to the University of Colorado and was my house guest for dinner one evening. Our conversation, of course, centered on Arthur and at one point turned to Riothamus, the Briton king recorded by Jordanes. This king "crossed Ocean" with an army to fight against the *Saxones*. We discussed in detail his book *The Discovery of King Arthur* and whether Riothamus might be the epithet for Ambrosius Aurelianus, a great king of the fifth century recorded by Nennius, rather than an "Arthur." Geoffrey was silently contemplative, then responded that it was possibly so. However, over the years when I personally communicated and interviewed him, he didn't consider that premise as probable.

In 1994, the American Library Association, in cooperation with the Arthurian collections of the Newberry Library and the New York Public Library, organized a traveling exhibition funded by a grant from the National Endowment for the Humanities. The library in Boulder, Colorado, hosted one of the exhibits in April of 1995, just prior to the publication of my first book, and I was invited to present a slide show, which I titled "Origins of Arthurian Romances." Thereafter, I gave presentations locally at schools, libraries, and bookstores, then became a member of the American Program Bureau, giving programs nationally. Independently, while I was in Pasadena, I gave an armchair tour titled "Arthurian Sites of Britain" at the Huntington Library, which drew an unexpected crowd of more than 400. After the event, I was granted access to do more research in their excellent library.

During this interim I had completed all coursework after my master's degree and was writing my first manuscript about the historic King Arthur, which was intended to be my dissertation. My advisor was impressed with the text, and after a great deal of discussion, the two of us concurred that, because my career was nearing its end and I was planning early retirement, I should seek a publisher. Shortly thereafter, my book, titled *The Historic King Arthur*, was published in 1996 by McFarland & Company. The key thesis is that Arthur was conflated with Ambrosius Aurelianus, and Riothamus is an epithet for Ambrosius, the Briton king from across Ocean.

Arthur, who acquires the title of king, makes his debut (three to four centuries) prior to Aneirin, who writes about a northern leader by that name. One of the requirements for seeking the "correct" Arthur who lies beneath the thick strata of the legendary romances is the investigation of any probable association between his name and a certain Lucius Artorius Castus in the histories, since several researchers suggest that Arthur's name might have derived from this individual's *nomen*, or middle name, normally indicating in Latin a person's *gens* or clan.

The profound subject of a historic Arthur continued to intrigue me. During the next four years I traveled to Great Britain, France, Brittany, and Italy to continue my research at Arthurian and Roman sites. Later, when I was in Britain, I invited Leslie Alcock, the archaeologist who participated in the Camelot Project and had written two texts — *Arthur's Britain* and *Was This Camelot?* — to an Arthurian get-together, but he graciously responded that he was making a distinction between "Arthur the legendary king and Ethelred the historic king." At this time he was professor emeritus in Glasgow, Scotland, and had bid an "ultimate farewell to Arthur, legendary persons, and south-west Britain."

Alcock's comments further supported my antithesis of a fifth-century King Arthur. After scouring sites and libraries and compiling data, another text titled *Historic Figures of the Arthurian Era* also came to fruition and was published by McFarland in 2000. Its content focused upon nine historical figures of the fifth century, associated not with Arthur, but with Ambrosius Aurelianus, who was conflated with Arthur.

In December of 2001, I was invited by the BBC to participate in a documentary titled *Arthur: King of the Britons*, and had the privilege of meeting the narrator, Richard Harris, conversing with him about his bygone days of *Camelot* and his role as Dumbledore, and watching him at work in the film. Unfortunately, the documentary did not clearly delineate an Arthur of the second century, nor did it give full credit to Ambrosius Aurelianus as the great Briton king of the fifth century. The ending then turned to myth, indicating that Arthur was not dead, but he lay sleeping until he was needed once more.

Little did I realize that the search for a historic Arthur in the fifth century had not yet been resolved. More questions had to be answered which would require a knowledge of chronological computation, the emendation of fifth-century British history, pitfalls stemming from interpolations inserted by scribes, the important distinction between epithets and proper names, the differences in translations, at least a rudimentary grasp of Latin, and a host of other impedimenta.

One of my favorite authors, John Steinbeck, offered a clue about the complexity of defining King Arthur, but I wasn't exposed to his book *The Acts of King Arthur and His Noble Knights* in tandem with *Steinbeck: A Life in Letters* (edited by his wife, Elaine, and Robert Wallsten) until around 1993. Although he was writing about Arthurian romances and not taking the path of a historic Arthur, he at first felt assured that he could finish his task quite quickly. By the following year, his attitude had changed and he knew that it was not going to be an easy job. When people asked when "the Artu thing would be ready," he chose a conservative figure of ten years. In 1959, he wrote, "This field and subject [of Arthur] is so huge, so vague, so powerful and eternal, that I can't seem to mount it and set spurs.... For the deeper I go, the more profound the subject becomes, always escaping me so that often I feel that I am not good enough nor wise enough to do this work. They [my efforts] seem puny in the face of a hideous subject, and I use the word in a Malorian sense." He died December 20, 1968, not having finished the book, which was later completed and copyrighted in 1975 by Elaine A. Steinbeck and Robert Wallsten.

The search for a historic Arthur is even more daunting than Steinbeck's claim. Like Steinbeck, I felt that I did not yet have a firm grip on the "Arthurian matter."

In the last several years, I've been privileged to present papers on a panel with three other colleagues — C. Scott Littleton, Linda Malcor, and Wolfgang von Chemielewski — at the Western States Folklore Society conferences at UCLA, UC at Sacramento, and the Otis College of Art and Design, Los Angeles. My horizon has been broadened by their judicious knowledge.

This present text continues the quest for Arthur, and separates fact from fiction. Leslie Alcock rightfully disclaimed an Arthur of the fifth century, but that does not forfeit the value of his text *Arthur's Britain*. Because he and the Camelot Committee were seeking a historic Arthur in the fifth century, he overlooked the Arthur of the second. Nevertheless, his book exonerates his oversight, particularly based upon two critical impacts. One is that Hengist and his clan were *not* contemporaries of an Arthur of the fifth century (see *Arthur's Britain*, pp. 59–60). The second is Alcock's discovery about three different kinds of chronological calibrations (see Pelican edition, Preface xvii, *Arthur's Britain*). Then check the entry "Arthur (Historic)" in this text. Alcock was also quite objective when he admonished researchers, scholars, and students that new perspectives of venerable manuscripts are the keys to distinguishing truth from fiction, fact from fantasy.

It is imperative that a person follow the proof of existence through evidence in order to transform a specter into reality. Depending upon discovery, truth is fluid. The bibliography in this text indicates the superfluity of research it takes to answer formidable questions diligently. Arthur as a *dux bellorum* deserves his historic niche in the second century and the romance tales which evolved in the twelfth century and thereafter. Ambrosius Aurelianus, whom Nennius lauds as the great king of kings, must be freed from his conflation with Arthur and recognized as Britain's savior in the fifth century.

Y Gododdin is an early poem penned by Aneirin (Uh-nigh'-rïn) sometime between 588 and 590, according to Kenneth Hurlstone Jackson. Two independent versions were recorded, Manuscript A, which is more detailed, and Manuscript B, which very concisely refers to Arthur, but the only surviving manuscript dates to the thirteenth century. Because of the passage of six centuries between the original and the existent manuscript, there were undoubtedly scribal errors and deliberate interpolations, and because only Manuscript B records the name of Arthur, the reliability of Arthur as a realistic figure is in question. In Manuscript B, Aneirin writes that he himself went into battle with his tribe and his great chieftain, Gwawrdder (Goo-wow'-er ther), who slaughtered many of the enemy on the rampart of the stronghold. Aneirin writes, even though Gwawrdder was a powerful warrior, "he was no Arthur." There is no hint of or allusion to whom this Arthur might be.

Later, two other ancient Briton manuscripts — the *De Excidio* penned by Gildas Badonicus (sixth century) and *A History of the English Church and People* attributed to Bede (eighth century) — have no reference to an Arthur. In the ninth century a fourth manuscript titled the *Historia Brittonum* named Arthur not as a king, but as a *dux bellorum* (a duke or leader of war), followed by an alleged list of twelve battles which he fought. Of the twelve battles, only the last one, fought on Badon Hill, is recorded in the two previous manuscripts of Gildas Badonicus and Bede, and these two, who do not acknowledge an Arthur of the fifth century, attribute that battle to a leader named Ambrosius Aurelianus.

It was Geoffrey of Monmouth's *History of the King of Britain* (twelfth century) which caused a firestorm, particularly Part Seven ("Arthur of Britain"). There were contemporaries who praised his manuscript, but others were incensed by his brazen distortion of history, denouncing his motives, criticizing his fabrications, and labeling him as "an impudent and shameless liar." Starting with Part Four, "The House of Constantine," Monmouth's so-called history, is deceptively fraudulent. His genealogy begins with Aldroneus's brother, Constantine, being sent to Britain with two thousand soldiers "to free the island from barbarian invasion." When he arrived, he was given a wife born of a noble family, and soon after the marriage, they had three sons, Constans, Aurelius Ambrosius, and Utherpendragon.

No other history mentions this particular Constantine. A careful scrutiny of Roman and British history, which lists a number of royalties named Constantine, Constantius, and Constantinus, shows that there were two Roman emperors of the West who went to Britain: Constantius I and his son Constantine I. Constantius I died in Britain at Eburacum in 306, and Constantine I died in 337, centuries before Monmouth's Arthur flourished.

An explicable suspicion arises when Monmouth's Constantine names his first-born son

Constans. It's more than a guess in the dark that Geoffrey is referring to Flavius Claudius Constantinus (also known as Constantine) and his son Constans. This particular Constantine crossed to Gaul with his son and British troops to overthrow the western emperor in 407. He was temporarily successful, but in 411 he was captured and beheaded. His son, who had been elevated to *caesar* in Spain, was also killed.

Monmouth meanders even deeper into a quagmire. He records Constans as Constantine's first son and Aurelius Ambrosius as Constantine's second son. Monmouth's second blunder (his first being that he doesn't correctly identify Constantius III) is that he does not name Constantine's third son. Lewis Thorpe, translator of Geoffrey's manuscript, explains in a footnote that Geoffrey takes the name Utherpendragon from a comet and two golden dragons which Geoffrey doesn't identify until fifty pages later. In other words, the term Utherpendragon literally appears out of a star "of great magnitude and brilliance," and the yet-unnamed brother of Aurelius Ambrosius is told by his wise men that he is to be "the king of all Britain," and that his son (Arthur?) will be a powerful man.

By adding that so-called third son, Monmouth's head is no longer above water and the believability of his genealogy disintegrates. Professor Michael Curley, in his text *Geoffrey of Monmouth*, writes that "the dramatic personae of the legend of Arthur's conception are Geoffrey's inventions," and among them is Utherpendragon. Not much more need be said: because Utherpendragon is bogus, Arthur's conception in this instance is make-believe. Four key figures, therefore, in Geoffrey's "history" must be stricken: Constantine, Constans, Utherpendragon, and Arthur himself.

Although the majority of historians and researchers admit that Utherpendragon is not a historical figure, there is yet a persistence by some individuals — claiming to be defenders of academia — who maintain picayune defenses that Utherpendragon is historic and fritter away time arguing that Pendragon translates to "head dragon" and not "chief dragon" or steadfastly claiming that Uther Pendragon (two words) is a combination of a proper name and epithet, with "Uther" being a Welsh name and not a Roman epithet. An important denial, however, is that in earlier centuries, Latin in Britain would have been more prevalent than Welsh, as attested by the extant manuscripts of Gildas Badonicus, Bede, and Nennius. The prefixes for Pendragon — Uther, Uthyr, Uthr, Uthir, and Uter — are therefore, irrelevant and unimportant points.

Attention must now turn to Arthur's *historical* identity. When Monmouth was writing his "history," there were dozens of other contemporaries penning manuscripts; one — Chrétien de Troyes — was outstanding and quickly became quite popular. Several historians and academicians of the twentieth century wrote this of Chrétien:

1. W.W. Comfort: "The man who, so far as we know, first recounted the romantic adventures of Arthur's knights" was Chrétien.
2. William Kibler: "Writing in the second half of the twelfth century, Chrétien de Troyes was the inventor of Arthurian literature as we know it."
3. D.D.R. Owen: "Chrétien de Troyes, commonly regarded as the father of Arthurian Romance and a key figure in Western literature, composed in French in the latter part of the twelfth century."
4. And even Lewis Thorpe writes that the date given for Monmouth's work by Acton Griscom — 1136 — "is much debated."

This is strong evidence that Monmouth borrowed an Arthur of *legend* from Chrétien. additionally, there is no doubt that Monmouth was also cognizant of the Arthur in Nennius's

Historia Brittonum, and that he, like Nennius, conflated Ambrosius Aurelianus with Arthur.

A more cogent thesis pertaining to the identity of a Constantine/Constantius is proposed by J.N.L. Myres in his text *Roman Britain and the English Settlements* and verified by two other colleagues — J.B. Bury and Dr. E. Stein. He offers convincing information about Constantius III, but it is independent of anything Arthurian. He writes that through the authority of the Western Roman Empire, the *Notitia Dignitatum* of Britain (*ca.* C.E. 395–430) established the new office of *Comes Britanniarum* in the fifth century, during the era of Constantius III, praefect for Emperor Honorius. This new command, *Comes Britanniarum*, came into existence in Britain *after* the supposed severance of the island from the Empire. Myres writes, "The beginning of such an office at such a time must certainly be associated with the work of the Patrician Constantius [III] who re-established Roman control in Brittany about 417." He concludes by adding, "The last phase of Roman government [in Britain] began about 417 and ended some years before 429. It may be some comfort to think that this much of historical reality, shadowy though it be, underlies the 'second vengeance' in the story of Gildas [Badonicus]. However it may have ended, both sides still no doubt believed that it [the Roman re-occupation of Britain] was to begin again; and it was only in 446, after the vain appeal to Aetius, that hope was abandoned."

This piece of Roman history tied to Britain profoundly impacts Arthuriana of the fifth century. In 417, the Western Empire wanted to reclaim Britain as a province by establishing the new office of *Comes Britanniarum* under the command of Constantius III. Ambrosius Aurelianus, the great king mentioned by Nennius in the *Historia Brittonum*, would have been born some time between 417 and 420. Monmouth writes that "Arthur [conflated with Ambrosius?] was bestowed the crown of the kingdom when he was a young man only fifteen years old." Historically there was constant warfare between Hengist's clan and the Welsh after Hengist slaughtered Vortigern's Council of the Province between the years 455 and 490. Near the end of that century, Arthur (Ambrosius?) is killed.

For other sources of information, see the Constantius III entry in this text, indicating that Constantius III dropped from sight in Gaul between 417 and 420. From a historical standpoint, it is important to resolve first whether or not Constantius III is the real person alluded to by Geoffrey of Monmouth, since Monmouth is simply an amanuensis and not a very astute historian.

Although Monmouth's "Arthur" and "Pendragon" were shams, C. Scott Littleton and Linda Malcor offer strong archaeological, geographical, and chronological evidence that there indeed was an Arthur in Britain near the end of the second century. His full name was Lucius Artorius Castus, a Roman *præfect* of VI Legion Victrix, comprised of Sarmatian troops and assigned by Rome to defend the frontier of Britain at Hadrian's Wall. The word "Sauromatae" is most likely translated as "lizard people," tying the "prominent role played by lizards (or dragons) into the symbolism associated with the Arthurian legends." Their probability is based upon the ancient bas-relief of a Sarmatian warrior carrying a serpentine banner, a venerated creature of the Sarmatian tribe which no doubt became the dragon insignia of Artorius and his troops, and later spread as the symbol for the Roman cavalry.

In the early fifth century, the dragon symbol might well have become an epithet for Constantius III, the supreme commander of Emperor Honorius's cavalry who was sent to Britain as *Comes Britanniarum* to try to reclaim Britain as a province. Pendragon would be an appropriate epithet — the head dragon or the chief dragon of the Roman Army. However, the important perspicacity is linking an epithet to a proper name, something easy to suggest but more difficult to accomplish. Perhaps this is the reason most researchers and historians will spend time defining or determining the meaning of an epithet, but commonly ignore who that individual might actually be. An educated guess, however, is better than avoiding the risk of being incorrect.

In *The Discovery of King Arthur*, Geoffrey Ashe claimed that Riothamus, the Briton king from across Ocean, was indeed an epithet meaning "supreme king," but more important, he did make an attempt to discover the proper name behind the epithet. Unfortunately, in his zeal to claim an Arthur of the fifth century (perhaps because he was an important member of the Camelot Committee), he skipped over evidentiary clues which would set him on the right path. Briefly, they are these: (1) he accepted all of Geoffrey of Monmouth's genealogy as fact; (2) he dismissed Professor Leon Fleuriot's claim that Ambrosius was the Briton king from across Ocean; (3) he bypassed Nennius's Section 48 in the *Historia Brittonum* which describes Ambrosius as "the great king among all the kings of the British nation"; (4) he accepted John of Glastonbury's praise of Arthur as truth instead of fraud; (5) he debased Ambrosius as a *gwledig*, interpreting that term as merely a "landowner" instead of "high chieftain"; and (6) the Battle of Badon is *Ambrosian* fact, not Arthurian. (See entry RIOTHAMUS.)

Welsh genealogies list three Romans: Tacitus, Paternus, and Æternus. The lineage thereafter gives Welsh names, sometimes appended with Roman ones. When necessary, to make some of the entries in this text easier to understand, variant spellings, in addition to clarifying Romano-Welsh names, are given: Vortigern is identified as Æternus, Vortimer is Vortigern's son Cunedda, Vitalinus is the Roman name for Guithelinus, Æsc is Octha, Ceredig is Cerdic, Cunedda is Brydw, and so on.

The purpose of this text is to clarify the distinction between Arthurian folklore and history, which requires the daunting task of emending fifth-century Britain, not bending it into an entirely different shape, but rightly extolling not only the fifth-century Emrys (Ambrosius Aurelianus), but other prominent figures who prevented Britain from annihilation, while at the same time reveling in the gamut of Celtic, Welsh, Scottish, and Irish tales and legends. In order to grasp the milieu of this era, an individual must be cognizant and open-minded enough to at least consider alternate perspectives and premises meant to structure a possible, probable, or even realistic set of circumstances.

Because both legendary and historical characters overlap each other, repetitions of events in some entries are a necessity. For example, in the entry about the legendary Arthur, episodes also must include other individuals such as Lancelot and Guinevere. In those instances, I've attempted to include only short extracts about the minor figure, and more detail about the major one.

Note on the Entries

The first name in each biographical entry is the one which is most commonly used, followed by variant ones. In the body of every other entry, these names are cross-referenced in small capitals at first appearance. The source or sources at the end of each entry lists the author's name followed by an abbreviation of the book's title. The entire bibliography is at the end of the text.

Although these biographical entries focus mainly upon Arthurian figures of history and legend, readers should be cognizant of a number of entries that help illustrate the depth and complexity of the subject in order to glimpse reality.

Among those entries are authors of antiquity who wrote on both sides of the question of Arthur's historicity or invention. Ranulf Higden, for example, was one of the few who questioned Arthur's historicity, accusing Geoffrey of Monmouth of inventing the story of Arthur. On the other hand, William Caxton, a pioneer printer of books, was adamant that Arthur was a joyous historical figure.

Other entries allude to Roman, Welsh, and Anglian definitions of words to clarify variants of meaning or importance. Britain was under Roman rule for nearly four centuries, and hence there are numerous entries explaining different terms. As an example, *præfectus* was a title used for a provincial commander. Welsh terms are extremely important because Roman occupation centered mainly around Wales, which extended farther to the east during the Roman era. Of the nine legionary fortresses in Britain, five of them are along the eastern border of Wales. Positions of importance, such as *gwledig*, must therefore be defined. Similarly, Anglian names overlap, especially the ones which parallel Welsh names: Esla, Elesa, Gewis, Hwiche.

The astuteness of early-century chronologists, whose work rectified calibrations, are also important attachments to entries in this text. Dionysius Exiguus is credited for the chronology based upon the incarnation of Christ. Victorius of Aquitaine calibrated dates upon the passion (death) of Christ, which is a difference of twenty-eight years. And a third calibration is ancient, calibrated by Meton of Athens, and termed lunar cycles.

Geographic factors are also crucial in these entries, since they profoundly affect historical changes in speculations of locales. Was Vortigern an overlord of Wales, or of Britain? Were Hengist and Horsa settled in Kent, or were they inhabitants of East Anglia? Where was Vortimer's battle by the Inscribed Stone fought, near Thanet in the extreme southeastern part of Britain, or in the northwestern section of Wales? Where was Arthur's battle of Badon fought, at Aquae Sulis or the abandoned legionary fortress at Wroxeter near the hillfort the Wrekin? Where is the distinctive location of Wessex? And was it invaded from the north or the south?

I hope the reader is as intrigued with this information as I was in recording it.

BIOGRAPHICAL DICTIONARY

Abloyc, Afloeg. Sixth son of Gwledig CUNEDDA. His kingdom became Afloegion, which included the northern half of the Lleyn Peninsula in northwest Wales.

Sources: L. Alcock (AB); P. Bartram (WG); S. Blake/S. Lloyd (KTA).

Accolon is introduced in Book II, Chapter 11 of *Le Morte D'Arthur* by SIR THOMAS MALORY. MERLIN warns King ARTHUR to keep the scabbard of Excalibur safe, for Arthur can lose no blood while it is strapped to him. For safekeeping, Arthur entrusts the scabbard into the care of MORGAN LE FAY, his treacherous sister, who loves not her husband King Uriens, nor King Arthur. She fashions another scabbard by enchantment and gives the scabbard instead to her lover, a knight named Accolon.

Unknown to Accolon, Morgan le Fay arranges a fight between Accolon and Arthur, providing Arthur with a fake Excalibur and scabbard. A furious fight follows, and when he is almost at death's door, Arthur's fake sword breaks. Arthur mightily hits Accolon with the pommel, and when the damsel of the lake witnesses Arthur's predicament, she causes the real Excalibur to drop from Accolon's hand.

Arthur recovers Excalibur, and after he subdues his foe, he asks who he is, and Accolon confesses that Morgan le Fay had plotted to kill her brother. Arthur forgives him, and the two are reconciled. Shortly thereafter they are treated for their wounds, but Accolon has lost so much blood that he cannot be saved.

Source: T. Malory (LMD'A).

Adam of Domerham, Adam of Damerham (*floruit* 1275–1305). In the late thirteenth century, Adam of Domerham, a monk at Glastonbury Abbey, held three main positions — one as a cellarer in charge of provisions for the abbey. He later became the sacristan, in charge of the sacristy where sacred vessels, ceremonial equipment, and clothes were kept. Most important, he was elevated to a primary task of transcribing manuscripts for the abbey.

Historically, Adam is a rather obscure personage who has only a gossamer connection to Arthuriana. Very little is recorded about him, except that he had a vested interest in the well-being of Glastonbury Abbey. When he was put in charge of scribal documentation, the abbey was passing through a particularly difficult financial crisis, Canterbury and St Davids were fierce competitors for pilgrimages, and even its rival municipality to the north at Wells was a threat. As the sacristan at Glastonbury, Adam was in an ideal position to metamorphose legend into history when he wrote his *Historia de rebus Glastonienbus*. Thomas Hearne, in reporting on Adam's manuscript, states that the monk's "avowed aim is an attempt to incite the manuscript's readers to protect and to increase the prosperity of Glastonbury Abbey."

Adam had access to the manuscripts penned by GIRALDUS CAMBRENSIS and GEOFFREY OF MONMOUTH, and, what turned out to be the most damaging to British history, WILLIAM OF MALMESBURY's *De Antiquitate Glastonie Ecclesie*, which Adam interpolated beyond recognition. In his book *The Glastonbury Legends*, R.F. Treharne writes in full detail how drastically Malmesbury's manuscript was altered, which would never have been exposed if Malmesbury hadn't kept a copy of his own to refute the one that had been left at Glastonbury Abbey. One legend which Treharne debunks — bordering on farce since it is so unlikely to be history — is the story of JOSEPH OF ARIMATHEA, a separate entry listed in this text.

Treharne also labels the link between Glastonbury Abbey and King Arthur as a hoax, including King Arthur's genetic link to Joseph of Arimathea, Arthur's burial on the grounds of the Abbey, and his exhumation so that he could be buried in front of the High Altar. Referring to Geoffrey of Monmouth's *History of the Kings of Britain*, Treharne writes "Geoffrey had provided the germ of the Arthurian Legend which the later Glastonbury revisers were to appropriate for the glorification of their ancient Abbey."

WILLIAM OF NEWBURGH agrees with Treharne's assessment. He infers that Geoffrey of Monmouth is the "Father of Lies" and claims "Geoffrey had given, in a Latin version, the fabulous exploits of Arthur, drawn from the traditional fictions of the Britons, with additions of his own, and endeavored to dignify them with the name of authentic history; moreover, he has unscrupulously promulgated the mendacious predictions of one Merlin, as if they were genuine prophecies, corroborated by indubitable truth, to which also he has himself considerably added during the process of translating them into Latin."

William continues his invective, blaming not only the perpetrator Geoffrey but his victims, the Britons: "It appears that whatever Geoffrey has written, subsequent to Vortigern, either of Arthur, or his successors, or predecessors, is a fiction, invented either by himself or by others, and promulgated either through an unchecked propensity to falsehood, or a desire to please the Britons, of whom vast numbers are said to be so stupid as to assert that Arthur is yet to come, and who cannot bear to hear of his death.... Since, therefore, the ancient historians make not the slightest mention of these matters, it is plain that whatever this man published of Arthur and of Merlin are mendacious fictions, invented to gratify the curiosity of the undiscerning."

John Scott, in his text *The Early History of Glastonbury*, apologizes to his readers about the forgeries and interpolations made to William of Malmesbury's *De Antiquitate*. He asks the readers' forgiveness for Glastonbury's transgressions in their deceptive interpolations, defending their actions by relaying that "other monasteries [also] tried to bolster their reputations by similarly elaborating stories." Scott also claims that the sham can easily be discerned by the use of different pens, by the use of simplistic grammatical structure contrasted to Malmesbury's more complex use, and by poor Latinity which shows that at least two different monks were involved in the interpolations, and Adam of Domerham is the monk who emerges as most likely and obvious candidate for accomplishing this task.

The widely held scholarly stance is that the 1191 exhumation of King Arthur and Guinevere was undoubtedly a hoax to lure pilgrimages to the abbey for financial gain.

Sources: J. Carley (CGA; GA: HHHMA); J.A. Robinson (TGL: KA&JA); J. Scott (EHG: ETSWM); R.F. Treharne (TGL: JA/HG/KA); William Of Newberg (HEA/HRA).

Addaon is the name used by Gwyn Jones and Thomas Jones for the son of TALIESIN, who is one of the main bards of Arthuriana.

See also AVAON.

Source: G. Jones/T. Jones (TM).

Ægidius, known as King of the Romans and as a temporary King of the Franks on the continent, is aligned with the Arthurian saga through RIOTHAMUS, an epithet which Geoffrey Ashe claims is a reference to King Arthur. History infers Ægidius established himself on the continent circa 457, but later assertions record Ægidius's reign from 461 to 464. In contrast, John Morris writes that Ægidius establishes his kingdom about the same time as the massacre of VORTIGERN's Council in Britain, which further ties this king to Arthuriana. Ægidius's definitive death date is set in 464 C.E.

When the Britons migrated across Ocean to the continent en masse with their king Riothamus, Morris asserts, "The survivors of the catastrophe [the Saxon incursions on the island followed by the massacre of the Council] despaired of their homeland, and sought security in the still Roman dominions of Ægidius. He welcomed them, and gave them estates 'north of the Loire.'" The historical conditions supply the motive for Riothamus's voyage across the channel; it was not simply a headlong flight from the Saxons ravishing the island: Riothamus was to aid the Romans by joining ranks with Ægidius to stem the barbaric onslaught in Gaul. In return, there was hope that the pacification of Gaul would allow a Roman re-occupation of Britain to reclaim it as a province.

With allegiances changing from day to day, the upheaval in Gaul shook the foundations of the Western Roman Empire; Ægidius, however, maintained his loyalty to Rome, and when, in 457, the Franks conflicted with their king, Childeric, they accepted Ægidius as their leader. He withheld his allegiance to Ricimer, whom he considered a traitor and not a bona fide emperor of Rome.

Nevertheless, rebellions by Childeric, Arvandus, the Saxons, and the Franks led to Riothamus's defeat by EURIC the Visigoth, caused by thinning Roman reinforcements which never arrived on the scene. Upon Ægidius's death, Childeric was reinstated as leader of the Franks. The years between 468 and 472 sounded the death-knell not only for the Western empire, but also for Britain's dissolution as a Roman province.

Sources: G. Ashe (DKA); E. Brehaut (GT: HOF); M. Holmes (KA: AMH); J. Morris (AOA); F. Reno (HKA); L. Thorpe (GOT: HOF).

Ælle. The Ælle listed in *The Anglo-Saxon Chronicle* who is recorded in Arthur's historic era is the House of Ælle, which falls between the House of Hengist and the House of the West Saxons.

There are only three entries allotted to this particular Ælle:

477 — In this year Ælle came to Britain and his three sons, CYMEN, Wlencing, and Cissa, with three ships at the place which is called Cymenesora, and there slew many Welsh and drove some to flight into the wood which is called *Andredesleag.*
485 — In this year Ælle fought against the Welsh near the bank of *Mearcrædesburna.*
491— In this year Ælle and Cissa besieged *Andredescester,* and slew all the inhabitants; there was not even one Briton left there.

There is an addendum in the Parker version of the *Chronicle* in entry 827 which states that Ælle, the King of Sussex, was the first king to rule so great a kingdom as Bretwalda.

A later entry about Bretwalda explains the importance of Ælle's title, which intimates three particular peculiarities:

1. Ælle's enemies are the Welsh *and* the Britons. In entries 477 and 485 of *The Anglo-Saxon Chronicle,* Ælle is fighting the Welsh, the first battle at Andredesleag (allegedly the Saxon Shore fort at Anderida), and the second at Mearcrædesburna (unidentified, but conjectured to be on the borders of Mercia). The peculiarity of the first battle is the Welsh fighting a battle on the southern shores of Britain, approximately a hundred and seventy-five miles from their homeland. The battle at Mearcrædesburna is more realistically set in the midlands, approximately thirty-five miles from their borders. Ælle's battle in 491 is fought against the Britons, and Andredescester is equated with Andredesleag.
2. Of the seven other Anglo-Saxons who were given the honorific title of Bretwalda, Leslie Alcock writes that four were East Anglian or Northumbrians; that is, their kingdoms were in the East Midlands, not in the south of Britain.
3. CEAWLIN was the second Bretwalda, identified, like CERDIC, as a West Saxon with a Welsh ancestry. Ceawlin was Cerdic's great-grandson; his father was Cynric, and his grandfather was Creuddyn.

In the last *Chronicle* entry of 491, Ælle and only his youngest son, Cissa, besiege the Britons (not the Welsh) in Andredescester. It is impossible to infer an accurate sequence. Was Ælle an English Anglian rather than a German Anglian entering Britain from Gaul? Did he fight his first two campaigns against the Welsh, as suggested? Do Andredesleag and Andredescester identify the same location? Were Ælle's two older sons killed by in battles prior to the 491 entry? Answers to these questions can only be conjectural.

See also BRETWALDA.

Sources: L. Alcock (AB); T. Forester (CHH); G.N. Garmonsway (ASC); F. Reno (HKA, HFAE); Whitelock Etal (ASC).

Æsc, Oeric, and Oisc are simply other names for OCTHA. In Chapter 5 of *A History of the English*

Church and People, BEDE refers to Æsc as Oeric, surnamed Oisc. Oeric's father was HENGIST, who first came to Britain with his son Oeric at the invitation of VORTIGERN.

In *The Anglo-Saxon Chronicle*, Æsc's name appears in five entries:

    455 — After his uncle Horsa's death, Æsc succeeded to the kingdom with his father Hengist and fought against King Vortigern.

    457 — Hengist and Æsc fought against the BRITONS.

    465 — Hengist and Æsc fought against the WELSH and killed twelve Welsh nobles.

    473 — Hengist and Æsc fought against the Welsh and captured innumerable spoils, and the Welsh fled from the English like fire.

    488 — Æsc succeeded to the kingdom, suggesting that Hengist was killed at an earlier time. The Parker Chronicle lists Æsc's reign as twenty-four years, but the Laud Chronicle lists his reign as thirty-four years. His name doesn't appear again in the *Chronicle*.

The above five entries aver a link between Octha and King Arthur. Although there are claims of a northern and a southern Arthur, scholarly consensus of Arthur's historicity sets him in the milieu of Wales. Lewis Thorpe's translation of the *ASC* is by far the most accurate, particularly because he makes a distinction between Octha's two enemies being the Britons and the Welsh, a differentiation which is crucial. It has been established beyond debate that Vortigern's domain is in Wales, and hence entries 455, 465, and 473 substantiate that Arthur and Hengist's clans were contemporaries in the same environs.

To further elucidate the connection between Octha and Arthur, one must first emend the discrepancies of entries as reported in *The Anglo-Saxon Chronicle*. The most obvious disparity is the length of Æsc's reign as recorded in the Parker Chronicle, opposed to the Laud Chronicle, but there are several other incongruities which are not as obvious without adjusting chronological calibrations.

Because Hengist and Æsc represent two successive generations, their two life-spans and floruits are best viewed simultaneously. As a standard rule of thumb of twenty years representing one generation, Hengist would have been approximately 40 years old in 455 when his son Æsc, presumably about 20 years old, joined him as a co-leader after Horsa's death. Entry 488 states that "Æsc succeeded to the kingdom, and was king of the people of Kent for twenty-four years" (Parker Chronicle). Since Hengist's name is not included in this entry it has been assumed that he died in 488.

Typically, however, in annals where a succession to the kingship is listed, as given in Entry 488, the preceding king's death is assumed to have occurred in the entry which last made reference to a particular king. In this instance, Hengist's name appears for the last time in Entry 473. If the "reasonable age" concept is ignored, then, as stated above, Hengist would have been 73 years old when he died.

However, following the lead of Thomas O'-Sullivan and Geoffrey Ashe, Frank D. Reno has proposed a "reasonable age" concept for the overlapping generations of Hengist and Æsc. Three other sources besides *The Anglo-Saxon Chronicle*— the *Historia Brittonum*, the *Tysilio*, and *The History of the Kings of Britain*— indicate that Hengist is in the prime of his life in the early half of the fifth century. The last recording of the name Hengist is in the year 473. If one rationally assumes, on the basis that regnal successions commonly assert that an entry listing a new king implies the death of the king named in the previous entry, then Hengist died in 473, not in 488 as *The Anglo-Saxon Chronicle* claims. Hengist's age at that time would have been realistically 58, just past his prime.

Æsc succeeded to the kingdom twice, once in 455 when he became co-chieftain with his father, and then when he was sole chieftain after Hengist was killed in 473. At that time, Æsc would have been 38 years old. The Parker Chronicle relates that Æsc ruled for 24 years: [473 + 24 = 497], an enigmatically astounding date in Arthuriana. The year 497 is the commonly ascribed date for the twelfth battle fought by Arthur, the Battle of Mount Badon, recorded by GILDAS, by Bede and by NENNIUS. The *His-*

toria Brittonum, in §56, notes that Octha (Æsc) came down from the north, and when Octha's clan was "defeated in their campaigns, they sought help from Germany ... and considerably increased their numbers, and brought over their kings from Germany to rule over them in Britain."

If Welsh tradition has nuggets of history embedded in it, then "The Dream of Rhonabwy" is a gold mine. In this tale, Arthur's huge army is on the move "to be at the Battle of Badon by noon in order to fight Osla Big Knife [i.e., Æsc]." Osla asks Arthur for a truce to be granted "to the end of a month and a fortnight." After consultation with his council, Arthur agrees to an armistice and Osla gives tribute.

Geoffrey of Monmouth provides the finale. In his own words, "Octa and Eosa escaped to Germany" and "returned to Britain with an immense fleet." When the two armies clashed, "there was great slaughter done on both sides, and in the end Octa and Eosa were killed and the Saxons turned tail." These fragments corroborate that Æsc was at the Battle of Badon at the very end of the fifth century, and that he was killed at age 62.

See also OCTHA and OSLA BIG KNIFE.

Sources: G. Ashe (DKA); J. Gantz (TM); G. Garmonsway (ASC); J. Morris (HB); J. Myres (RBES); T. O'sullivan (DEG: A&D); F. Reno (HKA); L. Sherley-Price (BEDE: HEC&P).

Æternus, Æternus's single entry into British history appears in the Welsh genealogies. He is listed as the son of PATERNUS PESRUT and the grandson of TACITUS, the only three Roman names appearing in Welsh texts. Perhaps most important, Æternus is identified as Cunedda's father, since CUNEDDA is the one true Celtic hero. John Morris makes a terse reference to the name of Æternus being "an ancestor who was installed to protect the Roman army against the Picts," and quotes a poem that "splendid was Cunedda in battle, with his nine hundred horse, Cunedda the Lion, the son of Æternus."

Æternus is a phantasm who becomes significant in British history only when the epithet VORTIGERN is applied to his persona. If indeed Æternus was also known as the Overlord and usurper Vortigern, then he must be viewed as Arthur's rival, a traitor who forsook his country and aligned himself with the Anglian Hengist and his clan.

Sources: P. Bartram (WG); L. Alcock (AB); J. Morris (AOA).

Æthelweard, Æthelwerd, Ethelweard, Ethelwerd (*floruit 968 – 998*). Not only was Æthelweard a chronicler of note, but he himself is listed in *The Anglo-Saxon Chronicle*, Year 994, as an ealdorman of Wessex who was sent to negotiate with Anlff Tryggvason. Charles Plummer lists him as "identical with the chronicler Etherwerd," then lists his son as Æthelmær, and Æthelweard (aka Ethelwerd) as his grandson. Translator G.N. Garmonsway concurs that "toward the end of the tenth century ealdorman Æthelweard used, as one of the authorities of his *Chronicon*, an early version of the original Ælfredian chronicle, and one which was apparently more authentic than any of those which the chronicle texts have preserved."

Æthelweard is of interest in Arthuriana because his chronicle is based upon a version of *The Anglo-Saxon Chronicle* which did not survive the ravages of time. Plummer indicates that the details in Ethelwerd's chronicle are not verbatim when compared with details in the $\overline{A}$ manuscript of the *ASC*, but are more accurate than the other existing chronicles. The following chart provides a comparison of the three different manuscripts.

A quick glance gives the impression that the three documents are similar. Two of the documents record the year as 494, and the other as 495, and as Plummer asserts, "It is a small matter that the Preface puts the invasion of CERDIC and CYNRIC in 494, while the *Chronicle* places it in 495." Plummer's choice of the word "invasion," however, is misleading; one document uses the word "landed," another "came," and the third "arrived." A closer scrutiny reveals even more serious discrepancies which an individual might overlook. The port named in the three manuscripts is Cerdicesora, but the locale differs. Two manuscripts claim Cerdic and Cynric fight against the Welsh, but Ethelweard writes that Cerdic and Cynric joined battle against the Britons, an important distinction.

The last major difference is that the *Chronicle*

Genealogical Preface of the ASC	Anglo-Saxon Chronicle	Ethelweard Chronicle (edited by Alistair Campbell)
In the year of Christ's Nativity 494, Cerdic and Cynric his son landed at Cerdicesora with five ships. In the year 500, they conquered the kingdom of Wessex from the Welsh.	In the year, 495 two aldormen, Cerdic and Cynric his son came to Britain at the place which is called Cerdicesora and the same day they fought against the Welsh. Entry 519: In this year Cerdic and Cynric obtained the kingdom of the West Saxons.	In the year 494 Cerdic and his son Cynric arrived in Britain with five ships at the port called Cerdiscesora, joined battle against the Britons the same day, and were victorious. In the year 500, they encircled that western area of Britain now known as Wessex.

claims Cerdic and Cynric's "victory" was won in the year 519, while the other two give the year as 500. The Genealogical Preface uses the word "conquered," the *Chronicle* the word "obtained." and the third "encircled," which is nondescript. Further differences are pointed out in other entries: Cerdicesora is a different location from Cerdicesforda; Welsh is distinct from Briton; Cerdic's son is CREODA and not Cynric; and West Saxons is more accurately described as Wessex.

The Historic King Arthur suggests three modifications when interpreting the dates proposed by these three documents in order to eliminate confusion:

1. the 494–95 dates of the three manuscripts being considered should list only that "the West Saxons (Cerdic and Cynric) arrived at Cerdicesora in western Britain," and that any reference to a battle being fought should be stricken;

2. the translation for the 500 date should replace the word "conquered" with a word such as "obtained" or "granted" so that it reads, "Six years (i.e., Year 500) after Cerdic and Cynric (Creoda) arrived, they *acquired* the kingdom of Wessex from the Welsh." Using the term "acquired" could infer by conquest, by negotiation, or by award, thus circumventing the issue of how the kingdom was attained;

3. the most profound and serious revision is accepting Plummer's assertion that the 519 entry is a doublet of the 500 entry, and hence the 519 entry should be deleted from history.

This last item is the most difficult to accept because it so profoundly changes the perspective of Arthur's historic era. This would mean that Arthur's battle of Badon would have been fought around 494–95, and that the battle of Camlann would have been fought six years later. As mentioned above, this changes the history of that period from conjecture to fact. Each reader can determine which scenario most satisfies his perspective.

Sources: G.N. Garmonsway (ASC); J. Giles (SOEC); C. Plummer (TSCP); F. Reno (HKA).

Aëtius, Agricius, Gittius, Agricius, Agitium, Agitius. To understand Aëtius' importance in British history, it is best to analyze his chronology in reverse order, following a pattern of flashback by beginning with the years 446 C.E. to 454 C.E. and then retrospectively tracing his role from birth onward.

There is only one thread of history which ties Aëtius to Britain, and even this gossamer connection is fragile. The oldest extant British manuscript which can be termed as history is Gildas Badonicus's *The Ruin and Conquest of Britain,* De Excidio et Conquestu Britanniae. The full title as provided by J.A. Giles in *Six Old English Chronicles* is "The Epistle of Gildas the most ancient British Author, who flourished in the yeer of our Lord 546. And who by his great erudition, sanctitie, and wisdome, acquired the name of Sapiens." It's a small wonder the full title is very seldom used.

Unfortunately, however, GILDAS BADONICUS does not properly use the name "Aëtius." In Latin, he writes, "*Sed ante promissum deo volente pauca de situ ... de epistolis C.E. Agitium,*" which translates to "But before I make good my promise, I shall try, God willing, to say a little about the situation [of Britain] ... and of the epistle [letter] of Agitium." He uses the name Agitium rather than Aëtius.

In a later section, Gildas writes, "*Igitur rursum miserae mittentes epistolas reliquiae C.E. Agitium Romanae potestatis virum, hoc modo loquentes: 'Agitio ter consuli gemitus Britannorum.'*" This translates to "So the miserable remnants [of the British] sent off an epistle [letter] again, this time to the Roman commander Agitium, in the following terms: To Agitio, thrice consul."

Gratuitously, the phrases "Roman commander" and "thrice consul" properly identify the individual Aëtius. Surviving Roman documents — plus later manuscripts produced by copyists — correctly associate the descriptors with the Roman Magister Aëtius of the Western Empire who had thrice been selected as a *consulibus*.

Echoing a great deal of material written by Gildas, the Venerable BEDE completed his *History of the English Church and People* around 731. He mentions Aëtius twice; in the first passage he records the year as 423, when Theodosius the Younger ascended to the throne, and in the twenty-third year of his reign (423 + 23 = 446), "Aëtius, an illustrious patrician, became Consul for the third time together with Symmachus. To him the wretched remnant of the Britons sent a letter, which commences: 'To Aëtius, thrice Consul, come the groans of the Britons.'" Bede provides a firm date of 446 in his first passage, but he only hints at a date in his second mention of Aëtius: "Not long afterwards, in the fifth year of Marcian's reign, Valentinian was murdered by supporters of the patrician Aëtius, whom he had executed, and with him fell the Empire of the West."

GEOFFREY OF MONMOUTH borrows almost verbatim the passage about Agitius from Gildas Badonicus, except Monmouth uses the name Agicius: "To Agicius, three times consul, come the groans of the Britons. The sea drives us into the hands of the barbarians, and the barbarians drive us into the sea. Between the two of them, we have two deaths to choose from; we can either be drowned or have our throats cut." Monmouth then adds, "For all this, the messengers returned sadly home, to explain to their fellow-citizens their lack of success, for they had received no promise of help." Shortly thereafter, the Britons sent the Archbishop of London, GUITHELINUS (Roman name VITALINUS) as an emissary to travel to Little Britain (Armorica/Letavia) to seek help from their kinsmen ALDRONEUS.

The *Tysilio* narrates a slightly different account. Translator Peter Roberts writes: "When the departure of the Romans was known to Gwnwas and Melwas, they assembled the greatest force they were able, landed in Albany, and renewed the war with the Britons, and ravaged the country as far as the Humber. The Britons being unable to repel the enemy, sent to implore the assistance of Gittius, the Roman General against their enemies. But the Roman Senate, having heard their petition, refused to comply with it, and renounced the tribute." In a footnote, Roberts explains that "Gittius" is "Agytyus in the Brut Gildas and Agitius in Geoffrey of Monmouth," then explains, "This must be Ægidius, the master general of Gaul." The reader can make a fair assumption that the *Tysilio* has a variant story.

Roman history, however, supplies the explicit details about Aëtius's associations and influences. The year of his birth is obscure, but he was born at Durostorum in Bulgaria near the end of the fourth century. His father was GAUDENTIUS, a *magister equitum*, a close friend and comrade of Constantius III, who was a fellow *magister*.

While in his early teens, Aëtius witnessed the sack of Rome by Alaric the Visigoth, and after the pillage, Aëtius and GALLA PLACIDIA, half-sister of Emperor HONORIUS, were taken as hostages in 410. Their captivity lasted approximately seven years, during which time CONSTANTIUS III became the negotiator for their return. After a consensual marriage between Galla Placidia and ATAULPHUS (the new king of the Visigoths), the hostages were finally released in 417. Upon their return to Rome, Constantius III became supreme commander, shortly thereafter marrying Galla Placidia and becoming co-emperor of the Western Empire with Flavius Honorius.

Aëtius was taken a second time as a hostage by the Huns, which by a twist of fate worked to his advantage in later life. After a period of up-heaval and eventual resolution between Aëtius and Galla Placidia, and after the deaths of both Constantius III and Honorius, Placidia became regent of the West for her son VALENTINIAN III and selected Aëtius as her *magister equitum*.

In 446 (the date matching Gildas's implication and Bede's recording), the Britons appealed to Aëtius during the magister's third consulate for help against the barbarian invaders of their island. Aëtius, however, was attempting to pacify Gaul from an onslaught of continental barbarians and was unable to offer aid to the British prov-ince.

In 451 Aëtius joined with the Visigoths in de-feating Attila the Hun in a fierce battle on the Catalaunian Plains, and although he was suc-cessful, Attila invaded Italy the following year and Aëtius could do little to deter the savage Hun and his tribe.

In 454, after the Romans were regaining a new foothold in Gaul, Emperor Valentinian III, who had inherited the throne from his mother, Galla Placidia, stabbed Aëtius to death in a fit of jealous rage. Shortly thereafter, Valentinian him-self was allegedly assassinated by supporters of Aëtius.

Sources: E. Duckett (MPFE&W); A. Ferrill (FOTRE); E. Gibbon (D&FORE); S. Oost (GPA); P. Roberts (CKOB); L. Sherley-Price (BEDE: HEC&P); L. Thorpe (GM: HKB); M. Winterbottom (G; ROB& OW).

Agitius is the name used by GILDAS BADONICUS for AËTIUS, who in Roman history becomes the *magister militum* and is thrice *consulibus* for GALLA PLACIDIA. The Britons appeal to him in his third consulate (in 446) for Roman aid after the legions withdrew from Britain, but no aid was forthcoming because of the insurrections in Gaul. Leslie Alcock pointed out that Agitius was the name used in the *De Excidio*, "but BEDE silently amends Agitius to Aëtius."

Sources: L. Alcock (AB); M. Winterbottom (G: ROB&OW).

Agloval, Aglovale. Sir Agloval is one of Sir GAWAIN's nephews, and brother of Sir Lamorak, Sir PERCEVAL DE GALES, Sir Dornard, and Sir Tor, all begotten of King Pellinor and Aries the cowherd's wife, save for Sir Tor, who was begot-ten afore Aries wedded Pellinor.

Source: T. Malory (LMD'A).

Agnomen. Freeborn Romans and Celts custom-arily bore three names, sometimes four. An ag-nomen is a surname often bestowed as a title of honor, or fondly as a nickname. Its plural is ag-nomina, pronounced ag-**nom'**-i-na. Example: EMRYS Ambrosius.

See also COGNOMEN, NOMEN, and PRAENOM.

Sources: Merriam Dictionary; Cassell's Latin Dictionary.

Agravain, Agravaine. In Malory's text, Agravain has three brothers—GAWAIN, GAHERIS, and GARETH. His mother is MARGAWSE, whom Malory equates with MORGAN LE FAY, Arthur's sister. ARTHUR has Agravain marry Dame Laurel.

In his most notable role Agravain is portrayed as a malicious villain. He and MORDRED ensnare GUINEVERE and LANCELOT in their love tryst. Though Gawain, Gaheris and Gareth try to stop them, he and Mordred conspire to catch the adulterers together. The two tell Arthur of the love affair, but Arthur insists upon proof.

Agravain and Mordred recruit twelve knights who pound on the queen's door and demand that Lancelot show himself. Lancelot opens the door and "at the first buffet he slew Sir Agra-vain, and the twelve of his fellows after." Sir Mordred was wounded and "fled with all his might."

Source: T. Malory (LMD'A).

Agricius, Agitio. Agricius is the name used by GEOFFREY OF MONMOUTH for AËTIUS, *magister militum* and thrice *consulibus* for GALLA PLACIDIA. Aëtius's name appears as Agitio in the manu-scripts of GILDAS BADONICUS.

Sources: L. Thorpe (GM: HKB); M. Winter-bottom (G: ROB&OW).

Agricola Longhand, Agricola the Pelagian. Agricola Longhand must not be confused with Gnaeus Julius Agricola, the Roman general noted for his conquests in Britain (specifically Scotland) between the years of 78 C.E. and 84 C.E. Agricola Longhand (the name used by John Morris) is known also as "Agricola the Pelagian" in Bede's work. This Agricola's floruit falls in the middle of King Arthur's historic era. In a terse passage, Bede writes

> A few years before [the Saxons'] arrival, the Pelagian heresy introduced by Agricola, son of Severianus a Pelagian prelate, had seriously infected the faith of the British Church. Although the British rejected this perverse teaching, so blasphemous against the grace of Christ, they were unable to refute its plausible arguments by controversial methods, and wisely decided to ask help from the bishops of Gaul in this spiritual conflict. These summoned a great synod, and consulted together as to whom they should send to support the Faith. Their unanimous choice fell upon the apostolic bishops GERMANUS OF AUXERRE and Lupus of Troyes.

From this passage the reader is informed that (1) Agricola and Germanus are contemporaries; (2) from a different source, the date of 429 is supplied for Germanus's first visit to Britain; (3) there would have been about a one-generation separation between Agricola and AMBROSIUS AURELIANUS, who would have been approximately seven years old; (4) from a different copy, VORTIGERN would have been in power approximately four years; (5) similarly, from a different manuscript there is a suggestion that Vortigern, too, may have been a Pelagian; and last but quite important, (6) there is a suggestion that the son of Agricola Longhand was VORTIPOR. This in turn would suggest that there was a strong bond between VORTIGERN, Agricola, and Vortipor, the last being one of the kings castigated by GILDAS.

Christopher Snyder points out that Germanus's first visit to Britain can be dated with certainty to the year 429 because of the evidence from an independent historian, Prosper of Aquitaine: "A.D. 429: The Pelagian Agricola, son of the Pelagian bishop Severianus, corrupted the churches of Britain through his underhanded ways, but on the initiative of the deacon Palladius Pope Celestine sent Germanus, bishop of Auxerre, as his representative to confound the heretics and guide the Britons to the Catholic faith." Embedded here is a subtle suggestion ("underhanded ways") of how Agricola might have acquired the epithet of "Longhand."

Sources: J. Morris (AOA); L. Sherley-Price (Bede: HEC&P); C. Snyder (AAOT).

Agwisance (Äg'-we-saunce), Angwyshaunce, Anguish, Anguisel, Agwisance. King of Ireland and father of Isoud first appears in Malory's *Le Morte D'Arthur,* Book 1, Chapter 12. Eleven kings make a pact, swearing that they would destroy Arthur, and Agwisance, King of Ireland, pledged that he would supply five thousand horsemen. During the first attack Agwisance aids in "putting to earth" GRIFLET and Lucan. When Lucan recovers, he attacks Agwisance with a spear and puts him to earth along with his horse.

Source: T. Malory (LMD'A).

Aldhelm of Almsbury. Because of the lack of ancient manuscripts, there is still controversy as to whom penned the *De Excidio,* but that point is moot because the important emphasis here is the structuring of a chronology tracing the alleged history of a King Arthur and establishing the role of AMBROSIUS AURELIANUS in the fifth century. Aldhelm of Malmesbury was an obscure monk — among several others — who is sometimes identified as the author of the *De Excidio.*

See also GILDAS BADONICUS and GILDAS ALBANIUS.

Aldor. Translator Peter Roberts uses the name Aldor in the *Tysilio,* whereas Geoffrey of Monmouth refers to the King of Brittany as ALDRONEUS.

Sources: P. Roberts (COKB); L. Thorpe (GOW: JTW/DOW).

Aldroneus, Aldor. In Monmouth's *History of the Kings of Britain,* Aldroneus is the King of Brittany, known in the *Tysilio* as Aldor. Aldroneus, "the fourth British King of Brittany," plays an important initial role in Arthuriana. At the beginning of Part Four, "The House of Constantine," Aldroneus enters Arthurian history when GUITHELINUS, the Archbishop of London, seeks his help to defend Britain from the onslaught of barbarians. Guithelinus complains that MAGNUS Maximus despoiled the island of its soldiers by conscripting them to sail to Gaul to fight, first against the barbarians, then treacherously against the Romans themselves. After a heart-rending speech, Guithelinus concludes that Aldroneus holds the kingdom of Britain in his hands.

Aldroneus graciously declines to help since his interests now lie in Brittany, where he rules with honor and does not have to pay homage to anyone. Nevertheless, out of respect for his heritage, Aldroneus agrees to place his own brother, CONSTANTINE of Brittany, under the command of Guithelinus, along with two thousand soldiers. The pact is forged and Guithelinus, along with his new recruitment, sails back to Totnes in Britain. When Constantine is elevated to King of Britain, he takes a Celtic noblewoman as his concubine and they have three children, CONSTANS, AURELIUS AMBROSIUS, and Utherpendragon. Utherpendragon (UTERPENDRAGON) seduces YGERNA, and ARTHUR is the result.

Aldroneus then drops from Monmouth's history. His role as reported in the *Tysilio* is equally as brief. The two additional pieces of information is that Aldor is 1) the son of Cynvawr, who succeeded to the throne after Cynan Meiriadawg, and 2) Totnes in Britain is in the province of Lloegria.

Sources: P. Roberts (CKOB); L. Thorpe (GM: HKB).

Alfred the Great, Aelfred. G.N. Garmonsway's introduction indicates that there are seven extant manuscripts of *The Anglo-Saxon Chronicle*, designated by Charles Plummer as Ā, A, B, C, D, E, and F. Between the years 894 through 924, however, Alfred the Great modified some of the entries which have become known, of course, as the *Alfredian Chronicle*. Plummer suggests Alfred's chronicle is an offshoot of the Orosius translation dating to the years 890–893. The first twenty-two lines of Giles's translation of Asser are important because it, too, uses the Genealogical Preface (or some other lost source) which differs from the body of the *ASC* itself, echoing the name of Creoda as part of the West Saxon genealogies, which is so vital in establishing dates for the Arthurian era.

Sources: M. Alexander (HEL); G.N. Garmonsway (ASC); C. Plummer (TSCP); F. Reno (HKA).

Ambrosius. In its shortened form, the name Ambrosius, as it applies to King Arthur, is either Ambrosius Aurelianus, as recorded by GILDAS BADONICUS, or Aurelius Ambrosius, his counterpart in Geoffrey of Monmouth's *History of the Kings of Britain*.

Only in the *Historia Brittonum* is this individual referred to by the simple appellation of Ambrosius. In §31 he is introduced in an informative passage which reads, "VORTIGERN ruled in Britain, and during his rule in Britain he was under pressure, from fear of the Picts and the Irish [Scotti], and of a Roman invasion, and, not least, from the dread of Ambrosius."

This was during the period of insular history when the Picts were ingressing southward and the Scotti were migrating to Britain and then into what became known as Scotland. The Romans had withdrawn the majority of troops around 410, but there was no intention for this to be a permanent abandonment, which caused Vortigern to fear their return. Vortigern also dreaded the return of Ambrosius, but Nennius does not give reasons why the king was so apprehensive of this man. It is only by inference drawn from later segments in the *Historia*, and from other independent sources, that the reader can speculate about the persona and power of Ambrosius.

A later heading—"The Tale of Emrys"—was affixed to Sections 40–42 in the *Historia Brittonum* to clarify that this story was about Ambrosius, who is identified by the epithet Emrys. When Vortigern asks the lad his name, the boy answers, "I am called Ambrosius." The passage which then follows is "That is, he was shown to be Emyrs (*Embries Guletic* in Latin) the Overlord."

Later, in Section 48 of the *HB*, he is described as the "great king among all the kings of the British nation." Numerous researchers equate Ambrosius and Emrys, but few explain why the connection is made or what explicitly the term EMRYS means. Jeffrey Gantz, in *The Mabinogion*, does label "emyrs" as a Welsh term (emhyr) meaning "emperor," but that title is given to Arthur, not Ambrosius, whose name does not appear in that text. E.K. Chambers alludes to Professor John Rhys, who also stresses the importance of titles applied to Ambrosius. He writes, "Wledig may have been the later representative of some Roman official, *dux* or *comes*, whose functions he [Ambrosius] assumed."

In *The Discovery of King Arthur*, Part II Chapter 6, Geoffrey Ashe points out that continental authors of the fifth and sixth centuries do not link Riothamus with Arthur, which he thinks is a paradox. Although he himself is assured that he knows Riothamus *is* Arthur, he does not want to jump to conclusions and sets up a process of eliminating "Vortigern, Vortimer, Ceredig, Uther, and (to keep the chief claimant to the last) Ambrosius Aurelianus."

Confusingly, he then cites Professor Leon Fleuriot as accepting that the Britons had a great leader in the third quarter of the fifth century, whose title was Riothamus, and whose exploits went into the making of the Arthur of legend. He believed, however, that the ruler was Ambrosius, and his deeds were credited later to somebody else named Arthur.

The Historic King Arthur agrees with Fleuriot and disputes what Ashe claims as "proof" that Ambrosius is *not* Riothamus. Ashe's case can be summarized and refuted on five counts:

1. Admittedly, Gildas Badonicus doesn't call Ambrosius a king, but he does acknowledge him as Roman royalty, and a victor, but Gildas does not even recognize an Arthur.

2. Nennius likewise does not call Arthur a king, even in the spurious §56 where Nennius refers to Arthur as a *dux bellorum*.

3. Why Ashe labels Ambrosius's kingship as "legend" is mystifying. Ambrosius is verified by both Gildas and Bede, whereby an Arthur of the fifth century is not. As a copyist, Nennius describes Ambrosius as "the great king among all the kings of the British nation." In that same passage, he indicates that Ambrosius had the power to grant kingdoms to Paschent.

4. Ambrosius is not merely a "landholder" as Ashe claims. Although a modern Welsh dictionary defines Gwledig as a landholder, the term as it was used implies royalty and rank, exemplified by five independent sources: E.K. Chambers, John Morris, John Rhys, Nora Chadwick, and Jeffrey Gantz. The epithets from those individuals label him as an Overlord, Supreme Ruler of the Land, Ruler of a Country, Ruler of South-Western Britain, and Emperor.

5. Indeed, the name of Ambrosius does not appear in either history or legend on the continent, but neither does Ashe's historic Arthur. In the continental historical manuscripts, the epithet Riothamus is not attached to a proper name but identifies him only as the *Briton king* from across Ocean. In the early 470s that Briton king ties in perfectly and historically with ANTHEMIUS, SYAGRIUS, and AEGIDIUS.

For other specifics of Ambrosius, there are various entries which provide different perspectives: MERLINUS AMBROSIUS, RIOTHAMUS, EMRYS, UTERPENDRAGON, and ARCTURUS.

Sources: G. Ashe (DKA); N. Chadwick (CB); E. Chambers (AOB); J. Gantz (TM); J. Morris (HB/AOA); F. Reno (HKA/HFAE/AAA) J. Rhys (CB); L. Thorpe (Gm: HKB); M. Winterbottom (G: ROB&OW).

Ambrosius Aurelianus, Ambrosius, Aurelius Ambrosius, Ambrosius Merlinus, Uter, Uterpendragon, Arthus, Arcturus, Arthur, Emrys, Emrys Wledig. The full name Ambrosius Aurelianus is recorded in only two ancient manuscripts, the *De Excidio* by GILDAS BADONICUS and *A History of the English Church and People* by BEDE. All the other appellations listed above were later designations assigned to him by different sources.

For an individual who was so greatly respected, Gildas surprisingly allotted Ambrosius only minimal space: "[The Briton] leader was Ambrosius Aurelianus, a gentleman who, perhaps alone of the Romans, had survived the shock of this notable storm: certainly his parents, who had worn the purple [a color of royalty], were slain in it. His descendants in our day have become greatly inferior to their grandfather's excellence. Under him our people regained their strength, and challenged the victors to battle. The Lord assented, and the battle went their way." Gildas makes no other mention of Ambrosius Aurelianus.

BEDE, who used Gildas as his source, was equally as terse:

> [The Briton] leader at this time was Ambrosius Aurelianus, a man of good character and the sole survivor of Roman race from the catastrophe. Among the slain had been his own parents, who were of royal birth and title.

Under his leadership the Britons took up arms, challenged their conquerors to battle, and with God's help inflicted a defeat on them. Thenceforward victory swung first to one side and then to the other, until the battle of Badon Hill, when the Britons made a considerable slaughter of the invaders. This took place about forty-four years after their arrival in Britain: but I shall deal with this later.

Only in the tenth century does Nennius supply details from an unknown source and record what was later titled as the "Tale of Emrys." Nennius identifies Ambrosius Aurelianus only as AMBROSIUS, but retains the characteristics given by Bede and Gildas Badonicus. Ambrosius claims his father was not only Roman royalty, but also a *consulibus*, an intriguing addition since historically Constantius III was twice appointed as a *consulibus* by Emperor Honorius of the Western Roman Empire. Nennius also gives scores of specific names, including barbarians, Britons, and Romans.

In §48 of the *Historia Brittonum*, Ambrosius, who was labeled "the great king among all the kings of Britain," gave Vortigern's son Pascent permission to rule, and in §66 there was discord between Ambrosius and Vitalinus (GUITHELINUS). Leslie Alcock, John Morris, and Robert Fletcher are among those who believe that Ambrosius and Vitalinus were opponents or rivals, but in *The Historic King Arthur*, Frank Reno proposes that Ambrosius and Vitalinus were allies but he disagrees on how to avert Vortigern's manipulations for the kingship after the Romans withdrew from Britain. There is no controversy, however, about the date when this occurred: twelve years from the beginning of VORTIGERN's reign, in 437.

Summarized, the reader learns these details about Ambrosius:

1. Vortigern fears the return of the Romans, but he dreads even more the return of Ambrosius;
2. Ambrosius is a respected and competent leader;
3. Ambrosius pulls the Britons from the brink of destruction;
4. as a young boy, Ambrosius confronts Vortigern at a northern fortress which the usurper king is attempting to construct;
5. Ambrosius takes on the appellation of Merlinus;
6. Ambrosius is also known as Emrys, the Overlord;
7. Vortigern flees and gives Ambrosius his fortress, along with all the kingdoms of the western part of Britain;
8. Ambrosius's parents "wore the purple"— that is, they were Roman royalty;
9. Ambrosius's father was a *consulibus*;
10. Ambrosius was a powerful king in western Britain, specifically Wales;
11. there was discord between Ambrosius and Vitalinus in 437.

Three important things are controversial about Ambrosius:

1. Ambrosius Aurelianus is conflated with the historic King Arthur;
2. by implication, Gildas Badonicus and Bede infer that Ambrosius was the leader at the Battle of Badon, but Nennius ascribes Arthur as the *dux bellorum*;
3. whether Ambrosius and Vitalinus were allies or adversaries.

Without Nennius's, Gildas's, or Bede's treasure trove of information, piecing together early medieval Briton history would be impossible.

HENRY OF HUNTINGDON (*floruit*, 1103–1133) re-tells the story of Ambrosius, but some of his details vary from the preceding three sources. He writes:

When, however, the army of the Saxons, having entirely routed the natives, returned to their own territory, the Britons, emerging from their hiding-places, began to take heart, and assembling a great force, marched into Kent against HENGIST and HORSA. They had for their leader at that time Ambrosius Aurelian, an able man, the only one of Roman extraction who had chanced to survive the late troubles, in which his parents, who had been invested with the name and the ensigns of royalty, both perished. Two sons of Vortigern, Gortimer [VORTIMER] and Catiger [CATIGERN], acted as generals under him. Ambrosius himself led the first rank, Gortimer the second, Catiger the third; while Horsa and Hengist, though their troops were inferior in numbers, led them boldly against the enemy, dividing them into two bodies, of which each brother commanded one.

Ambrosius is given the name Ambrosius Aurelian, which is a cross between the name as it appears in the works of Gildas and Bede, and the name Aurelius Ambrosius, which is in Monmouth's manuscript.

As further clarification, in Henry's retelling

1. it is controversial whether Hengist and Horsa ruled in Kent or in Anglia;
2. it is possible Vortimer was a "general" under Ambrosius, since Vortimer violently opposed his father's (Vortigern's) alliance with Hengist;
3. Henry might have made the assumption that Catiger was also one of Ambrosius's generals based upon information derived from the *Historia Brittonum* and *History of the Kings of Britain*.

See also AMBROSIUS.
Sources: T. Forester (CHH); J. Morris (HB); F. Reno (HKA/HFAE); L. Sherley-Price (Bede: HEC&P); J. Stevenson (N: HB); L. Thorpe (GM: HKB); M. Winterbottom (G: ROB&OW).

Amerauder and Amherawdyr are titles. John Rhys, a forerunner to both Leslie Alcock and John Morris, gives one of the titles used by Arthur: "The Welsh have borrowed the Latin title of *imperator* 'emperor' and made it into *amherawdyr*, later *ameraudur*, so it is not impossible that, when the Roman imperator [Honorius] ceased to have anything more to say to this country [Britain], the title was given to the highest officer in the island, namely the COMES BRITANNIAE, and that in the words *Yr Amherawdyr Arthur* 'the Emperor Arthur' we gave a remnant of our insular history."
Sources: J. Rhys (STAL); L. Alcock (AB).

Amfortas. *see* ANFORTAS, which is listed as Amfortas in Ronan Coghlan's Legends.

Amhar, Amr, Amir, Anir. Amhar, son of Arthur, is listed in the tale "Gereint and Enid" of *The Mabinogion*. Arthur and his retinue are preparing for a hunt, and Amhar is one of four chamberlains whose job is to guard Arthur's bed.

He is also mentioned in the "Wonders of Britain" of the *Historia Brittonum* in Section 73: "There is another wonder in the country called Ergyng.... There is a tomb there by a spring called Llgad Amr; the name of the man who is buried in the tomb was Amr [who] was the son of the warrior Arthur [who] killed him there and buried him." The tomb is strange because it changes sizes, affirmed by Nennius himself.
Source: J. Gantz (TM); J. Morris (BH).

Amlaud, Amlawd the Great, Amlawd Wledig, Amlawdd, Amlaudd, Amlaut. Amlawd is identified as "a ruler" in "How Culhwch Won Olwen" of *The Mabinogion*, but other than revealing that Culhwch's mother is "Goleuddydd, daughter of Amlawd," nothing more is said about him. Geoffrey of Monmouth does not use the name Amlawd, but the *Tysilio* does, recording that Eigr (Ygraine/YGERNA) is the daughter of Amlawdd the Great. A third work, the "Life of Saint Iltud," records that RHIEINWYLDD (pronounced Hree-in-WOOL-idd) was Amlawd's daughter and Iltud's mother. Piecing this information together, Amlawd had three daughters, Goleuddydd, Eigr, and Rhieinwyldd, meaning that Arthur's mother, Culhwch's mother, and Iltud's mother were sisters, making ARTHUR, CULHWCH, and Iltud cousins.

Amlawd's mother was named Gwen, which means "white" or "pure" in Welsh.
Sources: E. Chambers (AOB); J. Gantz (TM); P. Roberts (COKB); W. Rees (HAW); W. Rees (LC-BS); W. Stokes (LS).

Amren is the son of BEDIVERE, as is listed in the *Mabinogion* tale "How Culhwch Won Olwen."
Source: J. Gantz (TM).

Anator. *see* WOLFRAM VON ESCHENBACH.

Aneirin, Aneurin, Nwirin, Neirin. Only a thirteenth-century manuscript of Aneirin's *Y Gododdin* survives. Most experts suggest the date of composition circa 600 C.E., but agree that the original poem may have been composed much earlier and the language modified during oral transmission. In its original form, *Y Gododdin* is a poetic elegy containing 99 to 103 stanzas, depending upon the translation. The title names an ancient territory, Manau Gododdin, near what is now Edinburgh, at the head of the Firth of Forth extending southward to Lothian. Aneirin was among the Gwyr y Gogledd (the Men of the North) who battled the enemy.

The poem is difficult to identify because the number of stanzas vary, but the important one which relates to the purpose of this entry records the name "Arthur":

He [Gwawrddur] charged at the head of three
    hundred, most bold of the finest.
He cut down both centre and wing.
He excelled in the forefront of the noblest host.
He gave gifts of horses from the herd in winter.
He glutted black ravens on the rampart wall
    though he was no Arthur.
Among the powerful ones in battle,
In the front rank, Gwawrddur was a palisade.

This is a poetic way of saying that Gwawrddur was a magnificent warrior who killed so many enemies during the battle that ravens had a gluttonous feast. Yet in spite of this, Gwawrddur did not match the prowess of Arthur.

It is surprising that Aneirin, one of two acknowledged as a Welsh bard and signified as *cynfeirdd* (early poets) incidentally influences Arthuriana. Because only a thirteenth-century manuscript of *Y Gododdin* exists, the original text of the sixth-century, passing through so many centuries, could be heavily interpolated and altered, and thus the reference to Arthur might be an interpolation, an enigma which cannot be resolved.

Who might this famous Arthur be in such an early reference? That question has baffled researchers for over eight centuries, with different ones making different claims. Richard Barber, in *The Figure of Arthur,* believes that "it would seem reasonable to assume that Arthur belongs to the same period [when *Y Gododdin* appeared], as there are no other references to earlier heroic figures. All of the comparisons are immediate, to figures whom the poet's audience would have known personally."

There is nothing, however, to substantiate this claim. There is no Arthur of any substantial fame during the fifth or sixth centuries, and the omission of an Arthur in the works of GILDAS BADONICUS and BEDE significantly stresses that there was no such figure in British history during the fifth century. Based upon this erroneous deduction — that an Arthur must have been a contemporary of the poet Aneirin — Barber rejects the idea that the name of Arthur might refer to

a hero of bygone centuries, a Roman cavalry commander during late second century named LUCIUS ARTORIUS CASTUS, a well-known figure to Arthurian enthusiasts.

In a later segment Barber writes,

> Any connection between [this commander] and the Irish and Welsh Arthurs must be extremely tenuous. We can only conjecture that distant memories of L. Artorius Castus's campaigns, perhaps stray inscriptions on Roman sites, might have encouraged later writers to embellish the legend of Arthur in otherwise unsuspected ways. To build a bridge of tradition from second-century Roman Britain to ninth-century Wales with no other support is a daring feat of imagination, but not admissible evidence. Nor are the "coincidences" such as L. Artorius Castus's Breton expedition and the idea of an overseas expedition by the mythical Arthur any stronger than the supposed links between the Roman general and the occasional use of the name Artor near York in the eleventh century recorded in the Domesday Book.

Barber implies that Lucius Artorius Castus was a Breton, or perhaps a Roman commander campaigning only in Brittany, but there is enough circumstantial, archaeological, and Romano-historical evidence to establish that Artorius Castus did campaign in northern Britain, from Bremetennacum (Ribchester) and Eburacum (York), across Hadrian's Wall and to the Antonine Wall.

C. Scott Littleton and Linda Malcor offer a scenario that Aneirin's "Arthur" is Lucius Artorius Castus, a Roman commander in charge of the VI Legion Victrix, "headquartered at York and charged with the defense of northern Britain." This would have been in Aneirin's vicinity, though not during the same era. The co-authors cite Dio Cassius's *Roman History,* which chronicled that "8,000 *cataphracti* [heavily armed auxiliary cavalry] from a Sarmatian tribe known as the Iazyges were impressed into the Roman legions. Of these Iazyges 5,500 were sent to Britain."

Several modern-day authors comment about the name "Arthur" as it appears in the *Y Gododdin*:

1. Graham Phillips and Martin Keatman theorize that Arthur was named because the

warrior chief Gwawrddur was one of Arthur's descendants, or that "Arthur" might not have been a real name but could signify a by-name or title.

2. Rodney Castleden cites "Oliver Padel, who denies the historicity of Arthur, saying that the line may have been added in the ninth century."

3. Geoffrey Ashe, in *The Arthurian Handbook*, simply writes that "the stanza is interesting, although it cannot be proved to be Aneirin's own rather than an addition by another poet."

As a conclusion, Aneirin survived the devastating battle at Catterick, and a Welsh triad explains his later death:

Three Unfortunate
Assassinations of the Island

1. Heidyn son of Engyan, who slew Aneirin of Flowing Verse, Prince of Poets.

2. Llawgad Trwm Bargod Eidyn, who slew Afaon son of Taliesin.

3. Llofan Law Ddifo, who slew Urien son of Cynfarch.

Ef gwant tra thrichant echasaf,
Ef laddai a pherfedd ac eithaf,
Oedd gwiw ym mlaen llu llariaf,
Goddolai o haid meirch y gaeaf.
Gochorai brain du fur caer
Cyn ni bai ef Arthur.
Rhwng cyfnerthi yng nghlysur,
Yng nghynnor, gwernor Gwawrddur.

This stanza is from the *Llyfr Aneirin*, a sixth-century copy which is housed in the Cardiff Library. The fifth and sixth lines are touted to be the earliest British reference of Arthur. It was translated from the Welsh by A.O.H. Jarman. Briefly, the Welsh hero Gwawrddur and his tribe are battling against the barbarians and he has killed so many enemies that black ravens are glutting themselves with corpses on the ramparts. And although he is a hero, he is not as great a warrior as Arthur.

Welsh translation by A.O.H. Jarman

Sources: G. Ashe (DKA); G. Ashe (K&QEB); G. Ashe (MBI); C. Barber/D. Pykitt (JTA); R. Barber (FOA); R. Castleden (KA: TBL); R. Collingwood/J. Myres (RB&ES); J. Davies (HOW); N. Lacy/G. Ashe (AH); C. Littleton/L.

Malcor (FSTC); J. Markale (KOTC; J. Morris (AOA); G. Phillips/M. Keatman (KA: TS); G. Williams (E: SFA).

Anfortas, Amfortas. Anfortas is the name given to the Fisher King in WOLFRAM VON ESCHENBACH's *Parzival*, one of King Arthur's knights.

Parzival first meets Anfortas fishing in a boat and is invited to the king's castle (Book 5). When they dine in the Great Hall, Anfortas is carried in. A squire appears carrying a lance with blood dripping from the point and running down the shaft. The Queen appears later, carrying the Grail, a flat stone which is placed before Anfortas and which magically provides all the food and drink. Heeding the advice given to him earlier by Gurnemanz (GORNEMANT OF GOHORT), Parzival doesn't ask about the lance, the Grail, or Anfortas's injury.

In Book 9, TREVRIZENT, the holy hermit, tells Parzival about Anfortas' wound in the thigh. Anfortas was chosen to become Lord of the Grail, but that position required that he love no woman but instead was to love Christ and the Grail. When he broke that vow, he was struck with a poisoned lance during a joust with a heathen, punctured through his testicles. The point was embedded in his flesh and his wound festered. Trevrizent tried to help but even the remedies of a pelican's blood, a unicorn's ear, or dragon-wart didn't help.

Yet Anfortas is kept alive against his will and in great pain. His agonized screams reverberate throughout the castle, and his room must be continually ventilated because of the stench. An inscription on the Grail itself tells of Anfortas' eventual healing by Parzival, who finally asks a question and Anfortas is healed with the Lord's help. Parzival is selected to be the new Lord of the Grail.

Sources: A. Hatto (WVE:P); E. H. Zeydel (PWVE).

Angles. Entry 449 in *The Anglo-Saxon Chronicle* provides the basic information of the barbaric influx into Britain during the era of the fifth century. One segment states,

These men came from three nations of Germany: from the Old SAXONS, from the ANGLES, from the JUTES. From the Jutes came the people of Kent and the people of the Isle of Wight, that is the race which now dwells in the isle of Wight, and the race among the West Saxons which is still called the race of the Jutes. From the Old Saxons came the East Saxons and the South Saxons and West Saxons. From Angel, which has stood waste ever since between the Jutes and the Saxons, came the East Angles, Middle Angles, Mercians, and all the Northumbrians.

Prior to this, in Entry 443 of the *Chronicle*, the reader is informed that the Britons made an appeal to the Angles to join forces with them and fight against the northern Picts. This entry, although there is a three-year discrepancy from 443 to 446, also refers to a letter of appeal the Britons addressed to AËTIUS as described in the manuscript of GILDAS BADONICUS for the year of 446.

The entry of 449 specifies the two major Anglian chieftains solicited by the Britons: HENGIST and HORSA. Entries 455 and 457 then relate that Hengist and Horsa treacherously fight *against* the Briton king VORTIGERN.

These are indispensable pieces of information to consider because of the effect on Arthurian history and legend. Hengist, Horsa, and OCTHA are the primary enemies of the Britons and the Welsh in the 450s. Gildas Badonicus refers to Hengist's clan as the "sacrilegious easterners."

These barbaric chieftains, thence, settle in East Anglia, not in southeastern Kent. Unfortunately, the heading of this section in the Gildas manuscript was added by later translators who incorrectly labeled the segment as "The Coming of the Saxons" instead of "The Coming of the Anglians." The Anglians (later termed the English) and the Britons (accurately the Welsh) were separated by the Cornovii territory, which the Romans militarily occupied until 410, when the withdrawal of Roman troops began.

There is one other distinction which must be made about the Angles. The Angles of East Anglia had been settled in Britain for at least a generation — perhaps two — prior to the middle of the fifth century. Those Anglians became known as the English Saxons. When NENNIUS writes about the campaigns of Arthur against Hengist and Octha, he specifically describes the Battle of Mount Badon, in which the Welsh were victorious: "[After their defeat] the English sought help from Germany, and continually and considerably increased their numbers, and they brought over their kings from Germany to rule over them in Britain, until the time when Ida reigned, who was the son of Eobba. He was the first king in Berneich." Stated differently, after that defeat, the English "Saxons" recruited help from their kinsmen, the German "Saxons" across the Channel. These German Anglians began inhabiting and settling in the territory listed in *The Anglo Saxon Chronicle*: Mercia and Northumbria, Lindsey, Deira and Bernicia.

Sources: G.N. Garmonsway (ASC); J. Morris (BH); L. Sherley-Price (BEDE: HEC&P).

Anglians are King Arthur's generic enemies. When GILDAS BADONICUS uses the broad Latin term *Saxones*, he is including Saxons, Anglians, Jutes, and Frisians, but connotatively the context of his manuscript identifies the Anglians, referring to the SACRILEGIOUS EASTERNERS (*orientali sacrilegorum*) settled in East Anglia. Gildas stresses that external wars in Britain have ceased but the civil ones continue. The explicit enemies he is referring to are the English *SAXONES* who have been settled on the island, not the GERMAN *SAXONES* who sometimes invade from across the Channel.

BEDE becomes even more specific, identifying the enemy as the Angles, those who came from the country known as "Angulus, which lies between the provinces of the Jutes and Saxons and is said to remain unpopulated to this day — are descended the East and Middle Angles, the Mercians, all the Northumbrian stock (that is, those peoples living north of the river Humber), and the other English peoples. Their first chieftains are said to have been the brothers Hengist and Horsa." It was not long before such hordes of these alien peoples vied together to crowd into the island that the natives who had invited them began to live in terror.

Based upon this information, the entries from Year 449 to Year 560 in *The Anglo-Saxon Chronicle*— and its Genealogical Preface — are crucial sources for identifying Arthur's prime enemies. Bede echoes Gildas Badonicus, but NENNIUS and GEOFFREY OF MONMOUTH add significant details about the enemy. Nennius explains that the English (i.e., the Angles) "increased their numbers and grew in Britain." He also writes that the English were defeated in some of the campaigns which sometimes favored the Britons and sometimes the English. The English sought help from Germany (the German "Saxons") and "considerably increased their numbers, and they brought over their kings from Germany to rule over them in Britain."

Monmouth completes the story, becoming very specific about HENGIST, HORSA, RENWEIN, OCTHA, and scores of others opposed to ARTHUR. Likewise, oral tradition supports what these early antiquarians recorded.

Sources: J. Gantz (TM); L. Sherley-Price (BEDE: HEC&P); J. Morris (HB); L. Thorpe (GM: HKB); M. Winterbottom (G: ROB& OW).

Anguish. *see* AGWISANCE.

Anna. In Geoffrey of Monmouth's work, Anna is identified as Arthur's sister, the first-born child of Utherpendragon and Ygerna:

> Utherpendragon set out and made his way towards his own army, abandoning his disguise as GORLOIS and becoming Utherpendragon once more. When he learned all that had happened, he mourned for the death of Gorlois; but he was happy, all the same, that YGERNA was freed from her marital obligations. He returned to Tintagel Castle, captured and seized Ygerna at the same time, she being what he really wanted. From that day on they lived together as equals, united by their great love for each other; and they had a son and a daughter. The boy was called Arthur and the girl Anna.

Geoffrey's portrayal of Anna then becomes a comedy of errors. One page later, Geoffrey states that Anna marries LOTH OF LODONESIA. As the days lengthened into years, the Saxons came back to Britain with an army so huge that the men could not be counted. Utherpendragon (UTERPENDRAGON) put the British army under the command of Loth of Lodonesia, who was rewarded by the king by giving the general his daughter Anna in marriage.

Several episodes later, Geoffrey writes that Anna is married to King BUDICIUS of Brittany, and had a son by him named Hoel I: "Arthur dispatched messengers to King Hoel in Brittany to explain that a great disaster had befallen Great Britain. This Hoel was the son of Arthur's sister; and his father was Budicus, King of Armorican Britons." Several pages later Geoffrey explains, "Arthur was determined to grant his allies their hereditary right. He returned the kingships of the Scots to Auguselus; to Urian, the brother of Auguselus, he gave back the honour of ruling over the men of Moray; and Loth, who in the days of Aurelius Ambrosius had married Aurelius's sister and had two sons by her, Gawain and Mordred."

In one instance, therefore, HOEL would be Arthur's nephew, but in the other, Loth is first married to Anna (Arthur's sister), followed by a claim that Loth is married to Aurelius's sister and they have two sons, GAWAIN and MORDRED. If Geoffrey mistakenly wrote "Aurelius's sister" for "Arthur's sister," then Gawain and Mordred would be Arthur's nephews. There's also a twist that in some Arthurian stories Mordred is Arthur's nephew, but in others Mordred is Arthur's son by an incestuous relationship between Arthur and Morgana.

Source: L. Thorpe (GM: HKB).

Anonym. A specialty term which applies to King Arthur, indicating that ARTHUR is an epithet referring to an anonymous person, in this instance AMBROSIUS AURELIANUS.

Source: F. Reno (HKA).

Antanor. In Chrétien de Troyes' *Perceval*, KAY throws an unnamed dwarf into the fire because the midget empathizes with Perceval. However, in Wolfram von Eschenbach's *Parzival*, the dwarf's name is Antanor.

Sources: R. Cline (P: SG); A. Hatto (WVE:P).

Anthemius. Anthemius is linked to Arthuriana through RIOTHAMUS, a Briton king from across Ocean who allegedly is either King ARTHUR of the fifth century or AMBROSIUS AURELIANUS. LEO I, who ruled over the united Eastern and Western Roman Empire for nearly two years, appointed Anthemius as Emperor of the West in an attempt to quell the insurrections threatening the East in Africa and the West in Gaul. The newly-appointed patrician, son-in-law of the former Eastern emperor Marcian, was caught up in deceit, trickery, and treachery throughout his short reign from 467 to his murder in 472.

One year prior to Anthemius's instatement as Emperor of the West, EURIC had become king of the Visigoths and foresaw an opportunity to seize Gaul. By giving command of his contingency to Marcellinus in Gaul, Anthemius alienated Ricimer, who plotted against him, thus weakening the emperor's position and strengthening the Gothic's power. Euric seized Arles, raided along the Rhone, and then turned his attention to Berry, the heartland of the Gallic empire.

Anthemius tried to stem the waves of insurrection, but he was overwhelmed by the Visigoths and Saxons, plus the treachery of the Franks. JORDANES writes about Anthemius making a plea to the Brittones for aid and obtaining an army commanded by Riotimus (Riothamus), who was received in the vicinity of Berry. But Riotimus was overwhelmed and before Roman allies could come to his rescue, Euric routed Riotimus and destroyed a large part of the Briton army. Riotimus fled with survivors into Burgundy.

After that resounding defeat, in 472 Ricimer besieged Rome to overthrow Anthemius and raise Olybrius to the throne. Anthemius attempted to escape by disguising himself and hiding among the peasants, but he was discovered and beheaded. Anthemius became known as the last true Western Roman emperor.

Sources: G. Ashe (DKA); E. Brehaut (GT: HOF); A. Ferrill (FOTRE); C. Littleton/L. Malcor (FSTC); C. Mierow (J: O&DG); F. Reno (HKA/HFAE); C. Snyder (AAOT).

Arcturus. It is surprising that "Arcturus" as a root for King Arthur is suggested by so many authors interested in the King Arthur's historicity; a quick survey yields at least a dozen modern researchers who suggest that possibility. Two independent historians, who have no ulterior motive attempting to verify Arthur's historic origins, are E.K. Chambers and R.G. Collingwood. Others have devoted their efforts attempting to clarify or somehow explain why the name of Arthur was bypassed in early insular manuscripts.

Collingwood devotes his last chapter, 19, to Britain during the fifth century, which, of course, demands some kind of comment about King Arthur. Citing the *Historia Brittonum* as the oldest stratum to record the name Arthur, Collingwood then mentions that, if Gildas alludes to Arthur obliquely, then one has to focus upon someone nicknamed The Bear, Ursus. On the grounds of possibility, Arthur's names may have been twisted through the Celtic *artos*, bear. The Cambridge thirteenth-century manuscript of Nennius glosses the passage of the *Historia* by observing that "Artur, translated into Latin, means *ursus horribilis.*" The key word is "bear" because of its link with "*arth-.*"

Chambers spends much more time on Arthur as a mythical or cultural hero, but inevitably, Arthur's name is connected with "god," "bear," or the Cornish word *aruthr*, or the Greek/Latin Arcturus. He also tersely suggests its derivative from LUCIUS ARTORIUS CASTUS, but adds, "It is a rather fantastic notion that an expedition of this Artorius to Armorica was the germ of Arthur's fabulous continental empire." Yet there is line of association suggesting perhaps that Castus is the individual who gave rise to the battlelist in the *Historia Brittonum*.

After this slight detour, Chambers cites several researchers who conjecture that Arthur's name is a doublet of a divine Uthyr Ben, due to a confusion between the Welsh *uthr*, "cruel," and a variant form of *aruthr*. Further on, he goes into great detail about Professor Rhys's label of "Culture Hero" for Arthur.

In his book *King of the Celts*, Jean Markale remarks that "most scholars agree that Arthur's name comes from the Latin Artorius, based on the derivation from Lucius Artorius Castus," but then adds that this is a simplistic way of looking at the origin of Arthur's name, claiming that the name Arthur can be traced back to other, equally convincing etymological manuscripts. He cites the name Arcturus as a more likely candidate than Artorius, since Arctus is associated with the Great Bear and Little Bear.

Gwyn Williams (*Excalibur: The Search for Arthur*) offers a rationalization that the king's name was sometimes written as Arcturus, the star in the constellation which never falls below the horizon. This, he surmises, could imply that "Arthur was a man of bear-like quality — Arthur the Terrible known to later Welsh writing."

Richard Barber follows a similar track in his book *King Arthur: Hero and Legend*. In writing about a particular monk, that monk cited a tale "about some Arthur (Arcturus)." He also points out that Ben Johnson's *Prince Henry's Barriers* claims Arthur appears in the guise of the star Arcturus.

In *Journey to Avalon* Chris Barber and David Pykitt express these their contention effectively. They write, "In the Welsh language Arth Fawr means the 'Great Bear' and in ancient times this was the name given to the polar god who symbolised all the forces which come to us from the region of the seven main stars of the constellation called Ursa Major, which is Latin for Great Bear. The word Arctus comes from the two celestial constellations which are commonly called Ursa Major and Minor, and Arcturus is a star near the tail of the Great Bear. Accordingly, Arcturus seems a more likely Latin root for Arthur than Artorius for it dates back to pre–Roman times and is derived from the early Celtic form — Artorix meaning 'Bear King.'"

See also LUCIUS ARTORIUS CASTUS and CERNE ABBAS for differing and interesting points of view and contrasts.

Sources: C. Barber/D. Pykitt (JTA); R. Barber (KA:H&L); E. Chambers (AOB); R. Collingwood (RB&ES); J. Markale (KA: KOK/KOTC); G. Williams (E: SFA).

Arnive is Wolfram von Eschenbach's equivalent of Igerna (Ygerna) in the Arthurian tales. In Book 4 of *Parzival*, she is identified as being married to Uterpandragun.

See also WOLFRAM VON ESCHENBACH.

Arthur (Historic). It is imperative at the onset to clearly state that there is *not* convincing proof of a historical figure named King Arthur who existed in Britain during the fifth century, four hundred years prior to an extract recording the name "Arthur" by NENNIUS, and eight hundred years prior to GEOFFREY OF MONMOUTH's segment on "Arthur of Britain." The only other extant hallmarks of British history — the *De Excidio*

penned by Gildas in the sixth century and *A History of the English Church and People* penned by Bede in the eighth century — make no mention whatsoever of Arthur. How Arthur emerged as a heroic King of Britain during the fifth century is mired in a morass of circumstances, obscuring historical reality because so much documentation has been lost over the centuries. Lacking those resources, researchers and historians must rely mainly on oral tradition and possibility. To date, archaeology has provided geographic and chronological hints and clues about Arthur's alleged milieu or particular era, but nothing confirms King Arthur's historic Briton persona.

The *Historia Brittonum*, ascribed to Nennius, is the earliest written record of a British hero named Arthur. In §56 — which was titled "The Campaigns of Arthur" at a much later date — claims that Arthur fought against HENGIST, HORSA, and OCTHA, these latter three figures who are also recorded in *The Anglo-Saxon Chronicle*. A list of twelve battles follow, naming sites which some modern scholars have identified with archaeological and historical assurance. The section ends in praise of Arthur's victory, but the English *Saxones* seek more help from German *Saxones* across Ocean to increase their numbers in Britain.

Arthur's name appears one more time in the *Historia Brittonum,* §73, a section which, like §56, acquired a later title, "Wonders of Britain," a marvel having to do with Arthur's dog and its paw-print. There is no other information about Arthur.

It is Section 56 which provides some astounding revelations. In *Arthur's Britain,* Leslie Alcock doesn't pretend to have ironclad answers, but he cautions serious scholars, researchers, and historians that "the difficulties of distinguishing between authentic and interpolated material form one of the major cruxes of Arthurian scholarship." This leads Alcock to his admonishment that "consequently the major task of research consists in looking at the existing texts in new ways."

It is vital to peruse §56 in its commonly translated style in order to show how mundane the passage appears to the casual reader:

~~THE CAMPAIGNS OF ARTHUR~~

At that time the English increased their numbers and grew in Britain. On Hengist's death, his son Octha came down from the north of Britain to the kingdom of the Kentishmen, and from him are sprung the kings of the Kentishmen. Then Arthur fought against them in those days, together with the kings of the British but he was their *dux bellorum* (leader in battle).

However, Alcock points out how the format appears in the original version of *British Historical Miscellany* (folio 187A). First, the title "The Campaigns of Arthur" must be stricken (as above), because it was a much later addition, in the 1800s. In English, the extant *British Historical Miscellany* is structured in this manner:

> I n those times the English increased their numbers and grew in Britain. On Hengist's death, his son Octha came down from the north of Britain to the kingdom of the Kentishmen, and from him are sprung the kings of the Kentishmen.
>
> T hen Arthur fought against them in those days, together with the kings of the British, but he was their leader in battle, the dux bellorum. The first battle was at the mouth of the river called Glein. The second, third, fourth, and fifth were on another river....

Ancient Roman manuscripts did not, of course, use capitals or punctuation, but what this designates, according to Leslie Alcock, is that there is a space prior to a lower-case "n," and another space in front of "unc" which were intended to contain respectively a red drop-cap letter "I" and a red drop-cap letter "T" to be inserted by an enlumineur.

Using modern script, with the addition of "enluminated letters" the passages should have appeared in this format:

> I n illo tempore Saxones invalescebant in multitudine et crescebant in Britannia. Mortuo autem Hengisto, Octha, filius ejus, transivit de sinistrali parte Britanniae ad regnum Cantorum, et de ipso orti sunt reges Cantorum.
>
> T unc Arthur pugnabat contra illos in illis diebus cum regibus Brittonum sed ipse dux erat bellorum. Primum bellum fuit in ostium fluminis quod dicitur Glein. Secundum, et tertium, et quartum, et quintum super

aliud flumen quod dicitur Dubglas, et est in regione Linnius.

Alcock writes about the first segment, "It even might be argued that there is no definite reference to the Saxons in general." Of the second segment on pages 59–60, he surmises, "We have seen that the phrase 'Tunc Arthur pugnabat' begins a new section of the *British Historical Miscellany* with its own colored initial. The implication is that *the information about Arthur is separate from that relating to Hengist and the Kentish kings* [italics added]. A separate source is inevitably implied if the list of Arthur's battles is based upon a Welsh poem, for it is unconceivable that it would have contained information about Kent."

The twelve battles are then listed: the first at the mouth of the river Glein; the second, third, fourth, and fifth on the river Dubglas; the sixth on the river called Bassas; the seventh in Celyddon Forest; the eighth in Guinnion fort; the ninth in the city of legion; the tenth on the bank of the river Tryfrwyd; the eleventh on the hill called Agned; and the twelfth on Baddon Hill.

Because Alcock was focused upon an array of other aspects, he overlooked the impact of this new information. For those who ascribe to a Briton King Arthur, the above emendation nullifies the only vestigial possibility of Arthur flourishing during the fifth century. Relying on other sources — a different section of the *Historia Brittonum*, *The Anglo-Saxon Chronicle*, and Bede's *History of the English* — Hengist and his clan are indeed of the fifth century. But the only other king of that era recorded by Nennius is Ambrosius Aurelianus, noted in Sections 31, 40, 42, 48, and 66. Ambrosius fits neatly into the same era as Hengist and his clan, but Arthur disappears.

In a paper this author presented at the University of California Davis during a Western States Folklore Society conference in April 2008, the ramifications that Alcock's "discovery" had on fifth-century British history was proffered. If indeed Hengist and his clan are of a different era from Arthur, a reader must envision a totally new perspective of personages, milieu, events, and outcome; the modifications profoundly change everything.

To simplify the nuances of those modifications, a comparative list gives the basics:

Data from the Historia Brittonum	*Modification*
Vortigern is referred to as the King of Britain.	Vortigern is overlord of a small kingdom in Wales.
§31, 36, and 43 are labeled "The Kentish Chronicles."	"The Welsh Chronicles" is more accurately limiting.
§44 Vortimer, Vortigern's son, fights a battle against Hengist and Octha at the Inscribed Stone on the shore of the Gallic Sea.	According to Alcock, there are 140 inscribed stones, mainly in Wales, but there are *none* in southwestern Britain near Kent.
§58 is titled "The Genealogy of the Kings of Kent."	The title should be emended to "The Genealogy of the Kings of East Anglia.
An Arthur never confronts Vortigern.	In §40, 41, and 42, it is Ambrosius who confronts Vortigern at Dinas Emyrs in Wales.

Because Geoffrey of Monmouth borrowed so heavily from the *Historia Brittonum*, a similar list is needed to point out his discrepancies. His book is called a "history," but controversy about its historicity and authenticity continues to rage more than 900 years after its inception.

There are two other emendations in Section 56, one which doesn't cause controversy, and the second which does. The first is a consensus among researchers that the segment which reads "On Hengist's death, his son Octha came down from the north." That segment should be changed to "On *Horsa's* death, Hengist's son Octha came down from the north." The *Historia Brittonum* contradicts itself, for in Section 44,

the reader is informed that the second battle which Vortimer (Vortigern's son) fought was at Rhyd yr Afael, and "there fell Horsa and Vortigern's other son Cateyrn," not Hengist. Two other ancient sources claim Horsa is killed. The first is Bede's *History*, which states Horsa was subsequently killed in battle against the Britons. The second is *The Anglo-Saxon Chronicle*, in which Entry 455 states, Horsa was slain at Agaelesthrep.

The second emendation focuses upon Hengist and his clan being "Kentishmen." Bede, on page 56, identifies Hengist and his tribe as Angle. Maps of early Britain label those territories as Mercia and East Anglia. Enigmatically, after

Data from Monmouth's HKB	*Modification*
Arthur is the son of Utherpendragon and nephew of Aurelius Ambrosius.	Because there is no proof of Arthur in the fifth century, and because Utherpendragon is an epithet and not historically verifiable, Ambrosius is the only historical individual listed in the extant manuscripts of that era.
Constantine is found in Roman histories of the fourth century, and Constantine the Usurper is recorded in British and Roman histories but neither is associated with Arthur.	The first Constantine died in the 300s and Constantine the Usurper was beheaded in 411. The only Constantian in the fifth century was Flavius Constantius III, who became co-emperor in the 400s.
The mysterious Constantine marries an unnamed Celtic queen.	Historically, Constantius III disappears from Roman history for a three-year period from 417 to 420 at the same time that a *comes Brittaniarum* (i.e., Constantius III) is sent to Britain.
Constantine's son (Utherpendragon) takes a concubine named Ygerna and has two children, Anna and Arthur.	In his confrontation with Vortigern, Ambrosius Aurelianus reveals that his father (i.e., Constantius III) is a *consulibus* who "wears the purple," a sign of royalty.
The enigmatic Arthur becomes the king of Britain.	Ambrosius Aurelianus becomes the "great king of all the kings of Britain."

Bede identifies the clan as Anglian, he writes that Horsa was buried in east Kent, which was *Saxon* territory, not Anglian. Gildas Badonicus (who doesn't mention Arthur) writes that enemies fighting the Britons on Baddon Hill were the *orientali sacrilegorum*— the impious easterners. Those easterners (Hengist's clan) are the inhabitants from East Anglia.

These addenda were written in 1972, twenty-two years prior to the publication of Doctors Littleton and Malcor's *From Scythia to Camelot*, a book which provides comprehensive evidence that Lucius Artorius Castus — who served in Britain as *dux bellorum* along Hadrian's Wall — is the historic Arthur of the second century recorded by Aneirin at the beginning of the sixth century. That text and Dr. Malcor's two articles published in *The Heroic Age* establish a reliable case that a Briton Arthur — not a king — points archaeologically and historically to Lucius Artorius of the second century.

William Skene unknowingly — almost prophetically — points in that direction. Writing about "The True Place of the Poems in Welsh Literature," he observes, "It is very remarkable how few of these poems contain any notice of Arthur. If they occupied a place, as is supposed, in Welsh literature, subsequent to the introduction of the Arthurian romance, we should expect these poems to be saturated with him and his knights, and his adventures, but it is not so. Out of so large a body of poems, there are only five which mention him at all, and then it is the historical Arthur, the Guledig, to whom the defence of the wall was entrusted, and who fights the twelve battles in the north and finally perishes at Camlan."

Arthur evaporates from history. Particularly surprising is that the locus for Lucius Artorius Castus was "in the north" at Hadrian's Wall, with his headquarters at Eburacum. Littleton and Malcor trace his movements, which in most instances match the battlelist supplied in the *Historia Brittonum*. Skene makes two errant comments: the Battle of Badon is not attributable to Artorius Castus, and the strife at Camlan doesn't account for Castus's death.

See the entry LUCIUS ARTORIUS CASTUS for more detail.

Sources: L. Alcock (AB); C. Littleton/L. Malcor (FSTC); J. Morris (BH); F. Reno's Two Papers "Ambrosius, Ambrosius, Wherefore Art Thou Not Arthur?" And "Emending Fifth-Century British History"; W. Skene (FABW); J. Stevenson (N: HB).

Arthur (Legendary/Euhemeristic). Whereby the historic Arthur is categorized in two eras — LUCIUS ARTORIUS CASTUS of the second century and a "pseudonymous Arthur" of the fifth century — the legendary or traditional Arthur is clustered in the eleventh and twelfth centuries. Although the name Arthur appears in ANEIRIN's *Y Gododdin* of the early 600s, the name is but a reference to earlier time; in this particular case, Aneirin's poem claims that although an important Celtic hero named Gwawrddur killed a great many enemies in battle, "he was no Arthur." Taking into account the date of this poem, the most logical deduction is that this allusion to Arthur must be a reference to Lucius Artorius Castus, the only known prior hero of eminence bearing the name Arthur.

The same condition can apply to the Arthur included in the *Historia Brittonum*. As listed in the entry ARTHUR (HISTORIC) of this text, all the rationale listed by William Skene points to Lucius Artorius Castus: this Arthur fought in the north, his arena of warfare was along Hadrian's Wall, and his headquarters were in Eburacum, according to the best evidence uncovered to date.

After the turn of the millennium, GEOFFREY OF MONMOUTH's *History of the Kings of Britain* made its debut in the mid-twelfth century, and has since been branded with a nonsense-term of "pseudo-history" by a number of scholars, apparently because the scribe he claimed he copied from — the notorious *liber vetustissimus*— has never been identified. Admittedly, numerous "historical" details which he writes of are inaccurate, but a gentler accusation would be that either the copyists or his interpretations were erroneous, not that he added creative scenarios to deliberately dupe his readers. Without Monmouth's history, the figure of a historic King Arthur during the fifth or sixth century disintegrates.

Monmouth has become the bridge between a historic era for Arthur and a profusion of romances, legends, folktales, and other oral traditions. In his chapter "The Coming of Arthur," Charles Squire writes that Arthur's sudden rise into prominence has created many problems in Celtic mythology, since Arthur is not mentioned in any of "The Four Branches of the Mabinogi" and the earliest references to him in Welsh literature "treat him as merely a warrior-chieftain." *The Red Book of Hergest*, which scholars claim was written between 1382 and 1410, contains two tales about Arthur, "Culhwch and Olwen" and "The Dream of Rhonabwy," but "The White Book of Rhydderch" penned in 1325 includes only the Culhwch material but not the Rhonabwy tale.

Squire explains, "The most probable, and only adequate explanation, is given by Professor Rhys, who considers that the fames of two separate Arthurs have been accidentally confused, to the exceeding renown of a composite, half-real, half-mythical personage into whom the two blended."

Written in 1891 and republished in 1901, John Rhys' hypothesis varies widely from new perspectives appearing a century later. Doctors C. Scott Littleton and Linda Malcor have firmly established an Arthur of the second century, a Roman officer who was sent to Britain and stationed near Hadrian's Wall, followed by two texts — *The Historic King Arthur* and *Historic Figures of the Arthurian Era* — which theorize that Ambrosius Aurelianus of the fifth century (verified in Gildas Badonicus's *De Excidio*, in Bede's *English History*, and in Nennius's *Historia Brittonum*) has been conflated with Lucius Artorius Castus of the second century.

Sources such as *The Mabinogion*, *The Welsh Triads*, *The Lives of Saints*, and the various ancient texts of Wales contribute details about Arthur from a literary viewpoint which evolved into oral tradition, or conversely. In "Culhwch and Olwen" of *The Mabinogion*, Jeffrey Gantz indicates that "this is probably the king's [Arthur] earliest appearance in Welsh prose." He is introduced as Culhwch's first cousin, who is also of royalty (signified by a purple mantle with a red-gold apple in each corner), and he beseeches Arthur to help him win Olwen,

daughter of Chief Giant Ysbaddaden. Although Arthur plays a minor role in the story, there is a "staggering catalogue of Welsh heroes," among them a few Arthurian figures including Kei, Bedwyr, Gwenhwyvar, Drystan, and Esyllt. Osla Big Knife makes an appearance paradoxically as one of Arthur's warriors.

"The Dream of Rhonabwy," another tale in *The Mabinogion*, focuses more directly upon Arthur. Jeffrey Gantz claims that this story "may have been the last to have taken shape." He assumes that it, like the Culhwch tale, places Arthur's court in Cornwall, not Wales. In the tale itself, however, Arthur is riding from his court, and he fords the River Severn at Rhyd y Groes, hoping to be at Baddon before noon. Baddon was typically associated with Bath, and if Arthur were coming from Cornwall, there would have been no need to cross the Severn.

In this author's point of view, "The Dream of Rhonabwy" surpasses the other three branches because of its poignant allegory. Owein allegorically represents one of Arthur's foes as a "Raven," perhaps a tribal name. The two sit down together to play a game of gwyddbwyll. During the first game, a young man approached them and addressed Owein, telling him that the emperor's (Arthur's) lad and servants were harassing and molesting Owein's ravens. Owein then asks Arthur to call the young men off the ravens.

During the second game, a different young man told Owein that the emperor's pages were stabbing the ravens, killing some and wounding others. Owein asks Arthur to call of the men, but Arthur doesn't answer.

At the beginning of the third game, a handsome young page with yellow hair told Owein that the noblest ravens had been killed. Owein once again asks Arthur to control his men, but Arthur does nothing. Owein turns to the young man and orders him to "go where you see the fiercest fighting and raise the standard, and let God's will be done."

During game four, a youth with a great gold-hilted one-edged sword approached Arthur and told him that the ravens were killing the squires and pages, whereupon Arthur ordered Owein to call off his ravens, but Owein did nothing. They began playing still another game. This rider approached the emperor and told him that the ravens had killed not only his squires and pages, but also the sons of the nobles of Britain.

In the sixth game the rider angrily approaches Arthur angrily and reports that the ravens have now killed Arthur's retinue. At this point Arthur squeezes the gold men on the gwyddbwyll board until they were nothing but dust, and Owein orders one of his men to lower the banner, and when this was done, there was peace on both sides.

After the games, news comes from OSLA BIG KNIFE (Octha) asking Arthur for a truce to the end of a month and a fortnight. Arthur seeks advice from his council — among them PEREDUR, Howell, CADWR Earl of Cornwall (Cador), and GILDAS (Albanius), son of Caw — and a truce is made.

In the other tales of *The Mabinogion*, in one, "Owein, Countess of the Fountain" (a different Owein from "Rhonabwy"), Arthur plays no role, because he claims, "Men, if you would not be offended, I would like to sleep until it is time to eat. You can tell stories to each other, and Kei will fetch you a pitcher of mead and some chops." Similar to the Countess story, the Peredur tale (a parallel to Chrétien's *Perceval*) doesn't relate much about Arthur. Peredur goes to Arthur's court, and he is immediately sent away to kill a knight who had slighted GWENHWYVAR. After his easy kill, he returns to court and is knighted by Arthur. Peredur departs once more to pursue his quests, sending each defeated knight to return to Arthur's court to beg forgiveness and absolution. The last branch is about Gereint and Enid. Comparable to Chrétien's "Erec and Enide," the Welsh tale is fictional and doesn't try to appear as fact. Arthur plays more of a role, but nothing in this saga shows the king in a different light.

This text offers further entries of Arthur's dimorphic roles by HENRY OF HUNTINGDON and WILLIAM OF MALMESBURY in the eleventh century, through CHRÉTIEN DE TROYES and WOLFRAM VON ESCHENBACH of the twelfth century, and to RANULF HIGDEN and JOHN OF GLASTONBURY in the fourteenth century, then culminates with THOMAS MALORY's classic in the fifteenth century.

As relayed by J. Armitage Robinson, who was using an untainted version of the *De Antiquitate*, William of Malmesbury claims to have seen a very ancient charter reporting that a king of Dumnonia (whose name was illegible) granted the Isle of Yneswitrin to the Old Church (Glastonbury). Linking Glastonbury Abbey to Yneswitrin is listed in the Grail manuscripts, but William of Malmesbury's uninterpolated manuscript of the *De Antiquitate* does not make the assertion which links the two. William references GAWAIN as Walwen and writes, "Walwen deservedly shared his uncle's fame, for they averted the ruin of their country for many years. But the tomb of Arthur is nowhere to be seen, for which reason the dirges of old relate that he is to come again."

This passage is of vital importance because it leaves no doubt that King Arthur's Avalon is not a synonym for Glastonbury. It was ADAM OF DOMERHAM who knowingly helped perpetrate the fraud that Arthur was buried at Glastonbury (i.e., Isle of Yneswitrin), and it was John of Glastonbury who passed on that information, which was then assumed as truth when GIRALDUS CAMBRENSIS wrote of Arthur's exhumation.

According to John Scott, the interpolations added to William's *De Antiquitate* are distinguishable from Monmouth's original because of different pens used by the scribes, simplistic grammatical structure which contrasted to Malmesbury's more complex use, and the poor Latinity added by the monks. Scott is confident about the interpolations when he writes, "It can be discerned easily that at least two different monks were involved."

J. M. Coles and B. J. Orme, in addition to Arthur Bulleid and General Pitt-Rivers, have determined conclusively that as far back as 2,500 B.C.E., Glastonbury and several other sites were islands in a bog, and even in present times, "the Levels still flood when the winter rains choke the river systems" (Coles and Orme, *Prehistory of the Somerset Levels*, page 64).

At this point, the curiosity is: "What does archaeology and the prehistory of the Somerset Levels have to do with the legendary Arthur?" Layamon offered a clue when he wrote that there was great sorrow at Arthur's departure to the Isle of Avalon with the fairest of fays. When Arthur would be "needed, he would come again." Glastonbury becomes one of the pivotal points of Arthur's milieu in Britain. Arthur's Avalon be-

Glastonbury Tor (foreground) and Chalice Hill (background) were at one time an island, similar to neighboring Nyland, Godney, Chedzoy, and Pitney. The terms King Arthur's Avalon and Ynis Witrin, however, were not synonyms for Glastonbury. That connection was not made until William of Malmesbury's manuscript was subjected to heinous interpolation by Glastonbury monks to benefit the abbey with money and pilgrimages. There is no evidence of a fifth-century King Arthur who was a benefactor to Glastonbury or who was buried there.

comes synonymous with Glastonbury because it was indeed at one time an "island."

Now that Glastonbury was claimed as an island where Arthur went when he was wounded in the battle against Mordred, where else but here would he be buried? Neil Fairbain claims that there are sixteen sites in southern England claiming Arthur as a "favorite son."

Since Arthur's gravesite was now attracting a great number of pilgrims who came to the abbey to mourn the loss of Arthur, there surely should be some attraction which would lure even more people to visit to the renowned abbey. Arthur wore an emblem of the Virgin Mary and Babe on his shoulder (perhaps shield?), so which historical religious figure would be most likely to draw huge crowds?

A close neighbor of Glastonbury is a village called South Cadbury, which became famous because of a hillfort descriptively acquiring the name Camelot by John Leland in the 1500s. He wrote, "At the very south ende of the chirch of South-Cadbyri standith Camallate, sumtyme a famose toun or castelle, apon a very torre or hille, wunderfully enstrengtheid of nature." The name Camelot was actually used first by Chretién de Troyes, perhaps evolving from two sites known as Camelodunum in ancient Roman maps, now known as Colchester and Huddersfield.

Other sites wanted to join in the melee, and succeeded. In his search, Fairbain also toured fifteen sites in Brittany, more than thirty sites in Scotland and northern England, an amazing fifty-four sites in Wales, and four dozen Arthurian sites in the southwestern peninsula. A huge attraction is, of course, Tintagel.

SITE OF THE ANCIENT GRAVEYARD
WHERE IN 1191 THE MONKS DUG
TO FIND THE TOMBS OF
ARTHUR AND GUINEVERE

Giraldus Cambrensis continued the Arthurian legend when he allegedly claimed he viewed the exhumation of Arthur's grave. Giraldus, however, did not view the exhumation, but simply copied the details from a different source. Glastonbury Tor is in the background, with St. Michael's tower to the upper left. Photograph taken with permission of the Custodian, Glastonbury Abbey.

When Gorlois the Duke of Cornwall tried to shield his Duchess Ygraine from Utherpendragon, the Duke was positive that no one would be able to enter his fortress at Tintagel. While he fought Utherpendragon's forces at Tregeare Rounds (Dimiloc), Utherpendragon was sneakily seducing Ygraine.

Arthur's Round Table has no singular locale. The only actual table that was an alleged meeting place where Arthur and his knights congregated was one which now hangs in the Great Hall near the cathedral at Winchester. The Round Table was first recorded by WACE in his manuscript *Roman de Brut* in 1155. However, recently Martin Biddle, in his book *King Arthur's Round Table*, indicates that investigation shows that the table hanging in the Great Hall was constructed in the 14th century, made of oak, eighteen feet in diameter, and weighing 1.2 tons. It was repainted in its present form for King Henry VIII "to reinforce his claim to a British imperium."

Those believers of an Arthur of the fifth century scoff at the probability of an actual table for all of Arthur's knights, but there are some who

SITE OF KING ARTHUR'S TOMB.
IN THE YEAR 1191 THE BODIES OF
KING ARTHUR AND HIS QUEEN WERE
SAID TO HAVE BEEN FOUND ON THE
SOUTH SIDE OF THE LADY CHAPEL.
ON 19TH APRIL 1278 THEIR REMAINS WERE
REMOVED IN THE PRESENCE OF
KING EDWARD I AND QUEEN ELEANOR
TO A BLACK MARBLE TOMB ON THIS SITE.
THIS TOMB SURVIVED UNTIL THE
DISSOLUTION OF THE ABBEY IN 1539

Arthur's second burial site in front of the high altar. There is no written information about the condition of Arthur's or Guinevere's remains in the years between 1191 and 1278. King Edward and Queen Eleanor might not have even seen the contents of the "casket." After 1539, only the cross was allegedly seen by John Leland, who said it was about a foot high. Both it and the skeletal remains disappeared thereafter. Photograph taken with permission of the Custodian, Glastonbury.

The Holy Grail was allegedly hidden in this well at Chalice Hill by Joseph of Arimathea, sparking all the romances about King Arthur and his quest for the Holy Grail.

On Wearyall Hill the hollythorn tree in the foreground is a symbol which, like the Chalice Well, links Joseph Arimathea to Arthur. The disciple supposedly planted his staff in the ground granted to him by the abbey, and from it sprang the hollythorn tree, one of two which survive in Britain. The other is on the Abbey grounds near the modern chapel.

profess the feasibility of a geographic "round table." There are two sites commonly mentioned.

One is a formation at Mayburg near Penrith at the base of the Cumbrian Mountains, dated to the third millennium BC. Geographic "round tables" make more sense, since as Wace writes, at Arthur's Round Table sat Britons, Frenchmen, Normans, Angevins, Flemings, Burgundians and Loherins.

A second geographic round table is at

The excavation at South Cadbury conducted by the Camelot Committee extended from 1966 to 1970. This group has been defunct for quite some time, but three major figures involved in the archaeological exploration were Leslie Alcock, Geoffrey Ashe, and Sir Mortimer Wheeler. After an extensive search to determine if this site was Arthur's Camelot, Alcock abandoned the venture. In a personal letter to this author on May 12, 1997, he wrote that he wanted his scholarly endeavors to focus not upon Arthur, the legendary king, but Ethelred, a historical king.

Because of this naturally formed silhouette on the cliff at Tintagel, townspeople have inherited the right to claim King Arthur as their "native son." To the locals, this is appropriately called King Arthur's Profile. Merlin's Cave is on the beach at the base, where Merlin and Uterpendragon plotted the seduction of Ygerna.

The long, narrow limestone steps would have made it perilous for enemies to try to take Tintagel by assault. Even though the arduous climb might not have deterred invaders, the fortress was still protected by a gateway. Gorlois, however, hadn't counted on the effectiveness of Merlin's magic.

Wace claimed that Arthur himself constructed the table, but others alleged that it was given to Arthur by Guinevere's father as a wedding gift. There are three things which bar the credibility of this physical relic as Arthur's historic Round Table. The first is the striking resemblance between Arthur and Henry VIII, especially because it was painted during Henry's reign to impress Charles V. The second suspicion is the table's center piece (not shown) which anachronistically bears the Tutor Rose, signifying a royal line from 1485 to 1603. The third is that the histories record nothing of this table until six and a half centuries after the historic time of King Arthur and two decades after Monmouth's work.

A formation at Mayburgh at the base of the Cumbrian Mountains, dated to the third millennium BC is one geographic round table professed to be feasible.

The second geographic "round table" is in southern Wales; during Roman times gladiators fought there.

There are several quoits which are supposedly Arthur's burial sites; one at Dorstone is impressive. According to Neil Fairbairn, it dates to 5,000 years before Arthur's time, but marks Arthur's battle with a giant. The top stone contains two depressions made by the giant as he leaned on the stone dying. A different legend narrates that the indentations were made by Arthur's knees as he prayed.

Caerleon in southern Wales. During Roman times this was actually an amphitheater where gladiators fought. It was outside the fortified walls, and would have been an excellent choice for war councils, military drills, parades, and jousts.

If all legendary material about Arthur were to be compiled, it would fill a huge library as well as a giant art gallery. Knowing that an attempt to cover the vast scope of legendary Arthuriana is folly, only four more aspects will be touched upon — two of several Arthurian-related quoits (or dolmens), and two claimants of where Arthur's battle of Badon occurred.

Just prior to the advent of Arthur, Geoffrey of Monmouth manufactures quite a legend of his own. Arthur's forefathers — namely Aurelius Ambrosius and Utherpendragon — lamented their comrades who had been slaughtered in the conflict. Aurelius wanted to have a monument which would stand forever as a memorial of his distinguished warriors.

The mysterious Merlin and Utherpendragon decided to steal the Giants' Ring which was located in Ireland. Many years prior the Giants had transported the huge stones from Africa. Fifteen thousand men were chosen for the task. Through Merlin's mystifying magic, he was able to steal the stones and deliver them to Aurelius at the base of Mount Ambrius. He followed the King's bidding and erected the stones in a circle precisely as they had been in Ireland.

Translator Lewis Thorpe explains in a footnote that Monmouth perhaps confused Ambrius with Avebury with Amesbury, and then "repeatedly treats Stonehenge/Avebury as if they were one place." Upon the deaths of Aurelius and Utherpendragon they were buried side-by-side inside the Giants' Ring.

Regarding Arthur's battle, the most popular

Based only upon Monmouth's narrative, some people believe that Stonehenge is the site where Arthur's father and uncle were buried.

The problem of Bath being considered as the site of Arthur's last battle is made worse because the baths, at least fifteen feet below the present city, have been renovated extensively over the centuries. To make matters worse, tourists who see the statues of Roman soldiers surrounding the baths believe they are from a much earlier era, but in fact there were erected during the Victorian era. And last, Bath was of no military significance in the fifth century.

supposition is that it was fought at Bath based on the gossamer thread that Baddon and Bath are the same.

The city of Bath was not known by that name until the 700s. During the alleged Arthurian Age in the fifth century, the area was known by the Roman term Aquae Sulis, in a sparsely settled countryside which was of no military consequence, and was known only as a spa.

The Historic King Arthur and *Historic Figures of the Arthurian Era* propose the battle of Badon was fought near Wroxeter, at a hillfort named The Wrekin, the highest hillfort in Britain. Wroxeter, in the Roman and early post–Roman period, was listed as the fourth-largest city in Britain. It had been the site of a legionary fortress, and once the Romans moved their legion to Chester-upon-Dee, Wroxeter became a *civitate*, a civil and administrative post. In the post–Roman period, Wroxeter retained its importance as the tribal center for the Cornovii tribe, which aligns with Arthur's epithet "The Boar of Cornwall."

Unlike Little Solsbury Hill, which is considered by supporters as "Mount Badon," archaeological digs have not uncovered any relics of consequence. On the other hand, The Wrekin has been extensively excavated and quite a number of artifacts have been discovered. The River Severn plays a crucial role in determining Badon's geography; whereby Aquae Sulis lies fifteen miles east of the river, the fortified walls of Wroxeter literally touched its banks. Carrying this rationale even further, the Mouth of the Severn near Aquae Sulis (later Bath) would be impossible to ford, because it is approximately four miles wide as it empties into Bridgewater Bay and eventually the Bristol Channel.

King Arthur's pervasive legends in Britain have stimulated John Rhys to write that topo-

Although Aquae Sulis — not known as Baddon (Bathon, Bath) until the seventh century — has erroneously become known as Arthur's twelfth battle site, in the fifth century it was not an important or strategic military installation. More likely the battle, attributed not to Arthur but to Ambrosius Aurelianus, would have been fought at Wroxeter near the Wrekin. There, the baths were huge, the size of an English cathedral.

graphically Britain has embedded Arthur with "no lack of Arthur's Hills, Arthur's Seats, Arthur's Quoits, and Round Tables." Enthusiasts can add to that hoof prints of Arthur's horse Llamrei, a burial site for his dog Cabal, Arthur's footprint at Tintagel, his ship named *Prydwyn*, a knife named Carnwennen, a shield named Rhongomyniad, and, of course, his sword Excalibur, which is also known as Caliburn, Caliburnus, and Caledvwlch. Arthur's court, too, has been labeled as Celliwig, Celliwic, Kelliwig, Kellicis, Kerriwig, Caerleon, Winchester, Killibury, Callington, Padstow, Kelly Rounds, and most commonly Camelot. His gravesite is difficult to identify because claims are widespread: St Davids Head, Dorstone, Preseli Mountains, Slaughter Bridge in Cornwall, and Glastonbury.

Sources: R. Bromwich (TYP/BWP); J. Gantz (TM); W. Rees (LC-BS); J. Rhys (STAL/CB); Squire (CMAL); L. Thorpe (GM: HKB).

Arthur of Dalriada. In his quest to identify the figure of Arthur, Richard Barber, writing in 1972, bypassed LUCIUS ARTORIUS CASTUS as a possibility because "to build a bridge of tradition from second-century Roman Britain to ninth-century with no other support is a daring feat of imagination, but not admissible evidence." The advent of *From Scythia to Camelot* and scholarly articles which followed in 1994, however, built a very strong case that Lucius Artorius Castus *was* the figure of Arthur.

Barber proposed that ANEIRIN, whose poem *Y Gododdin* was written around 600 and made the first reference to an "Arthur," was the son of Aedan mac Gabrain, based on the reasonable assumption that Arthur would have existed during the same time period as Aneirin. Evidence since then denies that assumption.

Sources: R. Barber (FOA); C. Littleton/L. Malcor (FSTC); F. Reno (HKA/HFAE).

Arthursus the Bear. Graham Phillips and Martin Keatman offer an interesting evolution of King Arthur's name. Quite aware that the name Arthur does not appear anywhere on record until the end of the sixth century, the co-authors theorize that "if Arthur was a form of by-name, what could it mean? The first syllable, *Arth*, from

the British language and also preserved in modern Welsh, means 'bear.' If the warrior who led the Britons in the late sixth century was called the Bear, he would not have been the only such warrior to be named after an animal, as this seems to have been a common Celtic practice of the period." Combining epithets in an attempt to unify the Britons, these co-authors claim this hero "may not only have used the Brythonic word *Arth*, but also the Latin word for bear, *Ursus*. His original title may therefore have been *Arthursus*, later being shortened to Arthur."

Indeed, it was common during this era to combine Welsh-Latin affixes. Additionally, the name which they proposed is strikingly close to the name ARCTURUS, a term quite a few scholars of the historic King Arthur suggest, independent of LUCIUS ARTORIUS CASTUS being the cognate appellation for the great king of Britain.

Source: G. Phillips/M. Keatman (KA: TS).

Arviragus, Arvirargus. Although Arvirargus (second spelling above) is seemingly a historic figure of the first century, it is questionable whether or not his name should appear in Arthuriana. However, this obscure individual has been linked to JOSEPH OF ARIMATHEA, and in turn, Joseph of Arimathea has become ingrained in King Arthur's ancestry, entering the legend of Arthur as history.

Judging by his writings, JOHN OF GLASTONBURY believed Arthur to be a historic figure, thus weaving this famed king into the history of Glastonbury Abbey, and in so doing, Joseph of Arimathea was likewise incorporated into British history and the Abbey. John of Glastonbury included the following extracts in his manuscript:

ON THE ANTIQUITY OF THE ANCIENT CHURCH OF ST MARY AT GLASTONBURY

In the thirty-first year after the Lord's Passion, twelve of the disciples of St. Phillip the apostle, among whom Joseph of Arimathea was chief, came into this land and brought Christianity to King Arviragus, although he refused it. They nevertheless obtained from him this place, with its twelve hides of land; here they constructed the first church in this kingdom, finishing the walls with wattles; in his own presence Christ dedicated this church in honour of his mother, and the ground nearby as a burial-place for his servants.

XVI: On The Lands And
Possessions Bestowed Upon The
Monastery Of Glastonbury By Various
Kings, Bishops, Dukes, And Others

At the very beginning, Arviragus, king of the Britons, although he was a pagan, gave this island, upon which the monastery is situated, to St Joseph, who buried the Lord, and to his disciples; at that time it was surrounded with forests, thickets, and marshes, and was called Ynswytryn by the natives. Later Lucius, king of the Britons, who was first among the British kings to receive holy baptism, benevolently confirmed this island's possession to Phagan and Deruvian, the cardinal monks who baptized him, when Pope Eleutherius had sent them, and to their disciples.

XVIIII

After this, St. Joseph and his son Josephes and their ten companions travelled through Britain, where King Arviragus then reigned, in the sixty-third year from the Lord's Incarnation, and they trustworthily preached the faith of Christ. But the barbarian king and his nation, when they heard doctrines so new and unusual, did not wish to exchange their ancestral traditions for better ways and refused consent to their preachings. Since, however, they had come from afar, and because of their evident modest of life, Arviragus gave them for a dwelling an island at the end of his kingdom, surrounded with forests, thickets, and swamps, which was called by the inhabitants Ynswytryn — that is "the glass island."

Geoffrey of Monmouth devotes several pages to Arvirargus, some of which is recounted in Geoffrey Ashe's book *King Arthur's Avalon*. Ashe's closing comment about Joseph of Arimathea and the account about him is: "How and why the legend grew, and when and under what circumstances, and how much truth may underlie it, are proper themes for dispassionate inquiry."

Sources: G. Ashe (KAA); J. Carley (CGA); L. Thorpe (GM: HKB).

Ataulphus, Ataulph. Although Ataulphus is not actually a figure who enters the inner circle of the historic or legendary King Arthur, his orbit is close enough to merit mention. If by default Constantius III were indeed the father of Ambrosius Aurelianus (conflated with "King Arthur") in lieu of the Constantine mentioned

by Geoffrey of Monmouth in *History of the Kings of Britain*, then Ataulphus would have had close contact with Ambrosius's/Arthur's father. Constantius III, therefore, becomes a shadow in Arthuriana particularly because of his convoluted connection to Galla Placidia and Ambrosius Aurelianus.

When Ataulphus became the leader of the Visigoths after Alaric was killed, his life became closely entwined with Roman Royalty of the fifth century because of a perilous set of circumstances created by Alaric, who had plundered Rome and taken hostages, including Emperor Honorius's half-sister (Galla Placidia) and Aëtius, the son of Gaudentius, who later became Constantius III's *contubernalis*.

There ensued a bizarre set of events over the course of the next several years. Constantius III continually negotiated for the return of the hostages but had little success. Ataulphus had been granted the abandoned hillfort at Carsac near Narbo Martius during an extended, uneasy truce. Unimpressed by promises, the Visigoth bargained for a permanent tribal city, *foederati* status, payment in gold for services, and shipments of grains, but there was no agreement and the negotiations collapsed. When Placidia and Ataulphus announced their intent to marry, Honorius was incensed, and ordered Constantius III to annihilate the Visigoths and free the hostages. Instead, the tribe, along with the hostages, fled to Hispania, where Placidia gave birth to a son, Theodosius, who mysteriously died in infancy. Shortly after his death, Ataulphus was murdered and Galla Placidia and Aëtius were returned to Rome.

Sources: E. Duckett (MPE&W); A. Ferrill (FOTRE); E. Gibbon (D&FRE); S. Oost (GPA).

Aurelius Ambrosius. The name of Aurelius Ambrosius was used by Geoffrey of Monmouth in lieu of Ambrosius Aurelianus as it appears in the manuscript of Gildas Badonicus.

According to Monmouth, Aurelius Ambrosius was one of three sons born to a certain obscure Constantine, and "a wife born of a noble family, whom Archbishop Guithelinus had himself brought up." Constans, the oldest son, was handed over to the church to join a monastic order, and both Aurelius Ambrosius and his younger brother, who later assumed the epithet Utherpendragon, were given to Guithelinus so that he would become their ward.

After Constantine died and Constans had been murdered at the behest of a usurper to the throne, Aurelius became king. Once the two brothers were grown, they came out of hiding on the continent and returned to Britain. Aurelius reclaimed the throne from the usurper VORTIGERN and began the process of expelling the Saxons from the British homeland. VORTIMER replaced his father, Vortigern, for a short while, but he was treacherously poisoned by RENWEIN, daughter of the Saxon chieftain HENGIST. Wars raged between Aurelius's army and the Saxons supported by Vortigern. When the entire Briton Council of the Elders were slaughtered by Hengist, with great determination Aurelius tried to root out the stubborn entrenched Saxons.

When his plans were foiled by Paschent, who instructed Eopa to poison Aurelius, Utherpendragon became king. GORLOIS of Cornwall was recruited to help drive off the Saxons, and success seemed to be within reach until Utherpendragon met Gorlois's beautiful queen YGERNA. With MERLIN's help, Utherpendragon claimed the queen, and two children resulted from their union, a girl named ANNA and a boy named ARTHUR, who were half-siblings to CADOR, Gorlois's son. Utherpendragon, too, was then poisoned by traitors.

Hence, it is Geoffrey of Monmouth's work which structures the foundation of Arthuriana: King Arthur is of the House of Constantine, traced through his father, Utherpendragon, to Constantine. His uncle is Aurelius Ambrosius.
Source: L. Thorpe (GM: HKB).

Aurelius Caninus is a name that distantly becomes linked with AMBROSIUS AURELIANUS and thus King ARTHUR. He is the second king castigated by GILDAS BADONICUS in the *De Excidio*. Gildas describes him as a "lion-whelp" and accuses him of parricide, fornication, and adultery. The specific transgressions which make this tyrant so noxious is that he "hates peace in our country" and has an "unjust thirst for civil war and constant plunder."

The kingdom of Aurelius is in southeastern Wales, extending slightly into what is presently part of the Midlands.

See map in the entry GILDAS BADONICUS.
Sources: A. Wade-Evans (EOE&W); M. Winterbottom (G: ROB&OW).

Avaon, Afaon. There are two individuals named Avaon in *The Mabinogion*, one in "The Dream of Maxen" and the other who is more directly associated with a historic Arthur, appearing in "The Dream of Rhonabwy." The former is identified as Avaon son of Eudav, and the latter is son of TALIESIN, the famous bard in Welsh tradition. Following is the literal description of Avaon's role from *The Mabinogion*:

> After that another troop was seen approaching the ford: from the pommels of their saddles upwards they were as white as the lily, and from that point downwards as black as jet. A rider forged ahead and spurred his horse into the ford so that the water splashed over the head of Arthur and the bishop and their advisers until they were as wet as if they had been dragged out of the river. As this rider turned his horse's head, the lad who was standing before Arthur struck the animal with the sword in its scabbard, so that it would have been a marvel if even iron had been unscathed, let alone flesh or bone. The rider drew his sword half out of its scabbard and said,
> "Why did you strike my horse — as an insult, or out of a desire to advise me?"
> "You need advice. What foolishness caused you to ride so recklessly as to splash the water of the ford over the heads of Arthur and the holy bishop and their advisers, until they were as wet as if they had been dragged from the river?"
> "I will accept that advice," said the rider, and he turned his horse and returned to his troop.
> "IDDAWG, who was that rider?" asked Rhonabwy.
> "A young man considered the wisest and most accomplished in the kingdom: Avaon son of Talyessin [Taliesin]."

In a later passage of the same story, he surprisingly appears as one of Arthur's advisors. A battle is taking place at Baddon in the valley of the Hafren, and Arthur's foe, Osla Big Knife, asks for a truce to the end of a month and a fortnight. Arthur rises and seeks out his council for advice. Avaon is one of the advisers.

Avaon son of Taliessin also appears at least three times in the Welsh Triads:

1. The three Bull-chieftains of the Island of Britain:
   a. Elinwy son of Cadegr;
   b. Cynhafal son of Argad;
   c. Afaon son of Taliesin.
   The three of them were bards.
2. Three Battle-Leaders of the Island of Britain:
   a. Selyf son of Cynan Carrwyn;
   b. Urien son of Cynfarch;
   c. Afaon son of Taliesin.
3. Three Unfortunate Assassinations of the Island of Britain:
   a. Heidyn son of Enygan, who slew Aneirin of Flowing Verse, Prince of Poets;
   b. Llawgad Trwm Bargod Eidyn ('Heavy Battle-Hand of the Border of Eiden'), who slew Afaon son of Taliesin;
   c. Llofan Law Ddifo ('Ll. Severing Hand'), who slew Urien son of Cynfarch.

Sources: R. Bromwich (TYP) J. Gantz (TM).

Beaumains. When Arthur was having his plenour feast on Pentecost (feast for everyone on the seventh Sunday after Easter commemorating the descent of the Holy Spirit on the apostles, also known as Whitsunday), there was a young man who requested three gifts from Arthur. The king gladly granted the first request, which was food and drink for a year. When Arthur asked his name and the other two gifts, the young man said he would tell only after the passage of a year. Arthur put his seneschal Kay in charge, and Kay named the young man Beaumains (Fair-hands) and made him a kitchen knave who could eat all he wanted.

When the twelvemonth was over and Whitsunday was being celebrated at Caerleon, there came a damosel who needed help to divert a tyrant from her castle. Beaumains volunteered and rode after the damosel, followed on horse by Sir Kay, who had beleaguered and belittled Beaumains during the young man's ordeal as a kitchen knave. Sir Kay demanded a joust and

Beaumains almost killed his tormenter. Launcelot (LANCELOT) also followed and Beaumains challenged him, too. They fought to a standstill, and Launcelot claimed that the young man proved himself a knight, and asked his name. Beaumains revealed himself as GARETH, brother of Sir Gawain.

Source: T. Malory (LMD'A).

Bede, Baeda (circa 673–738). Translator Leo Sherley-Price sets Bede's birth during the year 673 C.E. and his death May 25, 735 C.E., four years after completing *A History of the English Church and People,* the manuscript which is of interest because of its satellite connections to Arthuriana. Although Bede, like GILDAS BADONICUS, does not record the name of ARTHUR, there are several crucial points.

Historically, Maximus was a Spaniard who became a commander of the troops in Britain, where he pacified the Picts and the Scotti for a short while. Bede writes that Maximus "was well fitted to be an Emperor had not ambition led him to break his oath of allegiance." The British troops (not the Roman emperor) elevated Maximus to the purple because they were dissatisfied with Emperor Gratian on the mainland. Maximus amassed most of the British army, sailed to the mainland, and managed to kill Gratian at Lyons. He was caught and executed as a traitor by Theodosius of the East five years later.

Bede also confirms the historicity of CONSTANTINE— who is also commonly referred to as Flavius Claudius Constantinus or Constantine the Usurper. Bede refers to him as

> ... a common trooper of no merit, chosen as an Emperor solely on account of his auspicious name. Once he had obtained power, he crossed into Gaul, where he was hoodwinked into many worthless treaties by the barbarians and caused great harm to the commonwealth. Before long, at the orders of [Emperor of the Western Empire] Honorius, Supreme Commander Constantius III entered Gaul with an army, besieged Constantine in the city of Arles, captured him, and put him to death. His son Constans, a monk whom he had created Caesar, was also put to death by Count Gerontius in Vienne.

All the characters listed above are corroborated by Roman and British records as historic figures, but GEOFFREY OF MONMOUTH either miscopied or contrived the genealogy he structured for Constantine the Usurper and his son. This Constantine was the only Briton of the fifth century known by that name. Geoffrey also lists CONSTANS as Constantine's son, but at that point, the genealogy falls apart; Geoffrey adds two other sons, Aurelius Ambrosius and Utherpendragon, the latter who begets Anna and Arthur, two names not appearing in any genealogies elsewhere, but echoed in later centuries. Monmouth's Constantine might have been conflated with CONSTANTIUS III, whom Bede also mentions. R.G. Collingwood proposes an interesting probability that Constantius III is the most likely individual to be the *Comes Britanniarum* sent to Britain between the years 417 and 420, but no solid evidence has been forthcoming, only circumstantial speculation.

In his initial introduction to Bede, John Morris writes, "Before 597, Bede is a secondary writer; all the sources that he knew are extant, known to us independently; and many other texts are known which were not available to be Bede." Bede's readers "can learn nothing from his introductory chapters that they could not also learn elsewhere."

This, however, is not correct. Bede is more specific about several matters; he gives more details about the:

- migration patterns of the Saxons, the Angles, the Jutes; and the Frisians;
- older name Gewissae used for the West Saxons;
- distinction between Gewissae and Hwiccas;
- invitation from Vortigern to Hengist and his son Oeric;
- most complete and continuous history of the English;
- inception of East Anglia and Northumbria;
- Septimius Severus;
- reason for AËTIUS not sending aid to Britain;
- trips made to Britain by GERMANUS.

Nennius copied a great deal of information which was supplied by Bede. Bede presumes —

even more directly than Gildas — that Ambrosius Aurelianus was the leader responsible for the Briton victories, including the Battle of Mount Badon. It isn't until two centuries after Bede's era that Nennius associates Arthur, not Ambrosius, as the Briton leader at the siege of Badon. The nagging curiosity of what transpired to cause the discrepancy recorded about the Briton leader at the Badon conflict continues to plague modern scholars. Several hypotheses have been proposed, but no incontrovertible evidence has been forthcoming.

Neither Bede nor Gildas explains who the SAXONES specifically are or where their "dwelling" or "home" is. "*Saxones*" is a generic Latin term blanketing the SAXONS, the ANGLES, the JUTES, and the Frisians. But there is no distinction made which is the separate tribe attacking the Britons. The implication is that it is the Saxons from Chent (Kent) attacking central England, but it could also refer to the Angles attacking the Cornovii territory, which was at that time part of Wales.

Likewise, the natural assumption is that the *Saxones'* "homeland" is the continent, but that is indeed an assumption which can be very misleading. The *Saxones*, which includes the ethnic Angles, had been settled on the island and tolerated by the Romans for several generations. J.N.L. Myers addresses this problem when he writes, "It will be as well to indicate at the outset that the question, 'Where did the invaders come from?' is one which must be kept distinct from the question 'In what parts of England did they settle?' The two problems are no doubt intimately related, but any attempt to answer both at once is bound to raise more difficulties than it solves."

But Bede endeavors to clarify the issue of both questions. Later borrowed by the *Parker Chronicle*, Bede offers this explanation of the reinforcements who joined the migration to the island

> from three powerful German peoples, the Saxons, Angles, and Jutes. From the Jutes are descended the Cantuarii and the Victuarii, the people which hold the Isle of Wight and to this day is called the *Jutarum natio* in the province of the West Saxons set opposite the Isle of Wight. From the Saxons, that is from that region which is now called that of the Old Saxons, came the East Saxons, South Sax-

ons, and West Saxons. Moreover, from the Angles, that is from that country which is called Angulus, and from that time to this is believed to remain uninhabited between the provinces of the Jutes and the Saxons, are sprung the East Angles, Middle Angles, and Mercians.

Major tribes, including Angles and Saxons, migrated to (or invaded, if you will) Britain after the withdrawal of Roman troops in 410 C.E. and during the next five decades of the early medieval period. Roman military roads tend to be straight as arrows, and Thomas Codrington stresses the important legacy of these roads, which still mark the countryside two millennia later. Footsoldiers and cavalry could move at a fast pace along these well-structured thoroughfares, and they additionally mark the important sites occupied by the Roman military.

The invasions from the mainland during the fifth century were continuously raging not only on the continent, but in Britain as well. The tribes were nomadic, sometimes being forced from their homeland by both Romans and other tribes, causing original territories such as Angeln to disintegrate. By the latter half of the fifth century, the Western Roman Empire was reaching its death-throes, and the barbaric tribes had nowhere to establish what they called their "homeland." Mainlanders were spilling across the channel, and Britons were seeking refuge in Little Britain and along the western fringes of the northern shores. Emperors were being changed frequently and there was no loyalty between tribes and the empire.

The first-century writer Tacitus, second-century Ptolemy, and sixth-century Procopius record different ethnological regions on the continent, but it is well-established that by the middle of the third century the Saxons were "in full possession of the whole region between the lower Elbe and the Wesser," the Angles were "near neighbors in Scgleswig and Holstein," and the Frisians were northern neighbors of the Old Saxons. The origin of the Jutes is more obscure, but for the early-medieval period of history which is of interest here in this text, Bede's assessment is generally accurate.

Myers cautions that Bede's passage about migrations from the continent (quoted above) suggests that part of it

> was an insertion by Bede himself at a late stage in the revision of his work. For as it now stands the leadership of Hengist and Horsa is most naturally read as applying to the Angles who are discussed in the previous sentence rather than to the Saxons or Jutes. If, however, the three ethnological sentences are removed Hengist and Horsa become again the leaders of the Kentish *foederati* which Bede clearly took them to have been. His later insertion has thus broken the thread of his narrative, and confused its sense.

Myers, however, has assumed that Hengist and Horsa were indeed irrefutably part of Kentish *foederati*, a contentious proposition which is not accepted when viewing other evidence. Bede was a copyist and recorder of history whose major source was Gildas Badonicus, and Gildas unequivocally refers to the invaders as the *orientali sacrilegorum*, the impious easterners. Gildas (writing in Latin) used the generic Roman term *Saxones*, but his reference to the impious easterners is no doubt referring to those German immigrants who settled to the east of what is now Wales, in the Iceni territories which became known as East Anglia.

In Britain, the writings of Gildas Badonicus, Bede, and Nennius reflected this era. Typically, the Angles occupied the ancient territory of the Iceni, filtering westward into areas which became known as Middle Anglia and Mercia. Some of the Saxons settled in the Trinovantes territory between the Rivers Stour and Thames, denoted as the East Saxons and Middle Saxons. West Saxony is an aberration which is discussed in the entry about CERDIC.

Based upon evidence presented by Leslie Alcock in *Arthur's Britain*, there were three major *Saxones* (not Saxon) *adventi*: in 428 at the invitation of a *superbus tyrannus* to an unknown area; in 440 in circumstances wholly unknown; and to an area which Alcock calls "Kent," gleaned, no doubt from its appearance in Bede and Nennius. To fit into a workable chronology, Hengist and Horsa would have been leaders of their tribe during the last two *adventi*.

Sources: L. Alcock (AB); H. Bradley (PTOLEMY: A); H. Dewing (PROCOPIUS: HOW);

M. Hadas (HOR); M. Grant (TACITUS: AIR); J. Morris (AA); J.N.L. Myres (RB&ES); F. Reno (HKA); L. Sherley-Price (BEDE: HEC&P); M. Winterbottom (G: ROB&OW).

Bedivere, Bedevere, Bedwyn, Bedwyr, Bedour, Bediver, Baudoyer. Bedivere is known in Welsh tradition as Bedwyr, son of Pedrawd (Bedrydant). According to the *Mabinogion* tale, "How Culhwch Won Olwen," Bedwyr had a son named Amren and a daughter named Eneuawg. He was a constant companion of Kei (KAY). He goes on the quest for Olwen with CULHWCH and Arthur, and in one of the first episodes, when they meet Ysbaddaden, Olwen's giant father, he throws a poisoned stone at Arthur's men, but Bedwyr catches it, throws it back, and strikes Ysbaddaden in the kneecap.

Bedivere is described as the most handsome man at King Arthur's Round Table "save for Arthur and Drych," and "though he was one-handed no three warriors on the same field could draw blood faster than he; moreover he would make one thrust with his spear and nine counter-thrusts."

In yet another Welsh capacity, Bedwyr is recorded in the *Black Book of Carmarthen* as having fought in Arthur's tenth battle on the bank of the river called Tryfrwyd:

[The Dog-heads] fell by the hundred,
by the hundred they fell
before Bedwyr Bedrydant [of the Strong Sinews]
on the banks of Tryfrwyd
fighting with Garwlwyd.
Furious was his nature
With shield and sword.

In Geoffrey of Monmouth's *History of the Kings of Britain*— which is mirrored almost identically in the *Tysilio*— Bedwyr makes his debut as Bedevere nine years after Arthur slew Frollo and subjected all the regions of Gaul, giving Neustria (Normandy) to Bedevere, who becomes his cup-bearer. After a brief respite in Britain, Arthur leaves MORDRED to defend Britain and returns to the continent to wage war against LUCIUS HIBERIUS. During a lull in the conflict, Arthur, accompanied by Kay and Bedevere, fight and slay a giant residing at Mont Saint Michel. After that episode, at the battle of Saussy, Bedi-

vere is killed by King Boccus and is laid to rest at Bayeux.

In Thomas Malory's *Morte d'Arthur,* Bedivere assumes the role assigned to GRIFLET in an earlier work; Bedivere is the son of Corneus and brother of Lucan. Although Bedivere is rather ignored throughout most of Malory's monumental work, he and his brother become central figures in Book 21, Chapter 7, at the Battle of Camlann, which portends the end of Arthur's Golden Age. When Arthur knows he is near death, he asks Sir Bedivere to take Excalibur and cast it into the water. Bedivere departs, but cannot force himself to cast the beautiful sword into the water, so he hides it under a tree and returns to the king.

Arthur asks him what he saw upon casting the sword into the water, and Bedivere replies that he saw nothing except waves and wind. Arthur berates him, and asks him to do as he has been commanded.

Bedivere departs again, takes the sword in hand, but once again cannot throw the sword into the water. He hides the sword and returns again to Arthur's side, telling the king that he cast the sword into the water. Arthur once more asks him what he saw and Bedivere claims that he saw only the "waters wappe [lap] and the waves wanne [recede]." Arthur calls him a traitor and rebukes him for betraying him twice. Arthur, near death, chastises Bedivere and sends him away a third time.

Bedivere finally does as he was commanded, and when he throws the sword far into the water, an arm rises above the surface, catches it, brandishes it three times, and vanishes into the water. When Bedivere tells the king what he saw, Arthur asks his last surviving knight to place him in a barge. The king tells him he is going to Avilion (Avalon) to have his wounds healed. The ending of the tale is parallel to the outcome of the Griflet romance.

Sources: R. Barber (FOA); P.B. Ellis (COTC); J. Gantz (TM); T. Malory (LMD'A); P. ROBERTS (COKB); L. Thorpe (GM: HKB).

Bedwyr is a variant name for BEDIVERE in *The Mabinogion.* In "How Culhwch Won Olwen," Bedwyr, son of Pedrawd and father of Amren, is a close comrade with Kei (KAY). In the story of "Gereint and Enid," Bedwyr is only mentioned once, as a chamberlain guarding Arthur's bed, along with three other chamberlains.

Source: J. Gantz (TM).

Béroul. Béroul's era was one in which all authors associated with Arthurian material made very little or no autobiographical references to themselves, from Thomas D'Angleterre through Ralph of Coggeshall. Modern researchers can calibrate the penning of certain works, based only upon educated estimates which sometimes vary as many as three decades. Particularly during the twelfth century, generalizations about contemporary authors are sketchy at the very best.

In Béroul's case, Norris Lacy presumed that Béroul's *Tristan* romance reflected a "more primitive, noncourtly stage of the legend, whereas that of Thomas d'Angleterre integrates the work thoroughly into the current of courtly love." One can also confirm with some certainty that Béroul's other living contemporaries were William of Newburgh, Thomas d'Angleterre, Chrétien de Troyes, Giraldus Cambrensis, Layamon, and Gottfried von Strassburg. The immediate succeeding generation would have included Hartman von Aue and Wolfram von Eschenbach.

Although one might infer from Lacy's comment above that Béroul's writing slightly preceded that of Thomas D'Angleterre, in his (and Geoffrey Ashe's) *The Arthurian Handbook*, there is a clarification: "We know nothing about Béroul except that he wrote a romance of Tristan and Iseult, of which we now possess a single long fragment of some 4,500 lines, preserved in a single manuscript. Although his work ... belongs to the primitive version, it may well date from after 1190 or 1191, that is, after Thomas's work." Based upon this and other circumstances, Béroul's floruit and lifespan have been placed at a slightly later date than Thomas's in Appendix A of this text.

C. Scott Littleton and Linda Malcor echo Lacy's and Ashe's statement that "Béroul's Anglo-Norman romance *Tristran* (late 1100s) belongs to a noncourtly, primitive stage of the Tristran legend," then add a cogent addition as it applies to Arthuriana: "[T]he story of Tristan and Isolde, wife of King Mark, is not found in Celtic sources that predate the twelfth- and thirteenth-century Arthurian romances."

Jean Markale circuitously promulgates the same premise. He writes, "But Arthurian material was proving so successful that the authors of Tristan [Thomas and Béroul] showed no hesitation in artificially incorporating their tale into the Arthurian tradition.... The 13th-century prose *Tristran* links Tristan even more closely to Arthur, and by the 15th century, when Thomas Malory wrote his *Morte d'Arthur*, the Tristan legend has become an integral part of the Arthurian tradition."

Richard Barber likewise suggests that of the Arthurian stories, the TRISTRAM legend was seemingly based upon an original story by Thomas of Britain (Thomas d'Angleterre), but now "it is believed that [Thomas] shared a common lost source with Béroul, a contemporary French writer."

Béroul, therefore, becomes a key figure for modern researchers who strive to make a connection between Arthurian history and Arthurian legend. Rodney Castleden cites Béroul as placing King Mark's "lofty palace" at Lancien, and then points out that Lancien survived in Britain as Lantyan Manor, which then changed to Lantien in 1086. Castleden also indicates that "Béroul has Iseult going by a paved road to the monastery of St. Samson, to which she gave a gold-embroidered robe, converted into a chasuble and still in use in Béroul's time."

Sources: R. Barber (AA); R. Barber (KA: H&L); R. Castleden (KA: TBL); A. Fedrick (B: RT); N. Lacy (AE); N. Lacy (B: RT); N. Lacy/G. Ashe (AH); C. Littleton/L. Malcor (FSTC); J. Markale (KA: KOK); G. Mermier (B: RT: ENG-FR).

Blanchefleur. In Gottfried von Strassberg's romance of *Tristan and Isolt*, Blanchefleur is the sister of King Mark. Of all the fair maidens in Mark's court, there were none so fair as Blanchefleur, and of all the knights in Mark's service, there were none so valiant as RIVALIN. Love for the knight crept into Blanchefleur's heart, but she hid her secret until they both realized, with no words spoken, that they loved each other more and more as the days went on.

When Mark's kingdom was invaded, the king gathered together an army and defeated the enemy. But Rivalin was sorely wounded, which caused Blanchefleur great grief. Incognito, and with the help of her handmaiden, she entered Rivalin's chamber and "kissed him over and over again, till kisses brought him back to life and her love gave him strength to live."

News soon came that a foe had broken the truce and marched into Rivalin's territory. Blanchefleur wept when she heard the ill tidings, but the two lovers decided to elope, and they set sail together from Cornwall. Before he amassed his army, Rivalin sought counsel and wed Blanchefleur.

Rivalin was killed in battle and Blanchefleur died after giving birth to a son, Tristran. The two were buried in one grave, and the people of the kingdom thought that the child lay with them, but Rual, Rivalin's counsel, raised him as his own son.

See also BLANCHEFOR and ELIZABETH.
Source: R. Loomis/L. Loomis (MR).

Blanchefor. Whereby BLANCHEFLEUR is the name of TRISTAN's mother in the romance *Tristan and Isolt*, Blanchefor is Perceval's concubine in Chrétien de Troyes' *Conte du Graal*.

At a certain point in the story (lines 1830 to 2938), PERCEVAL has just left GORNEMANT of Gohort's castle and sought lodging at a fortress belonging to a damsel (Blanchefor) who turns out to be Gornemant's niece. In the course of events, a wicked knight, CLAMADEU, is attempting to subdue the castle and claim Blanchefor as his lady.

During the night Blanchefor stealthily sneaks into the bedroom where Perceval is sleeping, and when he awakens, she tells him, "Despite my being almost naked, I had no foolish, wicked, or base intention; for there's no living soul in all the world who is so grief-stricken or wretched that I am not more so."

She tells him her woeful tale, and he invites her into his bed, claiming it is wide enough for both of them. He promises to settle the siege at daybreak.

At the coming of dawn Clamadeu's seneschal Engygeron jousts with Perceval and is defeated. Blanchefor invites Perceval into her chamber for a respite and "shows no reluctance in embracing and kissing him: instead of eating and drinking, they sport and kiss and embrace and talk tenderly together."

Clamadeu, however, is confident that he can capture the castle, believing that Perceval will be too busy showing off his gallantry. Twenty knights attempt to storm the gates, but they are trapped by the portcullis and are annihilated by a barrage of arrows. Clamadeu meets his enemy in single combat and is defeated. Perceval sends the villain to King Arthur, who retains him all his days.

Blanchefor and Perceval take their pleasure, but anon Perceval's mind turns to his heartbroken mother and he sets off, promising to return.

Sources: R. Cline (P: SG); W. Kibler (CDT: AR); D. Owen (AR).

Bleise is Merlin's master, appearing only once in Malory's *Le Morte D'Arthur*. In a great battle against eleven kings, Arthur has slain, according to Merlin, of three score thousand of the enemy, all but fifteen thousand. (Of 60,000 troops, only 15,000 were still alive.) Merlin berates Arthur for wanting to continue the slaughter and orders him to cease. Merlin then goes "to see his master Bleise, that dwelt in Northumberland." Merlin describes the battle, and his master writes down the details.

Source: T. Malory (LMD'A).

Bragwaine, Brangwaine, Brangoene, Brangein. As with several other characters, Malory's Bragwaine is a parallel with Gottfried's Brangoene, Isolt's handmaiden. Bragwaine is a shrewd, intelligent servant, and unswervingly loyal to both La Beale Isoud and TRISTRAM, but she makes a blundering mistake of not protecting the two from a love potion given into her care by Isoud's mother. The potion, meant for Isoud and King Mark, is left unguarded and the couple inadvertently drink the elixir. Bragwaine deeply mourns her carelessness, and the trio become bonded for life.

In a frenzy, Isoud commits an atypical crime,

encouraging two squires to take Bragwaine into the forest and kill her. Bragwaine successfully pleads her case, and the squires bind her to a tree at a height where wolves won't devour her. When the squires return, Isoud repents her atrocious act, Bragwaine is rescued, and her life is saved.

Bragwaine becomes a key in all the future cover-up plots, beginning with Bragwaine crawling into the marriage bed with Mark so that Isoud could be with Tristram. The substitution worked, for Bragwaine herself was a beautiful virgin. In a later episode, Bragwaine tends to all of Isoud's and Tristram's needs while they are in the love grotto. and still further on, Bragwaine has an affair with KAHERDÎN (KEHYDIUS), son of King Howel (HOEL) of Brittany.

Sources: R. Loomis/L. Loomis (MR); T. Malory (LMD'A).

Brangoene. In *Tristan and Isolt* Brangoene is Isolt's handmaiden.

See also Bragwaine.

Breton. Breton refers to those inhabitants of Brittany, a country which at one time was known as Aremorica. Brittany is also referred to as Little Britain.

See also BRITONS.

Bretwalda, Brytwalda, Bryten Wealda, Bryrtenwalda, Brytenweald, Bretenanwealda. Because the term bretwalda is so vague in the ancient documents, some researchers circumvent any attempt of a definition. Bede does not actually use the word "bretwalda" in any form. Instead, in his description of King Ethelbert, he writes that Ethelbert was the third English king "to hold sway over all the provinces south of the River Humber," then adds, "The first king to hold such overlordship was ÆLLE and the second was Caelin, known in the speech of his people as CEAULIN." Hence, Bede suggests that these English rulers of British provinces were similar to overlords. He then lists four English kings who were endowed with this title, but he never records the actual term Bretwalda.

In the middle half of the twentieth century, J.N.L. Myres expresses his bewilderment of the term Bretwalda, but he does not question the authenticity of the title. He writes that Aelle's iso-lated and backward kingdom was the least likely of all the Teutonic kingdoms to have developed supremacy such as the term Bretwalda implies. Yet he asserts that no one "would hardly think of inventing such an unlikely tale [about Aelle's honorific of Bretwalda]; nor, if there was any suspicion of its authenticity, should we expect to find it reported without comment by Bede."

Several contemporary scholars touch upon the term and its Anglo-Saxon significance. In *Arthur's Britain*, Leslie Alcock discusses the hierarchy of English rulers and at the pinnacle of prestige he lists those kings known as *Bretwaldas*, those Anglo-Saxones who held *imperium* on the island, defining the term as "Ruler of Britain." He lists four Bretwaldas south of the River Humber, followed by three Northumbrian rulers. However, he does not elaborate upon a definition.

Geoffrey Ashe, in *The Discovery of King Arthur*, names three specific Bretwaldas, defining the term as "Britain-Ruler," but labeling the term as mainly honorific. He gives a fragmentary interpretation that no Bretwalda could rule over several regional domains, but instead were limited to establishing policies within their own kingdom, which essentially contradicts Bede's perception of the Bretwalda title.

John Morris, *The Age of Arthur*, adds additional detail. As does Alcock, Morris defines the term as "Ruler of Britain" but claims that Bretwalda is a variant of Brytwalda, "wide ruler," a term occasionally used by Roman emperors. In a footnote, he likens the term *bretwalda* to the Welsh title of GWLEDIC.

Morris undoubtedly borrowed the association between bretwalda and gwledig from John Rhys, who goes into some details about the title of bretwalda perhaps being a continuance of gwledig. In *Celtic Britain* Rhys gives a fairly lengthy etymological connection, concluding that surely the "English were in some measure guided in their choice of these terms [bretwaldas] by the term gwledig which was used among the Welsh."

Bretwalda, therefore, embodies a position of eminence, a special designation which should more likely be conferred upon powerful ealdormen such as Hengist or Octha. Concurring with J.N.L. Myres's astute perplexity of why so many obscure Anglo-Saxons have been bestowed with such a prestigious title, the *Historic Figures of the Arthurian Era* speculates that in order to resolve the discrepancy and most accurately define the term Bretwalda, one must first make a distinction between English Saxons and German Saxons.

In Section 56, the *Historia Brittonum* contributes the initial crucial information that after the *English Saxons* were defeated in all their battles, they sent for *German Saxons* to rule over them in Britain. Based upon other evidence, Hengist and Horsa were leaders of the second Saxon *adventus* who had been settled on the island for at least a generation, and hence they were considered English Saxons. Their tribes were the English Saxons who had been defeated, and Aelle, a German Saxon king who joined the remnants of his defeated English allies to fight against the Welsh, would have been the impelling force behind the reclamation of insular territories.

Hence, the most likely definition would bypass the traditionally accepted translation of "British Ruler" since that term implies that ethnically the ruler would be Briton. Precisely, Bretwalda would be "a German Saxon who allied himself with his English Saxon compatriots and conquered kingdoms in Britain. The title of Bretwalda for Aelle would be appropriate, not because he was a distinctive ruler in Britain, but because he was the first German Saxon to come to the aid of his English counterparts. To confirm this definition of Bretwalda as feasible, the *Historical Figures of the Arthurian Era* analyzes Ceawlin's role as the second Bretwalda.

Henry of Huntingdon lists the Bretwalda in this order: Aelle first, Ceaulin King of the West-Saxons second, Ethelbert as the third, and Redwald King of the East-Angles as the fourth; Edwin of the Northumbrians is fifth, Oswald of Northumbria is the sixth, and Oswy (Oswald's brother) is the seventh. Egbert (king of Wessex whose rule extended to the Humber) is the eighth, ALFRED (Egbert's grandson) is the ninth, and Edgar (great-grandson of Alfred) is the tenth. Peter Blair, in *Roman Britain and Early England*, provides a list of all the Bretwaldas in his Appendix A.

Sources: L. Alcock (AB); G. Ashe (DKA); T. Forester (CHH); L. Sherley-Price (BEDE: HEC&P); P. Blair (RB&EE); J. Morris (Aoa); J.N.L. Myres (RB&ES); F. Reno (HKA, HFAE); J. Rhys (CB).

Breunor. There is some confusion in MALORY's *Le Morte* about this particular character. The first appearance of this name is in Book 7, Chapter 2, when Sir Launcelot (LANCELOT) berates Sir KAY for calling a knight named "Breunor" by the sarcastic nickname of LA COTE MALE TAILE. However, in Book 8, Chapters 24 and 25, a knight named Breunor confronts Sir TRISTRAM, and in Chapter 26 Sir Tristram smote off this same Breunor's head. In Book 9 a certain Breunor le Noire makes his entrance, and Sir Kay admits that he has mockingly named him La Cote Male Taile, the knight with the "evil-shapen coat."

Because the Breunor mentioned in Book 7 is identified by Launcelot as "a good knight," and because Launcelot chides Kay for giving this honorable knight the name of La Cote Male Taile, the reader is alerted that this is not the same Breunor who is named in Book 8, a villainous knight who is known as the lord of Castle Pluere, the Weeping Castle. That Breunor is beheaded in Book 8, leaving no doubt that it is Sir Breunor le Noire who is mentioned in Book 7 and who appears once again in Book 9 with the appellation La Cote Male Taile. To be more precise:

1. Breunor in Book 7 should more specifically named Breunor le Noire, the honorable knight who is invited to join Arthur's Round Table;
2. Breunor in Book 8 is the evil Lord of the Weeping Castle who threatens to kill both Sir TRISTRAM and ISOUD, thus consigned to his own death by Tristram's blow.
3. Breunor le Noire is also known as La Cote Male Taile.

Breunor's role is extinguished as quickly as a falling star.

In Book 8, Sir Tristram, La Beale Isoud, and Dame BRAGWAINE her handmaiden are on a return trip to deliver Isoud from her father, King AGWISANCE, to King Mark, who would have her for his wife. They disembarked for the night at Castle Pluere, but as soon as they entered the castle, they were taken prisoners by Lord Breunor, who had the custom of making a righteous judgment of whose lady was more beautiful. The lady judged to be less beautiful would lose her head, and the knight would likewise forfeit his head.

Breunor judged Isoud to be more beautiful, and "therewithal Sir Tristram strode up to Breunor's lady and with an awke (back-handed) stroke he smote off her head clean." The two knights then jousted, and after Tristram unhorsed Breunor he threw him down groveling, "unlaced his helm, and struck off his head."

See also BREUNOR LE NOIRE and LA COTE MALE TAILE.

Source: T. Malory (LMD'A).

Breunor le Noire. In MALORY, Breunor le Noire is also known by the appellation LA COTE MALE TAILE, sarcastically given to him by Sir KAY. Wanting to avenge his father's death by a coward who had hacked him, Breunor le Noire came to Arthur's court to be knighted. On the morrow after his arrival, Breunor le Noire saved Queen Guenever from a lion. Arthur knighted him, but Breunor le Noire requested that he be called La Cote Male Taile, as Sir Kay had dubbed him.

See also BREUNOR and LA COTE MALE TAILE.

Source: T. Malory (LMD'A).

Britons. One of the most frustrating obstructions any researcher faces in attempting to accurately interpret Arthurian material is determining what the writer intended to convey. "Briton" is one such example. G. N. Garmonsway, in his translation of *The Anglo-Saxon Chronicle*, makes a distinction between "WELSH" and "Briton" for the twelve entries from 457 through 527. In six entries (457, 491, 501, 514, 519, and 527) the "*SAXONES*" were fighting the Britons; in the other six entries (465, 473, 477, 485, 495, and 508) the *Saxones* are fighting the Welsh. In Dorothy Whitelock's translation of the *Chronicle*, however, none of the manuscripts — A, B, C, D, E. F, or G — makes a comment on the term "Welsh" as opposed to "Briton."

The difference between "Briton" and "Welsh" is a crucial distinction in order to correctly interpret history of the era. In his text *The Emergence of England and Wales*, Wade-Evans discusses the plea made by the Britons to Aëtius in 446 after the Roman withdrawal. He explains what is meant by the term Britannians: "It was long the fashion to regard the pre–Roman inhabitants of Britain as ... 'Ancient Britons' ... [an] idea [which] derives from the *de excidio* which equates the *Britanni* (i.e., the general name given to the pre–Roman inhabitants of the Island of Britain in its most extended sense) with the self-styled Britons of Gildas' own day.... For though the *Britanni* ... were all of them Romans (Walas), they were by no means all of them 'Britons.'"

After the Romans had conquered Britain, they divided the island into five segments. The largest was Britannia Prima, which included all of what is now known as Wales (under Walas, i.e., Roman military control) and Cornwall, plus extended territory to the east. Of the nine legionary fortresses the Romans built, six of them were in Britannia Prima.

Not only should a distinction be made between Briton and Welsh, but also between BRETON (an inhabitant of Little Britain on the continent) and Briton. Of crucial importance, too, is that the Romans used the generic term *Saxones*, which didn't differentiate the SAXONS, the ANGLES, or the JUTES. All these distinctions are important in understanding the history of the period and its impact on Arthuriana.

Sources: G.N. Garmonsway (ASC); C. Plummer (TSCP); F. Reno (HKA/HFAE); A. Wade-Evans (EOE&W); D. Whitelock Etal (ASC).

Brude, Brudeus, Bruide, Brodjos, Bride, Bridei, Bridius. Brude is a satellite figure in Arthuriana, perhaps strengthening the chronological link if he is the son of Maelgwyn. The father-son relationship would tie to ÆTERNUS (VORTIGERN) and CUNEDDA (VORTIMER, BRYDW), during the time of Cunedda's migration to Wales, and to Cunedda's sons, namely Enniaun Girt, but most particularly to CERDIC.

John Morris unconditionally accepts the premise that Meilochon is Maelgwn and Bridei is his son. Nora Chadwick indicates that the two variants of Maelgwn are basically identical. On the other hand, Thomas O'Sullivan cites those who disagree: John Rhys believes that Maelchon and Maelgwn were two different entities; Kenneth Hurlstone Jackson claimed that Bruide mac Maelshom was a Pict and his father's name couldn't be regarded as Goidelic.

Sources: J. Morris (AOA); T. O'Sullivan (DEG: A&D); F. Reno (HKA/HFAE).

Brydw. Brydw is an obscure name appearing on Eliseg's Pillar, a memorial stone set up by Cyngen, the last king of Powys at a location near the Valley Crucis Abbey, about a mile and a half north of Llangollen. According to Jeremy Knight, its inscription is "at least 31 lines of capital letters in Insular script. This was a type of writing developed in the monasteries of sixth century Britain and Ireland for books of the Scriptures and other texts.... Each line consisted of a little under thirty letters and the text was divided into at least ten phrases, each beginning with an initial cross, though not necessarily on a new line."

Brydw's name appears near the end of the inscription and identifies him as "the son of Gwtheyrn, whom Germanus blessed and who was borne to him by Severa, the daughter of Maximus the king, who slew the King of the Romans." Gwtheyrn is the Welsh name for VORTIGERN, the overlord recorded in the *Historia Brittonum*. Maximus is the Spanish general who seized power in Britain in 383 C.E. and became a usurper in Gaul, where he maintained his power until 388, when he was deposed and beheaded after killing Gratian.

The *Historia* reveals that Vortigern had four sons, including Vortimer, Cateyrn, and Pascent, in that order. The fourth was Faustus, born to him by his daughter. The names Pasgen and Cattigirn (i.e., evidently Cateyrn) appear on the pillar, and because names were passed on from one generation to the next, it is likely the names Pasgen and Cattigirn refer to Vortigern's two sons of the fifth century.

The name Brydw is definitely linked to Vortigern, strongly suggesting that Brydw is Vortimer, Vortigern's first-born, because of two similarities. The first is that Vortimer is an epithet and not a proper name, and the second is because other manuscripts explicitly state that Vor-

timer was blessed by Germanus. There can be no mistake that Germanus never blessed Vortigern. That Brydw is another name for Faustus cannot be substantiated, since Faustus, although raised by Germanus, was born of Vortigern's daughter (Faustus's sister), not born of Severa.

Sources: J. Knight (VCA&POE); J. Morris (HB).

Brython. Although the words BRITON and Brython are considered cognates, Sir Ifor Williams give an interesting variation. He writes, "The dwellers in the three British districts called themselves Britons (*Brython*).... The Britons of Wales and Strathclyde, however, for some reason or other, began to call themselves also CYMRY, the plural of *Cymro*, a compound of *com* a prefix meaning "together" and *bro* "border, coast, district."...[S]o *Cymro* means a fellow countryman. Cornishmen were never known as *cymry*, but the people of Cumberland were; Cumberland means "the land of the *Cymry*."

A.W. Wade-Evans offers an explanation that substantiates a connection between Strathclyde Welsh and Saxon *foederati*: the Men of the North, GWYR Y GOGLEDD, structured a different province built upon the disintegrated portions of the Cornovii territory when the Romans left, and a new segment they called Mercia. He indicates the people were a mixture of English Saxons and Brython, but spoke both languages.

Sources: R. Bromwich (BWP); A. Wade-Evans (EOE&W).

Budic *see* BUDICIUS.

Budicius. Geoffrey of Monmouth's manuscript records a Budicius I and a Budicius II, the former being identified as the King of Brittany who raises AURELIUS AMBROSIUS and UTHERPENDRAGON when they are taken across the Channel from Britain to avoid assassination attempts by VORTIGERN, and the latter identified as a King of Brittany, but listed by Monmouth as the father of HOEL. Confusingly, however, Hoel's mother is listed as ANNA, Arthur's sister, who has also been identified by Monmouth as married to Loth of Lodonesia.

Attempting to extract more information about Budicius from the extant histories is rather futile. John Morris writes of a Budic and Maxentius, brothers and heirs to the British kingdom of

Quimper in southwestern Brittany who returned from abroad (Britain?) at the end of the 500s. Morris claims that that particular Budic died about 557. If that be true, then the time period is beyond a connection with Monmouth's Budicius, since the young Aurelius and Utherpendragon would have been handed over to Budicius I somewhere around the year 425.

Researchers Chris Barber and David Pykitt are two of the very few who address the issue of Budic/Budicius. They write, "The two brothers [Aurelius and Utherpendragon] remained in exile for many years and were brought up as princes by their cousin Budic, Emperor of Armorica, whose name in Welsh is Emyr Llydaw." This implies that Budic is Monmouth's Budicius II because of the appellations "King of Brittany" and "Emperor of Armorica," synonymous titles. The only other reference they make is that "all three of Meurig's daughters married sons of Emyr Llydaw (Budic, Emperor of Armorica) and thus achieved an important alliance between the two royal families."

The problem is compounded by the addition of the Welsh name Emyr Llydaw. Steve Blake and Scott Lloyd do not mention Budic in either of their two books, and refer to Emyr Llydaw only once: Gwrleis had two daughters by Eigyr, Gwyar and Dioneta. Gwyar was a widow and after the death of her husband, Emyr Llydaw, she dwelt at her father's court with her son Hywel. Gwrleis is a reference to Gwrlois, another name for GORLOIS of Cornwall, and Eigyr is, of course, YGERNA. Hywel is likely a variant of Hoel. But there is no further identification of Budic or Emyr Llydaw.

Evidence is too thin to draw an inference about Budicius and Budic. The source for Monmouth's claim is vague and contradictory, and fragments of Welsh tradition might have been extracted from Geoffrey's work.

Sources: C. Barber/D. Pykitt (JTA); S. Blake/S. Lloyd (KTA); J. Morris (AOA).

Cabal, Cafal, Cavall. Cabal is the name of Arthur's dog, considered important enough to merit an entry in §73, "The Wonders of Britain," in the *Historia Brittonum*:

There is another wonder in the aforesaid country called Builth. There is a heap of stones there, and one of the stones placed on top of the pile has the footprint of a dog on it. When he hunted Twrch Trwyth Cafal, the warrior Arthur's hound, impressed his footprint on the stone, and Arthur later brought together the pile of stones, under the stone in which was his dog's footprint, and it is called Carn Cafal. Men come and take the stone in their hands for the space of a day and a night, and on the morrow it is found upon the stone pile.

The passage referring to Arthur's hound hunting the boar Twrch Trwyth is associated with the tale "How Culhwch Won Olwen" in *The Mabinogion*. In that tale the dog's name is spelled C-a-v-a-l-l. Cavall is mentioned again in the tale "Gereint and Enid." The expression "Carn Cafal" is the dog's grave.

Sources: J. Gantz (TM); J. Morris (BM).

Cador, Cadwr. Cador is not only one of Arthur's major allies, he is Arthur's half-brother. Both are sons of YGERNA, but Arthur's father is Utherpendragon and Cador's father is GORLOIS. This relationship has given rise to the theory that Arthur, not his father, should be addressed as Utherpendragon. If translated as a Latin affix cognate with the word *uterine*, *uter-* means two siblings born of the same mother but of different fathers. His father then, would bear the epithet Pendragon, meaning Head Dragon, and Arthur would be UTERPENDRAGON, Son of Pendragon.

The stories about Cador are quite similar in the *Tysilio* and Monmouth's *History of the Kings of Britain*. Arthur was crowned at the young age of fifteen and immediately after the ceremony, it was necessary for him to collect an army and march to York to confront Colgrin and his army of Saxons, Scots, and Picts. After a victory against Colgrin, Arthur in turn had to face Cledric (CERDIC), choosing Cador, Earl of Cornwall, to head six hundred cavalry and three thousand infantry to intercept the enemy, which Cador did, routing the barbarians with great slaughter.

Cledric avoided death and mounted another attack at Caer-Vadon (Bath). Arthur put Cador, Earl of Cornwall, in charge with ten thousand men-at-arms. The enemies fled and Cador pursued them. He then "seized on the Saxon vessels, put part of his own men on board of them, and with the other part pursed the Saxons closely, so that Cledric was slain, and those who were not killed, taken and doomed to perpetual slavery."

Later, when Arthur has a great festival at Caerleon, the king dressed in his royal robes and was preceded into the cathedral by four sword-bearing generals, one who was Cador, his half-brother, called King of Cornwall for a second time.

When Arthur wages war with the Roman Lucius, Cador plays a major role. Having been ordered by Lucius to submit to Rome and pay tribute, Arthur consults Cador and the council for advice. Arthur decides to appear at Rome and demand tribute, not pay it. An extended battle follows, in which Cador is mentioned several times. Lucius is finally killed, and Arthur's troops return to Britain upon the news that Mordred has assumed the crown.

Cador drops from the history, and the reader is informed that "Constantine the son of Cador succeeded to the throne by Arthur's desire, for Cador was the son of GORLOIS, Earl of Cornwall, by EIGR, Arthur's mother, the daughter of Amlawd the Great."

The name Cador appears twice in *The Mabinogion* tale "The Dream of Rhonabwy," which is described in the AVAON entry. "Cador" becomes "Cadwr," who arms Arthur for battle and who is one of Arthur's counselors.

Sources: J. Gantz (TM); F. Reno (HFAE/HKA); P. Roberts (COKB); L. Thorpe (GM: HKB).

Cadwallon Lawhir, Cadwallon. *see* CATGOLAUN LAUHIR.

Cadwr. Cadwr is the Welsh spelling of Cador, who becomes the king of Cornwall. *See also* CADOR.

Sources: J. Gantz (TM); F. Reno (HFAE/HKA); P. Roberts (COKB); L. Thorpe (GM: HKB).

Cai. *see* KAY.

Calogrenant. Calogrenant is another knight of the Round Table who makes his first appearance in Chrétien's *Le Chevalier au lion* (*Yvain*, or *Knight with the Lion*). Surprisingly, he has more of a role in this work by CHRÉTIEN DE TROYES than he does in *Le Mort d'Arthur* by THOMAS MALORY.

During the feast of Pentecost at King Arthur's court in Carduel (identified as Carlisle in Wales) Calogrenant, Sagremor, and Dodinel are three knights in attendance. Calogrenant, described as very handsome, makes a point of honoring Queen Guinevere by jumping up from his seat. Sir Kay, who is portrayed in many of the tales as spiteful and abusive, chides Calogrenant for his ostentatious actions. The queen defends the handsome knight, calling Kay tiresome and base, but Kay continues his tirade, after which he implores that there be no more quarreling.

Calogrenant slights Kay with a barb, saying that a dung heap will always smell and a cad will always slander and vex others. He requests permission to entertain the queen by telling a story which might please her. The long tale, which happened seven years prior, begins with Calogrenant riding through Carduel in Wales and ends up in the forest of Broceliande in Brittany. After crossing open country, Calogrenant sees a fortress where he takes lodging for the night, and during dinner, meets a beautiful young maiden who is seated next to him. It seems as if a love tryst would follow, but the knight simply relates a pleasant evening.

When he resumes his travel, he meets a man resembling a Moor, an ugly and hideous giant who describes his job as controlling the beastly bulls in the field. When Calogrenant explains he is seeking adventure, the giant recommends that he visit a spring that boils and yet is colder than marble.

What follows is a description of Berenton Fountain near Merlin's tomb and the Fountain of Youth in Broceliande, Brittany. Calogrenant describes the site in such specific detail that it strongly suggests that Chrétien borrowed this material from the *Roman Brut* of WACE, a work which preceded Chrétien's by approximately five years.

While at the spring, Calogrenant is excited to witness "the miracle of the storm and tempest," so he recalls that "I saw the heavens so rent apart that lightning blinded my eyes from more than fourteen directions; and all the clouds pell-mell dropped rain, snow, and hail. The storm was so terrible and severe that a hundred times I feared that I'd be killed by the lightning that struck about me or by the trees that were split apart. You can be sure that I was very frightened until the storm died down." The end of the adventure fizzles, with Calogrenant fighting an angry knight and then returning to the fortress.

When Thomas Malory writes of this knight, the name changes from Calogrenant to COLGRE-VANCE.

Sources: W. Kibler (CDT: AR); E. Mason (AC:W&L).

Camden, William (*floruit* 1572–1602; *lifespan EB* 1551–1623). Whereby GIRALDUS CAMBRENSIS (in the early 1190s) and ADAM OF DOMERHAM (in the early 1190s) focus on the exhumation of King Arthur's grave at Glastonbury, Camden gives detailed information about the leaden cross.

Leslie Alcock states that most of the scribes who have written about the exhumations "have paid too little attention to the lead cross which was said to have been found beneath the coffin cover." Those antiquarians who have recorded the inscription on the cross vary in detail. Alcock admonishes the reader to accept the variations, not to defend a particular authenticity, but to stress the commonness of inadvertent errors. He cites Richard Robinson, a copier in 1582, whose version of the imprint on the leaden cross "differed at four points from [John] Leland's, despite the fact that he had Leland's printed text before him."

Camden's drawing is slightly under six inches in height. Alcock claims with certainty that the inscription "is not contemporary with Arthur's death in the first half of the sixth century," arguing that "various letter forms, in particular the Ns which look like Hs, and the squared Cs, are not of that early date." Similarly, Alcock avers, they are not traceable "to a date in the late twelfth century at the time of the exhumation and the supposed forgery." He makes a judgment that the best comparisons for the letters are provided by the inscription on Late Saxon coins,

Edmund Gibson's 1695 English translation of William Camden's 1607 edition of *Britannia* included Camden's drawing of the Glastonbury Cross. John Leland recorded the cross in 1542, and acording to Leslie Alcock, Camden's version differs on only one point, substituting an I for a Y in INCLITUS. The earlier recordings of Giraldus Cambrensis and Ralph of Coggeshall matched Camden's. Because Camden proclaimed, "Behold the cross itself and the inscription," Alcock asks the modern reader, "Does this drawing [of Camden's] depict the details of the lettering with such accuracy that we can use it to date the cross on epigraphic grounds?"

and on epigraphic grounds, a date in the tenth or eleventh centuries seems most likely.

From these contradictions — a cross dating to about the tenth century, a grave sixteen feet deep, a man allegedly buried at the end of the sixth century and exhumed by monks of the abbey in the twelfth century — Alcock proposes two possible scenarios, the first which supports forgery and the perpetration of a hoax so that the monastery could make grandiose claims about Arthur's burial at the abbey. He writes,

Twelfth-century monks ... were sufficiently scholarly to know that the script of their own day would be inappropriate ... to pass off as an ancient "burial.... The Glastonbury forger knew just enough to tell him that a contemporary script [of the twelfth-century] would not do. Casting around in the monastic library for ancient manuscripts to serve as models, his hand fell upon some work of the tenth or early eleventh century, and copying the capital letters from that, he produced an inscription which was colourably ancient."

The second scenario which Alcock conjectures "takes into account the total archaeological evidence from the area of exhumation." He explains several possible events:

- the discovery of the mausoleum in 1962;
- St. Dunstan's reconstructing of the cemetery by raising the cemetery grounds ten feet;
- evidence that mason's chips from the Doulton stone was used only in the building of the Lady Chapel in 1184–9; and lastly,
- St. Dunstan's crew forging a cross to put on the bottom side of the slab.

Archaeologist C. Ralegh Radford, in *The Quest for Arthur's Britain*, writes: "The emphasis placed on Camden's cross has always focused upon the epigraphy of the inscription, but nothing has been said about its configuration. It could very well be that Camden did not simply 'invent' the shape of the cross, but borrowed its appearance from what he knew of Merovingian crosses. There were crosses of that configuration on Merovingian graves dating from 480 to 730 C.E. and would therefore have been significant during Arthur's historic period."

The flange at the bottom signified a processional or a monumental cross of that era. It was first carried on a pole in a cathedral or through the town streets, honoring the important deceased individual, and then it was later attached to the monument for that individual. The circular underparts of the crossbars might have signified one of two things: that ornamental pieces were suspended from the cross, or the cross might have been suspended by nails or wooden plugs at one time to a vertical surface before it became part of a gravemarker.

Perhaps when Saint Dunstan refurbished the

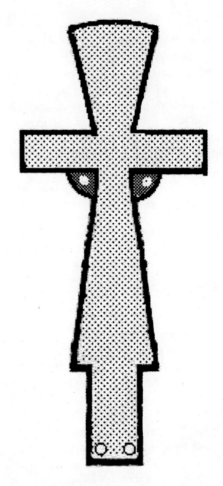

The authenticity of the leaden cross has long been a matter of doubt, and many have favored the solution that is was made by the monks in 1190. Epigraphically this is difficult to accept. There is no reason to doubt the basic accuracy of the letter form as engraved by Camden, though the arrangement of the words and the form of the cross are not necessarily correct. The letters are debased and straggling Roman capitals. The square C (two instances) and the N with a horizontal cross bar (three instances) are consistently used. These forms are proper to the eleventh century or earlier, rather than the twelfth. If the cross was really a fabrication of the late twelfth century, the maker was unusually consistent. It seems more likely that it was a genuine relic of pre–Conquest date.

Glastonbury graveyard in the 10th century, a deteriorated cross was also unearthed. Saint Dunstan and the monks might have forged a new one to take its place. This would be logical and could possibly explain why the cross was so designed, even though no one ever attested to it configuration.

Camden himself gives specific details that the monks "digged" 7 feet and ran across a stone, and on the back part was fastened a rude leaden cross. Under it (supposedly the cross) almost 9 feet deep in a coffin made of a hollow oak were reposited the bones of the famous Arthur. He writes that the letters on the cross are of antiquity, "a sort of barbarous and Gothic appearance." However, he writes nothing about the shape of his drawing.

The remarks of Alcock and Radford are tentative, as the verification of archaeologists should be. Likewise, Richard Barber is objective, but he lays down an argument supporting a hoax. He writes,

> Nor is a good motive for such a forgery lacking. Arthur's grave was an obvious attraction for pilgrims, and pilgrims were the abbey's chief source of income apart from its properties. They were the only way by which large additional sums could be made; and there was need of extra funds. In 1184, the buildings had been largely burnt down; but Henry II had provided the money for reconstruction. However, when he died in 1189 and Richard came to the throne, the Exchequer's resources were directed entirely to the fitting-out of the Crusade, and the supply of funds ceased. It is strange that within a few months of this, a new source of revenue should suddenly appear. Politically, too, it would suit Richard; for the hope of Arthur's return could be used to foment rebellion in Wales, and this discovery seemed to dispose of it. Giraldus tells us that Henry told the monks something about Arthur being buried at Glastonbury; this may be an oblique reference to a hint from Henry that such a discovery would suit him for this reason.

Sources: L. Alcock (AB); R. Barber (AA); E. Gibson (CB); C. Radford (GA: QFAB).

Caradoc of Llancarfan (circa 1140). When Caradoc penned his manuscript the *Vita Gildae* ("The Life of Saint Gildas"), he did not differentiate between GILDAS ALBANIUS and GILDAS BADONICUS, but coupled with research extracted from a variety of other documents, Caradoc's work — for those who ascribe to a distinction between the two Gildases — is identified as a biography of Gildas Albanius.

Josephus Stevenson presents a strong case that Gildas Albanius preceded Gildas Badonicus by at least two generations, and hence it was Gildas Albanius who had direct contact with Arthur. In this context, Caradoc's manuscript was written during WILLIAM OF MALMESBURY's era and John Scott even suggests that Caradoc was probably at Glastonbury when William was, or at least soon after. Therefore, in the transmission of his story, Caradoc connects King Arthur with Glastonbury. He describes the wicked King MELWAS of the Summer Region abducting Guennuvar (GUINEVERE) and holding her at Glastonbury.

Caradoc refers to Glastonbury as the "City of Glass," deriving its name from the Welsh *Yniswitrin*, but he gives no hint that this is identical to the Isle of Avalon. King Arthur travels with all of his forces from Devon and Cornwall to rescue Guennuvar and exact vengeance. The abbot of Glastonbury, accompanied by Gildas Albanius, intervenes as a mediator to prevent a serious battle. A solution is forged and peace is made, thus restoring the queen to Arthur. As a result of this mediation between the two kings, Glastonbury not only received land grants, but also extracted promises from the two kings that they would not violate the abbey any more.

James Carley explains that in JOHN OF GLASTONBURY's shorter account of the story, the Latin is made simpler, and "all references to Arthur as *rex rebellis* or *tyrannus* and the rape of Guinevere by Melwas are removed." John Scott suggests that William of Malmesbury was extremely cautious because of the Arthur connection, and since he, Malmesbury, wanted to report only reliable fact, he avoided the manuscript about Gildas.

About fifty years after Caradoc penned his manuscript, GIRALDUS CAMBRENSIS in his *De Principis Instructione* describes Arthur's exhumation at the abbey, strengthening King Arthur's association with Glastonbury. The Caradoc story stresses an aspect which should be given in more detail — that of equating Glastonbury with the Isle of Glass. In the twelfth century when Caradoc makes this association, the Welsh already had a tradition about *Ynis Witrin*, which was where Melwas lived. It is described as a water-surrounded fortress of glass where nine maidens dwelt perpetually. Carley established his connection:

> The Isle of Glass bears a close resemblance to the Isle of Apples described by Geoffrey [of Monmouth]. It would therefore be possible for someone familiar with both these traditions to make the equation: Glastonbury = Isle of Glass = Isle of Apples = the isle to which the wounded Arthur was conveyed. Certainly it is tempting to think that something similar to this was at least a partial cause for the choice of [Glastonbury as the] excavation site for [Arthur's exhumation]. Moreover, as E.K. Chambers points out, there were probably many places which were known as Avalon in local traditions. Glastonbury was, without a doubt, considered a holy island long before the advent of Christianity and it is quite possible that it enjoyed locally the reputation of being an Isle of Avalon even before the exhumation took place.

Sources: G. Ashe [Ed] (QFAB); J. Carley (CGA); E. Chambers (AOB); J. Scott (EHG: ETSWM); J. Stevenson (G: DEB); F. Reno (HKA).

Categern, Cateyrn, Cattigern, Katigern, Cynderyn. Categern is one of Vortigern's sons and brother of Vortimer and Paschent. He is, therefore, of the Arthurian era, but according to history and oral tradition, he has no direct bond with Arthur or Ambrosius Aurelianus.

His name is recorded in §44 of the *Historia Brittonum*, which describes Vortimer's battles against Hengist and Horsa: "The second battle was at the ford called Episford in their language, Rhyd yr afael in our, and there fell Horsa and also Vortigern's son Cateyrn." His name also appears in §48, which gives a brief genealogy of Vortigern's clan: "Vortigern had three sons, whose names are Vortimer, who fought against the barbarians, as I have described above, the second, Cateyrn; the third, Pascent."

The *Tysilio* records this same individual under the name of Cyndeyrn: "Cyndeyrn and Horsa slew each other." Geoffrey of Monmouth records a slightly different entry for Katigern after noting that Katigern, Paschent, and Vortimer were born of Vortigern's first wife. Several paragraphs later Monmouth describes Katigern's fate: in the second battle waged by Vortimer, "Horsa and Katigern met hand to hand and both died, for each was mortally wounded by the other."

The Anglo-Saxon Chronicle records the death of Horsa in 455, but mentions nothing of Categern.

Sources: G.N. Garmonsway (ASC); J. Knight (POE); J. Morris (BH); P. Roberts (COKB); L. Thorpe (GM: HKB).

Catgolaun Lauhir, Cadwallon Lawhir, Cadwallon. Catgolaun Lauhir is a satellite figure of the historic Arthurian era; he and his relatives were either directly or indirectly associated with Arthur and his clan. A partial genealogical tree for Catgolaun Lauhir, beginning with his father CUNEDDA Wledig, is shown in the chart below.

The genealogy in the chart is based on the assumption that Cunedda's fifth son is also CERDIC the West Saxon king recorded in *The Anglo-Saxon Chronicle*. For those who do not accept that premise, then the left-hand column should be discarded.

Because Catgolaun Lauhir is only indirectly associated, it is his son MAGLOCUNUS—described by GILDAS BADONICUS as the "dragon of

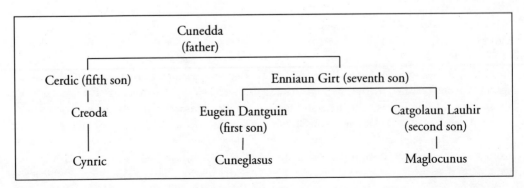

the island"—who is significant for the establishment of a genealogical calibration and a sequential timeline of Arthurian ancestry.

See also the entry about OWEIN DANTGUIN, since his role is directly tied to Arthur through Welsh oral tradition. See also GWYR Y GOGLEDD, the "men of the north."

Sources: C. Barber/D. Pykitt (JTA); P. Bartram (WG); J. Morris (AOA); G. Phillips/M. Keatman (KA: TS); F. Reno (HKA/HFAE).

Cattigirn. *see* CATEGERN.

Caw, Cau, Caunus, Cawr, Cadw. Caw is one of the most enigmatic figures whose role determines whether or not Arthur can be classified as a historic king of the fifth century. Two entries in this text—GILDAS ALBANIUS and GILDAS BADONICUS—have created an inferno in modern scholarship, which is a necessity when searching for truth, or the nearest thing to it. *The Arthurian Encyclopedia* doesn't lend credence to the significance of two Gildases. Curtly, it states there were not two Gildases, and hagiography treats them as the same person, "an assumption which may be allowed to stand." The two entries in this text supply an in-depth scrutiny based upon Josephus Stevenson's more astute analysis.

Caw plays a cryptic but rather detached minor role during the Arthurian age, but he is an important figure who clarifies a crucial piece of history as well as the identity of one of his sons, who became a sixth-century monk and scribe. Gildas Albanius's niche during this era defines other major characters in both history and oral tradition.

There is no ancestral background that records information about Gildas Badonicus, except what he records in the *De Excidio* about his birth being just prior to the Battle of Badon. There is no doubt that Gildas Badonicus was born in the late 500s. Gildas Badonicus does not give any recognition to an Arthur of that century, in spite of trumped-up charges that this Gildas ignored Arthur because Arthur had killed his brother Hueil. Hueil is listed as one of Caw's other sons.

Hence, for Gildas Albanius there is quite a bit of ancestral information supplied not only by Caradoc but by Welsh oral tradition. His Scottish ancestry is referred to quite often. Richard

Barber quotes segments of Caradoc's work, pointing out that Caw lived north of the Antonine Wall, not far from the territory of Dalriada, and that he had twenty-three sons, two of whom were Gildas and Hueil. Stevenson adds more information about Gildas Albanius, giving his birth as circa 425 C.E., and his journey to France at the age of thirteen when that territory was ruled by Childeric, returning after seven years. Caradoc then records the monk's death in 512.

The tale "How Culhwch Won Olwen" enumerates most of Caw's sons:

Dymig	Iusstig	Edmyg	Angawdd
Govan	Keyln	Conyn	Mabsant
Gwyngad	Llwybyr	Coch	Meilyg
Kynwal	Ardwyad	Ergyryad	Neb
Calcas	Hueil	GILDAS	

Later in the same tale, Caw's son Gwarthegydd (not named above) helps hunt the boar Twrch Trwyth, and in the "Dream of Rhonabwy" Gwarthegydd is with Arthur at the battle of Baddon. When OSLA BIG KNIFE calls for a truce in that tale, Arthur summons his advisors, two of them being Gwarthegydd and Gildas (Albanius). When Gwenhwyvar (GUINEVERE) has to be escorted back to court in the tale of "Gereint and Enid," Arthur selects Gildas, son of Caw, for the task.

Three other details are provided by *The Mabinogion*: Caw of Scotland reigns over sixty cantrevs; he is riding Arthur's mare Llamrei when he fights against Twrch; and when Arthur split the Black Hag in two, Caw captured and retained two vats of her blood.

For those researchers and historians who reject the concept of two Gildases, then the chronological discrepancy between Welsh tradition and British history remains unresolved.

Sources: R. Barber (FOA); S. Blake/S. Lloyd (KTA); J. Gantz (TM); J. Stevenson (G: DEB); M. Winterbottom (G: ROB&OW).

Caxton, William (circa 1422–1491). The work of this pioneer printer of Britain is sometimes criticized as not being original and producing books that had no lasting aesthetics, but he must still be considered a giant during his era and an inspiration for future generations. He printed monumental English works of literature such as

Geoffrey Chaucer's *Canterbury Tales* and RANULF HIGDEN's *Polychronicon* before taking on the formidable task of THOMAS MALORY's epic.

Although his preface to *Morte d'Arthur* doesn't attract much attention, it is worth citing extracts here, since Malory's work is the major bridge between King Arthur's historic era and all the modern works which have since evolved. Caxton didn't print *LeMorte* until 1485, and in his preface he explains why: "Divers men hold opinion that there was no such Arthur, and that all such books as be made of him be but feigned and fables, by cause that some chronicles make of him no mention nor remember him no thing, nor of his knights."

One of the "many noble and divers gentlemen of this realm of England" petitioned Caxton to print Malory's work by explaining that "those who think there was never such a king called Arthur, might well be credited great folly and blindness, for there are many evidences to the contrary." The gentleman then listed at least a dozen pieces of "evidence" that King Arthur was indeed a historical figure. Among the ones which he listed were: Arthur's sepulcher at Glastonbury; the book published about him by Galfridus (Geoffrey of Monmouth); Gawain's skull at Dover; the Round Table at Winchester; Arthur's popularity across the Channel; and his town of Camelot.

Caxton reconsidered, and concluded that "many noble volumes be made of him and of his noble knights in French, which I have seen and read beyond the sea, which be not had in our maternal tongue, but in Welsh be many and also in French, and some in English, but no where nigh all."

When he decided to accept the undertaking, Caxton hoped to succeed in capturing the joyous history of King Arthur by stressing "noble acts, feats of arms of chivalry, prowess, hardiness, humanity, love, courtesy, and very gentleness, with many wonderful histories and adventures." He divided Malory's work into twenty-one books and 507 chapters.

Source: T. Malory (LMD'A).

Ceaulin is the name Bede uses for Ceawlin, the Bretwalda named in *The Anglo-Saxon Chronicle*.

Ceawlin, Ceolwin, Caelin, Ceaulin. Ceawlin is a *Saxone* king of hidden significance. He is the son of CYNRIC, the grandson of CREODA, and the great-grandson of CERDIC, but his notability surpasses his association with his ancestors. Reconciling the discrepancy between the Genealogical Preface and *The Anglo-Saxon Chronicle* by adding Creoda's preceding sovereignty and subtracting Ceol's succeeding rule, Ceawlin's reign spans twenty-five years, from 560 C.E. to 585 C.E. His name first appears in 556 of the *ASC*: "In this year, Cynric and Ceawlin fought against the BRITONS at Beranburh," followed immediately by entry 560, "In this year Ceawlin succeeded to the kingdom in Wessex, and ÆLLE succeeded to the kingdom of the Northumbrians."

In addition to their face-value pronouncements, two other very important pieces of information are divulged. One, in the entry of 556, Ceawlin is explicitly fighting against the Britons and not the WELSH, signifying that Beranburh is in south-central Britain. Two, the entry of 560 indicates Ceawlin's kingdom is the enigmatic realm of Wessex. It is necessary to distinguish between the West Saxon territory and Wessex, since the former is a larger, more inclusive area than the latter, which commonly encompasses Wiltshire and Hampshire. Beranburh is the modern Barbury Castle, one of the few locales which can be identified, a site halfway between Swindon and Marlborough.

HENRY OF HUNTINGDON, who uses the name Ceaulin, writes that "in the sixth year of Ceaulin's reign (565), Ethelbert, that great king, began to reign in Kent." In a footnote, however, his biographer adds, "The *ASC* fixes the accession of Ethelbert in the first year of Ceawlin instead of the sixth, in which it appears to agree with the computation of Bede." Henry then names the Bretwalda, which are listed in that entry.

The *ASC* for 568 records the battle between Ceawlin and Ethelbert, whereby Ceawlin drove the latter into Kent, and they slew two princes, Oslac and Cnedda, at Wibbandun. Henry adds these details: "Ceawlin and his brother Chuta [Cutha in the *ASC*] were compelled by various causes to engage in war with Ethelbert, who had arrogantly intruded himself into their kingdom. In a battle fought at Mirandune, Ethelbert's two generals, Oslap and Cneban, thunderbolts of war, with a vast number of their followers, were slain, and Ethelbert himself was pursued as far as Kent. This is remarkable as the first international war among the English kings."

The succeeding entries of 577 and 584 indicate that Ceawlin was fighting the Britons, listing geographic sites as Dyrham, Gloucester, Cirencester, and Bath. The two remaining entries which refer to Ceawlin (592 and 593) are spurious. Relying upon the Genealogical Preface and its reconciliation with the *ASC*, Ceawlin's reign ended in 585. After Ceawlin's death, Ceol succeeded to the throne and ruled six years, from 585 until 591.

One other cogent piece of information is that Ceawlin succeeded Ælle as the second BRETWALDA, a title which provides not only interesting information of Ceawlin's whereabouts during his era, but also gives a clue about his ethnicity.

Sources: Bede (HECP); T. Forester (CHH); G. Garmonsway (ASC); C. Plummer (TSCP); F. Reno (HKA).

Cerdic, Three faces of. A 1957 movie *Three Faces of Eve* was based on a true story about Eve White, who suffered from Multiple Personality Disorder. Extensive therapy revealed to the psychiatrist three distinctive personas which he was

able to reconcile. Borrowing and modifying that title is a perfect lead-in to "The Three Faces of Cerdic," a fifth-century British figure whose three different roles in history and folklore point to one specific individual.

In Welsh genealogies and history, Cerdic's first face is the fifth son of Cunedda, born circa 436–400. Extracting material from the *Historia Brittonum*, Section 37, his second face is an interpreter for his grandfather, Vortigern, plus a link in Welsh folktales of *The Mabinogion*—specifically "How Culhwch Won Olwen" and "The Dream of Rhonabwy"—which record an individual named Gwrhyr Interpreter of Languages. His third and most mystifying face is Cerdic, the King of Wessex, recorded in *The Anglo-Saxon Chronicle*.

Genealogy is an important factor in tracing Cerdic's three personas. The names Paternus and Æternus are Roman ancestors; Peis Rut, Patern, Padarn, Guorthigirnus, Gwythern, Cunedda, Guorthimer, Cunedag, Ceredic, Ceredig, and Cerdic are Welsh/Celtic; Vortigern and Vortimer are epithets which commonly mean "overlord" and "overprince;" and Gewis, Esla, and Elesa are postulations for Paternus, Æternus, and Cunedda respectively, extracted from chronologies in *The Anglo-Saxon Chronicle*. All names are recorded on inscribed stones, in various Roman and Welsh histories, or in *The Anglo-Saxon Chronicle*.

Prior to 410 and at least two decades later,

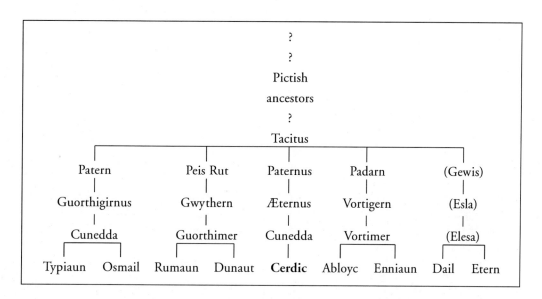

Cerdic's great-grandfather and his grandfather Æeternus had strong ties to the Romans, who still occupied the British province. When Cunedda reigned as a Welsh chieftain, parts of the Roman legions had been withdrawn, but the empire still considered Britain as its province.

Section 14 of the *Historia Brittonum* relates that "the sons of Liathan prevailed in the country of the Dementians, where the city of Mynyw is, and in other countries, that is Gower [and] Kidwelly, until they were expelled by Cunedda, and by his sons, from all countries in Britain." Section 62 is a parallel: "Cunedda, with his sons, to the number of eight, had come from the north, from the country called Manaw Gododdin ... and expelled the Irish from those countries, with immense slaughter so that they never again returned to inhabit them."

Although there has been some controversy about the historicity of Cunedda's dynasty, Leslie Alcock writes that there is nothing inherently improbable about Cunedda and Ceredic migrating to Wales, and "there's no reason why the account should be anything other than a record of fact" (Alcock, 1989, 126). After debating three dates for Cunedda's migration, Alcock selected the year 450 as the most plausible, organized by a sub–Roman authority which had sent Anglian *foederati* to Britain as allies. Cunedda's clan journeyed from the Antonine Wall, across Hadrian's Wall, and into northern Wales. He was granted a huge tract of land.

In addition to the *Historia Brittonum*, several others confirm Cunedda's trek. Nora Chadwick writes that Cunedda's function as chieftain was to protect the Antonine Wall, but he was later transferred to Wales. She uses a term of high distinction — Gwledig — to describe his son Ceredig (Chadwick 1965, 39–42).

Welsh historian John Davies claims that the story of Cunedda is "unlikely," but doesn't offer evidence indicating why he believes such. Surprisingly, his text contains a map depicting six territories named after Cunedda's sons.

Steve Blake and Scott Lloyd (2002, 101) catalogued all the territories occupied by Cunedda and his sons. Variant spellings of some of the occupied territories are: Meirion/Meriaun, Ceredigion/Ceredig/Cerdic, Afloeg/Abloyc, Dunod/

Dunaut, Rufon/Rumaun, Dogfael/Docmail, Edeirn/Etern, Einion Yrth/Enniaun Girt, and Ysfael/Osmail. The largest is Ceredigion; to the north is Creuddyn, a tract granted to Cerdic's son Creoda, verifying that *The ASC* erroneously labels Cynric as Cerdic's son instead of Creoda. *The BHM* avers Cunedda and his sons were granted land extending from the River Dee to the River Teifi.

J.N.L. Myres writes that Cunedda and his tribe were first employed by the Romans as *limitanei* on the Antonine Wall. The Roman Magister Stilico then transferred Cunedda and his clan to North Wales. The Roman government applied this policy of "enlisting a tribe from the north and planting it with the status of *foederati*" in Wales (288–290).

Overriding Davies's denial of Cunedda's genealogy and historicity, R.G. Collingwood writes,

> If certain late traditions current in Wales [during this era] are at all to be trusted (Cunedda's court at Carlisle; his horsemen on the Wall; his shadowy connexion with the office of *Dux Britanniarum*; and John Rhys' *Celtic Britain*), then Cunedda and his tribesmen were employed as frontiersmen on the Wall between its evacuation by the regular *limitanei* and his transference to North Wales by Stilicho ... then the story of Cunedda must indicate that, just before the close of the century, the Roman government applied this well-worn device to the Scotic problem: enlisting a tribe from the north and planting it with the status of *foederati* in the west, there to act as a local militia under its own king.... The transplantation of Cunedda was part of Stilicho's work [Collingwood, 1937, 119, 288–290].

A second factor which is as crucial as genealogy in establishing Cerdic's role in history is chronology.

It is fortuitous that when GILDAS BADONICUS computed his birth year based on the Battle of Mount Badon, he also provided future generations chronologies for the death of Cerdic and Octha in 497, and the victory of Ambrosius in the same year. The dates in bold print signify Cerdic's floruit, his rule-of-thumb lifespan, and the date of his death at the Battle of Camlann. Cerdic would have been ten to twelve years old in 440 when HENGIST and his clan infringed upon the Welsh. All three Cerdics fall within the

Fifth- and Sixth-Century British Chronology
± Two Years

426 — First Anglian Landing	*497 — **Death of Cerdic**
440 — Second Anglian Landing	*Death of Octha the Anglian
450 — Third Anglian Landing — *ASC*	Victory of Ambrosius
455–485 — Cerdic Floruit	502 — Battle of Camlann
440–500 — Cerdic Lifespan	Death of Ambrosius
497 — (Birth of Gildas Badonicus)	541 — Penning of the *De Excidio*
Battle of Mount Badon	570 — Death of Gildas Badonicus

listed lifespan. The asterisks signify suppositions extracted from probable sources or from folklore. This sums up the historic figure of Cerdic, fifth son of Cunedda.

The second persona of Cerdic — that of an interpreter — also appears in the existent histories. Josephus Stevenson translated Manuscript A (Nennius *HB*, 37) which records Cerdic in this manner: "In one of the Anglian keels came Hengest's daughter, a beautiful and very handsome girl. Hengest held a banquet for Vortigern, for his men, and for his interpreter, whose name was Cerdic, and he told the girl to serve their wine. They all got exceedingly drunk, and Satan entered into Vortigern's heart, and made him love the girl. Through his interpreter, he asked Hengest for her hand, saying, 'Ask of me what you will, even to the half of my kingdom.'"

Cerdic fades from British history, but finds a niche in Welsh folklore. In *The Mabinogion*, the quintessence of Welsh literature, Gwrhyr, Interpreter of Languages, appears in three tales — "How Culhwch Won Olwen" (Gantz, 1976, 147, 149–151, 161, 163–166, 171), "The Dream of Rhonabwy" (Gantz, 1976, 190), and "Gereint and Enid" (Gantz, 1976, 275). In the latter two he is only mentioned once, but in the Culhwch tale he plays a rather important role. Gwrhyr

knows all tongues, and also solicits help from animals. When he is on a quest to capture Twrch the pig and steal the "comb and shears between his ears," he tries to trap Twrch, but the pig escapes and swims to Ireland with Gwrhyr and Kay in hot pursuit. They fail.

The second quest is to rescue Mabon, a baby kidnapped at birth. Gwrhyr first talks to an ousel, who directs him to the Stag of Rhedenvre, who sends him to the Owl of Cwm Cawlwyd, who refers him to the Eagle of Gwernabwy, who recommends him to Salmon of Llyn Llyw. Mabon is finally rescued from his imprisonment. As a wondrous interpreter, Gwrhyr is an evocative name for Cerdic the Interpreter, who, in Section 37 of versions G, I, K, and N of Nennius's manuscripts, is the only "Briton among the Britons who knew Saxon."

Both Monmouth's *History of the Kings of Britain*, and the *Tysilio* are referred to as pseudo-histories, somewhere between history and folktale. Although the *Historia Brittonum* gives no information about the death of VORTIMER (NENNIUS, HB, 44), Monmouth lists Vortimer's four battles, the return of possessions taken from the Britons, Renwein's plotting his assassination, his death by poisoning, and his burial (Monmouth, vi 14–vi15).

History of the Kings of Britain Geoffrey of Monmouth	*Tysilio* (Peter Roberts/compiler)
CHERDIC comes to Britain with Octha at the invitation of his father Hengist.	CHELDRIC comes to Britain with Octha.
CHELDRIC is killed by Cador in the Battle of Baddon.	CLEDRIC is killed at Bath (Badon) by Cador.
CHELRIC is in league with Mordred against Arthur. He is killed in the Battle of Camblam.	

Does Cerdic have a role in either of these manuscripts? The answer is a tentative nod because both Geoffrey and Peter Roberts are amanuenses — copyists or scribes — and evidently at times, neither can decipher his own script. In the realm of these "pseudo-histories," then, the names Cerdic becomes a specter. As the chart shows, the name Cerdic or Ceredic or Ceredig (his most commonly known names) do not appear in either of the manuscripts.

The individuals named in the preceding table come to Britain, but from where? Wales? East Anglia? The mainland? And in other manuscripts, it is Cerdic who is in Britain with Octha, and it is Cerdic who is killed in the Battle of Badon. Chelric is an enigma, but the other names in the chart should no doubt be considered misspelled epithets for Cerdic/Ceredic/Ceredig.

The third persona of Cerdic — a king — is seemingly the simplest to unravel, yet for some reason it is the most complex to persuasively establish. The simplicity is that there is no doubt among serious scholars that Cerdic is a Celtic-British name, not an Anglian one, although the name appears in *The Anglo-Saxon Chronicle*. That fact is repeated in a number of texts: *The Discovery of King Arthur* (Ashe, 1985, 197–198), *King Arthur* (Castledon, 2000, 90), *Roman Britain and Early England* (Blair, 1963, 202–203), *Celtic Britain* (Chadwick, 1965, 39, 40, 42), *The Anglo-Saxon Age* (Fisher, 1973, 32–35, 46), *Two of the Saxon Chronicles Parallel* (Plummer, 1952, note 12), *The English Settlements* (Myres, 1945,

404 footnote 3, 446), *The Quest for Arthur's Britain* (Ashe, 1987, 158–159, 188), *Historic Figures of the Arthurian Era* (Reno, 2000, 60, 164), and *King Arthur: A Military History* (Holmes , 1996, 92–95).

The first item which must be stricken because it is so misleading is Cerdic being dubbed a West-Saxon king, and must be supplanted with the title of "Celtic King of Wessex," since the former presupposes that Cerdic is an Anglian (not a Saxon) from the mainland. Each of the books stresses that Cerdic, the traditional founder of the ruling dynasty of Wessex, is not the only name derived from a Celtic copyist in Anglo-Saxon history. As J.N.L. Myres admonishes, "We are face to face with the thorniest of all political problems in this period, the question of the origin of Wessex" (Myres, 1945, 393). He follows up (page 404) by pointing out that there are eight generations of Celtic names in the House of Wessex, more than any Anglian kingdom, which will be further considered later.

It is baffling why scholars and historians have skirted the probability that Cerdic son of Cunedda and Cerdic interpreter for Vortigern are also Cerdic the Wessex king. Michael Holmes (1996, 92) writes, "It is quite possible that Cerdic was a British leader who joined forces with the invaders and fought with them against his own countrymen." Unfortunately, he didn't follow through to establish his concept. Other authors claim there is no archaeological evidence that Cerdic invaded Wessex from the mainland and through Southampton Water.

The Three Histories ± Two Years	The Anglo-Saxon Chronicle
426 First Anglo-Saxon landing	495 Cerdic arrives and fights in Wales
440 Second Anglo-Saxon landing	508 Cerdic kills a Welsh king
450 Third Anglo-Saxon landing	*519 Cerdic obtains the kingdom in Britain
455–485 Cerdic floruit	527 Cerdic fights the Britons
440–500 Cerdic lifespan	530 Cerdic fights in the Isle of Wight
497 Battle of Mount Baddon	534 Death of Cerdic
497 Death of Cerdic	
497 Birth of Gildas Badonicus	
502 Battle of Camlann	
541 Penning of the *DE* by Gildas	
570 Death of Gildas Badonicus	

Upon investigation, those truisms indicate discrepancies between the three existent British histories (the *De Excidio, A History of the English,* the *Historia Brittonum*) and *The Anglo-Saxon Chronicle.* The *ASC,* appearing several decades later, differs markedly from what the histories record, deviating widely from commonly accepted chronologies. No doubt everyone knows the definition of a chronicle, but Charles Plummer (1952, xvi) adds one interesting clarification. He states, "A chronicle admits to alterations indefinitely." He defines histories as facts "which have undergone a new arrangement, have been re-examined, criticised, distributed, and grouped." Based upon these definitions, Plummer proposes that if alteration must be made, it is the chronicle which must be emended, not the history.

Several items must be noted in the table on the bottom of the previous page:

1. G.N. Garmonsway differentiates between "Wales" and "Britain" and between the "Welsh" and the "British" (Garmonsway, 1990, 14–16).
2. There is a 45-year discrepancy between the dates of arrival, 450 (Alcock, 1971, 108–109), and 495 (Garmonsway, 1990, 14).
3. There is a 37-year discrepancy between the death of Cerdic, 497 (based upon the satellite date of Gildas's birth-year) and 534 (Garmonsway, 1990, 16).
4. The starred year, 519, according to Plummer, "is very like a doublet of year 527" (Plummer, 1952, 12).

Another anomaly is the discrepancy between the Genealogical Preface, and the *ASC.* The table lists the date (500) when Cerdic conquered Wessex as opposed to the *ASC* date of 519, which Plummer identified as spurious. The reign of Cerdic's son Creoda is listed only in the Genealogical Preface (Garmonsway, 1990, 2) and not in the *ASC* (Garmonsway 1990, 14). The dates in brackets show the inconsistency between the dates in the Preface and those in the *Chronicle,* varying by as many as thirty-three years. In 1899 Plummer (1952, 3) claimed that it was impossible to "harmonize the two series of dates," and it was "lost labor to try to reconcile these inconsistencies between the *Chronicle* versus its Preface."

However, ninety-seven years later, in *The Historic King Arthur* (Reno, 1996, 55–65), I reconciled the dates from 494 through 675, and covered the reigns of ten West-Saxon kings, including Creoda, Cerdic's son, who was overlooked in the *Chronicle,* where Cynric is listed as Cerdic's son instead of his grandson.

According to Plummer, (1950, 2), "It's a small matter that the Preface puts the invasion of Cerdic and Cynric in 494, while the Chronicle places it in 495, but it is more serious that the Preface places the foundation of the kingdom of Wessex six years after their arrival, while the Chronicle places it in 519." He's not concerned with a possible ± two years. In the reconciliation table (see top of next page), three dates are an identical match and the others are within Plummer's set boundaries; numbers are bracketed.

Nor is another text, the *Historia Brittonum,* free of discrepancies by any means. For one, the titles which were inserted by Theodor Mommsen in the 1800s should be removed so that a reader realizes that the original manuscripts had no such

	Genealogy Preface	*A–S Chronicle*	*Discrepancy*
Cerdic	500–[516] (16)	519–[534] (15)	516–534=18yrs
Creoda		Not Listed	Nil
Cynric	516–[527] (27)	534–[560] (26)	527–560=33yrs
Ceawlin	543–[574] (31)	560–[591] (31)	574–591=17yrs
Ceol	574–[580] (6)	591–[597] (6)	580–597=17yrs
Ceowulf	580–[597] (17)	597–[611] (14)	597–611=14yrs
Cynegils	597–[628] (31)	611–[643] (32)	628–643=15yrs
Cenwahl	628–[659] (31)	643–[672] (29)	659–672=13yrs
Sexburg	659–[660] (1)	672–[673] (1)	660–673=13yrs
Aescwine	660–[662] (2)	674–[676] (2)	662–676=14yrs

Saxon Kings	Genealogy Preface	Anglo-Saxon Chronicle
Cerdic	500–516 (16)	519–[534] (15)
Creoda	517–[534] (17)	
Cynric	534–[560] (26)	534–[560] (26)
Ceawlin	560–[585] (26)	Ceawlin is combined with Coel in the *Anglo-Saxon Chronicle*
Ceol	585–[591] (6)	560–[591] (31)
Ceowulf	591–[608] (17)	597–[611] (14)
Cynegils	608–[639] (31)	611–[642] (31)
Cenwahl	639–[670] (31)	642–[671] (29) mss A, B, C, E
Sexburg	670–[671] (1)	671–[672] (1)
Aescwine	671–[673] (2)	673–[675] (2)

headings. Of particular importance for the elimination are "The Kentish Chronicles" (Nennius 31, 36, 43). Had Vortigern, who was a Dyfed Overlord, granted land to Hengist in Thanet (Nennius 58), the two allies would have been separated by 350 miles. Mommsen had no regard for accuracy of locations.

Similarly Vortimer's third battle (Nennius 44) is listed as being fought at an inscribed stone near the Gallic Sea in Kent. Archaeologist Alcock (1989, Map 7 239, 245–247) writes, "There are nearly 200 Group 1 inscribed stones of the fifth century, 140 located in Wales," and "their overwhelming distribution pattern is away from the lowland heart of Roman Britain, and lies instead in the Irish Sea zone." Following this information, Vortimer would be fighting the battle in northwest Wales, nearly 300 miles from Hengist's territory.

According to Gildas Badonicus (23.4 and 24.1–24.4), and BEDE (I. 15), plus Leslie Alcock (1989, 109–110), Hengist and his clan were not settled in Kent but in East Anglia, and they were not *German Saxones* (generic Latin term) but *English Saxones* who had been settled on the island as *foederati*. The Anglian incursions came from the east.

Ashe compared the inscriptions on the Eliseg's Pillar with Cerdic's ancestry recorded in the *ASC*, which reads, "Cerdic was the son of Elesa, the son of Esla, the son of Gewis" (Garmonsway, 1990, 16). He deduces that the name Elesa in the *ASC* is a lingual doublet of Eliseg, which is on the pillar (Ashe, 1968, 158).

The Historic King Arthur goes several steps further, claiming Elesa equates to Cunedda, Esla

equates to Vortigern, and Gewis equates to Paternus, based upon the Welsh genealogies, epithets, the three existent British histories, and *The Anglo-Saxon Chronicle*, plus its Genealogical Preface.

J.N.L. Myres supplies the most comprehensive information about the English settlements in fifth-century Britain. However, he immediately admits that the readers "are face to face with the thorniest of all political problems in this period, the question of the origin of Wessex" (Myres, 1945, 393). Because the controversy about Wessex has not yet been resolved, Myres is faced with objectively presenting a variety of suppositions and theories. The question of how and by whom Wessex was settled is not easily determined, but Leeds and Harden concluded that because of scarce archaeological finds, the route of approach into Wessex was not from the south but more likely from the north (p. 399). Several pages later (p. 402) Myres writes, "How the occupation [of Wessex] eventually took place, and from what point of the compass the settlers came, is, unfortunately a topic on which direct evidence is lacking, but there is at least one notable and material proof that the population of Wiltshire and Dorset [south-central neighbors] in this period anticipated invasion and conquest rather from the north than the south." He then points out (p. 403) that Fox-Pitt-Rivers confirmed that the Wansdyke in the Wessex territory "was thrown up against a northern enemy," not a Saxon approach from the south.

In conclusion, Cerdic's most absorbing aspect is his triadic persona. He was not an Anglian from the Continent, but a powerful, seditious,

Eliseg's Pillar is a stone monument in northern Wales near Valle Crucis, naming Vortigern and some of his ancestry. Geoffrey Ashe has linked the name Elesa recorded in *The Anglo-Saxon Chronicle* with Eliseg on the monument, since other names — including Cattigern, Pasgen, and Brydw — are listed as Gwrtheyrn's (Vortigern's) sons.

Celtic chieftain who for some reason betrayed his loyalty to father and country and followed in the footsteps of his grandfather Vortigern. A researcher must dig through a mountain of information, but the nuggets of discovery do point to three faces of Cerdic.

Sources: L. Alcock (AB); G. Ashe (DKA); G. Ashe [Ed] (QFAB); R. Barber (FOA); P. Blair (RB&EE); S. Blake/S. Lloyd (P); R. Castleden (KA: TBL); N. Chadwick (CB); R. Collingwood/J. Myres (RB&ES); D. Fisher (A-SA); J. Gantz (TM); G.N. Garmonsway (ASC); M. Holmes (KA: AMH); C. Littleton/L. Malcor (FSTC); J. Morris (BH); Pitt-Rivers (ECC); C. Plummer (TSCP); F. Reno (HKA/HFAE); H. Scullard (RB: OOE); L. Sherley-Price (BEDE: HEC&P); J. Stevenson (N: HB); L. Thorpe (GM: HKB); M. Winterbottom (G: RBOW).

Ceredig of Elmet. Ceredig of Elmet is many times confused with CERDIC map (son of) Cunedda (Cerdic A), Cerdic the Interpreter (Cerdic B) , and Cerdic the West Saxon King (Cerdic C). *The Annales Cambriae* lists this king's obituary in the year 616, outside the fifth century, the alleged era of the historic Arthur, approximately a century later than the other Cerdics.
Sources: L. Alcock (AB); J. Moris (BH).

Cerne Abbas. An interesting connection with absolutely no evidence to support its relationship is a parallel between Arcturus the Bear and the famous landmark in Britain, Cerne Abbas.

The constellation Boötes (Bo-'ot-teez), as depicted by the Greeks in the sixth century B.C.E., is shown in an accompanying map. Although the earliest Greek work by Eudoxus of Cnidus has been lost, Hipparchus later described the constellation system which was adopted by Ptolemy three hundred years later. Ptolemy made very few changes to the system, which is still in use today. The Greeks personified Boötes as a man walking with his right hand holding a club and his left extending upward, restraining two leashed dogs apparently barking at the Great Bear.

The Great Bear constellation itself — Ursa Major — has given rise to two Arthurian epithets. In the sixth century GILDAS BADONICUS uses the expression "Bear" for CUNEGLASUS, one of his contemporary kings whom he castigates. He describes Cuneglasus as "a bear rider of many and driver of the chariot of the Bear's stronghold."

The Great Bear as a totem or epithet for Arthur's clan has been a subject of debate since the time of Gildas Badonicus. The respected his-

Cerne Abbas, an alleged replication of the constellation Artos the Bear, with the addition of an obvious appendage.

torian R.G. Collingwood comments that Gildas does not mention Arthur except "in an oblique allusion." He writes,

> There was, among the British leaders whom Gildas took it upon himself to rebuke, someone named or nicknamed The Bear, Ursus; and if he is not identical with Cuneglasus named in the same passage (an obscure one) his name may represent Arthur's, twisted through the Celtic *artos*, bear. Yet this is unlikely, because forty-four years, Gildas says, had elapsed between the siege of Mons Badonicus and the date of writing: too long, probably, for the victory to be still alive.... But, for what this is worth, the Cambridge thirteenth-century manuscript of Nennius glosses the passage of the *Historia* by observing that "Artur, translated into Latin, means *ursus horribilis*." It must be left an open question whether Gildas refers to Arthur or not.

E. K. Chambers, another respected Arthurian of Collingwood's era, agrees with the latter's as-

sessment. He comments, "It has been suggested that Arthur may still have been alive when Gildas wrote, and even that he may have been Cuneglases, who is somewhat cryptically described both as a bear and a charioteer of a bear. But the Bear etymology for Arthur is very doubtful." However, more recent promoters of a historic King Arthur of the fifth century still consider the possibility that Arthur's name might attach itself to the "Bear" motif, pointing to the Welsh/Breton association of Arth or Arto meaning "bear."

The second association of Ursa Major perhaps linked to an epithet for King Arthur is the star ARCTURUS in the constellation Boötes. This connection is based upon the fact that Gildas Badonicus does not mention the name ARTHUR as a noted leader, but instead praises AMBROSIUS AURELIANUS as the hero of the fifth century who snatches Britain from the brink of annihilation. Arcturus, therefore, would be an epithet for Ambrosius Aurelianus. Arcturus, the brightest star in the constellation, never drops below the horizon, which would symbolize the "regeneration motif" of this great hero. Arcturus (i.e., Arthur) never dies, but he is only sleeping until he is once again summoned to human activity.

Nonetheless, there is no supportable link between Ursa Major and Britain's Cerne Abbas, located eight miles north of Dorchester. There is an interesting likeness between the drawing of Ursa Major and Cerne Abbas, *sans*, of course, the phallus of the "Rude Man," but the inspiration which lies behind the carving of this figure remains an enigma. A different story which has evolved about this figure is that it was created during the reign of Emperor Commodus between 180 and 193 C.E. because he considered himself a reincarnation of Hercules. Yet that is an explanation which seems more far-fetched than the figure being a representation of Ursa Major, or more specifically, a tribute to Arcturus.

Sources: C. Barber/D. Pykitt (JTA); R. Barber (FOA/KA: H&L); R. Castleden (KA: TBL); E. Chambers (AOB); R. Collingwood/J. Myres

(RB&ES); M. Holmes (KA: AMH); J. Markale (KA: KOK); G. Phillips/M. Keatman (KA: TS); F. Reno (HKA/HFAE); M. Winterbottom (G: ROB&OW).

Cheldric. In the opening segment of "Arthur of Britain," Arthur is fighting a major battle at the River Douglas, obviously part of the material Monmouth was copying, extracted from the battle list in the *Historia Brittonum*. The reader is informed that the Saxon Balduf, Colgrin's brother, is on the seacoast of Britain "awaiting the arrival of Duke Cheldric, who is on his way from Germany to bring the Saxons support." Cheldric lands in Albany with six hundred shiploads of Saxons. When the Saxons confront Arthur's army in battle, Cheldric escapes from Arthur at the Battle of Badon. CADOR, however, tracks Cheldric to the Isle of Thanet and kills the villain there.

As with CHERDIC, Cheldric seems to be another doublet of CERDIC.

Source: L. Thorpe (GM: HKB).

Chelric. Chelric is another Saxon leader who is listed in Monmouth's manuscript, appearing in the section "Arthur of Britain" at a later date than CHELDRIC. MORDRED sends Chelric back to Germany to conscript more troops to fight against Arthur. In return for this service, Mordred promises Chelric a portion of the island stretching from the River Humber to Scotland, as well as all of the lands Hengist and Horsa held in Kent during earlier days. The treaty is agreed upon and Chelric returns with eight hundred ships filled with armed pagans.

Arthur pursues Mordred across the island and into Cornwall, catching the traitor at Camblam. Succinctly, Monmouth writes, "On Mordred's side, there fell Chelric."

Chelric appears to be the same character as Cheldric, who was killed by CADOR several pages earlier in the same chapter. It's almost as if Monmouth checked his copy-work, and realized he had "killed" Cheldric. Was the simplest solution to drop the "d" in Cheldric's name and create another character? It's obvious that in Arthuriana — both historical and legendary — that a character's name might be spelled a dozen different ways. It would not be farfetched to assume

that the same process might have happened to the names Cherdic, Cheldric, and Chelric.

See also CERDIC.

Source: L. Thorpe (GM: HKB).

Cherdic. Cherdic is mentioned only once, very briefly, by Geoffrey of Monmouth in Part Four, "The House of Constantine," in *History of the Kings of Britain*. Hengist is attempting to convince Vortigern to let more German Saxons into Britain. When Vortigern finally agrees, "Messengers set off. Octa and Ebissa arrive, and a man called Cherdic, too, with three hundred boats filled with a fully-equipped army."

In and of itself, this name seems unattached to anything Arthurian, but Geoffrey's inadvertent misunderstanding of the passage he was translating suggests that he confused three characters: Cherdic, CHELDRIC, and CHELRIC. There is a supportable possibility that Cherdic is a reference to Cerdic, King of the West Saxon House, whose exploits on the island span several decades. Further, this particular individual might be linked to Cerdic the Interpreter recorded in the *Historia Brittonum*, and Cerdic son of Cunedda given in Welsh genealogies.

See also CERDIC.

Source: L. Thorpe (GM: HKB).

Chrétien de Troyes (*floruit* 1140–1180; *CE* = 1160–1191 / *lifespan* 1145–1204). Calculating a floruit or lifespan for Chrétien is only an approximation, and assigning specific years for the appearance of his romances, with only a few exceptions, must be given in probable decades. One work claims that Chrétien's manuscripts were completed between 1160 and 1180, while another asserts a larger span, from the late 1150s to 1190, two similar calculations. Chrétien's final romance, *Le Conte del Graal*, was dedicated to Philip of Flanders, who died in 1191, fitting into the asserted time-span. But there is a different claim that *Le Chevalier de la Charrete*, probably his most popular romance, was not finished in his lifetime but was apparently completed by Godefroy de Leigny, which means the passage of time suggested by the two above time-spans is a bit misleading. William Kibler claims that "Chrétien was the first to speak of Queen Guinevere's affair with Lancelot of the Lake, the first

Romance	Characters	Comment
Erec and Enide (1170)	Guinevere Gawain Erec Lancelot Girflet Yvain the Valiant Morgan (le Fay)	Guinevere appears in Geoffrey of Monmouth's work, first alias Ganhumara, and then plays a major role. In the scene opening in *Erec*, she is insulted by Yder's hunch back dwarf, and Erecbecomes one of her champions.
		Of all good knights of the Round Table, Gawain was the first, Erec the second, and Lancelot the third. Gawain is a major character in Monmouth, but Erec and Lancelot are not. Lancelot makes his debut in this tale, then becomes the hero in Chrétien's later romance, *The Knight of the Cart.* Yvain was one of the named and numbered knights. Chrétien describes Morgan's healing powers, but does not reveal her evil side.
Cligés (1176)	Iseut (Isolde) Tristan King Mark Lancelot Perceval Gawain	Kibler asserts "*Cligés* is a romance based on Græco-Byzantine material," which is sprinkled with Arthurian matter, including Arthur, Gawain, Tristan, and Isoud. Cligés is the son of Alexander II of Greece and a queen named Soredamors.
Le Chevalier de la Charette (Lancelot) 1177	Guinevere Gawain Kay Meleagant Lionel Yvain	Chrétien explains, "The subject matter and meaning are furnished and given by the countess [Maria de Champagne] and he [Chrétien himself] strives to add nothing but his effort and careful attention."
Le Conte del Graal (Perceval)	Kay Girflet Yvain Sagremor Agravain Gawain	This romance is deeply engrained in Welsh tradition. When Perceval prepares for his journey to be knighted, he is outfitted in the manner of the Welsh. His mother refuses to let him travel with three javelins "so that he wouldn't appear so markedly Welsh."

to mention Camelot, and the first to write of the adventures of the Grail — with Perceval, the mysterious procession, and the Fisher King."

Because we know virtually nothing about Chrétien's life, a comparison of his writing with that of other contemporary antiquarians becomes problematic. One case in point is Layamon's *Brut*. It is well-nigh impossible to determine who penned what, and when, or whose writing might have influenced the other. LAYAMON is quite specific that he wrote his manuscript based upon three major sources — BEDE, Albin/Augustine, and WACE — but in spite of acclamations that he was quite well-read, he does not mention Chrétien. It can be affirmed that Wace's writing preceded Layamon and that he was a contemporary of both Layamon and Chrétien, but no more can

be positively asserted, except that the Arthurian writings of all three antiquarians were preceded by GEOFFREY OF MONMOUTH's *History of the Kings of Britain*.

The unexpected termination of the two tales by Chretien — *Lancelot* and *Perceval* — has led D.D.R. Owen to surmise that

Chrétien apparently found it difficult to bring his romances to a satisfactory conclusion. *Erec*, though ending with fine pomp, gives the impression of having been stretched artificially over the last couple of thousand lines. *Cligés* finishes on a note approaching bathos. *Yvain*'s ending is better, though contrived and psychologically barren. *Lancelot* was not finished at all by Chrétien but by a colleague, Godefroi de Leigni. *The Conte du Graal* was likewise left incomplete; or, as I believe, neither of its two constituent poems (the one on Perceval, the other on Gawain) runs its distance. It looks as if Chrétien had a target length for each of his major romances of something near 7,000 lines, and that this put a strain on his endurance.

Sources: R. Cline (P: SG); W. Comfort (CDT: AR); W. Kibler (CDT: AR); D. Owen (CDT: AR); B. Raffel (P: SG).

Cinglas. The name Cinglas appears in the Welsh genealogy of Cunedda and his sons. He is listed as Enniaun Girt's grandson.

See also CUNEGLASUS.

Clamadeu. In the course of PERCEVAL's adventures, Clamadeu is one of his rivals vying for BLANCHEFOR. He is besieging the damosel's castle in hopes of capturing her, but Perceval interferes, defeating not only Clamadeu's counsel Engygeron, but Clamadeu himself. Both villains are sent to King Arthur's court, where they repent and become respectable knights.

Sources: R. Cline (P: SG); W. Kibler (CDT: AR); D. Owen (AR).

Clamide. *see* WOLFRAM VON ESCHENBACH.

Cognomen. From Latin, a family or last name. Its plural is cog-**nom'**-i-nah. Example: Ambrosius AURELIANUS.

See also AGNOMEN and NOMEN.

Sources: Meriam Dictionary; Cassell's Latin Dictionary.

Colgrevance, Calogrenant. In Book XVI, Chapter XV–XVI, Malory's Colgrevance is Chrétien's Calogrenant. Sir Lionel is in a rage and has already slain a hermit who tried to protect Sir Bors. When Colgrevance intervenes, he tries to persuade Lionel that he should not kill his own brother Bors. But Lionel has lost his sensibilities and hence challenges Colgrevance. Lionel strikes a mighty blow, splitting the intervenor's helm. When Bors witnesses this, he tries to help Colgrevance, but is still too weak after Lionel's first attack. Lionel vows he will kill both Colgrevance and Bors.

With his sword Lionel strikes the helmet from Colgrevance's head, then strikes him again, knocking him to the ground. After he slays Colgrevance, he turns back to his brother. As a sign

from God, a cloud and flame comes between them. The two men fall to the ground in a swoon. When they awake, Lionel asks forgiveness of God and Bors, and he and his brother separate.

Yet this is not the end of Colgrevance. In Book XX, Chapter IV he is alive when LANCELOT is caught in Queen GUINEVERE's bedchamber. When Sir AGRAVAIN, Sir MORDRED, Sir Colgrevance, and eleven other knights come to capture him, Lancelot blocks the door so that only one man at a time can enter. Colgrevance of Gore was the unfortunate first. He struck at Lancelot, but Lancelot "put aside the stroke and gave Colgrevance such a buffet upon the helmet that he fell grovelling dead within the chamber door."

Source: T. Malory (LMD'A).

Combrogi. Combrogi is a Welsh word for "countrymen." *See also* CYMRY.

Comes Britanniarum. The title of *Comes Britanniarum* attaches itself to CONSTANTIUS III of the Western Roman Empire and the possibility that this individual is the supreme commander whom Emperor HONORIUS sent to Britain to reclaim the island as a Roman province. There are theories that claim Constantius III might possibly be the *Consulibus*, whom Ambrosius identifies as his father, recorded in the "Tale of Emrys" in the *Historia Brittonum*, the patrician described in Monmouth's "House of Constantine," and therefore the hero known as PENDRAGON, Arthur's father, on the island.

R. G. Collingwood provides the most informative details about the inception of the office known as *Comes Britanniarum*. He writes: "As for military organization [of the Western Roman Empire], the *Notitia* enumerates three commands: the *Dux Britanniarum*, with headquarters at York, the *Comes Litoris Saxonici*, in command of the coastal forts, and the *Comes Britanniarum*, in charge of a field-army." He explains that the first two offices had been created early in the history of the Western Empire, but then states that the office of *Comes Britanniarum* didn't exist until the second decade of the fifth century.

He continues: "Among the officers ascribed to

Britain is the *Comes Britanniarum*. Unlike [two other comrades] — the count of the Saxon Shore and the duke of Britain, [the *Comes Britanniarum*] ... commanded a mobile field-army of six cavalry and three infantry units. No such officer and no such force are mentioned anywhere in our literary sources." There were four other such counts, but none of these offices existed before the fifth century. Collingwood deduces that "the conclusion stands that the Count of Britain's command must have come into existence after the supposed severance of Britain from the Empire." This is a reference to the withdrawal of Roman personnel in 410.

After more detailed explanation about the office of *Comes Britanniarum* and how it affected Britain, he writes that the office "must certainly be associated with the work of the Patrician Constantius [III], who re-established Roman control in Brittany about 417." Collingwood then ends his inquiry with this summary: "The last phase of Roman government, therefore, began in or about 417 and ended some years before 429. It may be some comfort to think that this much of historical reality, shadowy though it be, underlies the 'second vengeance' in the story of GILDAS BADONICUS. However it may have ended, both sides still no doubt believed that it was to begin again; and it was only in 446, after the vain appeal to AËTIUS, that hope was abandoned." The *Comes Britanniarum* would fit into a chronological slot about the time of Ambrosius's birth, as suggested in the *Historia Brittonum*.

Source: R. Collingwood/J. Myres (RB&ES).

Condwiramurs, Parzival's paramour in Wolfram's romance, has two sons, Kardeiz and Loherangrin, the latter who is Lohengrin in Wagner's work.

See also WOLFRAM VON ESCHENBACH.

Constans, Son of Flavius Claudius Constantinus. There are three figures identified by the appellation Constans. Only two, however, appear within the sphere of Arthuriana, in a bipolar historical role. One is Constans, the son of Flavius Claudius CONSTANTINUS, the latter who acquired the epithets of Constantine the Briton and Constantine the Usurper. In the year 407,

Constantine crossed the channel with a force of British soldiers and established himself as co-emperor with Honorius of the West, taking control of Gaul. Constans was appointed as caesar by his father, and was sent to Spain to quell a rebellion. After his success, he returned to Gaul to rejoin his father, but his father, overwhelmed by Roman troops, was dethroned and beheaded. Constans was killed a short time later at Vienne. Both met their fate in 411.

The second Constans reappears 625 years later in Geoffrey of Monmouth's alleged history. Constans is correctly identified as the son of Constantine, but then Monmouth adds two brothers for Constans, one being AURELIUS AMBROSIUS, borrowed from the *Historia Brittonum*, and the other, UTHERPENDRAGON, dragged out of mid-air. Utherpendragon takes YGERNA as a concubine, and as a result, two offspring — Anna and Arthur — perplexingly spring into history.

Constans becomes a monk in the church of Amphibalus in Winchester, but Vortigern dupes him to abandon the religious sect so that he might become king of Britain. Vortigern himself structures the ploy and crowns Constans as king. The naive monk becomes the puppet for VORTIGERN, and in short order, he is assassinated by Vortigern's Pictish henchmen. Vortigern then becomes the king of Britain.

Sources: E. Duckett (MPE&W); A. Ferrill (FOTRE); P. Roberts (COKB); C. Snyder (AAOT); L. Thorpe (GW: HKB).

Constantine (III). King Arthur's alleged successor. Constantine III — not to be confused with CONSTANTIUS III — is the first king castigated by GILDAS BADONICUS. Although Gildas does not use the appellation "III," Gildas's descriptions equate this individual with Geoffrey of Monmouth's Constantine III, King Arthur's successor. This is not the same Constantine listed as King Arthur's father, nor is he Constantine the Usurper. This "tyrant" is alive during Gildas's lifetime, calculated by *The Historic King Arthur* as 497 to 570, emendations of the dates given in the *Annales Cambriae*.

Gildas is scathing in his description of this "filthy lioness of Dumnonia (Cornwall). "He writes: "This very year [Constantine] bound himself by a dreadful oath not to work his wiles on our countrymen, ... then he most cruelly tore at the tender sides and vitals of two royal youth and their two guardians. Their arms were stretched out not to weapons ... but to God and the altar.... He tore them, I say, at the holy altar, using as teeth his sword and spear."

Gildas identifies Constantine by name, but he doesn't reveal who the "two royal youths" were. The reader knows only that Constantine killed these two young lads and their guardians at the altar of a church.

GEOFFREY OF MONMOUTH, through perhaps the fortuity of his ancient source or — as some scholars believe, through his creative imagination — supplies a detailed story. Adding numerals to the name Constantine (Constantine III), Monmouth reveals that Constantine III is the son of Cador, Duke of Cornwall, who succeeds Arthur to the throne. The time frame is, of course, perfect: Constantine III and Arthur are within two generations of each other, and Constantine III fits into Gildas's life span. Although unreliable, Geoffrey gives a date, 542 C.E.

When Constantine assumes the throne, the Saxons and two sons of Mordred revolt against him. They fail to overthrow him and after extended battles, his enemies flee. Geoffrey then describes what transpires. "First [Constantine, son of Cador] forced the Saxons to submit to his authority; and then he captured the two cities [London and Winchester]. He killed one of the young men in front of the altar in the church of St. Amphibalus, where he was taking refuge. The second hid himself in the monastery of certain friars in London. Constantine discovered him and slew him without mercy, beside the altar there."

There is just enough similarity between Gildas's sketchy information and Monmouth's account to make the story ring true. If Geoffrey manufactured the material after he read Gildas's passage, then his story demonstrates a great imagination, especially since Gildas's account definitely gives the impression that the two youths were killed in the same church, whereby Geoffrey records they were killed in separate incidents and in separate locations.

A matter of satellite interest is Gildas's description of the youths' deaths. As evident by his phrasing of the connection between Mons Badonicus and his own birth, Gildas's Latinity can be confusing. It recurs here when he structures this passage: "Constantine tore them at the holy altar, using as teeth his wicked sword and spear so that the place of divine sacrifice was touched by the purple cloaks (as it were) of their drying blood" (M. Winterbottom translation). Arthurian specialists know the significance of "purple" as a mark of Roman heritage and royalty, but even so this passage is confusing.

Winterbottom is an excellent translator, obvious by his meticulous and critically precise selection of synonymous words. He has translated this segment by sticking very closely to the original Latin passage, which itself obscures its meaning. *Historic Figures of the Arthurian Era* more liberally translates the passage thusly: "At the holy altar, the attacking Roman Constantine, armed with his abominable sword and spear, mauled and slashed the youths as with teeth, so that the heavenly altar was purple from clotted gore."

This translation does not reinforce Winterbottom's "purple cloak" which symbolically suggest the attire of Roman royalty, but it does suggest internal conflicts between the *Romanophils* and other *Britanni*. In the original Latin manuscript, *pallia* means "clad as a Roman," positively identifying Constantine as having Roman ties. The word *attingere* can connote "touch," as Winterbottom used it, or it can signify, surprisingly, "attack." D.P. Simpson explains that "touch" is a "transferred" definition — that is, used in an altered or metaphorical sense — but "attack" is a literal definition.

The passage can also be transvaluated, based upon the Latin words *ac si*, so that there is a slight change in perspective: "Constantine, with his abominable sword and spear, mauled and slashed the youths as with teeth, so that clotted gore tinged the heavenly altar purple, matching the cloak of the attacking Roman."

The Latin word *ac*, which is used before words beginning with consonants as opposed to *atque*, which is used before words beginning with *h* or vowels, means "and moreover" or "and even" when adding a new point which is to follow. The

Latin word which follows *ac* in Gildas's passage is *si*, a conjunction, and when this conjunction is preceded by *ac*, its specific use is for comparisons, in this instance comparing the purple gore on the altar with the purple of Constantine's cloak.

In any case, Gildas's account can be used to historically authenticate a Constantine whose floruit was approximately a generation *after* the fifth century. For those who accept Geoffrey's source, it verifies Geoffrey as a copyist/translator rather than a fiction writer.

Ironically, the final segments from Geoffrey's *The History of the Kings of Britain* closely parallels the five tyrants castigated by Gildas Badonicus in the *De Exidio*:

1. The first tyrant whom Gildas castigates is Constantine, and as mentioned above, when Constantine becomes king he murders two young boys. Geoffrey writes that after Arthur (Ambrosius Aurelianus?) passes, Constantine, the son of CADOR, Duke of Cornwall, acquires the throne.
2. Gildas then castigates AURELIUS CANINUS, who succeeds Constantine, which is then copied by Geoffrey as Aurelius Conanus.
3. Gildas identifies the next king as VORTIPOR, and Geoffrey uses the name Vortiporius.
4. The fourth tyrant in Gildas's manuscript is CUNEGLASUS, but Geoffrey lists the king as Malgo, akin to MAGLOCUNUS, listed as the *fifth* successor by Gildas.
5. The real irony is that Monmouth lists Keredic as the next king. Could it be that Cuneglasus (extracted from Gildas) is a reference to Cunedda, and Keredic is actually Cerdic who follows him as successor? Gildas calls Cuneglasus the "red butcher," and the *Historia Brittonum*, in Section 14, states the sons of Liathan were expelled by Cunedda from all countries in Britain. In Section 62, the *Historia* records: "King Maelgwn [Gildas's Maglocunus?] was reigning among the British in Gwynedd, for his ancestors, Cunedda, with his sons to the number of eight, had come from the north, from the country called Manaw Goddoddin, 146 years before Maelgwn reigned, and expelled the Irish from these countries, with immense slaughter, so that they never again returned to inhabit them." This appears as a parallel to Gildas's description "red butcher."

Sources: J. Morris (BH); F. Reno (HKA/HFAE); L. Thorpe (GM: HKB); M. Winterbottom (G: ROB&OW).

Constantine (GM's *History of the Kings of Britain*). This particular Constantine is the most enigmatic when attempting to link the House of Constantine to the historic or legendary Arthur.

After the withdrawal of the Romans from Britain circa 410, Geoffrey of Monmouth relates in his narrative that Guithelinus, the Archbishop of London, travels to Little Britain (Armorica) in a final attempt to recruit aid to drive out the influx of barbarians who are continuously invading Britain. Aldroneus, King of Armorica, rejects Guithelinus's plea that the king lead an army to Britain, but he agrees to send his brother Constantine, with two thousand soldiers, back to Britain under Guithelinus's command. Aldroneus describes his brother as "skilled in military affairs and well endowed with other virtues."

The scenario is concise. As soon as Constantine arrives in Britain with his troops, he attacks the enemy and is victorious. The Britons hold council and raise Constantine to the kingship and as soon as the crown is set upon his head, he is given a wife born of a noble family. When their marriage is consummated, the king has three sons by her, Constans, Aurelius Ambrosius, and a third unnamed for quite some time until he is bestowed with the epithet Utherpendragon. Ten years pass and a Pict stabs Constantine to death with a dagger. End of Monmouth's half-page plot.

Since the release of Monmouth's manuscript in 1136, there has been speculation and controversy during the last eight centuries as to whom this mystifying Constantine might be. The *Tysilio*—exposed to controversy as to whether the work preceded, succeeded or was contemporaneous with *The History of the Kings of Britain*—relates a tale which closely parallels Monmouth's. The *De Excidio* of Gildas Badonicus, written in the sixth century, provides only scant and gossamer clues about Monmouth's Constantine, independent of Constantine III, whom Gildas castigates as a king during his own era. In the eighth century Bede lists three Constantines in his *History*, but none of them is the Constantine named by Geoffrey: the first is Constantine the Usurper, whose real name was Constantinus Flavius, killed in 411 when he attempted to overthrow the Western Roman Empire; the second is Constantine I, emperor of the Roman Empire in the 300s; the third is Constantine, a pope of Bede's own century.

Sources: J. Morris (BH); P. Roberts (COKB); L. Sherley-Price (BEDE: HEC&P); L. Thorpe (GM: HKB); M. Winterbottom (G: ROB& OW).

Constantine the Usurper. *see* CONSTANTINUS, FLAVIUS.

Constantinus, Flavius (Constantine the Usurper). Flavius Constantinus was the true name for Constantine the Usurper. He was a private soldier elevated to Roman emperor by his army in Britain, acquiring the title from 407 C.E until 411. Conscripting his British army and depleting the forces on the island, he crossed to the mainland supposedly to help Gaul quell insurrection by Vandals and other barbarians. He succeeded in expelling the invaders from eastern Gaul, but Honorius sent *foederati* (mercenaries) led by Sarus the Goth, who was able to defeat Constantinus's army at Valentia. Reinforced by troops from Hispania led by his son CONSTANS and Gerontius, a *Magister Utriusque Militiae* (master of soldiers), Constantinus reclaimed the territory, and after Honorius had executed Stilicho, HONORIUS recognized Constantinus as his co-emperor in 409. A different usurper, known as Maximus, weakened Constantinus's position, and eventually led to the death of the Briton usurper and his son Constans. Constantinus was captured by Constantius III in September of 411, and in the usurper's deportment to Ravenna, the prisoner was beheaded.

Because Geoffrey of Monmouth's genealogy of the "House of Constantine" falls apart, the possibility arises that Monmouth, in translating and copying *The History of the Kings of Britain*,

confuses the Constantine/Constans issue. Historically, Constantinus (known more widely as the usurper Constantine) indeed had a son named Constans, whom Edward Gibbon asserts was an ecclesiastic. When Monmouth records his genealogy, he lists a Constantine whose firstborn (Constans) enters a monastery at a later age, but there is no such combination, other than Constantinus and his son Constans, who can be traced in history. This has led to one of two conclusions. Either Monmouth was a copyist and translator who was confused in his assertion that King Arthur's grandfather was named Constantine, or Monmouth's House of Constantine was fiction.

Sources: E. Duckett (MPE&W); E. Gibbon (D&FRE); S. Oost (GPA); L. Thorpe (GM: HKB).

Constantius III. Constantius is a well-known figure in Roman history. He was a native of Illyricum, and under the guidance and protection of Stilicho, he began working his way up the ranks, first in the Eastern Empire ruled by Theodosius the Great, then in the Western Empire ruled by HONORIUS when East and West split.

His career began in earnest during the second decade of the 400s. In 410 C.E. after Rome had been sacked by ALARIC and the Visigoth had secured GALLA PLACIDIA and AËTIUS as hostages, Constantius became the negotiator for Honorius. The negotiations spanned at least six years, during which time Alaric died, ATAULPHUS became leader of the tribe, the tribe was driven into Hispania from Gaul, Ataulphus and Galla Placidia married and had a son, and both Placidia's son and husband were killed.

Simultaneously, interspersed with these events, in 411 Constantius III led an army against Constantine the Usurper (Flavius CONSTANTINUS) who had established his headquarters at Arles in Gaul. Knowing he was to be overwhelmed, Constantine fled to a monastery to be ordained as a priest and hopefully be protected against the wrath of Honorius and Constantius. But Constantius tracked him, and once the usurper was subdued, Constantius promised him safe journey to Ravenna, where Honorius had set up court. Under mysterious circumstances, however, Con-

This recorded history gives a clear-cut image of Constantius III, except for one thin slice of intrigue which ties him to Arthuriana. It might be that Constantius III is confused with Geoffrey of Monmouth's Constantine in Parts IV and VI.

stantine was beheaded en route, and the de-curion in charge of the transfer disappeared.

In 412/413 Heraclian, the Count of Africa, also attempted to overthrow the government. Having complete control of Carthage, Heraclian must have concluded that with both Emperor Arcadius of the East and Stilicho dead, plus Honorius as a reputed weak emperor of the West, the entire empire was ripe for the pluck-ing.

However, he did not realize the power of Constantius III, who was further motivated because Heraclian had, according to Zosimus the historian, slain Stilicho, Constantius's superior and close comrade. The Count of Africa severed commerce between Africa and Rome, attacking Italy with an armada of over three thousand ships. Heraclian and Constantius clashed in a fierce battle on the Tiber River near Portus and Ostia. Defeated, Heraclian retreated back to Carthage, where he was captured and beheaded in March of 413. As a prize, Honorius awarded Constantius with Heraclian's sizeable collection of treasures.

Immediately following this disastrous toll on the strength of the West, only a few months later, in the autumn of 413, Jovinus, another Visigoth leader, was attempting to destroy the empire. After a failed attempt to join his tribe with that of Ataulphus, Jovinus was captured and his head was used to decorate the gates of Ravenna.

It is no wonder that, after successes in all these episodes, Honorius twice appointed Constantius III as *Consulibus*, made him praefect of Gaul, offered his half-sister's hand in marriage, and elevated him to co-emperor of the West. Constantius and Galla Placidia married and had two children. The first was a daughter, Justa Grata Honoria, and the second was a son, born in July 419, named Placidus Valentinianus (VALENTINIAN III).

Geoffrey correctly gives some details about Constantius I (Aurelius Valeriuis Constantius), who invaded Britain and later died in Eburacum (York), but he is obscure about the Constantine he describes as brother of ALDRONEUS and later King of Britain who sires Aurelius Ambrosius, the Ambrosius Aurelianus posted in the *Historia Brittonum*. The individual from Geoffrey's "House of Constantine" much more accurately depicts Constantius III, the *Comes Britanniarum* written about by R.G. Collingwood in his text.

See also PENDRAGON.

Sources: R. Collingwood/J. Myres (RB&ES); E. Duckett (MPE&W); A. Ferrill (FOTRE); S. Oost (GPA), F. Reno (HKA).

Creoda (Manuscripts Ā ß ß). Creoda is Cerdic's son, the "lost" generation who was omitted from the genealogy of the House of the West Saxons. Two impeccable researchers dealing with ancient

chronicles, J.A. Giles and Charles Plummer, are authoritative amanuenses who verify that Creoda should be firmly entrenched in the Anglo-Saxon histories. J.A. Giles specifically explains how the various surviving manuscripts of *The Anglo-Saxon Chronicle* should be approached: "It is commonly stated that the *ASC* is contained in seven MSS, those which are denoted by the letters Ā, A, B, C, D, E, F. It would be truer to say that these MSS contain four Anglo-Saxon Chronicles. A is a transcript of B, and as far as it goes, is identical to C, both having been copied from the same MS: F is an epitome of E. But C, D, E, have every right to be considered distinct Chronicles."

What is particularly important here is that the variants and the Asser annals must seriously be considered in assigning Creoda a generation because those manuscripts have preserved the true chronology which in all the other manuscripts "is disjointed."

Plummer has no doubt that the chronicles themselves ran a sequence of Ā = æ = Æ, with the earliest form of a national chronicle attributed to Alfred the Great. Plummer has no hesitation in declaring that Alfred supplied the earliest form for a national chronicle:

> It is the work of Alfred the Great.... The idea of a national Chronicle as opposed to merely local annals was his, that the idea was carried out under his direction and supervision, this I do most firmly believe.... I have chosen the symbol Æ for this original Chronicle partly because it is the initial of the great king's name, and partly because it expresses that this original stock branches out on the one side into our Ā, and on the other into our E, the two Chronicles which are the furthest apart from one another in character, as they are in time, of all our existing Chronicles.

As Leslie Alcock points out, *The Anglo-Saxon Chronicle* is further criticized because it seems to emphasize leap years, which makes the chronology artificial and inaccurate. However, for the specific period of the latter Arthurian era, the leap years are from 500, 504, 508, etcetera, to 536, 540. Yet the dates actually listed in the *Chronicle* over that same span are 495, 501, 508, 514, 519, 527, 530, 534, and 538. Only one entry, 508, falls on a leap year, which would not follow the pre–Christian artificiality.

Based upon these assertions, *The Historic King Arthur* rectifies the discrepancies of dates and firmly entrenches the Creoda generation in the chronology. Plummer devised a table to show the contrast of dates between the Genealogical Preface and the *Chronicle*, which is given in the first table below.

Plummer concluded that it was impossible to reconcile the discrepancy between the Preface and the *Chronicle*, but he overlooked three miscalculations, excluding those of only ± two years. The first is that Ceawlin's reign was followed by Ceol's, but the next scribe who copied the work did not omit Ceol's reign, but instead combined the two into 31 total years. Plummer then assigned the 31-year combined reign of the two West Saxon kings to only Ceawlin and then added an additional six years for Ceol's reign, giving a total span of 37 years for the two rulers. This, then, throws the calculation off by six years. The second discrepancy is during Ceolwulf's reign, which is listed as 17 years in the Preface, but as 14 years in the *Chronicle*.

Plummer's major oversight, however, is that Creoda is also missing from the Preface. Plummer himself recognizes the missing Creoda generation and that Creoda is CERDIC's son, but for some reason doesn't take that into account.

When those three discrepancies are corrected, the table in *The Historic King Arthur* gives the modification as shown in second table below.

This reconciliation alleviates some of the criticism leveled at the unreliability of chronology in *The Anglo-Saxon Chronicle*. Even better, it clarifies and validates several important factors, independent of attempting to verify (or deny) the historic Arthur. With these emendations, British history of the early medieval period changes quite drastically. Taking the Æthelweard chronicle into account plus the genealogies, these are the events which emerge:

1. Creoda was CERDIC's son who ruled for seventeen years after his father died.
2. Creoda was CYNRIC's father.
3. Cynric was Cerdic's grandson
4. The first two generations — at least Cerdic and Creoda — were on British soil in 494 or 495. *The Anglo-Saxon Chronicle* does not have a year-500 date for the West

	Genealogical Preface	*Anglo-Saxon Chronicle*
Cerdic	500 + 16	519 × 534 = 15 years
Cynric	516 + 27 (17)	534 × 560 = 26 years
Ceawlin	[543 + 31]	560 × 591 = 31 years
Ceol	574 + 6	591 × 597 = 6 years
Ceolwulf	580 + 17	597 × 611 = 14 years
Cynegils	597 + 31	611 × 643 = 32 years
Cenwalh	628 + 31	643 × 672 = 29 years
Sexburg	659 + 1	672 × 673 = 1 year
Æscwine	660 + 2	674 × 676 = 2 years

	Genealogical Preface	*Anglo-Saxon Chronicle*
Cerdic	500 + 16 = 516	34 years: 500–534
Creoda	517 + 17 = **534**	(Cerdic combined w/Creoda)
Cynric	534 + 26 = **560**	26 years: 534–560
Ceawlin	560 + 25 = 585	31 years: 560–591
Ceol	585 + 6 = **591**	(Ceol combined w/Ceawlin)
Ceolwulf	591 + (17*) = **608**	(14*) years: 597–**611**
Cynegils	608 + (31*) = **639**	(32*) years: 611–**643**
Cenwalh	639 + (*31*) = **670**	*29* yrs: 643–672 (Chron $\overline{A}$)
		29 yrs: 641–**670** (Chron A)
Sexburg	670 + 1 = **671**	1 year: 670–671
Æscwine	671 + 2 = **673**	2 years: 671–673

Saxon House, but Æthelweard's *Chronicle* for the year 500 states, "In this sixth year from their arrival in 494, they encircled the western area of Britain now known as Wessex." The arcane wording raises several questions. The word "encircled" is very different from the word "conquered" as it is reported in the Genealogical Preface, and "the western area of Britain" is certainly not the present-day Wessex on the south-central coast of the island. Instead, Æthelweard is suggesting that the "western area of Britain is the territory which was labeled as Ceredigion on the west central coast of Wales," which is more descriptive of the location of Wessex. Could this possibly imply that the original word "Cerdicesora" in entry 495 of the *ASC* is a reference to ancient territory of Ceredigion, rather than the scholarly interpretation that there is no differentiation between Cerdicesora and Cerdicesford, which is then identified as Charford in south-central England? Æthelweard, on the other hand, accepts Charford as Cerdicesford, but lists Cerdicesora as an "unidentified place." If one accepts Æthelweard's description, then Cerdic and Creoda would accurately be fighting the Welsh in west-central Wales, rather than them fighting the Welsh in south-central England.

5. *The Anglo-Saxon Chronicle* does not mention the West Saxons in either the 500 entry or the 514 entry. The West Saxons appear in the 519 entry as "obtaining" the kingdom of the West Saxons and "reigning from that day onward," conflicting with entry 516 in the *Annales Cambriae*, which tersely describes the Battle of Badon, "in which Arthur carried the Cross of our Lord Jesus Christ for three days and three nights on his shield, and the Britons were victorious."

Entry 534 gives notice that "Cerdic passed away and his son Cynric continued to reign for twenty-six years." Based upon the reconciliation of dates, however, that entry of 534 should read *Creoda* passed away and his son Cynric con-

tinued to reign for twenty-six years. With that emendation, Cynric would fit into the "reasonable age" concept spanning the years from 534 until 556.

Thus ends Creoda's reign. One other comment which further emphasizes the importance of Creoda is that his kingdom merits attention. John Davies, in his *History of Wales*, passes over Creoda, probably because he didn't recognize Creoda as a Welsh figure, not aware that the territory (or *commote*) of Creuddyn in Wales is named after Creoda. That kingdom is directly north of Ceredigion, his father's territory. In addition to this association strengthening the premise that Cerdic the West Saxon King is a triplet of Cunedda's son and Vortigern's interpreter, it raises the issue of why the Cunedda clan is considered bogus when five of the sons' territories were so entrenched in Welsh geography from the fifth century to the thirteenth. Creoda and Cerdic might have been Celts who abandoned their heritage and treasonously joined the *Saxone foederati*.

Sources: L. Alcock (AB); A. Campbell (COÆ); J. Davies (HOW); J. Giles (SOEC); C. Plummer (TSCP); F. Reno (HKA); G. Garmonsway (ASC); D. Whitelock Etal (ASC).

Creuddyn. Creuddyn is a variant of the name Creoda.

Culhwch is the main character in one of the five tales of *The Mabinogion* in which Arthur makes his first appearance. *The Mabinogion* is a Welsh compilation of what has become known as the "Four Branches of the Mabinogion," plus seven other tales, five of which include Arthur as a character. Translator Jeffrey Gantz suggests that "How Culhwch Won Olwen" is the earliest of the tales and has not been subjected to as much French influence as the others, and that both the romances of Chrétien de Troyes and *The Mabinogion* "derive from French reworking of Celtic originals." Because only fragments of the "Culhwch" tale are recorded in the *White Book of Rhydderch*, which dates to 1325, the "Culhwch" tale was undoubtedly extracted from the early fifteenth-century *Red Book of Hergest*.

The name Culhwch is interpreted as "Pig Run" because his mother gave birth to him near a pigpen. His name is a misnomer, however, and because Arthur is his first cousin and Amlawdd is his grandfather, he goes to Arthur's court and successfully beseeches the emperor to help him win the hand of Olwen, the daughter of Ysbaddaden. Among Arthur's comrades are Kei, Bedwyr, Gwrhyr Interpreter of Languages, Custenhin, Mabon, and enigmatically Osla Big Knife. After great tribulation, they succeed in their quest and Arthur returns to Kelliwic in Cornwall.

See also RHONABWY and PEREDUR.

Source: J. Gantz (TM).

Cundrie. see WOLFRAM VON ESCHENBACH.

Cunedag. see CUNEDDA.

Cunedda, Cunedag. Leslie Alcock is one of the few researchers who gives due consideration to Cunedda's impact in both Welsh history and Arthuriana. He first notes that Cunedag is an ancient spelling for Cunedda: "Although the *Historia Brittonum* as we have it is a compilation of the ninth century, the primitive spelling Cunedag argues that an early written source underlies this passage."

At the end of the Welsh genealogies, the *British Historical Miscellany* gives us further information about Cunedda and his sons. He then lists the nine sons, including TYPIAUN, who died in Manau Guodotin. Two other sons who made marks in history were CERDIC and Enniaun Girt, the former who assumes a major role in historical Arthuriana, and the latter who is important because he is the grandfather of MAELGWN and Cinglas, all of whom stress the historical aspect. When Cunedda and his sons come down from the north, they are given lands from the Dubr Duiu (the River Dee) to the River Tebi (Teifi) in Western Britain (Wales). There are two sections in the *Historia Brittonum* which refer to Cunedda. The first, §14, is in a segment describing Irish history and the migration of some tribes crossing the sea and settling on the main island: "Later came the Kindred of Eight and lived there with all their race in Britain until today. Istoreth son of Istorinus held Dal Riada with his people. Bolg with his people held the Isle of Man, and other islands about. The sons of LIATHAN pre-vailed in the country of the Dementians ... until they were expelled by Cunedda, and by his sons from all countries in Britain."

The second is §62: "King Maelgwn the Great was reigning among the British, in Gwynedd, for his ancestors, Cunedag with his sons, to the number of eight, had come from the north, from the country called Manau Guotodin, one hundred and forty-six years before Maelgwn reigned, and expelled the Irish from these countries, with immense slaughter, so that they never again returned to inhabit them."

Alcock acknowledges that "some scholars regard the whole account of Cunedda's sons as a confection, or at best as a piece of antiquarian speculation about the origins of certain Welsh place-names." Yet it is not easy to so quickly dismiss characteristics which have become so ingrained in history and geography; it seems presumptuous to disregard nine provinces in central and northern Wales recorded in ancient histories named after Cunedda's sons, and one province named after a daughter. It is quite rare for geographic sites to be named after fictitious individuals; the norm is that rivers, villages, mountains, valleys, and other topographical features acquire their names because of important figures who have inhabited those areas.

Alcock then attempts to establish a date for Cunedda's migration, arriving at one reckoning of 383. After explaining that possibility, he analyzes two other possibilities, one in the year 490, and the next around 450, the last which "suggests that the migration was organized by some sub–Roman authority like that which brought in the Anglo-Saxons as allies."

He then ties in extractions from the *Anglo-Saxon Chronicle* and the three separate *adventi* of Hengist and Horsa. For conviction, he points out that the three generations immediately ancestral to Cunedda all have Roman names: his father was Æternus, his grandfather *Patern Pesrut*, PATERNUS of the Red Robe, and his great-grandfather was TACITUS. In Alcock's words, "This has led to much speculation about the character of Roman influence which had made such names fashionable in this rather remote family. In particular, it has been suggested that Paternus's red robe or cloak was a mark of some

Romanized authority or office, or at least of recognition by the Romans."

Even though disputes have arisen about Cunedda's authenticity, Alcock stresses there has been no argument about where Cunedda evidently came from — the Manau Guotodin, distinguished from Manaw, the Isle of Man. Similarly, other documents indicate that Cunedda was granted territories of western Wales as far south as the River Teifi, and he may have been involved in military operations in southern coastal districts, based upon "statements in the *Historia* about the expulsion of the Irish from Gower and Kidwelly."

These territories of Wales do suggest blood relationships between Cunedda and VORTIGERN, whose ancestry is associated with the migration of the Dessi tribe from Ireland. There are other present-day scholars who identify Vortigern's southern fortress as Llanfihangel-ar-arth on the River Teifi, located twelve miles due north of Carmarthan.

Based on Alcock's research, *The Historic King Arthur* has drawn two parallels, one between

ÆTERNUS and Vortigern, and the other between Cunedda and Vortimer. If Cunedda's ancestry was not fictitious, then his father, Æternus (and his grandfather, Paternus), would indeed have had connections to Roman royalty which would have made that clan powerful enough to direct affairs in Wales. Without these parallels, the *HKA* infers, it seems odd that Cunedda would play such a minor role in British (particularly Welsh) history, especially when considering the upheaval caused by the supposed temporary Roman withdrawal extending to what the Welsh then perceived as a permanent condition.

Historic Figures of the Arthurian Era elaborates upon the parallel between Cunedda and Vortimer. The book devotes three chapters to the ascription that Cunedda is a proper name and Vortimer is an epithet for that individual. Because Cunedda is an obscure but pivotal figure of British history, Chapter 6 focuses upon his homeland and migration, a chronological computation, and both his ancestry and progeny.

In addition to Alcock's clarification of Cunedda's original homeland, Arthur Wade-

Vortimer	*Cunedda*
Vortimer's father = Vortigern (*HB* & Genealogies)	Cunedda's father = Æternus (HB & Genealogies)
Vortigern is associated with the Dessi tribe of Dementae in Wales, later called Dyfed.	Cunedda came from the north and was granted territories in Wales, from the River Dee to the River Teibi, which is the locale of Vortigern's territories.
The *Historia* doesn't provide specific dates, but does relate that Vortimer took over his father's kingdom and expelled the Anglians. Upon his death Vortigern once again resumed the throne.	The *Historia* records that Cunedda and his sons expelled the Irish from Dementae in Wales. In §62, the second section relates that King Maelgwn's ancestors came down from the north 146 years before he reigned. Maelgwyn's death-year, recorded in the *Annales Cambriae*, is 547, suggesting that his clan migrated south to Wales about 401.
The Anglo-Saxon Chronicle supplies the date of 449 for the Anglian entry, and the date of 455 when the Anglians rebel against Vortigern.	
The accepted date by scholars for the beginning of Vortigern's rule is 425. Based upon Vortigern's deposal between 449 and 455, Vortimer's rule would have been during that period of time, from 449 to 455.	Several scholars and historians write that Paternus—Æternus' father and Cunedda's grandfather—migrated from the north and was already settled in Wales. Cunedda would have been a Wledig in the 450s.
The *Historia* indicates that Vortimer was not killed during the four battles against the Anglians, but "died soon afterwards." When he died, the Anglians returned.	Cunedda drops from history.

Evans describes the little district to the west of Edinburgh, on the southern shore of the Firth of Forth. Sir Ifor Williams uses John Rhys as confirmation to validate Manaw Gododdin, but it is Kenneth Jackson who offers a core of explanation in the appendix of his book on the Gododdin: "on a narrow plain on the south side of the Firth of Forth, extending northwest to Stirling, south to Ochils, and eastwards past Alloa."

The motive for Cunedda's migration, as mentioned above, is discussed by Leslie Alcock, and extensive consideration pointed to the fourth or fifth decade of the fifth century as the most logical date, initiated by "some sub–Roman authority like that which brought in the Anglo-Saxons as allies."

By far the most convincing aspect is setting up a paradigm comparing Vortimer and Cunedda. Although it would appear nothing else could be deduced historically about Cunedda, not only history but oral tradition paint quite a comprehensive picture of his crucial contribution to his era. Additionally, both his ancestry and progeny intensify his clan's profound impact from the end of the fourth and into the fifth sixth century. Rachel Bromwich and Thomas O'Sullivan give sketchy information about the etymological significance of Cunedag's name, information which is more consequential than expected.

Sources: L. Alcock (AB); R. Barber (FOA); R. Bromwich (BWP); J. Giles (SOEC); K. Jackson (TG); J. Morris (BH); F. Reno (HFAE/HKA); I, Richmond (RB); W. Skene (FABW); J. Stevenson (N: HB); A. Wade-Evans (EOE&W).

Cunedda's fifth son. *see* CERDIC.

Cuneglasus, Keredic, Caredig. Cuneglasus is the fourth British tyrant whom GILDAS BADONICUS castigates in §34 of the *De Excidio.* This same individual can be found in Geoffrey of Monmouth as Keredic, and in the *Tysilio* as Caredig. The content, however, is very different between Gildas and the other two copyists.

In his writings, Gildas Badonicus labels four of the five tyrants he castigates as "leonine," calling them "whelp of the filthy lioness," "lion-whelp," and "leopard-like," then he scornfully describes Cuneglasus as *lanio fulve* (leonine/tawny butcher). He confronts Cuneglasus di-

rectly, leaving no doubt that Cuneglasus is still alive, and castigating him for committing heinous sins against both man and God. Gildas Badonicus rebukes the scoundrel for rejecting his wife and casting adulterous eyes upon his sister-in-law, inviting disastrous suffering which will someday befall him. This is followed by pleas that he change his ways, and through penance redeem himself before he spends eternity in perpetual fire.

However, the other two accounts are much longer and very different. After a reference to Cuneglasus, both tell the story of Gormund, King of Africa who is inhabiting Ireland, joining with the Saxons to defeat the Britons. The barbarians attack King Keredic, and after a long series of battles, they drive him to Cirencester. When Cirencester is burned, Gormund pursues Keredic across the River Severn into Wales. Gormund ravages most parts of the island, then hands over a considerable part of it to the Saxons. The Britons are deprived of their right to govern themselves, and civil wars continue.

Of interest are Monmouth's term Keredic and Roberts' term Caredig. Both names are very close to Cerdic, whose name appears in three historical documents of the Arthurian era: CERDIC, son of CUNEDDA in the Welsh genealogies, Cerdic the interpreter in the *Historia Brittonum,* and Cerdic the West Saxon king in *The Anglo-Saxon Chronicle.* The primary importance of the link between Keredic/Caredig and Cuneglasus is the *Cunos-* affix in the latter's name. Both MAGLOCUNUS and Cunedda are primary names of the Cunos clan, and Cuneglasus could have been a grandson of someone mentioned above.

To strengthen the possibility of this link between Cuneglasus/Keredic is the territory in Wales where most scholars place the kingdom of Cuneglasus. It is on the west-central coast of Wales, the same territory which became known as Ceredigion, the region of Ceredic.

See also CINGLAS.

Sources: L. Thorpe (GM: HKB); P. Roberts (COKB); M. Winterbottom (G: ROB&OW).

Cunneware. *see* WOLFRAM VON ESCHENBACH.

Cunorix. As with so many figures associated with Arthuriana, Cunorix's role is difficult to assess, especially since few historians, scholars, or archaeologists provide comprehensive information about him. Yet the few available details are invaluable in ascertaining his ancestry and endeavoring to clarify his role in Arthuriana, which in turn aid in configuring feasible history of fifth-century Britain.

Based upon several sources, there is no doubt that Cunorix was of Irish descent. Writing about Group I inscribed stones in Britain, Leslie Alcock provides an extensive background about their type and location. Summarized, he points out the difficulty of tracing the Goidelic language and its Ogham script, explaining that "in Gwynedd not more than two or three Ogham stones are known" and that the concentration of Ogham inscriptions are in Dyfed, where "the influence of the ruling dynasty of the Dési was obviously responsible."

Although the above comments might seem inconsequential, they point to other segments of Alcock's dissertation. First, VORTIGERN is linked to Irish descent of the Dési tribe, and second, Vortigern's province or kingdom was Dyfed, later known as Dementae. Of that, Alcock writes "The recent tendency has been to place the migration of the Dési at the very end of the fourth or the beginning of the fifth century, and to see it as a response to the evacuation of the Welsh frontier by MAGNUS Maximus in 383." When the Romans began evacuation of Britain in 410, there was no opposition to stop the Irish from settling in Wales. Vortigern and his clan were able to claim territory and establish kingdoms.

Alcock then writes, "Irish personal names are even more wide-spread than Ogham stones, and from as far inland as Wroxeter comes a memorial in partly Latinized Primitive Irish to *Cunorix macus Maquicoline*, 'Hound-king, son of Son-of-the-holly.'"

In 1967, just outside the walls of the ancient legionary fortress of Wroxeter, an inscribed stone, bearing the name of Cunorix, was unearthed. R.P. Wright and Kenneth Hurlstone Jackson dated the inscription between the years 460 to 475. Christopher Snyder point outs that several scholars label Cunorix as an Irish mercenary hired to protect the city, and that Margaret Gellings believes Cunorix was a high-ranking

visitor to a British court. Graham Phillips stresses that there cannot be any denial that the CU-NEDDA clan ruled Wroxeter (Viroconium) and Cunorix was one of the Irish chieftains; additionally Phillips writes, "The clan still ruled the kingdom of Powys in the mid–sixth century, as an analysis of Gildas and his tirade against Cuneglasus reveals."

Segments of the various sources have led this author to explore new perspectives in *The Historic King Arthur* and *Historic Figures of the Arthurian Era*. Because the Cunorix stone was damaged, the last name listed — Maquicoline — is conjectural only. There is no denial that *–rix* is a Celtic affix substituted for the Latin *–rex* (king), and that *macus* is a Celtic word taking the place of *filius* (son). It is Graham Phillip's book, *The Cornovii*, which induces an examination and connection to the manuscripts of GILDAS BADONICUS and NENNIUS.

Gildas Badonicus inadvertently sets up three dates which aid in establishing a chronology of the period. The first is his birth date, forty-four years prior to the Baddon Battle, which other scribes establish as approximately 497. The second is his castigation of Maglocunus, calculated to be 547. The third is his chastisement of CUNEGLASUS, who is alive when Gildas is penning the *De Excidio*, inferring that Cuneglasus flourished sometime between 533 (Alcock's estimate) and 541 (Reno's calculation). If Cunedda migrated from the north around 450— one of the dates proposed by Alcock — the migration was prompted by "some sub–Roman authority like that which brought in the Anglo-Saxons as allies." This rationally points to Vortigern allying himself with HENGIST and points to the *Historia Brittonum*.

In Section 37 of the *HB*, "Hengest took counsel with the elders of *Angul*," that is, Hengist's Anglians. However, of the eighteen extant manuscripts of the *HB*, Manuscript E defines the term as "Anglian." The manuscript which Josephus Stevenson used for his translation was Manuscript A, the Harleian MS. 3859, which refers to the elders not as Anglians, but as elders of *insula Oghgul*; that is, the island of the Irish. These elders, whose tribe was known as the Dési, originally came from Hibernia (Roman term for

The Cunorix Stone, discovered just outside the walls of Wroxeter, is, of course associated with the Cunos clan, and has been dated to the second half of the fifth century, precisely the era when Cunedda would have migrated from the north. During that period of time, Wroxeter was within the boundary of Wales.

Ireland), and settled in Dyfed, which is where Vortigern built his first fortress at Llanfinhangel-ar-arth. It is not surprising, therefore, that Cunorix — of the same clan — was identified as Irish, and that his grave marker was inscribed both in Ogham and Latin.

Because epithets play such a crucial role in establishing historiography, *The Historic King Arthur* and *Historic Figures of the Arthurian Era* have also promulgated the belief that:

1. VORTIGERN is an epithet meaning overlord (a common consensus) and referring to ÆTERNUS of Welsh history (Reno's hypothesis).
2. Vortimer is an epithet meaning overprince (a common consensus) and referring to Cunedda, Æternus's son (also Reno's hypothesis).

One last factor is emending the definition of *cunos*. In Welsh *cwn* is defined as "dog" or "hound," but in most instances, the affix used by Gildas Badonicus in the *cunos* name is feline. He describes Cuneglasus as "*Romana lingua lanio fulve.*" In Latin, *lanio* means butcher, executioner, or one who mangles. *Fulvus* means tawny, most commonly suggesting the color of a lion. Interestingly, in the *Pa Gur* poem, Llachau and Kei are fighting lions, a reference to the northern tribes bearing this symbol.

Cunorix could be either Cuno- (Cunedda) + rix (king) = King Cunedda, or the Lion King. Generically, it could be an epithet for the entire Cunedda tribe or any of Cunedda's sons.

Sources: Alcock (AB); G. Phillips/M. Keatman (KA: TS); F. Reno (HFAE); H. Scullard (RB: OOE); C. Snyder (AAOT); G. Webster (TC); G. Webster/P. Barker (W: RC); R. Wright/K. Jackson (AJ).

Cyfarwyddiaid (cue-far-ooith'-ee-ad). Cyfarwyddiaid is a reference to Welsh bards. In speaking of the Welsh Matter or the Welsh Triads, Rachel Bromwich defines the Welsh Triads, then adds, "It is clear that the Welsh historical and romantic triads are based on the debris of saga literature, the product of the professional storytellers known as *cyfarwyddiaid.*"

Several of these bards — part of the classification for druids — are listed in the *Historia Brittonum*, §62, "Then Talhaern Tad Awen was famed in poetry; and Aneirin and Taliesin and Bluchbard and Cian, known as Gueinth Guaut were all simultaneously famed in British verse." Avaon, the son of Taliessin, is listed as one of Arthur's advisors in *The Mabinogion.*

Sources: R. Bromwich (WT: ALMA); J. Gantz (TM); J. Morris (BH).

Cyhelin is the name for GUITHELINUS (VITALINUS) as it appears in the *Tysilio*. However, in the *Tysilio*, Cyhelin is not given the title of Bishop of Gloucester in his earlier years, nor is he given the title of Archbishop of London later, even though his role is the same as it is in GEOFFREY OF MONMOUTH's manuscript.

None of the above names — Cyhelin, Guithelinus, or Vitalinus — appears in the manuscripts of Gildas Badonicus. Instead, GILDAS BADON-

ICUS simply avers that "envoys" were sent to Rome. In §15 Gildas writes that the Britons "plaintively requested a military force to protect them, vowing whole-hearted and uninterrupted Briton loyalty to the Roman Empire so long as the island's enemies were kept at a distance." The Romans sent a legion as reinforcements, but then returned to the continent, after which, of course, Britain's enemies "re-appeared like greedy wolves."

In §17, Gildas continues that a second time envoys beseeched Rome for help, which was given, but in §18, Gildas Badonicus records that the Romans informed Britons that they would not again be able to send reinforcements; the Britons would have to learn how to fend for themselves. The Britons were too weak to defend themselves, and for a third time they solicited aid through Agitio (AËTIUS), but Rome was embroiled in its own conflicts throughout Gaul.

The *Tysilio* and Monmouth's *History of the Kings of Britain* echo the same events as those recorded by Gildas Badonicus. Only after the appeal to AËTIUS is Cyhelin referred to in the *Tysilio* as the Archbishop of London, the individual who solicits aid from "ALDOR, the son of Cynvawr, the King of Brittany." Confusingly, ALDOR is ALDRONEUS, and Aëtius is Agicius in Monmouth's manuscript.

Sources: P. Roberts (CKOB); L. Thorpe (GM: HKB); M Winterbottom (G: ROB&OW).

Cymen is one of ÆLLE's sons, whose name was recorded in the year 477 of *The Anglo-Saxon Chronicle*: "Ælle came to Britain with his three sons Cymen, Wlencing, and Cissa with three ships at the place which is called *Cymensora* [the Owers to the south of Selsey Bill], and there slew many Welsh and drove some to flight into the wood which is called *Andredesleag* [Sussex Weald]."

That passage contains weird contradictions when accepted at face value. To begin, Aelle is considered a *South Saxon*, but the oldest of his sons — Cymen — is a *Welsh* name. They arrive in Britain in 477 and land at a place which bears Cymen's name, *Cymenesora*. G.N. Garmonsway explains that there is doubt about identification when a name appears in italics. He then clarifies

that material in square brackets identifies the locale of the preceding word. In the first instance, Cymenesora at the very southern tip of Sussex, which means "Owers to the south of Selsey Bill" is an interpolation and merely someone's conjecture. "Sussex Weald" is the second conjecture identifying where Andredesleag is located.

The entry of 485 relates that Aelle fought against the Welsh near [the stream] *Mearcraedesburna*. There is no mention nor explanation of what happened to his sons. And once again, the location is an interpolation. In Entry 491 Aelle and Cissa besieged *Andredescester* [the Roman fort of Anderida, Pevensey] and slew every Briton there. According to Eilert Ekwall, Andreadesleag and Andreadescester are the same.

Upon further deliberation, the combined three entries become even more bizarre. Aelle and his sons kill many *Welsh*. Why, everyone must wonder, are there Welshmen fighting battles two hundred miles away from their country? Strangely, in 491 Aelle is fighting and killing *Britons*. And even more confusing, the name Adreadescester and Andreadesleag are a combination of the Brit prefix *ande-* and the Welsh root *rhyd*. All these inconsistencies appear to indicate that Aelle was not in the south of Britain (or England) but somewhere near Wales.

Sources: G.N. Garmonsway (ASC); E. Ekwall (CODEP-N).

Cymry, Cymri, Cymru, Combrogi. In *The Emergence of England and Wales*, Cymry is defined by Wade-Evans as "compatriots," claiming that Cymry derives from Kymery, a common noun "as old as the Welsh language itself." Henri Hubert defines Cymry as "the national name of the Britons," then adds, "The Cymry are the tribes who fight side by side, under the command of a chief called the *Gwledig*, against the Irish, Picts, or Saxons. The country of these Cymry is called Combrog in the British of that day, or Cambria." Peter Ellis, in his Celtic dictionary, states that Cymru is "the land of comrades or of fellow-countrymen, derived from the British *combrogos*, compatriots."

However, the clearest explanation comes from Steve Blake and Scott Lloyd: "Cymry is the Welsh name for Wales — any reader who has driven across the border into Wales will have been greeted by signs saying *Croeso I Cymru* (Welcome to Wales), for Cymru is the modern Welsh spelling of Cymry." They also give information that in the 12th century the word Britannia was not an allusion to all of Great Britain, but specifically referred to Wales.

Charles Squire relates an interesting tale about Edward Williams, known more widely by his pseudonym IOLO MORGANWG. From Iolo's manuscript comes this account of Wales: "A real building, constructed out of the bones of the 'Caesarians' (Romans) killed in battle with the Cymri, consisted of numerous chambers, some of large bones and some of small, some above ground and some under. Prisoners of war were placed in the more comfortable cells, the underground dungeons being kept for traitors of their country. Several times the 'Caesarians' demolished the prison, but, each time, the Cymri rebuilt it stronger than before." This tale is no doubt one of Iolo's "forgeries" criticized by Sir Ifor Williams.

Sources: H. Hubert (HOCP); P.B. Ellis (DOCM); S. Blake/S. Lloyd (KTA); C. Squire (CMAL); A. Wade-Evans (EOE&W);

Cynric, Cenric, Kenric. According to *The Anglo-Saxon Chronicle*, Cynric is the son of Cerdic, founder of the West Saxon kingdom. However, as discussed in other entries of this text, such as CERDIC and CREODA, Cynric is the son of Creoda, and therefore he is the grandson of Cerdic, as is verified by Charles Plummer and several other experts in the field of Anglo-Saxon genealogy. Additionally, as resolved in *The Historic King Arthur*, Cynric's reign should be modified from a range of 495–556 as recorded in the *ASC* to a range of 534–556 as calculated after inserting Creoda's reign.

Henry of Huntingdon's commentaries on the *ASC* closely follow the Parker and Laud renditions, but he does slightly vary certain entries, then appends material, allegedly from other sources. For example, he writes, "Cerdic and Kenric, his son, in the ninth year of his reign [527 C.E.] fought another battle against the Britons [agrees with the ASC] at Cerdicesford [*ASC* = Cerdicesleag in the Parker Chronicle;

Cerdicesford in the Laud Chronicle]." However, he then inserts, "in which there was great slaughter on both sides. At that time large bodies of men came successively from Germany, and took possession of East-Anglia and Mercia; they were not as yet reduced under the government of one king; various chiefs contended for the occupation of different districts, waging continual wars with each other; but they were too numerous to have their names preserved."

For entry 552 C.E., he follows the script for half of the first sentence, but then once again adds information, in italics here for clarification: "Kenric, in the eighteenth year of his reign fought against the Britons, who advanced with a great army as far as Salisbury; but having assembled an auxiliary force from all quarters, *he engaged them triumphantly, overthrowing their numerous army, and completely routing and dispersing it.*"

In the twenty-second year of his reign (556 C.E.), Kenric, with his son Ceaulin, had another battle with the Britons,

> which was after this manner: to avenge the defeat which they had sustained five years before, the Britons assembled vast numbers of their bravest warriors, and drew them up near Banbury. Their battle array was formed in nine battalions, a convenient number for military tactics, three being posted in the van [front], three in the centre, and three in the rear, with chosen commanders to each, while the archers and slingers and cavalry were disposed after the Roman order. But the Saxons advanced to the attack in one compact body with such fury, that the standards being broken, it became a hand-to-hand fight with the sword. The battle lasted until night-fall without either party being able to claim the victory. Nor is that wonderful, considering that the warriors were men of extraordinary stature, strength, and resolution.

Graham Phillips and Martin Keatman include a special detail about affixes to clarify Cerdic's genealogy. The name Cunedda and its variant Cunedag bear affixes peculiar to a particular clan. The meaning of the *-cunos-* affix is controversial and need not be addressed, since their concern is to emphasize that *cunos* and its variants *cyn-*, *cym-* are Welsh. The name Cynric, therefore, in *The Anglo-Saxon Chronicle*, suggests, they propose, a hybrid name, half-Saxon, half-Welsh, which in turn explains the Welsh name Cerdic in an Anglo-Saxon chronicle.

This is another example which supports the contention that Cerdic himself need not be viewed as an Anglian or a Saxon, but Briton, and this concept is further verified by both Creoda and Cynric not being foreigners or German Saxons who migrated to Britain as late as 495. CEAWLIN also fits into this line of reasoning.

Sources: T. Forester (CHH); G. Garmonsway (ASC); G. Phillips/M. Keatman (KA: TS); C. Plummer (TSCP); F. Reno (HKA).

Cynyr Farfog. In the Llanstephan manuscript 201, ECTOR is known as Cynyr Farfog. As with other narratives, Cynyr is selected by Merlin to raise Arthur, making this king-to-be a step-brother to Cai.

Source: S. Blake/S. Lloyd (P), Pages 249–255, Appendix 2.

Dagonet, Daguenet, Danguenes, Dangueneit. The name Dagonet appears on posters as well as on the Round Table hanging in the Great Hall at Winchester. He is center table to King Arthur's right. His heraldic shield is a silver dagger on a silver and sable background. According to the poster's caption, "in the *Galehaut* he was born insane, and was the most coward heart to be known. In *Guiron le Courtois* he is a foolish knight who administers the king's household with great inefficiency. The Vulgate *Lancelot* tells us that his madness developed after he lost his wife."

Malory portrays Dagonet as the fool at King Arthur's court. In Book IX, Chapter XVIII, Malory writes, "And upon a day Dagonet, King Arthur's fool, came into Cornwall with two squires with him, and as they rode through the forest they came by a fair well where Sir TRISTRAM was wont to be; and the weather was hot, and they alit to drink of that well, and in the meanwhile their horses brake loose. Right so Sir Tristram came onto them and first he soused Sir Dagonet in that well, and after his squires, and thereat laughed the shepherds."

In Book 10, Chapter XII, six knights sent Sir Dagonet to joust with King Mark. Sir MORDRED was injured and could not bear his shield, so Dagonet armed himself with Mordred's trappings to joust with Mark. When Mark beheld the shield of Mordred, he "ran his horse as fast as it might through thick and thin," with Dagonet chasing him. Two knights followed the fool to make sure he wasn't hurt, since "King Arthur loved Dagonet passing well and made him knight with his own hands." Sir Palomides happened to see Mark racing by and "bare a spear to Dagonet, and smote him so sore that he bare him over his horse's tail, and nigh he had broken his neck."

Source: T. Malory (LMD'A).

Didot-Perceval. This prose text of the PERCEVAL story by CHRÉTIEN DE TROYES derives its title from the Frenchman Ambroise Firmin-Didot. Because this version is so conflated — going through two redactions which perhaps stem from a prose retelling of a *Perceval* penned by ROBERT DE BORON but no longer extant — it is better for the reader to consult Robert's trilogy, Chrétien's *Perceval,* or *The Mabinogion*'s "PEREDUR."

Perceval, the son of Alain le Gros, bungles his way through a variety of adventures, eventually having his questions about the Grail answered, which heal the FISHER KING. The story then turns to Arthur, basically retelling Geoffrey of Monmouth's account of Arthur's conquest of France, the war against LUCIUS HIBERIUS, MORDRED's treason, and Arthur's departure to Avalon.

Sources: N. Lacy (AE); W. Roach (D-P).

Dinabutius is an obscure figure in Arthuriana, important only because his name is linked to MERLIN, and therefore the Emrys overlord, AMBROSIUS. In Geoffrey of Monmouth's *History of the Kings of Britain,* VORTIGERN was betrayed by the Saxon HENGIST, who treacherously slaughtered the king's entire council. Vortigern, kept as a hostage, ceded everything to Hengist, then fled to a site somewhere in northern Wales. He later summoned his magi to ask them what to do to protect himself against the deceitful Saxons, and he was given the advice that he should build a mighty citadel to protect himself.

The king selected a location on Mount Erith, but when the masons attempted to build the tower, the earth swallowed up the material.

When Vortigern consulted his magi, they told him that he must sprinkle the foundation of his tower with the blood of a lad without a father. The magi scoured the countries and finally came across two young boys, Merlin (Ambros) and Dinabutius, at play. As the boys argued, Dinabutius railed at his playmate, "Why do you try to compete with me, fathead? How can we two be equal in skill? I myself am of royal blood on both sides of my family. As for you, nobody knows who you are, for you never had a father." The messengers and magi then took Merlin to the King.

Dinabutius drops from history, but his name remains important because it is cited as a validation that certain segments of Geoffrey's *History* are historically reliable. Translator Lewis Thorpe points out that in Monmouth's work there is a long list of proper names, a large proportion which are the names of historical people. He admits that much of the material is twisted almost beyond recognition, but there are some elements of truth. Verified by J.S.P. Tatlock, Thorpe believes that the name Dinabutius is one of the rare names Geoffrey did not manufacture but took from an original source.

Source: R. Fletcher (AMC). L. Thorpe (GM: HKB).

Dionysius Exiguus was a reputable Roman theologian, mathematician and astronomer who flourished during the middle of the sixth century C.E. In humility he labeled himself Denis the Little, but he was a prolific writer in Holy Scriptures and canon laws. His greatest contribution to posterity, however, was his chronological calibrations based not upon the Passion of Christ proposed by VICTORIUS OF AQUITAINE, but upon the Incarnation (Birth) of Christ. Sixty-eight years after Victorius's calibrations, Dionysius developed the new system, and from that point onward, Christ's Incarnation became the base of reckoning.

Scribes not only calibrated entries according to the Dionysiac Table but began to replace computations which were done according to the Victorian Table. Unfortunately, however, the replacement was neither methodical nor documented, so that as time passed there was no record to show which calculations had been used — whether it was the Victorian Table or the Dionysiac system.

The difference between the Victorian and Dionysiac systems creates a 28-year differentiation. If the scribes who copied the *Annales Cambriae* consistently used the Victorian Table in calibrating the date for the Battle of Badon, then they recorded a date which is quite accurate, 516 C.E. If they used the Dionysiac system, however, the date is 28 years too late; Arthur's Battle of Badon (and the date of Gildas Badonicus's birth) should have been recorded as 488 C.E. The historicity of the victory at Mount Badon is undeniable because of Gildas's near-contemporary account. Nevertheless, the date supplied in the *Annales Cambriae* is questionable. Any attempt to select either 516 C.E. or 499 C.E. requires close analyses of other, solidly accepted historical events linked to the same time-frame.

Compounding the difficulty even more, Leslie Alcock discovered another commonly used method of calibration using lunar cycles. In his Preface to the Pelican edition of *Arthur's Britain*, he writes, "Confusion between Incarnation and Passion dating is not the only way in which chronological errors can occur in the records of the period; another cause of error is confusion between successive nineteen-year Easter cycles. If we assume such an error here, then the date of Badon might be corrected to C.E. 499 [Morris's date of 497]."

Using lunar cycles for calibration perhaps goes further back than METON OF ATHENS. It becomes evident why it is so complex to chronicle events during Arthur's alleged historic era.

Sources: L. Alcock (AB/WTC); J. Morris (AOA/BH); F. Reno (HKA/HFAE); M. Winterbottom (G: ROB&OW).

Docmail, Dogfael. Cunedda's eighth son. His kingdom becomes Dogfeilling, east of Rhufoniog in Wales.

Sources: L. Alcock (AB); P. Bartram (WG); S. Blake/S. Lloyd (KTA).

Dodinel, Dodinas. According to one of the tales of CHRÉTIEN DE TROYES, Dodinel is Arthur's ninth-ranked knight, a close comrade of SAGRE-

MOR. In *Le Mort d'Arthur,* Dodinel is known as Dodinas.

Sources: W. Kibler (CDT: AR); T. Malory (LMD'A).

Druids. Prior to the advent of Christianity, Druidism had a powerful impact in Gaul, Brittany, and the islands. Its importance here, however, is limited to the Druidic impact on Arthuriana. MERLINUS AMBROSIUS arises from somewhere deep within Geoffrey of Monmouth's psyche or the *liber vetustissimus* which has been lost in the swirls of mist. The word Druids doesn't actually appear in any of the five ancient major texts of Britain — *Y Gododdin, De Excidio, Tysilio,* or *Historia Brittonum.*

In *The Chronicle of the Kings of Britain,* after HENGIST slaughters VORTIGERN's Council of the Provinces, the king flees to Dinas Emyrs to build a fortress. After three failures, he calls upon his "twelve principal Bards," who go in search of a child born of no father. The Bards arrive at Caervyrddin (Caermarthen). At this point the story is interrupted to explain that Caermarthen was named from *myrddyn.* Peter Roberts clarifies what this means: a *myrddyn* is a legion of 10, 000 men, a definition which is set down "to exclude the idea that the town had its name from Merddyn or MERLIN."

The only other text which makes a shady reference to Merlin is the *Historia Brittonum.* In the tale of EMYRS, Vortigern's advisors are called Magi — defined in a modern dictionary as high priests of the Medes Persians. More commonly, the translations are wizards and magicians. When Monmouth uses the term Merlinus in reference to Ambrosius, he might have been suggesting that Ambrosius had druidic instruction as a young boy when he was in hiding.

Sources: J. Morris (BH) ; P. Roberts (COKB).

Drustan, Drust. Roger Loomis and Laura Loomis introduce the tale *Tristan and Isolt* by providing a background concerning the evolution of this tale:

> We now know a great deal about the history of that legend.... It began about 780. To him was attached a tale somewhat like that of Perseus and Andromeda, the outline of which was borrowed and incorporated into an Irish

saga, the *Wooing of Emer.* In that outline one still finds a Drust, though demoted to a subordinate role, and one can recognize clearly certain elements of the medieval romance of Tristan. From Pictland ... the legend passed south to Wales, where Mark, Isolt and the elopement of the lovers to the forest were added; thence again southward to Cornwall where Cornish racounteurs chose the romantic castle of Tintagel.

The legend then crossed the channel to Brittany (Gottfried von Strassburg's "Parmenie"), where Isolt of the White Hand was probably borrowed from an Arab love story about Kais and Lobna.

See also TRISTRAM.

Sources: G. Ashe (TGAB); R. Loomis (MR).

Dunaut is Cunedda's fourth son. His kingdom becomes Dunoding, the area surrounding Porthmadog, south of Afloegion in Wales.

Sources: L. Alcock (AB); P. Bartram (WG); S. Blake/S. Lloyd (KTA).

Dunstan (Saint). Unaware of the role he would play in history, Saint Dunstan became a critical and renowned figure associated with the exhumation of King Arthur, about 250 years prior to the description by GIRALDUS CAMBRENSIS of the exhumation in 1193. Sometime after the year 945, Dunstan, who was then the Abbot of Glastonbury Abbey, had the ancient cemetery enclosed with a masonry wall. The area itself was raised ten feet above the original ground level. Excavations show that a layer of clay had been packed as an embankment against the new wall and sloped toward the church.

Archaeologist C.A. Ralegh Radford surmised that the area within the cemetery was raised to form a pleasant meadow, removed from the noise of the passers by, so that it might truly be said of the bodies of the saints lying within that they repose in peace. A raising of the level of this whole area would have left the old church of St. Mary half-buried; the formation of an enclosing terrace, as discovered in 1954, is practicable and conforms to the words of Dunstan's biographer.

Similarly, Dr. Radford gives a verbal description matching the model which was commissioned by Glastonbury Abbey and constructed by Dr. A.M. Boyd and N.J.W. Gaffney: "The ancient cemetery ... lay on the south side of the Lady Chapel. The east wall ran just outside the late extension of the pre–Conquest church, through the south door of the thirteenth-century nave. The south wall ... was some hundred feet south of the Lady Chapel. The entrance, which coincided with St. Dunstan's Chapel, west of the Lady Chapel, was in the west wall. The position of the north side is unknown."

Radford then describes in detail the two pyramids in the cemetery south of the Lady Chapel, explaining that the term "pyramid" denoted a venerated tomb. He gives the heights of the two pyramids, indicating that the inscriptions on both could scarcely be read. He then turns his attention to the hole of the exhumation, forty feet south of the chapel and three to four feet in width: "It was irregular, which had been dug and filled in after standing open for a very short time. At the bottom, this hole had destroyed two, or perhaps three, of the slab-lined graves belonging to the earliest stratum. One of these destroyed graves was set against the wall of the mausoleum, a position likely to have been granted only to a person of importance."

Model of Glastonbury Abbey. The cemetery which was restructured by Dunstan is near lower center, with gravestones identified by the white markers. Nowhere in the history of Dunstan, however, is there a connection with Arthur nor the alleged king's gravesite at Glastonbury Abbey. Photograph taken with permission of the Custodian, Glastonbury Abbey.

He then gives specifics, as an archaeologist would:

The hole between the pyramids was dug through this bank and was immediately re-filled with soil containing many masons' chippings of Doulting stone. Into this filling was dug a later series of graves, one of which contained an early fourteenth-century token. Doulting stone was first used at Glastonbury after the fire of 1184; the facing of the Lady Chapel is of this material with dressings of local blue lias. It was therefore in use in the area during the period 1184–89, while the chapel was being built, and it is unlikely that mason's chippings in this quantity would have been lying about the ancient cemetery at any other period. It is therefore certain that the large hole discovered in 1962 represents the excavation for the bodies of Arthur and Guinevere.

It is crucial to understand that Dr. Radford is not claiming that the bones extracted from the grave are unequivocally those of Arthur and his queen; instead he is simply saying that this indeed is the hole dug by the monks at the end of the twelfth century in their search for what they deemed the great king, offering the Doulting stone chippings as evidence.

In a different document, Leslie Alcock comments on the bones themselves. In *Arthur's Britain*, he writes that several historians have gone to considerable lengths to try to strengthen the hypothesis that the monks perpetrated a hoax about the grave's contents. He writes that some historians were "even suggesting that the monks had dug up elsewhere a Celtic chieftain and his wife, buried over a thousand years earlier in a tree-trunk canoe or coffin, in order to 'salt' the grave. The only comment needed here is that no modern archaeologist would know where to dig up such a burial."

Alcock also surmises that "The demolition of the mausoleum may well have been part of Dunstan's work. Had there been a monument to Arthur standing just north of the mausoleum, it would have been removed at the same time. But it may have been felt that the grave of such a distinguished person should not go altogether unmarked, so a lead cross, inscribed in contemporary tenth-century Latin letters was placed in the grave."

These conditions — the raising of the cemetery, the depth of the exhumation, the chippings of Doulting stone, the difficulty of salting the grave with Celtic bones, and the discovery of a tenth-century cross — belie the perpetration of a hoax by the monks of the Abbey by explaining why Arthur's grave was at the unusual depth of sixteen feet. Additionally, it explains to the archaeologists why a tenth-century cross was found in a twelfth-century exhumation, a cross seen not only by WILLIAM CAMDEN but by JOHN LELAND. It seems odd that if a hoax was being perpetrated that such circumstances would be manufactured.

Several antiquarians of a later age comment about Giraldus Cambrensis's descriptions, including ADAM OF DOMERHAM, JOHN OF GLASTONBURY, and RALPH OF COGGESHALL. William Camden mainly gives information about the Glastonbury cross.

The major problem lies with the extant histories dealing with Saint Dunstan himself. Exclusive of those by Adam of Domerham, John of Glastonbury and Ralph of Coggeshall, there are no manuscripts or encyclopedias which do more than merely hint that Dunstan modified the graveyard at Glastonbury Abbey or sanctioned fastening a cross on the underside of a slab marker. All other material is marked as "legends" or "tales" about Arthur and his gravesite.

Sources: L. Alcock (AB); C. Radford (GA: QAB).

Dux Bellorum. The Latin title *dux bellorum,* meaning "leader of battles," is used frequently in Arthuriana and is applied to Arthur in the introduction of §56 of the *Historia Brittonum*: "At that time the English increased their numbers and grew in Britain. On Hengist's death, his son Octha came down from the north of Britain to the kingdom of the Kentishmen, and from him are sprung the kings of the Kentishmen. Then Arthur fought against them in those days, to-gether with the kings of the British; but he was their *dux bellorum.*"

In addition to other titles attached to King Arthur, Alcock also comments on the title of *dux bellorum* in Nennius:

> We must look closely at the words *dux bellorum* for which two alternative translations have been put forward: "Duke," as a specific rank or title, or "leader." The late Roman military system had two titles for high-ranking officers, *Dux* and *Comes,* which we may translate as "Duke" and "Count." ... Even in the late Roman empire a *dux* might command field units as well as garrison troops, and might have administrative duties of a civilian nature as well. In sixth-century Gaul, a *dux* was appointed by the king to administer a tribe or region, especially in an area of military importance, and he also undertook military duties in the field.

R.G. Collingwood clarifies his translation of the word *dux bellorum*. As it applies to King Arthur, he writes,

> To call [Arthur] *dux bellorum* implies that the governments of his day entrusted him with a special military command: in the same way Bede describes St. Germanus as *dux belli.* To say that he fought "with the kings of the Britons" implies that this commission was valid all over the country, and that he fought not in any one kingdom or region, but wherever he was wanted, co-operating with the local levies. His was, in fact, a mobile-field army of the kind which, early in the fifth century, had been commanded by the *Comes Britanniarum.*

Sources: J. Morris (BH); L. Alcock (AB); R. Collingwood (RB&ES).

East Anglians. *see* GILDAS BADONICUS.

Ebissa, Abisa. After Hengist had ensconced himself in Vortigern's favor, he tells the king, "You must not spurn what I say, for with the powerful support of my people, you will overcome all your enemies. Let us invite my son Octa to come here, and his younger brother Ebissa, both of them distinguished warriors. Give them lands which are in the northern parts of Britain, near to the Wall between Deira and Scotland." Messengers were sent off, and in this third *adventus* of the Anglians, Octa and Ebissa arrived, and a man called CHERDIC, too, along with three hundred keels filled with an army.

The echo of Monmouth's writing once again sounds borrowed from the *Tysilio* and relates an almost identical tale. Hengist tells VORTIGERN, "My advice is you send to Germany to invite hither my son Octa and his uncle Ossa, who is a valiant warrior. Give Scotland, which troubles you with so many wars, up to them, and they will preserve it from strangers." Vortigern agrees and sends a message to Germany, from whence came three hundred ships with men at arms, under the command of Octa, Ossa, and Cheldric (Cerdic).

Peter Roberts evidently made a slip and inadvertently called Ebyssa/Abisa by the name Ossa, but the footnote itself is garbled. Additionally, Roberts misspells the name CHELDRIC and uses Chledric, which still doesn't match Monmouth's Cherdic, and as if to clarify who this individual is supposed to be, Roberts uses the name Cerdic in parentheses.

The name Ebissa was probably borrowed from §38 of the *Historia Brittonum*, where Hengist said to Vortigern, "Never ignore my advice, and you will never fear conquest by any man or any people, for my people are strong. I will invite my son and his cousin to fight against the Irish, for they are fine warriors. Give them lands in the north about the Wall that is called Guaul."

Vortigern invited Octha and Ebissa along with forty keels and they sailed around the Picts, ravaged the Orkney Islands, and occupied the districts beyond the Frenessican Sea. Extracting and attempting to coordinate the details from these three different manuscripts demonstrates why it is so difficult to accept claims about insular history.

1. Ebissa is Octa's brother, or perhaps he is Octha's uncle, but he might even be Octha's cousin;
2. Octa and Ebissa are distinguished warriors, or perhaps Octa came from Germany with Ossa, and only Ossa is a valiant warrior;
3. Octa and Ebissa (or is it Ossa?) are accompanied by a third man, whose name is either Cherdic, Chledric, Cheldric, or Cerdic;
4. Octa and Ebissa (or is it Ossa?) come to Britain in three hundred keels (according to Geoffrey of Monmouth, p. 161) filled with an army, emended to perhaps forty keels;
5. These three men with their army conquered Vortigern's enemies and were victorious in every battle. No doubt this was an exaggeration, because the second source claims that the army of the Saxons was so numerous that the British kings were displeased, but Vortigern gave the Saxons wealth and landed property instead. But it indeed could be that the huge army ravaged the north as far as the borders of the Picts.

They fought against the Irish, which of course means the Scotti, because the migrants from Hibernia were known as the Scotti when they infiltrated into Wales and from there migrated to the north, not only to Hadrian's Wall but all the way to the Antonine Wall, which held the Picts in check, perhaps?

Incidentally, neither the name Ebissa nor its variants appear in the *ASC*.

Sources: Lewis Thorpe (GM: HKB); J. Morris (HB); P. Roberts (COKB).

Ector, Hector, Ectorius, Antor, Antour. Ector is Sir Kei's father and Arthur's foster father. When Arthur is born, Merlin takes the babe and gives him to Ector and his wife to raise. After Arthur draws the sword from the stone and becomes king, Ector asks as a favor that Arthur make Kay his seneschal.

Source: T. Malory (LMD'A)

Edern, Edeyrn. Edern is a variant of IDER and YDER. The name appears in several different tales of *The Mabinogion*. In "How Culhwch Won Olwen," he is described as Gwynn's brother and the son of NUDD. In "The Dream of Rhonabwy" his name is listed twice, first described as the leader of the men of Denmark and the son of Nudd, then as one of Arthur's advisors.

Whereby in the above two tales he is an incidental character, in "Gereint and Enid" he assumes a major role. Edern confronts Gereint, and after losing the challenge, he is sent to

Arthur's court to plead forgiveness for insulting Queen Guinevere. This is the same character, too, who fights three giants for Arthur. Upon Edern's death, Arthur bequeaths lands to Glastonbury Abbey in Edern's honor.

Sources: J. Gantz (TM); J. Carley (CGA).

Edyrn, Edern. *see* ETERN. There is sometimes a confusion between Etern the son of CUNEDDA, and an Edern, son of Nudd. In *The Mabinogion*, Nudd is equated with Nodons, a British deity.

Eigr, Eiger, Eigyr. Eigr and its variants are the Welsh names for IGRAINE, Uther's wife and Arthur's mother. Translated from the Welsh copy attributed to *Tysilio*, it appeared several centuries prior to Thomas Malory's *Le Morte D'Arthur*. There are disagreements as to whether the *Tysilio* preceded or succeeded Geoffrey of Monmouth's *History of the Kings of Britain*.

After a victorious battle planned by Uther and Gorlais (Gorlois), a night of entertainment was planned and "on this occasion Gorlois, Earl of Cornwall had brought with him his wife Eigr, daughter of AMLAWDD the Great, and who was considered the most beautiful woman then in Britain." Uther was impassioned by her, and Gorlois, sensing this, left the feast with Eigr. Uther became violently angry and sent orders for the earl's immediate return with his wife. Gorlois refused, and Merddyn planned his magical ruse for Uther to seduce Eigr.

See also YGERNA.

Source: P. Roberts (COKB).

Elaine, Lady of Shalott. When King Pelles and Sir Launcelot meet, Pelles invites the knight to his castle. While they are at the table for a repast, a dove flies in through the window with a censer of gold in its beak, which, when the censer is set on the table, transforms into a fabulous meal. Elaine, Pelles's daughter, enters with a vessel of gold, and they kneel for a prayer.

After Pelles and Launcelot spend the day together, Pelles secretly devises a scheme for Launcelot to lie with his daughter and get a child upon her named Galahad who at the age of fifteen would save the country and achieve the Holy Grail.

Pelles summons an enchantress named Dame Brisen. She meets with Launcelot and tells him that Queen Guenever has sent him a ring to wear. Launcelot asks where the queen is, and the enchantress tells him she's five miles away at the Castle of Case. Pelles has twenty-five knights accompany Dame Brisen and Elaine to the castle. Upon arrival, Dame Brisen gives Launcelot a cup of wine, and he becomes "so assotted and mad that he went to bed and thought that the maiden Elaine was Queen Guenever."

In the morning Launcelot realizes what has happened and he draws his sword to kill Elaine, but "she skipped out of her bed all naked, and kneeled down afore Sir Launcelot" and begs for mercy. Launcelot forgives her, and "therewith he took her up in his arms and kissed her, for she was as fair a lady, and thereto lusty and young." Galahad was conceived, and Launcelot returned to Camelot.

Years later, after Arthur's successful campaigns on the continent, the king returns to Britain and heralds a great feast for all the lords and ladies of the island. When Elaine hears of it, she goes to the festivities with a huge entourage, including Dame Brisen. Launcelot ignores Elaine, and, grief-stricken, Brisen comforts her by saying she will resolve the problem and bring Launcelot to Elaine's bed.

However, Queen Guenever knows not only of the tryst between Launcelot and Elaine, but also of the birth of Galahad, who has now passed pubescence. The queen demands that Elaine sleep in the chamber next to her. To insure that nothing will take place, the queen "sent for Launcelot and ordered him to come to her chamber that night" because she is sure that otherwise he would go to the "lady's bed, Dame Elaine, by whom he gat Galahad." Launcelot swears that he will be with the queen.

When all the others are abed, Brisen sneaks to Launcelot's bedside and tells him that Guenever is ready for him. Brisen grabs him by the finger and instead leads him to Elaine's bed. The two make love, "kissing and clipping (embracing)." Guenever is losing her wits because her lover does not arrive. As the hours pass, Guenever hears Launcelot's voice next door, and realizes from past escapades that Launcelot is talking in his sleep. She coughs very loudly, awakening

"How King Arthur and Queen Guinevere went to see the barge that bore the corpse of Elaine the fair maiden of Astolat." In Pollard's _The Romance of King Arthur_ (1917), illustration by Arthur Rackham.

Launcelot, who then realizes he's in the wrong bed. The two encounter each other in the hall, and Guenever rejects him and causes him to swoon. When he awakes, he goes mad, jumps out a window, and disappears for two years.

After that length of time, Launcelot, known now as a fool, ends up in the garden belonging to Castor, a nephew of King Pelles. That afternoon Elaine and three of her maidens go into the garden where Launcelot is asleep, and at once she recognizes him. Brisen casts a spell on him, and Launcelot names himself Le Chevaler Mal

Fet, the knight who has trespassed. He, King Pelles, Elaine, Brisen and a troupe live in the Castle of Bliant surrounded by deep, swampy water. Because Launcelot is so happy, he renames the castle Joyous Isle.

Skipping to the end of this tryst, Launcelot decides to return to Camelot with a couple of other knights who rescue him. Brazenly, Launcelot tells Elaine, "I will for your own good will and kindness show you some goodness, and that is this, that wheresomever ye will beset your heart upon some good knight that will wed you, I shall give you together a thousand and pound yearly to you and to your heirs."

Elaine refuses, shrieks loudly, and falls down in a swoon. Ten days later, she asks her father to laden her richest clothes into a barge covered in black samite, and have a trusted servant steer the barge down the Thames to Westminster. Thus did Elaine die of a broken heart.

Source: T. Malory (LMD'A)

Eldol, Eidiol. In the *Tysilio*, Eidiol, the Earl of Gloucester, becomes quite a hero in an Ambrosian episode, then fades like a shooting star. During a meeting of Vortigern's Council of the Provinces, the traitor Hengist slaughters four hundred and sixty earls, barons, and chieftains of the Britons, and in the aftermath seizes Vortigern for ransom. Eidol is the sole survivor, "who having found a pole lying on the ground, with it killed seventy men, and so escaped and returned safe home."

After the fiasco, Merlin prophesies to VORTIGERN that he would be burned in a tower of stone once Emrys AMBROSIUS lands in Britain and becomes king. The prophecy is fulfilled; Vortigern is burned in the tower, Aurelius Ambrosius becomes king, and attention then turns to HENGIST and his clan, who in fear "flee beyond the Humber and fortify themselves there." An interesting aside at this point is that Hengist is north of East Anglia, nowhere near Kent as recorded in the *Historia Brittonum*.

Ambrosius pursues Hengist and his army by following the path of destruction left by the barbarians. Hengist lies to his men, telling them that Ambrosius's army is small and weak in comparison to their own force of two thousand men.

A battle ensues at Maes-Beli, and after great slaughter of Hengist's army, the stragglers flee to Caer Cynan, but many are overtaken and killed. Eidiol voraciously seeks and finds Hengist, finally seizing him by his beard and helmet, then dragging him into the midst of the Briton army so that they can avenge themselves.

Ambrosius meets with his council to determine how to dispose of him, and with the sanction from the Bishop of Gloucester, Eidiol "took Hengist to the top of a hill and beheaded him."

Geoffrey of Monmouth's narrative is more detailed than the one in the *Tysilio*. During the massacre of the council, Eldol, as in the *Brut*, kills seventy men, but Monmouth's account becomes a bit more explicit. Nothing more is said about Eldol for approximately twenty intervening pages, diverting to the discovery of the boy MERLIN and the inserted text of "Prophecies of Merlin." A minor variant is that in the *Brut*, Eidiol is granted permission from the Bishop of Gloucester, and in *History of the Kings*, the Bishop of Gloucester is identified as Eldadus, Eldol's brother.

The *Historia Brittonum* describes the massacre of Vortigern's council in Section 46, but it differs on two counts from the other two manuscripts; it does not mention Eldol or Eidiol, and whereby both of those manuscripts record the number of slain council members as four hundred and sixty, the *Historia* claims that "all of the three hundred Seniors of King Vortigern were murdered, and the king alone was taken and held prisoner."

Sources: J. Morris (HB); P. Roberts (COKB); L. Thorpe (GM: HKB).

Elesa. In *The Anglo-Saxon Chronicle* and its Genealogical Preface, Elesa is listed as Cerdic's father. Beyond that, there is no other reference to him, but there has been broad speculation, based upon pedigrees which indicate that "Cerdic" is a Welsh/Briton name, quite unusual because it appears in the important House of the West Saxons. If the Briton Cerdic, fifth son of Cunedda, is equated with Cerdic the West-Saxon king, then Cunedda, a Celtic "man of the North," would be equated with Elesa.

See also ELISEG.

Sources: G. Garmonsway (ASC); F. Reno (HKA); F. Reno (HFAE).

Eliseg, Eliset, Elized. The pillar raised in honor of Eliseg dates to Cyngen, last of the kings of Powys, some time at the turn of the ninth century. The pillar is seemingly outside the arena of the historic King Arthur, but a number of individuals recorded in the inscription date to the fifth century, including BRYDW, VORTIGERN, GERMANUS, and Severa. MAGNUS Maximus and Gratian date to the fourth century.

The name Eliseg is more complex to trace, but its significance is intriguing. The historicity of Eliseg is verified by several researchers, who identify him as the tenth generation of the Powys dynasty, which places his floruit in the eighth century. A different researcher makes an eponymous connection between Eliseg and the Eglywseg Valley near Llangollen, which is where the pillar itself is located. In itself, this connection appears trivial, but when linked to an archaeological excavation which uncovered evidence of a Saxon building in this vicinity, a chain of circumstances unfolds to create an entirely new outlook on developments in early insular medieval history.

As related above, the first name in the chain is Eliseg, but there is nothing at first glance to elicit surprise. But as far back as 1982, Geoffrey Ashe, in *Kings and Queens of Early Britain*, penned this excerpt: "The Welsh king who asserted his descent from that marriage [between Vortigern and Severa], and is the subject of the inscription, was named Eliseg. Cerdic's father in his own pedigree is Elesa" as listed in *ASC*.

What Ashe has done in this terse passage is equate the Welsh king Eliseg with the name Elesa in *The Anglo-Saxon Chronicle*, a link which should have caused a wave of astonishment, but evidently didn't even cause a ripple, since that revelation remained buried for at least a decade and a half, and it is still not causing a stir. Where this proposition (or speculation) leads is through Cerdic's pedigree as it is given in the *ASC*, and it includes CERDIC himself, his father CUNEDDA, his grandfather ÆTERNUS, his great-grandfather PATERNUS, and his great-great-grandfather TACITUS, all of whom would be ancestors of the Eliseg named on the pillar.

Unaware of Ashe's lead, in 1996, *The Historic King Arthur* picked up on the same thread.

The next name from *The Anglo-Saxon Chronicle* which comes under scrutiny is Elesa. That particular name in the West Saxon genealogy aligns itself with the Eliset/Eliseg inscribed pillar in Valle Crucis, near Llangollen in northeastern Wales just east of Offa's Dyke. The pillar, one of the most famous of the Ogham stones, commemorates Eliseg, an adversary of Offa's....

Eliseg and his possible connection to Elesa appears three times in the *ASC*. There are two entries in the *Annales Cambriae*, years 814 and 943, which give the name Elized. The 943 entry is traceable back to the Clonmacnoise Chronicle which adds that Elized and his father Idwal (Iudgual) were killed by the West Saxons.

If the equation Elesa = Eliset/Eliseg is accepted, then Elesa is a Saxon name and Eliseg is the philological Briton counterpart. Approaching the equation in reverse, if Elesa is Cerdic's father in Saxon terms, then Eliseg is Cerdic's father in Briton terms.

This would establish the veracity of the inscription on the stone, and confirm its link with the West Saxon genealogy as listed in *The Anglo-Saxon Chronicle*. If the full genealogy of one is a template of the other, then the resulting new perspective is quite a revelation.

See the table in the CERDIC entry, and the translator EDWARD LHUYD about the importance of Eliseg's Pillar.

Sources: G. Ashe (K&QEB); C. Barber/D. Pykitt (JTA); S. Blake/S. Lloyd (KTA); J. Knight (POE); F. Reno (HKA).

Elizabeth is King Mark's sister and Tristram's mother in Malory's *Le Morte D'Arthur*. She is married to Meliodas, and by an unfortunate circumstance, she dies in childbirth, leaving their young son Tristram in the care of Meliodas. Meliodas remarries and shortly thereafter the stepmother attempts to poison Tristram, but accidentally poisons one of her own children. Tristram pleads with his father to forgive her, which Meliodas does.

See also BLANCHEFLEUR and RIVALIN for a variant of the Malory tale.

Source: T. Malory: (LMD'A).

Emrys, Emry, Embreis, Embries, Embres, Emhyr. The honorific title "emrys" is commonly used for AMBROSIUS Aurelianus in the *Historia Brittonum* as well as several other manuscripts of Welsh tradition. Josephus Stevenson's book includes all variations of this term: embries gluetic, embres gulethic, embreis gleutic. Stevenson then adds more detail, that "Ambrosius was thought to be Ambrosius the Royal, Glwledig, being anciently an epithet given to the Loegrian princes, expressive of supreme authority."

Charles Squire, in *Celtic Myths and Legends*, exclusively uses the term emrys as a title for Myrddin (MERLIN). Geoffrey Ashe, too, in *Mythology of the British Isles*, points out that commonly the expression emrys applies to Ambrosius and to Merlin. The term emrys is often followed by another epithet, GWLEDIG, which is a more common attachment to Welsh leaders.

Sources: G. Ashe (MBI); J. Morris (HB); C. Squire (CM&L); J. Stevenson (N: HB).

Emyr Llydaw. *see* BUDICIUS.

Esla. Like Elesa, Esla is recorded only once in *The Anglo-Saxon Chronicle*. He is of the House of the West Saxons, the father of Elesa and the grandfather of Cerdic, the latter who has a major role in Arthuriana. There are speculative claims which equate Esla with Vortigern/Æternus in Welsh genealogies, but no firm evidence corroborates this. See the third chart in the Ceredic entry.

See also ELISEG.

Sources: G. Garmonsway (ASC); F. Reno (HKA); F. Reno (HFAE).

Eslit. In a number of the Arthurian romances, Arthur's knights are listed according to importance. In Chrétien's works, Eslit is listed as Arthur's eleventh best knight, along with Brien and Yvain, the former who is also obscure and the latter who earns a major role as the Knight of the Lion. Eslit, however, doesn't play a major role in any of the Arthurian tales.

Source: P. Ryan (DKAK).

Etern, Edeirn. Cunedda's ninth son. His kingdom is east of Dunod's territory in Wales. Etern is sometimes confused with Æternus, son of Paternus, but Etern would be two generations re-

moved from Æternus. Similarly, a distinction must be made between Etern (Cunedda's son) and Edern (Yder/Ider, son of Nut).

Sources: L. Alcock; P. Bartram (WG); S. Blake/ S. Lloyd (KTA).

Ethelweard. *see* ÆTHELWEARD.

Eugein Dantguin. *see* OWEIN DANTGUIN.

Euric, Eurich (the Visigoth). Euric was one of six sons born of King Theodrid, a Visigothic King whose close ties with the Western Roman Empire extended through three generations.

Theodrid joined forces with Valentinian in the wars against Attila and the Huns. When those wars reached a crescendo, Theodrid sent four of his sons — Friderich, Eurich, Retemer, and Mimnerith — home, taking his two elder sons, Thorismud and Theodrid, with him. With AËTIUS as an ally, the wars against the Huns continued for quite some time. In one of the battles, Theodrid was killed, but history is muddled about his death, averring that he either fell from his horse in battle and was trampled by his own tribe, or he was slain by a certain Andag, an Ostrogoth who was allied with Attila.

Upon his death, his son Thorismud was convinced to return to Tolosa, which was the tribal city granted to him by Aëtius, to contain insurrection there while the Roman general continued his war with the Huns. Thorismud was once more summoned to clash with Attila, whom he defeated. After he returned to Tolosa, he fell ill in the third year of his reign. He was betrayed by a comrade during a blood-letting and bled to death.

Theodrid, named after his father, became king. History, however, is vague about whether this king retained close ties to the Romans, but when EURIC succeeded him, the alliance between the Visigoths began to crumble. According to Jordanes,

> His brother Eurich succeeded Theodrid with such eager haste that he fell under dark suspicion. Now while these and various other matters were happening among the people of the Visigoths, the Emperor Valentinian was slain by the treachery of Maximus, and Maximus himself, like a tyrant, usurped the rule. Gaiseric, king of the Vandals, heard of this

and came from Africa to Italy with ships of war, entered Rome and laid it waste. Maximus fled and was slain by a certain Ursus, a Roman soldier. After him Majorian undertook the government of the Western Empire at the bidding of Marcian, Emperor of the East. But he, too, ruled but a short time. For when he had moved his forces against the Alani who were harassing Gaul, he was killed at Dertona near the river named Ira. Severus succeeded him and died at Rome in the third year of his reign. When Emperor Leo, who had succeeded Marcian in the Eastern Empire, learned of this, he chose as emperor his Patrician Anthemius and sent him to Rome. Upon his arrival he sent against the Alani his son-in-law Ricimer, who was an excellent man and almost the only one in Italy at that time fit to command the army. In the very first engagement he conquered and destroyed the host of the Alani, together with their king, Beorg.

At this point, Euric debuts as a historical figure in the Arthurian saga, two or three steps removed from King Arthur. Jordanes continues with this compacted piece of history:

> Now Eurich, king of the Visigoths, perceived the frequent change of Roman Emperors and strove to hold Gaul by his own right. The Emperor Anthemius heard of it and asked the Brittones for aid. Their King Riotimus came with twelve thousand men into the state of the Bituriges by the way of Ocean, and was received as he disembarked from his ships.
>
> Eurich, king of the Visigoths, came against them with an innumerable army, and after a long fight he routed Riotimus, king of the Brittones, before the Romans could join him. So when he had lost a great part of his army, he fled with all the men he could gather together, and came to the Burgundians, a neighboring tribe then allied to the Romans. But Eurich, king of the Visigoths, seized the Gallic city of Arverna; for the Emperor Anthemius was now dead [239]. Engaged in fierce war with his son-in-law Ricimer, he had worn out Rome and was himself finally slain by his son-in-law and yielded the rule to Olybrius.

Riotimus (RIOTHAMUS) is the enigmatic Briton king from across Ocean whom Geoffrey Ashe theorizes is King ARTHUR. In *The Discovery of King Arthur,* after establishing his case, Ashe concludes that Arthur was the king known on the continent as Riothamus, to whom Sidonius wrote a letter. *The Historic King Arthur* takes a different path, theorizing that the Briton king was AMBROSIUS AURELIANUS, whose epithet was somehow conflated with Arthur. In either case, Euric's name becomes linked with insular history.

Sources: G. Ashe (DKA); C. Mierow (J: O&DG); F. Reno (HKA/HFAE).

Exuperantius is historically one of the most inscrutable figures indirectly attached to Arthuriana. Information about this particular individual is virtually nonexistent, recorded in mere fragments.

Peter Salway, one of the few authors who even acknowledges him, devotes one sentence to this figure: "In 417, for example, the first time that we hear of Romans using force in northern Gaul since the fall of Constantine's empire, Rutilius Namatianus' relation Exuperantius put down a slave revolt, 'restoring law and liberty;' in other words bringing back the normal order of things." He gives no clue whether Namatianus is a brother, father, grandfather, cousin, or uncle.

There are other fragments which border on the edge of impossibility to ferret out a firm basis. The only interest in this context is Exuperantius's chronological link to Arthuriana. Fortuitously, Salway provides the date, 417, and scattered references imply that Exuperantius was apparently praefectus praetorio Galliarum when killed in an army mutiny at Arles in 424; he participated in the revolt against the Western empire by Britain and Armorica in 409; the Armorican revolt which broke out in 409 is identical with the Armorican revolt which Exuperantius was suppressing in 417.

In *Romans and Barbarians: The Decline of the Western Empire,* E.A. Thompson traces the relationship between the Romans and the barbarians. He writes, "Exuperantius began to master the Bacaudae [barbarians] in 417 and had presumably completed the task by the end of that year."

The year 417 is the crucial element when the information by R.G. Collingwood is linked to the above data. Collingwood is establishing the likelihood that the Western Roman Empire, which had withdrawn the legions from Britain in 410, did so not as an abandonment of the island, but had the intention to re-occupy the island after Gaul had been pacified. His premise is based upon the establishment of a new military rank of *Comes Britanniarum*. He conjectures that a reorganization was underway by the Patrician Constantius (CONSTANTIUS III the Supreme Commander under Emperor HONORIUS), who had re-established control in Brittany in 417.

The corollary of assembling these segments of information and completing the puzzle wasn't proposed until F.D. Reno presented a paper entitled "Emending Fifth-Century British History" at the University of California, Davis. Constantius III mysteriously drops from Roman history between the years 417 and 420, and when he reappears, he becomes co-emperor with Honorius.

Considering the circumstances, it's likely that Exuperantius became the acting praefectus of Gaul while Constantius III was in Britannia Prima.

Sources: R. Collingwood/J. Myres (RB&ES); F. Reno (EF-CBH); P. Salway (TOIHORB); E. Thompson (R&B).

Felix is indisputably a historical figure, a Roman commander who became the chief minister of government for Galla Placidia, and, as Eleanor Duckett notes, "From 425 to 429 he rose higher: as Master of Both Services, as consulibus for the year 428, and as Patrician in 429." Galla Placidia was regent of the Western Empire for her son Valentinian III for approximately thirty years and during the early years of her reign, Felix and Aëtius vied for her favors to try to become her supreme commander.

Felix merits mention in an Arthurian context for several reasons. Galla Placidia was Emperor Honorius's half-sister, who was married to CONSTANTIUS III, the supreme commander for Emperor HONORIUS. If Constantius III was indeed the COMES BRITTANIARUM who was sent to Britain and became known as PENDRAGON, then Felix and Arthur's father would be comrades.

Probably more important, however, and more solidly based in fact, is that the consulship of Felix can be used to verify the reign of VORTI-GERN in Britain. The best information about Vortigern is a set of chronological computations recorded at the head of the Easter Annals, and Leslie Alcock supplies the details: "Vortigern held rule in Britain in the consulship of Theodosius and Valentinian. And in the fourth year of his reign the Saxons came to Britain in the consulship of Felix and Taurus, in the 400th year from the incarnation of Our Lord Jesus Christ."

Alcock explains that there is a major error in the chronological calibrations because "the consulship of Felix and Taurus was in fact in 428 C.E. and therefore four hundred years not from the Incarnation but from the conventional date for the Passion." This gives a firm fix for the beginning of Vortigern's reign.

Sources: L. Alcock (AB); E. Duckett (MPE&W).

Fisher King. The Fisher King originated with CHRÉTIEN DE TROYES in his romance *Conte du Graal* (*The Story of the Grail*), sometimes titled *Perceval*, which survives in fifteen versions. In later modifications of Chrétien's story, other writers dub this king as the Rich King, the Maimed King, the Grail King, or Pelle in the Vulgate Version.

Description of the Fisher King given by Chrétien is minimal. Perceval encounters two men fishing in a boat, one of whom invites PERCEVAL to his castle for a night's lodging. When Perceval enters the great hall filled with 400 people, the nobleman is seated on a large bed and apologizes to his new arrival for not rising. As the two are conversing, a squire enters and gives a sword to the nobleman, announcing that the weapon had been sent by the nobleman's niece, The nobleman gives the sword to Perceval, saying it is ordained and destined that the sword should be his.

As they continued conversing, a different squire enters bearing a white lance. Everyone in the hall could see that drops of blood were seeping from the tip and flowing down onto the squire's hand. Perceval refrains from asking any questions, for he had been admonished earlier in his travels not to ask questions lest he reveal his ignorance.

Two other squires enter holding candelabra of

pure gold. A maiden accompanies the two, carrying a grail, set with precious stones of all kinds. Again, Perceval does not speak. It is only later that Perceval learns he should have asked questions, for in addition to answers, the nobleman would have had his wounds healed and his domain productive again.

Chrétien does not use the epithet "Holy" attached to the grail, and evidently in the original script the word "grail" is not capitalized. Similarly, there are no details given about the bleeding lance because no questions had been asked. The Fisher King remains shrouded in mystery; only in later versions are details added about his wounds and how he and his kingdom could be healed.

In works following Chrétien's *Perceval*, the Fisher King assumes a variety of roles:

1. In a trilogy ascribed to ROBERT DE BORON, de Baron transforms the Grail into a Christian holy relic, given by Pilate to JOSEPH OF ARIMATHEA, who uses the vessel to collect Christ's blood at the crucifixion. When the exiled Joseph goes to a distant land, he sets up a table in memory of the Last Supper, where Hebron (Bron/Bran in Celtic mythology?/Rich Fisher) is instructed to catch a fish to be served at the table with the grail.

2. WOLFRAM VON ESCHENBACH modifies Chrétien's PERCEVAL into a character named Parzival. Arthur is related to Parzival through his father, and is related to the grail through his mother. The grail, which is solid gold and bedecked with jewels in Chrétien's story, has become stone — perhaps a slab with a concave surface — which miraculously provides food and drink. Wolfram also transforms the Fisher King into a character named ANFORTAS.

3. The Vulgate Cycle, which was compiled by anonymous scribes over a period of time, not only changed the format from verse into prose, but also became more historical and religious in tone. Rather than concentrating on literary plot, attention shifted to quests for the Holy Grail with emphasis on creating links between a hero's

evolution and Christian development. When Joseph of Arimathea is granted land in Britain at Glastonbury, tales evolve that the Holy Grail was hidden somewhere in Chalice Well. And when Joseph dies, he bestows the Grail to Alain, the first Fisher King. Perceval and GALAHAD are the final questers of the Grail.

4. Because there is such a similarity between Chrétien's Perceval and the Welsh story in *The Mabinogion* depicting PEREDUR, it is natural that there would likewise be a parallel between the Fisher King and Brân/Bron.

Sources: R. Cline (P: SG); J. Gantz (TM); E. Jung/M-L. Von Franz (TGL); W. Kibler (CDT: AR); D. Owen (AR); B. Raffel (P: SG).

Foederati. Frank Graham, author of *An Abbreviated Dictionary of Roman Military Terms*, presents only a brief comment about *foederati*, but it offers interesting affirmation for what transpired in Britain during the mid–400s. He writes, "The first settlement of *foederati* in Britain was in 417. They were tribes within the frontier allied with Rome." That particular year is significant because it was the year CONSTANTIUS III, supreme commander for Emperor HONORIUS, mysteriously disappeared from Roman history and didn't resurface until the year 420, at which time Emperor Honorius announced that Constantius III would become his co-emperor.

Leslie Alcock clarifies the definition of *foederati*, first classifying them as Germanic soldier-peasants, the *foederati* or *laeti*, settled by the Romans. He also claims "Literary sources [not indicating which specific ones] distinguish between *foederati*, who held their land by virtue of a *foedus* or treaty, and *laeti*, who were settled in return for military service." He attaches the name of VORTIGERN as one of the British *tyranni* "in the 420s and 430s who continued the Roman policy of settling Germans as *laeti* or *foederati* for the defence of Britain."

R.G. Collingwood, discussing various migrations, including the ones between Manau Gododdin and Wales, puts CUNEDDA's clan into the category of *foederati*. This would agree with Alcock's above comment about Vortigern, since there is evidence of a father-son connection between Vortigern (under his proper name ÆTERNUS) and Cunedda (whose epithet is VORTIMER). Both are given the edict by the Western Empire which Alcock theorizes when he suggests Vortigern invited "the coming of the English" in 428 to "an unknown area," and in 440 under "circumstances wholly unknown," provides the reason why Cunedda migrated and was given territories in Wales from the River Dee to the River Teifi, a vast expanse of approximately four hundred and fifty square miles. PATERNUS, Æternus's father, was also part of the *foederati*, and his tribal city was Chester, the legionary fortress which had been moved from Wroxeter.

Collingwood is one of the few historians who writes of Constantius III's gap in Roman history. He proposes that the Western Empire did indeed attempt to reclaim Britain as a province, and it was likely that Constantius III, under the newly established rank of *COMES BRITANNIARUM*, was assigned to repeat his success in Britain because he had re-established Roman control in Brittany. When he was prematurely recalled to Gaul because of more uprisings, the task fell to Vortigern to distribute other *foederati* to new locations. Collingwood does not place the blame on Vortigern for the influx of the East Anglians, but instead indicates that it was Roman policy which created the problem.

A more recent author, Christopher Snyder, begins his perspective by giving Gildas Badonicus's "portrayal of the military situation in Britain." He writes, "At first the Britons do not know how to fight, and have to be instructed by the Romans. Then the *consilium* and the *superbus tyrannus* decide to follow the standard imperial practice and hire Saxon *foederati* to fight for them. When this fails, they turn to the "last of the Romans," AMBROSIUS [AURELIANUS], and finally gain the upper hand against the invaders." Snyder uses the appropriate epithet *SUPERBUS TYRANNUS* instead of assuming Bede's replacement of "Vortigern." The Saxon *foederati* is no doubt the generic Roman term, since Gildas emphatically calls the enemy *ORIENTALI SACRILEGORUM*.

Hence, it should be agreed that the term *foederati* enhances the perspicuity of the events in fifth-century Britain. The two supreme powers of the Western Empire are Honorius and Constantius III facing a besieged Gaul, threatened by Visigoths, Vandals, Huns, Franks, Saxons, Alans, Bretons, and others. As segments of these tribes were subdued by the Romans, they were conscripted into the Roman army as *foederati*, and when Gaul was seemingly pacified, the West wanted to reclaim Britain, not only for additional military support, but mainly for Britain's supply of lead, tin, and iron. In 446, approximately thirty-six years after Rome began extracting troops from Britain, GILDAS BADONICUS writes of a letter to AËTIUS pleading for Roman support. And in the year 468 Emperor ANTHEMIUS of the West is pleading for help from the king across Ocean, both appeals signifying a bond which still existed between the empire and Britain. Not only does the chronology verify history of the period, but events and all the personages mentioned above also depict a clear scenario, to a point of verifying RIOTHAMUS as Ambrosius, the Briton king from across Ocean, and not a King ARTHUR.

Sources: L. Alcock (AB); R. Collingwood/J. Myres (RB&ES); F. Graham (ADRMT); C. Littleton/L. Malcor (FSTC); F. Reno (HKA/HFAE); C. Snyder (AAOT).

Frollo, who makes a cameo appearance in both Monmouth's *History of the Kings of Britain* and Roberts' *Tysilio*, merits a brief recognition in the Vulgate Lancelot and the Tristram romance, but then he disappears from history and legend.

Monmouth's narrative introduces Frollo as a Roman general appointed by Emperor LEO, prior to the time of LUCIUS HIBERIUS, procurator of the Roman Republic. Arthur, having decided he would conquer the whole of Europe, sailed to Gaul and confronted the tribune Frollo. When Frollo realized the strength of Arthur's army, he fled to Paris to reassemble and reinforce his own troops to meet Arthur a second time in battle.

Arthur, however, arrived unexpectedly and besieged Paris. After a month, when the troops inside the city were starving, Frollo sent a message to Arthur, recommending that they meet in single combat, and whoever won that conflict would take the kingdom of the other. The duel was agreed to, and the two met on an island outside the city.

They faced each other with lances in the air, spurred their steeds, and charged. Frollo missed his mark, but Arthur hit his adversary high on the chest and knocked him to the ground. Arthur quickly drew his sword and spurred his horse, but Frollo was prepared, leveling his lance at Arthur's steed and bringing down both horse and rider.

The hand-to-hand swordfight was ferocious, one trying to overcome the other. Frollo found an opening and swung at Arthur's head, but the blade hit his helmet. Enraged, "Arthur raised Caliburn in the air with all his strength, and brought it down through Frollo's helmet and so on to his head, which he cut into two halves. At this blow Frollo fell to the ground, drummed the earth with his heels and breathed his soul into the winds."

Sources: P. Roberts (COKB); L. Thorpe (GM: HKB).

Gaheris is one of the sons of King Lot and Morgause. His two brothers, Gawain and Agravain, are relatively major figures in Arthuriana. When he discovers that his mother is being bedded by Lamorak, he bursts into the chamber and beheads her, but lets Lamorak go free. King Arthur banishes Gaheris, but later allows him to return to court. During a foray when Lancelot and Guinevere's trysts are exposed, Lancelot kills Gaheris.

Source: T. Malory (LMD'A)

Gahmuret In Wolfram von Eschenbach's *Parzival*, Gahmuret is Parzival's father, whom Parzival never meets. While serving Baruch in the Middle East, Gahmuret is killed by the Babylonians prior to Parzival's birth.

See WOLFRAM VON ESCHENBACH.

Gaiseric, King of the Vandals and Alani from 428 to 477 C.E., is a satellite figure of the Arthurian Age, mainly through the epithet RIOTHAMUS, who is attached to the name ARTHUR by Geoffrey Ashe and to AMBROSIUS AURELIANUS by Frank Reno. In a spectacular reign of nearly fifty years,

Gaiseric was never defeated by the Romans, even when the empires of the East and West combined forces.

In the year after he assumed kingship, in 429, it is widely accepted that he transported all his people — listed as 80,000 — to Africa upon invitation by Boniface, the Roman governor of Africa who later became magister militum for GALLA PLACIDIA. The Vandal king turned on Boniface and defeated the joint forces of the East and West. He retained Carthage, the "Breadbasket of Rome," and in 441 a powerful Eastern army set sail to recapture the city, but the legion had to be recalled because of Attila's rampage on the Danubian frontiers.

Gaiseric's most daring political maneuver, however, is listed as the sack of Rome in June of 455. Pope LEO I attempted to stave off the destruction, but wasn't very successful; Rome was pillaged for a fortnight, losing countless treasures. Gaiseric also took with him as hostages Empress Eudoxia and her two daughters, Eudocia and Placidia, in addition to Gaudentius, son of AËTIUS. Twice more the empire tried to overthrow the Vandal king — by Majorian in 460 and by Basilicus, who had been empowered by ANTHEMIUS in 468 — but in both instances the Romans were defeated.

Sources: E. Duckett (MPFE&W); A. Ferrill (FOTRE); M. Hadas (HOR); C. Littleton/L. Malcor (FSTC); S. Oost (GPA).

Galahad, Galahallt, Galaat, Galehat. Galahad's introduction in Malory's *Le Morte* appears in Book 2, Chapter 16: "King Pelles lay so many years sore wounded, and might never be whole till Galahad, the Haut Prince healed him in the quest of the Sangrail, for in that place was part of the blood of Our Lord Jesus Christ, that Joseph of Arimathea brought into this land, and there himself lay in that rich bed."

According to editor Janet Cowen, who used Caxton's edition of *Le Morte*, printed in 1485, and at times referenced Eugene Vinaver's translation, the King Pelles passage doesn't appear in any of Malory's known sources. The mere mention of the Holy Grail, Christ's blood, and JOSEPH OF ARIMATHEA leaves no doubt that Galahad is a phantasm etched in folklore. In later

"How Galahad drew out the sword from the floating stone at Camelot." In Pollard's *The Romance of King Arthur* (1917), illustration by Arthur Rackham.

chapters, ELAINE begat Galahad from LAUNCE-LOT, who was under a spell of enchantment.

After Galahad is knighted at Camelot and the king with his knights return from the service, there are signs on each seat of the Round Table, the one at the Siege Perilous claiming that "four hundred winters and four-and-fifty accomplished after the Passion of the Lord Jesus Christ ought this siege to be fulfilled." Using calculations devised by modern scholars, the year would be 482, since the Passion of Christ is twenty-eight years later than the Incarnation. Interestingly, the advocates of a historic Arthur claim that Arthur was crowned king around 475, which means in this instance that Arthur would have been king for seven years.

A squire enters the hall of the Round Table and declares that a marvel has occurred. A great stone has arisen from the river, and a sword is sticking from the stone. Lettered in gold on the sword are the words that only the best knight in the world would be able to extract the sword. Launcelot refuses to try, but Gawain and Percival try and both fail. The knights return to feast at the Round Table.

Upon arrival, an old man brings Galahad into the hall and leads him to the Siege Perilous, and the message on the chair has magically changed to "This is the siege of Galahad, the Haut Prince." The knights "all marvelled greatly of Sir Galahad" and when the meal ended, the knights went to show Galahad the adventure of the sword in the stone. Galahad is not surprised and claims, "This adventure is mine, and for the surety of this sword I brought none with me, for here by my side hangeth the scabbard." He then grabs the sword, easily withdraws it, and sheathes it. A damsel rides up on a white palfrey and asserts that Galahad is indeed the best knight in the world, and berates Launcelot as being a "sinful man of the world."

Galahad becomes the noblest knight of the round table and the only one worthy to sit in the Siege Perilous. His shield is emblazoned with a red cross, painted in blood by a different kinsman named Joseph. He travels to the Holy Land, achieving the Quest of the Holy Grail, and with that accomplished, his soul is raised to Heaven.

Sources: T. Malory (LMD'A); A. Pollard (RKA).

Galla Placidia. Upon the deaths of her half-brother Emperor Honorius and her husband co-emperor Constantius III, Galla Placidia became regent of the Western Roman Empire for her young son, Valentinian III. Both she and her half-brother were born in the Eastern Empire, which their father, Theodosius the Great, ruled. It was her misfortune to be in Rome when Alaric, Judge (king) of the Visigoths sacked the city in 410. After three days, she, Aëtius, and another young Roman boy were taken as hostages when Alaric abandoned the city and headed south toward Regium, where he had planned to commandeer ships and sail to Africa to capture Carthago (Carthage).

Alaric's plans, however, were thwarted, and in the melee, he was killed. ATAULPHUS (Ataulph) became judge, and during the seven-year interim, Galla Placidia willingly married the new leader. They had a son, whom they named Theodosius, after her father. Although the infant was healthy, he died a mysterious death before his first year, and shortly thereafter Ataulphus was killed by a stablehand. Vallia then became the new judge.

During Aëtius's and Placidia's captivity, Constantius III unsuccessfully negotiated several times for their release. Finally, in 417 C.E. when Vallia had assumed command, the hostages were released. Constantius III not only became co-emperor, but he was selected as a consulibus, and Honorius gave his co-ruler Placidia's hand in marriage. Constantius and Placidia bore a son, Valentinian III.

Following the deaths of Constantius III and Emperor Honorius, Galla Placidia became an unprecedented female figure of the Western Roman Empire during the tumultuous fifth century, ruling for 27 years (423 C.E. to 450 C.E.) as regent for her son Valentinian. Placidia's connection to Arthuriana stems from her marriage to Constantius III after Honorius's decree that a *Comes Britanniarum* be assigned to reclaim Britain as a province. Intense research and scrutiny has not led to an ironclad reality, but based upon R.G. Collingwood's belief that the new office of

Comes Britanniarum "must certainly be associated with the work of the Patrician Constantius," its feasibility has been structured in *The Historic Arthur* and *Historic Figures of the Arthurian Era* as a hypothesis that Galla Placidia's second husband, Constantius III, was indeed AMBROSIUS, Aurelianus's father, and Arthur is conflated with Ambrosius, since Arthur is a phantom of the fifth century.

Galla Placidia would therefore be Ambrosius's stepmother, which would at least partially explain her intense interest in Britain as a province. Her major apprehension would be Ambrosius Aurelianus's claim to the Western throne.

Sources: R. Collingwood/J. Myres (RB&ES); E. Duckett (MPE&W); A. Ferrill (FOTRE); E. Gibbon (D&FRE); S. Oost (GPA); F. Reno (HKA, HFAE).

Gandîn. In *Le Morte D'Arthur*, Thomas Malory's character PALOMIDES replaces Gottfried von Strassburg's Gandîn in *Tristan and Isolt*.

Approximately halfway through the romance *Tristan and Isolt*, Gandîn is introduced as "a knight, a noble baron of Ireland, ... rich, handsome, and courteous; so manly and strong of limb that all Ireland spake of his valor." Gandîn is likewise a marvelous bard. He travels to King Mark's court in Cornwall because of the great love he has for Isolt, the daughter of Ireland's queen who has been betrothed to Mark, and in the Great Hall during festivities, he charmed everyone with his lute.

After singing several lays, Mark asks him to play more, and Gandîn agrees, on the condition that the king grant him a reward. The king knows not what the reward might be, and unthinkingly agrees that he will grant any possession the bard asks. When the lay has ended, Gandîn asks for Isolt. The king is shocked, but after some haggling, Mark knows he is bound by honor to grant the request. Because Gandîn is so strong and valiant, no one challenges him, and the bard takes Isolt to the seashore to await the tide.

Tristan returns from his hunt, and when he hears the news, he goes to Gandîn's tent, and through the trickery of music, he steals Gandîn's steed and rides off with Isolt. Brokenhearted, Gandîn sails on the tide back to his homeland.

Sources: R. Loomis/L. Loomis (MR); T. Malory (LMD'A).

Ganhumara, Guenhuvara, Guanhumara. Geoffrey of Monmouth uses the Latin term *Ganhumara* to identify GUINEVERE, Arthur's Queen.
Source: L. Thorpe (GM: HKB).

Ganieda. Through MERLIN, Ganieda has only a satellite connection to Arthuriana. Merlin is typically portrayed as a magus or wizard who has a major role in Geoffrey of Monmouth's *The History of the Kings of Britain*. As explained in a separate entry, Monmouth breaks off his narration of "The House of Constantine" and inserts "The Prophecies of Merlin," which in actuality has no connection to the historic King Arthur. In "The House of Constantine" Monmouth uses the name Merlinus, but it is attached as a nominative for Ambrosius, referring to him as Ambrosius Merlinus.

Because Monmouth's *Vita Merlini* was written in 1148, about twelve years after his *History of the Kings*, and because the story was no doubt built upon an entry in *The Annales Cambriae* from Harleian *MS* 3859 (which Leslie Alcock called the *British Historical Miscellany*), this Merlin appears in the late sixth century, not in the fifth century, normally labeled as "the historical era of King Arthur." The entry from the *AC* is the year 573: "The Battle of Arfderydd †*between the sons of Eliffer and Gwenddolau son of Ceidio; in which battle Gwenddolau fell; Merlin went mad.*† The italicized material between the daggers is explained by John Morris in *British History*: "These additional entries and details contained in MS 'B,' and absent from the Harleian text, are added between dagger symbols."

In the fictionalized tale *Vita Merlini* — separated from what Monmouth called "history" in his first manuscript — Merlin's sister is named Ganieda. She is married to King Rydderch of Cumbria, whom she dupes when she tells him she is chaste.
See also MERLIN.
Sources: Geoffrey of Monmouth (VM); J. Morris (BH); L. Thorpe (GM: HKB).

Gareth, Garethe, Cahariet, Gaharie, Gahariet. After Gareth drops his epithet BEAUMAINS, everyone realizes that he is son of King Lot and his brothers are GAWAIN, GAHERIS, AGRAVAIN, and (MORDRED?). The Queen of Orkney (unnamed), who has not seen her sons for fifteen years, comes to the Pentecost feast and orders of her brother King Arthur why he has treated her young son so poorly. The brothers and Arthur claim they knew him not. She rebukes them for keeping her son in the kitchen and "feeding him like a poor hog." Gareth is not there, but on a quest for the sake of the damosel Lynette.

Thereafter he becomes an honored knight of the Round Table. When his brothers Agravain and Mordred are pushing to disclose to Arthur the love affair between Launcelot (LANCELOT) and Guenever, Gawain, Gareth, and Gaheris are against it, realizing that the realm would crumble if that information were divulged. Agravain, Mordred and twelve knights catch Launcelot in Guenever's bedchamber. Agravain and the twelve knights are killed. Mordred escapes.

The feud continues, and when the queen is put to justice, Arthur approaches Gawain and tells Sir Gawain, "Dear nephew, I pray you make you ready in your best armour with your bretheren, Sir Gaheris and Sir Gareth, to bring my queen to the fire, there to have her judgment and receive the death." Gawain refuses, defending the queen and claiming that he will not be present for such a grotesque affair. Arthur then commands Gawain to require his two brothers be there. The two brothers say that they will do so against their will, but they will go in peace and not make war. However, there is great melee, and in all the rashing and hurling, both are slain.

Source: T. Malory (LMD'A).

Gaudentius. There were two figures named Gaudentius in Roman history of the mid–fifth century. The elder Gaudentius became the magister equitus (master of the cavalry) of Rome for Emperor HONORIUS during the early decades of the fifth century. Gaudentius would have known and been a comrade with CONSTANTIUS III, who was Honorius's supreme commander. This elder Gaudentius's son AËTIUS became magister utriusque militiae (magister of both services/ magister of soldiers) during Regent GALLA

PLACIDIA'S reign. The younger Gaudentius was Aëtius's son, who was taken and held hostage along with Empress Licinia Eudoxia and her two daughters, by Gaiseric, the Ravager of Rome in 455.

Sources: E. Duckett (MPE&W); E. Gibbon (D&FRE).

Gawain, Gawaine, Gauvain, Galveins, Walwain, Gagain, Gauen. Sir Gawain is a knight with multiple personalities: one appearing in Thomas Malory's text *Le Morte D'Arthur*, a second in Geoffrey of Monmouth's *History of the Kings of Britain*, and a third in a manuscript titled *Sir Gawain and the Green Knight*. In Malory's text, Gawain is one of four brothers—GAHERIS, AGRAVAIN, and GARETH. His mother is MARGAWSE, and his father is King Lot (LOTH) of Orkney. In Book 2, Chapter 10, Malory evidently confuses Margawse with MORGAN LE FAY and mistakenly adds another son, MORDRED. Gawain plays an important role not only in Malory's work, but also in GEOFFREY OF MON-

Gawain's blazon with a purple background and a gold double-headed eagle.

MOUTH's *History of the Kings of Britain.* In this latter manuscript, Gawain's mother is ANNA, the sister of AURELIUS AMBROSIUS, ostensibly Arthur's first cousin for those individuals who believe that ARTHUR was a historic figure of the fifth century.

Monmouth's version of Gawain in Arthuriana is convoluted beyond comprehension. His first reference to Gawain is: "Loth, who in the days of Aurelius Ambrosius had married that King's own sister and had two sons by her, Gawain and Mordred." The interpretation is that Aurelius Ambrosius had a sister named ANNA; Anna married Lot (Loth), and the couple had two sons, Gawain and Mordred. Aurelius Ambrosius would therefore be Gawain and Mordred's uncle, which in itself is distorted in later Arthurian material, because Arthur is listed as Mordred's uncle.

Translator Lewis Thorpe points out the chaos Monmouth perpetrated. In the index about Anna, he writes: "Anna: Arthur's sister, like him the child of Utherpendragon and Ygerna, 208 (on page 209 Geoffrey says that she marries Loth of Lodonesia; on page 214 he says that HOEL I, King of Brittany, is the son of Anna and BUDICIUS, King of Brittany; on page 221 he again contradicts the former statement, making Loth of Lodonesia marry the sister of Aurelius Ambrosius)." This contortion points out why Monmouth's genealogy is bogus — there is no historic Arthur of fifth-century Britain, as stated in the *Historia Brittonum.* Ambrosius is king of that era. The folktales of Arthur are mistakenly following a historic path when they record Mordred as a nephew of "Arthur" and Morgan (or Margawse) as "Arthur's" sister, with whom he unknowingly committed incest.

Tracing Gawain in Monmouth's manuscript, Gawain is with Arthur when he attacks the powerful Roman general LUCIUS HIBERIUS. He fights valiantly against the Roman general but cannot conquer and kill him. The battle lasts for three days, and Lucius is finally slain by an unknown hand. Bedevere and Kay are also killed in the battle.

Shortly after that victory, Arthur receives news that his nephew Mordred (Gawain's brother?) had placed the crown of Britain on his own head, and the "treacherous tyrant was living adulterously and out of wedlock with Queen GUINEVERE." As soon as Arthur's troops land in Britain, a fierce battle ensues, and "Gawain, the King's nephew, died that day."

The epic *Sir Gawain and the Green Knight* is unrelated to Arthuriana. According to A.C. Cawley, this narrative poem is made up of two independent stories, one which is known as "The Beheading," and the other "The Temptation." Cawley writes that the first can be traced to the eighth-century Irish saga of *Bricriu's Feast* and that neither "beheading nor Temptation had anything to do with the Arthurian legends originally, and possible that both stories go back to ancient Irish and Welsh sources."

Sources: A. Cawley (SGGK); T. Malory (LMD'A); L. Thorpe (GM: HKB).

Geoffrey of Monmouth (*floruit* 1112–1139 / *lifespan* circa 1095–1155). Geoffrey of Monmouth might seem displaced when considering the fifth century, because his book's content spans a millennium and a half, from the Trojan War to the Saxon domination of Britain. However, fifty-eight percent of *The History of the Kings of Britain* is focused upon the Arthurian matter, a 150-year legacy of the Arthurian Age claiming most of the emphasis. In *The Historic King Arthur*, F. D. Reno writes,

> No discussion of King Arthur, serious or otherwise, can deny Geoffrey his rightful position in Arthuriana. No single author — with perhaps Thomas Malory as the exception — has been as quoted, as analyzed, as praised or as scorned as Geoffrey; scholars have ranged from accepting everything Geoffrey writes as either covert or explicit truth to denouncing him as a fraud; there are very few fence-sitters. A person at the former end of the continuum has to apologize and rationalize for some of the things he writes, while the latter refuse to waste time trying to sort through his distorted claims. But the patient few who are the fence-sitters glean the most from his work.

Geoffrey offers a wealth of crucial information about Arthur, whether it be explanations of the legendary king or a genealogical background for the historic figure, providing crucial details which cannot be offhandedly discarded. Only a sampling of material can be presented here to reveal a shadowy silhouette of the controversial legendary/historic Arthur. Proponents defend Geoffrey by claiming: "Geoffrey meant to say..."; "Geoffrey's understandable error is..."; "Geoffrey misunderstood his sources when he...." However, Geoffrey cannot accurately be labeled as a marvelous visionary, an apocalyptic diviner, or a flawless interpreter.

As a twelfth-century writer, he had at his disposal GILDAS BADONICUS, BEDE, NENNIUS, the *Tysilio*, HENRY OF HUNTINGDON, WILLIAM OF MALMESBURY, and undoubtedly other works which have been lost to modern scholars, notwithstanding his sole claim of a *liber vetustissimus*. Based upon detailed lists of identifiable historical people, he cross-referenced Cicero, Juvenal, Lucan, Bede, and King ALFRED, as well as archaeological evidence. Thorpe concludes, "What nobody who has examined the evidence carefully can ever dare to say is that Geoffrey of Monmouth simply made up his material."

To the detriment of his veracity, Geoffrey erred at the very onset of his treatise on the historic Arthur. In Part Four, "The House of Constantine," GUITHELINUS crosses to the mainland to solicit help from Aldroenus, the king of Armorica. His plea opens with a reference to CONSTANTINE and Maximianus, the former obviously being an allusion to Flavius Claudius Constantinus, also known as Constantine the Usurper, who attempted to wrest the Western Empire from Honorius.

Although Aldroneus graciously refuses Guithelinus's entreaty, he offers to send his own brother, also named CONSTANTINE, commanding two thousand soldiers to free Britain from barbarian invasion.

The soldiers are chosen, and the army lands in Britain, where a council is immediately held and Constantine is raised to the kingship of Britain. The new king is also given a wife "born of a noble family, whom Archbishop Guithelinus had himself brought up. When their marriage had been consummated, the King had three sons by her. Their names were Constans, Auelius Ambrosius, and Utherpendragon. The King [Constantine] handed Constans his first born over to the church of Amphibalus in Winchester, so that

he might enter a monastic order. The other two, Aurelius and Utherpendragon, he gave to Guithelinus, so that he might bring them up."

This is Monmouth's inception of the Constantinian Dynasty, or the House of Constantine, a lineage which creates confusion and consternation even present-day. A close perusal of Roman and Breton history uncovers no Constantine who fits into this particular time frame. Constantine (the Briton usurper) was beheaded by Honorius in 411 C.E., four years after he invaded Gaul and tried to overthrow the West. According to Monmouth, this usurper had a son named Constans who followed his father to Gaul and was killed during a revolt in Spain.

Roman history of course records prolific information about Constantine I (the Great) dating to the beginning of the 300s, more than a century prior to the era Monmouth is narrating. Constantine I also had a son named Constans, and Constans had two brothers — Constantine II and Constantius II — both whose floruits are the 350s. Geoffrey might have confused not only the three Constantines (Constantine the Great, Constantine II, and Constantine the Usurper), but also misidentified the two Constanses.

There is only one patrician appearing in Roman history through the second decade of the fifth century who would match or correspond with the "Constantine" in Geoffrey's story. That figure is Flavius Constantius III, a patrician who became Honorius's supreme magister and later co-emperor of west. Constantius III was instrumental in securing the release of Aëtius and Galla Placidia after they were taken as hostages by the Visigoths, and later he married Placidia, thus becoming Honorius's brother-in-law. Constantius III is the individual who R.G. Collingwood postulates is the officer who is assigned to Britain as the *COMES BRITANNIARUM*. Based on the fact that this office was not in existence prior to the fifth century, Collingwood writes, "It has been conjectured that [this position] originated with the reorganization carried out by the patrician Constantius [III] in the second decade of the [fifth] century. The comes Britanniarum, therefore cannot have existed until after [italics added] the rescript of Honorius."

Collingwood cites a number of other historians — J.B. Bury, Dr. Ernst Stein, GILDAS BADONICUS, GERMANUS — then points to two other sources, the first being the *Gallic Chronicle* of 442, stating that "Britain, distressed by various defeats and other happenings, becomes subject to the Saxons." He concludes by commenting, "However [the reoccupation] may have ended, both sides [Britons and Romans] still no doubt believed that it [the reoccupation] was to begin again; and it was only in 446, after the vain appeal to Aëtius, that hope was abandoned."

Stewart Oost writes, "About 415 or 416 Roman authority appears to have been restored in Armorica by EXUPERANTIUS, probably a lieutenant of Constantius [III]; this revolt had either been connected with or identical with a revolt of the peasants, Bacaudae. Constantius may even have been able to restore some measure of control over a part of Britain." This suggests a link between Flavius Constantius III and "Arthur of Britain" as written in Monmouth's work. Constantius III drops from Roman history after his marriage to GALLA PLACIDIA and he doesn't reappear until late 419 or early 420. In the interim, Exuperantius becomes acting praefectus of Gaul. Constantius himself might have filled the new office of *Comes Britanniarum* (Monmouth's Constantine, the royal nobleman from the House of Constantine), and sailed to Britain after Gaul had been pacified to try to reclaim Britain as a province. While there, he took as a concubine a Celtic woman "born of a noble family, whom Archbishop GUITHELINUS himself had brought up," to use Geoffrey's own words.

This might well be a reference to YGERNA (Ygraine), an enigmatic identification which carries over to her children. According to Geoffrey, Constantine had three sons by her: Constans, Aurelius Ambrosius, and Utherpendragon. In Roman histories of the early 300s, Constantine the Great (Costantine I) sired four or five sons, two of whom were Constantine II and Constans. In a struggle for the empire, these two brothers fought a battle in northern Italy in 340, where Constantine II was killed.

Constans became ruler of the Western Empire, and did visit Britain in 343, but he was killed in Gaul in 350, which eliminates this Constans as the person Monmouth was referring to nearly a century later. Because there is no clear-cut history which Monmouth might have been using, he must have confused genealogical lines when he wrote, "Constantine had three sons by a noble Celtic wife," labeling one of the sons as Constans. Other than Constans the son of Constantine the Great, the only other Constans associated with Britain was Constans the son of Flavius Claudius Constantinus — Constantine the Usurper — mentioned earlier.

Equally off the mark is Monmouth's reference to a second son of Constantine, Utherpendragon. However, translator Lewis Thorpe adds a footnote about the advent of Utherpendragon on page 151 of the text. The addendum notifies the reader that "Utherpendragon (*Jesus*, Ythr ben dragwn) takes his name from the Comet and the two Golden Dragons which he [one of Constantine's sons] had made on page 202 [51 pages later]. Geoffrey calls him Utherpendragon from his first appearance."

It is crucial to recall that Geoffrey is translating his material directly into Latin from early Welsh. This is the very first identification of King Arthur's father — not an actual proper name, but an epithet — and unfortunately, an epithet which is extremely controversial in its translation. In Thorpe's footnote, *Jesus* is a reference to the manuscript, and "Ythr ben dragwn" is allegedly the early Welsh term which Monmouth copied, Anglicized to Utherpendragon.

There is no dissention about the root *-dragon* of the epithet; the purple dragon was a long-standing icon for the Roman cavalry. However, the two prefixes, *uther-* and *pen-*, have caused heated controversy, especially the former. To understand the thread more thoroughly, the reader is encouraged to look first at the entry titled PENDRAGON for clarification of the prefix *Pen-*, then read the entry UTERPENDRAGON.

Thorpe, who must be viewed as the leading modern translator of Monmouth's work, writes about Jacob Hammer's involvement in interpreting Monmouth's intent. Thorpe writes:

> In a book published in 1951, Jacob Hammer printed a variant version of the *Historia*, which differs in many ways from the standard or Vulgate text. Hammer's suggestion was

that this variant version was an adaptation of what Geoffrey himself had written, made by some other contemporary author. Concerning this variant version, Robert A. Caldwell has now put forward a startling theory that this variant version possibly preceded the standard text. Monmouth's "certain very ancient book" might be this variant.

Thorpe also acknowledges Acton Griscom's contributions to the Monmouth manuscript. In 1929, Griscom listed nearly 200 Latin manuscripts which had survived, including 48 from the twelfth century. Of all those, Thorpe chose to use Griscom's text, the Cambridge University Library, manuscript 1706.

See also WACE, LAYAMON, and CHRÉTIEN DE TROYES.

Sources: E. Chambers (AOB); A. Griscom (HRBGM); N. Lacy (AE); K. Malone (JE&GP: HOA); L. Thorpe (GM: HKB).

Geraint, Gereint. The name Geraint or Gereint can be found in at least a score of manuscripts, and upon perusal, the only conclusion which can be reached is that there is considerable confusion over this name because it was a such a popular one in the early medieval period. Richard Barber touches upon the dilemma, but it is stated in more detail by Chris Barber and David Pykitt. Because literature and history can be haphazard in recordings of who's who in genealogical tracts, not only is chronology entangled, but pinpointing geographic sites can be misleading and inaccurate.

There is no difficulty in Erec's evolution from Chrétien de Troyes's *Erec and Enide* through Hartmann von Aue's *Erec and Enite*, to Gereint and Enid in *The Mabinogion*, but the links become very tenuous after that. In *Kings and Queens of Early Britain*, Geoffrey Ashe, among others, accepts the premise that "'Geraint' is a Welsh form of 'Gerontius.'" This might have been borrowed from E.K. Chambers's book *Arthur of Britain*, where Gereint is identified as the son of Erbin in the ancient *Black Book of Carmarthen* and recurs in both the *Red Book of Hergest* and the *White Book of Rhydderech*. Chambers writes, "A Gerontius is known to history, and may very well have fought at Langport.

He was the last independent Celt King of Dumnonia, and was conquered by Ina of Wessex in 710. This was nearly two centuries after the time of Arthur, but the Celtic historic muse cares little for chronology." Chambers is referring to a poem in the above-mentioned books which celebrates the death of Gereint of Devon at the battle of Llongborth. The difficulty with geographic identities is evident when Llongborth is equated with Langport; other scholars and researchers surmise that Llongborth is the Severn estuary, or that it is Portchester. The Gerontius/Gereint mentioned here is the same Geraint, King of Dumnonia, who was defeated by the West Saxons in 710, recorded by Peter Hunter Blair.

In *The Figure of Arthur*, Richard Barber picks up on "Gereint of Devon" and comments that this Gereint could be "'Gereint from the south' in *The Gododdin*, a distant memory of [Gereint and Arthur's] alliance in the north."

For the "Gerrans" entry in *The Traveller's Guide to Arthurian Britain*, Geoffrey Ashe gives an excellent nutshell commentary on Geraint:

> Gerrans [a village in Cornwall] on the promontory over the water east of Falmouth is supposed to have been named after the West Country ruler Geraint — an Arthurian character (husband, in some stories, of the Lady Enid) who almost certainly existed.
>
> Several Geraints are on record in the West Country, and it is hard to tell which is which. One of them, maybe the Arthurian one, figures in a poem about the battle at Llongborth. Another, probably senior, is said to have been the father of Cadwy, Arthur's co-prince at Dunster....
>
> [T]he Geraint buried at Gerrans ... may have been younger than the Arthurian one, and the village was named after him in the belief that he was a saint himself. Much later again, a Geraint is mentioned as fighting at Catterick, in the battle commemorated by Aneirin.

The tale "Gereint and Enid" in *The Mabinogion* is, according to Jeffrey Gantz, "by far the least obtrusively marked by mythological motifs, ... the most thoroughly refined and rationalized, ... and the best narrated."

The tale opens in the typical fashion of the original *Erec et Enide*. Gwenhwyvar and Gereint encounter a knight, a damsel, and a dwarf, the latter who insults both Gwenhwyvar's hand-maiden and Gereint. These details are given:

1. Gereint is the son of Erbin;
2. the knight is Edern, son of Nudd;
3. Arthur's dog Cavall is mentioned;
4. Gildas son of Caw [i.e., GILDAS ALBANIUS] escorts Gwenhwyvar back to court;
5. Howel is the son of Emhyr of Brittany; and
6. the Earl Limwris is *li mors* (death) in Chrétien's *Erec*.

See also GERONTIUS and GEREINT.

Sources: G. Ashe (TGAB); C. Barber/D. Pykitt (JTA); R. Barber (FOA); P. Blair (RB&EE); E. Chambers (AOB); J. Gantz (TM); N. Lacy/G. Ashe (AH).

Gerald of.Wales. *see* GIRALDUS CAMBRENSIS.

Gerbert de Montreuil (1226–1230). Gerbert de Montreuil is another Continuator of CHRÉTIEN DE TROYES' *Le Conte du Graal* (*Perceval*). W. Kibler writes, "An independent conclusion composed by Gerbert de Montreuil ... is inserted after the Second Continuation, although the MANESSIER conclusion is also retained. Gerbert did not know Manessier's work and probably wrote a conclusion to the Grail story that was independent of his; however, in the manuscripts the ending has been altered slightly to lead into Manessier's continuation."

Gerbert's addition runs thusly. Because PERCEVAL had not asked pertinent questions, he awakes the next morning in a meadow. He returns to Arthur's court, where he is given the honored seat in the Grail Knight's chair. Shortly afterwards he begins a quest, going to the court of King Mark in Cornwall, where he wins victories against his rivals. When he returns, he marries BLANCHEFLOR, but they pledge not to consummate their marriage so that they can attain Paradise. He is deemed an honorable knight and is to have the secrets of the grail revealed to him, but then Gerbert's tale is superseded by Manessier's ending.

Source: W. Kibler (CDT: AR).

Gereint. Of the three tales in *The Mabinogion* traditionally known as Welsh Romances, Jeffrey Gantz characterizes "Gereint and Enid" as the one "least obtrusively marked by mythological motifs," but is also "the most thoroughly refined, rationalized ... and best narrated." He then points out that the tales — dated to the thirteenth century — are euhemerized, mythical or legendary figures interpreted as historical people, which is no doubt why he immediately labels Gereint in this particular tale as "not a historical figure."

D.D.R. Owen, in his Introduction of Chrétien de Troyes's *Arthurian Romances*, iterates the parallel of the Welsh "Gereint and Enid" and Chrétien's "Erec and Enide." He writes that the collection of prose tales in *The Mabinogion* were written down over a century after Chrétien's death. He then clarifies: "After many years of debate, the question is still far from being resolved to everybody's satisfaction. There are those, though their ranks are now depleted, who hold that the Welsh tales are all corrupt and abbreviated versions of Chrétien's. It is more usually supposed that each pair [the three tales which have parallels] is derived from a common source; but a refinement in the discussion is to claim that the Welsh author or authors knew Chrétien as well as the shared models."

Owen inserts two other comments in an attempt to resolve the dilemma; the first is that "*Erec* [and *Enide*] is currently thought to have been composed in about 1170," and the second is, "Chrétien appears to have reorganized and elaborated one [Erec] already fairly well developed tale of ultimately Celtic origin." Gantz writes, "Our earliest written fragments of *The Mabinogion* date only to the thirteenth century, by which time it is clear that the material has been greatly altered." The "thirteenth century" is a broad span of time, and with all the continuations which have been written, there is no resolution.

Chronological calibrations are crucial considerations when attempting to separate fact from fiction in ancient manuscripts. Because the purpose of this text is to delineate material as accurately as possible, it is necessary to heed axioms by De La Rouchefoucauld and Jean Markale. De La Rouchefoucauld reminds us that history never embraces more than a small part of reality and truth, and Jean Markale remarks that we can look for evidence either in history or in legend, for both will give us clues of reality.

Aware of the complexity of specifically defining the categories of literature, fiction, legend, and folklore (excluding mythology because of its religious context) as opposed to fact, reality and history, the purpose of this text is to separate Arthurian fiction from historical fact, particularly as those distinctions apply to the fifth century. If, as Brynley Roberts wrote in his entry about Geraint [*sic*] for *The Arthurian Encyclopedia* that Gereint "is of the late sixth- or early seventh-century king of Dumnonia," then the tales of Gereint and Erec must be classified as fiction, since both are outside the era ascribed to an unfounded historic King Arthur and an attested King Ambrosius.

An entry by Brynley Roberts in *The Arthurian Encyclopedia* supplies an excellent synopsis of the Gereint folktale:

> Geraint, one of Arthur's knights, wins Enid's hand after successfully competing for the prize of a sparrow hawk in a tournament. After their marriage, the couple are recalled to Geraint's patrimony because of the feebleness of his father the king, but the young husband neglects his duties as a ruler and knight because of his overriding affection for his wife. One morning, she inadvertently reveals the courtiers' criticism of their prince to Geraint, who mistakenly (and inexplicably) takes her words to mean that she is unfaithful to him. He orders her roughly to ride out with him, but through a series of trials she eventually convinces him of her constancy and care for him. On the return journey to their court, Geraint in a final adventure overcomes the knight of the hedge of mist and destroys its enchantment.

He elucidates the end of the story by stating that the first segment is well-constructed and the ending more rambling. He then concludes that "whatever its immediate origins may be, Chrétien's romance or its source, the story has been successfully put into a Welsh mold."

Sources: J. Bartlett (FQ); J. Gantz (TM); N. Lacy (AE); D. Owen (CDT: AR).

German *Saxones* are those relatives of ENGLISH SAXONES living on the continent. When civil war broke out on the island, the English *Saxones* sought aid from their German counterparts. In Section 56 of the *Historia Brittonum*, Nennius writes about the English seeking help from Germany to defeat the Welsh.

Germanus of Auxerre (b. circa 378; d. 31 July 448 in Auxerre, France). Germanus is an important historical figure of the fifth century, both on the continent and the role which is attributed to him in the *Historia Brittonum* as a historical personage as well as an individual who apparently affects the Arthurian era. Josephus Stevenson applauds Constantius Hericus as Germanus's biographer,

> an author of considerable reputation [who] wrote an account of the Life and Miracles of St. Germanus, which he dedicated to the Emperor Charles the Bald, in C.E. 876 or 877. In his manuscript Hericus cites, as his authority for several miracles wrought by Germanus, the testimony of "a certain old man named Mark," a bishop of the British nation, and a native of that island. Nor should we fail to remark that this Hericus quotes, as from dictation of Mark, the adventures of Germanus and the Cowherd, which find a place in *The Historia Brittonum*.

Shunning an earlier life of profligacy, Germanus became Bishop of Auxerre on July 7, 418. In 429 he was dispatched to Britain to combat the Pelagian heresy flourishing there. One of the proponent's leaders was Agricola at a synod in Verulamium (St. Albans), where the two men confronted each other. An assault by the Scotti from the west interrupted the debate, and Germanus, who was a military commander prior to becoming bishop, blessed the Briton troops and frightened away the Scotti in the famous "Hallelujah" encounter.

He returned to Britain around the year 447 with a certain Severus of Trèves, which the *Historia Brittonum* records as "The Life of Saint Germanus, Parts 2 and 3." When he left the island and arrived in Gaul, the Armoricans in Brittany faced destruction for evidently rebelling against the Western Empire. Germanus pled for a stay of execution until they could be pardoned by Empress GALLA PLACIDIA, Regent for her son VALENTINIAN III.

Germanus's involvement with contemporaries in Britain is not as openly accepted as history. Yet AMBROSIUS AURELIANUS, CERDIC, Cateyrn

(CATEGERN), CUNEDDA, HENGIST, HORSA, Maelgwyn, OCTHA, PASCENT, VORTIGERN, VORTIMER, and VITALINUS (GUITHELINUS) all appear in either Gildas's *De Excidio*, the *Historia Brittonum*, *The Anglo-Saxon Chronicle*, or Welsh genealogies. Similarly, the chronology is a perfect fit, from the Roman withdrawal circa 410 until Germanus's death in 448. Ambrosius's birth is estimated as 421, Vortigern's reign as beginning in the second decade of the 400s, Cunedda, Hengist, Horsa, Categern, and Pascent being clustered within a generation, Vitalinus as having a disagreement with Ambrosius at the end of the third decade in the 400s, Cerdic and Octha being in a succeeding generation, and Maelgwn (MAGLOCUNUS) being a contemporary of Gildas.

See also MARK THE HERMIT.

Sources: T. Forester (CHH); J. Morris (BH); J. Stevenson (N: HB); E. Thompson (GA& ERB).

Gerontius. The Gerontius/Geraint connection is one of the most complex and circuitous trails to follow in Arthuriana. Not only is the name GERAINT difficult to trace, but the name Gerontius can be equally as confusing. Added to the mix, which Steve Blake and Scott Lloyd in their most recent book *Pendragon* try to resolve, is Geruntius of Dumnonia. In reference to the battle of Llongborth titled "Geraint filius Erbin," they write: "Scholars trying to identify Geraint as a man named Geruntius of Dumnonia, mentioned in a letter from Bishop Aldhelm of Wessex in 705, have obscured the identification of this Welsh hero."

Blake and Lloyd are attempting to accurately identify the site of Llongborth, but by doing so, this casts a shadow of doubt about a Gerontius, Celtic king of Dumnonia conquered by Ina of Wessex in 710, mentioned by E.K. Chambers and by Geoffrey Ashe in *Kings and Queens*. Two questions, therefore, come to mind; 1) is the date 710 applicable to Geraint/Gerontius, and 2) is Dumnonia a reference to Devon, or should it be considered an older reference to the Roman Cornovii territory and not to Cornwall?

As mentioned in the Geraint entry, some scholars claim that the Welsh name Geraint derives from the Roman Gerontius. E.K. Chambers doesn't list Gerontius as a Roman, but he does claim the man's historicity, associating him with the Geraint who was one of Arthur's followers killed at the battle of Llongborth. Although Chambers seems aware that the date of the historic Arthur is commonly set in the mid–fifth century, he facetiously comments that this was nearly two centuries after the time of Arthur, "but the Celtic historic muse cares little for chronology."

John Morris covers this meandering inquiry in the most detail. Encapsulated, it is:

1. Morris geographically sets Constantine the Usurper and Gerontius (both common names used for many centuries) in the Roman territory of Cornovii, i.e., the central midlands encompassing Wroxeter (Viroconium);
2. one medieval Welsh poem (the Llongborth battle?) appears to echo a tradition that a commander who fought with Germanus was named Gerontius;
3. near Llangollen (central midlands) Moel-y-Geraint bears the name Gerontius;
4. the Cornovii homeland was the upper Severn with the capital at Wroxeter, not Cornovia (Cornwall), which was a later reference for Dumnonia and included Devon;
5. Cunedda's migration, Docco, and Gerontius are all dated to the mid–fifth century and could be associated with the Llongborth battle;
6. the Cornovii poem accepts Arthur as emperor and superior ruler over its own hero Gerontius during the wars, and after the wars the "life of Carantoc" accepts Arthur as well as the local king, Gerontius's son Cato, as rulers of Cornovii;
7. the enlisted barbarians fought against Arthur and killed his ally, Gerontius, and had perhaps fought and fallen in alliance with the English at Badon;
8. on the continent, after the second migration of 458–460, Riwal, known by the Roman name of Pompeius Regalis, was linked to the dynasty of Cornovii and was referred to as a descendant of Arthur's Gerontius and Cato.

This collated material is scattered throughout Morris's *Age of Arthur,* but how Geraint interlocks with Gerontius and therefore Arthur remains obscure. Gerontius of 410 also falls into this entanglement. He is undoubtedly an influential historic figure in the Western Roman Empire, contemporary with Emperor Honorius, Constantine the Usurper from Britain, and Constantius III (who some believe was Arthur's father, Pendragon). Christopher Snyder, for one, informs us that Ammianus Marcellinus records Gerontius as a Briton, but no one elaborates what his direct connection is to the island.

Sources: G. Ashe (K&QEB); S. Blake/S. Lloyd (P); E. Chambers (AOB); J. Morris (AOA); C. Snyder (AAOT).

Gewis appears in *The Anglo-Saxon Chronicle* as the great-grandfather of CERDIC, the West Saxon king. If an individual accepts the premise that Cerdic is a Briton/Celtic name of an individual who forsakes his heritage and aligns himself with the West Saxons and becomes a king, then Gewis would be equated with PATERNUS, father of ÆTERNUS, father of CUNEDDA, father of CERDIC in Celtic history.

BEDE records in his history that there were two ancient territories known as GEWISSAE and HWICCA, which were labeled as an "older name for West Saxons" and a "branch of the West Saxons" respectively.

See also ELISEG.

Sources: G.N. Garmonsway (ASC); F. Reno (HKA); F. Reno (HFAE); L. Sherley-Price (BEDE: HEC&P).

Gewissae is an "ancient term for the West Saxons" which appears in *A History of the English Church and People* by BEDE, who mentions this territory three different times, first identifying Cynegils as a king of Gewissae, who was baptized by Bishop Birinus, then describing Cadwalla as "a daring young man of the royal house of the Gewissae," and third as Agilbert being Bishop of the Gewissae.

J.N.L. Myres, in "The English Settlements" as part of the text *Roman Britain and the English Settlements,* makes this comment about GEWIS as part of a genealogy in *The Anglo-Saxon Chronicle* and the clan of the Gewissae itself:

The usual explanation of the Gewissae as meaning "confederates" would be applicable enough to the mixed traditions of the West Saxon folk here envisioned. Its acceptance, however, involves the rejection of Gewis himself as a fictitious personage interpolated into the West Saxon pedigree. No adequate ground has ever been given for such an interpolation, and the increasing tendency of scholars to treat the genealogies as archaic and primitive documents makes it safer to believe that the Gewissae owe their name to an historic Gewis than that he owes his existence merely to their name.

The observation that Myres makes here is extremely important in piecing together not only the West Saxon genealogies, but it also gives a clue to fifth-century Briton genealogies. The use of the word "confederate" historically fills in what Roman policy was not only on the continent, but on the island of Britain. It avers that the *Saxones*— a generic Roman term for Angles, Saxons, Jutes, and Frisians — were indeed *foederati* assigned to Britain by the Romans. Equally as important, Myres views Gewis as a historical figure and not a fictional one. By extension, it verifies that other individuals (Esla and Elesa) succeeding him in the genealogies provided by *The Anglo-Saxon Chronicle* up to the mythical Woden would likewise be historical figures.

Another reservation could be the confusion which evolved about where the Germanic tribes had settled when they migrated to Britain. Leslie Alcock listed the specific tribes Bede had written about, and adds two more: the Franks and the Suevi. The discrepancy of Hengest and his Anglian clan being settled in Kent — despite the surmises of place-names — could very well be the reason why Myres questioned the location of Gewissae and whether Gweissae and Hwicca are interchangeable terms.

See also HWICCA, HYRPE, GEWIS, ESLA, and ELESA.

Sources: L. Alcock (AB); G.N. Garmonsway (ASC); J.N.L. Myres (RB&ES); L. Sherley-Price (BEDE: HEC&P).

Gildas Albanius, Gildas Son of Caw (lifespan circa 425–512). In the Preface of his book about Gildas, Josephus Stevenson addresses the controversy of whether there was only one individual bearing the name of Gildas during the Middle Ages. He presents a cogently persuasive case that at least two individuals were named Gildas, and that they were not contemporaries. Stevenson cites a *vitae* for Gildas Albanius which establishes the birth of this particular Gildas circa 425, and when thirteen, he left his Scottish homeland and sailed to France, which at that time was under the rule of identifiably historic Childeric, the son of Merovius, eventually founding a monastery at Ruys.

Stevenson contends that the *Life of Gildas*, penned by CARADOC OF LLANCARFAN, is an account of Gildas Albanius, not GILDAS BADONICUS, based upon contextual evidence that Gildas "was reconciled with Arthur." According to this same account, Gildas Albanius died in 512. For those who ascribe to a historic Arthur, his ascendancy to kingship at age fifteen took place circa 475. Arthur's floruit, therefore, would be 460–490, overlapping that of Gildas Albanius. A lifespan commonly assigned to Gildas Badonicus, however, is 497–570.

The Mabinogion, one of the most comprehensive oral-tradition Welsh tales, interestingly supports the notion that not only was Gildas Albanius a contemporary of King Arthur, but that they were comrades. In the tale "How Culhwch Won Olwen," Culhwch invoked Olwen in the name of Gildas, son of CAW, King of Scotland. In the tale "The Dream of Rhonabwy," Gildas son of Caw is listed as one of Arthur's advisors at the battle of Baddon. In the story of "Gereint and Enid" Arthur asks Gildas son of Caw to accompany Gwenhwyvar back to court. These episodes link Arthur and Gildas Albanius as contemporaries, in addition to pointing out that Gildas's homeland was Scotland.

Geoffrey of Monmouth in the *History of the Kings of Britain* also writes of a Gildas, but he identifies Gildas as the author of a brilliant book, a reference to *De Excidio Britanniæ*. However, the author of *De Excidio Britanniæ* (Gildas Badonicus) is irreconcilable with events: the Pelagian heresy and Germanus's visit to Britain took place between the years 429 to 437, a half century before Gildas Badonicus was born.

Section 32 of John of Glastonbury's *Cronica* gives a capsulated biography of Gildas — obviously Gildas of Albanius because he is immediately identified as the son of Caw:

In those days flourished St Gildas, the excellent teacher and historian of the Britons. He was the son of a king of Scotland named Kau who also had twenty-three other sons who were warlike soldiers. St Gildas, however was set by his parents upon a course of literary studies. As a youth he crossed to Gaul, where he studied in the best fashion for the space of seven years. When this period was over, he sailed back to Great Britain with a great supply of books of all sorts. Scholars came together from everywhere when they heard of the splendid teacher's fame; he abundantly poured forth for them what he had learned in a far land by excruciating labour and sleepless nights. The piety of this wisest of teachers was extolled by all, and he was praised for his excellent merits. He fasted and prayed assiduously while clothed in a hairshirt. He ate barley bread mixed with ash, and spring water was his daily drink. He slept little, lying upon a rock, and content with only one garment; he was, moreover, the most outstanding preacher in the whole kingdom of Britain. Not much later, he crossed to Ireland, where by his teaching he converted many to the catholic faith. Meanwhile his elder brother Hueil often plagued King Arthur: coming from Scotland, he would burn villages and carry off all sort of spoils. King Arthur therefore grew angry, pursued the youth, and killed him. When Gildas heard of this he wept and moaned in his grief. He returned from Ireland to Britain, and Arthur came to him with many great men; he granted pardon to him who humbly asked it. After the space of a year St Gildas and St Cadoc, Abbot of the church of Llancarfan, came to two islands, "Renech" [Steep Holm] and "Echni" [Flat Holm]. Cadoc landed upon the island closer to Wales, and Gildas on that lying nearer England. They knew of no better counsel than to abandon human wealth and to go to some secret place on an island; and while St Gildas persevered there, intent upon fasting and prayer and other exercises of spiritual warfare, pirates from the Orkney Island came and laid him low, snatching away all those who were attached to him, along with all his moveable property. Exceedingly weighed down as he was with cares, therefore, he climbed into a little ship and came to Glastonbury. He was received by the abbot of Glastonbury with the honour due him, and he taught the people, sowing with the seed of heavenly doctrine the place where he also wrote his histories of the kings of Britain. Then the most religious Gildas again desired to lead a hermit's life; and going away to the bank of a river near Glastonbury, he built a church in the name of the holy and undivided Trinity, which is called the "chapel adventurous," where he prayed and fasted assiduously, clothed in a hairshirt and providing to all an example of living well. After a short time he fell into sickness, and, knowing that the day of his burial was approaching, he called the abbot of Glastonbury and asked him that, when the course of this present life was finished, the abbot would have his body taken to the monastery, to be buried there. The abbot agreed, and after the saint had passed on, many saw an angelic brightness about the fragrant body. When the tearful funeral service had been completed, the holy remains were carried by the brothers to the monastery and buried, with great lamentation and the worthiest honour, in the midst of the Old Church's pavement. This was in C.E. 512; in the same place where he had lived as an anchorite there is now a parish church dedicated in the saint's name.

John's main source of this information is Caradoc of Llancarvan's "Life of Gildas," dated about 1140.

One other decisive factor is that Gildas Albanius has a brother named HUEIL, who figures prominently into the Arthurian saga. The reconciliation between Gildas and Arthur stemmed from a dispute over Hueil's death.

Sources: J. Carley (CGA); J. Gantz (TM); Saints' Lives (LG); J. Stevenson (G: DEB); L. Thorpe (GM: HKB).

Gildas Badonicus (lifespan circa 497–570). The *De Excidio* of Gildas Badonicus is the oldest extant manuscript, a critical document penned in the sixth century soon after the close of what has been termed by some scholars as the Arthurian Age. Josephus Stevenson names this scribe Gildas Badonicus to distinguish him from a certain GILDAS ALBANIUS, who was a different historical figure of several generations earlier. Although Gildas Badonicus makes no direct allusion to King Arthur, his manuscript is crucial in defining fifth-century Britain, clarifying segments of British history which would have otherwise been lost in this dark age.

Gildas Badonicus was Welsh, writing about Wales. The Anglians (identified by Gildas as the "impious easterners") were *foederati* troops sent as allies to VORTIGERN by the Romans, which would have been the Anglians invading Vortigern's territory in northern Wales. When Gildas writes about the Battle of Mount Badon, he would have been referring to the hillfort known as The Wrekin near Wroxeter, not Bath, which wasn't in Vortigern's jurisdiction. Gildas wasn't familiar with Kent or the Jutes.

Gildas's wording alerts the reader to events, characters, and geography: "A fire heaped up and nurtured by the hand of the *orientali sacrilegorum* spread from sea to sea. It devastated town and country round about, and once it was alight, it did not die down until it had burned almost the whole surface of the island and was licking the western ocean with its fierce red tongue.... So a number of the wretched survivors were caught in the mountains and butchered wholesale.... Others made for lands beyond the sea."

Later, the Welsh rallied around a savior: "Their leader was Ambrosius Aurelianus, a gentleman who, perhaps alone of the Romans, had survived the shock of this notable storm: certainly his parents, who had worn the purple, were slain in it. His descendants in our day have become greatly inferior to their grandfather's excellence. Under him our people regained their strength, and challenged the victors to battle."

Gildas makes no allusion to a King Arthur of the fifth century, nor is there any piece of information suggesting he deliberately ignored Arthur. Surely, if Arthur had killed one of Gildas's brothers as some scholars surmise without evidence, Gildas would have added the name of Arthur in his castigation of the five Welsh tyrants. Two centuries after Gildas, BEDE reiterated that the enemies were not the SAXONS infringing on the BRITONS, but the ANGLIANS invading the WELSH. What caused the confusion was that during Roman times, *SAXONES* was a generic term applicable to Anglians, Saxons, Jutes, and Frisians.

The enigma of territorial name-changing also created problems for later historians and schol-

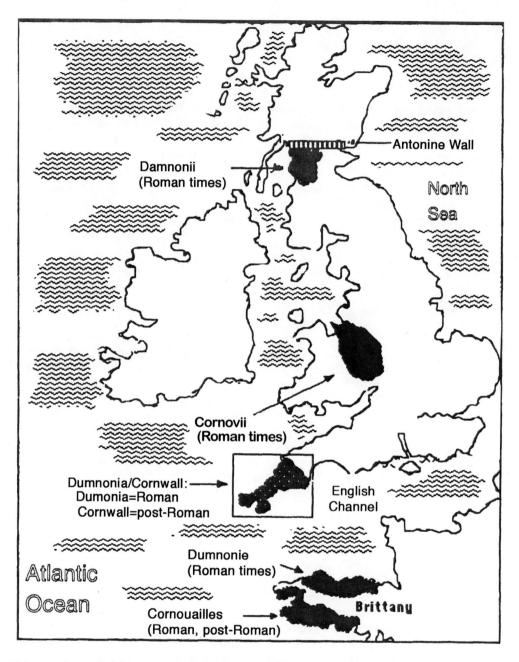

This map shows that there were three Cornish territories on the island and two Dumnoniis, all which appeared on the ancient Roman ordnance surveys. This is part of the reason why modern historians and scholars confuse territories and claim the alleged King Arthur of the fifth century was associated with Tintagel in Cornwall rather than Cornovii in the Welsh midlands.

ars. Gildas points out that many of the Welsh migrated to other territories and even "lands beyond the sea." Many migrated to the southwestern peninsula which in Gildas's time was known as Dumnonia. The Welsh settlement there became known as *Cornwealas*, inhabited by people from Cornovii, and the peninsula eventually acquired the name Cornwall in the 700s.

The Ordnance Survey Map of Roman Britain shows there is even a Cornovii territory at the very northern tip of the island. Migrants who crossed the sea to escape the wars settled in Brittany, and there, too, with the passage of time, the southwestern coast became known as Cornouailles.

AMBROSIUS AURELIANUS fits into the scenario perfectly: he is associated with Wales and Cornovii, he is in the correct era of the fifth century, and he is fighting against East Anglians and not Saxons. With the exception of his castigation of the five tyrants, Gildas rarely identifies an individual by name. His one exception is Ambrosius Aurelianus. In §25 he praises Ambrosius:

> After a time, when the cruel plunderers [Saxones] had gone home, God gave strength to the survivors [Britons].... Their leader was Ambrosius Aurelianus, a gentleman who, perhaps alone of the Romans, had survived the shock of this notable storm; certainly his parents, who had worn the purple, were slain in it. His descendants in our day have become greatly inferior to their grandfather's excellence. Under him our people regained their strength, and challenged the victors to battle. The Lord assented, and the battle went their way.

In the Gildas manuscript, the very first part of §26 states, "From then on victory went now to our countrymen, now to their enemies.... This lasted right up till the year of the siege of Badon Hill, pretty well the last defeat of the villains, and certainly not the least. That was the year of my birth; as I know, one month of the forty-fourth year since then has passed."

Gildas gives the date accepted by the vast majority of researchers: the last decade of the fifth century C.E. Meton in the fifth century B.C.E. calculated chronology in moon phases. In 457 C.E. VICTORIUS OF AQUITAINE devised a chronology based upon the Passion of Christ. In 525 C.E. DIONYSIUS EXIGUUS devised a chronology based upon the Incarnation of Christ. Over the centuries there were no set times when scribes decided to convert to a different system, and because primitive communications were haphazard and many times inaccurate, the dates listed for certain events could vary by at least twenty-eight years. Being aware of this, the most astute researchers have accepted scribal dates with a jaundiced eye and taken great pains when establishing chronological sequences. It has been through the labor of Leslie Alcock that the time frame pertaining to fifth-century Britain has become balanced and accurate.

To whom else would Gildas be referring, other than Ambrosius Aurelianus? And wouldn't a battle of this magnitude obviously be fought in a coveted territory? No doubt many historians based the answer to these questions upon the *Historia Brittonum* ascribed to NENNIUS, answering the first question with "Arthur," and the second with "a hill near the city of Bath." Littleton and Malcor have built a convincing case that the name ARTHUR is a reference to LUCIUS ARTORIUS CASTUS of the second century; there is no evidence of such a renowned king of the fifth century in any of the ancient documents.

As to the locale of Badon, Little Solsbury Hill, adjacent to the City of Bath, has often been identified as Badon. However, similar to the confusion between the Cornovii territory and Cornwall, the city of Bath in Roman times was named Aquae Sulis; it didn't become know as Bath until the 700s. As to its importance, Barry Cunliffe writes, "The 18th and 19th century buildings in the centre of Bath today bear no relation to the Roman remains which lie six metres (20 feet) below them." Beginning in the year 367 Aquae Sulis and the surrounding area were being destroyed and the "baths became increasingly derelict." It wasn't until the late 900s that the baths were being reconstructed. Aquae Sulis was a spa and was not a coveted region.

Chapter 5 (140–178) of *The Historic King Arthur* gives detailed rationale pointing to why Wroxeter was the site where the battle of Badon was fought. At one time, Wroxeter was a prominent legionary fortress, and the walled city was the fourth largest in Britain.

Summarized, the reasons are:

- The city of Bath was not known by that name until the 700s. During the fifth century the area was known by the Roman term Aquae Sulis.
- Aquae Sulis was sparsely populated, whereby Wroxeter became a *civitate,* a civil and administrative post.
- In the post Roman period Wroxeter

Even after the legion moved to Deva, the city remained a thriving tribal center. The only standing wall of the bath at Wroxeter is known as the "Old Work." In the background is the Wrekin, the highest tor in Britain.

retained its importance as the tribal center for the Cornovii tribe, and the Anglians were determined to drive them from their homeland.

- Little Solsbury Hill was excavated by W.A. Dowden, who indicated that the hill had been abandoned well before the Roman period, and there was no trace of Roman influence.
- The River Severus plays a crucial role in determining Badon's geography; whereby Aquae Sulis lies eighteen miles east of the river, at Wroxeter the river literally touched the wall of the city.
- Carrying the rationale further, the Mouth of the Severn near Aquae Sulis would be impossible to ford because it is approximately three miles wide as it empties into Bridgewater Bay and eventually the Bristol Channel.

Besides using the epithet of ORIENTALI SACRI-LEGORUM, Gildas uses quite a number of others. He blames the SUPERBUS TYRANNUS for allowing the Anglians into Britain, but never names who he is. The term is commonly translated as supreme tyrant, supreme ruler, proud ruler, pre-eminent ruler, outstanding ruler and haughty tyrant. Bede assumed that the *superbus tyrannus* was equated with VORTIGERN, and ever since that time antiquarians, historians, and most modern scholars have followed his lead, translating that name as great king, overlord, and over-king. However, in the two extant Gildian manuscripts which have survived (the thirteenth century F. f. i. 27 and the late-fourteenth century D. d. i. 17), Gildas makes no mention of Vortigern. Following Bede's lead, the majority of researchers have equated *superbus tyrannus* and Vortigern, but others who deny that connection stand on the claim that Vortigern was a petty chieftain, an overlord who follows an edict from someone much more powerful. In the Western Roman Empire, it was a common practice to send *foederati*—captured and Roman-trained barbarians—out of Gaul and to distant provinces, and in this instance it might well be that Emperor VALENTINIAN III, under the regency of his mother GALLA PLACIDIA, ordered Vortigern to accept Hengist and his clan as allies.

In Sections 28 through 36 of the *De Excidio*, Gildas uses proper names attached to epithets in his castigations of five Welsh tyrants: CONSTANTINE III is the whelp of the filthy lioness of

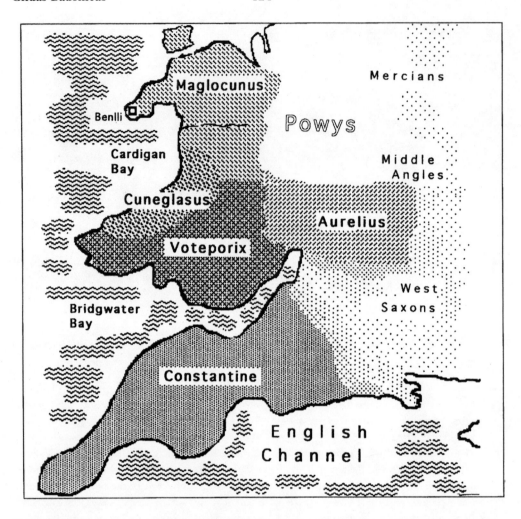

Domains of the five tyrants castigated by Gildas Badonicus: Maglocunus = Gwynedd; Cuneglasus = Ceredigion; Aurelius Caninus = Dobunni/Catavellauni; Voteporix = Dementae; and Constantine III = Cornwall.

Dumnonia, AURELIUS CANINUS is likewise a lion-whelp and slime like sea-water. VORTIPOR is a leopard spotted with wickedness, and CUNE-GLASUS is a red butcher. Gildas heaps scorn on the last in his list. MAGLOCUNUS MAP CATGO-LAUN LAUHIR is a dragon of the island, a wolf in lamb's clothing, a sick hound returning to his disgusting vomit, a despiser of Christ, and dog that is dumb and cannot bark.

Although two of the tyrants — Aurelius Caninus and Vortipor — cannot specifically and historically be verified, the names of two others, Constantine and Maglocunus, appear in other records. The remaining one, Cuneglasus, can be identified by clan. The geographic area Gildas

writes about are areas commonly known to antiquarians as Britannia Prima during Roman occupation. Broadly, those areas once encompassed all of Wales, some of the Midlands, and the southwestern peninsula of England.

By far, the most important contribution of the *De Excidio* is the chronological calibrations which can be gleaned from it. Unfortunately, a vast number of historians and academicians have elided over the difficulties of establishing reckonings during the early and central medieval period. One of the dates already noted is the battle of Mount Badon. As alleged Arthurian Matter relates to Gildas Badonicus, there are two other dates which are of utmost importance to confirm: the year of the *Saxones* landing, and the year in which Gildas penned the *De Excidio*.

As explained above, *Saxones* is a generic Latin term identifying at least five different tribes, and to use the term loosely leads down the wrong path. When Arthur's enemies are identified as the *Saxones* in other ancient manuscripts, the astute historian must carefully weigh evidence before concluding who Arthur's enemies are. The English *SAXONES* are those who have been on the island for a generation or two. The German *SAXONES* are invaders from across the Channel not sanctioned by the Britons, Welsh, or Romans. Of similar importance is the distinction between Briton and Welsh. The Welsh are inhabitants of Britanniae Prima, which extended into part of the Midlands, while other natives known as Britons normally settled in Britanniae Secunda and Britanniae Flavia.

Two other problems cause difficulty in interpreting Gildas's history. The first is that there were three separate *Saxone adventii*, not just one *Saxone adventus*. Leslie Alcock has clearly delineated the three: the first was in 428 at the invitation of Vortigern to an unknown area; the second was in 440 in circumstances wholly unknown, and the third near 450–455. Gildas does not give any clues as to which ad*ventii* he refers to. The second is that Gildas's garbled passages present even more problems, caused by Gildas himself and not by translators of a future era. A crucial passage in this category has to do with Gildas's two references, one to the Battle of Mount Badon, and the other to the coming of the *Saxones*. In this enigmatic passage, scholars debate whether Gildas claimed that the Battle of Badon was 44 years prior to his birth, or whether Gildas was suggesting that the advent of the Saxones was 44 years prior to his birth.

Fortunately, that problem becomes moot for those who have expended energy establishing a reliable chronology. Careful calculations show that Gildas was writing the *De Excidio* in 541. That being the case, the Battle of Mount Badon would have been fought in 497, 44 years earlier. And carrying that one step beyond, forty-four years prior to the Battle of Badon would be 453, the third Saxone *adventus*. There is very strong possibility, therefore, that Gildas's convoluted

passage meant to convey both dates: 44 years prior to his birth the battle took place, and 44 years prior to that was the last *Saxone* adventus. Other ancient manuscripts and calculations by many researchers accept the dates of 497 for the Battle of Mount Badon and 453 as the dates for the third *adventus*.

In addition to the territorial name-changes, there has been continuous confusion about the locale of the battle on *Badonici montis* (Badon Hill) which Gildas recorded. The date is solidly confirmed by historians, but the location remains contentious in spite of Gildas's clues. Judging by Section 25, there should be no doubt that Gildas's main focus is Wales.

There were eight legionary fortresses built by the Roman military in Wales, confirming the extreme importance of the region, known by the Romans as Britannia Prima. A controversial north-south defensive line in Wales is called Offa's Dyke by some scholars and the Wall of Severus by others. The Romans also established a demarcation line between Gloucester in the west and London in the east to separate the military zone in the north from the civilian zone in the south. Bath, as a part of the southern civilian zone, was not an important strategic military site, whereas Wroxeter, in Wales, was a vital position in the war zone.

The five kingdoms of the tyrants castigated by Gildas are all in Wales, which included the southwestern peninsula. Ambrosius Aurelianus — recorded also by Bede — is the hero who stems the tide of Anglians. And yet there is no consensus among historians and scholars that the Badon battle must have been fought somewhere in Wales, a military territory coveted by the enemy. There is even more evidence listed in Section 25 of the *De Excidio* which further describes Ambrosius's victory against the Saxones, and Section 26 briefly describes the "last defeat the villains."

Three centuries later, that battle re-appears in the *Historia Brittonum,* unfortunately conflated with a historic King Arthur. Relying upon the history of Gildas Badonicus, the baths at Wroxeter were much larger and the size of the exercise hall as large as a medieval cathedral. The baths at Wroxeter were much larger than those at the

The Romans divided Britain into what was called the Five Britains. Britannia Prima was the most crucial of the military area, including Wales (which at that time was larger to the east than present-day), and all of the Dumnonian peninsula to the southwest. Britannia Secunda was sometimes called the heart of Britain, and Britannia Flavia was occupied mainly by the Anglians and the Mercians. To the north was Britannia Maxima, the entire territory between Hadrian's Wall and the Wall of Antonine. Britannia Valentia was all of Scotland, mainly inhabited by the Scotti (mainly migrants or invaders from Ireland), and the Picts.

spa of Bath. Perhaps historians and scholars of a later time set the site of the Badon battle at Little Solsbury Hill because the spa at Bath increased in size over the centuries and the great baths at Wroxeter are now only a pile of rock and *pilae*. The only wall left standing is called the "Old Work."

Leslie Alcock unravels the misconceptions and unknowingly makes a crucial discovery. In relation to Section 56 and Arthur, he writes that the paragraph beginning with "Then Arthur fought against the Saxons" is not related to the previous segment about Hengist and his clan. The discrepancies are:

- Bede makes it explicitly clear that Hengist and his clan are Angles, not Saxons.
- Evidence shows that there was not a King Arthur in fifth-century Britain, nor was there a renowned Arthur during that era.
- The battlelist, excluding the Badon Battle, which was attributed to Arthur, points not to a fifth-century king of that name, but to a Roman *dux* named Lucius Artorius Castus who was sent to Britain and stationed along Hadrian's Wall during the second century. Ambrosius Aurelianus was a Briton king during the fifth century, correctly reported in the histories of Nennius, Gildas Badonicus, and Bede, but conflated with a non-extant King Arthur.
- Contrary to the material in the *Historia Brittonum*, Hengist and his clan were not chieftains in Kent. Vortigern, who was Welsh and established his first fortress in Dyfed, and who treasonously allied himself with Hengist, would not have the power to grant Hengist territory in the Isle of Thanet, three hundred and fifty miles away.

Sources: L. Alcock (AB); B. Cunliffe (RB: BO2000/COB); (BHM FOLIO 187A); J.A. Giles (SOEC); C. Littleton/L. Malcor (FSTC); Meton of Athens (IAJ); J. Morris (BH); (ORDNANCE SURVEY RB); F. Reno (HKA/HFAE); L. Sherley-Price (BEDE: HEC&P); J. Stevenson (G: DEB); A.W. Wade-Evans (EOEW); G. Webster/P. Barker (W: RC); M. Winterbottom (G: RBOW).

Ginover is Hartmann von Aue's name for Guinevere in his romance *Erec*.

See also Hartmann von Aue.

Giraldus Cambrensis, Gerald of Wales (*floruit* 1178–1208 / *lifespan*1147–1218). Two eminent scholars — James Carley and Lewis Thorpe — focus upon Giraldus Cambrensis and his involvement with stories of a historic King Arthur. Carley approaches the connection through his interest of Glastonbury Abbey's history, and Thorpe gives an in-depth commentary about two of Giraldus's manuscripts, *De Principis Instructione* and *Speculus Ecclesiae*, which has memorialized Giraldus in the hallmark of Arthur's reality.

Carley reports Giraldus's description of Arthur's exhumation on the grounds of Glastonbury Abbey from a relatively neutral and straightforward position, whereby Thorpe critiques Giraldus's two manuscripts from a realistic viewpoint.

Thorpe begins his critique from the first four words. He questions, "What does Gerald mean by his tantalizing 'In our lifetime?'" Giraldus wrote the *De Principis* some time between 1193 and 1199, and Henry II died 1189 — four to ten years before Giraldus witnessed the discovery. Adam of Domerham writes in his interpolation of William of Malmesbury's *De Antiquitate* that Arthur's body had lain in his tomb at Glastonbury for 648 years which, when subtracted from the date of Arthur's exhumation, would be the date claimed by Geoffrey of Monmouth as Arthur's death-year.

Thorpe conjectures that

> Henry II's motives for persuading the Glastonbury monks to dig up what could plausibly be taken for the bodies of King Arthur and Queen Guinevere would be obvious enough: the discovery would, he might have hoped, put an effective end to Welsh dreams that their hero would come back one day to help them in their resistance to the Norman kings. How could he possibly know that these

James Carley's
*Glastonbury Abbey: The Holy House
at the Head of the Moors adventurous*

Now the body of King Arthur which legend has feigned to have been transferred at his passing, as it were in ghostly form by spirits to a distant place, and to have been exempt from death, was found in these days at Glastonbury deep down in the earth and en-coffined in a hollow oak between two stone pyramids erected long ago in the consecrated graveyard, the site being revealed by strange and almost miraculous signs, and it was after-wards transported with honor to the Church and decently consigned to a marble tomb.

Now in the grave there was found a cross of lead, placed under a stone and not above it, as is now customary, but fixed on the underside. This cross I myself have seen, for I felt the letters engraved thereon, which do not project or stand out.

Lewis Thorpe's extract from
De Principis Instructione

In our own lifetime Arthur's body was discovered at Glastonbury, although the legends encouraged us to believe that there was something otherworldly about his ending, and he had resisted death and had been spirited away to some far-distant spot. The body was hidden deep in a hollowed-out oak-bole and between two stone pyramids which had been set up long ago in the churchyard there. They carried it into the church with every mark of honour and buried it decently there in a marble tomb. It had been provided with most unusual indications which were little short of miraculous, for beneath it and not on top, as would be the custom nowadays, there was a stone slab with a leaden cross attached to its underside. I have seen this cross myself.

---

bones lay there sixteen feet in the ground, and all the attendant circumstances? The monks may have known that some very distinguished man and woman had been buried centuries before in their ground.... They may have been clever enough to plant the remains there.

He also mentions that the leaden cross with an inscription might also be spurious, a comment which Leslie Alcock independently surmised that the comparison of the letters N (which look like Hs) and the squared letters C "argue against a date of the late twelfth century," and that the best comparisons for the letters indicate "on epigraphic grounds to be from the tenth or eleventh centuries." In both the *De Principis* and the *Speculum*, Giraldus claims to have personally seen the cross, and John Leland — around 1542 — also purported to see the cross. It was last seen in the eighteenth century at Wells, but after that, it disappeared.

Giraldus is one of the major individuals who transmogrifies Glastonbury into the Isle of Avalon, known in Welsh as Ynys Avallon, the Isle of Apples, and also referred to as Ynys Gutrin, the Isle of Glass. He describes it as having been an island where, after the Battle of Camlann, Morgana (Morgan Le Fay) and other queens ferried Arthur to heal his wounds. Based upon the

booklet *Prehistory of the Somerset Levels* by J.M. Coles and B.J. Orme, Glastonbury and several other sites were indeed islands in what was once surrounded by the encroaching waters of Bridgewater Bay.

On the southern side of Lady Chapel is the cemetery which Saint DUNSTAN had elevated ten feet. Arthur's first burial was allegedly sixteen feet deep, close to the chapel. He and Guinevere were exhumed almost three centuries later and reburied in the Choir near the High Altar, approximately 130 paces from the original gravesite. Thorpe explains that there is only one copy of Geraldus's *Speculum*, and it is badly damaged.

Arthur's exhumation has become a very complex and divisive issue involving antiquarians and modern archaeologists, some labeling the disinterment as a Glastonbury hoax in an attempt to increase funds after a devastating fire, others pointing to the renovation by Saint Dunstan in the tenth century as evidence that the excavation was real even though the discovery might not have been Arthur's bones. There are varying accounts given by ADAM OF DOMERHAM, WILLIAM CAMDEN, JOHN OF GLASTONBURY, JOHN LELAND and RALPH OF COGGESHALL. William of Malmesbury, too, was dragged into the controversy, but fortunately there are

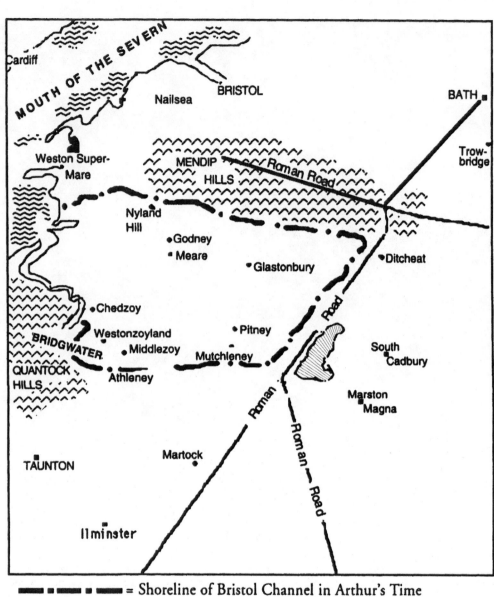

━ ▬ ▪ ▬ ▪ ━ = Shoreline of Bristol Channel in Arthur's Time

▨▨▨▨▨▨ = Marshy area near Marston Magna

This map shows other islands besides Glastonbury. The suffix *-ney* or *-ny* is an Old English term meaning "island" which etymologically translates "Nyland Hill" as "island hilltop." The village Meare is derived from the affix *-meare/-mere/-mearc*, which means "lake." According to Eilert Ekwall, the suffix *-zoy* also means "island." Not only does Arthur become attached to Glastonbury, but only a short distance to the southeast is South Cadbury, which becomes identified as Arthur's Camelot.

two of his surviving manuscripts which show that the manuscript left at Glastonbury was very heavily interpolated and therefore can't be used as proof of Arthur's exhumation.

Sources: L. Alcock (WTC); J. Carley (GA: HHHMA); E. Gibson (CB); William of Newberg (HEA/HRA); F. Reno (HKA); J.A. Robinson (TGL: KA&JA); J. Scott (EHG: ETSWM); L. Thorpe (GOW: JTW/DOW); R.F. Treharne (TGL: JA/HG/KA).

By recording both Arthur's first burial to the left of Lady Chapel, pictured here, and then recording Arthur's exhumation and reburial in front of the high altar, Giraldus boosted Glastonbury's fame even more. The alleged burial site was in view of Glastonbury Tor and St. Michael's at the top. Photograph taken with permission of the Custodian, Glastonbury Abbey.

Gloius. According to GEOFFREY OF MONMOUTH, Gloius is the son of Emperor Claudius.

See also GLOUI for the individual associated with King Arthur and Ambrosius Aurelianus in fifth-century Britain.

Gloui. The name Gloui appears twice in the *Historia Brittonum*. Chapter 49 provides this piece of genealogy: "This is his genealogy traced backwards to the beginning.... son of Guitolin [VITALINUS/GUITHELINUS], son of Gloui. Bonus, Paul, Mauron, Guitolin were four brothers, sons of Gloui, who built a major city upon the banks of the river Sabrinae, which the Britons call Cair Gloui, the Saxons Gloescester [Gloucester]. Enough has been said about Guorthigirno [VORTIGERN] and his clan."

GEOFFREY OF MONMOUTH records a certain Gloius, but identifies this individual as the son of Emperor Claudius in the first century and comments that "Claudius ordered a town to be built which should be called Kaerglou or Gloucester. Down to our day it retains its site on the bank of the Severn, between Wales and Loegria. Some, however, say that it took its name from Duke Gloius, whom Claudius fathered in that city and to whom he granted control of the duchy of the Welsh after Arvirargus."

This cannot be the Gloui recorded in the *Historia Brittonum*, for "Gloui" and "Gloius" are separated by nearly four centuries. The importance of Gloui to Arthuriana is that he sired Vitalinus/Guithelinus.

Sources: J. Morris (HB); J. Stevenson (N: HB); L. Thorpe (GM: HKB).

Goeznovius, Goueznou, Gwyddno. Goeznovius has never attained a well-deserved niche in Arthuriana. Several avoidable circumstances might have caused him to fade into near-anonymity, but to have him relegated to such an indistinct position is an unfortunate transgression, especially since the historical narrative about him verifies so poignantly other manuscripts about the Arthurian era of the mid–fifth century.

The unfortunate circumstances that could have caused conditions for Goeznovius to sink into obscurity are:

1. The narrative about Goeznovius was ascribed by someone named William, but the manuscript was labeled as *The Legend of Saint Goeznovius*, which immediately suggests that anything historical would tend to be discounted.

2. The manuscript was one of several documents which initially appeared in a fourteenth-century compilation titled *Chronique de Saint Brieuc*, which partially survives in a fifteenth century work, where a preparatory statement gives the name of the scribe as William and its date as 1019. J.S.P. Tatlock denounced the date of 1019 as spurious, claiming that the manuscript was penned by GEOFFREY OF MONMOUTH as a prelude to *History of the Kings of Britain*. The manuscript fell from favor and was spurned, until decades later Leon Fleuriot made a counter-claim that the date of 1019 was correct.

3. The author William makes a fatal blunder by recording that "the king of the Britons who came across Ocean" was Arthur, when indeed Goeznovius made no such historic connection to Arthur. The king of the Britons who came across Ocean — as documented by Jordanes — was known as RIOTIMUS. It was URISCAMPUM, in 1175, who made the suggestion that Riothimir was Arthur.

William writes about the Britons' migration to Gaul and the colonization which began in Brittany. Known as Gwyddo in Wales, Goeznovius was one of those migrants who helped settle the territory which went through name changes from Little or Lesser Britain to Armorica to Brittany. Goeznovius' floruit is broadly given

as the sixth or seventh century, most likely the sixth century, which would be nearer the time about which William is writing, the fifth century, when there was a mass migration of British saints.

It is through the initial research by Geoffrey Ashe that Goeznovius became attached to the Arthurian matter. The prologue of William's work is an early historical narrative which, Geoffrey Ashe asserts, "has no obviously dubious or fantastic touches" and "gives local information that carries some weight." The one exception is that William inserts the name of Arthur for the name Riothamus. Because of this switch, the solid history in the tale of Goeznovius becomes tainted.

In his *Ystoria Britanic*, William explains how Vortigern, as the usurper in Britain, invited the Saxons into the island, evidently either borrowing material from the Nennius manuscript or using some other technique borrowed from Geoffrey of Monmouth in a later century. But the *faux pas* William commits is his description of the British wars with the Saxons, in which the enemy was reduced to subordination "by the great Arthur, king of the Britons." He is referring to a passage from Jordanes's *Gothic History* in which Anthemius asks the Brittones for aid, and the Briton King Riotimus with twelve thousand men sails to Gaul.

Geoffrey Ashe salvages the *Goeznovius* manuscript from sinking into a morass of indifference, doing so in spite of labeling Arthur as an "unknown factor" and assuming that the reference in the William manuscript equates Riotimus with Arthur. Accepting that equation, Ashe writes in the Goeznovius entry in *The Arthurian Encyclopedia*,

> *Goeznovius* therefore tells a story that fits history quite well and is nowhere in outright conflict with known facts. The story makes Arthur prominent in the 460s, and perhaps a little before and after. This agrees with Geoffrey [Monmouth's] single but repeated chronological fix for him, putting his Gallic warfare in the reign of the eastern emperor Leo I (457–74).... The concurrence is one of several facts suggesting that both Geoffrey [of Monmouth] and the *Goeznovius* author are thinking of the "king of the Britons" who is

documented in Gaul ca. 468–70 as Riothamus and for some shared and older reason are calling him Arthur.

Ashe discusses the Goeznovius thread in a number of his books, including *Kings and Queens of Early Britain*, *King Arthur's Avalon*, *The Quest for Arthur's Britain*, *The Discovery of King Arthur*, and *Mythology of the British Isles*.

Sources: E. Chambers (AOB); R. Fletcher (AMC); N. Lacy (AE); C. Littleton/L. Malcor (FSTC); C. Mierow (J: O&DG); F. Reno (HKA).

Gogyrfan, Gogfran, Ogfran Gawr. Gogyrfan is an ancient name for Guinevere's father, who becomes LEODEGRANCE in the later romances. His name is linked to the ancient hillfort Old Oswestry, previously known as Maes Cogwy, meaning Cogwy's Boundary, on the borderlands between Wales and Cornovii. Peter Clayton in his book *Guide to the Archaeological Sites of Britain* identifies the site as one of the oldest Iron Age hillforts of the Welsh Marches with a history dating back to the mid–third century B.C. Of interest because of its Arthurian link, Clayton notes that "evidence has been found of squatters during the Dark Ages."

Source: P. Clayton (GASB); F. Reno (HFAE); J. Rhyr (CF); P. Roberts (COKB).

Gorlois, Gwrlais, Gwrleis, Gorlais. Gorlois is figuratively and physically short-lived in the Arthurian saga. He is not recorded in BEDE's *History*, or NENNIUS's *Historia Brittonum*, or in GILDAS BADONICUS's *De Excidio*. His name does appear in the *Tysilio* and Monmouth's *History of the Kings of Britain*, but because those two manuscripts are swamped in skepticism, he is relegated to the realm of Arthurian legend.

The *Tysilio* records that, upon the approval of the traitorous Pasgen (PASCENT)— one of the sons of VORTIGERN — a Saxon named Eppa poisoned Emrys AMBROSIUS. At that time a star appeared as "a ball of fire resembling a dragon, and from the jaws of the dragon two beams ascended," one toward France, and the other toward Ireland. Merddyn later interprets it as an omen signifying that Uther was the head of the dragon, indicating that the Saxons should be attacked with full fury. That same night, Uther convened a council which included Gorlais, Earl of Cornwall. The Britons scored a victory, and afterwards he toured the country, establishing power, law and justice throughout the kingdom. They celebrated Easter "by a great festival, to which all the earls and barons and their wives were invited for mirthful entertainment." Gorlais had with him his wife Eigr, and when Uther beheld her, his passion was so strong that he could not be absent from her. Merddyn makes magic so that Uther can seduce Eigr, Gorlais is killed in a separate foray, and shortly thereafter ANNA and ARTHUR were born. Arthur's name does not reappear until fifteen years later.

The story provided by Geoffrey of Monmouth is basically the same, except it includes more detail. The Earl of Cornwall Gorlais transforms to the Duke of Cornwall Gorlois, and Eigr becomes YGERNA. Whereby the ending of the Tysilio story relates that Uther married Eigr in secret, Monmouth's account is a bit more brazen:

> Uther set out and made his way towards his own army, abandoning his disguise as Gorlois and becoming Utherpendragon once more. When he learned all that had happened, he mourned for the death of Gorlois; but he was happy, all the same, that Ygerna was freed from her marital obligations. He returned to Tintagel Castle, captured it and seized Ygerna at the same time, she being what he really wanted. From that day on they lived together as equals, united by their great love for each other; and they had a son and daughter. The boy was called Arthur and the girl Anna.

Sources: P. Roberts (COKB): L. Thorpe (GM: HKB).

Gornemant of Gohort. In Chrétien's romance *Conte du Graal*, Gornemant is one of PERCEVAL's mentors, teaching him lessons of life that will be useful (and sometimes detrimental because of Perceval's interpretations) during his adventurous quests. His niece BLANCHEFOR becomes Perceval's concubine for a short time.

Sources: R. Cline (P: SG); W. Kibler (CDT: AR); D. Owen (AR).

Gottfried Von Strassburg (*floruit* 1185–1215 / *lifespan* 1170–1230). Nearly every Arthurian researcher has listed the *Tristan* penned by Gottfried as being by far the most artistic, complex, and meticulous version. Richard Barber labels his work as a masterpiece of erotic literature, infused with pure passion; Lacy and Ashe refer to Gottfried as a learnéd and cultured poet with superior talent, an admirable stylist who created a classic version of the legend.

Details of Gottfried's life are quite sketchy, as are so many biographies of antiquarians during this period. One can surmise, however, that Gottfried's work was based upon that of THOMAS D'ANGLETERRE, and that he was a contemporary of HARTMANN VON AUE and WOLFRAM VON ESCHENBACH. His "literary excursus" indicates that he favored versions such as Hartmann von Aue and the more courtly version written by Thomas D'Angleterre over the more primitive version by BÉROUL; whereby Thomas focused upon courtly pleasures and romance, Béroul wrote of battles and quests. Gottfried's excursus also criticizes an unnamed poet, referred to only as a consort of the hare hopping about in a meadow of words. The poet who is the object of scorn is commonly identified as Wolfram von Eschenbach.

Gottfried's tale ends just prior to Tristan's marriage to Iseult of the White Hands, not to be confused with Iseult the Blond. By fortuitous circumstance, however, Thomas D'Angleterre's surviving fragments relate that Tristan and Iseult do not consummate the marriage. Plagued by his poisonous wound, Tristan sends for Iseult the Blond. The ship she takes is supposed to hoist a white sail if she is aboard, or a black flag if she refused to come. Iseult of the White Hands is aware of the arrangement and she lies to Tristan, telling him that the ship has a black sail. Tristan dies of grief, and when Iseult the Blond arrives, she embraces her true love and she, too, dies.

Sources: R. Barber (AA); R. Barber (KA: H&L); Gottfried (T); N. Lacy (AE); N. Lacy/G. Ashe (AH); R. Loomis/L. Loomis (MR).

Gregory of Tours. Similar to JORDANES but more sketchy and disjointed, Gregory of Tours attaches to a minuscule piece of the Arthuriana puzzle through Riothamus. In Book I, §18 and §19 of the *Historia Francorum*, Gregory writes:

Now Childeric fought at Orleans and Odoacer came with the Saxons to Angers. At that time a great plague destroyed the people. Egidius died and left a son, SYAGRIUS. On his death Odoacer received hostages from Angers and other places. The Britanni were driven from Bourges by the Goths, and many were slain at the village of Déols. Count Paul with the Romans and Franks made war on the Goths and took booty. When Odoacer came to Angers, king Childeric came on the following day, and slew count Paul, and took the city. In a great fire on that day the house of the bishop was burned.

Section 19 adds information about the Romans before turning its attention to the Saxons and the Franks: "After this, war was waged between the Saxons and the Romans; but the Saxons fled and left many of their people to be slain, the Romans pursuing. Their islands were captured and ravaged by the Franks, and many were slain. In the ninth month of that year, there was an earthquake. Odoacer made an alliance with Childeric, and they subdued the Alamanni, who had overrun that part of Italy."

Source: E. Brehaut (GT: HOF).

Griflet. Gerflet, Girflet, Girflez. Griflet is a minor knight who appears in the romances of Chrétien de Troyes, specifically *Erec et Enide* and *Le Conte del Graal* (*Perceval*), and in the Vulgate Cycle. He transmutes to Bedivere in Book XXI of Malory's *Morte d'Arthur*. However, it is in the Vulgate Cycle where he acquires the most prominence because he is given the task of returning Arthur's sword to the Lady of the Lake. After the battle between Arthur and Mordred in which Mordred is killed, only Lucan, Griflet, and Arthur — who is sorely wounded — are alive. Lucan is mourning and weeping because of Arthur's distress, and when Arthur takes him in his arms to comfort him, Arthur crushes him to death. Distressed at causing Lucan's death, Arthur orders Girflet to return the sword to Lady of the Lake. Like Bedivere, Girflet makes three trips before he obeys Arthur's will.

When the task is completed, Arthur orders him to leave. Griflet asks if he will see him again. Arthur answers that he will not; Griflet asks where he will be going, and Arthur responds that he cannot tell. Heavy of heart, Griflet mounts his horse, and after he has ridden a distance, he stops under a grove of trees atop a hill to wait until the rain stops. He looks back to the area where he had left Arthur and sees a ship approaching the shore. When the queens aboard beckon Arthur to join them, Arthur recognizes his sister MORGAN, arises, and boards the ship with his horse and armor.

Griflet panics and hurries back as fast as he can, but by the time he reaches the shore, the ship is too far afloat. He, too, recognizes Morgan, but no one acknowledges him. Griflet bemoans the loss of the king, knowing that, indeed, he will never see his beloved leader again. He remains prostrate on the ground for two days and two nights, neither eating nor drinking.

On the third day, he returns to the Black Chapel. When he enters, he sees a magnificent tomb which is inscribed "Here lies King Arthur who through his valour conquered twelve kingdoms." The knight collapses in despair, remaining at the side of the tomb until eventide. A hermit who attends to the chores of the church arrives, and Griflet beseeches the hermit to tell him the truth: does the king lie here? The hermit nods assent, saying that the king was brought to the chapel by ladies he did not know. Griflet realizes who the queens are, and that his lord and king has left this world. He begs the hermit to receive him as a companion, and after the passage of eighteen days, Griflet himself dies.

In *Le Morte d'Arthur* by THOMAS MALORY, Griflet appears in a different role. In Book I, Chapter XXI, he is introduced as squire, about the same age as Arthur, and he seeks the king so that he can become a knight. In Chapter XXII–III Arthur grants knighthood to Griflet, and in return Griflet must agree to joust with the Knight of the Fountain. Griflet does what the king has requested, and is nearly killed:

> The two knights ran together that Griflet's spear all to-shivered; and there-withal he smote Griflet through the shield and the left side, and brake the spear that the truncheon stuck in his body, that horse and knight fell down.
>
> When the knight saw him lie so on the ground, he alighted, and was passing heavy, for he weened he had slain him, and then he unlaced his helm and gat him wind, and so

with the truncheon he set him on his horse, and so betook him to God, and said he had a mighty heart, and if he might live he would prove a passing good knight. And so Sir Griflet rode to the court, where great dole was made for him. But through good leeches he was healed and saved.

In Book XX, Chapter VIII, Griflet is killed by LANCELOT when Lancelot is saving Queen GUINEVERE from the fire.

Sources: J. Cable (LMA); T. Malory (LMD'A).

Guendoloena. In MERLIN (*VITA MERLINI*), Geoffrey of Monmouth's manuscript dated 1148, Guendoloena is Merlin's wife. Because GANIEDA, Merlin's sister, cannot keep her poor brother from going continually insane, she solicits the help of Guendoloena. But Merlin wants to be free from both his sister and his wife, and orders Ganieda to tell Guendoloena that he will profusely endow his wife when she is ready to marry another man. His only condition is that the man who marries her be careful that he never comes near the wizard.

He seems complacent when she is to marry and calmly tells himself, "So I lose; so another enjoys her. So my rights are taken away from me while I dally. So it is surely, for a slothful lover is beaten by one who is not slothful or absent but is right on hand. And when tomorrow's sun shall shine, I will go and take with me the gift I promised her when I left." His gift is a line of stags and she-goats, and he mounts the lead stag and forces the stags to wait patiently at the gate when he arrives. Guendoloena comes quickly, but unfortunately the bridegroom is at a loft window, and when Merlin sees him, he "wrenched the horns from the stag he was riding and shook them and threw them at the man and completely smashed his head in, killing him and driving out his life into the air." He then tries to escape into the woods, but servants capture him and return him to his sister.

Source: Geoffrey of Monmouth (VM).

Guennuvar. *The Life of Gildas* (*Vita Gildas*), penned by Caradoc of Llancarvan, records Guinevere's name as Guennuvar.

Guinevere, Ganhumare, Ginover, Guenhuvara, Guennuvar, Gwenhwyfar, Gwennhwyfar,

Gwynnevar, Wenhaver, Wenneveria, Wenor. Guinevere's personality — or portrayal in history or legend — is as varied and the spellings of her name. She's been depicted as a solemn Christian queen with high moral standards, a constant object of kidnap and rape; an Isis worshipper, a Celtic warrior queen, a vindictive and jealous mate, a meek and obedient young woman betrothed to an older king, an unfaithful wife, and even a participant in a ménage à trois affair.

She is also precariously balanced between history and legend, a dilemma which Jeffrey Gantz describes: "Inasmuch as the Celts, true to their escapist nature, tended to view history as what ought to have happened rather than as what actually did, fact and fiction in *The Mabinogion* are not easy to distinguish." Guinevere's earliest appearance occurs in the *Mabinogion* tale of "How Culhwch won Olwen." Gantz presumes that the tales were formed between 1000 and 1250, an unfortunate broad span because "Welsh scholars want to maximize the extent of their ancestors' contribution," and French scholars prefer the later date. The CULHWCH tale is considered the earliest one to take shape.

There are claims that Guinevere's name first appears as the Latinized Ganhumara in GEOFFREY OF MONMOUTH's *History of the Kings of Britain*, but although she cannot be placed in Arthur's historical age of the fifth century, her name — or its variants — legitimately appears prior to 1135. A specific, narrow time span is unrealistic, particularly since researchers must rely upon early oral tradition rather than the written word from which perceptive thinkers build a circumstantial case strong enough to set chronological parameters for such an obscure period of insular and continental history. Monmouth himself stresses his role as a copyist and translator of British history, not as a creative storyteller, and his use of the name Ganhumara for Arthur's Queen helps substantiate his claim. Through an overabundance of instances such as this, Monmouth indirectly exhibits that he indeed must be copying and not inventing material. Monmouth is allegedly translating material from an earlier Welsh source into Latin, and what he has done is use the Latin term Ganhumara for the Welsh term Gwenhwyfar.

Opinions are sharply vituperative not only about Monmouth's "very ancient book" (the infamous *liber vetustissimus*), but also what he meant when he wrote that he was translating directly into Latin from that very ancient book "written in the British language." Lewis Thorpe explains that *Britannicus* can mean British, Welsh, or Breton, but according to John J. Parry and Robert A. Caldwell — two giants in the field — Monmouth's words can only mean "in the Welsh language." There are modern researchers who claim that Monmouth couldn't even speak Welsh, but that assertion must be dismissed as extreme. Monmouth was translating from a manuscript that was written in his native language, and he had also visited Brittany.

There is no firm evidence that knowledge of a Gwenhwyfar preceded the publication of Monmouth's book in 1135, since — as Jeffrey Gantz asserts — "Peniarth 6, the earliest manuscript to preserve even fragments of the Four Branches [of *The Mabinogion*], dates only to *c.* 1225, and so offers nothing to scholars who feel that *The Mabinogion* achieved written form by 1100 or earlier." However, there are still claims that Guinevere is linked to a parallel, the Irish Findabar, which preceded Monmouth by about thirty-five years.

The earliest collection of the Welsh triads is in the National Library of Wales, MS Peniarth 16, dating to 1235. They are a collection ostensibly used by ancient Welsh bards (*cyfarwyddiaid*) to more easily recall traditional tales (*cyfarwyddyd*) of their repertoire. There are four pertinent to Guinevere. Because numbering varies so widely, they are randomly listed here.

The first triad is titled "Three Unrestrained Ravagings of the Island of Britain:"

- When Medrawd (MORDRED) came to Arthur's Court at Celliwig in Cornwall, he left neither food nor drink in the court that he did not consume. *And he dragged Gwenhwyfar from her royal chair, and then he struck a blow upon her.*
- The second Unrestrained Ravaging was when Arthur came to Medrawd's court; he left neither food nor drink in the court.

- And the third Unrestrained Ravaging occurred when Aeddan the Wily came to the court of Rhydderch the Generous at Alclud [Dumbarton]; he left neither food nor drink nor beast alive.

The second triad is "The Three Faithless Wives of the Isle of Britain:"

- Three daughters of Culfanwyd of Britain: Essyllt Fair-hair, mistress of Trystan, and Penarwan.
- Wife of Owain son of Urien, and Bun, wife of Fflamddwyn.
- *And one was more faithless than those three: Gwenhwyfar, wife of Arthur, since she shamed a better man than any of them.*

The third triad is "The Three Harmful Blows of the Island of Britain:"

- The first of them Matholwch the Irishman struck upon Branwen, daughter of Llyr.
- The second *Gwenhwyfach struck upon Gwenhwyfar and for that cause there took place afterwards the Action of the Battle of Camlan.*
- The third Golydan the Poet struck upon Cadwaladr the Blessed.

The fourth is "Three Great Queens of Arthur:"

- *Gwennhwyfar daughter of Cywryd Gwent.*
- *Gwenhwyfar daughter of Gwythyr son of Greidiawl.*
- *Gwenhwyfar daughter of Gogfran the Giant.*

The violence to Gwenhwyfar in the first-listed triad is covered in a bit more detail by Geoffrey of Monmouth. While Arthur is on the continent fighting a war against Lucius Hiberius, he gets news from the island that his nephew Mordred, in whose care he had left Britain, "had placed the crown upon his own head, and what is more, this treacherous tyrant was living adulterously and out of wedlock with Guinevere, who had broken the vows of her earlier marriage." It is impossible to state with surety whether the "faithless wife triad" was "borrowed" from Monmouth, or conversely.

In addition to this violence against Guinevere, CARADOC OF LLANCARFAN writes of another episode in *The Life of Gildas* [Albanius]. He describes the wickedness of King MELWAS of the Summer Country, who abducts her and holds her for ransom at Glastonbury. King Arthur travels with all his forces to effect her release. In JOHN OF GLASTONBURY's shorter account, James Carley writes that "All references to Arthur as a *rex rebellis* or *tyrannus* and to the rape of Guennuvar by Melwas are removed." A later tale is a close parallel to this, in which a synonymous miscreant — Meleagant — abducts Guinevere.

The depiction of Guinevere in the second triad appears in so many accounts — with Lancelot — that they would be too numerous to list. What happens when Arthur accepts the "False" Guinevere is one example of the trysts between Arthur's actual queen and LANCELOT.

GWENHWYFACH, listed as Gwenhwyfar's sister in the third triad, is mentioned in one microscopic ten-word passage — *the first lady of the island Gwenhwyfar and her sister Gwenhwyach* — during Culhwch's incredibly lengthy invocation in the tale "How Culhwch Won Olwen." The name of Gwenhwyfar's sister is spelled differently, but it is actually a reference to Gwenhwyfach. Caitlin and John Matthews explain the two different suffixes in the names: *Fach is the mutated Welsh suffix meaning bach or 'small': the far part of Gwenhwyfar's name is probably derived from the Welsh fawr or 'big.' The similarly named pair of sisters might be called 'Little Gwen and Big Gwen.'*

The fourth triad above presents an enigma. Most of the tales claim that Arthur married Guinevere, daughter of Gogfran. Steve Blake and Scott Lloyd suggest that "In Welsh tradition Gwenhwyfar is the daughter of Ogrfan Gwar, whose name is associated with the hill fort known as Old Oswestry on the Welsh border," but point out there is no certainty that Gwenhwyfar is a reference to Arthur's queen, since that name was so common in medieval Wales. Her father's name goes through a cycle of Ogrfan to Gogfran to GOGYRFAN, to Leodagran to LEODEGRANCE.

That Arthur married three women named Gwenhwyfar is compounded by GIRALDUS

CAMBRENSIS in the early twelfth century when he describes the exhumation of Arthur's grave:

> Now in the grave was found a cross of lead ... which I myself have seen ... and reads as follows: "Hic jacet sepultus inclitus rex Arthurus cum Wenneveria exore sua secunda in insula Avallonia." ... For he had two wives, the last of whom was buried with him, and her bones were found together with his, but separated from them as thus: two parts of the tomb, to wit, the head, were allotted to the bones of the man, while the remaining third towards the foot contained the bones of the woman in a place apart; and there was found a yellow tress of woman's hair still retaining its colour and freshness; but when a certain monk snatched it and lifted it with greedy hand, it straightway all of it fell into dust.

In the romances and legends, Guinevere is Arthur's queen, daughter of Leodegrance and therefore, as heir-apparent, also Queen of Cameliard in her own right.

Sources: G. Ashe (K&QEB); S. Blake/S. Lloyd (P); R. Bromwich (TYP); H. Butler (AGC); P. Clayton (GASB); R. Coghlan (EAL); J. Gantz (TM); A. Hopkins (BOG); N. Lacy (AE); C&J. Matthews (LOTL); F. Reno (HKA); P. Roberts (COKB); L. Thorpe (GM: HKB).

Guinevere (False), Gwenhwyfar. Although the name GUINEVERE doesn't appear earlier than the turn of the millennium and does not attach to the historic King Arthur of the fifth century, her name permeates legends in a variety of ways. Her half-sister was dubbed in the romances as the False Guinevere because she was conceived by Leodegan (LEODEGRANCE) and his unnamed seneschal's wife, whereby Arthur's "True Guinevere" was conceived by King Leodegan and his legitimate queen. The half-sisters were conceived on the same night, born on the same day, given the same name, Gwenhwyfar, and looked like twins. The only means of distinguishing between the two was a birthmark of a king's crown on the "true" Guinevere's back, while the "false" Guinevere had none.

In the *Vulgate Merlin*, the false Guinevere plots with Sir Bertholai of Camelide to convince Arthur she is his wife. In a letter she tells him he must accept her or return the Round Table to her. Because the true Guinevere is gone, Arthur decides to meet her to determine if she is indeed his wife. Bertholai and his knights capture Arthur and give him a potion so that he falls in love with the false Guinevere. Arthur rejects the true Guinevere, convicts her of treason, and sentences her to the stake.

News of the threat spurs LANCELOT to rescue the true Guinevere. Lancelot and his knights challenge Bertholai's army and Lancelot is the victor, but Arthur, still under a spell, refuses to take back his true wife. Lancelot and Guinevere resort to Sorelois, where they continue their tryst unheeded. After a year, the false Guinevere and Bertholai both become immobile from a strange illness. They assume it is God's punishment for lying and putting a spell on Arthur. They confess to the crime and die an inexplicable death. Arthur and the true Guinevere re-unite, and Lancelot remains a knight of the Round Table, since Arthur has been such a cuckold.

Source: P. Korrel (AAT).

Guithelinus, Cyhelin (Tysilio), Vitalinus. Although Guithelinus, the Celtic name for the Roman VITALINUS, appears in only a cursory and incidental role in the *Historia Brittonum*, GEOFFREY OF MONMOUTH elevates him to a major status in establishing the PENDRAGON dynasty on the island.

As an introduction, Guithelinus enters British history independent of the Arthurian cycle. In *The History of the Kings of Britain*, Guithelinus addresses the BRITONS at the moment of Roman evacuation, which occurs sixty-seven pages prior to the chapter about Arthur of Britain. When HONORIUS announces to Britain that the Romans can no longer defend the island as a province, Guithelinus addresses his countrymen and encourages them to protect their own liberty.

When the Britons can no longer stave off the onslaught of the barbarians, Guithelinus crosses the sea to Little Brittany to seek aid from King ALDRONEUS. The king refuses, but agrees to send his own brother CONSTANTINE with two thousand soldiers. Constantine is crowned king after he lands on the island.

The new king of Britain is given a wife, raised by Guithelinus himself, and she bears three sons—CONSTANS, AURELIUS AMBROSIUS, and one who becomes known as Utherpendragon (UTERPENDRAGON). Constans is handed over to the church, and Guithelinus becomes the ward responsible for raising the two others. After Constantine's death and the succession of VORTIGERN as king, those in charge of Aurelius and Utherpendragon, who "still lay in their cradles, fled with their charges to Little Britain, just in case the two should be murdered by Vortigern." By this time Guithelinus is dead.

Peter Roberts's translation of the *Tysilio* is a close parallel to Monmouth's history. Both Roberts and Monmouth use the name CYHELIN with the title or noun of address "Archbishop of London," Roberts also includes Guithelinus's speech to the Britons, but in a footnote he additionally claims that "the speech has every appearance of authenticity, as far as truth of feeling can give it. The ideas, the spirit, and the eloquence of language are so far superior to those of the writers of the Brut as to exempt them from all suspicion of having composed an address, which gives so fine an impression of the character of Cyhelin."

The major variance from Monmouth's text is that Roberts' text of the *Tysilio* records that "The Archbishop Cyhelin, when he heard of the death of [Constantine], became apprehensive of treachery to his wards, and fled with them to Emyr king of Armorica, by whom they were joyfully received." According to Monmouth, Guithelinus was dead by that time and other wards took the two brothers across the sea for protection.

Sources: L. Thorpe (GM: HKB); P. Roberts (COKB).

Gurnemanz, Gornemant. In WOLFRAM VON ESCHENBACH's *Parsival*, Parsival's mentor is Gurnemanz, a doublet of Gwawrddur.
See also GWAWRDDUR.
Source: K. Jackson (TG).

Guttyn Owain. A copy of the *Book of Basingwerke Abbey* was written by Guttyn Owain in the year 1461. This particular manuscript affects not only the *Tysilio* but also Geoffrey of Monmouth's *History of the Kings of Britain*.
See also WALTER, ARCHDEACON OF OXFORD.

Gwawrddur. In *Y Gododdin*, Manuscript B, verse 38, there is a reference to Arthur which does not appear in other translations. ANEIRIN, the poet, makes a comparison between Gwawrddur, chieftain of the Gododdin territory, and Arthur. The passage is about Gwawrddur's valor: "He stabbed over three hundred of the finest ... he behaved worthily in the forefront of the most generous army.... He glutted black ravens on the rampart of the stronghold, though he was no Arthur."

Kenneth Jackson writes, "There is of course no guarantee that [this verse] was in the original Gododdin, but if it was, and if the poem was composed about the year 600, it is by far the oldest known reference to King Arthur and dates from a time when people who remembered him would still be alive. Arthur was the great national hero of the entire British people, from Scotland to Brittany, and there is therefore no logic whatever in the idea that this reference can be used to support the theory that he was a Northern leader."
Source: K. Jackson (TA).

Gwenhwyfach, Gwenhwyvach, Gwenhwy. Gwenhwyfach is Guinevere's sister, mentioned only once in "How Culhwch Won Olwen" of *The Mabinogion*. Her name also appears in two separate Welsh triads. The first is Triad 58:

Three Harmful Blows of the Island of Britain

The first of them Matholwch the Irishman struck upon Branwen daughter of Llyr;

The second Gwenhwyfach struck upon Gwenhwyfar: and for that cause there took place afterwards the Action of the Battle of Camlan;

And the third Golydan the Poet struck upon Cadwaladr the Blessed.

The second is Triad 84:

Three Futile Battles of the Island of Britain

One of them was the Battle of Goddue: it was brought about by the cause of the bitch, together with the roebuck and the plover;

The second was the Action of Arfderydd, which was brought about by the cause of the lark's nest;

And the third was the worse: that was Camlan, which was brought about because of a quarrel between Gwenhwyfar and Gwen-hwyfach.

Commenting on early Welsh genealogies, C. Barber and D. Pykitt aver in their book that Gwenhwyfach was the wife of Medraut ap Cawrdaf, Arthur's adversary. This connection could suggest that Medraut (MORDRED) was therefore an adversary of Arthur, a fact not suggested in the *Annales Cambriae*. This exhausts the information recorded about Gwenhwyvach.

See also GUINEVERE, THE FALSE.

Sources: C. Barber/D. Pykitt (JTA); R. Barber (FOA); R. Bromwich (TYP); R. Coghlan (EAL); J. Gantz (TM).

Gwenhwyvar is a commonly-used spelling for Guinevere.

Source: J. Gantz (TM).

Gwledig, Gwledic, Guledig, Guletic, Guleticus, Wledig, Wledic. Similar to emrys, gwledig is a title which expresses Welsh royalty. In the case of AURELIANUS, his title bears both honorifics, emrys gwledig, or its variations. Gwledig, however, is more common than emrys, and suggests Welsh kings.

One of the few researchers who comments on this title is Geoffrey Ashe. In *Kings and Queens of Early Britain*, he writes, "'Wledig' is a rather cryptic title which occurs as *gwledig* in early texts. Derived from the Welsh for 'land,' it seems to mean an army commander who attains a more or less legitimized power—a 'land-holder.' Four or five men are styled so who flourished during the last phase of the Western Empire. All but Maximus are native to the island, so the bestowal of the title on him is another token of his adoption as a compatriot." Ashe is referring to MAGNUS Maximus, the commander who attempted to overthrow the Western Empire from 383 to 387. Other gwledigs besides Ambrosius are CUNEDDA, MAELGWN, and Urien.

E.K. Chambers labels all these different titles or epithets as a "federation of *reges*," then claims that these particular Welsh terms apply to "outstanding personages in Welsh writings." Generically, he asserts, gwledig is a Welsh epithet meaning "ruler of a country," "prince," or "chieftain," depending upon which translation one uses. The word *gwledig* does seem to be a cognate

of *gwlad*, meaning "land" in Welsh. If one were to accept the modern definition of *gwledig*, then these warriors would be described as "rural; rustic; boorish." However, *gwladig*— in more modern terms, *gwladgarwr*— would be a patriot or a protector of the "land of my fathers." Based upon the *Historia Brittonum*, in ancient terms "shires" were commonly referred to as "countries," which would have implied that a *gwledig* was the ruler-protector of a territory, realm or country. In Giraldus Cambrensis's *Journey*, translator Lewis Thorpe agrees that the term *gwlad* is a cognate of *gwledig*, then gives the meaning of *gwlad* as a country or tribe of free people.

Sources: G. Ashe (K&QEB); R. Castleden (KA: TBL); E. Chambers (AOB); L. Thorpe (GOW: JTW/DOW).

Gwrhyr the Interpreter. *see* CERDIC (Interpreter of Languages).

Gwrtheyrn is the name used by Jeremy Knight in his article "The Pillar of Eliseg." The name is a variant of VORTIGERN.

Of the legible lines deciphered by Edward Llwyd in 1696, Gwrtheyrn's name was recorded in line 8: "But BRYDW was the son of Gwtheyrn, whom GERMANUS blessed and who was borne to him by Severa, the daughter of Maximus the king, who slew the king of the Romans." Jeremy Knight then explains that Gwrtheyrn was associated in Welsh oral tradition with the downfall of Britain when he invited the Saxons into the island.

Source: D. Evans (VCA).

Gwyar is one of Gwrleis's daughters, and sister of Kioneta. She was widowed after the death of Ymer Llydaw and thereafter lived in the court of Gwrleis with her son Hywel. Lleu (known in other manuscripts as King Lot or Loth) later married her and they had two sons, Gwalchmai and Medrawd, and three daughters, Gracia, Graeria, and Dioneta, the last daughter having the same name as one of Gwrleis' daughters.

Source: S. Blake/S. Lloyd (P), Page 245–246, Appendix 2.

Gwyr y Gogledd (Goo-EAR ee Gogleth) is a Welsh term meaning "men of the north," a common reference to an ancient territory known as

Manau Gododdin near Edinburgh, Scotland. ANEIRIN's work, surviving in a thirteenth-century manuscript known as *Llyfr Aneirin*, was originally titled *Y Gododdin*. Upon their initial migration mainly to northern Wales, these men — such as the PATERNUS/ÆTERNUS/CUNEDDA clan — become extremely important figures in Welsh history as well as quite influential in the saga of Arthuriana, some as allies to the historic Arthur and others as his adversaries.

Charles Thomas in *Celtic Britain* wrote "[T]he transfer of so much of British tradition — of kings and battles, bards and magicians — from Gwyr Gogled, 'the People of the North,' to still-British Wales as the Northumbrians and Scots made inroads upon the former, brought to the principalities (and indeed, faintly, to distant Cornwall) a shared past. When in the 9th–10th centuries the native historians put together what they could find of times past, that of British Wales was not fully distinguishable from British Cumbria."

Nora Chadwick, in *Ancient Peoples and Places: Celtic Britain*, viewed the Welsh of Wales as recognizing the Gwyr y Gogledd as "close kin and spoke of them familiarly in later records." In the Welsh poem *Armes Prydein* (*The Prophecy of Britain*), probably composed early in the tenth century, the Gwyr y Gogledd "are distinguished from the Gwyr Deheu, the 'Men of the South,' i.e., the Welsh of Wales," from whence came the name of the ancient territory of Deheubarth.

Sources: R. Barber (FOA); P. Bartram (WG); N. Chadwick (CB); J. Morris (BH); F. Reno (HKA/HFAE); J. Stevenson (N: HB); C. Thomas (CB); A. Wade-Evans (EOE&W).

Hartmann Von Aue (*floruit* 1190–1215 / *lifespan* 1175–1235). Hartmann is one of several important poets clustered in the last half of the twelfth century who contributed to the development of Arthurian romances. His first epic poem, *Erec*, which was based upon Chrétien de Troyes' *Erec et Enide*, was not merely a translation, but more of a reconstitution, expanding some episodes and modifying the sequence of various events, both suggesting that Hartmann was also cognizant of *Geraint*, a Welsh romance of the tenth century

which had much earlier roots. The king GERAINT is the equivalent of Chrétien's Erec, and his wife was likewise named Enid.

Most scholars suggest that Hartmann's second Arthurian work, *Iwein*, was completed around 1205. *Iwein* more closely follows Chrétien's *Le Chevalier au Lion* (*Yvain*) and hence is often categorized as an adaptation. After the hero Iwein marries Laudine, Arthur and his court visit the newlyweds, and Gawein (Gawain) convinces Iwein to go on a year's quest. The deadline is ignored, and Iwein, accused of a breach of untruth upon his belated return, goes mad until he is cured by Feimorgan (MORGAN LE FAY).

Sources: T. Keller (E: HVA); N. Lacy (AE); N. Lacy/G. Ashe (AH); P. Mcconeghy (I: HVA); J. Thomas (E: HVA).

Heinrich Von Freiberg (*floruit* 1272–1302 / *lifespan* 1257–1317). Heinrich completed his continuation of GOTTFRIED VON STRASSBURG's unfinished *Tristan* some time between 1285 and 1290, following Ulrich von Türheim's earlier continuation of the same work.

Heinrich's tale opens with Tristran's marriage to Isolde of the White Hands (Isoud la Blanche Mains), not to be confused with La Beale Isoud, the latter also known as Isoud the Blonde. Tristram doesn't consummate the marriage because he has given a vow to the Virgin Mary to live celibately for a year. Tristran still yearns for La Beale Isoud, and at their deaths King Mark plants a rose over Tristran's grave and the vine over Isoud's.

Source: N. Lacy (AE); M. E. Kalinke.

Hengist, Hengest. The earliest British historical document, the *De Excidio*, written by GILDAS BADONICUS, does not record any names of Hengist's clan. Gildas uses the common but misleading Latin term SAXONES, which is equated with the expression ORIENTALI SACRILEGORUM and translates to "sacrilegious or impious easterners." The generic term *Saxones* was used by the Romans to refer not only to the SAXONS, but also to the ANGLES and the JUTES, which has created serious problems for successive generations of historians in their attempt to identify Hengist's ethnic origin.

Some translators of four specific texts which followed Gildas —*A History of the English Church and People* by BEDE, *British History* by NENNIUS, *The Anglo-Saxon Chronicle* compiled by numerous scribes, and *The History of the Kings of Britain* by GEOFFREY OF MONMOUTH—label Hengist as a Saxon, while others describe him as an Anglian, and others confusingly identify him sometimes as an Anglian but assign him migration patterns of a Saxon, contradictions which have far-reaching implications when linking Hengist and his clan to Arthur and his forebears.

As barbaric Germanic tribes migrated to Britain to escape conquest by the Romans, historians recorded migration patterns which became the accepted routes down through the centuries. These early histories described Germanic tribes as coming from three nations: the Old Saxons, the Angles, and the Jutes. The Saxons settled in what became known as Kent and Wessex, the Angles settled in East Anglia, Mercia, and Northumbria, and the Jutes settled in Kent and the Isle of Wight.

In the early eighth century, Bede, who borrowed some of his material from Gildas, gives the routes used by the above-named Germanic tribes, identifies Hengist's ethnic origin, and provides the names HORSA and Oisc as two others of Hengist's clan. Very succinctly, in two separate sections, he writes: "And from the Angles ... are descended the East and Middle Angles, the Mercians, all the Northumbrian stock (that is, those peoples living north of the river Humber, and other English [Anglian] people). Their first chieftains are said to have been the brothers Hengist and Horsa." Approximately fifty pages later, he writes that OISC was the son of Hengist, who came to Britain at the invitation of VORTIGERN.

But for whatever his reason, Bede vacillates about whether Hengist is an Anglian or a Saxon. On a jarring note, he mentions in passing that Hengist's brother Horsa was killed in battle and buried near Kent, which would have been, by Bede's own admission, Jutish territory. In the very next sentence, Bede switches once again and later avers that "Suddenly the Angles (including Hengist) made an alliance with the Picts." An appendix at the back of the text gives a genealogy of English kings, listing Hengist and Horsa as Kentish chieftains. It is unknown whether the genealogical trees were created by Bede or by later scribes or translators.

In the *Historia Brittonum*, attributed to Nennius, Hengist's name is listed in eight separate sections, or "chapters:"

§31— After the Romans had left Britain, there came three keels which bore Hengist and Horsa. Vortigern welcomed them, and handed over to them the island that in their language is called Tanet, in British Ruoihin.

§37 — Realizing Vortigern's incompetence as a king, Hengist convinces the Briton king to invite more of the barbarian clan. Hengist's daughter (unnamed) also arrives. Vortigern falls in love with her and strikes a bargain with Hengist, giving the barbarian leader the territory of Cantguaralen in trade for his daughter.

§38 — Hengist then invites his son OCTHA to Britain with forty keels and they go to the north.

§43 — VORTIMER replaces his father, Vortigern, as king and drives Hengist back to Tanet. Hengist and Horsa summon more keels from Germany and they fight against the British, sometimes advancing and sometimes being defeated.

§44 — Vortimer fights four battles against Hengist and Horsa. Horsa is killed in battle, along with the Briton Categirn. Soon after the four battles, Vortigern dies.

§45 — The barbarians return in force, and Vortigern calls a council to make peace.

§46 — Hengist treacherously slays the Council of the Provinces, and King Vortigern alone is taken and held prisoner.

§56 — On Hengist's death, Octha comes down from the north and fights against ARTHUR, together with the kings of the British.

There are several items worthy of note: 1) unlike Bede's implication, Vortigern initially does not invite Hengist into Britain, but welcomes Hengist and his exiled clan when they arrive; 2) Section 36 — which doesn't contain the name

Hengist — relates that the English were encamped on the island of Tanet, placing the Angles at the southeastern tip of Kent, which is normally considered Jutish territory; 3) Bede does not include Hengist's daughter, whereby Nennius mentions the daughter but does not name her; 4) in that same section, Vortigern grants Hengist land in Canturguoralen, which is defined as Kent, inferring once again that Hengist is given land in Jutish territory; 5) Hengist's son Octha — apparently synonymous with Bede's Oisc — is invited to the "north" near an unidentified wall called Guaul; 5) Section 31 is titled "The Kentish Chronicle, Part I," Section 36 is titled "The Kentish Chronicle, Part 2;" and Sections 43, 44, 45, and 46 are labeled "The Kentish Chronicle, Part 3," but John Morris in his translation specifically admonishes the readers to be aware that these headings were later additions. In particular, Sections 31, 37, 43, and 44 suggest that Wales and not Kent are the locations of battlesites recorded in their content.

Near the turn of the millennium, *The Anglo-Saxon Chronicle*, particularly the Parker Chronicle ms Ā, and mms E and F, which carried at least through the Norman Conquest, made its first appearance. Hengist and his clan are recorded in the following entries:

> 443 — ms Ā: The Britons sent to the princes of the Angles and asked them for troops against the Picts.
>
> 447 — ms F: At that time the Angles came to Britain, invited by king Vortigern, to help him overcome his enemies. They came to this land with three warships, and their leaders were Hengest and Horsa. First they slew the enemies of the king and drove them away, and afterwards they turned against the king and against the Britons, and destroyed them by fire and by the edge of the sword.
>
> 449 — mms Ā and E: In their days Hengest and Horsa, invited by Vortigern, king of the Britons, came to Britain at a place called Ypwinesfleot at first to help the Britons, but later they fought against them.
>
> 455 — mms Ā and E: In this year Hengest and Horsa fought against king Vortigern at a place which is called Agælesthrep, and his brother Horsa was slain. And after that Hengest succeeded to the kingdom.
>
> 456 — ms E: In this year Hengest and Æsc (his son) fought against the Britons at a place which is called Crecganford and there slew four companies; and the Britons then forsook Kent and fled to London in great terror.
>
> 457 — ms Ā: In this year Hengest and Æsc fought against the Britons at a place which is called Crecgranford and there slew four thousand men; and the Britons then forsook Kent and fled to London in great terror.
>
> 465 — mms Ā and E: In this year Hengest and Æsc fought against the Welsh near Whippenesfleot and there slew twelve Welsh nobles.
>
> 473 — ms Ā: In this year Hengest and Æsc fought against the Welsh and captured innumerable spoils, and the Welsh fled from the English like fire.

Several points are noteworthy: G.N. Garmonsway in his translation makes a crucial distinction between the Welsh and the Britons, whom Hengist is fighting against; there is a claim that Vortigern invited the Angles Hengist and Horsa into Britain; after Horsa's death, Æsc came down from the north; entry 456 claims that Hengist was fighting Britons in Kent; and the last appearance of Hengist is in 473. These entries, therefore, indicate that Hengist's reign spanned about thirty years, from 443 to 473.

Approximately a century later, Monmouth wrote the *History of the Kings of Britain*, in which Hengist plays a major role, but his adversary is not Arthur but Aurelius Ambrosius.

Hengist's story unfolds thusly:

- "About this time there landed in certain parts of Kent ... two brothers named Hengist and Horsa."
- "Vortigern made peaceful overtures to them ... and is delighted by their arrival" because "my enemies harass me on every side and if you share with me the hardships of my battles, I will welcome you in all honour to my kingdom and

enrich you with gifts of all sorts and with grants of land."

- Vortigern gave to Hengist "many lands in the neighborhood of Lindsey." Hengist then asks Vortigern to grant him as much land as can circled by a single thong, "so that I can build there a fortress into which I may retreat in time of need."

  Hengist then took the hide of a bull and cut from it one single, thin strip of thong, then marked out a site atop a certain precipice so that he could build a fortress. Once the fortress was complete, "it took its name from the thong, since it had been measured with one. This place which we call Castrum Corrigie in Latin, was ever afterwards known as Kaercarrei in the Welsh tongue and as Thanceastre in Saxon."

- Vortigern allows Hengist to import more kinsmen from Germany, who also "brought with them the daughter of Hengist, a girl called Renwein.... When Vortigern saw the girl's face, he was struck with her beauty and was filled with desire for her."

- A short time later Octa and Ebissa and Cerdic arrive with three hundred keels filled with a well-equipped army. The Britons rebel against their king for allowing such a thing, and promote Vortimer to the kingship. Renwein "collected all the information she could about noxious poisons," and poisons Vortimer to restore Vortigern to the kingship.

Peter Roberts, who translated the *Tysilio*, adds a footnote in his text, calculating that if the hide were six feet square and cut into a thong of one-tenth of an inch, the thong would enclose a circular space of nearly 480 yards in diameter.

Independent of attempting to pinpoint some of the locales that Hengist might have occupied, Ekwall adds this information about Thanceastre as recorded in Monmouth's work. He defines *ceaster* as an Old English loan-word borrowed from the Latin word *castra*, which means a walled fortress or waystation. Of villages named "Thong," he traces the origins to *Thwong* and *wong* and notes that these prefixes can be used in a transferred (figurative) sense, such as in *wong-Chastre*.

Thanceastre, therefore, can be offered as a different possibility where Hengist settled rather than on the isle of Thanet. Of course, no site can be solidly identified for Hengist's settlement in Britain. Only shreds of details can be collated about the mysterious Hengist, what his associations were with Vortigern, and where he might have settled upon his migration to the island. There is no birth-year or death-year given for Hengist, but *The Anglo-Saxon Chronicle* gives a long span of time for his reign, outside the range of what scholars label the "reasonable-age concept." Hence, this entry requires citations with differing opinions, none of which can be characterized as utterly neutral or factual.

Later, Hengist slaughters the Council of the Provinces, and only one man, Eldol, escapes. When Hengist later makes war with Aurelius Ambrosius, Hengist is captured and Eldol has the pleasure of beheading the savage.

As with the works about Hengist which preceded Monmouth, Monmouth's manuscript also contains the befuddling confusion first labeling Hengist as an Angle, but then establishing him in Kent. Similarly, some manuscripts state that Vortigern invited Hengist to Britain, and some, like Monmouth's, indicate Vortigern does not invite Hengist to Britain, but when the Angles land, Vortigern "makes peaceful overtures."

Monmouth, however, is the only amanuensis who gives interesting insights into Hengist's milieu in Britain. Commonly, what is exemplified in the early manuscripts such as the *De Excidio* and *The Anglo-Saxon Chronicle* is that widely spaced events are reported back-to-back, a technique which scholars and researchers refer to as "compacting." This practice can often be confusing because it tends to lead the reader to believe that events might be separated by only months when indeed the separation might be years or even decades. One case in point is the 457 entry about Hengist which relates that he fought against the Britons at Crecganford, and the next reference about Hengist is the date 465, when Hengist fights against the Welsh near Wippedesfleot. "Compacting" is easy to spot in this instance, but many times there isn't a clue that there is such a gap between events.

In his copy-work, Monmouth might have faced that situation when he records material about Hengist being granted land near Lindsey. Lindsey — the Latin term is Linnuis — appears in several works, not only as the locale which was granted to Hengist when he first arrived, but it is also listed as one of Arthur's battle sites on the River Dubglas.

A careful check in Eilert Ekwall's *Concise Oxford Dictionary of English Place-names* presents this information: "Lindsey *Lindissi, Lindesig* is a Brit derivative of *Lindon*, the old name of Lincoln, to which was added O[ld] E[nglish] *eg* 'island.'" The entry about Lincoln reads thusly: "Lindon is identical with Welsh *llyn* 'a lake' and refers to a widening of Witham." These two entries offer an interesting suggestion that Monmouth might have been referring to Lindeseg — that is, an "island" near present-day Lincoln — and not to Thanet, which is likewise not truly an island.

Sources: L. Alcock (AB); P. Blair (RB&EE); R. Collingwood/J. Myres (RB&ES); E. Ekwall (CODEP-N); G.N. Garmonsway (ASC); J. Morris (BH); C. Plummer (TSCP); P. Roberts (COKB); L. Sherley-Price (BEDE: HEC&P); J. Stevenson (N: HB); L. Thorpe (GM: HKB); M. Winterbottom (G: ROB&OW).

Henry de Blois. After WILLIAM OF MALMESBURY finished his manuscript *De Antiquitate* for Glastonbury Abbey, it was left in the hands of Henry de Blois, the abbot of that time. The offshoot, over the next 150 years, was a manuscript laden with interpolations and rewritten to include material that had not been sanctioned by William of Malmesbury, and in most instances did not remotely approach the truth. Modern-day scholars would have been ignorant of Malmesbury's original *DA* and would have forever perpetuated untruths, manipulations, and deliberate deceits had not William himself included large segments of the *DA* in his revision of *Gestis Regum Anglorum*.

In all, excluding William's original text, there are at least six major distinctive revisions and rewrites inserted by the monks. There was a revision one year later, in 1230, followed by manuscripts bearing the initials B, C, L, M, and T. These have nothing to do with an alphabetical chronology but instead indicate abbreviations of where each particular manuscript was housed. John Scott gives detailed information about these manuscripts, then uses Manuscript T in presenting his translation, specifying deviations and interpolations.

R.F. Treharne's scholarly work predates Scott's text by 15 years. His text is titled *The Glastonbury Legends*, and the last word, "*Legends*," should be emphatically stressed, since the focus is upon JOSEPH OF ARIMATHEA, the Holy Grail, and KING ARTHUR, each legendary topic depicted as truth by the abbot and monks of Glastonbury Abbey.

Armitage Robinson's text, titled *Two Glastonbury Legends: King Arthur and St. Joseph of Arimathea*, also denotes the fictionalized material housed at Glastonbury Abbey. In addition to denying King Arthur and St. Joseph of Arimathea as having a connection with Glastonbury, Robinson asserts that the term *Yneswitrin* — similar to what appears in the Grail manuscript — is not synonymous with the term Avalon. Hence the Isle of Avalon is not historically linked to Glastonbury during the time when it was surrounded by water.

In summary, the following items are what Malmesbury thought to be credible history:

- Gildas spent several years at the abbey, a place of sanctity, holiness, and reverence, but he does not make a distinction between GILDAS BADONICUS and GILDAS ALBANIUS, probably because he wasn't aware of the duo.
- Glastonbury was a holy shrine which not only attracted many pilgrims but became a coveted resting place for many saints.
- Over the centuries, the shrine was also revered by conquerors and therefore left intact rather than being destroyed.
- He accepted the stories about St. Patrick, St. David, and the Lord himself consecrating the Old Church of Wattles.

He makes no claim that Glastonbury is factually or historically tied to King Arthur, and he states that "*the tomb of Arthur is nowhere to be seen*, for which reason the dirges of old relate that he is to come again." [Italics mine.] This in itself casts serious doubt that King Arthur's grave was "discovered" in 1191, that King Arthur and GUINEVERE were exhumed, and that they were then buried in front of the high altar in the year 1278.

See also JOHN OF GLASTONBURY and ADAM OF DOMERHAM.

Sources: J. Carley (CGA/GA: HHHMA); F. Reno (HKA/HFAE); J.A. Robinson (TGL: KA &JA); J. Scott (EHG: ETSWM); R.F. Treharne (TGL: JA/HG/KA).

Henry of Huntingdon (*floruit* 1103–1133 / *lifespan* 1080/1085–1155). As with so many antiquarians, little is known of Henry of Huntingdon's life. One item of importance which pinpoints his locale is that in 1109 or 1110 he was made archdeacon of Huntingdon, only about seven miles south of the Benedictine Ramsey Abbey, founded in 969 and headed by the abbot he called Lord. When he made a trip to Rome in 1139, he met a Norman historian named Robert de Torigny who introduced him to the history written by GEOFFREY OF MONMOUTH, a history which Henry came to view as based totally on fact. Henry writes: "In those times Arthur the mighty warrior, general of the armies and chief of the kings of Britain, was constantly victorious in his wars with the Saxons. He was the commander in twelve battles, and gained twelve victories."

He lists the twelve battles, obviously extracted from NENNIUS, then adds his own commentary: "In our time the places are unknown, the Providence of God, we consider, having so ordered it that popular applause and flattery, and transitory glory, might be of no account."

E.K. Chambers writes,

Henry [of Huntingdon] did see the *Historia* [of Geoffrey of Monmouth] for the first time in Bec [on the continent] in January 1139, and in the course of the same year he notified his discovery in a letter to his friend Warinus Brito, giving him a short abstract of the contents of the book. Copies of the letter

are preserved in some of the manuscripts of Henry's *Historia Anglorum* and others in those of a chronicle by Robert de Torigny, who has added explanatory interpolations of his own. Certain details of Henry's abstract do not quite agree with those of [Monmouth's] *Historia* as we have it. Thus Uther Pendragon is made the son and not the brother of Aurelius [AMBROSIUS]. There is no mention of MERLIN.... These discrepancies have been taken as evidence that what Henry saw was a first draft of [Monmouth's] *Historia* and that it was afterwards revised by Geoffrey.

Henry's segment about Arthur's Battle of Camlann were extracted from the *Annales Cambriae*, the *Historia Brittonum*, and *The Anglo-Saxon Chronicle*. The *Chronicle* provides more information and is of course biased, but Henry offers this pronouncement: "[T]hat same year some of the most powerful of the British chiefs joined battle against [CERDIC]. It was fought bravely and obstinately on both sides; when the day was declining, the Saxons gained the victory; and there was great slaughter that day of the inhabitants of Albion [Britain], which would have been still more terrible had not the setting sun stayed it."

James Carley writes "Henry of Huntingdon is the first author I can locate who places Cerdic and Arthur in the same period." As suggested in the RANULF HIGDEN entry of this text, Carley's statement holds true. Geoffrey of Monmouth only vaguely mentions a CHERDIC who travels to Britain with Octa, but he records that the battle of Badon (Bath) was fought between Arthur and CHELDRIC, and that CHELRIC was in league with MORDRED against Arthur at the battle of Camblam (Camlann). Cherdic, Cheldric, and Chelric are most likely references to a CERDIC.

Huntingdon's *Historia* is so rich in detail that it is worth reading, independent of any Arthurian connection. As Thomas Forester points out in footnote 1 on page 43, "From the date of C.E. 465 to the year 527, Henry of Huntingdon introduces many recitals, for which it is not known whence he collected materials." That span of sixty-two years covers the heart of King Arthur's historical era for those researchers who ascribe to Arthur as an authentic figure.

Sources: R. Barber (AA); J. Carley (CGA); E.

Chambers (AOB); R. Fletcher (AMC); T. Forester (CHH); F. Reno (HKA/HFAE).

Herzeloyde is Gahmuret's wife and Parzival's mother in Wolfram's romance *Parzival*. Her husband dies while she is still pregnant with Parzival, and while her son is growing up, she shields him from the outside world. Parzival eventually meets knights and wants to become what they are. After he leaves for Arthur's court, unknown to him, she dies of grief.

See also WOLFRAM VON ESCHENBACH.

Higden, Ranulf (Ranulph, Ralph) (Higdon, Hydon, Hygden, Hikeden) (*floruit* 1325–1355 / *lifespan* 1310–1370). Like RALPH OF COGGESHALL, Ranulf Higden is rather obscure about Arthurian Matter. E. K. Chambers mentions him only in passing while discussing WILLIAM CAXTON, the first English printer who produced almost all of the English literature of his time. including Thomas Malory's *Morte d'Arthur*. Caxton had expressed that "there are those who hold opinion that there was no Arthur, and that all such books as been made of him been feigned and fables, because that some chronicles make of him no mention, ne remember him nothing, ne of his knights."

There is virtually nothing known of Higden's personal life except that he was a Benedictine monk at St. Werberg Abbey in Chester some time in the fourteenth century. Researchers generally agree that Higden died around 1363 or 1364. Some suggest that he entered the abbey in 1299, and if this be true, Higden's lifespan would have been approximately eighty-four years. There is also a consensus that a Cornish scholar named name John Trevisa (1342–1402) translated and annotated the *Polychronicon* in 1387, and one source estimates that Higden penned his chronicle between 1327 and 1340.

The Arthurian Encyclopedia avers that Higden's Arthurian Matter is primarily based upon HENRY OF HUNTINGTON and WILLIAM OF MALMESBURY. Ranulf Higden was one of the few individuals of the period who questioned Arthur's historicity. Caxton seemingly echoes Higden's stance, for Higden himself accuses GEOFFREY OF MONMOUTH as inventing the story of Arthur: "Since Geoffrey is the only writer to extol Arthur, many have wondered how it is possible to learn the truth about what is said about him, because if Arthur (as Geoffrey writes) had acquired thirty kingdoms, if he had conquered the kingdom of the Franks, and killed Lucius procurator of the republic of Italy, why do all Roman, French, and Saxon historians utterly fail to mention such a man, while recording the minor deeds of lesser men?"

John Trevisa's translation is more difficult to understand. His interpretation is written in the vernacular and becomes confusing. Higden might be following William of Malmesbury's lead of skepticism about Arthur's historicity, but this fact is not obvious:

> Here William telleth a maggle tale without evidence; and Ranulf's reasons, that he moveth against Arthur, should move no clerk that can know an argument, for it followeth not.... Though Geoffrey [of Monmouth] speak of Arthur's deeds, that other writers speak of darkly, or make of no mind, that disproveth not Geoffrey's story ... and in the third book, chapter 9, [Higden] sayeth himself that it is no wonder though William of Malmesbury were deceived, for he had not the British book. It may well be that Arthur is oft overpraised, but so be many other. Sooth saws be never the worse though mad men tell maggle tales — and some mad men will mean that Arthur shall come again, and be afterward king here of Britain, but that is a full maggle tale, and so be many other that be told of him and others.

It is undeniable that Higden is questioning the veracity of GEOFFREY OF MONMOUTH's tale of Arthur, but references to William telling "maggle tales," to William being "deceived," and to William not having "the British book" are confusing. If William is telling fairy tales or tales of magic because he has been deceived, then it is possible that Higden was reading what E.K. Chambers calls the "Pseudo William of Malmesbury" — that is, the heavily interpolated *De Antiquitate* which William left at the Glastonbury monastery. Only in this interpolated version does the manuscript make any references to Arthur. (*See also* WILLIAM OF MALMESBURY.)

At any rate, the major premise Higden conveys is that he specifically does not accept the Arthurian story as presented by Geoffrey of

Monmouth, and hence he rejects the historicity of Arthur based upon the lack of continental evidence, particularly Roman history. The controversy continues, six and a half centuries after his death.

One other point about Higden must be mentioned lest it remain obscure. Higden and JOHN OF GLASTONBURY were contemporaries, with an estimate that John of Glastonbury wrote *Cronica sive Antiquitates Glastoniensis Ecclesie* in 1342 and Higden wrote supplements down to 1339. Both record that ARTHUR gave Wessex to CERDIC, but it remains an enigma if one borrowed from the other. More than likely, however, Higden and John might have read material from Henry of Huntingdon, whose work appeared about two centuries prior. It doesn't seem as plausible that these antiquaries — Ranulf, John, or Henry — extracted the Arthur/Cerdic link from Geoffrey of Monmouth, because Monmouth confuses three characters (CHELDRIC, CHELRIC, and CHERDIC) who could be associated with Cerdic.

Sources: C. Babington/J. Lumby (PRH); E. Chambers (AOB); S. Blake/S. Lloyd (KTA); R. Castleden (KA: TBL); D. Fowler (TBGAS); V. Galbraith (AMSP: HLQ); N. Lacy (AE).

Hoel, Howel. Even when limiting the search for Hoel to the fifth century, there's still a great deal of confusion in relation to his association with Arthuriana. Lewis Thorpe, translator of Monmouth's *History of the Kings of Britain*, lists three different Hoels in the index, and the first one listed — Hoel I — causes the most confusion. Thorpe's translation reads, "This Hoel was the son of Arthur's sister, and his father was Budicus the King of the Armorican Britons." Thorpe then adds a footnote: "'Arthur's sister' must read 'the sister of Aurelius Ambrosius,' making Hoel I Arthur's first cousin. In Monmouth's narrative, Arthur's sister Anna is first listed as being married to Loth of Lodonesia and later has two sons, GAWAIN and MORDRED, who would thus be *Ambrosius's* nephews." Perhaps this explains the mix-up in legend of why Mordred was identified as Arthur's nephew, not Ambrosius's nephew.

A short time later, Monmouth writes that Arthur and Hoel were cousins. Thereafter, for many years, Hoel becomes Arthur's powerful and invaluable ally fighting wars both on the continent and on the island. R.F. Treharne summarizes Arthur's great achievements against the enemies, summoning Hoel to his aid during "a vigorous northern campaign, winning victory after victory, defeating the Saxons, Scots and Picts again and again, exterminating or expelling most of them from Britain, and so subjugating the remaining Scots and Picts that Hoel and Arthur are able to embark on a tour of the beauties of Loch Lomond and the surrounding Highlands."

Sources: R. Barber (AA); S. Blake/S. Lloyd (KTA); R. Coghlan (EAL); L. Thorpe (GM: HKB); R.F. Treharne (TGL: JA/HG/KA); G. Williams (E: SFA).

Honorius, Emperor of the Western Empire. Honorius's father was the Roman Emperor of the East, Theodosius the Great, and his mother was Aelia Flaccilla. His older brother was Arcadius, who later became Emperor of the East, and his half-sister was GALLA PLACIDIA.

Honorius reigned as Emperor of the West during the second decade of the fifth century. He was elevated to the rank of augustus at the age of nine when his father, Emperor Theodosius, died, and because he was so young, Stilicho was actually the ruler of the West until Honorius became of age.

Honorius had many eccentricities which crept into Roman history of the period, including raising chickens as "royal" pets, refusing to eat eggs, building a "chicken palace," and having servants flogged if they abused his "advisors" who were more intelligent than his senators. It's rumored that he had a pet rooster named "Rome," and when the city of that name was plundered by Alaric in 410, a messenger reported to him that "Rome was no more." Assuming that his rooster had died, Honorius went into a raging fit, but calmed considerably when he learned the truth.

The emperor's public displays of kissing his half-sister (Placidia) on the lips created a great deal of gossip in his court, and when he sent two successive wives, neither whose wedding vows had been consummated, back to their mothers, rumors about Honorius's sexual preferences were rampant.

These oddities caused Honorius to be labeled weak, feeble, and ineffective, but his 30-year reign (including Stilicho's regency) was considered effectual. With CONSTANTIUS III as his supreme commander, he was able to pacify Gaul, ridding the province of the British usurper CONSTANTINE (aka Flavius Claudius Constantinus) and his son CONSTANS, killing the Visigothic king Jovinus, and overthrowing Priscus Attalus and Maximus. He elevated his supreme commander to praefectus of Gaul, and offered his half-sister's hand in marriage to his future co-emperor. His worst political blunder was the murder of Stilicho.

Honorius also had close ties to Britain. Although he was forced to withdraw Roman soldiers from the province, his intention was to reoccupy the island. He bade the British to look to their own defenses, but according to R.G. Collingwood, Honorius created a new office termed COMES BRITANNIARUM in order to reclaim Britain as a province. Between 417 and 420, his supreme commander, Constantius III drops from the political and military scene on the mainland, and EXUPERANTIUS, the General's second, assumes the role of Praefectus in Gaul. Though unsuccessful, the Britons still hoped for Rome's return until approximately 446.

Honorius died on August 15, 423. He was childless, but because of his foresight, Constantius III and Placidia had a son, VALENTINIAN III who succeeded to the throne of the Western Empire.

Sources: E. Duckett (MPE&W); A Ferrill (FOTRE); E. Gibbon (D&FRE); S. Oost (GPA).

Horsa, Horsus. Horsa plays only an incidental role in the Arthurian saga. His name is recorded twice in *The Anglo-Saxon Chronicle*. The first is Entry 449 C.E.: "In their days HENGEST and Horsa, invited by VORTIGERN, the king of the Britons, came to Britain at a place which is called Ypwinesfleot." The second, in Year 455 C.E., relates that "In this year Hengest and Horsa fought against king Vortigern at a place called Agæles-threp and his brother Horsa was slain."

Those details about Horsa are echoed in the *Historia Brittonum*. However, new information about Horsa appears in Section 44, which states that in the second *Saxone* battle against the Britons "there fell Horsa and also Vortigern's son Cateyrn," adding three more details not included in *The Anglo-Saxon Chronicle*: where the battle was fought (Rhyd yr afael), who the adversary was (VORTIMER), and the Briton chieftain besides Horsa who was killed.

In his narrative, Bede adds that Horsa, who was killed in the battle against the Britons, "was buried in east Kent, where a monument bearing his name still stands." Evidently, from a manuscript which no longer survives, Bede was under the impression that Hengist's and Horsa's homeland was Kent, even though he previously stated that "in the country known as Angulus [on the continent] which lies between the provinces of the Jutes and Saxons and is said to remain unpopulated to this day — are descended the East and Middle Angles, the Mercians, all the Northumbrian stock, and the other English people. Their first chieftains are said to have been the brothers Hengist and Horsa."

Bede correctly labels Hengist and Horsa as Anglian, but then sets their homeland in Kent. The monument or the burial site for Horsa is a puzzle. Nennius lists the battlesite where Horsa fell as Episford, Rit Hergabail, Rithergabail, Sathenegahabail, Satenhegabail, Set Thergabail, or Saissenaeg-haibail, depending upon which copy of the *Historia Brittonum* is being used. G.N. Garmonsway, translator of *The Anglo-Saxon Chronicle*, gives the name as Agælesthrepe, italicizing the words and explaining that "the modern form of the place-name is given in *italic* if there is some doubt about the identification." Ronan Coghlan in his encyclopedia claims that Horsa's memorial was thought to have been a flint heap near Horsted Kent, citing Geoffrey of Monmouth, but Monmouth simply names the site of the battle. Similar to Coghlan, Chris Barber and David Pykitt record that Horsa was entombed at "the flint heap near Fort Horsted."

One last fragment of information pertaining to Horsa should duly be noted. In Section 56 of the *Historia Brittonum*, the title "The Campaigns of Arthur" is in brackets. Editor John Morris explains in his Introductory Notes that "titles in brackets enclose words not found in the text." Additionally, in the second sentence of that segment there is undoubtedly a scribal error stating "On *Hengist's* death, his son Octha comes down from the north of Britain," which should actually read, "Upon *Horsa's* death, Hengist's son Octha came down from the north." According to *The Anglo-Saxon Chronicle*, Horsa was killed in 455, which accounts for OCTHA coming down from the north and succeeding to the kingdom with his father Hengist. Thereafter, Hengist and Octha are listed as co-rulers in the entries through 473. The narrative of Geoffrey of Monmouth verifies the modification of this sequence.

Sources: C. Barber/D. Pykitt (JTA); G. Garmonsway (ASC); R. Coghlan (EAL); J. Morris, (BH); J. Stevenson (NHB); L. Thorpe (GM: HKB).

Howel. *see* HOEL.

Hueil, Cuill, Huail. Hueil is the most common spelling used by Jeffrey Gantz and co-authors Gwyn Jones and Thomas Jones, while Steve Blake and Scott Lloyd use the variant Huail. This character, who is relegated to an incidental position in Arthuriana through British tradition, appears very briefly in the tale "How Culhwch Won Olwen." In Culhwch's extensive invocation to Arthur at the beginning of the story, Hueil is identified as "son of CAW, who never submitted to a lord's hand." Two pages later Hueil's confrontation with Gwydre is tersely reported: Gwydre, son of Llwydeu, was stabbed by his uncle Hueil, and became "the source of the feud between Hueil and Arthur."

The next reference to Hueil is in *The Life of Gildas* penned by Caradog in 1130. In an opening passage, CARADOC writes, "St. Gildas was the contemporary of Arthur, the king of the whole of Britannia, whom he loved exceedingly, and whom he always desired to obey."

That brief statement is crucial and indispensable when interpreting the era of Arthur. The extract "St. Gildas Albanius was the contemporary of Arthur" cannot be overly stressed, although it is ignored or denied by a large number of researchers. Without a doubt, Caradoc emphatically states that St. Gildas was a contemporary of Arthur. If that statement is true — and there is no evidence to suggest that it isn't — then this particular Gildas is GILDAS ALBANIUS and

not GILDAS BADONICUS who penned the *De Excidio*.

In the *De Excidio*, Gildas explicitly writes that he was born in the same year that the Battle of Mount Badon was fought, which most scholars have assigned to a period between 497 and 500 C.E. He does not name the victor against the *Saxones*, which would have been slightly more than one generation prior to Gildas' birth, nullifying that this particular Gildas was a contemporary of Arthur. Josephus Stevenson provides sound logic that a different Gildas, one of the sons of Caw, was Arthur's contemporary. Caw was a king of Scotland, and hence his son Gildas has been ascribed the name Gildas Albanius, a prince of Scotland. The antiquarian who penned the *De Excidio* was, for discretion, called Gildas Badonicus.

Caradoc goes on to describe the attributes of Gildas Albanius, which later scholars and researchers have unfortunately ascribed to Gildas Badonicus: "Nevertheless, [Gildas'] twenty-three brothers constantly rose up against the aforementioned rebellious king [referring to a local chieftain named Gwydre], refusing to own him as their lord; but they often routed and drove him out from the forest and battlefield. Hueil, the elder brother, an active warrior and most distinguished soldier, submitted to no king, not even Arthur. He used to harass the latter, and to provoke the greatest anger between them both."

In 1188 GIRALDUS CAMBRENSIS penned the *Descriptio Kambriae*, three years prior to his most famous passage which appeared in both the *De Principis Instructione* and *Speculum Ecclesiae*. In the *Descriptio* (*Description of Wales*), he writes this passage about Hueil, making no distinction as to whether Gildas and Hueil were sons of Gildas Albanius or Gildas Badonicus: "The Britons maintain that, when Gildas criticized his own people so bitterly, he wrote as he did because he was so infuriated by the fact that King Arthur had killed Gildas's brother Hueil, who was a Scottish chieftain. When Gildas heard of this brother's death, or so the Britons say, he threw into the sea a number of outstanding books which he had written in their praise and about Arthur's achievements. As a result you will find no book which gives an authentic account of Arthur." In this short passage, Giraldus identifies Gildas and Hueil as sons of the Scottish King Caw (thus suggesting a Gildas Albanius), but then offers rationale why Gildas Badonicus did not include the name of Arthur in his manuscripts.

It is oral tradition which further traces Hueil's connection with Arthur. In their book *Pendragon*, Steve Blake and Scott Lloyd record a chronicle written by a certain Elis Gruffudd in 1530 which explains the enmity between Hueil and Arthur. Paraphrased, Hueil was sporting with one of Arthur's mistresses, leading to a vicious fight in which Hueil wounded Arthur's knee, an injury which caused Arthur to slightly limp forever thereafter. An uneasy truce ensued, based upon the condition that Hueil would never make reference to the injury nor how it occurred. On a later occasion, Arthur disguised himself as a girl to visit another female who lived in Ruthin. Hueil saw the two dancing, recognized Arthur, and facetiously called out that his dancing was acceptable, except for his injured knee. Arthur returned to court and had his cohorts apprehend Hueil, who was beheaded. The large stone, known as Maen Hueil, is still on display in the town square of Ruthin.

Sources: G. Ashe (TGTAB); R. Barber (FOA); S. Blake/S. Lloyd (P); Caradoc (LOG); N. Fairbairn & M. Cyprien (TGTKOA); J. Morris (AOA); J. Gantz (TM); G. Jones/T. Jones (TM); F. Reno (HKA/HFAE); L. Thorpe (GOW: JTW/DOW); G. Williams (E: SFA).

Hwicca. The name Hwicca first appears in *The History of the English Church and People* by BEDE. In an entry dated C.E. 603, he writes, "Meanwhile, with the aid of King Ethelbert, Augustine summoned the bishops and teachers of the nearest British province to a conference at a place still known to the English as Augustine's Oak, which lies on the border between the Hwiccas and the West Saxons."

A second reference relates that Queen Eabae was baptized in her own province of the Hwiccas, and in a third, dated 680, the reader is informed that the province of Hwicca was ruled by King Osric. The last entry, dated 716, tells of Wilfrid as being bishop of the Hwiccas.

The name Hwiccas then disappears from history.

Whether or not the Hwiccas are linked in some way to the historic King ARTHUR, to AMBROSIUS AURELIANUS, or to the fifth century remains obscure. Bede does not clearly or emphatically make a distinction between the Hwicca tribe and the GEWISSAE, but J.N.L. Myres lists them as different provinces. According to him, Gewissae is located south of the West Saxon country and north of the Isle of Wight; he locates Hwicca farther north and west, between Gloucester and Stratford on the borderlands of Wales.

Resolving the difference between Gewissae and Hwicca — if there is one — is essential in determining whether one of these territories had an impact on the alleged historic Arthurian era of the fifth century, specifically, in relation to Arthur's (i.e., Ambrosius's) adversaries, Hengest, Octha, and Cerdic. If an individual accepts Bede's records as correct, then

1. HENGIST, OCTHA, and HORSA would have settled to the east, in East or Middle Anglia.
2. CERDIC as a "West Saxon" would have had some connection with Hwicca.
3. The *SUPERBUS TYRANNUS* (or VORTIGERN) would have had the authority to allow the Anglian foederati to settle in the Hwicca territory, adjacent to his own kingdom in Wales.
4. GEWISSAE would have been misplaced by later historians who would have been following the suggestion that Hengist's kingdom was in Kent.
5. Vortimer would have driven Hengist's clan out of Hwicca and back to Anglia.

See also HYRPE.

Sources: J.N.L. Myres (RB&ES); L. Sherley-Price (BEDE: HEC&P); M. Winterbottom (G: ROB&OW).

Hyrpe, Hræfn. An ancient tribe by the name of Hyrpe might well be the origin of the Gewissae and the Hwicca clans recorded by BEDE. In explaining a piece of history about Alchfrid, son of Oswy, Bede wrote, "Alchfrid had given [Wilfred] a monastery with four hides of land at In-

Hrypum." Translator Leo Sherley-Price adds a footnote that In-Hyrpum is a reference to Ripon. *The Historic King Arthur* traces that site which is buried in a great deal of etymology. Simply put, however, the trail leads in this direction: Ripon, Ripum, Hryopan, Onhripum, Hyrpsatna, Hripis, Hrypadun. Eilert Ekwall, in *The Concise Oxford Dictionary of English Place-names*, writes, "No doubt *Hyrpa stan* is 'the stone of the *Hyrpe*.' The stone may have been a boundary stone marking the territory of the Hyrpe tribe, or a stone at the meeting-place of the tribe. An intervocalic change *p > b* is found early in other names, for instance, in hebden."

If indeed *Hyrpe* derivations mark a boundary, sites from the mouth of the River Ribble to the River Humber delineate a chain: Ribble, Ribchester, Ripley, Ripon, and Riplingham. Similarly, there are such names north-south in the midlands.

Scholars and historians evidently do not equate Bede's tribal reference "Hwicca" with "Gewissae." Ekwall traces the Hyrpe tribe through several sources, one prior to Bede in a monastery during the year 715. Peter Clayton, in his *Guide to the Archaeological Sites of Britain*, writes that Ribchester "was a small cavalry fort in the territory of the Brigantes tribe. When a group of Sarmatian cavalry veterans were given land to settle here on their retirement about C.E. 200 it was Brigantian land taken from the tribe." At that time, however, the site was known as Bremetannacum Veteranorum, and according to Ekwall, it was not known as Ribchester.

See also Lucius Artorius Castus.

No other document is specific about hyrpe.

Sources: P. Clayton (GASB), E. Ekwall (CODEP-N), L. Sherley-Price (BEDE: HEC&P); F. Reno (HKA).

Iddawg. In "The Dream of Rhonabwy," Iddawg is introduced as "the Churn of Britain," and Rhonabwy asks him why he is called that. Iddawg responds,

I was one of the messengers at the Battle of Camlann between Arthur and his nephew Medrawd. I was a high-spirited young man, so eager for battle that I stirred up bad feeling between them: when the Emperor Arthur sent me to remind Medrawd that Arthur was his

uncle and foster-father, and to ask for peace lest the sons and nobles of the island of Britain be killed, though Arthur spoke as kindly as he could I repeated his words to Medrawd in the rudest possible way. Thus I am called Iddawg the Churn of Britain, and that is how the Battle of Camlann was woven.

During the trip to Baddon, Rhonabwy asks Iddawg a series of questions. An important question he asked was the reason for such a large army, and he was told that they were to be at Baddon by noon to fight against OSLA BIG KNIFE. The narrative turns to several games of gwyddbwyll between Arthur and an unexplained opponent named Owein Dantquin (OWEIN DANTGUIN). After Rhonabwy questions the outcome of the six games, twenty-four horsemen came from Osla Big Knife and asked Arthur for a truce. The truce is granted by Arthur after a conference with his council, and once Arthur receives tribute, the armies disperse and Arthur returns to Cornwall.

In his narrative, Jeffrey Gantz uses the name "Owein," Peter Ellis uses "Owain ap Urien" (Owain son of Urien), and Frank Delaney calls Arthur's gwyddbwyll opponent "Owen."

Sources: F. Delaney (LOTC); P. Ellis (COTZ); J. Gantz (TM).

Ider, Yder, Edern, Isdermus. The variant of Ider for Yder occurs in JOHN OF GLASTONBURY's *Cronica Sive Antiquitates Glastoniensis Ecclesie*, penned in first half of the fourteenth century. In Section 33, John writes

When, one Christmas festival at Caerleon, King ARTHUR had decorated Ider, the son of King Nuth and a very strong youth, with the insignia of knighthood, he sent him, as a rest, to the mountain of Areynes in North Wales, where, he had learned, there were three giants famed for their misdeeds, and he charged him to fight against them. With swift steps Ider pursued the giants and, bravely advancing against them, killed them in a marvelous slaughter. When the giants were dead Arthur came and found Ider, who, being worn out by his great labour and wholly out of control of his faculties, had collapsed unconscious. He and his companions mourned him as though dead; and so, returning to his territories with unspeakable sadness, he left his body behind, which he thought lifeless, until he had sent some transportation to carry him back from there. Thinking himself the cause of Ider's death, because he had come to his aid too late, when he came at length to Glastonbury he established twenty-four monks there for the sake of the young man's soul, and he abundantly bestowed possessions and territories for their support, as well as gold, silver, chalices, and other churchly adornments. He gave, namely, Brent Marsh, Polden, and many other holdings which the pagan Saxons later took away when they occupied this land, but which they restored along with many other territories, as will be clear below, when they were subsequently converted to the faith of Christ.

There is no way to determine if John was copying the interpolated version of WILLIAM OF MALMESBURY's *De Antiquitate*, if he was adding details of his own, or if he had another manuscript available. One discordant note above all others is John's claims that Ider fought the giants on Mount Areynes in North Wales, far away from Arthur's court at Caerleon and even farther from Glastonbury, where Arthur granted Brent Marsh/Knoll and Polden to the abbey in Ider's honor.

Geoffrey Ashe, in *The Landscape of King Arthur*, adds some detail about the connection between Ider and Arthur, citing a thirteenth-century scholar, a reference to the Yder romance edited by Alison Adams. He writes that Arthur knighted Ider at Caerleon, then told Ider of three notorious giants who lived on Brent Knoll, which was then known as the Mount of Frogs. Arthur was marching against them and invited Ider to join the troop. "Ider over-zealously galloped ahead and slew all three [giants] single-handed. When Arthur caught up, he found the giant-killer lying unconscious and apparently dead or dying. The king returned sadly to Glastonbury blaming himself, appointed some monks to pray for Ider's soul, and endowed the Abbey with lands around the hill."

Ashe speculates that "there are hints that Ider was once actually reputed to be GUINEVERE's lover," but there is not much credence granted to that supposition.

One other variant, however, leads to a more interesting consideration. JOHN OF GLASTON-BURY records that the Ider episode occurred in north Wales, atop Mount Areynes, while Ashe labels the location as Brent Knoll, once know as the Mount of Frogs — in Latin, Mons Ranae/Renarum. Geographically, Ashe's supposition makes more sense, since Brent Knoll is much closer to Arthur's court at Caerleon and much closer to Glastonbury for the logic of Arthurian adventures. Independent of the Arthurian matter, an analysis of Anglo-Saxon land grants would lend more credence to John of Glastonbury's observation that Arthur donated Brent Marsh, Brent Knoll, and Polden to Glastonbury Abbey in honor of Ider; the Saxons took that land away after Arthur's demise, but later restored it when they converted to the faith of Christ. It explains, too, that the "Mount of Frogs" might have been metamorphosed into the "Mount of Spiders," probably through the misreading of *mons aranearum* for *mons renarum*.

Sources: G. Ashe (LKA); J. Carley (CGA); C.W. Carroll (CT: AR); E. Chambers (AOB); N. Faribairn (TGKOA); N. Lacy (AE); J/. Markale (KA: KOK); D.D.R. Owens (CT: AR).

Igraine, Igrayne. Igraine is the name used by Thomas MALORY in *Le Morte D'Arthur* for Arthur's mother. Through a magical spell, MERLIN changed himself into Sir Jordans, changed a knight of Uther's into Sir Brastius, and changed Uther himself into GORLOIS, promising Uther that he would lie by Igraine, get a child upon her, and take the babe. It came to pass, and the babe was handed over to Sir Ector, christened by a holy man, and named Arthur.

Upon Uther's death Arthur was coronated and Merlin defended Arthur as king because the young man was begotten in wedlock between Igraine and Uther. It is much later that Merlin, disguised as a fourteen-year-old child, tells Arthur that he was begotten by Uther and Igraine. Sir Ulfius blames Merlin and Igraine for the deception, but Igraine defends herself by replying, "Merlin and you knoweth well how King Uther came to me in the Castle of Tintagel in the likeness of my lord and thereby gat a child that night on me, and after the thirteenth day, King Uther wedded me, and by his commandment when the child was born it was delivered unto Merlin and nourished by him, and so I saw the child never after, nor wot was his name for I knew him never yet."

See also YGERNA and EIGR.

Source: T. Malory (LMD'A).

Impious Easterners. GILDAS BADONICUS uses this term *ORIENTALI SACRILEGORUM* to refer to the Britons' Anglian enemies who had settled to the east of the Cornovii territory along the coast. In §24 he describes how those enemies were destroying the island: "In just punishment for the crimes that had gone before, a fire heaped up and nurtured by the hands of the impious easterners spread from sea to sea. It devastated town and country round about, and, once it was alight, it did not die down until it had burned almost the whole surface of the island and was licking the western ocean with its fierce red tongue."

The above passage, coupled with §26.2/.3, alerts the reader that it is not foreign wars destroying the island:

> But the cities of our land are not populated even now as they once were; right to the present they are deserted, in ruins and unkempt. External wars may have stopped, but not civil ones. For the remembrance of so desperate a blow to the island and of such unlooked for recovery stuck in the minds of those who witnessed both wonders. That was why kings, public and private persons, priests, and churchmen, kept to their own stations. But they died; and an age succeeded them that is ignorant of that storm and has experience only of the calm of the present.

Honorable Britons have disappeared, and Gildas feels that Britain kings have become tyrants, judges are wicked, and the citizens have become thieves and adulterers. From here, Gildas then launches into the castigation of the five tyrants governing Wales.

Source: J. Stevenson (G: DEB).

Iolo Morganwg (Jolo Morganoog), aka Edward Williams, was a Glamorganshire stonemason in the 1770s who became an enthusiast of Welsh druidry. He adopted the pseudonym of Iolo Morganwg, and, as Stuart Piggott writes, became immersed in "fancy and fabrication." Piggott describes him as being a misguided patriot who

> declared that the Glamorganshire bards had preserved, virtually intact, a continuous tra-

dition of lore and wisdom going back to the original prehistoric Druids.... With the prevailing low standards of scholarship in early Welsh linguistics and paleography it was unfortunately not difficult for Iolo to forge documents to prove his case, and these were in fact a part only of his large corpus of fabrications of early Welsh literature which was to cause so much confusion when more exact scholarship came to be applied to the texts.

Peter Ellis echoes the same sentiment about Iolo, dubbing his writing as "radical and even republican in nature." Ellis's comments are almost identical to those by Piggott when he writes Iolo claimed that he could prove that the cult of the literary Druids had continued unbroken in Glamorgan. But Ellis is not as severe in his condemnation of Iolo: "Although, on a scholastic level, one can criticize Iolo Morganwg, as Professor Piggott has done, for his inventions, nevertheless, his inventions have now been given two hundred years of tradition and are an integral part of the Welsh, Breton, and Cornish national life. Having created Druids for a 'never-never' world, the Gorsedd and its values, particularly its recognition of cultural endeavours of the Celtic communities, has taken on a serious and respected life of its own."

Sir Ifor Williams sides with Piggott in relation to Iolo. He writes, "Iolo was the greatest forger of Welsh documents that Wales has ever known. The mischief that that man has done! Perhaps he was mad — let us be charitable. Any way, if any one should persist in using Iolo's faked manuscript to support any theory or thesis, he does so at his own risk and peril."

Rachel Bromwich, too, in her discussion of Welsh triads, cautions against the collections of Iolo, but she states that in the reliable versions of the triads, the increasing popularity of Arthur and Arthurian material is evident.

William Skene writes a three-page prescript about Iolo, ending with: "It is a peculiarity attaching to almost all of the documents which have emanated from the chair of Glamorgan, in other words, from *Iolo Morganwg*, that they [the documents] are not to be found in any of the Welsh MSS. contained in other collections, and that they must be accepted on his authority alone. It is not unreasonable, therefore, to say that they must be viewed with some suspicion, and that very careful discrimination is required in the use of them."

On the converse side of the coin, Lewis Spence writes in the Preface of his book, "Especially do I believe the writings preserved by Iolo Morganwg in Barddas to have been handed down from an immemorial antiquity, as his editors maintained, and to enshrine the beliefs, ideas, and practices of the Secret Tradition of Britain, and I feel that the unbiassed [sic] reader will, after having perused the evidence relative to this, find himself in general agreement with this view."

The vast majority, however, regarded Iolo Morganwg's material to be factual until 150 years after his death, when an "inquisitive scholar" found versions of most manuscripts written in Iolo's hand. The scholar who discovered this was most likely Damian McManus.

Sources: R. Bromwich (WT: ALMA); P.B. Ellis (TD); D. Mcmanus (GTO); S. Piggott (TD); W. Skene (FABW); L. Spence (MOB); I. Williams (LEWP).

Iseult. *see* ISOUD.

Isoud La Blanche Mains. This Isoud (Isolt) is also known as Isolt of the White Hands. She is a princess of Brittany, daughter of King Howel and sister of Kahedin (KEHYDIUS). She marries Tristan (TRISTRAM), but the marriage is never consummated. When Tristan is on his deathbed, she lies to him about Isolt (La Beale Isoud) not being aboard the ship coming into the harbor. Tristan dies and Isolt throws herself on him and she herself dies.

Sources: R. Loomis/L. Loomis (MR); D. Owen (GVS: T).

Ither. *see* WOLFRAM VON ESCHENBACH.

John of Glastonbury (John Seen; Johannes Sene) (*floruit AE* 1327–1357/ *lifespan* 1312–1372). John of Glastonbury's *Cronica sive Antiquitates Glastoniensis Ecclesie* (*Chronicle or History of Glastonbury Church*) is difficult to categorize because it falls into the shadowy realm between history and oral tradition. Its intent is serious, localized history, yet at times the content borders on the fantastic. Structurally, the *Cronica* can accurately

be termed a treatise, since it is a systematic exposition, methodically organized and presenting a great number of facts. Yet contextually it cannot easily be catalogued by genre. Even though the terms "oral tradition" and "legend" don't necessarily mean that the material is devoid of fact, those two classifications still do not adequately describe some of the entries. Likewise, "fantasy" and "fiction" are not appropriate descriptors. Fantasy implies a tolerance of unrestrained creative imagination, and fiction connotatively suggests an invented creation lacking a base in reality. None of these terms describes the *Cronica*.

As the title of the manuscript implies, the term "history" has to suffice — a *history* of Glastonbury Church. Yet there has to be an addendum or some kind of a subtitle, perhaps a qualifier. The genre "apocrapha" suffices, especially since John is writing about ecclesiastic affairs, including material about JOSEPH OF ARIMATHEA. By definition, this genre is "writings or statements of dubious authenticity." Even though a great deal — perhaps most — of what John recorded was indeed verifiable and factual, there are segments which are of a spurious nature, their origin falsified or erroneously attributed.

Some of John's material draws heavily on GEOFFREY OF MONMOUTH, whose *History of the Kings of Britain* is sometimes generously labeled as "pseudo-history" and at other times frequently classified as something much less laudatory. He also uses *The Mabinogion*, an intriguing mixture of oral tradition sprinkled with tidbits of historical fact. In that same shadowy realm, he draws upon material from WILLIAM OF MALMESBURY — not considered fiction either — but unfortunately John used a version of the De *Antiquitate Glastonie Ecclesie* at Glastonbury Abbey which had been heavily interpolated. In the Prologue of the *Cronica*, John also names ADAM OF DOMERHAM's *Historia de rebus Glastoniensibus*, which compounded the misinformation because not only was Adam's work spurious, but as scholars John Scott and E.K. Chambers report, Adam was probably the one who manipulated Malmsebury's *DA* which had been left at the abbey.

Without going into detail, John of Glastonbury was probably John Seen, the well-known historian and writer of chronicles during the fourteenth century. John Seen was selected as proctor for Walter de Monington, who became the abbot at Glastonbury Abbey. There are allusions and clues which suggest that John Seen was the one who penned the so-called earlier history of the monastery prior to 1290.

It is likely that John himself was unaware that the abbey's history had become so convoluted, verified by the Prologue which enumerates the specifics of his organization. In the first division, he writes, "If I have followed the lead of the monk William of Malmesbury, I have also followed that of brother Adam of Domerham, another monk of this said monastery of ours." John's assumption was that Adam had recorded William of Malmsebury's history meticulously.

In the second division John reiterates that "Adam carried the account forward from the time of the said Henry, bishop and abbot, when William cut the web of his history — that is, from C.E. 1126 — to the demise of Abbot John of Taunton in C.E. 1290."

The next reference to Arthur is §IX, which lists the relics of Saint Mary the Mother of the Lord: pieces of her sepulchre from the Valley of Josaphat, some of the Blessed Mary's milk, a thread from one of Her garments, and a lock of Her hair. John then adds that there was also "a crystal cross which the Blessed Virgin brought to the glorious King Arthur."

Overlooking the distorted portrayal of Joseph of Arimathea's fanciful migration to Britain and the allusions to the Virgin Mary's relics, and instead focusing upon references to King Arthur, John's first passing reference to King Arthur occurs in §V, "On the Saints that Rest in the Church of Glastonbury." John lists 91 people, excluding King Arthur, who rest in front of the high altar, then writes, "The virgin St Aelswitha rests there, whole and untouched in flesh and bone, buried between the high altar and the tomb of King Arthur."

Arthur accepts Christianity, changes his arms in honor of the Lady Virgin and her son, and receives the crystal cross to commemorate his conversion. John writes that the relic "to this day is honourably housed and guarded in the treasury of Glastonbury and is carried every year during Lent through the convent." Malmesbury, however, does not verify this preserved relic, nor does it actually appear in the abbey relic lists.

All of the avowals about Saint Mary's relics allegedly housed in Glastonbury Abbey seem outlandish, and Carley attaches this footnote about the crystal cross: "It is very interesting to note that the crystal cross which Mary gave to King Arthur, and which became his emblem, is not mentioned in the relic lists," yet he adds, "The cross was an intrinsic part of Arthurian tradition; the two relic lists, however, seem fairly conservative and exclude possible 'romance' items." This seems to be an indirect way of suggesting that Arthur's cross might have been omitted in order to keep official church documents "clean" of any Arthurian references, since all (or at least most) of the relics lists for *all* the saints are anomalous or extraordinary claims which could be labeled as "romance" items.

The name of Arthur then appears in §XIIII, seemingly linked to §V since it continues to name additional famous people buried at the Abbey. It is labeled by John as

ON THE SANCTITY OF THE CHURCH OF GLASTONBURY AND ITS CEMETERY, AND ALSO ON THE KINGS, BISHOPS, DUKES AND OTHER NOBLES BURIED THERE

Also in this island of Avalon, which is called the tomb of saints, rest Coel, King of the Britons, father of St Helen, the mother of the great emperor Constantine, and Caradoc, duke of Cornwall. The glorious King Arthur rests there with his queen, Guinevere; in the year of the Lord's Incarnation 542 Arthur was fatally wounded by Mordred in Cornwall near the river Camlann, was brought to the island of Avalon for the healing of his wounds, died there in summer, around Pentecost, and was buried in the monks' cemetery. There he rested 648 years and was afterwards translated into the larger church.

The date of the Lord's Incarnation echoes material from Geoffrey of Monmouth. Arthur resting in his original burial site for 648 years before he was buried in front of the high altar probably came from Adam of Domerham's manuscript. The one curiosity is that John, unlike other early recordings, identifies Arthur's last battle at Camlann as being a river site.

John then records:

XVI
ON THE LANDS AND POSSESSIONS BESTOWED UPON THE MONASTERY OF GLASTONBURY BY VARIOUS KINGS, BISHOPS, DUKES, AND OTHERS

The glorious Arthur, King of the Britons, gave Brent Marsh and Polden, along with many other lands located in the neighborhood. The Anglo-Saxons, who arrived as pagans, took these holdings away but afterwards, converted to the faith, restored them along with others. Thus a king by the name of Domp restored five hides in that land which is called Ynswytryn, and he confirmed the grant to the brothers who dwelt there.

The information which John provides in this section is quite easy to omit or suppress in an Arthurian context. In addition to this section, John Scott in Chapter 69 of a text about William of Malmesbury also describes land grants given to Glastonbury Abbey, not in itself unusual because John of Glastonbury's manuscript was most likely copied from William of Malmesbury. As suggested in F. D. Reno's *The Historic King Arthur*, "Studying annotated lists and bibliographies of Anglo-Saxon charters appears at first too divorced from Arthurian matters to be of any significant consequence. These land grants are records from various sources compiled for the purpose of tracing land grants throughout British history. Each entry, marked by a coded number, gives the year of the charter, the Saxon king bequeathing the land, the recipient of the grant, the manuscripts which contain the translation, and comments on the degree of the authenticity."

These land grants are briefly mentioned here, since there is a possibility that, because these documents are listed by dates, geographic location, and conditions, the historically recorded land grants might be linked to Arthur's pledges. Describing the tale of Ider, John of Glastonbury writes that King Arthur granted Brent Marsh and Poweldone to Glastonbury as remorse and penance for Ider's death. This passage links three seemingly discrete and independent elements which could possibly help dispel — not prove by any means — Arthur's Glastonbury exhumations

as hoaxes. Those interested in pursuing this in more detail should consult Peter Sawyer's *Anglo-Saxon Charters*, particularly Charters 238 and its repetition, 1671, and Charters 248, 250, 253, and 1680. *The Historic King Arthur* gives a synopsis of this information on pages 253 to 256.

Although §20 is titled "The Deeds of the Glorious King Arthur," the introductory sentence declares Arthur's lineage: "The book of the deeds of the glorious King Arthur bears witness that the noble decurion Joseph of Arimathea came to Great Britain, which is now called England, along with his son Josephes and many others, and that there they ended their lives." That same section then deviates to Arthurian legend, which John handles as if the material is history:

This is found in the portion of the book dealing with the search carried out by the companions of the Round Table for an illustrious knight called LANCELOT du Lac — that is, in the part of the book where a hermit explains to GAWAIN the mystery of a fountain which keeps changing taste and colour; in the same place it is also written that that miracle will not end until a great lion comes whose neck is bound in heavy chains. It is also reported practically at the beginning of the quest for the vessel which is there called the Holy Grail, where the White Knight explains to Galahad, son of Lancelot, the mystery of a miraculous shield which he enjoins him to carry and which no one else can bear, even for a day, without grave loss.

Since John gave the specific date of 542 C.E., there is no doubt that he extracted it from Monmouth's work. Yet John mentions the Round Table which didn't appear in literature until Wace's manuscript *Roman de Brut* of the mid–twelfth century. Lancelot was a creation of CHRÉTIEN DE TROYES dating to the late twelfth century, at which time Chrétien wrote *Le Chevalier de la charrete* (*The Knight of the Cart*), also known as *Lancelot*, a work de Troyes dedicated to Marie de Champagne.

Additionally, the Holy Grail is directly attributable to Chrétien de Troyes in his work *Conte del Graal*, and indirectly to ROBERT DE BORON, who continued the tale of PERCEVAL which de Troyes left unfinished. In his manuscript, de Boron described the Graal as the chalice of the Last Supper, the vessel which Joseph of Arimathea carried with him to Ynis Witrin. John of Glastonbury, therefore, has incorporated several fragments of narrative into his sections of the *Cronica*.

Section XXI of John's *Cronica* carries on with the introductory sentence of §20; that is, §21 is titled "This Passage Bears Witness that King Arthur Descended From the Stock of Joseph," and then gives the entire genealogy for Joseph of Arimathea, bypassed here because this lineage blends into Arthurian legend.

Because all of Chapter 32 deals with Arthurian material, the reader should check each of the following separate entries in this text: GILDAS ALBANIUS, CERDIC, CYNRIC, UTERPENDRAGON, AURELIUS AMBROSIUS, YGERNA, ARTHUR, JOSEPH OF ARIMATHEA, and HUEIL.

Section 32 opens in this manner: "**The kingdom of Wessex began about the year of grace 495** under Cerdic and his son Cynric. **In the eleventh year of Cerdic**, when Utherpendragon, the brother of Aurelius Ambrosius, had been killed with poison, his son Arthur, youth of fifteen years, began to reign over the Britons. He was born of his mother Igerna in Cornwall, in a castle called Tintagel" (boldface added).

The two most inscrutable segments above are boldface. There is no substantiation to indicate how John of Glastonbury acquired this information. J.N.L. Myres explains how archaeologists arrived at this conclusion, "The population of Wessex anticipated invasion and conquest rather from the *north* than from the *south*." This is one piece of evidence which led this author to aver that Cerdic the individual named in *The Anglo-Saxon Chronicle* and Cerdic the interpreter recorded in the *Historia Brittonum* are references to the same person.

John's second comment, "in the eleventh year of Cerdic," is an even more puzzling addition which occurs in no other document. Does this mean that Cerdic was eleven years old when Utherpendragon was poisoned? Or might it mean that Cerdic had been reigning eleven years when Utherpendragon was murdered? How do these statements relate directly to the specific date of 495 which is given, especially since it is so closely related to Arthur's battle at Badon and the birthdate of Gildas Badonicus?

Adding to the complexity, or perhaps, approaching it from a different viewpoint, Section 33 of John's *Chronica* relates that "King Arthur fought mightily against the Saxons and wore them down; he waged twelve battles against them, conquering and routing them in all twelve instances. **Often he struggled with Cerdic, who, if one month Arthur vanquished him, rose up the next fiercer for the fight. Finally, when Arthur tired of the conflict, he accepted Cerdic's fealty and gave him Hampshire and Somerset, which Cerdic called Wessex**" (boldface added).

The name King Arthur in this section indicates that once more John has unknowingly reverted to legend, since he is using a tainted version of Malmesbury's *De Antiquitate*. The "different viewpoint" is this: if the name "Arthur" is replaced by "Ambrosius Aurelianus"—the bona fide Briton king of the fifth century as listed in the *De Excidio*, in *A History of the English Church and People*, and in the *Historia Brittonum*—and if Cerdic indeed has three faces, then British history of the fifth century is set aright.

Thus ends the complex history of Glastonbury Abbey as recorded by John of Glastonbury, a mixture of fact and fiction, although John might have believed that all of what he had salvaged and narrated was the truth.

Sources: L. Alcock (AB); J. Carley (CGA); E. Chambers (AOB); W.W. Comfort (CDT-AR); J. Davies (HOW); G.N. Garmonsway (ASC); N. Lacy (AE); J. Morris (AOA); J. Morris (BH); E. Mason (AC-W&L); J.N.L. Myres (RB&ES); C. Plummer (TSCP); C. Radford (GA: QAB); F. Reno (HKA); J.A. Robinson (TGL: KA&JA); P. Sawyer (A-SC: AL&B); L. Thorpe (GM: HKB).

Jordanes (*floruit 535–565*). Jordanes earns his niche in Arthuriana because of his entries in *Gothic History* about Riotimus (RIOTHAMUS), a Briton king from across Ocean, who has been identified by several scholars as either King ARTHUR or AMBROSIUS AURELIANUS.

Jordanes, himself a Goth, was a historian of the mid–sixth century. He modestly claimed that he was uneducated, but wrote a great deal of history, in Latin. He was persuaded by his friend

Castalius to summarize in one volume the encyclopedic twelve volumes written by Cassiodorus on the history of the Goths. He undertook the formidable project, claiming that he added material from other Greek and Latin authors, and that the beginning and the end of the book were his own. He finished the manuscript in 551, and now his book is commonly referred to, simply, as *Gothic History*, which Charles Mierow translated and titled as *Jordanes: The Origin and Deeds of the Goths*. Theodor Mommsen also edited the book under the title *Monumenta Germaniae Historica*.

The two passages which catapulted Jordanes into Arthuriana are brief, but powerful and convincing:

> Now EURIC king of the Visigoths, perceived the frequent change of Roman Emperors and strove to hold Gaul by his own right. The Emperor ANTHEMIUS heard of it and asked the Brittones for aid. Their King Riotimus came with twelve thousand men into the state of Biturges by way of Ocean, and was received as he disembarked from his ships.
>
> Euric, king of the Visigoths, came against them with an innumerable army, and after a long fight he routed Riotimus, king of the Brittones, before the Romans could join him. So when Riotimus had lost a great part of his army, he fled with all the men he could gather together, and came to the Burgundians, a neighboring tribe then allied to the Romans.

Geoffrey Ashe has equated Riothamus with King Arthur as the Briton king from across Ocean, while Frank Reno professes that there is no Arthur who can be associated with the "great king among all the kings of Britain" during the fifth century. That honorific, Reno claims, must be bestowed upon Ambrosius Aurelianus, who is touted by Nennius in the *Historia Brittonum*.

Sources: G. Ashe (DKA); C. Mierow (J: O& DG); J. Morris (BH); F. Reno (HKA/HFAE).

Joseph of Arimathea. A separate entry for the story of Joseph of Arimathea rightfully belongs in this text because it touches upon the fringes of Arthuriana, particularly Arthurian legend. James Carley, in his book *The Chronicle of Glastonbury*, deals in some depth with both Joseph of Arimathea and King ARTHUR because JOHN

OF GLASTONBURY—the scribe of the above work—is a pivotal contributor to both subjects. However, because the contextual timeframe in this book focuses mainly upon Arthur's *historical* origins during the fifth century and into the beginning of the sixth, legendary and satellite aspects—such as the story of Joseph of Arimathea—are abbreviated. The biography of Joseph of Arimathea has its roots almost four centuries prior to Arthur's historic floruit, but the legendary aspects of Joseph's story aren't associated with Arthur or Glastonbury Abbey until the early sixteenth century. The copy of WILLIAM OF MALMESBURY's *De Antiquitate* which was given to Glastonbury Abbey was severely interpolated by the monks not only about Joseph of Arimathea but also about Arthur's burial on the Abbey's grounds. The appalling exaggerations by the monks—no doubt by Adam of Domerham and later copied by John of Glastonbury—led the successive generations to accept the accounts of Joseph and Arthur as absolute truth.

James Carley reinforces those sentiments when he writes that "until sometime after the 1220s ...

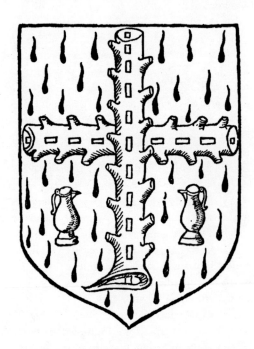

In the south window of St. John's Church in Glastonbury is Joseph's blazon: two cruets in the lower quadrants on either side of a cross made from the Glastonbury Thorn.

William of Malmesbury's story that unknown disciples of St Philip might have come to Glastonbury remained the accepted account of Glastonbury's foundation — although [the story of Joseph] changed in the late twelfth century from a possibility to a clear fact." Treharne terminates the Joseph story in a different manner by verbalizing William's judgment: "William's professional standards of historical criticism assert themselves, and he tactfully indicates his skepticism of this part [about Arthur and Joseph] of the Glastonbury story."

ADAM OF DOMERHAM was a resident monk of some stature who was not only the cellarer at Glastonbury Abbey, but he was also put in charge of the monastery's documents. When he wasn't busy writing his own manuscript, the *Historia de rebus Glastoni*e*nbus*, he was undoubtedly engrossed in adding marginal notes to William of Malmesbury's *De Antiquitate*. Over the centuries, Adam has become the primary suspect — with good reason — for the heavy interpolation. His motive, although it might have been justifiable, unfortunately distorted not only the abbey's veracity, but modified British history, and John of Glastonbury copied much of Adam of Domerham's work almost verbatim.

In his Introduction, Carley writes, "The first official recognition of Joseph at Glastonbury is not recorded until John wrote his *Cronica* in the early 1340s.... In Trinity College Cambridge MS R. 5. 33 (which is mid-thirteenth century) the material on Joseph is printed as a marginal note. In the British Library version, however, it is actually incorporated into the text. Since this latter manuscript almost certainly belongs to Adam of Domerham, one can assume that the note must have been written sometime before the 1290s." This is an excellent example of how an interpolation — a notation in the margin of a manuscript — becomes incorporated into a later copy and is presumed by later generations to be actual history, an indisputable fact.

Despite the lack of solid evidence, the deceptive trail linking the historic King Arthur and Joseph of Arimathea led to the two claims that

"Joseph of Arimathea among the Rocks of Albion." Engraving by William Blake.

Joseph was Arthur's ancestor, and that the quest for the Holy Grail was historically associated with Glastonbury Abbey, specifically based at Ynswytryn. How this Joseph-Arthur relationship evolved is encapsulated by Carley, who suggests that the popularity of this connection began expanding during the second half of the fourteenth century, attributable to "information about St Patrick being added to William of Malmesbury's *De Antiquitate*, and various other details being tidied up in William's manuscript." Carley adds that in 1350 anonymous additions linking Arthur's descent to Joseph of Arimathea appeared in a manuscript titled *Historia de mirabilibus gestis Edward III* by Robert of Avesbury.

R.F. Treharne, in his text *The Glastonbury Legends: Joseph of Arimathea, The Holy Grail, and King Arthur*, furnishes a concise yet adequate evolvement from the inception of the Holy Grail into British history until its demise. He writes that the Holy Grail "never had any historical substance, but was pure myth and fantasy, grafted on to the Arthurian Legend at a fairly early stage well before 1240."

The story of Joseph of Arimathea was carried on not only by writers such as Edmund Spenser, William Blake, and Alfred, Lord Tennyson, but also flourished into the twenty-first century through Arthurian tales.

Sources: J. Carley (CGA); E. Jung/M-L Von Franz (TGL); Magna Tabula Oxford. Bodleian Library, Ms Lat. Hist. A. 2; J. Robinson (TGL: KE&SJA); J. Scott (EHG: ETSWM); W.W. Skeat (AJOA, 37–52); R.F. Treharne (TGL: JA/HG/KA).

Jutes. According to *The Anglo-Saxon Chronicle*, the tribes or clans known as Jutes migrated from Germany to Britain, and "from the Jutes came the people of Kent and the people of the Isle of Wight." Although this is the only mention of Jutes, it is an important revelation that they settled in the southwestern part of Britain.

As translated by R.G. Collingwood, BEDE, of the eighth century, gives this information in *A History of the English Church and People*: "From the Jutes are descended the Cantuarii and the Victuarii, that is, the people which holds the Isle of Wight and that which to this day is called the *Jutarum natio* in the province of the West Saxons set opposite the Isle of Wight." These two early passages suggest two things: first, that the entry in *The Anglo-Saxon Chronicle* was extracted from Bede because of similar wording, and second,

that HENGIST, HORSA, OCTHA and their tribe would not have settled in Kent.

For further clarification, refer to the three ealdormen listed above, as well as the ANGLES' entry and the SAXONES' entries.

Sources: R. Collingwood/J. Myres (RB&ES); G.N. Garmonsway (ASC); L. Sherley-Price (BEDE: HEC&P).

Kahedîn. Because GOTTFRIED VON STRASSBURG's *Tristan and Isolt* ends just prior to the episode about ISOLT OF THE WHITE HANDS,* Kahedîn's name appears in what is termed a "continuation."**

Kahedîn, Duke of Parmenie (Gottfried's variation of Armorica, known also as Little Britain or Brittany) is Isolt of the White Hands' brother, responsible for the marriage between his sister and Tristan (TRISTRAM).

Even in his youth, Kahedîn loved an unnamed lady of the land whose husband was Nampotenis. Kahedîn took counsel with Tristan and the two were able to make entry into Nampotenis' castle when the knight was away. While Kahedîn and his lover were involved in their tryst, Tristan kept watch until the dawning.

Upon arrival the next morning, Nampotenis knew something was amiss and extracted the truth from his wife. Unknown to Tristan and Kahedîn that they were being pursued, they were taken unawares. Nampotenis attacked Kahedîn and ran him through the body with a spear, killing him instantly. In wrath, Tristan drew his sword and smote the knight dead, but in the process, Nampotenis pierced Tristan through the thigh with a poisoned spear.

* Isoud la Blanche Mains, not to be confused with La Beale Isoud.

**In this instance there were two continuations written, one by HEINRICH VON FREIBERG and the other by Ulrich von Türheim. Jessie Weston's translation has been used for the information in this entry.

See also KEHYDIUS.

Sources: R. Loomis/L. Loomis (MR).

Kay, Kei, Cai. Kay is recorded early in Welsh tradition, estimated by R.S. Loomis to be in the tenth or eleventh century. In *The Four Ancient Books of Wales* compiled by William Skene, Cai makes his first appearance in "Translations of the Poems," section B, Arthur the Guledig, VII Black Book of Carmarthen XXXI. Because of the complexity of the poems, suggested indirectly by Loomis from another text to be "elaborately incomprehensible," with all the allusions "recognized only by the *cognoscenti*," only fragments can be extracted. The opening segment is quoted below:

> What man is the porter?
> Glewlwyd Gavaelvawr.
> Who is the man that asks it?
> Arthur and the fair Cai.
> How goes it with thee?
> Truly in the best way in the world.
> Into my house thou shalt not come,
> Unless thou prevailest.
> I forbid it.

Loomis evidently misinterprets the above segment when he writes, "The first is a fragmentary dialogue between ARTHUR and a gate-warden, who demands that Arthur name his companions. Arthur complies and also tells the exploits of some of them."

In relation to the above quotation, a segment of "Culhwch and Olwen" in *The Mabinogion* unravels some of the confusion. When CULHWCH reaches the gate to petition Arthur to help him win the hand of Olwen, he shouts to the gatekeeper — Glewlwyd Strong Grip — who refuses him entry because "knife has gone into meat and drink into horn," but the gatekeeper offers to go to the dining hall to seek Arthur's permission. The gatekeeper does not demand that Arthur name his companions as Loomis states, because Glewlwyd *is* Arthur's gate-warden. Kay advises Arthur not to let Culhwch enter, but Arthur disagrees and sends word to admit the young man.

Kay has a role in all the "other tales" of *The Mabinogion*. In the Culhwch tale, Kay is fast friends with BEDWYR and Gwrhyr (CERDIC) Interpreter of Languages. At one point, Arthur belittles Kay for killing Dillus the Bearded, and there was no peace thereafter between Arthur and Kay. In the Rhonabwy narrative, Kay is described as the most handsome man in Arthur's kingdom and praised as a magnificent horseman. He is not personally mentioned in the list of Arthur's advisors, but Kay does follow Arthur back to Cornwall.

Kay's rudeness and harshness costs him dearly in the PEREDUR episode. Peredur strikes him under the jaw with a spear and unhorses him, breaking his arm and collar bone. Arthur has evidently mended the distance between him and Kay; the king was upset over the hurt Kay had suffered, for "he loved him very much."

Centuries later, several manuscripts describe Arthur's and Kay's childhood and adolescence. After Uther seduces Ygraine and Arthur is born, Merlin takes the baby and delivers him to Sir Ector, a trustworthy and honorable man whose wife was in childbed with her own infant son. Merlin arranged with Ector that his wife give her own son, Kay, to another woman to be suckled, so that she and her husband could nourish and keep the new child for which they would be rewarded and blessed in later life.

When entering manhood, Sir ECTOR took his son Kay and foster-son Arthur to the jousts, but Kay had left his sword at home. Arthur backtracked to retrieve the sword, but the women were gone and the house locked up. On his return trip, Arthur passed a churchyard and there saw a sword buried in a stone, and since there was no one in sight, he extracted it and then gave it to Kay, who was aware of the sword's significance. Ector is obliged to reveal that Arthur is not his biological son. Arthur becomes king, and Ector asks only that he make Kay his seneschal.

Kay's role is minimal in Malory's *Le Morte D'Arthur*, sometimes cruel, scornful, and pitiless, but he and Arthur remain bonded. In Monmouth's manuscript, during the battle between Arthur and LUCIUS HIBERIUS, Kay is severely wounded and carried away to Chinon, the town which he himself had built, and shortly thereafter he died.

Sources: J. Bruce (EAR); J. Gantz (TM); R. Loomis (DOAR); R. Loomis/R. Willard (MEV &P); T. Malory (LMD'A); W. Skene (FABW); J. Weston (CMEP).

Kehydius, Son of Howel. Kehydius is Malory's name for KAHEDÎN in GOTTFRIED VON STRASSBURG's work. Whereas KAHEDÎN is identified only as the brother of Isoud of the White Hands in Gottfried, Malory lists him as the son of King Howel (HOEL) of Brittany. Also, Kahedîn is short-lived, killed by his lover's husband almost immediately after his introduction into the story.

In Malory's epic, Kehydius is elevated from an incidental character to the slightly higher level of a very minor character. TRISTRAM weds Kehydius' sister ISOUD LA BLANCHE MAINS. During a sailing excursion, high winds blow the three off course and they end up on the coast of Wales. By chance they meet Segwarides then Lamorak (GAHERIS) who both recognize Tristram. They have an adventure, after which they sail back to Brittany.

Later, La Beal Isoud piteously writes Sir Tristram, begging him to return to Cornwall even though he is married to Isoud la Blanche Mains. Kehydius, knowing that Tristram has never consummated the marriage with his sister, agrees to accompany him. Malory then gives a preview of what happens next: "The French book maketh mention, at the first time that ever Sir Kehydius saw La Beale Isoud he was enamoured upon her that for very pure love he might never withdraw it. At the last, as ye shall hear or the book be ended, Sir Kehydius died for the love of La Beal Isoud."

Source: J. Cowan (STM: LMD'A).

Kindred of Eight. The Kindred of Eight is an expression in the *Historia Brittonum* used to describe a certain clan which migrated from Ireland to Britain. Josephus Stevenson uses the term Damhoctor, literally translating to "Clan of Eight." There are four other variants in Manuscripts D, H, P, and I. Translated, §14 reads, "Later came the Kindred of Eight and lived there with all their race in Britain until today. Istoreth son of Istorinus held Dal Riada with his people. Bolg with his people held the Isle of Man, and other islands about. The sons of Liathan prevailed in the country of the Dementians, †where the city of Mynyw is†, and in other countries, that is Gower and Kidwelly, until they were expelled by CUNEDDA, and by his sons, from all countries in Britain."

The daggers (†) indicate an interpolation — information added by a later hand — and Mynyw is an early term for Saint Davids. The core importance of this entry is, of course, Cunedda's involvement with this clan.

Sources: J. Morris (HB); J. Stevenson (N: HB).

Kyot. In Book 8 of his romance *Parzival*, WOLFRAM VON ESCHENBACH claims that the origin of the story — particularly the Grail segment — came from the scribe Kyot, in an Arabic manuscript found in Toledo. After Kyot had allegedly learned Arabic and read the story, he discovered that its author was the astronomer Flegetanis, and the contents told of the Grail and the Grail family. He followed up on Flegetanis's assertions, and after perusing Latin chronicles, he pieced together the entire tale.

Sidney Johnson's entry in the *Arthurian Encyclopedia* voices the opinion, which has now become widely agreed upon, that this account is "patently a fantastic fabrication to impress the gullible and to delight the *cognoscenti* in Wolfram's audience."

Sources: A. Hatto (WVE: P); N. Lacy (AE); E. H. Zeydel (PWVE).

La Cote Male Taile is an epithet for Breunor le Noire, not the single name Breunor as suggested in Book 7, Chapter 2 of Malory's *Le Morte*. In that passage where Sir Launcelot is berating Sir Kay, it should read, "Ye called Breunor *le Noire*, Sir Dinadan's brother, La Cote Male Taile, and that turned you to anger afterward." Breunor (no appositive) is a different character (an evil knight), but Breunor le Noire is a respectable individual knighted by King Arthur himself.

La Cote Male Taile is the highlighted character in Malory, Book 9, Chapters 1 through 10. La Cote wants to be knighted to avenge his father, which Arthur promises to do the following day. While Arthur and his troupe are chasing hart the next morning, La Cote Male Taile proves his valor by saving Queen Guinevere from an escaped, rampaging lion. When Arthur returns, he immediately dubs the brave lad as a knight. La Cote Male Taile begins a series of adventures accompanied by Damosel Maledisant, who continually rebukes him until the end of his quest, after he avenges his father's death.

See also BREUNOR LE NOIRE and BREUNOR.
Source: T. Malory (LMD'A).

Lady of the Lake. As with so many other enigmas in Arthuriana, the Lady of the Lake is steeped in folklore on the continent (specifically in Broceliande, "The Enchanted Forest") and in Britain. VIVIANE and NIMUË have been endowed with the epithet "Lady of the Lake," but at least one other nameless lady has been given that title.

In Malory's *Le Morte*, Book 1 Chapter 25, after MERLIN takes the wounded ARTHUR to a hermit, Arthur reminds Merlin that he has no sword. They ride to a lake, and in the middle of it is an arm clothed in white samite, holding a sword in the hand. When a damosel appears on the water, Merlin explains she is Lady of the Lake, and within the lake is a rock castle. As they approach, Arthur addresses her.

"Damosel," said Arthur, "what sword is that, that yonder the arm holdeth above the water? I would it were mine, for I have no sword."

"Sir Arthur, king," said the damosel, "that sword is mine, and if ye will give me a gift when I ask it you, ye shall have it."

"By my faith," said Arthur, "I will give you what gift ye will ask."

"Well!" said the damosel, "Go into yonder barge, and row yourself to the sword, and take it and the scabbard with you, and I will ask my gift when I see my time."

In *Medieval Romances*, "The Book of Balin, Section III" narrates "How the Lady of the Lake demanded the knight's head that had won the sword, or the maiden's head." The story begins when the Lady of the Lake rode into Arthur's court and asked of the king a gift that he promised her because she had given him Excalibur. Arthur cannot remember the pledge, so the damsel asks for the head of Balin, who had slain

Excalibur is returned to the mere. When Arthur is mortally wounded, he commands Bedivere to return the sword to Lady of the Lake, but Bedivere disobeys twice before he finally casts Excalibur into the lake, where an arm clothed in samite catches it and disappears beneath the water. Illustration by Aubrey Beardsley.

her brother. At that point, Balin, who was ready to leave on a quest, recognized the lady as his mother's murderer. He strides up to her and bellows, "Evil be you found; ye would have my head, and therefore you shall lose yours." And with his sword he smote off her head before King Arthur. It is Merlin who later tells Arthur that the damosel who was murdered was the "False Lady of the Lake."

Sources: B. Harris (CDAB); R. Loomis/L. Loomis (MR); T. Malory (LMD'A).

Lamorak. *see* GAHERIS.

THE LADY OF THE LAKE TELLETH ARTHVR OF THE SWORD EXCALIBVR

The Lady of the Lake tells Arthur of the sword Excalibur. When Arthur's first sword breaks, Merlin leads him to a new one. The two go out onto a lake where the Lady appears, and when she hands him Excalibur, she admonishes him that when Arthur has no more use for it, he must return it. Illustration by Aubrey Beardsley.

Lancelot. In "Celtic Elements in Arthurian Romance: A General Survey," Rachel Bromwich emphatically states, "I would certainly not go so far, for instance, as to claim any Celtic antecedent for the name and character of Lancelot — still less for that of his son Galahad. These are French creations, and they originated entirely in the post–Celtic development of the Romances."

C. Scott Littleton and Linda Malcor devote a chapter in their text, *From Scythia to Camelot*, to "Lancelot and the 'Alan of Lot.'" Malcor supports the claim that Lancelot de Lac first appears in Breton stories and legends, initially introduced as a knight in Arthur's court but with none of his adventures being recorded. She states, "Prior to these lays of the mid–twelfth century Lancelot, as a name, simply does not exist in surviving texts," adding in a footnote that, according to

In Breton and Briton legends, Meleagant (Melwas) is a wicked son of King Bagedmagus, sometimes portrayed as Guinevere's half-brother. He abducts Queen Guinevere and imprisons her in his castle at Trécesson, where Sir Kay, who had been entrusted to protect the queen, lay wounded. Lancelot discovers where she is being held captive and attempts to rescue her by somehow entering through a barred window. Guinevere pleads with him to break in and make love to her, and Lancelot finally succeeds, cutting his hand in the process. When Meleagant comes into the room the next morning, he reports to his father what has transpired, and a joust is set up. It's not too difficult to guess who won.

The rescue of Guinevere by Lancelot. Illustration by William Hatherell.

Ernst Soudek, Lancelot is named in Chrétien's "Erec and Cligés," and Lancelot's name is of Germanic origin even though his character takes on the role of a Breton knight.

According to D.D.R. Owen, Lancelot makes his first appearance in Chrétien de Troyes's "The Knight of the Cart" around 1177. Chrétien is allegedly the first to associate Lancelot with Arthurian material, claiming in his prologue that a segment of "The Knight of the Cart" was given to him by the Countess Marie. If this is fact, then she probably conveyed to him the popular Celtic abduction story [similar to the abduction story of Guinevere by Melwas (Meleagant)]. When Lancelot appears in Chrétien's work, he becomes Guinevere's heroic lover.

Chrétien did not complete the Lancelot tale; there were continuations of it, one supplied by a colleague, Godefroi de Leigni. Ulrich von Zatzihoven translated "The Knight of the Cart" into German sometime between 1194 and 1205.

William Kibler asserts that the manuscripts of Chrétien's work all date from at least a generation after the time he composed them. The "Knight of the Cart" was left unfinished, perhaps because Chrétien was dissatisfied with the material, which may have been imposed on him by his patroness Marie de Champagne. There are those, though their ranks are diminishing, who hold that the Welsh tales are all corrupt and abbreviated versions of Chrétien's work.

In Malory's tale, Lancelot performs another rescue when Guinevere is to be burned at the stake.

Sources: R. Bromwich (CEAR: LAMA); W. Kibler (CDT: AR); C. Littleton/L. Malcor (FSTC); D. Owen (CDT: AR).

Lawman. *see* LAYAMON.

Layamon, Lawman (*floruit* 1180–1210; *AE* 1189–1200 / *lifespan* 1165–1225). What little is known about Layamon's life is included in the verses of his text. An Anglo-Saxon, he was the son of Leovenath, and lived in Earnley (recorded as Ernlege in the *Cartularium saxonicum*, now Arley, Worcestershire) on the banks of the River Severn. In the opening verses, he writes that he traveled widely and had read several books, including Saint BEDE's book, segments of a book written in Latin by Saints Albin and Augustine, and a book written by WACE, a French cleric. Likewise, he then explains the personal manner he uses to peruse a text, as follows:

Layamon laid these books out, and he
  turned the leaves;
With love he searched them, the Lord be
  to him gracious.
He took feathers in his fingers, and he
  composed on parchment;
And these three books he condensed into
  one.

Layamon's chronicle survives in two manuscripts, B.L. Cotton Caligula A.ix, and B.L. Cotton Otho C. xiii, written between 1250 and 1350.

Henry Cecil Wyld highly praises Layamon's work: "The intensity of feeling, the wealth of imagery, the tender humanity, the love of nature, the chivalrous and romantic spirit, which distinguish the poetry of Layamon would give him a high place among the English poets of any age."

Layamon's *Brut* cannot be characterized as a translation of Wace's *Roman de Brut* even though he (Layamon) records events, people, and places which were directly extracted from works by Wace. Layamon's episodes are laden with elaborate, lengthy details, and when he borrows lines from Wace, he has the proclivity to extend to several pages while adding a tinge of Welsh influence or passages about Arthur's journey to the Isle of Avalon.

As one example, whereby Wace is credited for the introduction of the Round Table, Layamon is the one who embellished it with details. In Layamon's tale, Arthur journeys to Cornwall, where he meets a craftsman who made for him a most skillful board (table):

That there may sit at it sixteen hundred
  and more,
All in succession, that none may sit at the
  end,
But without and within, man beside man.

Whenever thou wilt ride, with thee thou
  mayst take it,
And set it up where thou wilt after thine
  own will;
And thou needest never dread throughout
  the wide world
That ever any proud knight at thy board
  stir a fight;
For there shall the high be equal to the
  low.

Layamon writes that Arthur extols this table at length, describing all the attributes of a great knight, and Arthur's "regeneration motif" is also attributed to Layamon.

See also GEOFFREY OF MONMOUTH, CHRÉTIEN DE TROYES, and WACE.

Sources: R. Brengle (A: KOB); N. Lacy (AE); R. Loomis/R. Willard (MEV&P); E. Mason (AC:W&L); H. Wyld (LEP).

Leland, John (Leyland) (*lifespan EB* 1506–1552; *AE* circa 1503–1552). John Leland, whose active life coincided almost exactly with the reign of Henry VIII, developed an interest in ancient documents and antiquarian studies, receiving a royal commission "to make a search after England's Antiquities, and peruse the Libraries of all Cathedrals, Abbeys, Priories, Colleges, etc. as also all places wherein Records, Writings and secrets of Antiquity were reposed."

Most significantly, Leland is cited for two Arthurian mainstays: Arthur's burial site and Arthur's court, although he does mention in his *Itinirarium* the Pomparles Bridge "wher men fable that Arture cast his swerd" and a Round Table which he had seen in Wales at Llansannan, a small village three miles northeast of Vortigern's fort known as Gwytherin. Steve Blake and Scott Lloyd claim that John Leland came upon a record and copied notes which were originally penned by a certain Melkin. Allegedly, Melkin had written a book entitled *De Arthurii Mensa Rotunda* (*Of Arthur's Round Table*), a manuscript which evidently did not survive the Dissolution and didn't come to Leland's attention prior to compiling his own work. Even though Melkin's book seems to be verified by John Bale, John Pits, Capgrave, and Hardyng, and even though Geoffrey Ashe and James Carley make reference to Melkin (which might be an epithet for MEL-

WAS or Mailcunus), there's no further evidence which throws light upon John Leland's Arthurian observations.

Leland's details about Arthur's exhumation at Glastonbury Abbey are more explicit. In his *Assertio* of 1544, he claimed that the inscription on the leaden cross was "*Hic iacet sepultus inclytus rex Arturius in insula Avallonis*," translated as "Here lies buried the famous king Arthur in the isle of Avalon." Leslie Alcock notes that Leland's inscription is "stripped of the reference to Guinevere for which GIRALDUS CAMBRENSIS is the only authority." Alcock provides two more pieces of information about the Glastonbury cross: one, Leland purportedly saw the cross about 1542, and second, the cross was allegedly traced into the "eighteenth century, when apparently it was in Wells." R.F. Treharne writes that Leland supposedly handled the cross and estimated its size as about a foot. Thereafter the cross disappears.

Leland's version of King Arthur's exhumation differs from RALPH OF COGGESHALL'S on two counts — the spelling of "inclytus," and the location of the word "sepultus" in the inscription. Alcock is very forgiving of these minor variations, as one should be, explaining that Richard Robinson published an English translation of John Leland, and although he had Leland's version in front of him, he differed from it at four points. It is very easy and not at all uncommon to make minor errors in transcription.

E.K. Chambers makes one last comment about Leland seeing Arthur's gravesite in front of the high altar. When Leland visited Abbot Whiting between 1534 and 1539, he wrote that "the tomb was of black marble. There were two lions at each end, and an image of the king at the foot; and there were epitaphs bearing the name of Abbot Henry, which is here given as Henricus Swansey." Chambers adds that Leland allegedly saw and handled the leaden cross which lay upon the tomb.

Leslie Alcock remains the significant focus about the subject of Camelot, since he was one of the major archaeologists on the Camelot Committee which supervised the excavations at the hillfort near South Cadbury (pictured in the distance at the base of the hillfort) between 1966 and 1970. The publication of that material came out in Alcock's *Was This Camelot?* Even at the onset of this text, Alcock warns, "It is as well to say outright that Camelot has no historical authenticity: it is a place that never was. The basis for this assertion is that it is not mentioned in the earliest traditions or earliest evidence about Arthur."

In addition to Leland's commentary on Arthur's interment and exhumation at Glastonbury, his itinerary impelled him to visit a hillfort near South Cadbury, only twelve miles to the southeast of Glastonbury. Whether he had heard tales that this fortress was the court of King Arthur or whether he had deduced this because of the nearness of West Camel, Queen Camel, and the River Cam is uncertain, although the former is most likely.

Sources: L. Alcock (WTC); S. Blake/S. Lloyd (KTA); J. Chandler (JL: TTE); (COL-E); L. Smith (IOJL).

Leo I (Emperor). Leo I was proclaimed Roman Emperor of the Eastern Empire in 457 C.E. by the powerful patrician Aspar, after the death of Marcian, and ruled until 474. In that same year, Majorian was recognized as Emperor of the West, but with the passage of Majorian in 467, Anthemius was sent to the West and became emperor.

The most noteworthy event which links itself to the Arthurian age was Leo's joint campaign with Anthemius against GAISERIC and his Vandals, who had conquered the northern coast of Africa, including Carthage. A powerful Roman force of allegedly over a thousand ships and 100,000 men attacked the combined tribes of Vandals and Alani. However, Anthemius had made the grave mistake of entrusting the campaign to his brother-in-law, Basiliscus. Basiliscus had incompetent military skills and was totally outmaneuvered by Gaiseric, and the entire imperial force was torched. This episode marked the rapid decline of the Western Empire. Anthemius became weak, and insurrections in Gaul continuously increased, causing irreparable cracks in the West's infrastructure.

In desperation, Anthemius solicited aid from the Briton High King from beyond Ocean, known in history only by his epithet RIOTHAMUS. Because Riothamus is undoubtedly linked to history through Emperor Leo I, Anthemius, and the Vandals, solving the enigma of Riothamus's identity becomes a factor in addressing the reality of a King Arthur in the fifth century.

To pursue this thread further, *see also* RIOTHAMUS, ARTHUR, and AMBROSIUS AURELIANUS.

Sources: G. Ashe (DKA); E. Duckett (MPFE&W); A. Ferrill (FOTRE); A. Griscom (HRBGM); M. Hadas (HOR); N. Lacy (AE); L. Thorpe (GM: HKB).

Leo I (Pope). Pope Leo, also know at Saint Leo I the Great, flourished as the head of the Roman Catholic Church from September 29, 440 C.E., to November 10, 461 C.E. The year and place of his birth are unknown, but his death date matches the end of his pontification as pope. During his time in office, the Western Roman Empire was in rapid decline. Prior to his floruit, Rome had been plundered in 410 C.E. by ALARIC the Visigoth, and then once again Rome was captured in 455 C.E. by GAISERIC and the Vandals when Leo was Pope.

During his era, he vigorously opposed the Pelagian sect both on the continent and in Britain, and he had direct influence upon Valentinian III. Other Arthurian contemporaries were GALLA PLACIDIA (mother of VALENTINIAN III), Magister AËTIUS (Military General under Galla Placidia), and Attila the Hun. Near the end of his papacy, Leo had the misfortune of seeing the Western Empire crumble because of four disastrous happenings: the murder of Aëtius ("the last Roman soldier") at the hands of Emperor Valentinian III, the death of Valentinian III, the Vandals under the leadership of Gaiseric sacking Rome, and the disintegration of Roman power in Gaul.

One very important legacy left by Pope Leo was his establishment of the pivotal point in chronological calibration. The *Annales Cambriae* at Year 453 gives notice that "Easter is altered on the Lord's Day by Pope Leo, Bishop of Rome." This is the date of C.E. 455 as proposed by Leslie Alcock.

John Morris writes of Pope Leo, "The Annals record that Patrick was 'approved' by pope Leo Great, who ruled from 440 to 467." Morris's technique of citations is, to say the least, disquieting, because nowhere does he indicate which "annals" he is writing about. To further compound the problem, Morris lists Leo's papacy as 440 to 467 instead of 440 to 461, although he corrects his oversight later. There is no historical Roman record of Pope Leo ever having visited Britain, and if Morris is suggesting that the "approval was via correspondence," there is no evidence of it being properly documented.

On the other hand, Geoffrey Ashe, in *The Discovery of Arthur,* offers interesting tidbits about Leo the Great. He writes, "The Vandals sacked the city [Rome] as the Goths had in 410, if not quite so ruinously, thanks to a plea from Pope Leo." The episode is detailed by Eleanor Shipley Duckett in *Medieval Portraits from East and West*: "Gaiseric was soon within sight of Rome, left undefended by its guards. Outside the gates, as he was about to enter, he came face to face with Pope Leo the First. Again a Pope had come to plead with a barbarian king. Like Attila, Gaiseric could not but listen; he gave his royal word not to set fire to the city, not to murder its men. On the third day following, he entered Rome."

Yet for fourteen days Rome was robbed and pillaged; when Gaiseric finally ordered his soldiers to the ships, they bore with them captives without number, treasure without end. Among the captives were the Empress Licinia Eudoxia herself and her two daughters, Eudocia and Placidia, together with Gaudentius, son of Aëtius, the murdered commander-in-chief.

Duckett's Gaiseric account is much more severe than Ashe's terse notice of 410. Alaric only remained three days when he sacked Rome, and the Visigoth took only three hostages.

In Ashe's second citation about Leo, he perhaps answers the question which John Morris failed to quote. Ashe is writing about Alberic's placing King Arthur's reign in the 460s and clarifies the claim about Arthur's reign by adding, "Nor does [Alberic] stand alone. In another chronicle, the *Salzburg Annals,* someone a little later than Alberic has inserted an Arthurian reference. The main entry for the year 461 notes the death of Pope Leo the Great ... [a]nd after it is an addition: 'At this time Arthur, of whom many stories are told, reigned in Britain.'"

Whether or not it is safe to assume that John Morris might perhaps have discovered the information about Saint Patrick (and Pope Leo) in the *Salzburg Annals* remains unclear.

Sources: L. Alcock (AB), G. Ashe (DKA), R. Collingwood (RB&ES); E. Duckett (MPFE& W), A. Griscom (HRBGM); M. Hadas (HOR); J. Morris (AOA/BH).

Leodegrance, Leodegraunce, Leodegan. Leodegan is the name used for Leodegrance in *The Arthurian Handbook* by Norris Lacy and Geoffrey Ashe, where he is listed as the father of GUINEVERE and the False Guinevere (GUINEVERE, FALSE). He allegedly gave the Round Table to Arthur as a wedding present. Extracting material from the Vulgate *Merlin,* Richard Barber makes a reference to Leodegrance when Arthur offers his services to this king who is being besieged by King Ryence of North Wales. Merlin helps Arthur succeed in defending Leodegrance's kingdom, and for the first time Arthur meets Guinevere, who has an illegitimate half-sister. After the true Guinevere and he marry, Arthur and Leodegrance become allies, binding Cameliard and Camelot.

In Malory's *Le Morte D'Arthur,* Leodegrance makes two brief appearances in Books 1 and 3. In Book 1, King Rience of North Wales makes war on King Leodegrance, which makes Arthur angry because "he loved Leodegrance well and hated King Rience." Joining Arthur, King Ban and King Bors make war on King Rience, and within six days, King Rience is defeated. Arthur meets Guenever of Camelerd, and forever after Arthur loves her, "as it telleth in the book." Book 3 reiterates Arthur's marriage to Guenever with Leodegrance's approval.

See also GOGYRFAN and Malory's Index.

Sources: R. Barber (AOA); N. Lacy/G. Ashe (AH); T. Malory (LMD'A).

Lhuyd, Edward, Edward Lhwyd, Llhwyd, Llwyd (1660–1709). According to historian John Davies, "Edward Lhuyd was the first Welshman to train himself in the experimental ideas of the new science and the first to place Welsh studies on a firm foundation. He visited all the countries where Celtic languages were spoken and anaylsed the linguistic links between them; he offered considered theories concerning the monuments of his country and through a vast correspondence collected an abundance of material relating to the customs and traditions of the Welsh. In addition, he was an expert geologist and botanist and won recognition as 'the finest naturalist now in Europe.' He was unable to complete his work (he died in his forty-ninth year) and only a tiny proportion of his writings was published."

Lhuyd's works are of interest to historical Arthurian enthusiasts because he was the individual who took the responsibility to translate Welsh documents and historic monuments before the ravages of time had destroyed the inscriptions on these precious relics. He contributed to the completion of the *Britannia* by WILLIAM CAMDEN in the hope of encouraging support for his own projects. He completed only a portion of the *Archaeologia Britannica* in 1707, two years before his death. He was the first to compare Germanic, Celtic, Greek, and Latin words.

One of Lhuyd's major contributions was translation of the inscription on Eliseg's Pillar, a ninth-century cross recording the ancestry of the kings of Powys, the lower portion which is still standing a quarter of a mile north of the Valle Crucis Abbey.

Jeremy K. Knight, under the patronage of Cadw, provides a brief history and description of the pillar:

> The cross was thrown down during the Civil War and lay in two broken pieces when the inscription was recorded by the scholar Edward Llwyd in 1696. The upper part of the shaft was re-erected in its original socket in 1779, as is recorded in a Latin inscription on its back. But the original inscription, already partly illegible in Llwyd's day, is now so badly weathered as to be only visible in good light. We have to rely on Llwyd for its text, though parts can be checked against the original and confirm his accuracy.

As Leslie Alcock stresses, inscribed stones are absolutely essential keys in interpreting the early historical records of the island; otherwise the history becomes distorted beyond recognition. These inscribed and carved stones are normally described as simply "early Christian monuments," but Alcock categorizes them into three broad groups, only one of which is of interest to Arthurian scholars who focus upon Arthur's possible historical origins. Those stones are in Group I dating to the fifth, sixth, and seventh centuries. Alcock writes that there are nearly two hundred monuments in Group I, then goes one step fur-

ther and avers that "a handful of early examples has led us to postulate of Group I stones ... their overwhelming distribution pattern is away from the lowland heart of Roman Britain, and lies instead in the Irish Sea zone."

Eliseg's Pillar, which falls into that category, indicates that VORTIMER and VORTIGERN were active in the region. Lhuyd's translation is as follows, with the obscure fragments in parentheses.

1. Cyngen son of Cadell, Cadell son of Brochwel, Brochwel son of ELISEG, Eliseg son of Gwylog.
2. Cyngen, therefore, the great-grandson of Eliseg, erected this stone in honour of his great-grandfather Eliseg.
3. It was Eliseg who united the inheritance of Powys (laid waste for nine years) out of the hand of the English with fire and sword.
4. Whosoever shall read this writing, let him give a blessing for the soul of Eliseg.
5. It was Cyngen (who united ... to his kingdom of Powys) ...
6. ...
7. (Cadell) the great (ruler) of Britain (son of) CATTIGIRN, Pasgen, (Maugan held) the monarchy (after him).
8. But BRYDW was the son of GWRTHEYRN, whom GERMANUS blessed and who was borne to him by Severa, the daughter of Maximus the king, who slew the King of the Romans.
9. Cynfarch painted this lettering at the command of his king, Cyngen.
10. The blessing of the Lord be upon Cyngen and upon all his household and upon the whole land of Powys until (the Day of Judgement. Amen).

The discussion which Knight includes is also important enough to repeat because it gives an overview of some of King Arthur's contemporaries of the fifth century. Additionally, those names occur in Welsh genealogies and histories; Brydw must be considered a Welsh name substituted for Vortimer, since the only son of Vortigern who is "blessed by Germanus" in other documents is known as "Vortimer." One needs only look at the variants of Edward Lhuyd's name to realize the disparity of proper names.

Sources: L. Alcock (AB); J. Davies (HOW); D. Evans/J. Knight (VCA); J. Morris (BH); A & W O'sullivan (EL: AB); F. Reno (HFAE).

Liathan, Liethan, Liethali, Bethan, Keianus, Ui Liathain. The Irishman Liathan and his sons encroached upon Dyfed, Gower, and Kidwelly until "they were driven out by CUNEDDA and his sons from all parts of Britain." Theodore Mommsen's addition in the *Historia Brittonum* adds that Liathan and his sons settled in the country of the Dementians, "where the city of Mynyw (Mineu, St Davids) is."

John Morris explains that in the term "Ui Liathain," Ui indicates a tribe, and Liathain is the clan, also adding that the *Historia Brittonum* records the clan was driven from Dementia by Cunedda. Other British and Irish manuscripts record that the Ui Liathain ruled in Dementia for another two generations.

Sources: L. Alcock (AB); P. Bartram (WG); J. Morris (AOA); J. Morris (HB); J. Stevenson (N: HB).

Libius Severus, Livius Severus, The Lucanian, Serpentius. One of the most obscure Roman emperors who ever ruled was Libius Severus during the sixth decade of the fifth century. Known also as Livius and Serpentius, he was a puppet emperor of the West, controlled by the Suebian Ricimer. Considered as a usurper, he was never legitimately recognized by Emperor LEO I of the East. When he was no longer useful, Ricimer eliminated him, one account claiming that he had been poisoned, and another recording that he died a natural death.

Source: R. Mathisen (OERE).

Llamrei. Arthur's horse is mentioned twice in the tale "How Culhwch Won Olwen" from *The Mabinogion*. In the quest for Culhwch's mate, Arthur and his mare Llamrei chase down a boar, which Arthur's dog Cavall kills. Later in the same episode, some of Arthur's men are injured by the Black Hag and are loaded onto Llamrei to be carried away.

Source: J. Gantz (TM).

Lleu is the name used in Llansepthan Manuscript 201 and refers to King Lot of Orkney and also the name Loth. Lleu's father is listed as Cynvarch in this same manuscript.

Source: S. Blake/S. Lloyd (P), Page 246, Appendix 2.

Loth of Lodonesia, Lot of Lothian and Orkney, Lot, Leudonus, Lleu ap Cynfarch. Steve Blake and Scott Lloyd are among the very few historians or scholars who refer to Lot. In *The Keys to Avalon*, under a segment titled "The Death of Uthyr Pendragon," they write that in Welsh, Lot is known as Lleu ap Cynfarch.

In GEOFFREY OF MONMOUTH's *History*, Loth is part of a "who's who" entanglement. At one point ANNA is listed as Arthur's sister and therefore the daughter of UTERPENDRAGON and YGERNA, and she marries Loth of Lodonesia. Later, Geoffrey writes that Anna is married to Budicus, King of Brittany, and still later he claims that Loth of Lodonesia marries Anna, but Anna is not ARTHUR's sister; she is AURELIUS AMBROSIUS's sister. This conflation between Arthur and Ambrosius continues throughout the Arthuriad, based on the assumption that the historic Arthur is of the fifth century in lieu of Ambrosius, who is the great king of all the kings of Britain during that century.

Loth is not a significant figure in Arthuriana, but is a major factor because of his offspring. According to Monmouth, Loth (Arthur's uncle/brother-in-law?) or (Ambrosius's uncle/brother-in-law?) and Anna have two sons, GAWAIN and MORDRED. However, in Malory's *le Morte*, Anna drops from view, Margawse displaces her as Lot's wife, and in Book 1, Chapter 2, the reader is told that Lot and Margawse have one son, Gawain. In Book 1, Chapter 19, King Lot sends his unnamed wife (evidently Margawse), along with her four sons — Gawain, Gaheris, Agravain, and Gareth — to spy on Arthur. In Chapter 8, King Lot with 500 knights, and other kings with large numbers, come to Arthur's coronation. Arthur is pleased, thinking that they had come out of great love for him, but the kings of the north (including Lot) rebuke him because "he was a beardless boy come from low blood." They laid siege to him, but with Arthur's army and Merlin's advice, the northern armies are repelled.

Later, several battles ensue, Lot is killed by Pellinor, and in revenge, Gawain kills Pellinor. Then there are more entanglements. As mentioned above, Book 1, Chapter 2, states that Margawse is Lot's wife. In Book 2, Chapter 9, King Arthur "lay by King Lot's wife and gat on her Mordred;" that is, King Arthur sired Margawse's son Mordred. In the very next chapter, Margawse and her four sons — Gawain, Agravain, Gaheris, and Gareth — attend the interment of several of Lot's knights. Also in attendance is "King Uriens, Sir Uwain's father, and Morgan le Fay his wife that was King Arthur's sister." Not only is Margawse conflated with Morgan le Fay, but in Book 1, Chapter 17, Merlin advises Arthur to put to death all children born on Mayday (Mordred's birth date) and Mordred is sent by King Lot's wife (Margawse), but previously four sons are listed for Lot and Margawse, and Mordred is not one of them.

Throughout the millennium, the persona of Loth has become garbled, very difficult (or perhaps impossible) to track through the existent manuscripts.

See also Morgana (MARGAWSE), Morgan le Fay, AND Mordred (MEDRAWT)

Sources: T. Malory (LMD'A).

Lucius Artorius Castus. The only Artorius ever documented as serving in Britain is the Roman soldier Lucius Artorius Castus who commanded the Sarmatian horsemen of Britain from roughly 175 C.E. through 177 C.E. and again from 181 C.E. through 186 C.E. Artorius Castus had a long and colorful career in the Roman military, and many of his adventures seem to have found their way into Arthurian tradition. His *gens nomen*, Artorius, has long been recognized as the potential source for the name Arthur/Arthyr as well as its many variants: Arturius, Arturus, Artus and so forth.

The Sarmatians whom Artorius Castus commanded looked very much like medieval knights. They rode horses, wore scale armor, fought with a lance-like weapon called a *kontus* as well as with long swords, and carried shields. They also fought beneath a dragon-head banner, something that may account for Arthur's association with the name PENDRAGON. Additionally, they ate at round tables, almost certainly worshiped a war god who was symbolized by planting a sword into the ground above a grave, and likely told stories of a magical golden cup that appeared at feasts and was kept by the bravest warrior as well as of a hero who died after his sword was thrown into a lake.

Although the Artorii as a family seemed to have been trained to kill Sarmatians, Castus was a rare exception who seemingly made a career out of commanding Sarmatian auxiliaries for the Romans. While Castus was in Britain, *ca.* 185, the Caledonii (the ancestors of the Picts) raided south of Hadrian's Wall and killed the governor of Britain at York. The pattern of destruction for this invasion stops roughly at a fort on a pass through the Pennines that leads to Ribchester, where the Sarmatians were stationed under Castus, who was promoted to the office of *dux*, the rank traditionally associated with Arthur in the *Historia Brittonum*. This suggests that it was Castus and his Sarmatian troops who drove the Caledonii back north of the Antonine Wall. It is possible that this campaign took the form of at least twelve battles, which roughly match the twelve battles associated with Arthur: one near the fort at Ribchester (cf. Bregouin), one near the mouth of the Ribble River (cf. Tribruit), four on the River Douglas (cf. Dubglas), one at York (cf. the "City of the Legions"), one at Binchester (cf. Castle Guinnion), one on the River Glen (cf. Glein), one in the Cat Coit Celidon, and one on the River Bassas.

The battle at Binchester would have required Castus to assume the rank of *dux* because he was leaving the territory officially controlled by his unit. The symbol of a *dux* was a brooch in the shape of a four-lobed rosette, the sign of the goddess Flora.

Castus's family supplied many priests and priestesses to the religion of Flora, and Castus himself put many repetitions of her rose on his tomb. During Castus's lifetime, Flora's religion was absorbed by the worship of the Virgin Mary, including the use of this particular rose. So at Binchester, for the first time, Castus would have worn the symbol of the Virgin Mary on his shoulder, something long associated with Arthur at the battle of Guinnion.

The final battle in the sequence given in the *Historia Brittonum*, Badon, was probably fought by AMBROSIUS AURELIANUS rather than by Arthur and attached to the battle list at a later date as tales of Arthur became more popular than tales of Ambrosius. GEOFFREY OF MONMOUTH, however, preserves another battle fought by Arthur, which may have originally belonged in this penultimate place on the battle list. This is the battle against the "Picts" at Dumbarton, which Arthur supposedly fought using attacks both on land and from the sea. Castus, the former commander of the Misenium fleet, may well have been the only Roman officer in Britain during the Caledonian invasion who had the training necessary to carry out such an ambitious battle plan. Whatever Castus and the Sarmatians did, though, the Caledonii did not give the Romans any trouble for several decades after the battle, which is consistent with tales about Arthur and the outcome of his battles.

Castus most likely had one final encounter with the Sarmatians of Britain after he left his post as their commander. About a decade later, in 197 C.E., Castus probably accompanied SEPTIMIUS SEVERUS to Gaul to fight a civil war against Albinus of Britain, who was using the Sarmatians among his troops. While all of Albinus's troops were slaughtered after his defeat, roughly half the Sarmatian unit appears to have survived. The Sarmatians were notorious for changing sides during battle, and it is quite possible that Castus, either during or after the first battle between Severus and Albinus, convinced at least half of the Sarmatian garrison to back Severus. Here, then, is the possible seed for stories of the civil war that splits the Round Table and results in the death of roughly half the knights.

Castus may have been mortally wounded in the final battle. His own account of his career, found on his tomb, ends just prior to the civil war. He apparently never returned to Dalamatia to report on the events, and he certainly held no further posts, either military or civil. Castus was born in Campania, Italy, not too far from a town called Avellinum, which may have been his mother's hometown. Avellinum, like Arthur's Avalon, had a strong association of women who performed magical healing and who were connected with water. If Castus did receive a serious injury in Severus's final battle, he could well have been trying to go back to his childhood home to be healed, something he could have done by boat, as Arthur is said to have done.

In the figure of Lucius Artorius Castus, then, we not only have the possible source of Arthur's name but also of many of the historical battles and other events associated with King Arthur. Later battles and events would have been added to Castus's tales in the oral tradition, a narrative cycle likely born at Ribchester that then spread to Wales (which the Sarmatians also helped to defend) as well as to the region of Hadrian's Wall. Some early insular poems describe heroes as "although he was no Arthur" or in other language that compares them to a figure in the past. Over time, tales of "someone like Arthur" doing something would become tales of Arthur doing something, and the cycle would grow. Eventually any number of heroes, real and imagined, contributed to the figure we know as King Arthur, but his humble beginnings are most likely found in the career of a resourceful Roman *dux* named Lucius Artorius Castus and the Sarmatian warriors who fought under his command.

(Graciously written and submitted by Dr. Linda Malcor. Dr. Malcor has also contributed several articles to *The Heroic Age* on the Internet.)

Sources: C. Scott Littleton/Linda Malcor (FSTC).

Lucius Domitius Aurelianus. Lucius Domitius Aurelianus enters the realm of Arthuriana as a probable ancestor of AMBROSIUS AURELIANUS, the individual who has been conflated with King ARTHUR of the fifth century. A partial rationale is the naming of Roman families through the use of *praenomen, nomen, agnomen* and *cognomen*. In the rolls of Roman emperors, Lucius Domitius is listed as Aurelian, who ruled from 270 until 275 during a time when the Roman Empire was on the edge of total collapse. Rival emperors preceded and succeeded Aurelian, making it almost impossible to reunite the empire.

To some extent he was able to quell the insurgents. In 274 he began fortifying Rome by constructing a wall which was named after him, but he then turned his attention to unifying religions, focusing upon the cult of the Unconquered Sun. He went to the extreme by having his subjects kissing his toe instead of his cheek. In 275 rumors spread that he was planning to execute that part of his army not loyal to the cult, and in fear a group of his officers assassinated him.

If there is a connection between Lucius Domitius and Ambrosius, Lucius would be Ambrosius's great-great-great grandfather.

Sources: J.R. Morris (EB-LDA); F. Reno (HKA).

Lucius Hiberius, Lucius, Lucerius. In Monmouth's *History of the Kings of Britain*, when Arthur fought in Gaul and then returned to Britain, Lucius Hiberius, a procurator of the Republic, sent a communiqué to Arthur, demanding that Arthur pay tribute to Rome for his tyrannical and criminal behavior on the continent. Arthur handed over the task of defending Britain to his nephew MORDRED and to his queen, GUINEVERE, then embarked from Southampton.

During the voyage across the channel, Arthur dreamed of a flying bear, growling so loudly that the shores shook. A dragon was flying from the west, his fiery eyes lighting up the countryside. A ferocious fight ensued with the dragon continuously attacking his adversary until, scorched, the bear fell to the ground. Those who were with Arthur interpreted the dream for him: he was the dragon, and the bear was a giant opponent. The dragon would be victorious.

Arthur's army pitched camp at Barfleur to await the arrival of the other kings of the islands. In the interim, news arrived that a monstrous giant had kidnapped Helena, the niece of Duke Hoel, and taken her to Mont-Saint-Helen. Arthur, KAY and BEDIVERE slew the giant, but unfortunately not before Helena died. This tale is also told in the *Tysilio*.

After this episode, both armies — Arthur's totaling about 183,000 men and Lucius' numbering to 400,160, according to Monmouth's calculation — established camps across the river from each other. Arthur sent three messengers (Boso, Gerin, and GAWAIN) to tell Lucius to either withdraw from Gaul or fight for the province the next day. In the heat of the moment, Gawain killed Gaius Quintillianus, Lucius's nephew, thus starting the war between the two super-powers.

The battle raged for days. "Many thousands of the Romans were killed. In the end Lucius himself, their general, was brought to bay in the midst of his troops. He fell dead, pierced through by an unknown hand." On Arthur's side many were killed, among them Hyreglas, Leodegarius, Cursalem, Guallac, and Urbgennis. Slain also were Bedivere and Kay. The body of Lucius was sent to Rome with a message that no tribute would be sent by Britain.

Monmouth's episode about Lucius and his battle with Arthur is an anomaly, since Arthur is typically portrayed as having Roman heritage and being an ally with Rome, not an adversary. Geoffrey Ashe is the only researcher who in several of his books touches upon this particular Lucius. In *The Discovery of King Arthur*, Ashe writes, "Lucius, Arthur's chief opponent, is a strange person. In the first campaign he is not mentioned; in the second his status is unclear. His title, "procurator," was given to deputies of the Emperor in minor provinces. That makes him sound less than absolute, and, in fact, the Senate in Rome has power to give him orders. Later Geoffrey [of Monmouth] calls him an Emperor a few times."

Ashe, however, concludes that no such emperor as Lucius ever existed, and then theorizes that Monmouth might well have known of the chronicle by Sigebert of Gembloux and an individual in that work who was known as Lucerius. Ashe then deduces that the Lucius in Monmouth could have been the Lucerius in Sigebert, adding that "nothing is historical here, only the names and the offices held. But the way all three coincide, within a small span of time, is striking."

In *The Kings and Queens of Early Britain*, Ashe comments on Lucius's title, which he thinks odd because there was a period when western Europe was still officially Roman, but its "'emperors' had been reduced to a point where they scarcely counted as such." Once again, in *Mythology of the British Isles*, Ashe suggest that Lucius is confused with Lucerius by Geoffrey of Monmouth. He adds, however, that THOMAS MALORY "adopts and improves the campaign against Lucius" and "transfers it to an earlier phase." In his article "Origins of the Arthurian Legends," Ashe reiterates that "there was never a Lucius," and repeats what might be a misinterpreted connection between the name Lucius and Lucerius for the years 469–470.

The common criticism, therefore, is that the figure of Lucius in Monmouth's work is just another instance in a series of the author's imagination distorting history. However, a precise reporting of events of that era by R.W. Mathisen, independent of an attempt to verify that Arthur fought a major war against a Western Roman emperor, offers yet another speculation that Monmouth was basically accurate in copying such a circumstance.

Writing of that same era — 460 to 470 C.E — Edward Gibbon, in *The Decline and Fall of the Roman Empire*, discourages a reader from wasting time adding details to fill the void after the death of Majorian. He gives this bare-bones report:

> At Ricimer's command [Ricimer being a Suebian chieftain who became a powerful patrician and "kingmaker" of the Western Empire] the obsequious senate of Rome bestowed the Imperial title on Libius Severus, who ascended the throne of the West without emerging from the obscurity of a private condition. History has scarcely deigned to notice his birth, his elevation, his character, or his death. Severus expired as soon as his life became inconvenient to his patron [Ricimer]; and it would be useless to discriminate his nominal reign in the vacant interval of six years between the death of Majorian and the elevation of Anthemius.

This is precisely the period of time Geoffrey of Monmouth writes about Arthur's war against Lucius.

Arther Ferrill, in *The Fall of the Roman Empire,* provides even fewer details, stating that "Ricimer appointed a new emperor, Libius Severus (461-5), an Italian who was never recognized by Leo I in the East." Worse still — but not

a transgression because her emphasis was upon other emperors — Eleanor Duckett, in *Medieval Portraits from East and West*, fails to provide Severus's first name: "In 465 Severus dies; in his *Chronicles* Cassiodorus tells of a rumor that Ricimer killed him by poison."

Ralph Mathisen supplies enough details about Libius Severus to draw a sensible inference about whom Monmouth's Lucius might be. In an abbreviated list:

1. Little is known of the origins of the emperor Libius Severus (sometimes, apparently incorrectly, referred to as Livius Severus). He was described in the *Gallic Chronicle of 511* and the *Chronicle* of Cassiodorus as a Lucanian, and ... had the cognomen ("nickname") "Serpentius." As the fourth of the so-called "shadow" or "puppet" western emperors, Severus came to power at a time when the western empire was beset by a multitude of problems.

2. Eventually, on 19 November 461, ... Libius Severus was proclaimed emperor at Ravenna at Ricimer's instigation. Theophanes (5955 s.a. 455) reported, "In this year Majorian was killed by Ricimer at Tortona, and on the *nones* of July Severus, nicknamed "Serpentius," was raised to the culmination of rule." The *Gallic Chronicle of 511* noted, "Severus, from Lucania, was raised to the rank of emperor and at the same time consul," although Severus's consulate was in fact not until 462. And Hydatius adds, "Severus was named emperor by the Senate at Rome in the fifth year of the emperor Leo" (*Chron.* 211).

3. Subsequently, Ricimer acted as the "power behind the throne" and assumed a role unequalled by previous generals.

4. Severus was never recognized by the eastern emperor Leo (457–474), and thus would have been viewed in the east as a usurper; the eastern chronicler Marcellinus, for example, asserted that Severus had "appropriated" Majorian's position, and referred to him as one "who had snatched the rule of the west" ("*qui Occidentis arripuit principatum*": s.a. 465), and

Jordanes noted that after the death of Majorian, "Severus invaded his place without the permission of the emperor Leo" ("*locoque eius sine principis iussu Leonis Severainus invasit*": *Romana* 336). By this time, moreover, the direct authority of the western Roman emperor was limited primarily to Italy.

5. Britain, Spain, and Africa had been lost, and Severus was faced by a revolt in Gaul, where an old ally of Majorian, the Master of Soldiers Aegidius, refused to acknowledge him. In 462, in a successful effort to gain the support of the Visigoths against Aegidius, Severus turned over to them the city of Narbonne, having found an ally in Aegidius's rival, Count Agrippinus.... Aegidius was killed in 465, and what was left of Roman authority in Gaul was shakily restored.

6. The carrying out of one [Beorgor's death] of the few actions known to have occurred during Severus' reign was, typically, attributed to Ricimer.

7. Severus's reign also saw renewed raids upon the coast of Italy by the Vandals, whose king Gaiseric still hoped that Olybrius would become western emperor.... It is in this context that one finds Severus's only attested diplomatic contact with the eastern court, as reported by Priscus.... [T]he imperial efforts to restrain the Vandals came to naught, and the Vandals continued to raid the Italian coast. It was only in 467, when their raids extended to the Peloponnesus, that the eastern emperor stepped in and named Anthemius as western emperor.

8. Severus ruled just about four years (pace Jordanes, Getica 236, who gives him only three years: "tertio anno imperii sui Romae obiit"), and died in Rome in the fall of 465. The Fasti vindobonenses priores, which give his date of death as 15 August, seem to be in error given that one of Severus's laws was issued on 25 September, although it might be possible that the law was issued posthumously. In the sixth century, it was said that he had been poisoned by Ricimer, ... but Sidonius Apollinaris, a much more contemporary source, asserted in 468 that he died a natural death.... PLRE II, p.1005, suggests a date of death of 14 November, but provides no evidence or justification for it.

9. The historian Priscus did not even deign to mention Severus's name, merely commenting, "There were, moreover, still other emperors in the west, but although I know their names well, I shall make no mention of them whatsoever. For it so fell out that they lived only a short time after attaining the office, and as a result of this accomplished nothing worthy of mention...." Severus is eminently deserving of his place among the "shadow" emperors.

Each reader individually must decide whether the account of Livius/Libius/the Lucanian Severus is similar enough to the jigsaw pieces of Monmouth's Lucius to be a match. Does this comparison indeed address Arthur's battle against Lucius, the Emperor of Gaul, who is also labeled by Monmouth as Procurator of the Roman Republic?

Sources: G. Ashe (DKA/K&QEB/MBI/OAL); E. Duckett (MPE&W); E. Gibbon (D&FRE); R. Mathisen (OERE); P. Roberts (COKB); L. Thorpe (GM: HKB).

Mabon, Mabuz, Mabonagrain. Mabon is one of Arthur's comrades. Peter Ellis describes him as a member of the cult Maponos, the Divine Youth, "which existed among the pre–Christian Celts ... in the north of Britain and in Gaul."

Source: P. Ellis (DOCM).

Maelgwn, Maglocunus Map Catgolaun Lauhir, Mailconum. Even though scholars agree that Maglocunus map Catgolaun Lauhir is entrenched in Welsh history also as Maelgwn, it's important to separate fact from fiction as it is given in the short notice of the *Annales Cambriae*. The entry states, "A great death in which Maelgwn, king of Gwynedd died. Thus they say 'The long sleep of Maelgwn in the court of Rhos.' Then there was yellow plague."

The date given is the first item to come under scrutiny. The *Annales Cambriae* entry is derived from an antecedent script, the Irish Annals, where the date is listed as 548, a slight discrepancy which is inconsequential. That date is verifiable because of "mortalitas magna," or the "Great Death." Thomas O'Sullivan gives an adequate clarification of the generic definition for the term *plague*, attached to an equally detailed explanation, which is normally associated with the Bubonic one, but does not necessarily have to be associated with the Maelgwn entry. Even if "plague" were used in its specific sense of the Bubonic plague, the date would still be acceptable. The Bubonic plague of the Justinian reign began in the East around 542, and assuming approximately five years for the disease to spread throughout Europe and across the Channel, the year 547 or 548 is not an unreasonable assumption.

That both the name Maelgwn and the "great death" appear twice in the same terse passage suggests that the original entry was interpolated. It is likely that the first sentence was the original entry because it supplies all necessary information. The second sentence simply offers the euphemism "long sleep" for "death," and then explicitly inserts the cantref Rhos in the kingdom of Gwynedd. The further addition of "yellow plague" creates confusion rather than clarification. Rather than *equate* "great death" and "yellow plague," the last sentence suggests that there were two separate diseases during the year — the first, the "great death," which was followed by the "yellow plague."

Thomas O'Sullivan suggests that other records should verify which epidemic killed Maelgwn, in order to confirm the accuracy of the king's death-year. Some accounts in the Welsh vernacular relate that Taliesin was deprived of certain property and cursed Maelgwn and all his possessions, whereupon "Vad Velen came to Rhos, and whoever witnessed it became doomed to certain death. Maelgwn saw the Vad Velen through the keyhole in the Rhos church, and died in consequence." However, since there is evidence that this material passed through unreliable hands, it cannot be used as corroborative evidence.

Fortunately there are other sources that provide verifiable evidence, such as the *Saints' Lives*.

These manuscripts contain reliable information not only because the scribes' main interest lay in precise recording of contemporary and previous events, but also because privileged access to church data and church methods created more reliable reckonings. O'Sullivan cites the Evans-Rhys edition of the *De vita sancti Teiliavi*: "Pestis autem illa flava vocabatur, eo quod flavos et exangues efficiebat universos quos persequebatur ... Traxit enim Mailconum regem Guenedotiae, delevit et patriam suam." This passage basically describes the universal (universos) outbreak (exangues) of the affliction (persequebatur) called the Yellow Pestilence (pestis flava). Maelgwn, the King of Gwynedd, is delivered to our Father on High by this epidemic. Gildas Badonicus refers to this king of northwestern Wales as "the dragon of the island," which Leslie Alcock conjectures was an emblem borne by later Welsh kings and "perhaps adopted at this time, whence ultimately the Red Dragon of Wales."

Whether or not Gildas's severe castigation of this king is accurate cannot be verified. The accounts of Maelgwn in the *Saints' Lives* tend to confirm some of the contentions and are accepted since Gildas himself had ties to Gwynedd. Yet Gildas's aspersions might be tainted by his overzealous religious base.

Sources: G. Ashe [Ed] (QFAB); R. Castleden (KA: TBL); N. Chadwick (CB); J. Davies (HOW); J. Morris (AOA); T. O'sullivan (DEG: A&D); F. Reno (HKA/HFAE).

Maglocunus map Catgolaun Lauhir, Mailcus, Mailcunus, Maelgwn. The figure of Maglocunus, son of Catgolaun Lauhir, is well-entrenched in British history. GILDAS BADONICUS, who was his contemporary, depicts him as the most heinous of tyrants in post–Roman Britain. Of the five tyrants whom Gildas castigated, he writes only one section about three of the tyrants, two sections about one, but four detailed sections about Maglocunus. In Gildas's words, Maglocunus's crimes can be outlined as

1. "wallowing like a fool in the ancient ink of your crimes, like a man drunk on wine pressed from the vine of the Sodomites;"

2. "in the first years of your youth using sword and spear and flame in the cruel

despatch of the king your uncle and nearly his bravest soldiers;"

3. "deceiving everyone by pretending to convert to a godly life;"
4. "returning to your wickedness like some sick dog returning to his disgusting vomit;"
5. "spurning your wife and seeking solace with the wife of your brother's son, followed by killing both your brother's son and your own wife;"
6. "turning a deaf ear to Christ, prophets, and neighbors, and living in wickedness with no signs of repentance for your sins."

Because Gildas and Maglocunus were living contemporaries, Gildas knew nothing of Maglocunus's death, which was recorded later in the *Annales Cambriae*. That manuscript records the wicked king's death: "547 A year of great death in which Maelgwn, king of Gwynedd died. †Thus they say 'The long sleep of Maelgwn in the court of Rhos.' Then was the yellow plague.†"

Maglocunus (recorded by Gildas Badonicus as MAELGWN) is of importance to Arthuriana for several reasons. One is that the date recorded by the *Annales Cambriae* gives a clue of when CUNEDDA, Maglocunus's ancestor, might have migrated from the North (Manau Gododdin). Another is that MAGLOCUNUS MAP CLUTOR would also have been one of Maelgwn's ancestors, living during the era of VITALINUS and AMBROSIUS AURELIANUS. A third is that Maglocunus provides a specific milieu of where certain events occurred; that is, Gwynedd in Wales.

See also MELWAS and Appendix B.
Source: M. Winterbottom (G: ROB&OW).

Maglocunus map Clutor is one of only two figures appearing in a Welsh context who can be even remotely connected with Arthuriana. At St. Brynach's Church in Nevern on the west-central coast of Wales, there is a stone marker, now set as a windowsill, for a certain Maglocunus map Clutor.

The brochure supplied by the church explains that this bilingual marker is 62.5 inches long and dates to the fifth century. Its inscriptions read: "Latin: Maglocvni (miscut Maglocvvi) fili Clutor. Ogham: Maglicunas maqui Clutor."

The fifth century Maglocunus stone was discovered by the Cambrian Archaeological Association in 1906 in the walls of the passage leading to the priests' chamber. It later became a windowsill in the church. The visible slashes are Ogham inscriptions. The translation of both Ogham and Latin is "Maglocunus son of Clutorius."

The slashes (Ogham inscription which is the Irish branch of the Celtic language called Goidelic) are read from right to left. The meaning of both is "The monument of Maglocunus (Maelgwn) son of Clutor."

No more information is provided about this stone. However, for those researchers familiar with the era and with Arthuriana, the name MAELGWN (*sans* appellations) is recorded in the *Annales Cambriae* and in Welsh genealogies. Additionally, GILDAS BADONICUS in the *De Excidio* castigates a Maelgwn, albeit not Maelgwn son of Clutor. This Maglocunus would have flourished in the fifth century, during the era assigned to the "historic" King Arthur.

See also MAGLOCUNUS MAP CATGOLAUN LAUHIR and MAELGWN.

Source: "Church of St. Brynach, Nevern, Pembrokeshire." Distributed Pamphlet Under the Guidance of the Vicar, Churchwardens & Parishioners. Wales: Cardigan, E.L. Jones & Son, Third Edition, May.

Magnus, Magnus Maximus, Macsen Wledig, Maxen. Magnus was a historic figure recorded in Bede's *A History of the English Church and People.* The *Historia Brittonum* also records Magnus in §27: "He went forth from Britain with all the troops of the British and killed Gratian, the king of the Romans, and held the empire of all Europe.... They are the Armorican British, and they never came back, even to the present day. That is why Britain has been occupied by foreigners, and the citizens driven out, until God shall give them help."

Additionally, Magnus makes a debut in Welsh tradition. His name appears on Eliseg's Pillar in northwestern Wales. Jeremy Knight asserts that the son of VORTIGERN (VORTIMER/BRYDW) was the grandson of Magnus, inferring that Vortigern was Magnus's son-in-law. Leslie Alcock devises a chronology that states, "The first consulship of Theodosius [who executed Magnus] was in 425 ... so the fourth year of Vortigern's reign would be 428 ... which incidentally this date for Vortigern's accession fits well enough his relationship as son-in-law of Magnus Maximus."

One of the four branches in *The Mabinogion*—"The Dream of Maxen"—tells the entire story of Magnus. Jeffrey Gantz describes "Maxen" as a mixture of history and pseudo-history, reflecting traditions found in GEOFFREY OF MONMOUTH. When linked with the inscription on Eliseg's Pillar, Vortigern married Severa, Maximus's daughter, who gave birth to Brydw (VORTIMER).

Sources: L. Alcock (AB); G. Ashe [Ed] (QFAB); J. Knight (POE); J. Morris (BH); L. Sherley-Price (BEDE: HEC&P).

Malory, Sir Thomas (*c.* 1416–March 14, 1471). Because there were several individuals known as Tomas Malory in the mid–fifteenth century, Malory's identity was obscure, but in 1894 the American scholar George L. Kittridge identified the author of *Le Morte D'Arthur* as the knight Thomas Malory (Maleore) of Newbold Revel, in the parish of Monks Kirby, Warwickshire. Based upon Kittridge's probe, which has been confirmed by subsequent scholars, a biography can be sketched for the author of the most notable Arthurian prose account written in English. More recently, P.J.C. Field, in *The Life and Times of Sir Thomas Malory*, leaves no doubt that "No-one but Sir Thomas Malory of Newbold Revel could have written the *Morte d'Arthur*."

In the seventeenth century Sir William Dugsdale linked Malory to Earl Richard Beauchamp of Warwick in the year 1436, suggesting Malory's birth-year to be approximately two decades prior, perhaps between 1414 and 1418. Born into Lancastrian gentry, he gained knighthood in 1445 and joined Edward IV's expedition into Northumbria in 1462. Records show, however, that his life was not exemplary, and he was accused of attempted murder, rape, robberies, escapes from prison, and scams — the antithesis of his subject matter.

He evidently fell from Edward's favor because in 1468 and again in 1470 Malory was excluded from pardons by the king. Malory was initially imprisoned in London in 1452, but when the Yorkists ascended to power he was obviously freed, for it was two years later when he joined Edward in his campaign to the north. Somewhere in the interim between 1442 and 1468 Malory must have expressed his loyalty to Henry VI.

William Caxton's edition of *Le Morte* was

completed in the ninth year of Edward's reign, which would have been in the year 1470, coinciding with the year in which Henry VI was restored to the throne. At or near this time Malory would have been a free man, because when he died in March of 1471 he was buried in the elite church of landed gentry in Greyfriars, Newgate.

The reign of Henry VI lasted only seven months, from October of 1470 through April of 1471. He was murdered in the Tower of London in May of 1471 and Edward reclaimed power until 1483.

Sources: J. Cowan (STM: LMD'A); P. Fields (L&T STM); A. Myers (EDWARD IV); T. Pugh (HENRY VI); F. Whitehead (STM).

Manessier (1214–1227). Because CHRÉTIEN DE TROYES never completed *Le Conte du Graal,* known also as *Perceval,* several scribes who are now referred to as continuators and sometimes more intriguingly called terminators wrote addenda to the story. Sometime between 1214 and 1227, Manessier was one such individual. He wrote the *Third Continuation,* adding 10,000 additional lines to Chrétien's tale. In the appendix of his book, William Kibler writes that Manessier's addendum "begins with the Fisher King's explanation of the Grail mysteries: the lance is that of Longinus; the grail was used by Joseph of Arimathea to catch Christ's blood; the trencher covered the grail so the holy blood would not be exposed; the sword had been broken when the traitor Partinial of the Red Tower slew the Fisher King's brother, and in his grief the Fisher King had crippled himself with the broken pieces."

The story then goes into details about knights who later appear in Book 16 of Thomas Malory's *Le Morte D'Arthur*— SAGREMOR, GAWAIN, Bors, Lionel, and Calgogrenant (COLGREVANCE) — before returning once again to PERCEVAL. When Perceval slays Partinial, the FISHER KING is healed. Perceval returns to King Arthur's court, but shortly afterwards, he is summoned to reign because of the Fisher King's death. When Perceval himself dies ten years later, the Grail, lance, and trencher accompany his soul to heaven, never to be seen again on earth.

Source: W. Kibler (CDT: AR).

Margawse. When attempting to distinguish the different personas of Margawse and MORGAN LE FAY, the latter individual seems to be Arthur's nemesis. Although Malory claims in Book 2, Chapter 10, that Arthur lay with Margawse and begat MORDRED, Margawse's death is too premature to blame her for Mordred's birth and tragic role. In Book 10, Chapter 24, Sir Lamorak laid with Margawse. Her son GAHERIS was aware of the affair, and at the proper time, he armed himself, entered the queen's bedroom, grabbed her by the hair, and cut off her head. Lamorak is dismayed that Gaheris killed his own mother and that he didn't extract his retribution on Lamorak himself, but instead Gaheris lets his mother's paramour go free.

See also MORGANA and MODRON.

Source: T. Malory (LMD'A).

Marhaus is Thomas Malory's doublet for Gottfried von Strassburg's MOROLT. In Book 4, Chapter 20, of Malory, Marhaus is initially identified as the King of Ireland's son who slays two knights and hates the women of the castle, for he believes them to be sorceresses and enchantresses. He jousts with Gawaine (GAWAIN) and Uwaine, unhorsing both of them. He then befriends them and they take adventure, joined by three damsels. He is challenged by a lord and his six sons, dueling with four of them. He has shown his prowess and he is made a knight of King Arthur's Round Table.

In Book 8, Chapter 4, Marhaus is portrayed in a strikingly similar parallel as Gottfried von Strassburg's Morolt. Marhaus comes out of Ireland to Cornwall for Mark's truage (tribute). He is described as a knight of the Round Table and brother to the Queen of Ireland, the latter being contradictory to the passage describing him as the King of Ireland's son in Book 4.

Thereafter, the two stories (Gottfried's and Malory's) are basically the same, except for the ending. In Gottfried's, Morolt is killed on the small island where he and Tristan duel, but in Malory's story, Marhaus retreats to Ireland and dies there from his wounds. (Book 8, Chapter 8).

Sources: R. Loomis/L. Loomis (MR); T. Malory (LMD'A).

Mark of Cornwall. *see* TRISTRAM.

Mark the Hermit, Mark the Ascetic, Marcus Eremita. One of the difficult issues to resolve is the authorship of the *Historia Brittonum*, a vital ancient rendition of British activity, particularly during the fifth and sixth centuries. NENNIUS has been granted that honor, but Mark the Hermit is a feasible contender.

Little is known about this particular individual, although he allegedly wrote a number of texts about spiritual law. Various vague references indicate that he was "probably an abbot of a monastery in Ankara, Turkey (ancient Ancyra)" before withdrawing to a solitary life. He is also described as a "theological polemicist author of the fifth century on Christian asceticism."

In his Preface of *Nennius: Historia Brittonum*, Josephus Stevenson suggests that Mark is a possible candidate of the authorship rather than Nennius.

Source: J. Stevenson (N: HB).

Maugantius. After Hengist murders all members of the Council of the Provinces except for VORTIGERN and ELDOL (who escapes), Vortigern flees to northern Wales, where he attempts to build a fortress. He fails three times and when he consults with his wizards, they advise him to find a lad without a father, and he should kill the boy, afterwards sprinkling his blood on the foundation to make it stand firm.

Messengers search the countries and finally come upon two boys who are quarreling, one named Merlin and the other DINABUTIUS. The messengers learn that Merlin has no father and immediately take him and his mother to Vortigern. The mother claims that she had never been with a man and must have been duped by an incubus. Vortigern then sends for Maugantius, an authority about incubi. Maugantius claims that "in the books written by our sages, and in many historical narratives, I have discovered that quite a number of men have been born this way. [These men] have partly the nature of men and partly that of angels, and when they wish they assume mortal shapes and have intercourse with women."

R.H. Fletcher, among other scholars, claims

that Maugantius is make-believe, picked without any kind of explanation.

Sources: R. Fletcher (AMC); L. Thorpe (GM: HKB).

Medraut. *see* MORDRED.

Medrawt. *see* MORDRED.

Meleagant. The name Meleagant is sometimes spelled as Melegrance, Maelwys, Melegraunce, Melegraunt, Meliagraunce, or Meliagaunce.

See also MELWAS and GUINEVERE.

Melwas, Maelwas, Maelwys, Maheloas, Medrawt, Melegraunce, Melegraunt, Meliagraunce, Meliagaunce, Melvas. Charles Squire, in his text *Celtic Myths and Legends*, typifies Melwas in a variety of ways: a Briton of Cornwall, the king of Avallon (the Land of Summer), the "dark god," a doublet of Sir Melias, a different doublet of Meliagraunce, and a parallel to MORDRED. Similarly, Jean Markale equates Maelwas with Maheloas in *Érec et Énide*, a god of the Other World who is also referred to as Lord of the Isle of Glass.

E.K. Chambers summarizes the story of Melvas in "The Life of St. Gildas" by CARADOC OF LLANCARFAN in this manner:

> The saint was at Glastonbury, preaching and writing his histories of the kings of Britain. Melvas, who was then king *in aestive regione* [the Summer Country], by which we must clearly understand Somerset, had carried off Guennuvar (GUINEVERE), the wife of the *tyrannus* Arthur, and brought her for security to the marshengirt sanctuary. The *rex rebellis* sought his wife for a whole year, before he learnt of her whereabouts. Then he gathered the forces of Cornwall and Devon and made war on Melvas. But Gildas Albanius and the abbot of Glastonbury made peace between the kings. Guennuvar was restored, and the kings recompensed the abbey with lands and privileges.

For whatever reasons, in writing *Arthur's Britain*, Chambers's attention was elsewhere, and he does not make a distinction between GILDAS ALBANIUS and GILDAS BADONICUS, as Josephus Stevenson does in the preface to his book on Gildas Badonicus. And that distinction is very important, whether an individual is considering King Arthur as a historical figure or as a legendary one. Caradoc of Llancarfan's manuscript was penned in the 1140s and focuses upon Gildas Albanius, who was son of CAW, King of Scotland, and flourished during Arthur's historical era. Gildas Badonicus himself gives his birth-year, which has been calibrated as approximately 497, a generation later than Gildas Albanius. Making this distinction between the two Gildases not only separates the Arthur of oral tradition and the Arthur of history, it also negates the contention that Gildas Badonicus ignores mentioning Arthur in the *De Excidio* because Arthur killed HUEIL. Hueil was Gildas Albanius's brother, another son of Caw, King of Scotland, and was not brother of Gildas Badonicus.

Later in his text Chambers adds more detail about Melvas:

> There is another version of [Gwenhwyvar's] rape, apparently independent of Geoffrey [of Monmouth], in which the agent is not called Medraut, but Melvas. Here Melvas is King of Somerset and Arthur recovers Gwenhwyvar from Glastonbury. The *Vita* [Life of Gildas] or some common source must be behind the *Conte de la Charrete* of Chrétien de Troyes, in which the same story is told at great length, and the rescue of the queen is ascribed to Lancelot. Chrétien's ravisher [of Gwenhwyvar] is Meleagant.... Meleagant son of Bagdemagus must be the Maelwys son of Baeddan of *Kulhwch and Olwen*.

Marion Zimmer Bradley, in her historical novel *The Mists of Avalon*, gives a graphic, gory account of Meleagrant's [Bradley's spelling] rape of Guinevere and Lancelot's subsequent murder of Meleagrant. The only twist which Bradley adds is that Meleagrant claims to be the bastard son of Leodegrance and hence a half-brother of Guinevere.

The incredible distortion of this character — Melwas and all his epithets — is a common occurrence of inextricably entwining Arthurian myth and history.

Sources: G. Ashe [Ed] (QAB); M. Bradley (MOA); R. Castleden (KA: TBL); E. Chambers (AOB); R. Coghlan (EAL); T. Malory (LEMD'A); J. Markale (KA: KK); C. Squire (CM&L); G. Williams (E: SFA).

Meriaun, Meirion. Typiaun's son; Cunedda's grandson, who migrated south with Cunedda and shared land with his uncles. His kingdom became Meirionydd, which encompasses Dolgellau in Wales.

Sources: L. Alcock (AB); P. Bartram (WG); S. Blake/S. Lloyd (KTA).

Merlin, Merlinus, Myrddin, Merddyn (Ann ap Lleian?). As with other Arthurian figures, Merlin is an enigma. Legends of him have sprung up in Brittany and tied to the Forest of Brocéliande, and one tells of his origin this way: "Satan was desirous of having on this earth a representative devoted entirely to his interests, who would deceive men and win their souls by acquiring a great authority over them by magic and using his knowledge of past and future. Satan sent one of his devils to this world with the mission of creating such a child."

Merlin was the babe born of a very religious mother who was raped in her sleep by that devil. Satan's plan went awry, however, because when the baby was born, the mother baptized him immediately, an act which destroyed the evil powers which would have been bestowed on him. Instead, Merlin was given powers which aided the righteous and oppressed the wicked.

Because the mother could not claim a father, she was sentenced to burn at the stake after she ceased the need to suckle the babe. Merlin, however, began to speak, explaining his origin which was forfeited because of his baptism. The child spoke so convincingly that the mother was exonerated and allowed to join a nunnery. Merlin became a magus for Uter.

In a "historical" rather than a literary or spiritual sense, the name Merlin appears only once, in the *Annales Cambriae*, at Entry 573. Translated by John Morris, the passage reads, "The battle of Arfderydd †between the sons of Eliffer and Gwenddolau son of Ceidio; in which battle Gwenddolau fell; Merlin went mad.†

However, it appears that the original entry read "573 an. Bellum Armterid." Nothing more. In an Introductory Note to Morris's translation, *British History*, R.B. White explains, "The text here printed is that of [E.] Faral (*La Légende Arthurienne*, Vol. 3, 1929) with some corrections of substance and additional passages supplied from Mommsen's edition (*Chronica Minora*, Berlin, 1892), these are enclosed with dagger symbols, thus †... ...†. Square brackets enclose words not found in the text, including corrected errors as, for example, where the text mistakenly reads 'filius' for 'frater,' the translation is given as [brother]."

This explanation is suggesting that Faral's work contains additions from Mommsen. The original (not the translation) gives the same information in Latin: "*Bellum Armeterid [inter filios Elifer et Guendoleu filium Keidiau; in quo bellow Guendoleu cecidit; Merlinus insanus effectus est].*" The same additional material is bracketed. This in turn suggests that the original was only two words long — Bellum Armterid — and that the remainder was interpolation. In an abstruse way, this negates the name of Merlin in any historical sense. The material enclosed in daggers, where Merlin's madness occurs, is therefore spurious.

Since GEOFFREY OF MONMOUTH in *The History of the Kings of Britain* records nothing about Merlin going mad, the extract in the *Annales Cambriae* seems to have been borrowed from the work of ROBERT DE BORON, the Vulgate cycle of Merlin. It is this "False Merlin" who is commonly equated with Lailoken, someone independent of the Merlin who evolves as a separate character in the Monmouth narrative. As an aside, in Monmouth's manuscript Merlin at one point is described as the "prophet of Vortigern." After VORTIGERN's flight, Ambrosius summons Merlin to erect a special monument in honor of those Welsh who were killed by the treacherous HENGIST, a task which entails moving Stonehenge from Mount Killarus in Ireland to Mount Ambris in Britain. Merlin and Utherpendragon (UTERPENDRAGON) complete the assignment, and later Merlin, after the death of Ambrosius, becomes Utherpendragon's magus. In Geoffrey's story, Merlin and "Arthur" never meet.

Geoffrey of Monmouth's *History of the Kings of Britain*, including his insertion of "The Prophecies of Merlin" splitting his section on "the House of Constantine," predates Robert de Boron's work by six and a half decades. Originally, "The Prophecies of Merlin" was printed as a separate volume containing a brief preface of its own, but in any event the name Merlin made its debut in print around 1136. The date of inception for this name, however, doesn't resolve the

mystery behind Merlin, nor does it resolve the reliability of Monmouth's book as authentic history.

Lewis Thorpe, one of the foremost authorities about Geoffrey, rhetorically asks what Monmouth's source might have been for his so-called history, then answers the question: "He either took his material from a [*liber vetustissimus*] very ancient book, or he made his material up." As a translator, he admits that much of the information in the *History* is fictional and "someone did invent it," and later on in his introduction he reasserts that a great deal of Geoffrey's material is unacceptable as history.

Thorpe is well aware that there are sundry researchers who believe not only that Merlin is pure fiction created by Geoffrey, but also that *The History of the Kings of Britain* is a grievous deceit, a subterfuge of the worst kind. Yet in spite of this, he's aware that history keeps peeping through the fiction. In support of Geoffrey's role as a historian, he writes, "Geoffrey may be said to have created the figure of the prophet Merlin as he appears in later romance, even though, according to Celtic scholars, it can now be regarded as certain that he derived the outline of the Merlin story from anterior Welsh sources." In a broader defense of the *HKB*, he adds, "What nobody who has examined the evidence carefully can ever dare to say is that Geoffrey of Monmouth simply made up his material."

Geoffrey himself claims that he was translating directly into Latin from a *liber vetustissimus*, a very ancient book written in early Welsh. For those who grant the concession that this is the case — as it appears to be — there are some fascinating revelations about Geoffrey's history in general and the figure of Merlin specifically. Therefore, it is worthwhile to explore some of the contextual clues in the Merlin section of the *HKB*.

One of the most glaring oddities is Geoffrey's account of the "Tale of Emrys." Upon the first reading, an individual might assume that Geoffrey borrowed this particular extract from Nennius's *Historia Brittonum*. But for some reason Geoffrey made one very mysterious and perplexing change; he uses *Merlin* as the main focal point of this tale rather than AMBROSIUS AURE-

LIANUS, who is also known as EMRYS the Over-lord.

Upon deeper reflection, a modern reader must wonder why Geoffrey would alter the name of the story's main figure. Geoffrey's learnéd contemporaries would certainly have read the "Tale of Emrys" in the *Historia Brittonum* and realized that Merlin was a fanciful insertion. Was Geoffrey truly translating prophecies for Alexander, Bishop of Lincoln? Was he inferring that Ambrosius had acquired Druidic powers in his younger years, and thus called him "Ambrosius Merlinus?" Or was he extracting the material

One oddity which seems to point to Geoffrey's use of an ancient book is the name Maugantius. Because Vortigern was confounded by the story which Ambrosius's mother tells about being impregnated by an incubus, "he summoned Maugantius to him." In the Introduction to his text, Lewis Thorpe states that there is ample evidence to sway us toward the conviction that Monmouth did indeed have at his disposal something closely related to ms. Harl. 3859. Drawing by Paul Honeywill, reproduced with permission of Paul White, Bossiney Books, Ltd.

from his very ancient book? Whatever his motive, he did infuse Merlin into Ambrosius in the "Tale of Emrys." Geoffrey does not mention where the prophecies came from, and he skirts the issue of the original language of the manuscript.

The tale of Ambrosius in Sections 40, 41, and 42 of the *Historia Brittonum* is a close parallel to Monmouth's passage of Merlin, which is more detailed. Capsulated, the story is this: Hengist deviously slaughters Vortigern's Council of the Province and forces the king to relinquish all of his territories in exchange for his life and those of his magi.

Vortigern flees to Wales and asks his magi what he should do next, and they tell him to build a fortress with a very strong tower. Stonemasons are assembled and they begin to build the foundation. However, each day they build the foundation, by the next morning it is swallowed up. Vortigern consults his magicians, who tell him that he must find a fatherless young man, kill him, and sprinkle his blood on the base.

The magi travel through various countries and finally come upon Merlin, whose father was a incubus; that is, a person without a real father. The magi take the young man to the governor of the town and order him to release the young man and his mother into their custody. When the two are brought into Vortigern's presence, Merlin amazes and frightens the king because of his supernatural powers. Intimidated, Vortigern and his magi flee farther north.

As stated earlier, Thorpe admits that much of the information in Monmouth's *History* is fictional, which someone did invent, but obversely, he comments that there is archaeological evidence that Monmouth's work is not all fanciful. He writes:

> The connexion of Vortigern and his son Pacentius with Ireland (viii.14) is, for example, allegedly supported by the ogham stones with Vortiger's name on them which have been discovered at Ballybank and Knockaboy. As fate caught up with him, Vortigern, in Geoffrey's account (viii.2), fled to the fortified camp of Genoreu, on the hill called Cloartius, in Erging, by the River Wye. Here "Gonoreu" is Ganarew and "Cloartius"

Top: Merlin's Cave, lower center. The cave, unfortunately in the shadows, may be entered from either side of the isthmus. Tintagel is allegedly the spot where Merlin transforms Uterpendragon into Gorlois in order to have him seduce Ygerna. To the left is Arthur's Profile. *Bottom:* Merlin's Tomb, Brittany. Prayers and supplications to Merlin are continuously stuffed into the crack of the large stone to the right. On the smaller stones to the left are beads, mementoes, and lighted candles.

a misspelling for the modern Little Doward, with its hilltop camp, all of it very near to Monmouth.

Thorpe comments on one other interesting discovery: "In v.4 Geoffrey tells how the Venedoti decapitated a whole Roman legion in London and threw their heads into a stream called Nantgallum or, in the Saxon language, Galobroc. In the 1860s a large number of skulls with practically no other bones to accompany them, were dug up in the bed of the Walbrook by General Pitt-Rivers and others."

Credit must be given to historians and researchers such as Lewis Thorpe, Acton Griscom, Edmond Faral, Jacob Hammer, Theodor Mommsen, and W.M. Flinders Petrie for their insightful discoveries, since it is scholars such as they who have offered fresh perspectives and interpretations to ancient manuscripts. Without their tireless efforts, Merlin might be summarily dismissed and Geoffrey of Monmouth's work denounced *in toto*.

The complexity of Merlin as a character becomes even more paradoxical as twentieth and twenty-first century researchers delve deeper into the persona of this formidable figure. Merlin is inextricably bound to King Arthur both "historically" and legendarily, since some recent research equates King Arthur to AMBROSIUS AURELIANUS, similar to Merlin being equated to AURELIUS AMBROSIUS.

Sources: O.-L. Aubert (CLOB); S. Blake/S. Lloyd (KTA); R. Clinch/M. Williams (KAIS); A. Griscom (HRBGM); J. Morris (HB/AC); W.M.F. Petrie (NBH); J. Hammer (GM: VV); Rb (M); F. Reno (HKA/HFAE); L. Thorpe (GM).

Merlin (*Vita Merlini*). Because Merlin is represented as a historical figure in Geoffrey of Monmouth's *History of the Kings of Britain*, and because "The Prophecies of Merlin" are inserted in that same manuscript, an addendum is needed to portray Merlin as a mythical figure in another of Monmouth's work, titled *The Life of Merlin*, written in 1148. Undoubtedly, Monmouth was cognizant of an entry in the *Annales Cambriae* recorded for the year 573: "The battle of Arfderydd †between the sons of Eliffer and Gwend-dolau son of Ceido in which battle Gwenddolau fell; Merlin went mad.†"

The material between the two daggers is an added interpolation penned by some unknown scribe, which is why scholars and historians have labeled this segment as mythological.

Monmouth's *Vita Merlini* begins with an extract from the *Annales*: "Peredur, king of the North Welsh, made war on Gwenddoleu, who ruled the realm of Scotland." GANIEDA, Merlin's sister who is married to King Rodarch of Cumbria, discovers that Merlin is skulking in the woods, insane because of the recent battle he had fought. Ganieda entices him to come to her court, but Merlin must be restrained and bound because crowds of people cause him to go mad again.

In this condition, Merlin sees Rodarch kissing his sister and plucking a leaf from her hair. When Merlin smirks and chuckles, Rodarch demands an explanation, which Merlin gives: "When just now you removed the leaf that Ganieda had in her hair without knowing it, you acted more faithfully toward her than she did toward you when she went under a bush where her lover met her and lay with her; and while she was lying there supine with her hair spread out, by chance there caught in it the leaf that you, not knowing this, removed."

Brazenly, Ganieda denies the accusation by claiming Merlin's fantastic madness. Three times she calls a young boy into the room in different guises and asks Merlin to predict how the lad would die. When Merlin gives three different answers, Ganieda ridicules him and convinces Rodarch that Merlin is indeed insane. It is years later, after the boy has become a man, that the anomaly is resolved.

Much of the remaining *Vita*, in this author's opinion, borders on absurdity: Merlin's insanity coming and going, repetition of Monmouth's material in *History of the Kings* (especially the prophecies), long passages about lakes, similarly long passages about birds, and Merlin's association with Taliesin. Caitlin and John Matthews, in their book *Ladies of the Lake*, Chapter 5 on Nimuë, properly label *Vita Merlini* as a myth.

Sources: C&J. Matthews (LOTL); J. Parry (GM: VM).

Merlinus Ambrosius. Merlinus Ambrosius is an expression used for Ambrosius, also known as Ambrosius Aurelianus (in the *De Excidio* of Gildas and *English History* of Bede), and as Aurelius Ambrosius (in Monmouth's *History of the Kings of Britain*). Referring to the *Historia Brittonum* of Nennius, Josephus Stevenson avows that Merlin, also known as Ambrosius, is the central figure in §41 (Vortigern's interview with Merlin), and in §42 (Merlin's confrontation with Vortigern, later known as the "Tale of Emrys"). In the latter instance, Stevenson states that Merlin was named Embries Guletic; that is, Merlinus Ambrosius is the "great king among all the kings of Britain."

When Geoffrey of Monmouth penned his manuscript, he called Aurelius Ambrosius by the name of Merlin. He began the tale with the discovery of Merlin, who had no father, but his mother was the daughter of the king of Dementia. When the young boy was taken to the spot where Vortigern was attempting to build a citadel, the king was alarmed by the lad's powers.

Near the end of the tale, Monmouth then revised the name to Merlin, who was also called Ambrosius. Vortigern is seated upon the bank of the pool when two dragons appear, one white and one red.

> And when the one had drawn anigh onto the other, they grappled together in baleful combat and breathed forth fire as they panted. But presently the white dragon did prevail and drave the red dragon onto the verge of the lake. But he, grieving to be thus driven forth, fell fiercely again upon the white one and forced him to draw back. And whilst that they were fighting on this wise, the King [Vortigern] bade Ambrosius Merlin declare what this battle of the dragons did portend.

Ambrosius Merlin rebukes Vortigern and his magicians for wanting to kill him.

Thus Monmouth ends the chapter "The House of Constantine." At this point he stops writing his narrative about the kings of Britain and inexplicably writes and inserts "The Prophecies of Merlin." He then picks up on the continuation of "The House of Constantine," at which point Merlin has become a separate individual.

Obviously, Monmouth partially copied material from the *Historia Brittonum*. E. K. Chambers adds the following about Merlin: "Professor Rhys goes so far as to construct for Merlin an elaborate mythological personality as a Brythonic representative of a Celtic Zeus or Heaven God. But in fact the name Merlin is untraceable in any assured pre–Galfridian document."

Chambers then goes into great detail about where Merlin's name does not appear. He is not with Taliessin or Aneirin; he is not in *The Mabinogion* or in "Culhwch and Olwen" or in any other Welsh manuscript, including the *Black Book of Carmarthen* and the *Red Book of Hergest*, because those documents are post–Galfridian and void of the name Merlin. Chambers concludes, "Geoffrey, casting about for a mouthpiece of the *Prophecies*, in which he proposed to give literary form to the vague rumours of a British hope, invented Merlin, and deliberately identified him with the prophet of Nennius."

For those, however, who believe that Monmouth tried to be an accurate amanuensis — although he certainly added his own inventive imagination and made inaccurate assumptions — Monmouth, like Nennius, knew not why the epithet Merlinus was assigned to Ambrosius. The *Prophecies* most certainly look like Monmouth's personal addendum, but there are other speculations — not hard evidence — which can logically fill the void. Between the story of Ambrosius the Wonder Boy and Ambrosius the great king of all the kings of Britain, there is a dark void of many years.

Monmouth writes that Aurelius Ambrosius and Utherpendragon, who were too young to rule, were taken out of Britain so that Vortigern could not assassinate them. They were secreted in Brittany. And what might Ambrosius have done during those years between infancy, puberty and manhood? *The Historic King Arthur* speculates that Ambrosius might have been sequestered with druids at a monastery such as Mount Dol or Augustonemeton. Had that been the case, he would have been exposed to the enigmatic inner circles of druidism. In his later years he indeed would have been a formidable opponent — a savvy war-leader and a druid priest with awesome spiritual powers.

One last notation: In Monmouth's manuscript, Merlin never comes into contact with Arthur. For a short time he is Ambrosius's wizard, and when Ambrosius dies, Merlin becomes Utherpendragon's wizard, but he never consorts with Arthur himself.

See also Merlin and Merlin (*VITA MERLINI*).

Sources: E. Chambers (AOB); S. Evans (GM); F. Reno (HKA); J. Stevenson (N: HB).

Meton of Athens. Meton, an astronomer and mathematician, developed what is now known as the Metonic cycle of 235 lunar months equaling 19 years; that is, a lunar cycle. The Council of Nicaea recognized this variant in 325 C.E., but it was not accepted until the eighth century. Recorded dates in ancient manuscripts could be off by at least twenty-eight years. This method of chronological calibration, plus the two reckonings by VICTORIUS OF AQUITAINE and DIONYSIUS EXIGUUS are indispensable aids in determining the accuracy of dates recorded in ancient manuscripts.

Source: M. Davidson (FDDE).

Modron, Matrona, Morrigan, Morgen/Morgan. In Celtic genealogies, Modron is one of Afallach's daughters, referred to as a fay (fairy). In "How Culhwch Won Olwen" of *The Mabinogion*, during the quest to win Olwen, one of Culhwch's tasks is to retrieve the pup of Greid son of Eri, but evidently no one can handle the hound except Modron's son. Attached to her son, Modron's name appears four more times, each indicating that Mabon son of Modron was stolen when he was three nights old. The combined names appear twice more: when he was imprisoned by an unnamed person, and then when Mabon mounted Gwynn Dun Mane, the horse of Gweddw. In the tale "Dream of Rhonabwy," Mabon son of Modron is in ARTHUR's army fighting against OSLA BIG KNIFE at Badon.

See also MORGAN LE FAY.

Sources: F. Delaney (LOTC); P. Ellis (DOCM); J. Gantz (TM); C. Littleton/L. Malcor (FSTC).

Mordred, Modred, Medraut, Medrawt, Medrod. Mordred is probably portrayed as the most repugnant villain in Arthuriana, though the brief comment about him in the *Annales Cambriae* (supposedly a historical document) is dispassionately mild. The confusion caused by GEOFFREY OF MONMOUTH between the kinship of AURELIUS AMBROSIUS, ANNA, HOEL, and ARTHUR recurs in the relationship between Mordred, Anna, Aurelius Ambrosius, and Arthur. Monmouth first writes that Aurelius Ambrosius is Anna's brother and that Mordred is Anna's son; that is, Ambrosius is Mordred's uncle; later, however, he calls Mordred *Arthur's* nephew. Tradition and legend portray Arthur as Mordred's uncle, but in later literature, unaware that they are brother-sister, Morgan le Fay (Morgause) and Arthur fornicate and a son, Mordred, is born, giving rise to the incest motif.

To add to the confusion, different dates are given for the entry in the *Annales Cambriae*. As explained in *The Historic King Arthur*, Leslie Alcock calculated an *anno Domini* date, but then discovered a possible two-year discrepancy by the time the Pelican edition of his book came out, and gave the year 539. In *Nennius: British History*, John Morris uses the date 537. The variance of date notwithstanding, the entry reads thusly: "The battle of Camlann, in which Arthur and Medraut fell: and there was plague in Britain and Ireland."

It has not been resolved whether the *Tysilio* preceded Monmouth's *History of the Kings of Britain*, but Acton Griscom suggests that possibly the *Tysilio* preceded Monmouth's text and could be part of the *liber vetustissimus* referred to several times by Monmouth. In *The Chronicle of the Kings of Britain* (which includes the *Tysilio*), Medrod, Arthur's nephew, seizes the king's crown and seduces Gwenhwyfar while the king is fighting wars on the continent. Arthur leaves Howel (HOEL) in charge and sails to Britain, where Medrod and leagues of Picts, Scots, and Irish attempt to prevent Arthur from landing. The king finally succeeds and puts Medrod to flight, and after pursuit, Medrod makes a stand on the River Camlan. Medrod is finally killed, but Arthur receives a wound which proves mortal after he is taken to the Isle of Afallach. Here the history of Arthur and Medrod ends, but there is one last comment that "Medrod's two sons, in conjunction with the

"How Mordred was slain by Arthur, and how by him Arthur was hurt to the death." In Pollard's *The Romance of King Arthur* (1917), illustration by Arthur Rackham.

Saxons, made an unsuccessful attempt to oppose Constantine III, Cador's son who had been coronated king after Arthur's death."

Monmouth's narrative closely parallels that of the *Tysilio*, but gives more detail about Mordred's sons. He writes, "But Constantine pursued the Saxons and subdued them into his allegiance; and took the two sons of Mordred. The one youth, who had fled into the church of St. Amphibalus at Winchester he slew before the altar; but the other, who was in hiding in the monastery of certain bretheren in London, he did there find beside the altar and slew by a cruel death."

The irony of this passage has been addressed only in the *Historic Figures of the Arthurian Era*, pages 61–63, since its date of publication in 2000. GILDAS BADONICUS never mentions the name Arthur, yet praises Ambrosius Aurelianus. More relevant in this entry is that his first castigation is a criticism of a tyrant named Constantine, who was still alive during Gildas's time, which would have been the same era when Constantine III, Cador's son, was King of Dumnonia.

The description of Constantine's actions in the *De Excidio* match Monmouth's narrative beyond mere coincidence. Gildas does not identify the two young men as Mordred's sons, but his passage relays that Constantine "most cruelly tore at the tender sides and vitals of two royal youths and their two guardians. Their arms were stretched out not to weapons — though almost no man handled them more bravely than they at this time — but to God and the altar.... [Constantine] tore them, I say, at the holy altar, using as teeth his wicked sword and spear, so that the place of divine sacrifice was touched by the purple cloaks (as it were) of their drying blood."

At times Gildas's graphic descriptions hinder his grammatical precision. *Historic Figures of the Arthurian Era* transvaluates the passage based upon the Latin words *ac si*, which specifically indicates comparisons, so that a different translation, suggested by Leslie Alcock's admonition to look at existing texts in new ways, allows a different perspective. F.D. Reno suggests, "Constantine, with his abominable sword and spear,

mauled and slashed the youth as with teeth, so that clotted gore tinged the heavenly altar purple, matching the cloak of the attacking Roman."

It is crucial to recall that there is no proof of a fifth-century King Arthur of Britain. Monmouth himself writes that Mordred was the second son of Loth of Lodonesia and the sister (Anna) of Aurelius Ambrosius. Gildas Badonicus is writing about Constantine, King of Dumnonia at a time when they were both living. Mordred would have been killed at the end of the fifth century, and his sons would be young men when Gildas was penning the *De Excidio*.

See also MORGANA and MORGAN LE FAY.

Sources: L. Alcock (AB); S. Evans (GM); A. Griscom (HRBGM); J. Morris (BH); F. Reno (HFAE/HKA); P. Roberts (COKB).

Morgan le Fay, Morgan le Fey, Morgana, Morgen, Morgan le Fee, Modron. Morgan le Fay is another complexity bonded to Arthuriana. Geoffrey of Monmouth does not mention a Morgan or Morgan le Fay in *The History of the Kings of Britain*, but approximately thirteen years later, around 1150, his *Vita Merlini* (*The Life of Merlin*) records the Isle of Apples (which he calls the Fortunate Isle) and then writes of nine sisters who ruled there. The first of them "is more skilled in the healing art, and excels her sisters in beauty of her person. Morgen is her name and she has learned what useful properties all the herbs contain, so that she can cure sick bodies. She also knows an art by which to change her shape, and to cleave the air on new wings like Daedalus." After the battle of Camlan, the sisters took the wounded Arthur to the island, had him laid on a golden bed, and carefully inspected his wound. At length, Morgen claimed that he could be restored to health if he stayed on the island and allowed her to use her healing arts.

Steve Blake and Scott Lloyd supply a concise, comprehensive explanation which traces Morgen's development through a variety of manuscripts which labeled her as Morgen, Morgan, and most importantly through her title Morgan le Fay. They write that the nine sisters appear in very early Welsh poetry titled "The Spoils of Annwn," which is a reference to the Celtic Otherworld. Summarized, they write that

- circa 1160 Morgen's name appears in the French romance *Roman de Troie* as a fairy who fell in love with Hector (ECTOR, Arthur's foster father) and hated him when he did not return her love;
- circa 1168 in Chrétien de Troyes' *Eric et Enide* she is called Morgan la Fee, the mistress of Guigomar, Lord of Avalon, and in the same work is named as Arthur's sister;
- in Chrétien's *Yvain*, she appears as Morgan the Wise;
- circa 1189–1205 in Layamon's *Brut*, she appears as Argante (Margante) "in the words spoken by the mortally wounded Arthur to Constantine after the Battle of Camlann, when Arthur utters that he is going to Avalun to be with the Elf queen;"
- circa 1216 GIRALDUS CAMBRENSIS writes that Morgan was Arthur's cousin;
- circa 1220 Morgan appears in the Cistercian Vulgate Cycle as the youngest daughter of HOEL (Gorlois), Duke of Tintagel (Dindagol), and therefore half-sister of Arthur.

After the passage of a little more than two centuries, when Thomas Malory penned *Le Morte D'Arthur*, there was still confusion about who was Margawse, Morgan, or Morgan le Fay, and Malory was not able to clarify the issue. In Book 1, Chapter 2, he writes, "King Lot of Lothian and of Orkney then wedded Margawse that was Gawain's mother," first implying only one son. In Book 1, Chapter 19, Malory records that "King Lot's wife came thither to King Arthur's court to espy on Arthur, and with MARGAWSE came her four sons GAWAIN, GAHERIS, AGRAVAIN, and GARETH."

Details become confused in Book 2, Chapter 10, when the reader is informed that King Lot was wedded to the sister of King Arthur, and Arthur lay by King Lot's wife "and gat on her MORDRED." In the very next section, Chapter 11, when twelve kings are being interred, Margawse and her four sons attend, as well as King Uriens along with his wife "Morgan le Fay that was King Arthur's sister."

Although Morgan le Fay is at times portrayed as a beneficent individual, she is continuously malevolent to Arthur. One segment in Book 4 will suffice to show her malice. By Morgan le Fay's magic, she gives her paramour, Sir Accolon, King Arthur's sword, Excalibur, and scabbard, so that unknown to both Arthur and Accolon, Accolon would slay Arthur because of Morgan le Fay's hatred for Arthur since "he was most of worship and of prowess of any of her blood."

With the aid of the Lady of the Lake, Arthur wins he battle, and though he spares Accolon when the discovers who he is, Accolon dies from his wounds. When Morgan le Fay thinks Arthur is dead, she plans to slay her husband, King Uriens, but her ruse goes astray and her son Uwain stops her. Because she is his mother, he doesn't behead her, but chides her that "Merlin may have been begotten of a devil, but I may say that an earthly devil bare me."

Sources: S. Blake/S. Lloyd (KTA); GOM (VM); T. Malory (LMD'A); L. Thorpe (GM: HKB).

Morgana, Margawse. It is difficult (probably impossible) to determine if the name Morgana evolved from Margawse or MORGAN LE FAY, the latter whose name is based upon the Celtic goddess Modron. Another option is that the suffix -*ana* might have been based on GEOFFREY OF MONMOUTH's Anna, Arthur's sister, who has only an incidental role in Arthuriana as compared to Morgan le Fay's major one.

Morolt, Morholt, Morhot, Morlot, Morold. In the medieval romance *Tristan and Isolt* by GOTTFRIED VON STRASSBURG, Morolt is introduced as a mighty champion of Ireland, acclaimed as the fiercest warrior of his time, and as uncle of ISOLT (LA BEALE ISOUD in Malory). Based upon his prowess, Morolt is sent yearly from Ireland to Cornwall to exact tribute which became increasingly demanding, from tin to silver to gold, and finally thirty lads of noble birth each year. As the tale progresses, four important details are revealed: 1) Morolt is the brother-in-law of King Gurman of Ireland, 2) Gurman's Queen is Isolt, 3) Morolt's sister (the Queen) is named Isolt, and most important, 4) Queen Isolt has a daughter whose name is also Isolt. It is this daughter who marries King Mark and who falls in love with Tristan.

Upon his return to Tintagel, Tristan hears of the marriage and rejects the arrangement when Morolt and King Mark are at council. Morolt is enraged, but because he has come on peaceful terms and has no army with him, it is decided that the matter will be settled by single combat between Morolt and Tristan.

The encounter will take place on a small isolated island, and the fight will be to death. The battle begins, and both exhibit the strength of four men. Morolt deals the first serious blow, cutting through Tristan's armor and slicing through his thigh. Morolt tells Tristan that this is a death-wound, for the sword was poisoned and only his sister could heal the wound.

Tristan refuses to concede and ferociously attacks, cutting off Morolt's sword hand and rendering Morolt weaponless and powerless. Tristan's second blow "clave through" Morolt's helmet, and when Tristran drew his sword back with a mighty heave, "a piece of the blade brake, and remained sticking in the skull." His third blow smote off Morolt's head.

The small troupe of men who had accompanied Morolt to Cornwall sailed to the small island to bear Morolt's body back to the King of Ireland. They gathered his body, head, and hand, then set sail for their own country.

The opening of this episode which focuses upon the tribute demanded between one country and another has overtones of the myth about Theseus and the Minotaur, suggested by Sigmund Eisner.

See also MARHAUS, who is a parallel of Morolt in Thomas Malory's *Le Morte D'Arthur.*

Sources: S. Eisner (TL: SS); R. Loomis/L. Loomis (MR).

Nennius (*floruit* 825–855). The *Historia Brittonum*, although severely criticized by certain sectors of scholars, is one of the most important surviving documents of early British history. Not only has it become sacrosanct because of its age, but it is the only resource melding Roman and insular details during an otherwise dark and silent void. Because there are scant manuscripts to verify or nullify what is recorded, dismissive-

ness and disdain for its shortcomings must be set aside, and any interpolations or additions must be tolerated and forgiven.

At the very onset, it must be stated that Nennius is the *presumed* author, since the *Historia* is ascribed to Nennius based solely upon prologues which are introductions for only a few of the surviving manuscripts. It is important, therefore, to read the Prologue in its entirety:

> I, Nennius, pupil of the holy Elvodug, have undertaken to write down some extracts that the stupidity of the British cast out; for the scholars of the island of Britain had no skill, and set down no record in books. I have therefore made a heap of all that I have found, both from the Annals of the Romans and from the Chronicles of the Holy Fathers, and from the writings of the Irish and the English, and out of the tradition of our elders.
>
> Many learned scholars and copyists have tried to write, but somehow they have left the subject more obscure, whether through repeated pestilence or frequent military disasters. I ask every reader who reads this book to pardon me for daring to write so much here after so many, like a chattering bird or an incompetent judge. I yield to whoever may be better acquainted with this skill than I am.

Like GEOFFREY OF MONMOUTH several centuries later, Nennius is direct in saying that he is not the historian, he is not the scholar, but only the copyist. He names each of the "writings" he is copying — chronicles, annals, and traditions.

Only one prologue in a twelfth-century manuscript gives a date when it was written, C.E. 858. William Skene surmises in *The Four Ancient Books of Wales* that an addition of the *Historia* might have been written in 823 by MARK THE HERMIT, but the date 858 is ascribed to Nennius.

Meticulous researchers compensate for the shortcomings of the *Historia* by

1. being cautious to remind readers that historical information has to be analyzed very carefully, separating it from oral tradition which is interspersed;
2. using Manuscript A in their investigations because it is the basis for all the other texts and because it is the text which Stevenson

states is "least vitiated by extraneous material;"

3. paying particular attention to Welsh place-names and Welsh personages;

4. admonishing readers and other researchers that most, if not all, of the headings are much later additions, and these interpolations tend to be misleading;

5. checking the body of the text for clues which indicate that glosses might have been contextually modified;

6. reading the original Latin to verify that place-names and individuals have not been superceded with translations to English or some other language.

These precautions will aid in separating carefully considered circumstantial evidence from wild guesses or suppositions.

Attempting to determine if the copyist of the *Historia Brittonum* was Nennius, Gildas, or Mark the Hermit leads into an insoluble chronological maze. Beginning with the earliest surviving Manuscript A of the tenth century and working through Manuscript M of the seventeenth century, with a great deal of intertwining, the puzzle leads to a dead-end. A more important question shifts the emphasis to "Where did all this information come from, between Gildas of the sixth century and BEDE of the eighth century, and between Bede of the eighth century to Nennius of the ninth century?"

Focusing upon material relating to Arthur and his milieu, the progression is this: In the *De Excidio*, GILDAS BADONICUS does not mention Hengist or his clan, nor does he record information about VORTIGERN and his offspring, nor does he supply the name of ARTHUR. Gildas offers only three major keys: the name AMBROSIUS AURELIANUS, the Roman royalty of his parents, and a battle at Badon which reverses the fortunes of war in Britain's favor. Bede does not use the epithet *superbus tyrannus*, but instead attributes the misfortune to Vortigern because he was responsible for the Saxon entry into the island. Bede does not give details about Vortigern's clan, and he mentions HENGIST, HORSA, and Oisc only in passing.

What specific material was at the disposal of the individual who penned the *Historia Brittonum*? Roman histories would have been the most likely for 1) Constantine the Great, 2) the extracts about Maximus, 3) SEPTIMIUS SEVERUS, 4) Constantine the Briton usurper, and the withdrawal of Romans from the island of Britain. The three segments of the life of GERMANUS could have come from the work of Constantius Hericus, also known as Constantius of Lyons, who wrote an account of Saint Germanus with but one irregularity: Constantius dedicated his book to Emperor Charles the Bald in either 876 or 877, fourteen or fifteen years after the Prologue.

This means that a reconciliation concerning the Germanus material in the *Historia* has to take one of two paths. One is that dates would have to be structured to properly arrange the events in chronological alignment, which is plausible, since in this particular era there were three ways to determine reckonings and no one knows specifically which method antiquarians used. The second is that some researchers assert that the accounts of Germanus were not part of the original work, but were later interpolations.

Whatever that situation might have been, questions still remain. Where did the scribe find the very detailed information about Hengist's clan recorded in Sections 36, 37, and 38, about the tale of Ambrosius in Sections 40, 41, and 42, and about Vortigern's son Vortimer in Sections 43, 44, 45, and 46? The crowning achievement, however, answers the question "Where did the scribe find the material in Section 56 which is commonly titled 'The Campaigns of Arthur?'"

After the advent of the *Historia Brittonum*, what the earlier two centuries lacked in previously recorded accounts was offset by an inundation of information during each century either side of the new millennium: *The Annales Cambriae*, ÆTHELWEARD's chronicle, *The Anglo-Saxon Chronicle*, WACE's *Brut*, HENRY OF HUNTINGDON, WILLIAM OF MALMESBURY, the *Tysilio*, GEOFFREY OF MONMOUTH, CHRÉTIEN DE TROYES, WILLIAM OF NEWBURGH, LAYAMON, and *Robert de Baron*, roughly in that order. Geoffrey of Monmouth's *History of the Kings of Britain* is the bridge, both figuratively and literally. His book is at a chronological crossroads, somewhere between history and fiction, not factually reliable, and not truly belonging to legend or folklore, but instead occupying a niche which has commonly been labeled as pseudo-history.

Josephus Stevenson issues this admonition in the first paragraph of his Preface: "The information which is extant concerning Nennius, the presumed author of the work entitled 'Historia Britonum,' is so scanty, and the literary history of that production, external and internal, is so obscure and contradictory, that we may despair of being able to decide, with any degree of accuracy, either as to the age, the historical value, or the authorship of this composition."

In spite of this caution, it is worthwhile, especially for Arthurian enthusiasts, to peruse the material about Hengist and his clan, Vortigern and his clan, and Ambrosius, in addition to the antiquarians listed above. Readers will have to accept or reject details in these works depending upon their propensity.

Sources: L. Alcock (AB); R. Collingwood (RB&ES); J. Davies (HOW); K. Jackson (AOH); F. Reno (HKA); W. Skene (FABW); J. Stevenson (N: HB).

Nimuë, Niniane, Nyneue, Nynyue, Nymue, Viviane, Vivien. Nimuë first appears in William Caxton's edition of Malory's manuscript *Le Morte D'Arthur* and is given nominatives of Damosel of the Lake, or Chief Lady of the Lake. In Book 3, Chapter 13, Pellinor is in search of a lady kidnapped from Arthur's court, and when he finds the culprit, Hontzlake, he challenges him to a fight. Hontzlake kills Pellinor's horse, and in a rage, Pellinor draws his sword and gives the villain "such a stroke upon the helm that he clave the head down to the chin," and Hontzlake falls to the earth dead.

When Nimuë is taken back to Arthur's court, MERLIN is besotted by her. Since he would never leave her side, she decides to take advantage of him and have him teach her everything he knows, although Merlin is aware of her purpose. He accepts his destiny, and it happens one day that he shows her a rock wrought by enchantment. Nimuë convinces Merlin to go under the stone, and she devises it so that (allegedly) in spite of Merlin's craft, he can never free himself from the stone.

Nimuë (Vivien), however, is not evil; it is she who loved and saved King Arthur from the wrath of MORGAN LE FAY, who attempted to have ACCOLON kill Arthur with Excalibur, which Morgan had given him. Nimuë intervenes several other times to save Arthur and his knights from dire consequences:

- she warns Arthur of a beautiful mantle sent by Morgan which would "burn him to coals if he were to wear it;"
- she retrogressively causes Lady Ettard to love Pelleas and Pelleas to hate Lady Ettard, and in so doing Nimuë and Pelleas "loved together during their life days;"
- she makes sure that Pelleas becomes a knight of Arthur's Round Table, but arranges that he never has to encounter stronger knights at jousts and tournaments;
- she once again saves Arthur's life by recruiting Tristram's aid in rescuing him from Annowre, a very powerful, evil sorceress.

Oddly, in *Le Morte*, when Arthur is ferried to Avalon, there are three queens in the boat—Queen Morgan le Fay, the unnamed Queen of Northgales, and another unnamed Queen of the Wastelands. But then Malory includes one more, Nimuë, the Chief LADY OF THE LAKE, and concludes that he knows no more of Arthur's death. In *Ladies of the Lake*, Caitlin and John Matthews cite an explanation of Nimuë's final appearance in *Le Morte* which claims she's on the barge specifically to counter-balance Morgan le Fay. Then they comment that (Nimuë) and her chief opponent (Morgan) "are brought together to cancel each other out, as well as add to the ambiguity of Arthur's fate."

In order to understand why Nimuë encases Merlin, the co-authors proffer a reason based on a passage from *The Didot Perceval*: "And then Merlin came to Perceval and to Blayse his master, and he took leave of them and told them that Our Lord did not wish that he should show himself to people, yet that he would not be able to die before the end of the world; ... 'and I wish to make a lodging outside your palace and to

Because Merlin is beguiled by Nimuë, she persuades him to teach her all he knows before she coaxes him into the crystal cave. Illustration by Gustave Doré, 1868.

dwell there and I will prophesy whatever Our Lord commands of me. And all those who will see my lodging will name it the *esplumoir* [a moulting cage for predatory birds] of Merlin.'"

The Matthewses conclude, "When one views the Merlin-Nimuë story in the light of [*The Didot Perceval*], one sees a story with a very different emphasis and motivation. Merlin, tired of the world and of the need to constantly intervene in its concerns, retires to his *esplumoir*, accompanied by his faery lover or sister (who was perhaps both!) where he remains. Nimuë, prepared by him for the role, takes Merlin's place as helper and adviser to Arthur, whom she continues to protect until his passing to Avalon."

Sources: T. Malory (LMD'A), C&J Matthews (LOTL); D. Skeels (DP).

Nomen. A *nomen* generally indicates an individual's *gens*, or clan. For instance, Ambrosius's last name appears in Gildas Badonicus's manuscript as "Aurelianus." The ending *-anus* or *-us* is *nomen* derived, which is why Ambrosius Aurelianus may appear as Ambrosius Aurelian or Aurelius Ambrosius, the name used by Geoffrey of Monmouth. *The Historic King Arthur* conjectures that Ambrosius's ancestry stems from Lucius Domitius Aurelianus, an emperor of the Western Roman Empire who ruled from 270 to 275. The wall around Rome was built by him, which is named the Aurelian Wall. He was also known as *Restitutor Orbis,* Restorer of the World.

Sources: Encyclopedia Britannica; F. Reno (HKA); L. Thorpe (GM: HKA).

Northumbrians were those tribes or clans who settled north of the River Humber. Part of this group was also known as GWYR Y GOGLEDD, "Men of the North," who had remained loyal to the Roman way of life in spite of Roman withdrawal several decades earlier. Some of the Gwyr y Gogledd tribe assimilated with the Welsh.

Nut, Nudd, Nodens, Nuth, Lludd, Lear. Yder/ Ider's father is named Nut in the romances of CHRÉTIEN DE TROYES, Nudd in *The Mabinogion*, and Nuth in JOHN OF GLASTONBURY's manuscript. John Davies lists the Nodens/ Nudd/Lludd shrine as dating to 367 C.E., and Collingwood links the name to King Lear.

Geoffrey Ashe writes, "I am not sure who Nuth was, or what he was king of. He may be the same as Nudd, the father of Gwyn, Glastonbury Tor's uncanny resident. Nudd in turn was originally the god Nodons, who had a temple at Lydney in the Forest of Dean. But Sir IDER emerges from the mists as a human character."

Sources: G. Ashe (LKA); P. Clayton (GASB); R. Collingwood (RB&ES); J. Davies (HOW); P.B. Ellis (DCM).

Octha, Octa, Osla, Osla Big Knife, Æsc, Oisc, Oesc, Oeric. Whereby Hengist's son appears as ÆSC/OISC/OESC/Oeric in *The Anglo-Saxon Chronicle* and Bede's work, the name Octha is used in the *Historia Brittonum*, and Octa is the variant in *The Chronicle of the Kings of Britain* and *The History of the Kings of Britain*. In all instances, however, the names are equated with Hengist's son.

Octha is accepted as a historical figure. His name first appears in *The Anglo-Saxon Chronicle*, entry 456/457, when HENGIST and ÆSC fought against the Britons at a place called Creganford. Thereafter his name is listed in entries 465, 473, and 488, the last entry stating that Æsc succeeded to the kingdom. One variant of the *Chronicle* (the Parker version) claims in Year 488 he ruled for twenty-four years, another (the Laud Chronicle) that he ruled for thirty-four years. Those differences, of course, would offer two separate death-years for Octha, but after meticulous investigation and comparative analyses, the discrepancy can be resolved.

One other seeming oddity is that there are two separate years for Octha's succession to kingship. One is the year 455, and the second is 488. This discrepancy, however, can also be resolved. The first date states outright that Æsc succeeded to the kingdom as a co-ruler with his father Hengist after HORSA— Hengist's brother—was killed. The second date, in 488, implies that Octha succeeded to the kingdom as the sole ruler. From this last succession, it is safe to assume that his father, Hengist, was either killed in 488 or perhaps in the year 473, the last entry which names him.

Four Welsh/Briton texts also record Octha's name: Bede's *English History*, Nennius's the *His-*

toria Brittonum, the anonymous *Tysilio*, and Geoffrey of Monmouth's *The History of the Kings of Britain*. BEDE simply states that Oeric first came to Britain at the invitation of VORTIGERN. The *HB* provides more details, recording that 1) Octha was brought over upon invitation of Hengist; 2) Octha came down from the north of Britain after Hengist's (more likely Horsa's) death; and 3) the English leaders sought help from Germany. By the turn of the millennium, Octha's battles against AURELIUS AMBROSIUS and UTERPENDRAGON are recorded in the *Tysilio* and *HKB*. Interestingly, the *HB* lists Octha in the introductory section of Arthur's battlelist, but the more detailed later manuscripts do not have Octha waging wars against someone named Arthur.

Combining all the resources, a comprehensive story about Octha emerges. After Hengist had allied himself with Vortigern, he invited more English, including his sons Octha and Ebissa, into Vortigern's territory. Octha was sent to a vague location in the north, identified in the *Historia Brittonum* somewhere near a wall, and in Monmouth's work somewhere between Deira and Scotland. Continuing with Monmouth's narrative, Octha and Ebissa revolt against Utherpendragon and ravage northern Britain, defeating the son of Constantine at York. In a subsequent battle Octha and Ebissa are defeated at the battle of Mount Damen, captured, and imprisoned in London. The two English leaders escape to Germany and return to the island with a large army.

Once again, the *Historia Brittonum* picks up the narrative by sketchily adding that upon Horsa's death, Octha came down from the north and fought against Arthur. The saga of Octha ends with only a vague reference: "When the English had been defeated in all their battles, they brought German kings to the island to rule over them." Monmouth concludes by recording that Utherpendragon defeats Octha and sees him killed.

Sources: Bede (HECP); J. Gantz (TM); G. Garmonsway (ASC); G. Monmouth (HKB); P. Roberts (COTKB); J. Stevenson (N: HB).

Offa. Although King Offa of Mercia — who ruled from 757 to 798 C.E.— is seemingly anom-

alous in a framework pursuing King Arthur's history and legend of the second and fifth century, what is consequential is that a 130-mile dyke has been attributed to him, which conflicts with an ancient manuscript describing that the remains of this particular earthwork is the Wall of Severus, dating to the beginning of the second century. If indeed the earthwork is of Roman origin, then it aligns itself with SEVERUS, who was the third emperor to cross to Britain at the very same time that LUCIUS ARTORIUS CASTUS was the *dux bellorum* sent to Hadrian's Wall.

It is Nennius's *British History* which raises disputatious circumstances. In Section 23 of Manuscript A under the heading of Roman Britain, Nennius records:

> Severus was the third [emperor] to cross to the British. To protect the subject provinces from barbarian invasion, he built a wall rampart there, which is called Guaul in the British language, from sea to sea across the width of Britain, that is for one hundred and thirty-two miles = *from Penguaul, a place which is called Cenail in Irish, Peneltun in English, to the estuary of the Clyde and Caer Pentaloch, where it finishes. The said Severus built it ruggedly, but in vain. The emperor Carausius rebuilt it later, and fortified it with seven forts, between the two estuaries, and a Round House of polished stone on the banks of the river Carron which takes its name from him; he erected a triumphal arch to commemorate his victory.* = Severus ordered the wall to be built between the British and Pictos and Scottos, because the Western Scotti and the Northern Picti were fighting against the Brittones, for they were at peace with each other. Not long afterwards, Severus died in Britain. [Italics indicate Mommsen's addition, 1892.]

What the *British History* reveals requires some important rationale. That the wall (Guaul) was built for protection from barbarian invasion doesn't elicit skepticism. Of the nine legionary fortresses, five form an arc along the borders of Wales because of the stated fact that the Irish were intruding into Wales from the west, and the Anglians invading from the east.

The one discrepancy is the Wall of Severus described by its "width" instead of its "length." Yet the very next segment of the *Historia Brittonum* indicates the wall was one hundred and thirty-two miles long. Some critics of the "Severn Wall" theory vilify this crucial fact by attempting to refute that distance because it would be so easy for a scribe to make an error by recording something other than cxxxii *millia* (one hundred and thirty-two miles). However, the manuscript of Paulus Orosius, circa 415, writes out that number — *centum triginta due millia* — as does Nennius's Manuscript A of the tenth century, the latter being the manuscript which Stevenson claims is the "least vitiated" by extraneous material and thus the one adopted by him as the basis of its text. Unfortunately, both John Morris in *British History* and the *Annales Cambriae* record the date numerically.

The italicized material above, between the crosses (= *from Penguaul ... to ... his victory* =), signify an interpolation and explanation. The location of Penguaul is self-explanatory; *Pen-* means head, top, end, or mouth, and *-guaul* means wall. Combined, then, Penguaul would be "the top or end of the wall." The English version (Peneltun) means the "town at the top or end." For further clarification, this locale is near the estuary of the Cluth, translated to River Clyde. The modern spelling for that particular river is now Clwyd, and its location is unmistakably the northern coast of Wales at the Irish Sea near Prestatyn. At the southern end, during the occupation of the island in Roman times, that body of water was called the Severn Outlet.

Interestingly, what Nennius copies about "seven forts between two estuaries" shows prior knowledge of the area. Whoever penned the original did not specifically name each fort, but Peter Clayton in his *Guide to the Archaeological Sites of Britain*, published in 1976, provides those names independent of his knowledge of Nennius's history. It cannot be merely coincidental that Clayton names the seven forts:

> On the other side of Conwy Bay and along the high ground of Gwynedd, is a long line of Iron Age hill forts. They are all situated on high ground which, in many instances, provides their defence by virtue of steep cliff faces rather than strong walls. While for the avid collector of hill forts they are in most instances worth visiting, there is little to describe except the number of their ramparts

and the extent of their acreage. The notable ones amongst this series running from Colwyn are: Pen y Corddyn-mawr, Parc y meirch (Dinorben), Moel Hiraddug, Moel y Gaer Flint, Pen y cloddiau, Moel y Gaer Ruthin, and Foel Fenlli.

Very few modern archaeologists write about the Round House, but Christopher Snyder gives this information:

> More that fifty years of excavation at the multivallate hillfort of Dinorben in Denbighshire revealed several periods of discontinuous occupation spanning the early Iron age to the sub–Roman period. Around 260, a large round house was built at the northern end of the site, followed by the construction of small curvilinear huts at the southern end. Associated items include a large number of Roman coins, the latest being two very worn House of Valentinian bronzes from Arles. By the fourth century, Dinorben appears to have become a rural estate, akin to a southern villa, with the round house possibly representing the residence of a Romano-Celtic noble. The round house was succeeded, probably in the early fifth century, by a roughly constructed aisled timber dwelling (identified from a system of post-holes) at the northern end, associated with fragments of late Roman flanged bowls of fine pink ware. A sub–Roman reoccupation thus seems likely, though it is not yet possible to trace the continuity between this early fifth-century community and the latest objects from the site, which include several "Anglo-Saxon" ornamental bronze items, a bronze stud (similar to those found at Dinas Powys), and a polychrome glass bead fragment.

The obverse side of the coin — that this linear earthwork is Offa's Dyke and not the Wall of Severus — is addressed by Ian Bapty, Offa's Dyke archaeological management officer. He cites Steve Blake and Scott Lloyd's book *The Keys to Avalon*, which proposes the theory that the earthwork is the Wall of Severus. Conceding that there is an "absence of any concrete archaeological material to support the conventional Anglo-Saxon association for the Dyke," Bapty writes,

> Scott and Steve are quite right to indicate how little detailed understanding we have both of Offa's Dyke and the wider historical period to which it belongs. However, that

should not cloud the fact there are really very good archaeological reasons for thinking Offa's Dyke to be Anglo-Saxon rather than Roman. The ancient written sources are potentially insightful but also present a minefield of interpretative and paleographic problems for modern historians, and it is crucial to look rigorously at the evidence on the ground as a balance in this process.

He concludes by summarizing: "In short, the archaeological and historical anomalies become simply intractable in relation to any attempt to interpret the Dyke as a Roman structure. The stratigraphic sequence from Ffridd tells us no more than that the Dyke is later than the second century in date; what the broader picture indicates is that it must be much later and almost certainly post–Roman."

Bapty is positive enough to state, "Ultimately, I'd be ready to wager my granny on the fact that Offa's Dyke is Anglo-Saxon and not Roman," but then he adds this conundrum:

Although I'd also have to say that I'd be keeping granny firmly out of the stakes when it comes to betting on most other aspects of our understanding of the Dyke, including key issues such as exactly why it was built, how it was built, and what it's original appearance and total extent was. I think it is the process of trying to answer these questions which may throw up some real and lasting revelations concerning not just Offa's Dyke itself, but the very origins of Welsh and English culture and society.

There is one last consideration about the possibility of Offa's Dyke being the wall built by Severus, and that would be whether or not King Offa would have the technology, manpower, and finances for such a formidable undertaking. A comparison of what David Breeze writes about Hadrian's Wall provides an incisive reason why a 130-mile earthwork would most likely be a Roman project: "The construction of Hadrian's Wall would not have been a costly venture for the imperial treasury. The builders were soldiers already employed by the state while the materials were there for the taking, if not actually imperial property. If built by civilian contractors, the cost of the Wall would have been astronomical, perhaps 100 million pounds sterling at today's prices."

Archaeologists have not yet been able to confirm or deny either assertion about the dyke's origin. Hopefully, further excavations will resolve the mystery in the near future.

Sources: P. Clayton (GASB); P. Blair (RB&EE); S. Blake/S. Lloyd (KTA); R. Collingwood/J. Myres (RB&ES); J. Davies (HOW); L. Sherley-Price (HECP); C. Snyder (AAOT); J. Stevenson (N: HB); M. Winterbottom (G: ROB&OW).

Oisc. Oisc is Bede's name for the son of Hengist, found in other works as Octha, Octa, and Æsc.

See also The Entry Octha.

Source: L. Sherley-Price (BEDE: HEC&P).

orientali sacrilegorum. A term used by GILDAS BADONICUS in the *De Excidio* to refer to English Anglians settled in East Anglia on the island, defined as "impious easterners."

See also IMPIOUS EASTERNERS.

Osla Big Knife, Octha, Æsc. Under a variety of names, Hengist's son is listed in at least five manuscripts, but of primary intrigue is the appearance of Octha's name as Osla Big Knife in two different tales of *The Mabinogion*, the major source of Welsh tradition. The honorific appellation of "Big Knife" derives from the Saxon term *seax*, meaning "broad sword," a slightly different description for Big Knife. Throughout Saxon manuscripts, many references refer to the Saxons as "the Longknives." The name Osla Big Knife is as out of place in a Welsh context as CERDIC is in an Anglo-Saxon one.

Osla Big Knife first appears in the "Culhwch and Olwen" tale as one of Arthur's favorite soldiers, a comrade important enough to be included in an invocation of many Welsh heroes. His importance is further magnified in a major role when he is individually identified fighting against Arthur's enemy, Twrch Trwyth. In that battle Osla follows Twrch Trwyth into a river, where Osla loses his knife, his sheath fills up with water, and Osla is dragged to the bottom.

This seems to unequivocally suggest that Osla drowns. Yet, even more bizarre than Osla's name appearing as an ally in Welsh tradition, Osla reappears (even though he has drowned) in a later Welsh tale known as "The Dream of Rhonabwy." In this latter tale, Arthur's huge army is on the move "to be at the Battle of Badon by noon in order to fight *against* Osla Big Knife." Not only is Osla still alive, but now he is Arthur's enemy at the Battle of Badon, the singular most important battle attributed to a historic Arthur. If Welsh tradition is considered as a supplement of history, then Octha is initially a comrade of Arthur's — perhaps as *foederati* — but later he becomes an enemy who fights against Arthur and is killed at the Battle of Badon.

Sources: J. Gantz (TM); F. Reno (HKA/HFAE).

Osmail, Ysfael, Osbald. Cunedda's second son, born circa 420–424. His kingdom becomes Ysfeillion (also known as Maes Osmeliaun), a portion of the Isle of Anglesey, just off the coast of Wales.

Sources: L. Alcock (AB); P. Bartram (WG); S. Blake/S. Lloyd (KTA).

Outigern, Dutigern. In the index of the *Historia Brittonum*, John Morris includes Outigern with entries of Vortigern. Yet Outigern appears in the section commonly headed "The Northern History, Part 2," which deals with Deira and Bernicia. Section 62 gives notice that "At that time Outigern then fought bravely against the English nation. Then Talhaearn Tad Awen was famed in poetry; and Aneirin and Taliesin and Bluchbard and Cian, known as Gueinth Guaut, were all simultaneously famed in British verse."

Josephus Stevenson lists the name as Dutigern who fights against the Anglians. And, like Morris, he gives no more information. Later scholars, however, provide more detail about Outigern's floruit. Leslie Alcock mentions this king several times, associating him with Ceredic of Elmet and Ida, stating that Outigern fought against the Northumbrians, which would have been the late sixth century, later than King Arthur's historic era.

Sources: L. Alcock (AB); J. Morris (HB); J. Stevenson (N: HB).

Owein Dantguin, Owain Ddantgwyn, Eugein. In Welsh genealogies, Owein Dantguin (Eugein Dantguin) is of the Cunos clan. In addition to the above variants of his name, the Archaic

Welsh Eugein is rendered in a number of ways during the Old-Middle Welsh period: Ewen, Quein, Iguein, Yuein, and Huweyn, all of which are found in the *Liber Landavensis*. (*See also* the partial genealogy in the entry for CATGOLAUN LAUHIR.) He succeeds his father, Enniaun Girt, and his grandfather CUNEDDA, and precedes his son Cineglas (CUNEGLASUS), whose name appears in the *De Excidio* as one of the castigated kings after AMBROSIUS AURELIANUS's death. His nephew is MAGLOCUNUS (Maelgwn), whose obituary is recorded in the *Annales Cambriae*.

His name appears only once in the genealogies, but because Owein is a popular figure in Welsh tradition, there is a great deal of speculation about the Owein who might be associated with Arthur. As a matter of fact, some researchers — most notably Graham Phillips and Martin Keatman — have proposed the name Owein Dantguin as a doublet for Arthur himself. In their book *King Arthur: The True Story* they write, "Cuneglasus' father [i.e., Owain Ddantgwyn] is therefore the most credible contender for the warrior who bore the title Arthur."

They correctly point out that with the exception of one section of the Welsh genealogies, there is nothing else recorded of Owain Ddantgwyn, suggesting that this Owain was Arthur:

- Owain ruled in the last decade of the fifth century, the period in which the *Historia Brittonum* locates "Arthur."
- He was the son of one of the Gwynedd kings known as the *head dragons*, similar to the title of Arthur's father.
- He was the most powerful ruler in Britain at the time of the Battle at Badon, where the British were led to victory by "Arthur."
- He was the father of Cuneglasus, whose predecessor was called the "Bear," the origin of the name "Arthur."
- He may have died in the valley of Camlan near Dolgellau.

Another researcher who focuses upon the historic King Arthur builds a case against Phillips and Keatman's proposal, but of the five points made by the latter authors, three are valid, one is dubious, and the last is unfounded speculation. *The Historic King Arthur* establishes a comprehensive 100-year chronology of the sixth century, and Owein Dantguin's floriut/lifespan would indeed have been 495–525/480–440, during the era of Arthur. Similarly, Maglocunus of the Cunos line is termed the "dragon of the island" by GILDAS BADONICUS, an epithet also acquired by Arthur's father. Furthermore, as a grandson of Cunedda, Owein would have been a powerful ruler in Britain, most likely inheriting his father's kingdom of Rhos, a domain on the northern coast of Wales. Owein Dantguin's floruit/lifespan also coincides with the date most commonly proposed for the battle of Badon.

Yet the epithet of the "Bear" for Arthur is highly debatable, and the site of Arthur's fatal battle at Camlann is even more tentative. Phillips and Keatman qualify their response by the use of "may have," but the Afon Gamlan near Dolgellau is only one of several other strong contenders: Camboglanna at Hadrian's Wall, the River Cam in Cornwall, the River Cam near Slimbridge east of the River Severn, and Caman Llan near Nevern, Wales.

However, the most telling discrepancy in the proposal that Owein Dantguin is Arthur appears in only one other genre, which is literary tradition. What makes this particular segment of the quest for the historic Arthur so difficult is that the only names we have to rely on are the variables Owein/Owain/Eugein.

One such Owain is Owain Finduu, mentioned by Arthur Wade-Evans in *The Emergence of England and Wales*. But Owain Finduu is the brother of Constantine and Peblig and son of Maxen and Elen; his chronological timeframe would be before the Roman withdrawal, prior to the historic Arthurian era. Another possible Owain is Owain ap Hywel Dda, but his era is in the mid–tenth century. The closest candidate would be Owain ap Urien, whose floruit is in the second half of the sixth century.

"The Dream of Rhonabwy" in *The Mabinogion* lists Owein as Owein son of Uryen, but Owein, Uryen, and their kingdom of Rheged wasn't established until the late 500s, and Owein ap Uryen therefore would be misplaced in a battle which is commonly dated between 490 and 500. An in-depth search shows that the only

Owein listed in insular history and Welsh genealogies who was alive during that chronological timeframe is, as Phillips and Keatman asserted, Owein Dantguin. The flaw of Phillips-Keatman scenario, however, is that Owein and Arthur are adversaries in that conflict at Badon, which means that if Owein is in fact Arthur, then Arthur is fighting himself.

Logistically, Owein Dantguin can be cast as himself in the role of Arthur's enemy at the Battle of Badon. Of the entire Rhonabwy tale, at least a third of it is devoted to four gwyddbwyll matches between Arthur and Owein, which is an allegory within the story. While the two are playing their first game, a page approaches and complains to Owein that Arthur's young lads are harassing Owein's ravens, but Arthur refuses to interfere and continues the game. During the second match, a different squire approaches and complains to Owein that Arthur's pages are killing and wounding the ravens. Again, Arthur refuses to interfere and continues playing. In the third game a page interrupts and complains to Owein that the noblest of the ravens had been killed, and those surviving had been severely wounded. For the third time, Arthur ignores the complaint.

In the same match a great turmoil erupts and a page hurries to Arthur and tells him that now the ravens are killing Arthur's squires and pages. Arthur tells Owein to call off his ravens, but Owein ignores the request. At the beginning of the fourth match there is another uproar, men screaming and ravens cawing. An angry rider complains that the ravens have killed Arthur's retinue and the sons of nobles from the island. Arthur tells Owein to call off his ravens and squeezes the gold figurines on the gwyddbwyll board until they become dust. Owein orders a warrior to lower the banner, and there was peace on both sides.

If Rhonabwy's dream is interpreted symbolically, it tells a superbly accurate story of the carnage and slaughter during the Badon battle. If Owein (Dantguin) is a symbol of kingship for the GWYR Y GOGLEDD (the Cunos clan of the North) and allied with OSLA BIG KNIFE, and if his tribe the Gwyr y Gogledd are the Ravens (Hræfn) of the Hyrpe tribe, the Black Warriors, then Owein and Osla are allies who are locked in a deadly battle against Arthur, a battle which will determine the fates of the two powerful kingdoms. The Britons are "victorious" when Osla Big Knife calls for a truce.

Sources: P. Bartram (WG); R. Castledon (KATBL); J. Davis (HW); J. Gantz (TM); Phillips/Keatman (KATS); J. Morris (HB); F. Reno (HKA/HFAE); J. Stevenson (N-HB); A. Wade-Evans (EOE&W).

Palomides, Plomyd, Palamides, Palamedes, Pallamedes. Palomedes, whom Gwynn Williams calls "another innovation," is the name used by Gottfried von Strassburg in the *Prose Tristan* during the first half of the thirteenth century. Palomedes, like Tristan, develops an unrequited love for Iseult when he sees her. According to Williams, Gottfried's *Prose Tristan* "achieved a popularity almost without peer; it blotted out the poems and became the only recognized form of the Tristan story. It greatly influenced Sir Thomas Malory's *Sir Tristram* and its impact can still be felt in Tennyson and Swinburne in the nineteenth century." Richard Barber writes of the impact suggested by Gwynn Williams, and includes references to Palomides first in his text *Arthur of Albion* and later echoes the same material in *King Arthur: Hero and Legend*.

Palomides (sometimes referred to as Palamides in some of Malory's texts) appears in Books 8, 9, 10, and 11 of Malory's *Le Morte d'Arthur*. In Book 8 Palomides is described as a Saracen who was "drawn onto La Beal Isoud (Isolt) and proffered her many gifts, for he loved her passingly well." He demonstrates his prowess by unhorsing nine knights (among them GAWAIN, KAY, and Sagramore) the very first day of jousting so that he had great worship and many called him the Knight with the Black Shield.

On the second day of the tournament he smote down two kings, but then TRISTRAM came onto the field. Twice he unhorsed Palomides, the second time smiting him on the head. Tristram then ordered Palomides to stay away from Isoud or Tristram would kill him.

In Chapter 29 of Book 8, two ladies at court seek to kill Isoud's maiden, Bragwaine. Bragwaine is bound feet and hands in the forest, where Palomides accidentally comes upon her. He returns her safely to Isoud, who grants Palomides a boon for rescuing the maid.

Isoud, realizing her mistake in granting Palomides a boon, complains to her husband, King Mark, and asks him to resolve the issue. After listening to both sides, Mark rules that Isoud must honor her boon, which is that he shall take the queen and "govern her as he pleases." But the king warns that upon Tristram's return, Palomides will have to deal with a death-struggle.

When Tristram returns, he tracks Palomides. A strong battle ensues for the love of the lady, in which both "were wounded passing sore, but Palomides was much sorer wounded." Isoud intervenes, pleading with Tristram that he should not kill Palomides because he is a Saracen and has not been baptized. Palomides is sent "onto the court of King Arthur" where Palomides will declare that "within this land there be only four loves, Sir Launcelot du Lake and Queen Guenever, and Sir Tristram de Liones and Queen Isoud."

In Book 9, when DAGONET, posing as Mordred, is chasing King Mark, Palomides (unknown by name to the knights at this point) intervenes, unhorsing Dagonet, Brandiles, Uwaine, Ozana, GRIFLET, and AGRAVAIN. Palomides's varlet then goes to a castle to seek meats and drinks from the lady who resides there. Palomides is identified as the knight following the glatisant beast, and the lady swoons, knowing this knight is her son.

In Book 10, Chapter 73, Tristram, Isoud, and Palomides are in Arthur's court. Arthur is taken by Isoud's beauty, and when he rides to greet her, Palomides challenges and unhorses him, not knowing he is Arthur, but mistaking him for an errant knight. Tristram, realizing that it is Lancelot who comes to the rescue, settles the matter amicably.

Later, Palomides betrays Tristram and under a different banner fights against him. Isoud knows that Palomides is battling Tristram incognito, but when she tells him of it, he accepts Palomides's word against hers.

Palomides eventually identifies himself as son and heir unto Astlabor and confesses to Epinogris that he is in love with Isoud, King Mark's queen. Epinogris cautions him of Tristram, a fact which is already known to Palomides.

The enmity between Tristram and Palomides is not resolved until the passage of many adventures. In Book 12 they attack each other like wild boars and fight for more than two hours. Tristram knocks the sword from Palomides's hand, but when Palomides is ordered to fetch his weapon and fight onto death, he refuses. He beseeches Tristram to forgive him and to allow him to be shriven and baptized. In the end, Palomides is baptized at Carlisle and the two ride to Arthur's court and feast at the Round Table with the other knights, after which "Sir Palomides followed the Questing Beast."

Although the Questing Beast (the glatisant beast) is also associated with Pellinore, Palomides is mentioned only three more times, in Book 20 of Malory, in which he allies himself with LANCELOT against Gawain.

Sources: G. Ashe (MBI); R. Barber (AA/KA: H&L); T. Malory (LMD'A); Gottfried (T); N. Lacy/G. Ashe (AH); G. Williams (E: SFA).

Pascent, Paschent, Pasgen. Very little is written about Pascent, and in the three manuscripts where he appears (the *Historia Brittonum*, Monmouth's *History of the Kings of Britain*, and the *Tysilio*), his roles are diametrically opposed. According to the *Historia Brittonum*, Pascent is Vortigern's third son, brother of VORTIMER and Catigern. Pascent is listed as the ruler of two countries, Builth (Buellt, Buelt, Guelt) and Gwerthrynion (Gwrtheyrnion, Guorthigirniaun), "by permission of Ambrosius, who was the great king among all the kings of the British nation." The supposition is that Ambrosius is a reference to AMBROSIUS AURELIANUS and that Pascent must have been Ambrosius's ally, or at least ingratiated to him.

Builth and Gwerthrynion were two of the clan's countries in the central Midlands, east of Ceredigion, the territory granted to Cerdic, Cunedda's son.

Monmouth's Pascent, however, is entirely different. Instead of being Ambrosius's ally, he is an adversary. In the *HKB*, Paschent is identified as "the third son of Vortigern by his first wife," but the similarity with the Pascent of the *HB* ends there. In *HKB*, Paschent flees to Germany and stirs up the Germans against Aurelius Ambrosius. With a great troop of German reinforcements, he lands in northern Britain and is defeated in battle, retreats to Ireland, and recruits the help of the Irish king. Paschent then hires a Saxon to poison Aurelius and upon the great king's death, Utherpendragon tracks down both Paschent and the Irish king and kills them.

Sources: J. Morris (HB); P. Roberts (COKB); J. Stevenson (N: HB); L. Thorpe (GM: HKB).

Pasgen. *see* PASCENT.

Paternus Pesrut, Paternus of the Red Robes, Padarn Peisrudd, Padarn Redcoat. Information about Paternus Pesrut is quite scarce, and what exists offers very general statements which aren't verified as reliable.

The Welsh genealogies as reflected by Leslie Alcock assert that Paternus's father was TACITUS, his son was ÆTERNUS, and his grandson was CUNEDDA. The names Tacitus, Paternus, and Æternus imply Roman heritage, and the epithet "Red Robes" for Paternus suggests his royalty status in Wales.

Brynley Roberts, in an article appearing in *The Arthur of the Welsh*, includes the name Padarn Peisrudd when listing the thirteen treasures of the island of Britain, referring to him as *pais Padarn Peisrudd*, the coat which fitted only a nobleman.

H.H. Scullard is one of the very few who makes comments about Padarn. In discussing the events of mid–fourth century and the ensuing repairs required because of assaults by the enemy, Scullard writes:

> The outlying forts were abandoned, and the system of *areani* [frontier scouts] abolished, but it is very far from certain that *vici* [civilian settlements outside the walls of fortresses] on the Wall were also abandoned and the civilians moved into the forts. Also controversial is the status of some kings in the Lowlands of Scotland who had Roman names, such as Cluim (Clemens), Cinhil (Quintilius), Annwn (Antoninus), and Padarn (Paternus). Since Padarn was also called Pesrut (The Man of the Red Cloak) some scholars suppose that these kings were set up by Rome as buffer rulers between the Picts and the Wall; others ... suggest that they were anti–

Roman and owed their Roman names merely to conversion to Christianity.

John Morris also names four dynasties established north of Hadrian's Wall, but his names differ from the listing by Scullard. Morris lists one dynasty under the leadership of Quintilius Clemens, while Scullard lists those names as two separate dynasties. Morris and Scullard agree on Antoninus and Paternus, but Morris lists the fourth as Catellius Decianus, which seems to be corrupt. Morris explains that these four names were Roman, containing the "old-fashioned form of *nomen* and *cognomen*, family and personal name, that in the later fourth century remained principally in vogue. Men so named were not native kings to whom Rome granted recognition, but Roman officers placed over border barbarians."

Although some scholars seem to aver that these dynasties were indeed native kings, Morris cites what Theodosius had devised in Africa several years later, which was to "put reliable *praefecti* in charge of the peoples he encountered." Morris therefore claims Theodosius applied this policy to the British frontier in 368.

Concerning the object of this search, Paternus was then transferred to Wales, and his dynasty didn't "expire until the thirteenth century, in the person of Llewellyn the Great."

When Morris writes of Cunedda, he explains, "Cunedda was the grandson of the Paternus who had been appointed, probably by Valentinian, to rule the Votadini of the north-east coast, between the Tyne and the Forth. Like Vortigern's sons, he [Cunedda] is one of the first persons in authority in Britain who were known only by a native personal name."

Sources: L. Alcock (AB); R. Bromwich (AOW); R. Bromwich (TYP); R. Coghlan (EAL); J. Morris (AOA); B. Roberts (C&O-SL); H. Scullard (RB: OOE).

Pendragon. Without making an unfounded quantum leap, it is possible to attach an array of circumstances to identify the undisputedly historical CONSTANTIUS III as King Arthur's father. Graham Phillips and Martin Keatman clarify the epithet Pendragon when they assert, "Surely it is no coincidence that GEOFFREY OF MON-MOUTH calls Arthur's father Pendragon, from the Welsh meaning 'head (or chief) dragon.'"

At the core of this equation — that Constantius III of Roman history can plausibly be linked to Pendragon of Arthurian history — is material drawn not only from history and Geoffrey of Monmouth, but also from Welsh sources and oral tradition which lead to the epithet "Pendragon." If an interpreter-translator modifies Geoffrey of Monmouth's proposition from "The House of Constantine" to "The House of Constantius," new perspectives emerge.

The name Pendragon does not appear in the writings of GILDAS BADONICUS, BEDE, or NENNIUS. Neither is it used in the *Annales Cambriae* or *The Anglo-Saxon Chronicle*. It is difficult to corroborate a specific date when this epithet was coined, but its initial use can be traced to either the *Tysilio* or Geoffrey of Monmouth's *History of the Kings of Britain* around the first triad of the eleventh century.

Most scholars attribute the epithet UTHERPENDRAGON to Monmouth. Translator Lewis Thorpe records the name "Utherpendragon" for the very first time when listing Constantine's three sons, Constans, Aurelius, and Utherpendragon. Interestingly, the first two sons are given proper names, the first one unidentifiable as an uncle of the historic King Arthur, and the second equated with AMBROSIUS AURELIANUS. Curiously, the third son is given an epithet, which Thorpe explains in a footnote on page 151 of the text: "Utherpendragon (*Jesus*, Ythr ben Dragwn), takes his name from the Comet and the two Golden Dragons which he had made on p. 202. Geoffrey calls him Utherpendragon from his first appearance."

Jesus is a reference to one of the surviving manuscripts about Monmouth's *History*, and the Welsh epithet used in that manuscript is Ythr ben Dragwn, not unusual because Monmouth was transcribing and translating from a Welsh text. "Ythr" offers a controversial playground for scholars, with no resolution in sight. Some Welsh linguists contend that this term (and its variants) are traceable to a Welsh poem known as *Pa Gur*, and that the term also appears in the Welsh Triads, but the dates of inception for these sources vary as widely as a century, and there's no solid evidence that these works pre-date Monmouth.

The second word in the *Jesus* manuscript, "Pen" (sometimes seen as "Ben"), literally means "head" in Welsh. The third word, of course, means "dragon." The epithet, therefore, literally means "something head dragon." (*See also* UTER-PENDRAGON.)

It's odd, to say the least, that Monmouth has no name for the third son (Constans being the first and Aurelius Ambrosius being the second) on page 151, and the epithet isn't created until page 202. Hence this alleged third son creates a great deal of skepticism and speculation.

It is similarly difficult to extract any type of conclusion from Peter Roberts's translated copy of the *Tysilio* from 1811. A notation by Llanerch, the publishers, cautions that the translation dating from 1811 is a work which "has been taken from a larger one of which the contents are indicated on the sub-facsimile of the title page overleaf." Roberts's title is *Chronicle of the Kings of Britain*, but the subtitle and explanation reads, "translated from the Welsh copy attributed to Tysilio." On the next overleaf, under his own title, he writes, verbatim, "This Book is called The Brut; that is to say, *The History of the Kings of Britain*, from the first to the last." The latter title, is, of course, Monmouth's title.

At any rate, the *Tysilio* gives this account of "Constantine." The names in brackets are Monmouth's variants. "The Britons sent Cyhelin [Guithelinus], the Archbishop of London to solicit assistance from Aldor [Aldronius] ... the king of Brittany. Aldor was much grieved for the Britons, and granted an aid of two thousand men at arms, giving the command to his brother Constantine, who set sail as soon as vessels for them could be got ready."

Roberts includes a footnote explaining the error about Constantine's name being confounded with someone else. He then continues with his narrative: "Constantine married a lady who was the daughter of a Roman chieftain [noble family], and had been educated by Cyhelin [Guithelinus]. By her Constantine had three sons, Constans, Emrys [Aurelius Ambrosius], and Uther-pen-dragon [Utherpendragon]."

The confusion about Constantine carries over to the above passage, but with more intense perplexity. This is the abyss where readers and researchers alike stand and gaze across the breach separating Roman and Welsh history on the one side, and oral tradition and legend on the other (see chart, page 208). Each must decide to either take the leap (significant but not lethal), or be content with Arthurian apologues.

It's very difficult to place the advent of the *Tysilio* in written form; some scholars claim it appeared subsequent to Geoffrey of Monmouth's *HKB*, although Acton Griscom builds a strong case that *Tysilio* came prior to Monmouth, and was, perhaps, even a segment of his "very ancient book." For those who believe the latter, however, Geoffrey could not have had an "ancient" book. Geoffrey might have believed that it was an old manuscript, but it wouldn't have preceded him by more than 20 or 40 years.

Sources: R. Collingwood (RB&ES); E. Duckett (MPE&W); A. Ferrill (FOTRE); G.N. Garmonsway (ASC); J. Morris (BH); G. Phillips/M. Keatman (KA: TS); F. Reno (HFAE); P. Roberts (COKB); L. Sherley-Price (BEDE: HEC&P); L. Thorpe (GM: HKB); M. Winterbottom (G: ROB&OW).

Perceval, Parsifal, Parzival. Although CHRÉTIEN DE TROYES is the creator of Perceval—the first to write about Perceval, the bleeding lance, the Grail, and the Fisher King—there is general consensus that a distinction must be maintained between Perceval and PEREDUR, the hero of the Welsh tale recorded in *The Mabinogion*.

In Chrétien's romance, Perceval is also given a Welsh background. He is a naïve and rather obtuse lad, to say the least, who takes everything literally and stolidly. Upon his first encounter with three knights, he is frightened and assumes they are devils, based on what his mother once described to him. After a number of doltish questions, Perceval believes they are angels, and asks one of them if he is God. When the mounted man explains he is a knight, the boy immediately sets out for Arthur's court, ignoring his mother's pleas.

A brief description of the convoluted story follows: the red knight arrives at court uninvited

Roman History

As detailed in the entries FLAVIUS CONSTANTINUS and CONSTANTIUS III there is no record of a father and son with names of Constantine and Constans from 417 C.E. to the end of the century. Constantine I (the Great) had a son named Constans, but the floruit for that occasion was 318–348. Between the floruit of 400–430, Constantius had two children by Galla Placidia, Justa Grata Honoria and Valentinian III.

In combination, GALLA PLACIDIA and her son VALENTINIAN were in power during the three *adventi* of the *Saxones*, who warred with the Britons.

Technically, Valentinian was emperor from Honorius's death in 423 until his own death in 455.

According to R.G. Collingwood, there is a blank in history between 418 and 421, when Constantius III disappears from Roman history, and Exuperantius becomes acting Praefectus in Gaul. Collingwood conjectures that during this period, Constantius, as the new *Comes Brittaniorum* created by Honorius, might possibly have gone to Britain to reclaim it as a province, since insurrections had been quelled in Gaul.

Welsh History and Oral Tradition

Constantius III falls within the floruit/lifespan for King Arthur.

As the entry UTERPENDRAGON explains, GILDAS BADONICUS does not provide a name for AMBROSIUS AURELIANUS's father, but does relate that Ambrosius's father "wore the purple" and was Roman royalty. This would equate with "Arthur's" father as Roman aristocracy.

Typical of Gildas, he does not name the *superbus tyrannus*, but does describe the plight of the Britons, continually fighting internal wars with the *Saxones*, who were let into the island by the SUPERBUS TYRANNUS, a conventional Roman practice of sending *foederati* to various provinces to ease the conflicts in Gaul.

Bede proposed that VORTIGERN was the *superbus tyrannus* in Gildas's manuscript. Surprisingly — perhaps beyond coincidence — Valentinian's reign is identical to Vortigern's, as is listed in the *Anglo-Saxon Chronicle*.

It is during this period when Pendragon makes an entry into Monmouth's history and into Welsh oral tradition. "Constantius III" marries (or takes) YGERNA as a wife or concubine and they have two children, Anna and Arthur.

---

and challenges all, including King Arthur. When no one takes up the gauntlet, the red knight insults the queen, then hastily departs as the clumsy youth Perceval enters and announces that he wants to be a red knight. A beautiful young maiden and the court jester immediately proclaim that Perceval's destiny is to become a great knight, whereupon Sir KAY roars insults at the awkward youth, slaps the maiden, and kicks the fool into the fire. However, King Arthur recognizes that the boy is slow-witted, overlooks his foolishness, and encourages Perceval to seek out the red knight and kill him.

Thus begins Perceval's adventures, meeting and falling in love with Blancheflor, then spending time with the FISHER KING in his castle, but being too naïve to ask about the bleeding lance or the grail. After defeating the Proud Knight, Perceval returns to King Arthur's court. The

story then switches to GAWAIN and his episodes, returns to Perceval's quests covering a five-year period, then once again picks up on Gawain's ventures. Gawain has accepted Guiromelant's challenge and sends a message to Arthur's court requesting witnesses at the combat, and there the text abruptly ends.

Because the romance was obviously unfinished, subsequent antiquarians wrote endings which have becomes known as "Continuations." Juliette Wood writes,

> Chretien de Troyes died before finishing this romance, but the story was completed by other writers. The Continuations, as they are referred to in critical literature, expand several themes and the grail gradually acquires a more "sacramental" character. The First Continuation is also incomplete and the author is unknown, but it can be dated before 1200. Besides Perceval, Gawain also has a grail ad-

venture (the womanizing Gawain is the type of the perfect worldly knight and regularly forms a contrast to Perceval in these romances). During a procession which Gawain sees, the "rich grail" (as it is now called) floats about the hall and provides food for all; the bleeding lance is later identified as the Lance of Longinus (beginning the trend to see these objects as relics); and the broken sword belongs to a dead knight who is laid out on a bier. He who mends the sword will know the secrets of the grail castle (thereby strengthening the link between sword and grail). A new adventure, the Chapel of the Black Hand, is added in which a mysterious hand snuffs out the candles in the chapel.

The Second Continuation, written by Gauchier de Donaing (c. 1200), is also unfinished but pushes the story even further into the realms of mysterious supernatural happenings. Perceval plays with a magical chess board; and a lady offers him a hunting dog and white stag's head, which he loses and has to recover before returning to the Grail Castle. He fails to mend the sword completely.

The Third Continuation (c. 1230), written by Manessier, completes the story of Perceval and Gawain. The Fisher King explains the items in the grail procession: the spear was used by Longinus to pierce Christ's side at the Crucifixion; the cup belonged to JOSEPH OF ARIMATHEA; the trencher covered the cup to protect the blood; and the sword wounded both the Fisher King and his brother. Perceval undergoes the adventure of the Chapel of the Black Hand. When the sword is mended, Perceval as grail ruler heals the land. After seven years, he retires to a hermitage, and when he dies, the grail, lance and dish go with him.

Unfortunately, Manessier's explanation of the grail was replaced by yet another, and final, continuation of the story. The Fourth Continuation by Gerbert de Montreuil (c. 1230) has a strong moralizing tone. It takes up the story after Perceval's first failure and introduces a long series of adventures before Perceval returns to the Grail Castle to mend the sword.

There are two excellent translations of *Perceval*. The first, by Burton Raffel, is written in a poetic format, but it is neither octosyllabic or rhyming couplets. As Raffel himself avers, "I will be content if this translation allows the modern English reader some reasonably clear view of Chrétien's swift, clear style, his wonderfully inventive story-telling, his perceptive characterizations and sure-handed dialogue, his racy wit and sly irony, and the vividness with which he evokes."

Ruth Harwood Cline's translation is in Chrétien's octosyllabic, rhymed-couplet format, a delightful masterpiece which no doubt took great skill and perseverance to write, exemplified in the opening passage when Perceval meets the knights:

> Once, in the season of the year
> When fields grow green, and leaves appear,
> And birds, in their own idioms,
> Sing sweetly when the morning comes,
> and all things are aflame with joy,
> at daybreak there arose a boy
> Who was a widowed lady's child.
> Deep in her forest lone and wild
> He saddled up his hunter, and
> He took three javelins in his hand.
> So armed with this accoutrement
> Out of his mother's manse he went.
> He planned to visit, where he rode,
> His mother's harrowers, who sowed
> The fields of oats by light of dawn:
> Six harrows by twelve oxen drawn.

Sources: R. Cline (P: SG); B. Raffel (P: SG); J. Wood (HG: FRMTMG).

Peredur. In Welsh tradition, the story about Peredur is a parallel to PERCEVAL in the romance of CHRÉTIEN DE TROYES. Both tales open in a strikingly similar manner, but the Peredur story is much more abbreviated, and, of course, contains no aspersions about the Welsh or *Britones*. The main character encounters three knights, but unlike the French version, the names of the knights are given: Gwalchmei son of Gwyar, Gweir son of Gwestyl, and Owein son of Uryen. Whereby Chrétien's prose translation covers six pages or more, *Peredur Son of Evrawg* sketches the details in less than a page: Peredur is told by his mother that these people are angels, and he then asks only about the saddle, and the rest of the accoutrements are summarized in one short sentence. Peredur discovers they are knights and mounts his "bony dapple-grey nag" (called a "hunter" in Chrétien's romance) and departs for Arthur's court.

Jeffrey Gantz's introduction explains where the two stories diverge, *Peredur* having an extended sequence of "unintegrated exploits," whereby *Perceval* presents the adventures of GAWAIN, as follows: "In the most important matter, though, these stories are sadly at one, for neither fully illuminates the mystery of the lance and Grail seen at the castle of the hero's (Fisher King?) uncle. Crestiens, of course, did not live to finish *Perceval*, and the ending of *Peredur*, while corroborating the revenge motif of Manessier (in his continuation of *Perceval*), seems horribly contrived, and leaves much unexplained too."

Gantz is of the opinion that "inasmuch as Crestiens admits that Perceval is a Welshman, and inasmuch as the name Perceval means little, it seems likely that Peredur is the more original form of the hero's name. Peredur, moreover, looks suspiciously like Pryderi (from the Four Branches). According to Welsh history Peredur and Gwrgi were companions in northern Britain of the fifth century, just as Pryderi and Gwrgi are companions in [the story] of Math."

Source: J. Gantz (TM).

Præfectus. When Rome's emperors ruled the world, a Præfectus (or Præficio) was a provincial commander assigned to conquered territories.

Source: Cassell's Latin dictionary.

Prænomen. The first name of a Roman, followed by a nomen (clan), a cognomen (family surname), and sometimes an agnomen for achievement or circumstance.

Source: Cassell's Latin dictionary.

Ralph of Coggeshall (*floruit* 1192–1222 / *lifespan* 1190–1224). Ralph of Coggeshall, a contemporary of GIRALDUS CAMBRENSIS, is one of several antiquarians who wrote of Arthur's exhumation at Glastonbury Abbey. In *Chronicon Anglicanum*, Ralph, too, records the inscription on the leaden cross, which reads, "*Hic iacet inclitus rex Arturius in insula Avallonis sepultus.*" It varies from JOHN LELAND's in two minor respects. The word "sepultus" in Leland's version comes after the word "iacet" rather than at the end, and whereas Ralph spells "inclitus" with an "i," Leland spells it with a "y." Literally trans-

lated, Ralph's inscription is "Here lies the famous king Arthur in the Isle of Avalon buried."

E.K. Chambers notes that Ralph does not provide the in-depth details supplied by Giraldus; Ralph neither writes about Guinevere and the yellow tresses, nor does he explain the size of the bones in the oak-bole. His account agrees that the gravesite was between two pyramids whose inscriptions were illegible, then gives an abbreviated account that Glastonbury was surrounded by marshes, that it was called the island of Avallon, and that "avallon" translated to "apples." Additionally, there are several differences. One is that Ralph claims that the gravesite was discovered inadvertently "to bury a monk who had urgently desired in his lifetime to be interred there [between the two pyramids]." A second is that Ralph claims the cross was atop the oak-bole, while Giraldus specifically describes the cross as being attached to the underside of a stone slab. And last, in relation to the cross itself, Giraldus's account uses the spelling of "Arthurus" for the great king, whereby Ralph uses the spelling of "Arturius."

Rather surprisingly, Geoffrey Ashe doesn't mention Ralph of Coggeshall's variations in his book *King Arthur's Avalon*.

Sources: L. Alcock (AB); R. Barber (FOA); E. Chambers (AOB); A. Jarmin (LOAMA); R. Loomis (ALMA); J. Markale (KA: KOK); F. Reno (HKA); J. Stevenson (RC: CA).

Renwein, Renua, Rowena. Rowenna, Ronwen, Ronwenn. Although Renwein is seemingly an incidental character, she plays a significant role in the opening scenes of the Arthurian saga. Her name is not given in the *Historia Brittonum*, but she comes with an envoy from across the sea and is described in this way: "In one of the keels came Hengest's daughter, a beautiful and very handsome girl. Hengest held a banquet for VORTIGERN, and he told the girl to serve them wine and spirits. When they were drinking, Satan entered into Vortigern's heart and made him love the girl." Vortigern bargains for her and gives Hengest a great deal of land.

Renwein, therefore, is Vortigern's concubine, HENGIST's daughter, and OCTHA's sister. In the *Vita Merlini* her name is recorded by translator

J.J. Parry as the Welsh Ronwen, incorrectly listed as Hengist's sister rather than his daughter. In Basil Clarke's translation her name is given as Renua. She plays no further part in the *Historia Brittonum*, but in GEOFFREY OF MONMOUTH's *History of the Kings of Britain*, her role is influential. She is described as Vortigern's wife rather than his concubine, but she remains fiercely loyal to her father while she manipulates Vortigern. Because VORTIMER, Vortigern's son, is opposed to the Anglian encroachment on British soil, Renwein plots Vortimer's death and has him poisoned by a Pict. She is instrumental in reporting to her father, who then treasonously slaughters all of Vortigern's Council of Elders except ELDOL, who escapes.

See also GANEIDA.

Sources: S. Blake/S. Lloyd (KTA); J. Morris (BH); G. Monmouth (HKB); J. Parry (LOM); P. Roberts (COTKB).

Rhieinwyldd. Rhieinwylydd (pronounced Hree-in-WOOL-ith) appears in the actual manuscript as Rieingulid and has one other variant, Riengulid. She has two sisters, YGRAINE (mother of Arthur) and Goleuddydd (mother of CULHWCH). Her father is Amlawd the Great, and her mother is Gwen.

See also AMLAUD.

Rhonabwy. The Welsh tale "Dream of Rhonabwy," in *The Mabinogion*, is intriguingly cogent when analyzed as an allegory or perhaps an offshoot of an apologue. Allegorically, characters and events are symbols used to express history and reality rather than mere fiction. Viewed as an apologue, the story is intended to convert oral tradition into history through the use of totems, icons, or animals — in this instance, using ravens to represent enemy warriors.

This story, perhaps the last of the "other tales" in *The Mabinogion*, begins with reminiscent overtones of the Cain and Abel episode in the Bible. Two brothers — Iowerth and Madawg — are at odds with each other, and when dissension arises, Madawg is willing to offer his brother equal rank, honor, arms, and horses, but Iowerth rejects the truce, and in anger raids England, slaughtering people and their stock, burning houses, and taking prisoners. In an attempt stop his brother's rampage, Madawg gathers some of his troops, one of whom is Rhonabwy.

When night comes, the troops seek shelter at the house of a companion, but the floor is "so slimy with cow dung and urine," and the straw is so flea-ridden that the troops cannot sleep. Rhonabwy, however, does fall into a deep sleep which lasts three days and three nights, filled with visions.

Concisely, his visions begin with him and his companions riding toward the River Havren (Severn), and he joins the Emperor Arthur's massive army riding to fight the Battle of Baddon against OSLA BIG KNIFE. After the various armies amass and cross the river, Arthur sets up camp, and he invites OWEIN to play a game of gwyddbwyll with him.

At this point, Rhonabwy's dream turns into the allegory/apologue mentioned above. The emperor and Owein play six games of gwyddbwyll. During the first three matches, pages come to the campsite to tell Owein that his ravens were being killed by Arthur's forces. The last three pages ride into camp to tell Arthur that Owein's ravens were killing the emperor's best and bravest men. The assumption is that Arthur and Owein are enemies fighting the Battle of Badon.

Shortly after the six games have ended, "twenty-four horsemen came from Osla Big Knife to ask Arthur for a truce to the end of a month and a fortnight." Arthur calls for his council to seek advice, and among those he gathers are Caw, father of Gildas; GILDAS; PEREDUR; Cadwr (CADOR of Cornwall); Gwrhyr (CERDIC) Interpreter of Languages; AVAON son of Talyessin, and HOWEL son of Emhyr. Arthur grants the truce, receives the tribute, and departs for Cornwall, inviting "whoever wishes to follow."

Source: J. Gantz (TM).

Richard of Cirencester (d. circa 1400). According to the *Catholic Encyclopedia*, Richard of Cirencester compiled a chronicle titled *Speculum Historiale de Gestis Regum Angliae* spanning the years 447 to 1066. The following is from a *CE* overview:

> The work, which is in four books, is of little historical value, but contains several charters granted to Westminster Abbey. Nothing is known of Richard's life except that

he was a monk of Westminster, who made a pilgrimage to Jerusalem in 1391, was still at Westminster in 1397, and that he lay sick in the infirmary in 1400. Two other works are attributed to him: "De Officiis," and "Super Symbolism Magus et Minus," but neither is now extant. In the eighteenth century his name was used by Charles Bertram as the pretended author of his forgery "Richardus Copenensis de situ Britanniae," which deceived Stukeley and many subsequent antiquarians and historians, including Lingard, and which was only finally exposed by Woodward in 1866–67.

In the development of place-names, Avalon became inextricably bound to Glastonbury. Different tales of Celtic lore label Avalon as a vague, misty afterworld governed by Avallach, Lord of the Dead, and from this lore springs Avalon. Although free of any reference to King Arthur, Richard of Cirencester, in *Six Old English Chronicles*, equates Glastonbury and Avalonia as the geographic location of the Hedui tribe covering nearly all of Somersetshire. As the above extract states, however, Richard of Cirencester's name was deceitfully used in a forgery, yet this spurious chronicle still appears under Richard's name in Giles's work.

Sources: (CE); J. Giles (SOEC); F. Reno (HKA).

Riothamus, Riothamo, Riotamus, Riothimir, Riotimus, Riatham, Rigotamos, Regula, Rhiadaf. Three continental writers — Jordanes, Gregory of Tours, and Sidonius — include the name Riothamus in their writings, independent of any attempt to corroborate King Arthur's historicity or his era. His meteoric flash in history occurs prior to the seventh decade of the fifth century.

The scholar Charles Mierow writes of Jordanes *and The Origin and Deeds of the Goths*: "Now Eurich, king of the Visigoths, perceived the frequent change of Roman Emperors and strove to hold Gaul by his own right. The Emperor Anthemius heard of it and asked the Brittones for aid. Their King Riotimus came with twelve thousand men into the state of the Biturges by way of Ocean, and was received as he disembarked from his ships."

Gratuitously — which is atypical for early medieval manuscripts — the reader is provided with several important pieces of information — EURIC is the leader of the Visigoths; ANTHEMIUS is the emperor of the Western Roman Empire; Riotimus is king of the Brittones and he sails to Gaul from across "Ocean," that is, the English Channel; and he comes with 12,000 men. The only detail which is questionable is the number of men he brings with him, a gross exaggeration of military strength so common in the ancient manuscripts. For example, GEOFFREY OF MONMOUTH, although he might be copying his information, lists Arthur's troops against Lucius as numbering 273,200 as tallied by translator Lewis Thorpe.

As the entry for Emperor LEO relates, after Majorian's death in 467 C.E., Anthemius was granted the throne as emperor of the Western Empire on April 12, 467 C.E. and ruled until he was beheaded by Ricimer on July 11 of 472. The date is not specific, but the reader is notified that Riothamus sailed to Gaul, specifically the Biturges territory, sometime between 467 and 472.

Jordanes's narrative continues: "Eurich, king of the Visigoths, came against them [Riothamus and his troops] with an innumerable army, and after a long fight he routed Riotimus, king of the Brittones, before the Romans could join him. So when he had lost a great part of his army, he fled with all the men he could gather together, and came to the Burgundians, a neighboring tribe then allied to the Romans. But Eurich, king of the Visigoths, seized the Gallic city of Arvenera; for the Emperor Anthemius was now dead."

The chronological timeframe becomes even more specific. Riothamus's defeat would be close the death of Anthemius, perhaps between 470 and 472. When Riothamus disappears into Burgundy with the survivors of his army, his name drops from the histories. Because there is no mention of his death, there remains a small window that perhaps he and his remaining troops straggled back across Ocean to Britain.

As for the two other brief notices in history, GREGORY OF TOURS contributes one other detail about the conflict between Euric and Riothamus: "The Britanni were driven from Bourges by the Goths, and many were slain at the village of Déols." SIDONIUS doesn't supply anything of the

Goth-Britanni conflict, but he does give a personal insight into Riothamus. Judging from the introduction of the letter, Sidonius has communicated with Riothamus previously, knowing him as an impartial, compassionate, and honorable ruler.

The letter *in toto* reads:

> I will write once more in my usual strain, mingling compliment with grievance. Not that I at all desire to follow up the first words of greeting with disagreeable subjects, but things seem to be always happening which a man of my order and in my position can neither mention without unpleasantness, nor pass over without neglect of duty. Yet I do my best to remember the burdensome and delicate sense of honour which makes you so ready to blush for others' faults. The bearer of this is an obscure and humble person, so harmless, insignificant, and helpless that he seems to invite his own discomfiture; his grievance is that the Bretons are secretly enticing his slaves away. Whether his indictment is a true one, I cannot say; but, if you can only confront the parties and decide the matter on its merits, I think the unfortunate man may be able to make good his charge, if indeed a stranger from the country unarmed, abject and impecunious to boot, has ever a chance of a fair or kindly hearing against adversaries with all the advantages he lacks, arms, astuteness, turbulences, and the aggressive spirit of men backed by numerous friends. Farewell.

In addition to giving insight into Riothamus's *persona* (reminiscent of Gildas's praise of AMBROSIUS AURELIANUS), the letter is important because it verifies the date listed in Jordanes's history. Sidonius is in Gaul, and in reference to his "order and position," Sidonius is intimating that he has already been installed as bishop, showing that the letter was written after his appointment in 469. Riothamus, therefore, had been summoned by Anthemius just prior to the end of the seventh decade.

Objectively summarized, the scant evidence about Riothamus reveals that he

1. was invited to Gaul—specifically Biturges—by Anthemius to quell the insurrection by Euric the Visigoth sometime near 470;
2. was Briton;
3. crossed Ocean from Britain;
4. was routed by EURIC before the Roman army could join him as reinforcement;
5. lost a great part of his army in Bourges near the village of Déols;
6. fled into Burgundy with the remnants of his army.
7. was not killed or captured.

No more information is given about Riothamus.

Geoffrey Ashe, in *The Discovery of King Arthur*, is the first researcher to explore who this mysterious king is. Jordanes lists positively that Riothamus is a Briton king and not a Breton one, since he had to travel across Ocean. Piqued by a parallel, Ashe answered the question by theorizing, "Maybe Riothamus was Arthur." In order to show that the two names referred to the same individual, he spoke of evidence that prior historians and researchers had also linked Riothamus with Arthur.

Using a concept he terms "lateral thinking," Ashe comprehensively compares characters and events of Riothamus's historic milieu, then draws parallels of Arthur's Gallic campaigns as described by others. He gives background credence to figures embedded in Gallic history, such as ÆGIDIUS, SYAGRIUS, Avitus, Ricimer, Arvandus, Odavacer, and Childeric, in addition to ANTHEMIUS and LEO I. Ashe agrees with Leon Fleuriot that Riothamus is a title meaning "king-most" or "supreme king," a close similarity to Kenneth Jackson, who also concurs that Riothamus is a title, but slightly adjusts the translation as "supremely royal."

In addition to exploring information provided by Jordanes, Gregory of Tours, and Sidonius, Ashe cites two other individuals. One is William of 1019, author of a manuscript titled *Legend of St. Goeznovius* who, Ashe claims, "embeds Arthur in history as no one else convincingly does." The second is Sharon (pronounced Sha-'RON) Turner, who wrote *History of the Anglo-Saxons*. In one fleeting passage he writes, "at this very period the Britons were so warlike that twelve thousand went to Gaul, on the solicitations of the emperor, to assist the natives against the Visigoths." He draws no inferences in the textual passage, but in a footnote he adds,

"Either this Riothamus was Arthur, or it was from this expedition that Geoffrey, or the Breton bards, took the idea of Arthur's battles in Gaul."

Ashe selects Arthur as the name behind the epithet Riothamus through a process of elimination. It is indeed odd that the most important British king of the time is recorded in continental history, yet there is not a single mention of that king in Britain. He never appears in GILDAS, BEDE, NENNIUS, nor parent Irish manuscripts. Geoffrey of Monmouth doesn't refer to him, there are no branches of *The Mabinogion* praising him, and he has no role in the works of CHRÉTIEN DE TROYES, WACE, or LAYAMON.

The Historic King Arthur and *Historic Figures of the Arthurian Era* offer a modification to Ashe's Riothamus theory. Both of the above texts ascribe to the theory that Riothamus is an epithet for Ambrosius Aurelianus, a twist of Ashe's theory because those texts also ascribe to the theory that the word "Arthur" is another epithet for Ambrosius. To clarify the divergence, Ashe contends that the term "Riothamus" is an epithet referring to the proper name "Arthur." The above two texts contend that the term "Riothamus" is an epithet referring to Ambrosius, who has already been titled as "the great king of all the kings of Britain." Likewise, because there is no evidence of an Arthur of the fifth century, the name "Arthur" has been conflated with Ambrosius.

In my two books cited above, I do not view my theories as a polarity to Ashe's hypothesis. On the contrary, in the quest for Riothamus's identity, my foundation was based upon a great deal of Ashe's work, using his concept of "lateral thinking." Whereby Ashe's approach was a "parallel" approach of similarities between Riothamus and Arthur, I added my tenet that one must break away from "patterned thinking" in the quest to discover Riothamus's role in Arthuriana. "Patterned thinking" is a term which other researchers and scholars sometimes refer to as "thinking outside the box."

Surprisingly, my conjecture that Riothamus is an epithet for Ambrosius Areulianus was provided by Geoffrey Ashe in *The Discovery of King Arthur*, because it was Ashe himself who cited Leon Fleuriot's belief that Riothamus was an epithet meaning "supreme king" and asserted that Riothamus was an epithet for Ambrosius Aurelianus. Ashe, however, maintained his stance that Riothamus was a title for *Arthur*, and set up a terse process of elimination of the five insular Briton leaders of the fifth century who might have acquired the epithet "Riothamus."

His first four rejections are simple and compact:

- "Vortigern is out of the question" because "he is too early, and while we may discount the blackening of his character, his historic role was quite different." Ashe doesn't explain how Vortigern is "different."
- "Vortimer is a shade more interesting" but "all we are really told of him is that he fought Saxons in Britain and died in Britain, and that it all happened well before Vortigern's death."
- "Cerdic ... was certainly real but he is ruled out by his remoteness and unimportance."
- "Uther is neither remote nor unimportant, but he is not real."

His fifth rejection — Ambrosius Aurelianus — is the crucial one. Ignoring that there is no evidence of an Arthur of the fifth century and contending that "Ambrosius has not carried conviction," Ashe gives four reasons for eliminating Ambrosius:

1. "Gildas does not call him a king," but "speaks of him purely as a war leader."

   Refutation: Gildas doesn't refer to anyone as "king." He uses that word generically, but in his castigations, he uses the word "tyrannus." When he writes "superbo tyranno," he does not identify a particular individual; it is Bede who mistakenly assumes that it's a reference to Vortigern. Even more baffling is that Ashe evades the fact that Gildas does not refer to an Arthur.

2. "Nennius, in a passing phrase, does make him a king ... but this is legend."

   Refutation: Nennius does *not* "make him king." Although Section 48 deals with Vortigern's genealogy, it is Ambrosius's role which is significant. "Pascent (Vortigern's son), who ruled in the two countries called Builth and Gwerthrynion after his father's death, by permission of Ambrosius, who was the †great† king among all the kings of the British nation...." The word "great" between the daggers is an addition by Theodor Mommsen in the 1800s. Ambrosius had the power not only to grant territory but to appoint rulers. If Ambrosius had that power to grant territories to historic people, how can that be labeled as "legend?"

When Ambrosius is first introduced in the *Historia*, "Vortigern ruled in Britain, and during his rule he was under pressure from fear of the Picts and the Irish, and of Roman invasion, and, not least, from dread of Ambrosius. Why would Vortigern be in such fear from a fictional character, even more feared than Roman reoccupation or the enemies?

3. Ashe adds, "Elsewhere Nennius preserves [Ambrosius's] rank in its Welsh form, calling him Emrys *gwledig*, and those who had this "landholder" office were regional rulers only."

Refutation: The *Historia Brittonum* does *not* refer to Ambrosius as Emrys or *gwledig*. The *Historia*, in Sections 40, 41, and 42, does contain the heading "The Tale of Emrys," but that heading was a later insertion not in the original manuscript. The term *gwledig* is sometimes defined as "landowner," but scholars have defined it as a term much more important and elevated. (*See also* AMBROSIUS entry.)

4. Ashe concludes, "Finally, even legend says nothing about Ambrosius campaigning in Gaul."

Refutation: It is true that Ambrosius is not recorded by his proper name in continental history. From the evidence, however, Ambrosius *is* mentioned as an important figure in *insular* history. Where, in continental or insular *history*, is *Arthur* mentioned? Since there is no evidence of an Arthur of the fifth century, the only logical premise left is that Ambrosius must have been the Briton king from across Ocean. Ambrosius's chronology matches perfectly with that of Emperor ANTHEMIUS, who solicited help in Gaul.

See also ARTHUR and AMBROSIUS AURELIANUS for a continuation of this discussion.

Sources: W. Anderson (S: P&LVI); W. Anderson (S: P&LVII); G. Ashe (DKA); R. Fletcher (AMC); N. Lacy (AE); C. Littleton/L. Malcor (FSTC); Sir J. Lloyd (HOW); C. Mierow (J: O&DG); J. Morris (HB); F. Reno (HKA/HFAE); J. Stevenson (N: HB/G: DEB); M. Winterbottom (G: ROB&OW).

Riotimus is the name used by JORDANES in *Gothic History* to identify Riothamus, the Briton king from across Ocean.
See also Riothamus.

Rivalin is Tristan's father in Gottfried von Strassburg's *Tristan and Isolt*. In addition to the name variances — BLANCHEFLEUR is the name of Tristan's birthmother instead of ELIZABETH, and the son's name is Tristran instead of Tristram — the story varies slightly. In an opening scene, Rivalin and Blanchefleur (King Mark's sister) fall deeply in love, and when they elope from Cornwall, Rivalin marries her "in the presence of all his nobles so that if harm befell him in the war all should know that Blanchefleur was his wedded wife and their liege lady." Instead of Tristran's father being on a hunt in the woods, his father in this story is sorely wounded in battle with a neighboring kingdom. He dies from that wound, and Blanchefleur dies because her heart brast (burst).

Rivalin and Blanchefleur are buried in the same grave, and Tristran is raised by Ruan, Rivalin's second-in-command. Tristran doesn't discover the tale of his mother's and father's deaths until he is seven, at which time Ruan turns him over to a learnéd man named Kurwenal, who travels with him abroad for seven years.
Source: R. Loomis/L. Loomis (MR).

Robert de Boron (*floruit* 1172–1202 / *lifespan* 1157–1217). As with so many of the antiquarians of this period, there is very little known of their lives, and Robert de Boron is no exception. There is consensus that he was from Burgundy, but whether or not Robert was born or lived in the village of Boron is based upon a presumption extracted from his manuscript that Gartier was his patron, a nobleman who lived in Montbéliard, a short distance from Boron. It has become accepted as fact that Robert was associated with Gartier Montbéliard before this Lord of Montfaucon joined the Fourth Crusade in 1202 and never returned to his homeland.

Like his near-contemporary CHRÉTIEN DE TROYES, Robert wrote his trilogy not in prose but in octosyllabic verse. More than likely, he completed the trilogy between 1190 and the end of the century, when his patron left. Robert would therefore have written the first of his trilogy after Chrétien's *Le Conte del Graal* (*Perceval*), prior to the death of Philip, to whom Chrétien dedicated his work. By uncanny circumstance, Philip's death occurred in 1191, the same year ascribed to the exhumation of King ARTHUR and Queen GUINEVERE in Britain, as described by GIRALDUS CAMBRENSIS. More than likely, Robert was aware of that work, since his Vale of Avalon seems to describe Glastonbury and Somerset.

The trilogy attributed to Robert includes *Le Roman de l'Estoire dou Graal* (*Joseph d'Arimathie*), *Merlin*, and *Perceval*. Richard O'Gorman writes in his article for *The Arthurian Encyclopedia* that Boron's *Perceval* is in all probability the generally-known Didot-*Perceval*, and a "prose adaptation of the three romances was made by an anonymous redactor shortly after composition. "It was this prose version," he continues, "that gave rise to the vast cycle of Arthurian prose romances known as the Vulgate Cycle."

Robert de Boron, therefore, is evidently the antiquarian who was so influential in structuring crucial elements of the Arthurian legend, specifically the roles of JOSEPH OF ARIMATHEA and MERLIN, the Holy Grail, the bleeding lance, the introduction of the sword in the anvil, and the refinement King Arthur's Round Table. Although the Grail and the lance appear in Chrétien's *Perceval*, it is Robert who labels the Grail "Holy" and adds significance to the bleeding lance.

Boron's *Joseph*, the only romance which has survived in its original poetic form, opens with a prologue giving information about the frailty of man and his fall from God's graces and relating the development of Christ's Passion. Pilate gives Joseph the *graal* used by Christ at the Last Supper, and after Joseph is imprisoned by the Jews, the resurrected Christ visits him and explains the secrets bound to the vessel. When Joseph is released, he and his followers journey to a distant land (interpreted as Britain). This sets the stage for closely linking ancestry of Joseph and King Arthur.

Joseph is instructed by the Holy Spirit to construct a second table to honor Christ and the graal. Joseph's disciples, who are untainted by sin, are seated at the table, but one man, named Moysés, begs to be seated, and when Joseph relents, the man is swallowed up in the abysmal depths of the earth.

This occurrence is the forerunner of King Arthur's Round Table and the Siege Perilous (overtones of Moysés's catastrophic fate in de Boron's work) which is later occupied by GALAHAD. Of even more significance, approximately a century and a half later, JOHN OF GLASTONBURY writes the *Cronica sive Antiquitates Glastoniensis Ecclesie* (*Chronicle or History of Glastonbury Church*), and the link between King Arthur and Joseph of Arimathea becomes permanently entrenched as supposedly legitimate history. Joseph is granted several hides of land, plants his staff in the earth from whence springs the hollythorn trees still existent on Glastonbury Tor and the Abby grounds, and hides the Holy Grail in Glastonbury Well. Thus Arthur's ancestry is traced back to the era of Christ.

Only 504 lines of Robert's Merlin story survives in its original form. Like the two other romances in the trilogy, this tale gave rise to two other later continuations, *Les Prophécies de Merlin* and *Suite du Merlin*, both of the thirteenth century. These works describe Arthur's attainment of Excalibur, Mordred's birth, Merlin's enchantment by Niniane, and the progressive development of the Round Table.

Merlin describes the history of the first two tables, the original of the Last Supper and the second which Joseph constructed from the guidance of the Holy Spirit. Merlin then advises Uther to create a third table, symbolizing the Trinity. The table is to be installed at Cardueil (probably a reference to Carlisle) for use at Pentecost. At this time Merlin chooses "fifty of the worthiest men of the land" to occupy seats at the third table, and informs UTHERPENDRAGON that the vacant seat will be occupied by the son of Alain li Gros.

Sources: N. Bryant (M&TG); E. Chambers (AOB); N. Lacy (AE); N. Lacy/G. Ashe (AH); G. Phillips/M. Keatman (KA: TS).

Rumaun, Rhufon, Rumanus. Cunedda's third son, born circa 426–430. His kingdom becomes Rhufoniog, east of Afloeg's territory in northern Wales.

Sources: L. Alcock (AB); P. Bartram (WG); S. Blake/S. Lloyd (KTA).

sacrilegious easterners is used only by Gildas Badonicus in the *De Excidio*. It refers to the *Saxones*, a generic Latin term which includes Angles, Saxons, Jutes, and Frisians who had been settled in Anglia on the island of Britain for a couple of generations. This ethnic group was also labeled as ENGLISH *SAXONES*, as opposed to newcomers known as GERMAN *SAXONES* from the continent.

In §24 Gildas writes, "In just punishment for the crimes that had gone before, a fire heaped up and nurtured by the hand of the *orientali sacrilegorum* (sacrilegious easterners) spread from sea to sea." Gildas is so repulsed by the saxones that he utters the word only once, a name so abominable it should not be spoken. In addition to the term, he uses deprecations such as barbarian lions, dogs, and degenerates.

Bede more accurately identifies these sacrilegious easterners as East Anglians, and specifically mentions that their first chieftains were Hengist and Horsa.

Sources: L. Sherley-Price (BEDE: HEC&P); J. Stevenson (G: DEB); M. Winterbottom (G: ROB&OW).

Sagremor, Sagramore. Sagremor makes his first entry as one of Arthur's knights in the works of CHRÉTIEN DE TROYES. In *Cligés*, the hero after whom the story is named traveled to Wallingford in Britain. He learned that King Arthur had organized a tournament to be held just outside Oxford. When Arthur's men had assembled, Sagremor the Unruly rode out and Cligés accepted the challenge. Chrétien writes, "[T]he two of

them delayed no longer, but gave rein to their horses, for they were inflamed and eager to meet in the joust. With his first blow Cligés smashed Sagremor's shield against his arm and his arm against his body, stretching him out flat upon the ground."

In *Erec and Enide*, Sagremor the Unruly is mentioned at one point only in passing as one of the noble barons of the Round Table, although he is not ranked as one of the top ten. In another passage, Erec and his comrades are at a tournament near Edinburgh, and among them is Sagremor, who "captured and struck down many."

Sagremor is also named in the opening passage of *Le Chevalier au Lion* (*Yvain*), along with DODINEL, the ninth-ranking knight of Arthur's Round Table. In the *Perceval Continuation* by MANESSIER, Sagremor helps PERCEVAL avenge the FISHER KING by defeating ten knights.

Sagremor then gains most of his reputation from the Continuation written by Manessier for Chrétien's unfinished *Le Conte du Graal* (*Perceval*). In that story, the Fisher King's brother has been slain by the villain Partinial, and Perceval sets out with Sagremor to avenge the death. They have a series of adventures before the story once more reverts to episodes by GAWAIN before focusing upon Perceval.

After his appearance in the Chrétien stories, Sagremor makes a second more noteworthy debut in Book 10 of Malory's *Le Morte d'Arthur*. On his way to do battle, Sir TRISTRAM encounters Sir Sagramore le Desirous and Sir Dodinel, who has now become Sir Dodinas le Savage. When they meet, the two question Sir Tristram, then ask if he would joust with them.

Tristram refuses, but Sagramore and Dodinas push the issue. Almost effortlessly, Tristram unhorses his two rivals, leaving them lying on their backs on the earth. Sir Tristram passes with his squire Gouvernail, but immediately after he passes, Sagramore and Dodinas mount their horses and give chase. Tristram turns his horse to face them again.

Sources: R. Coghlan (EAL); W. Kibler (CDT: AR); T. Malory (LMD'A).

Sangive. *see* WOLFRAM VON ESCHENBACH.

Saxones. The Latin term *Saxones* has created more confusion and misinformation about King Arthur's major enemy than any other word in the early and middle medieval era. Pressured by the Western Empire attempting to pacify Gaul, the Saxon, Anglian, Jutish, and Frisian kingdoms were disintegrating on the mainland during the fifth century, causing hordes of migrants to flee to Britain. For simplicity's sake, the Romans infused tribal identities and generically referred to all those tribes as *Saxones*.

J.N.L. Myres reflects the commonly held beliefs of where these individual tribes settled in Britain. Through a series of maps, he suggests that the Jutes settled in the area around Southampton Water and on the Isle of Wight, presently known as Hampshire. Farther to the north of Jutish territory was the area of the West Saxons, encompassing Cirencester to the west and Dorchester to the east. The East Anglians settled in what became known as Norfolk and in an area south of The Wash, while the Middle Anglians were located to the east of their kin, in the area of Leicestershire. The East Saxons settled to the north of the River Thames, bounded by the Middle Saxons to the west and the South Saxons along the coast.

The information from Myres is partially based upon Bede's description in the eighth century and also reflected in the recorded material of the Parker version of *The Anglo-Saxon Chronicle*. The Old SAXONS, the ANGLES, and the JUTES are identified as the three nations of Germany. From the Jutes came the people of Kent and the people of the Isle of Wight, and the race among the West Saxons which is still called the race of the Jutes. From the Old Saxons came the East Saxons, South Saxons and West Saxons. From Angel came the East Angles, Middle Angles, and Mercians, plus all of Northumbrians. Myres's placement of the Hwicca territory matches that of Bede's and BEDE simply identifies Gewissae as another term for the West Saxon territories.

The enigmatic areas of GEWISSAE and HWICCA territories pose more of a problem for geotopographers. Gewissae allegedly was sandwiched between the West Saxons and the Jutes, now known as Wiltshire and part of Berkshire. The Hwicca territory was identified as the area around Worcestershire and Gloucestershire. There is also suggestion, based upon Bede's geography, that Gewissae and Hwicca name the same strip of north-south territory, once a domain of the southern HYRPE tribe.

One other crucial consideration affecting the identification of Arthur's enemies is the distinction between ENGLISH *SAXONES* (not Saxons) and GERMAN *SAXONES* (not Saxons). The English Saxones were those Saxones who had migrated to Britain during Roman occupation, and had hence become known to the Romans by the generic term Britanni, since they had been there for at least a couple of generations. Arthur's battles are mainly against the English Saxones, which is why GILDAS BADONICUS refers to these conflicts as "civil" or "internal" wars. The German *Saxones* are those relatives who lived on the continent. When civil wars broke out on the island, the English *Saxones* sought aid from their German counterparts.

Sources: Bede (HEC&P); G. Garmonsway (ASC); J.N.L. Myres (RB&ES); F. Reno (HFAE).

Saxons. Henry of Huntingdon, whose floruit is 1103–1133, offers an interesting twist about the influx of barbarians into Britain from the continent. Henry records an account of the battle of Stamford and the first settlement of the Saxons in Britain, which comes from some other authority, now unknown.

A battle was fought by the Saxons against the Scotti and Picts, who had penetrated as far as Stamford, in the south of Lincolnshire, 40 miles from the town of that name. But as the Northerners fought with darts and spears, while the Saxons plied lustily their battle-axes and long swords, the Picts were unable to withstand the weight of their onset, and saved themselves by flight. The Saxons gained the victory and its spoils; their countrymen receiving tidings of which, as well as of the fertility of the island and the cowardice of the BRITONS, a larger fleet was immediately sent over with a greater body of armed men, which, when added to the first detachment, rendered the army invincible. The newcomers received from the Britons an allotment of territory on the terms that they should defend by arms the peace and security of the country against their enemies, while the Britons engaged to pay the auxiliary force. The immigrants belonged to three of the most powerful nations of Germany, the SAXONS, the ANGLES, and JUTES.

The strong implication given by Henry's account is that the first advent against the Britons (the Picts and the Scots) was by the Saxons. Immediately following this account at Stamford, Henry echoes what is recorded in *The Anglo-Saxon Chronicle* about the Angles, Saxons, and Jutes, which significantly changes the perspective of an invasion of the Germans. The first is that the initial advent into Britain was by the Germanic *Saxons* and not by the Germanic *Angles*. The second is that HENGIST is undeniably an Angle, and hence he would have been the leader of the *second* advent. The misfortune is that all the Germanic tribes were collectively labeled as *SAXONES* by the Romans, and the term *Saxones* should not be considered as synonymous with the word Saxons.

Henry then continues his narration, which reflects borrowings from Bede, Nennius, and the *Anglo-Saxon Chronicle*:

> Before long such swarms of the nations we have just mentioned spread themselves throughout the island, that the foreign population increased exceedingly, and began to alarm the native inhabitants who had invited them over. A certain author says that King VORTIGERN, from apprehension of their power, married the daughter of Hengist, a heathen; others, that as a climax to his wickedness, he married his own daughter, and had a son by her; for which he was excommunicated by ST. GERMANUS and the whole Episcopal synod.

Source: T. Forester (CHH).

Seen/Sene, John. *see* JOHN OF GLASTONBURY.

Severus, Lucius Septimius. Severus is associated with Arthuriana in an oblique way. He and Lucius Artorius

Castus — the historic Arthur of Britain — were in Britain during the same era, Severus as Emperor of the West attempting to pacify the northern segment of the island, and Artorius Castus as a *DUX BELLORUM* protecting Hadrian's wall. Moreover, Severus is historically associated with a third British wall — named, of course, the Wall of Severus.

In the *De Excidio*, GILDAS BADONICUS ostensibly records a third wall, but most historians and researchers are of the opinion that Gildas confused a reference to a "turf wall" as the Antonine Wall and mistakenly recorded that its

Septimius Severus was one of the few Roman emperors who traveled to the Isle of Britain. In the early 200s he took personal command of Britain and is credited by historians with building the Wall of Severus. He was in Britain at the same time of Lucius Artorius Castus. Emperor Severus died in February of 211 C.E.

construction preceded Hadrian's Wall. There are others, however, who conjecture that Gildas is describing a turf wall that preceded both the Hadrian and Antonine walls.

In Section 15, Gildas writes that a Roman legion, dispatched from the mainland, fought against the Scotti and the Picts, and constructed across the island "a wall linking the two seas; properly manned, this would scare away the enemy and act as a protection for the people. But it was the work of a leaderless and irrational mob, and made of turf, rather than stone: so it did no good."

The Romans therefore informed the country that they could not go on being bothered with such troublesome expeditions; the Roman standards, that great and splendid army, could not be worn out by land and sea for the sake of wandering thieves who had no taste for war. Rather, the British should stand alone, get used to arms, fight bravely, and defend with all their powers their land, property, wives, children and, more important, their life and liberty.

As a boon, the Romans built a wall quite different from the first. This [second wall] ran straight from sea to sea, linking towns that happened to have been sited there ... [and the Romans] employed the normal method of construction, drew on private and public funds, and made the wretched inhabitants help them in their work.

Regrettably, Gildas doesn't give a date or identify either of the two seas, which allows speculation of a third wall in Britain. Those who ascribe to this option cite confirmation from varying sources.

Bede seemingly clarifies construction of a third wall. In Book One, Chapter 5, he writes:

> In the year of our Lord 189, Severus ... was compelled to come to Britain by the desertion of nearly all of the tribes allied to Rome, ... and after many critical and hard-fought battles he decided to separate that portion of the island from the remaining unconquered peoples. He did this, not with a wall, as some imagine, but with an earthwork. For a wall is built of stone, but an earthwork ... is constructed with sods cut from the earth and raised high above ground level, fronted by the ditch from which the sods were cut. Severus built a rampart and ditch of this time from sea to sea and fortified it by a series of towers.

However, in Chapter 12 of Book One, the first section of Bede's narrative parallels Gildas's record (§18), but then becomes sharply divergent in the latter segment. Gildas is no doubt writing about the construction of the Antonine Wall which was distinctively different from the construction of Hadrian's Wall, whereby Bede has corrupted Gildas's information by stating outright that the wall was built with stone.

Sources: L. Sherley-Price (BEDE: HEC&P); P. Blair (RB&EE); M. Winterbottom (G: ROB&OW); J. Morris (BH); C. Barber/D. Pykitt (JTA); S. Blake/S. Lloyd (KTA); J. Davies (HOW); M. Holmes (KA: AMH); J. Morris (AOA); I. Richards (RB); P. Roberts (CKOB); H. Scullard (RB: OOE); C. Snyder (AAOT).

Sidonius. In addition to JORDANES and GREGORY OF TOURS, Sidonius is a third historical figure to verify the reality of RIOTHAMUS. A letter from Sidonius to Riothamus helps establish an important date during this confusing period of history. In late 469, Sidonius was installed as bishop of the Arverni in Clermont, which is at the same time when Arvandus, ANTHEMIUS's seditious viceroy, was on trial.

As a high-ranking official, Sidonius was asked to make a plea to Riothamus on behalf of a humble rustic whose slaves were being enticed away by soldiers of Riothamus's army. He writes,

> Here is a letter in my usual style, for I combine complaint with greeting, not with an express intention of making my pen respectful in its superscription but harsh in the letter itself, but because things are always happening about which it is obviously impossible for a man of my rank and cloth to speak without incurring unpleasantness or to be silent without incurring guilt.... However, I am a direct witness of the conscientiousness which weighs on you so heavily, and which has always been of such delicacy as to make you blush for the wrong-doings of others.

By the tone of his introduction, Sidonius's compliment to Riothamo (his salutation in the letter) suggests that the cleric has had previous contact with the "King from across Ocean."

Source: W. Anderson (S: P&LVI&VII).

Sigebert of Gembloux is author of *Chronicon sive Chronographia*, which attaches itself to Arthuriana only because of interpolations added to his manuscript.

See also URISCAMPUM and LUCIUS HIBERIUS.

superbus tyrannus is an epithet which has been translated in numerous ways by scholars and historians, causing confusion by their antonymous nature. A quick review shows that *superbus tyrannus* has been defined as high king, supreme ruler, great king, overlord, haughty tyrant, preeminent ruler, high chief, and most commonly, proud tyrant.

In the eighth century BEDE inadvertently mislead his readers when he wrote "the Angles or Saxons came to Britain at the invitation of King Vortigern." VORTIGERN cannot be designated as a king: more accurately he was a tribal chieftain, or a provincial ruler, or an overlord in Wales. Bede certainly must have known of and recorded material written by GILDAS BADONICUS, two of which have survived, Manuscript A of the thirteenth century (F. f. i. 27), and Manuscript B of the fourteenth/fifteenth century (D. d. i. 17). The former manuscript is what exonerates Bede from calling Vortigern a king.

The translation is this author's, but it closely follows Stevenson's account, and, most importantly, his is the section which clarifies the crucial need for explicit synonyms.

> Then all of the councilmen and the superbus tyrannus **Gurthrigerno Britannorum duce** were struck blind. They turned over our land, not to guardians, but to destroyers, the ferocious *SAXONES*, a name not to be spoken, despised by man and God, who were let into the island like wolves into the fold, to drive away the peoples of the north....
>
> On the orders of the pernicious tyrant, they first fixed their dreadful claws on the eastern part of the island, supposedly to fight for our country, but instead fought against it.

This is the only record this author is aware of which records the bold detail. Stevenson is explicit that the proud tyrant is Gurthrigerno Britannorum duce, which states precisely that the superbus tyrannus is Vortigern (Gurthrigerno) the Briton (Britannorum) leader (duce). Later translators and interpreters were not cognizant of the importance for accuracy.

Historic Figures of the Arthurian Era takes the stance that the term *superbus tyrannus* implies a much more powerful authority than Vortigern, who is a tribal overlord of a British province. During that era, the *superbus tyrannus* of the western Roman Empire was VALENTINIAN III. Rome's typical policy was to use *FOEDERATI* to supplement their legions, and hence with legionary strength at a low ebb, it would not have been unusual for Valentinian to send Saxon mercenaries to Britain in an attempt to subdue the Irish and Picts.

Leslie Alcock also makes several interesting observations about the similarity of Valentinian's and Vortigern's reigns, and how these two individuals might have been conflated; that is, Valentinian, as the emperor of the Western Empire was the *superbus tyrannus* in Britain, and was hated by Gildas Badonicus because of the *foederati* Anglians who had been sent to the island. Both individuals were elevated to a position of authority in the same year, 425 C.E., when Theodosius and Valentinian began their first consulship, and Vortigern became the leader of the Council of the Province.

The introduction of Vortigern in the *Historia Brittonum* certainly does not portray this "king" of a territory in Britain as proud, haughty, supreme, or great. Section 31 describes him in this manner:

> ... after the killing of the tyrant Maximus and the end of the Roman Empire in Britain, the British went in fear for 40 years. Vortigern ruled in Britain, and during his rule in Britain he was under pressure, from fear of the Picts and the Irish, and of a Roman invasion, and not least, from dread of Ambrosius.

The name Maximus in the above passage is a reference to the usurper in 383 C.E. who gathered together the troops of Britain and traveled to Gaul to overthrow the western emperor. He remained in that country for five years before he was finally captured and beheaded. Maximus can rightly be called a tyrant, particularly since he was recognized for a short while as the emperor of Gaul. But Vortigern could not be described by any of the adjectives listed above, with the exception perhaps of the term overlord, which is how he is described in Norris Lacy's *Arthurian*

Encyclopedia. Lacy offers an explanation that "Though found later as a name, it is probably a title here, or at any rate, a designation. In the British language it would have meant 'over-chief' or 'over-king.'"

See also VORTIGERN, VALENTINIAN III.

Sources: L. Alcock (AB); Bede (HEC&P); N. Lacy (AE); J. Morris (BH); F. Reno (HFAE); L. Thorpe (GM: HKB); J. Stevenson (GDE: ROB&OW).

Syagrius is the son of ÆGIDIUS, who also had ties to RIOTHAMUS in the sixth decade of the fifth century. There is a difference of opinion, however, about Syagrius's role. At one point John Morris writes that "Ægidius found himself transformed to 'king of the Romans,'" but Geoffrey Ashe contends that *Syagrius* adopts the title "king of the Romans." In either instance, both father and son were loyal to the Western Roman Empire, and if it had not been for both these people, Gaul and the empire would have crumbled earlier than history records. This was an era when "armies changed allegiance so rapidly and events were so jumbled that modern readers are dazzled by the confusion."

Upon Ægidius's death, Childeric was re-instated as king of the Franks, but Syagrius's army was still on good terms with the neighboring tribe. When the immigrant Britons under the leadership of Riothamus confronted the Saxons along the Loire, they were supported by Syagrius and the pro–Roman Burgundians.

Paraphrasing Ashe's and Morris's accounts, Riothamus was defeated because of these mitigating circumstances:

1. Around 468, two events evidently took place in rapid succession: ANTHEMIUS, who has historically been regarded as the last true Western emperor, negotiated an alliance with Riothamus, a Briton from across Ocean; the Gothic king EURIC, observing the frequent changes of Roman emperors, decided to master Gaul in his own right.
2. According to one account, Ægidius's death was attributed to a great plague, whereupon his son Syagrius ascended to the throne and carried on the Roman loyalty of his father, maintaining alliances with the Franks and the Burgundians.
3. Odovacer the Saxon made his mark in the Loire Valley, raiding Angers and taking hostages from the city and surrounding towns.
4. GREGORY OF TOURS relates that the Romans (ostensibly with the aid of the Briton troops) and the Franks battled the Saxons. "The Saxons fled and left many of their people to be slain, the Romans pursuing. Their islands were captured and ravaged by the Franks, and many were slain."
5. It is unclear where this occurrence falls in the sequence, but because of the context, logistically it suggests that the Franks, up to this point, were loyal to the Romans, Britons, and Burgundians. The Romans and the Franks under Count Paul (one of Syagrius's generals?) attacked the Goths and took booty (no locale mentioned).
6. When Childeric returned as the chieftain of the Franks, the loyalty of the tribe shifted from the Romans and Britons to the Saxons. Childeric killed Count Paul.
7. The Britons advanced up the River Loire to the northeast, crossed into Berry, the heartland of Gaul, and occupied Bourges (the Roman site of Avaricum).

Jordanes writes, "Euric, king of the Visigoths, came against them with an innumerable army, and after a long fight he routed Riotimus, king of the Britons, before the Romans [presumably under the leadership of Syagrius] could join him. So when Riotimus had lost a great part of his army, he fled with all the men he could gather together, and came to the Burgundians, a neighboring tribe then allied to the Romans."

The Britons are expelled from Bourges and driven by the Goths to Déols (the Roman site of Argentomagus, near Châteauroux), and from there they retreat into Burgundy. *From Scythia to Camelot* provides an accurate map of Riothamus's route.

Sources: G. Ashe (DKA); A. Ferrill (FOTRE); C. Littleton/L. Malcor (FSTC); C. Mierow (J: O&DG); J. Morris (AOA); F. Reno (HKA); L. Thorpe (GOT: HOF).

Tacitus. In Welsh genealogies, Tacitus is father of PATERNUS of the Red Robes. His grandson is ÆTERNUS, whom some equate with VORTIGERN, and his great-grandson is CUNEDDA, considered the proper name for the epithet VORTIMER.

It has been suggested but never pursued that Tacitus is the Roman officer who became known as Magnus Maximus in Welsh tradition.

Sources: L. Alcock (AB); F. Reno (HKA, HFAE).

Taliesin. Taliessin. Attempting to track the bard Taliesin is a daunting task. William F. Skene, who collated *The Four Ancient Books of Wales*, provides the most comprehensive material, but condensing it is as formidable as Theseus being in a maze. Skene amassed material from a Mr. Jones (no first name) and Robert Vaughn, whose manuscripts were combined at Hengwrt and hence named the Hengwrt collection. It is not known how the *Book of Taliesin* was acquired, but Skene designates its date as the fourteenth century.

Skene also had Robert Williams, author of *Biography of Eminent Welshmen* and *The Cornish Dictionary*, translate the seventy-seven poems attributed to Taliesin. Previous to this, Algernon Herbert claimed that the poems of Taliesin did contain a "mystic philosophy," but he did not generally recognize Taliesin's poems as genuine, as he did those of Aneirin's *Y Gododdin*.

The historicity of Taliesin is contestable, with some of the reliable sources leaning in the direction of his reality, and others pointing out what has to be legendary fantasy. Skene reminds that the reader must do the work of an editor before relying on a critic, and require the original orthography of the oldest manuscript. In *The Figure of Arthur*, Richard Barber labels Taliesin as a famous bard, "master of his craft" and a contemporary or near-contemporary of Aneirin. Barber conjectures that Taliesin was a man of the North, and his poetry "seems to have been brought south during the seventh and eighth centuries."

According to the Introduction of *The Arthur of the Welsh*, the editors claim *The Book of Taliesin* (NLW Peniarth MS 2) "was written by a single scribe during the first quarter of the fourteenth century. Its contents are a disparate collection of religious, prophetic, and historical poems purporting to comprise the collected works of the sixth-century poet Taliesin, as these were envisaged in the later Middle Ages."

The name Taliesin is used once in Section 62 of the *Historia Brittonum* along with five other bards: "At that time Outigern then fought bravely against the English nation. Then Talhaern Tad Awen was famed in poetry; and ANEIRIN and Taliesin and Bluchbard and Cian, known as Gueinth Guaut were all simultaneously famed in British verse."

Although Raymond H. Thompson expresses doubt about Taliesin's historicity in an entry of Lacy's *Arthurian Encyclopedia*, Lacy and Geoffrey Ashe described the bard in *The Arthurian Handbook* as a historical character who "flourished toward the end of the sixth century. Both [he and Aneirin] left poetry that has survived, in verse forms already well-developed and meant to be sung, a fact implying musical composition. Bards like these were honored figures attached to royal courts, and, supposedly, gifted with inspiration denied to most mortals."

E.K. Chambers devotes most of his material about Taliesin on *Preiddeu Annwfn*, then turns his attention to the role of a bard who encompassed "a double aspect of itinerant entertainer and household appanage. Each chieftain had a bard, but the bard of each kingdom was linked to a guild.... [They] had the status and privileges analogous to those of priests."

One Welsh vernacular text tells a tale that Taliesin was deprived of certain property and because of his loss, he cursed MAELGWN (a verifiable historical figure) and all his possessions, whereupon "Vad Velen came to Rhos, and whoever witnessed it became doomed to certain death. Maelgwn saw Vad Velen through the keyhole of the Rhos church, and died in consequence." It was, however, penned by an unreliable individual, a certain IOLO MORGANWG, whom Sir Ifor Williams condemns as "the greatest forger of Welsh documents that Wales has even known." Skene, too, cautions the reader that almost all the documents which have emanated from Iolo cannot be found in any of the Welsh MSS contained in other collections, then writes that "very careful discrimination is required in the use of them."

Sources: R. Barber (FOA); R. Bromwich (AOW); E. Chambers (AOB); J. Gantz (TM); N. Lacy (AE); N. Lacy/G. Ashe (AH); F. Reno (HKA); W. Skene (FABW); T. Stephens (LOK); I. Williams (LEWP).

Taurus. *see* FELIX. The two were Roman *consulibii* simultaneously.

Thomas d'Angleterre (*floruit* 1155–1185 / lifespan 1140–1200). Thomas d'Angleterre appears in Arthurian literature as Thomas of Brittany or Thomas of Britain. The *Encyclopedia Britannica* estimates his floruit in the smaller time period of 1160–1170 and offers a time span of 1170 to 1175 for his work. In the *Arthurian Encyclopedia*, William Kibler, who also edited *Chrétien de Troyes: Arthurian Romances*, introduces Thomas as writing the legend of Tristan in Old French verse which is variously dated "from ca. 1150 to 1200," adding that "most critics today place it around 1175."

Unfortunately, only fragments of Thomas's work has survived. Kibler notes that

1. the Cambridge fragment recounts King Mark's discovery of Tristan and Iseut in the garden;
2. the Sneyd fragment relates TRISTAN's marriage to Iseut (ISOUD) LA BLANCHE MAINS in Brittany;
3. the Turin fragments describe Tristan's starcrossed fate and Iseut's resistance of Mark;
4. the Strasbourg* fragments include KAHEDIN's (brother of Iseut la Blanche Mains) awe of Iseut the Blond's beauty, and the death of Tristan and Iseut the Blond.

*These are probably from GOTTFRIED VON STRASSBURG, a latter contemporary of Thomas d'Angleterre.

Sources: S. Gregory (TB: T); N. Lacy (AE); R. Loomis (RT&Y); R. Taylor (EB: GVS).

Thomas of Brittany. *see* THOMAS D'ANGLETERRE.

Trevrizent is a holy hermit in WOLFRAM's *Parzival* who relates the tale of Anfortas to Parzival. He preaches to the hero PARZIVAL about Cain and Abel, about Cain's grandmother, and about the purity of Jesus, then admonishes Parzival to atone for his sins.

Source: A. Hatto (WVE: P) Book 9.

Tristram, Tristan, Drustan, Drust. It was GOTTFRIED VON STRASSBURG who penned the *Tristan and Isolt* romance as it appears today, but the roots stretch much further back in time, to a historical king of the Picts named Drustan who ruled in the late eighth century. Roger Loomis writes that sometime around 1154 a famous troubadour sent a poem to Eleanor of Aquitaine which named Tristan "l'amador and Izeut," and even prior to that time the romance about Tristan and Isolt must have "crystalized in either an oral or a written form before 1150." Gottfried's work appeared about 1210, but remained unfinished and ended prior to Tristan's marriage to Isolt of the White Hand, not to be confused with Isolt of Ireland. Two continuations were written, one by HEINRICH VON FREIBERG and the other BY ULRICH VON TÜRHEIM. The romance as it appears nowadays is Gottfried's tale plus the addition of one of the continuations.

The tale is quite long, taking place in Ireland, Wales, Cornwall, and Brittany; both Gottfried's Tristan and Malory's Tristram are involved in many adventurous quests and jousts, and he kills scores of knights, sometimes eighty in one fell swoop; there are many trysts, a great deal of subterfuge, and sub-plots involving a long list of minor characters.

Even highlights must be curtailed, but Tristram's life runs thusly:

1. Tristram's father is killed before his son's birth, and Tristram's mother dies at her son's birth;
2. he is kidnapped and eventually ends up with King Mark, who turns out to be his uncle;
3. Queen Isolt heals Tristram's wound, unaware that Tristram killed her brother;
4. he meets Queen Isolt's daughter whose name is also Isolt;
5. In the process of delivering the young Isolt to Mark for a marriage, Tristram and Isolt accidentally drink a potion which causes them to fall deeply in love with each other, which causes many problems;

6. Tristram goes to Brittany and marries another Isolt, Isolt of the White Hand, but the marriage is never consummated;

7. Tristram is sorely wounded and secretly sends for Isolt;

8. ISOLT OF THE WHITE HAND discovers what is transpiring and tells Tristram that Isolt is not coming, which causes Tristram to give up the ghost;

9. Isolt enters (where's Isolt of the White Hand?), falls upon the body of her lover, and she also dies.

10. Mark buries them, putting a rose on Tristram's grave and a vine on Isolt's.

In Malory's version (Book 20, Chapter 6) Mark kills Tristram: "How shamefully that false traitor King Mark slew Tristram as he sat harping afore his lady La Beale Isoud, with a grounden glaive [broadsword] he thrust him in behind to the heart." And likewise in Malory, Mark puts a vine on Tristram's grave and a rose on La Beale Isoud's.

Sources: R. Loomis/L. Loomis (MR); T. Malory (LMD'A).

Typiaun, Typipaun. According to the Welsh genealogies, and sometimes included in the *British Historical Miscellany*, Typiaun was Cunedda's "first born who died in the region called Manau Guodotin and did not come hither with his father and aforesaid brothers."

Source: L. Alcock (AB).

Tywyssawc Llu. Although *dux bellorum* has remained a title for Arthur since its usage in the *Historia Brittonum* and many modern-day researchers have clarified its definition, Alcock cautions that the term might be distorted since the Nennius manuscript is not a Latin document which would retain the term's precise meaning. He admonishes the readers and translators:

> But when we recall that our ultimate source [the *Historia Brittonum*] is not a Latin document in which *dux* might have retained some precise meaning, but instead [the *Historia* is] a Welsh poem, and it becomes doubtful whether this interpretation is valid at all. Our doubts on this point are reinforced when we look at other Welsh evidence. In the elegy on Gereint of Devon, Arthur is called *ameraudur*

llwiaudir llawus, emperor, battle-ruler. And in the Llwarch Hen poems, we have *tywyssawc llu* and *tywyssawc cat*, leader of the host or army or, in the second case, since *cat* may mean either "army" or "battle," leader of the battle.

Source: L. Alcock (AB).

Uriscampum, Ourscamp. Uriscampum, a chronicler of 1175, jostles his way into Arthuriana in quite a disreputable way — he interpolated the manuscript of a certain Sigebert of Gembloux, whose original work contained no references to Arthur.

Except in ecclesiastical circles, Sigebert was a Benedictine historian born in what is now Belgium circa 1035. One of his most important works — other than his biographies of Bishop Theodoric I and King Sigebert III, and his poetry about saints and sainthood — was *Chronicon sive Chronographia*, a "chronicle of the world." It was not really a history, but more of a survey, including a period during the last years of his life from 1105 to 1110.

Since this chronicle was widely distributed, it is probably to this work which Uriscampum added his interpolations. The Sigebert manuscript had already been slightly interpolated between 1138 and 1147, but Uriscampum added a modified tidbit of information which he had evidently gleaned from Geoffrey of Monmouth's *History of the Kings of Britain*. Rather than just accepting Monmouth's history, Uriscampum suggests that Riothimir (one of the variants of the name) should be identified as Arthur.

No other Arthurian connection can be made with either Uriscampum or Sigebert.

Sources: G. Ashe (DKA); G. Ashe (OAL); R. Fletcher (AMC).

Uterpendragon. There is strong resistance to this term being accepted as an epithet for King Arthur because of the prefix *Uter*. The name Utherpendragon coined by Geoffrey of Monmouth was probably translated by Geoffrey from *Ythr ben dragwn* in the *Jesus* manuscript. Geoffrey was translating from Welsh into Latin, so there is some speculation that he used the prefix *Uther* to substitute for the Welsh noun *uther*, meaning "terrible" or "awful." This term does not appear in the seventeen or so variants of the *Historia Brittonum*, but the term *Uther* or *Uthr* is a marginal addition (interpolation) in the Sawley Glosses of the overlapping twelfth to thirteenth centuries. The full expression was *Uthyr mab Pendragon*, translating in English to "Terrible son Pendragon."

Richard Barber, in *The Figure of Arthur*, writes that the term *uthyr* could also mean "marvelous," which would cause the expression to become the "Marvelous son Arthur," suggesting that perhaps "terrible" has a positive connotation and is therefore synonymous with the word "marvelous."

There are those scholars, however, who adhere to the belief that Monmouth was a copyist, using various Breton and Briton manuscripts to translate those works into Latin. Since that was his primary function, he would therefore be looking for and selecting Latin words which would be equivalent or synonymous to the Welsh documents, not the other way around. For those advocates who concur that Monmouth was not grossly fraudulent, the word that he chose was therefore more accurately defined as the appellation "Pendragon's son." He might have selected the *Latin* prefix *Uter* from the cognate *uterine*, meaning "two siblings who share the same biological mother but have different biological fathers. This expression, Uterpendragon, would perfectly apply to Arthur: Arthur and Cador's mother was Ygerna, but Arthur's father was Constantius III (Pendragon), and Cador's father was Gorlois, the Duke of Cornwealas.

Regardless which viewpoint is more accurate, one characteristic is glaringly obvious: Monmouth was woefully confused in his segment about the House of Constantine, about Pendragon's identity, about AURELIUS AMBROSIUS'S role, and about the existence of a son named Utherpendragon. If that puzzle could be verifiably unraveled, the Dark Age of King Arthur would become the Enlightened Age of King Arthur.

Sources: R. Barber (FOA); J. Morris (HB); G. Phillips/M. Keatman (KA: TS); F. Reno (HKA); L. Thorpe (GM: HKB).

Valentinian III. Although a cursory glance would lead an individual to overlook Valentinian III as having a direct influence on King Arthur's era in Britain, there are some interesting assertions based upon two different premises which suggest that Valentinian could possibly have had a direct hand in controlling Britain's affairs during the middle decades of the fifth century. Additionally, there is interesting speculation that Valentinian might have been ARTHUR's (that is, AMBROSIUS's) half-brother.

Roman history categorically confirms that Valentinian III was the son of GALLA PLACIDIA and CONSTANTIUS III, who was a Roman Patrician, supreme commander, consulibus, *praefectus* of Gaul, and co-emperor.

There are enigmatic linkages, however, which emerge if an individual closely compares parallel events occurring in Britain and circumstances in the Western Empire during the same time period.

In Britain, the *De Excidio Britanniae* (*The Ruin of Britain*), written by GILDAS BADONICUS, is the earliest manuscript to have survived the ravages of time. Although there have been academic denials that Gildas can rightfully be termed a historian, there are others who believe the creed of a recent researcher who writes,

> It is most unfair to say, as many modern writers do, that Gildas was not a historian. Historical analysis was a crucial part of his work and he was considered a historian by later generations. He analysed the past for clues about the present, examining trends and patterns rather than individual episodes. As such, he has rather more in common with modern historians, particularly those studying the early Dark Ages, than writers like Bede and Nennius.... For Gildas, the analysis was everything.... We should not expect to find exact dates, regnal lists, or genealogies.... It is historical trends which are important to Gildas, and the model he uses to analyse them is a religious one.

Whereby BEDE and NENNIUS had previous Briton manuscripts and documents to rely upon, Gildas had none; there were no insular documents which he could rely on. Gildas provides very few names, and it is this characteristic which should warn interpreters of history and translators to use extreme caution when assigning a proper name to an epithet which Gildas has used in his work.

Unfortunately, Bede may have obscured the truth of British history by doing precisely that. Gildas Badonicus wrote that the *superbo tyranno* let the ferocious *SAXONES* into the island. Yet Bede substituted the Welsh moniker *Vortigern* for *superbo tyranno*, seemingly a harmless switch from one epithet to another, but in reality altered Briton/Welsh history.

The Historic King Arthur and *Historic Figures of the Arthurian Era* both advance the proposition that *superbo tyranno*, which translates to "proud tyrant" or a number of other synonyms, could be a reference to Valentinian III. As with all the preceding emperors, it was commonplace to send *foederati* (mercenaries paid by Rome) to quell insurrections. Britons were being overrun by *Saxones* (a generic Latin term referring to Angles, Saxons, and Jutes), and since the empire was short on legionnaires because of Gaulish rebellions, it would be natural of Valentinian to send mercenaries to the island in an attempt to retain Britain as a province.

What makes this possibility even more intriguing is that Valentinian as the representative of Rome and VORTIGERN as a Welsh overlord have strikingly similar floruits—a period between 425 C.E. and 455 C.E.

Sources: E. Duckett (MPE&W); A. Ferrill (FOTRE); E. Gibbon (D&FRE); S. Oost (GPA); F. Reno (HKA/HFAE).

Victorius of Aquitaine. Without a doubt, one of the most formidable hurdles for anyone interested in the early medieval period is chronological calibration. Prior to an understanding of various systems of calibration, the Christianized ecclesiastics were the only sect which attempted to sequence time. In order for individual churches to celebrate the Christian year uniformly, ecclesiastic scholars devised various tables which became known as Easter Annals, showing the dates on which Easter should fall over a number of years.

Because all documents were laboriously written by hand, scribal errors were common and in addition to these inadvertent mistakes, a copyist—as Leslie Alcock asserted—couldn't "resist the temptation to insert his knowledge" into the document being copied. Through centuries of recopying, these addenda led to corruptions that were indistinguishable from the original, since the originals unfortunately didn't survive the rigors of time. Events became distorted, dates became unreliable, historical figures became displaced. Alcock points out that modern-day researchers may have a "twelfth-century copy of a tenth-century compilation which includes annals written down in the fifth century; or a thirteenth-century copy of a poem composed orally in the sixth [century] but not written down before the ninth century."

Victorius of Aquitaine was the vanguard of systematic calibration. In 457 he calculated an Easter Table giving the date of Easter for every year from the Passion (Crucifixion) of Christ to his own era. However, he didn't stop with his own time, but continued his calculation into the future, and discovered that 532 years after the Passion, Easter would fall on the same day of the same month and at the same phase of the moon as in the year of the Passion itself. That repetition became known as the Great Easter Cycle.

Folios 190A to 193A of the *British Historical Miscellany* cover the 532 years, but according to Leslie Alcock, the Easter Table does not use *anno domini* dates for the single entries. Propitiously, however, decades and centuries are marked. Year ix gives information about a significant Christian event: "Easter is changed on the Lord's Day by Pope LEO, Bishop of Rome." This alteration took place in 455 C.E., so that if the ninth year is calibrated as 455 C.E., then the first year would be 447 C.E. Hence, for example, the date ascribed for Arthur's Battle of Badon is Year 72, which when calculated would be 446 + 72 = 518 C.E., a two-year discrepancy from the *Annales Cambriae* date of 516 C.E.

The Historic King Arthur compresses the explanation of why there is this variation between Alcock's computation and the date listed in the *Annales Cambriae*:

In his book *Arthur's Britain*, Leslie Alcock equates Year 9 with C.E. 455, the Easter change by Pope Leo, and then uses that beginning to compute the *Annales Cambriae* date for Badon as C.E. 518, since 518 is in Year 72 of the cycle. The calculation therefore follows this process: if Year 9 = 455, then year 1 = 446. Seventy-two years beyond 446 is 518 C.E., the date provided by Alcock's interpretation of the *Annales Cambriae*. However, other computations have different starting points. John Morris, for example, picked up on this differential when he edited and translated *British History*. The dates which he provides for the *Annales Cambriae* begin the cycle with C.E. 444 [not 446]. Thus, Morris's calculation is 444 +72 = 516 C.E., which coincides with the date found in the *Annales Cambriae*.

However, a discrepancy of ± 2 years is negligible when considering a time span of a millennium and a half. Even so, calibrating dates during the early medieval period is not that simple. As Alcock relates, calculations were not always determined by using Victorius of Aquitaine's Passion of Christ, since the church's method of reckoning changed because of DIONYSIUS EXIGUUS. After the release of Alcock's *Arthur's Britain*, Alcock himself also discovered that the ancients used a third method of calibration by lunar cycles.

Sources: L. Alcock (AB/WTC); J. Morris (HB); F. Reno (HKA).

Vitalinus, Guithelinus, Cyhelin. Vitalinus is the Roman equivalent of GUITHELINUS. His name is recorded in two different sections of the *Historia Brittonum*. In §49, which lists a genealogy traced backwards, Vitalinus is listed as one of four brothers, "son of Vitalis, son of Vitalinus, son of Gloui. Bonus, Paul, Mauron, and Vitalinus were four brothers, sons of Gloui, who built the great city on the banks of the river Severn that is called in the British Caer Gloui, in English Gloucester." In §66, the third segment states, "And from the (beginning of the) reign of VORTIGERN to the quarrel between Vitalinus and AMBROSIUS AURELIANUS are 12 years, that is Wallop, the battle of Wallop. Vortigern, however, held empire in Britain in the consulship of Theodosius and Valentinian (C.E. 425), and in the fourth year of his reign the English came to Britain, in the consulship of Felix and Taurus (C.E. 428), in the 400th year from the (Passion) of our Lord Jesus Christ."

Commonly, the material in parentheses indicates an interpolation — that is, an addition inserted later by a different hand. Many of the older manuscripts begin with "From the reign of...." assuming that the suggested year is at the beginning of the king's ascension. The dates in parentheses have to be verified, if possible, because one of three different methods of chronological calibration could have been used. The word "Passion" in parentheses indicates that a later hand is recording that the date given is based upon the year of Christ's death, and not the year of Christ's birth.

The choice of words in translation must also be carefully analyzed. The best example in the above passage is the word "quarrel" in the first sentence. The actual word in the original is the Latin word "discordium," which most accurately is defined as quarrel, discord, or argument. It is evident that in the above passage, "quarrel" is defined as a battle, specifically, the battle of Wallop.

This passage is spurious for a variety of reasons:

1. Quarrel and battle are not close synonyms, while quarrel, discord, and argument are much better.
2. The expression "That is" is a warning flag signaling a gloss (an interpolation) added by the later hand, prior to the scribe copying the manuscript.
3. The method of calibration more than likely is incorrect. The differential between the "Birth of Christ" Incarnation and the "Passion of Christ" is traditionally set as twenty-eight years. Hence, for example, if the beginning of Vortigern's reign is set according to the Birth of Christ, the date would be 400 C.E., but if determined by the Passion of Christ, the date would be 428 C.E. There is a third method of calibration calculated by lunar cycles which lies in the middle, one of nineteen years.
4. Assumptions by later readers such as antiquarians and later researchers are very dangerous pitfalls. Again using the above passage as an ideal example, antiquarians assumed that Vitalinus and Ambrosius were enemies, and conversely that Vitalinus and Vortigern were allies. This as-

sumption has carried over to the modern era. Because there is no firm evidence for this presumption, it very well could be Vitalinus and Ambrosius were allies but had a disagreement or dispute over some particular detail.

5. Lastly, the greatest majority of geographic sites listed in the ancient manuscripts are well-nigh impossible to trace. No one, for instance, can definitively determine where or what Wallop is. As a different example, when a manuscript lists an event as taking place in the "City of Legion," an individual can only guess (perhaps an "educated" guess) where that might be, since there were nine "Cities of Legion" in Britain.

The commonly accepted date for the beginning of Vortigern's reign is 425 C.E., which means the discord between Vitalinus and Ambrosius occurred in the year 437 C.E. What the circumstances were can only be conjectural.

The interested reader can peruse the books listed below for various conjectures about Vitalinus, Guithelinus, Cyhelin.

Sources: L. Alcock (AB); C. Barber/D. Pykitt (JTA); G. Phillips/M. Keatman (KA: TS); F. Reno (HKA/HFAE); P. Roberts (COKB); J. Stevenson (N: HB).

Viviane, Vivian, Vivien, Vivienne. Viviane and NIMUË are doublets, the first more commonly associated with the continent, and the second with Britain; in Thomas Malory's *Le Morte D'Arthur*, Nimuë is called the Chief Lady of the Lake. *See also* LADY OF THE LAKE.

Vortigern, Guorthigirn, Gwrteneu, Gwrtheneu, Gwrtheyrn, Uuertigerno, Uurtigernus, Vertigier, Vor Tigern, Vawrtighern, Vertigernos, Wyrtgeorn, Wortigernos. The term Vortigern — assumed to be a proper name by some scholars, and an epithet by others — has been so shrouded throughout centuries that no definitive evidence has yet led to a consensus or widespread agreement among researchers. There are a number of plausible speculations supporting his historicity, but there are two debates which have not been resolved.

The first focuses upon the question, "Was the term 'Vortigern' used by GILDAS BADONICUS in

A gravemarker near the door of St. Brynach's Church at Nevern is engraved for a *Vitalianus*. The inscriptions are: Latin: *Vitaliani Emereto*; Ogham: *Vitaliani*. In Latin and Ogham alike, the meaning is "The Monument of Vitalianus." The word "emereto" is unexplained, but is conceivably a territorian adjective. Alternatively it may be a corrupt and ungrammatical derivative of emeritus, "discharged with honor."

the *De Excidio*, the oldest Briton manuscript which has survived a millennium and a half?" Some aver that BEDE was the first historian to substitute the appellation Vortigern with SUPERBUS TYRANNUS and that Gildas Badonicus never mentioned the name Vortigern. Untangling an answer is a bit complex. Josephus Stevenson, a scholar and historian of the mid–nineteenth century, used two ancient manuscripts in his translation of Gildean material, one which is (F. f. i. 27) of the thirteenth century, and the other which is (D. d. i. 17) at the commencement of the fifteenth century. He does indeed record the name of Vortigern, aka Gurthrigerno (Welsh)—

one of at least a dozen others — in Manuscript A. What makes it problematic is that Stevenson writes "superbo tyranno Gurthrigerno Britannorum duce"; that is, "superbo tyranno = Vortigern the Briton leader." Those five words give an entirely different perspective. Cassell defines "superbo"—(in what he terms "a transferred, metaphorical, or bad sense")— as arrogant, overbearing, puffed up. "Tyrannus" is defined as ruler, prince, lord, usurper, despot. "Gurthrigerno" is, of course, Welsh for Vortigern, and "duce" is a leader. To make matters worse, some translators (for instance, Michael Winterbottom) do not record Gurthrigerno Britannorum duce, which explains why readers were, and perhaps still are, unaware that Gildas Badonicus records the information in the sixth century about two centuries prior to Bede, who unfortunately calls Vortigern "King Vortigern."

The second query probes the dilemma "Is the term 'Vortigern' the name of a particular individual extracted from British history, or is it an epithet which was so commonly substituted during that era? If it is considered as an epithet, can the identity of the historical figure be traced?" The answer is a cautious "yes." When Leslie Alcock writes about the probable three dates of CUNEDDA's migration, the most likely is the date of 450, which "may have been organized by some sub–Roman authority like that which brought in the Anglo-Saxons as allies." He then avers that Cunedda's very distant ancestors bore Pictish names, but his three immediate ancestors all had Roman names: ÆTERNUS his father, PATERNUS Pesrut his grandfather, and TACITUS his great-grandfather. He also writes about "British nicknames," which infers that the British nickname of Cunedda's father Æternus was Vortigern, a chieftain under Roman domain.

Summarized, Vortigern is an arrogant usurper under Roman dictate, specifically recorded in the *Historia Brittonum*, §31. Vortigern ruled under pressure because he feared the Picts and Scotti, feared the Roman invasion even though some legions had departed in 410, and mostly feared Ambrosius. The arrival of three keels from Germania was not because Vortigern invited them, but because the Romans had exiled those barbarians in an attempt to pacify Gaul.

In all fairness, some researchers do cite an edition of MS Avaranches A 162 in which the "Uortigerno" is substituted for Gildas' epithet *superb tyranno*. Another manuscript is MS Cambridge X, which does contain the expression "Gurthrigerno Britannorum duce." A third is MS Rheims 414, which echoes the Avaranches manuscript. Using the variances of the Welsh names assuages the debate by not inferring superbo tyrannus as an equivalent of "King" for Vortigern.

The equation, therefore, that the *superbus tyrannus* = Vortigern as a king remains in limbo. A partial list of respected researchers follows:

- Geoffrey Ashe, defines the term as "overking";
- H.H. Scullard equates Vortigern with "High King";
- Leslie Alcock uses the term "high chief;"
- David Dumville among others suggest that Vortigern means an "overlord";
- Chadwick writes that there is no name for a *superbus tyrannus* except for Bede;
- Richard Barber in *The Figure of Arthur* states Vortigern is a proud ruler;
- In *Arthur of Albion*, Barber generically states that the so-called British kingdoms "consisted of loose overlordships in civil and military matters";
- Blake and Lloyd (*Pendragon*) label Vortigern as a usurper, and in *The Keys to Avalon* as a ruler "of the Gewissi";
- Michael Holmes, *King Arthur: A Military History*, interestingly writes "There is still a query as to the ruler's actual name," not his epithet.

When methodical investigators come to credible definitions for *superbus tyrannus*, and also conclude whether "Vortigern" is an epithet or a proper name based upon cogent and realistic data, very enlightening history will be unveiled.

Gildas Badonicus has laid out a difficult puzzle by setting aside proper names and instead using a plethora of epithets. It is important to know that John Morris was a general editor for Michael Winterbottom's text, and it was Theodor Mommsen who added the titles in Gildas's work as he did in the *Historia Brittonum*; it is for that reason that titles such as "The Victory at Badon

Hill," "The Complaint of Kings," and "The Five Tyrants" can be overlooked. In §23 and 24, the proud tyrant and all the members of his council were struck blind by the ferocious Saxons who were supposed to beat back the peoples of the north. On the orders of the ill-fated tyrant, a pack of cubs from the cave of the barbarian lioness fixed their claws on the east side of the island. The mother lioness sent for another contingency of satellite dogs. When they arrived, a fire leaped up from the hands of the IMPIOUS EASTERNERS and spread over almost the entire island and licked at the western ocean.

Section 25 relates that although the plunderers had gone home, the Welsh selected AMBROSIUS AURELIANUS as their leader; he had survived the notable storm, but his parents who wore the purple had been slain in the conflict.

In §28, CONSTANTINE, the tyrant whelp of the filthy lioness of Dumnonia, cruelly tore at the tender sides and vitals of two royal youths and their two guardians, then using as his teeth wicked sword slew them at the altar.

If all of Gildas's epithets are replaced, a much more sensible story emerges. In these four sections alone, when specific names and locations are inserted, the historic era becomes much clearer. Substituting individual names and locales, events unfold as follows:

- In §23 and 24, Vortigern (Æternus) and all the members of his Council of the Province) were duped by the ferocious East Anglians who were supposed to beat back the Picts and Scotti from the north. On the orders of Vortigern, the barbarians occupied East Anglia. German Anglians were sent for and when they arrived, the EAST ANGLIANS (impious easterners, i.e., Hengist, Horsa, and their tribe) ravaged almost the entire island from Oceanus Germanicus to Oceanus Hibernicus.
- Section 25 relates that the Roman AMBROSIUS AURELIANUS (a name!) had become the leader of the conflict, perhaps the only Roman to survive, whose parents were Roman aristocracy.
- Constantine, who became the leader of

the Dumnonian province after ARTHUR's death (Ambrosius' death?), feared usurpation by the two sons of MORDRED and murdered them. Constantine was later succeeded by Aurelius Conanus (AURELIUS CANINUS in Gildas's *De Excidio*).

Gildas does not include the names OCTHA, HENGIST, HORSA, or East Anglians instead of ORIENTALI SACRILEGORUMAND; as illustrated above, he *suggests* Mordred and his two sons. The name MAGLOCUNUS MAP CATGOLAUN LAUHIR appears in a number of ancient manuscripts and annals, and MAGLOCUNUS MAP CLUTOR is engraved on a monument in the Nevern church.

Bede undoubtedly followed portions of Gildas's manuscript and might have either erroneously assumed that Gildas equated Vortigern with the epithet superbus tyrannus, or he might have been using a manuscript which didn't include Gildas's "Gurthrigerno Britannorum duce." The definition "duce" is a crucially different from "superbus tyrannus." Bede parallels Gildas's commentary that Vortigern granted eastern land to the Anglians, but he did it as a *duce* (provincial leader) upon the order of a *superbus tyrannus*. He makes one other single reference to Vortigern. In Book Two, Chapter 5, Bede writes, "The father of Oeric (OCTHA) was Hengist, who first came to Britain with his son Oeric at the invitation of Vortigern."

Vortigern appears no fewer than sixteen times in the *Historia Brittonum*, the work attributed to NENNIUS in the 9th century. In §37, Hengist invites sixteen keels of his kinsmen into Britain, including his unnamed daughter, "a beautiful and very handsome girl." During a banquet, Vortigern is served spirits by her, and as all the crowd gets exceedingly drunk, "Satan entered into Vortigern's heart and made him love the girl." Vortigern barters with Hengist and a deal is struck: Hengist is granted great tracts of land, and Vortigern is given the girl, "and he slept with her, and loved her deeply."

In §38 and §39, Hengist invites a third wave of Anglians into the island, this time including his son Octha and a nephew named EBISSA. Vortigern compounds his misdeeds by taking his own daughter as a wife and begat a daughter upon her. His own daughter gives birth to a son, thus validating Vortigern as the boy's father *and* grandfather. These transgressions introduce GERMANUS, who comes from the mainland to confront Vortigern. In fear, Vortigern flees somewhere to the north.

His flight sets the stage for "The Tale of Emrys," §40. In his panic to avoid the wrath of Germanus, Vortigern seeks refuge in the mountains of Eryri at a country called Gwynedd. He attempts to build a stronghold, but after his masons assembled timbers and stones, the materials disappeared in a single night. Three times Vortigern orders his stronghold to be built, and three times his supplies disappear. The king summons his magi, and they tell him he must sprinkle the blood of a fatherless child on the ground before the citadel can be built.

Section 41 continues the tale. The magi search the whole of Britain and finally enter the province of Glywysing, where two boys are arguing, and one of the boys reproaches the other about not having a father. The magi question the mother, who claims she has never lain with a man and swore to them that the boy had no father. The magi take the boy to King Vortigern.

When the boy reveals himself as Ambrosius the Overlord, Vortigern gives him "all the kingdoms of the western part of Britain," then flees with his magi.

Sections 43 and 44 side-track to Vortigern's son VORTIMER, whose reign against the Saxons is brief. When Vortimer dies, the Saxons return in full force. Vortigern makes a comeback in Sections 45 and 46, makes peace with Hengist, and convenes his council of elders. Hengist and his followers treacherously slaughter all the council (except ELDOL) and take Vortigern as a hostage, who cedes vast tracts of land.

Section 47 jumps to Germanus's second visit to "preach at Vortigern," who withdraws in disgrace and escapes to Dementia and in §48 Vortigern is denounced for his sins. One tale claims that his heart breaks and he dies in dishonor; a second says that he is swallowed up when his fortress burns around him.

In addition to Norris Lacy's assertion that Vortigern did exist, appearing in unaffected Welsh

legends, Leslie Alcock goes into much greater detail, admitting from the onset that Vortigern's historicity is uneven. He points out that the most reliable information about Vortigern is the set of chronological computations that stand at the head of the Easter Annals in the *British Historical Miscellany*: "Vortigern held rule in Britain in the consulship of Theodosius and Valentinian (Passion, 425)." The fourth year of Vortigern's reign would be 428, the same year as the consulship of Felix and Taurus, and a coming of the Saxons into Britain. Vortigern's accession fits well with his relationship as son-in-law of MAGNUS MAXIMUS.

According to Alcock, this is significant because it establishes a chronological calibration. If Vortigern's reign began in 425 and Vitalinus's discord with Ambrosius took place twelve years later, then the date for the discord would be set in 437, a date which is consistent with Gildas's information in *De Excidio* and the Tale of Emrys in the *Historia Brittonum*.

These calibrations verify the authentic information found in the factual annals called *Chronica Gallica a. CCCCLII*, the Gallic Chronicle for 452, which is influenced by or derived from *Chronica Gallica a. DXI*, Gallic Chronicle for 511. The first, *Chronica Gallica a. CCCCLII*, contains this information: "Britain, which up to this time had suffered manifold devastations and accidents, was subjected to the domination of the Saxons." The 19th year of THEODOSIUS—after the death of HONORIUS which occurred in 423—would be the year 442 when the Saxons "came into Britain." The second, *Chronica Gallica a. DXI*, reports this: "A.D. 441: Britain, abandoned by the Romans, passed into the power of the Saxons."

Some of this information might seem irrelevant, but it ties into Alcock's theory about the "coming of the Saxons." Although in actuality there were continuous comings and goings of the Saxons, Alcock ascribes to the hypothesis that there was not one Saxon *adventus* but three: the first at the invitation of Vortigern at the beginning of his reign around 425 C.E., the second between 440 and 442 C.E. which suggests CUNEDDA's migration from the north, and the third somewhere around 450 C.E., coinciding with Vortimer's demise, Vortigern's reinstatement, and Vortigern's death.

Approximately three centuries after the *Historia Brittonum*, Geoffrey of Monmouth's *The History of the Kings of Britain* made its debut. Geoffrey's narrative gives specific information about Vortigern, some evidently borrowed from the *Historia Brittonum*, some no doubt extracted from his enigmatic *liber vetustissimus* including the *Tysilio*, and — according to some critics — perhaps bits and pieces from his imagination.

For calibration chronologers, see DIONYSIUS EXIGUUS and VICTORIUS OF AQUITANINIA.

Sources: R. Castleden (KA: TBL); R.G. Collingwood/ J.N.L. Myres (RB& ES); N. Lacy (AE); J. Markale (KA: KOK); J. Morris (HB); P. Roberts (CKOB); L. Thorpe (GM: HKB); H. Scullard (RB: OOE); Sherley-Price (BEDE: HEC&P); C. Snyder (AAOT).

Vortimer, Gwrthefyr, Gortimer, Guorthemir. Gwrtheyrn, Gwytherin. Although Vortimer is not mentioned in the BEDE history, he acquires at least a minor role in the *Historia Brittonum* attributed to NENNIUS. With no introduction to this heretofore obscure figure, Vortimer, Vortigern's son, "fought vigorously against Hengest (HENGIST) and HORSA and their people, and expelled them as far as the aforesaid island called Tanat, and there three times shut them up and besieged them, attacking, threatening and terrifying them." His demise takes place several sentences later in a very terse obituary: "But Vortimer soon after died." The reader is, however, notified that "before he died he told his followers to set his tomb by the coast, in the port from which [the English] had departed, saying 'I entrust it to you. Wherever else they may hold a British port or may have settled, they will never again live in this land.' But they [meaning his followers] ignored his command and did not bury him where he had told them. If they had kept his command, there is no doubt that they would have obtained whatever they wished through the prayers of saint [*sic*] GERMANUS." The last notice given of Vortimer in the *Historia* is in Section 43, where he is verified in the Welsh genealogies as being the eldest son of VORTIGERN.

There are several versions of the Welsh Triads (Trioedd Ynys Prydein), the major ones being *The Black Book of Carmarthen* (*Llyfr du Caerf-* *yrddin*, c. 1250), *The White Book of Rhydderch* (*Llyfr Gwyn Rhydderch*, early 1300s), and *The Red Book of Hergest* (*Llyfr Coch Hergest*, 1400s). The segment of interest about Vortimer's triad is "Three Concealments of the Island of Britain." One is, "The bones of Gwrthefyr the Blessed are buried in the Chief Port of this island." The second is, "The bones of Gwrthefyr were buried in the chief harbour of this island and while they remained there hidden, all invasions were ineffectual." The third addenda was that Vortigern (his father) revealed where Vortimer's bones were because of love for Hengist's daughter, and by that revelation the Anglians were able to return.

There is no doubt that the Triads were modified — if not directly extracted — from *The History of the Kings of Britain* by GEOFFREY OF MONMOUTH. Of Vortimer, Geoffrey also adds:

- Vortimer was born of Vortigern's first wife;
- Vortigern was deposed from his kingship by the Welsh in favor of Vortimer;
- after battles with Hengist and his clan, Vortimer restores the Britons' possessions; his stepmother Renwein plots his death and poisons him;
- Vortimer asks to be buried in a pyramid at a port used by Hengist, but is buried instead at Trinovantum.

Near the end of the eleventh and the beginning of the twelfth century HENRY OF HUNTINGDON seems to be the first to link Vortimer and Ambrosius, which Geoffrey doesn't do. In the fight against Hengist, Henry writes that Gortimer was in charge of the second rank, but writes nothing of Vortimer in the battle, except that he was valorous and commanded superior forces. He then writes, "When LEO was emperor, Gortimer, the flower of the youth of Britain fell sick and died," whereby Monmouth indicates that Vortimer was poisoned, thereby allowing the Saxons back into Britain.

See also BRYDW.

Sources: J. Morris (BH); J. Stevenson (N: HB); L. Thorpe (GM: HKB); R. Bromwich (TYP); T. Forester (CHH).

Vortipor, the "bad son of a good king," tyrant of Demetae, is the third king rebuked by GILDAS

BADONICUS. As the name Vortipor suggests, VORTIGERN is one of his ancestors whose homeland became Demetae after the Dessi migration from Ireland.

Gildas accuses Vortipor of murders and adultery, but the king's most heinous sin is "the rape of a shameless daughter after the removal and honourable death" of his wife. Gildas beseeches him to seek salvation, or "otherwise, the worm of your torture will not die, and the fire of your burning will not be extinguished."

Source: M. Winterbottom (G: ROB&OW).

Wace (Robert) (*lifespan AE* 1110?–1176?). Wace was Norman, born on the isle of Jersey. One of his most important manuscripts, which survives in twenty-four versions and fragments, is *Geste des Bretons,* more commonly known as *Roman de Brut.* This manuscript, which Wace himself claims he completed in 1155, provides an important fundamental base to Arthuriana. The *Brut* is written in octosyllabic verse and closely follows the content of GEOFFREY OF MONMOUTH's *History of the Kings of Britain.* R.H. Fletcher describes this particular work by Wace as "a free paraphrase of Geoffrey's *History,* which closely reproduces the substance of the original."

However, Fletcher goes on to explain that "Wace was very far from being a servile translator, and the great differences which distinguish his race, character, occupation, aim, language and literary form from those of Geoffrey reappear as fully as was to be expected of his work." Whereas Geoffrey structured his work as history, Wace maintained Monmouth's veracity but framed it more as a romance. Those who critique Wace's writing style characteristically describe it as vivid, precise, and personal, sometimes injecting his opinion into the narrative.

It is also important to recognize how Wace emphasizes aspects in his narrative differently from Geoffrey. Wace removes some of the barbarity of wars — the bloodshed, anguish, and cruelty (particularly to animals), while Geoffrey meticulously enumerates the number of troops, who battles whom, and explicit details of someone's death.

Wace's presentation of Merlin, too, is quite different. Geoffrey borrows MERLINUS AMBRO-SIUS from the *Historia Brittonum,* but then molds MERLIN into a separate figure, depicting him as sage or seer but trying to minimize or at least rationalize his power. Wace, on the other hand, personifies Merlin as the romances do: he is a great magician/sorcerer with powers far beyond human capabilities.

It is in Wace's adaptations of Geoffrey that the first allusions occur about courtly love, manners, and chivalry. As Fletcher remarks, Wace "takes pains to expunge from the story certain suggestions of barbarity or lack of chivalrousness on the part of Arthur or his knights which occur in Geoffrey's version."

Two other significant Arthurian motifs are credited to Wace. The first is that Wace modifies Geoffrey's Caliburn or Caliburnus to Excalibur. Geoffrey for the first time mentions Caliburn at the Battle of Bath: Arthur "drew his sword Caliburn, called upon the name of the Blessed Virgin, and rushed forward at full speed into the thickest ranks of the enemy." He describes the sword several more times, stressing that it was forged in the isle of Avalon. The difference between the two terms, Excalibur and Caliburn — plus a third, the Irish form Caladbolg — have given rise to etymological controversies which are still debated.

The second addition which appears first in Wace is the Round Table: "For the noble barons he had, of whom each felt that he was superior — each one believed himself to be the best, and no-one could tell the worst — King Arthur, of whom the Britons tell many stories, established the Round Table. There sat the vassals, all of them at the table-head, and all equal. They were placed at the table as equals. None of them could boast that he was seated higher than his peer." Its physical configuration is difficult to conceive, for it sounds as if it is shaped like a doughnut, with the knights sitting around its interior. And unlike the table at Winchester, Arthur is not necessarily seated at the table, suggesting he *is* superior, but the knights themselves are all equal.

Fletcher also suggests that Wace must have been aware of previous stories about the Round Table, "which may be considered substantially proved by the nearly certain fact that round tables were a very ancient pan-Celtic institution.

The antiquity of the thing being admitted, there is no reason to doubt that its close association with Arthur goes back to a stage of the tradition anterior to Wace and Geoffrey."

William Kibler, in Norris Lacey's *Arthurian Encyclopedia*, aptly stresses Wace's importance in Arthuriana: "Wace is noted for his skill in description and lively style. He had great influence on subsequent French authors of Arthurian materials; on Chretién de Troyes and Marie de France, as well as on the anonymous authors of the Vulgate *Merlin,* the *Mort Artu,* the Didot-*Perceval,* and the *Livre d'Artus.*"

See also GEOFFREY OF MONMOUTH, CHRÉTIEN DE TROYES, and LAYAMON.

Sources: R. Brengle (A: KOB); R. Fletcher (AMC); N. Lacy (AE); E. Mason (AC:W&L); L. Thorpe (GM: HKB).

Walter, Archdeacon of Oxford. Although Archdeacon Walter at first might be judged as an incidental figure in the Arthurian arena, his name merits recognition because his role is a pivotal point in the quest for a British heroic figure of the fifth century. Geoffrey of Monmouth writes in his dedication of *The History of the Kings of Britain*: "For the satisfaction of the curious, will I add onto this prologue a letter of Archdeacon Henry, where he doth briefly enumerate all the Kings of the Britons from Brutus as far as Cadwallo, who was the last of the puissant Kings of the Britons and was father of Cadwallader whom Bede calleth Cedwalla.... I offered [Archdeacon Henry] a copy of the whole history of the Britons when he was on his way to Rome."

This is the infamous lost *liber vetustissimus* which has confounded scholars ever since Monmouth's book was distributed nearly nine centuries ago. And the mystery does not stop here. There have been many scholarly comments as to whether or not this *liber vetustissimus* was a reference to a manuscript called the *Tysilio,* which is basically a combination of the *Tysilio* and another manuscript known as the *Book of Basingwerke Abbey,* attributed to Guttyn Owain.

Walter's role becomes very confusing. At the end of the *Tysilio* is a postscript which states, "I, Walter, Archdeacon of Oxford, translated this

book from the Welsh into Latin, and in my old age have again translated it from the Latin into Welsh." Translator Peter Roberts adds a footnote explaining that this probably means Walter had given his original Welsh copy to Geoffrey of Monmouth and hence had to re-copy his Latin version into a Welsh one.

Geoffrey of Monmouth has normally been considered the individual who translated and copied this *liber vetustissimus* (the *Tysilio* and *Book of Basingwerke Abbey*), which became the basis for Monmouth's *History of the Kings of Britain.* It is definitely mislabeled as a "very ancient book" when measured by Monmouth's century.

In an attempt to unravel the confusion, John Bruno Hare offers this explanation of what perhaps transpired:

So far we may extricate some facts:— all the MSS of the first text agree that it was a translation by Walter the Archdeacon from Latin to Welsh; on the authority of the Hengwrt MS, we may pronounce the third to be a translation into Welsh, by Geoffrey of Monmouth, of his Latin edition; the text probably represents an intermediate stage of the work; all seem to imply that Walter's book was at all events in Latin before it reached Geoffrey; but whether the original was in Breton, in Cymraec, or in Latin, or whether there ever was an original, there is certainly no text, either in Welsh or Latin, which now represents it; and all of these texts must be placed in the first part of the twelfth century.

Based upon the final paragraph in *The Chronicle of the Kings of Britain* by Peter Roberts, we can say with trepidation and no assurance that Walter, in whose possession was the *Tysilio* and the *Book of Basingwerke Abbey,* translated his Breton copy into Latin, and thereafter he gave that Breton or Welsh copy to Geoffrey of Monmouth, who translated it once again into Latin.

Sources: S. Evans (GM); P. Roberts (COKB).

Welsh, Combrogi. An age-old, recurring dilemma focuses upon which terms appropriately describe Britain's inhabitants during the Arthurian age. Of all the terms used for aboriginal/indigenous insular tribes, there are two which are most problematic in attempting to resolve specific groups of allies or adversaries. In *The*

Anglo-Saxon Chronicle, there are two common terms used to describe the SAXONES' adversaries: the Welsh and the BRITONS. Some researchers contend that there is no difference between the Welsh and the Britons and the two terms are sometimes used synonymously and interchangeably.

Those with an opposing view, however, strongly believe that a distinction is imperative if one expects historical and geographic locales to match accurately the events on the island, and by appropriately differentiating between Welsh and Briton, their different contexts modify interpretations of the Arthurian period.

Writing about the five languages of Britain, Plummer explains that if Manuscript D of the *ASC* breaks "Brytwylsc into two parts, Brittisc and Wilsc, then there are six languages of the period, not five." What Plummer is suggesting is that by BEDE's time there was no distinction between words like Brittisc and Wilsc. Instead, the word Briton had become a generic term, and therefore it, rather than the more precise term Welsh, was used in some translations of the ancient manuscripts.

He further explains that the variations for the terms Briton/British/Britain and Welsh/Wales indicate that Briton/Wilsc was used more in the entries up to about the middle of the sixth century, and thereafter, in the later entries, the Welsh terms began to blend with the British. Plummer suggests that the terms Briton/British as opposed to Welsh were used in the specific sense for entries 449, 457, 491, 501, 508, 514, 519, 552, and 556. Conversely, the specific use of the term Welsh identified the Saxones as enemies in entries 465, 473, 477, 485, 495, 508, all within the Arthurian era. He then makes a distinction that Wessex was conquered from the Welsh and that Wilsc was one of the languages of Britain.

Sir Ifor Williams writes that the process by which Welsh words were combined with Latin suffixes is a significant fact which hasn't yet been fully realized and claims that they are proofs of the old British declension systems going to pieces in Wales long before 540. Williams offers no explanation why the Britons of Wales began calling themselves Cymry (plural Cymro), but those terms applied *not* to Cornishmen of a later period but to Wales itself and to Cumberland, which means "land of the Cymry."

The translator G.N. Garmonsway is meticulous in distinguishing Welsh from Briton in all variants of the *ASC* and in each entry. Garmonsway's distinction is supported by Clark Hall's Old English dictionary. *Bryttwealas* are the Britons of Wales — that is, Welsh, and *Bryttons* are Britons — that is, those others who are indigenous to the island.

The Welsh/Briton question leads to other entanglements. For those who believe that the terms are synonymous, then the geographic locations of Cerdicesora and Cerdicesford are also evidently synonymous. However, as only one example, since the *ASC* records in one entry that CERDIC fought the Welsh at Cerdicesora, and in another entry that Cerdic fought a different battle against the Britons at Cerdicesforda, then Cerdicesora and Cerdicesforda must be two separate locations.

Sources: R. Bromwich (BWP); G. Garmonsway (ASC); C. Plummer (TSCP); F. Reno (HKA); D. Whitelock (ASC); I. Williams (LEWP).

West Saxon King. *see* CERDIC, West Saxon King.

William of Malmesbury (*floruit* 1110–1140 / *lifespan* circa 1095–1143). As an impartial antiquarian, William of Malmesbury does not give historical credibility to King ARTHUR even though he was consigned as a principal authority for the early history of Glastonbury Abbey. His manuscript *De Antiquitate Glastonie Ecclesie* has not survived the ages without heavily biased interpolations; the edition of Hearne from the manuscript at Trinity College, Cambridge, shows that the book is filled with self-serving and unscrupulous accretions for a hundred years after Malmesbury's death. Luckily, however, Malmesbury himself had included the first part of the *De Antiquitate* in a subsequent edition of another of his works, titled *Gesta Regum Anglorum*, which was revised several times. The passages from *Gesta Regum Anglorum*, then, come from Malmesbury himself, unencumbered by the interpolations inserted by the Glastonbury abbot and monks in his *De Antiquitate*.

Before looking at John Scott's translation, however, a terse chronology will illustrate the complexity of scrutinizing the Malmesbury material in order to extract only that material which he truly wrote. William visited Glastonbury Abbey around 1129, commissioned in the specific sense of the term to chronicle an accurate record of the abbey's long religious history, using manuscripts and charters that were made available to him. William accepted his charge by the abbot and monks, but as a serious historian, he remained remarkably impartial in his recordings, although the pressures to paint a more biased history must have been enormous. He suggests, for instance, that Glastonbury's apostolic origin is a possibility, but he does not wholeheartedly accept that premise, in spite of pressure from his hosts. To borrow some of Scott's words, Malmesbury writes of "fulfilling the monks' expectations, submitting to their commands and following their orders, and offering his work to them as the required token of his obedience." Yet, as another example, William fulfilled only part of the expectations expressed by the monks in validating the association between Saint DUNSTAN and Glastonbury Abbey. A longstanding feud had been going on between Glastonbury and Canterbury over Saint Dunstan's relics, but William omits a great deal of Saint Dunstan's life and the performance of miracles, thus side-stepping the issue without satisfying the Glastonbury contingencies while at the same time avoiding direct insult or denial.

Because of the Saint Dunstan issue, the monks at Glastonbury were dissatisfied with Malmesbury's writings. He offered them the *De Antiquitate*, attempting to convince them that the many things which the manuscript set forth would bring glory and prestige to the monastery, but they remained unhappy with the results. William wrote a Preface to the work, and submitted it to Abbot Henry de Blois, in hopes of mollifying him, but even this appeal did not seem to placate the monks.

As a consequence, Malmesbury's manuscript of the *De Antiquitate* was left in the hands of Henry de Blois and the Glastonbury monks. The offshoot, over the next 150 years, was a manuscript laden with interpolations and rewritten to include material that had not been sanctioned by William, and in most instances did not remotely approach the truth. Modern-day scholars would have been ignorant of Malmesbury's original *DA* and would have forever perpetrated untruths, manipulations, and deliberate deceits had not William himself included large segments of the *DA* in his revision of *Gesta Regum Anglorum*. We know now, independent of the Glastonbury manuscripts, what Malmesbury left for posterity in writing the *De Antiquitate*.

In all, excluding William's original text, there are at least six major distinctive revisions and rewrites. In addition to a revision around the year 1230, one year later, there are manuscripts which bear the letters B, C, L, M, and T. These have nothing to do with the alphabetical chronology but instead indicate abbreviations of where each particular manuscript is housed. There are also hybrids with such labels as CL, indicating that C was written using L as its base. Scott relays some fairly detailed information about these manuscripts, then uses Manuscript T in presenting his translation. Likewise, he is specific in pointing out where the interpolations are.

R.F. Treharne's scholarly work in 1966 predates Scott's translation by 15 years. On the one hand, Treharne humbly apologizes to the devout believers in the full legends of JOSEPH OF ARIMATHEA and King Arthur at Glastonbury, but indicates that his impartiality as a historian was not meant to be either impious or irreverent. Scott, in Section 4 — "Forgery and the Interpolations in the *De Antiquitate*" — offers an apology of a different sort. He asks the reader's forgiveness for Glastonbury's transgressions in their deceptive interpolations, defending their actions by saying that "other monasteries [also] tried to bolster their reputations by similarly elaborating stories" and averring that Glastonbury was no different from other abbeys in Britain; the abbeys had to maintain "their places in a world that was increasingly unsympathetic." However, both authors — Treharne and Scott — display an integrity of the truth and an impartiality of reporting.

William himself writes of his own integrity in what modern-day scholars now know to be his untainted version of the *DA*. In addition to it and *Gesta Regum Anglorum*, other manuscripts to his credit are *De Gesta Pontificum Anglorum*, around the year 1125, and *Vita Sancti Dunstani*, probably no later than 1135. What demonstrates his integrity, however — despite his allegiance to the monks and the abbot of Glastonbury — is what he writes in the original version of the *De Antiquitate*: "Since this is the point at which I must bring in the monastery of Glastonbury, let me trace from its very beginning the rise and progress of that church so far as I can discover it from the mass of source-material.... But lest I should appear to deceive the expectations of my readers with trifling fancies, let me come on to narrate facts of solid truth, leaving aside all these discrepancies."

While writing the *DA*, William of Malmesbury stayed at Glastonbury Abbey around 1125. He personally studied the records of the monastery, looking in great detail at the early charters of the church, and gleaning from the monks as many traditional stories as he could. He conveys the feeling that no documents were withheld from him, and he separates the historical data obtained from the written documents and the literary claims of traditional lore. He was aware of claims that the Old Church of Wattles, dedicated to the Blessed Virgin, was the most ancient sanctuary on the island and had been built by missionaries whom the Pope sent from Rome at the request of King Lucius in the year 166. He was likewise aware that an earlier date was claimed for it, allegedly built by the disciples of the Lord. In writing his history, however, he would not commit to any proposition that was merely hearsay or pious opinion.

As relayed by J. Armitage Robinson, who was using the untainted version of the *DA*, Malmesbury claims to have seen a very ancient charter reporting that a king (whose name was illegible) of Dumnonia (which then included not only Devon but also the greater part of Somerset) granted to the Old Church (Glastonbury) land in the Isle of Yneswitrin. The interesting term is Yneswitrin, linked to Glastonbury. This implies the same connection made between Glastonbury and Yneswitrin in the Grail manuscripts, but unfortunately it does not make an association between Avalon and Yneswitrin. Therefore, King Arthur's Avalon does not appear as a synonym for Glastonbury.

In summary, the following items are what Malmesbury thought to be history of credible account:

1. Gildas (no distinction made between GILDAS ALBANIUS or GILDAS BADONICUS) spent several years at the abbey, a place of sanctity, holiness, and reverence.
2. Glastonbury was a holy shrine which not only attracted many pilgrims but became a coveted resting place for many saints.
3. The shrine was also revered by the conquerors and therefore left intact rather than being destroyed.
4. Malmesbury accepted the stories about St. Patrick, St. David, and the Lord himself consecrating the Old Church of Wattles.

What must be accentuated because of its implication in relation to King Arthur's historicity is that Malmesbury makes no claim that Glastonbury is factually or historically tied to King Arthur. William refers to Gawain as Walwen, the son of Arthur's sister, who "deservedly shared his uncle's fame, for they averted the ruin of their country for many years. But the tomb of Arthur is nowhere to be seen, for which reason the dirges of old relate that he is to come again."

It is important to stress that the above quotation is the totality of William of Malmesbury's reference to King Arthur. All of the allusions linking Glastonbury (as Avalon) to King Arthur come *after* Malmesbury. Modern scholars know without a doubt that Malmesbury's *De Antiquitate* underwent a great deal of change during the subsequent century, with the two major additions being the exhumation of King Arthur and the inclusion of the Arimathea story. According to Scott, these interpolations are traceable because of the use of different pens, because of the use of simplistic grammatical structure contrasted to Malmesbury's more complex use, and because of poor Latinity. Scott is confident about interpolations when he writes, "It can be discerned easily that at least two different monks were involved." ADAM OF DOMERHAM is the monk who emerges as one of the most likely and obvious candidates for accomplishing at least part of this hoax.

Three specific interpolations should be addressed before concluding the material about William of Malmesbury. One focuses upon the pair of pyramids which GIRALDUS CAMBRENSIS describes. Malmesbury, too, describes the pyramids at Glastonbury, although he is unsure about the significance of their structures, tentatively suggesting that within the hollowed stones are the bones of those whose names can be read on the outside. He writes, "The nearer [one] to the church is twenty-six feet high and has four storeys," but makes no other claims about them, evidently neither reading about them in charters nor learning of them through oral tradition.

The second is the interpolation inserted into Malmesbury's manuscript which confuses Arthur's twelfth battle at Mount Badon and his eighth battle at Castle Guinnion. E.K. Chamber notes that the interpolation reads, "Finally at the siege of Mount Badon, relying upon the image of the mother of the Lord, which he had sewn on his armor, rising alone against nine hundred of the enemy he dashed them to the ground with incredible slaughter." In actuality, the passage which refers to "Our Lord's Mother" is not the Badon passage, but the passage in NENNIUS describing the battle at Guinnion, in which Arthur is carrying the image of Saint Mary either on his shoulder or on his shield.

And the last is an anonymous interpolator of the 1250s, cited by J. Armitage Robinson: "Arthur, in the year of our Lord's Incarnation 542, was wounded fatally by MORDRED in Cornwall, near the river Camba; and thence he was carried for the healing of his wounds to the island of Avallon; and there he died in the summer, about Pentecost, being well nigh a hundred years old or thereabout." The first line supplies the date 542 for Arthur's death, which is the same year used by GEOFFREY OF MONMOUTH; the Mordred, Cornwall, and Camba material also comes from Monmouth. The last segment perhaps echoes LAYAMON, who wrote the *Brut* around the 1200s.

Sources: E. Chambers (AOB); F. Reno (HKA);

J.A. Robinson (TGL: KA&JA); J. Scott (EHG: ETSWM); R.F. Treharne (GL: JA/HG/KA).

William of Newburgh (*floruit* 1152–1182 / *lifespan* 1136–1198). William of Newburgh and RANULF HIGDEN, his predecessor by approximately a century and a half, both stand apart in history because of their sharp criticism of GEOFFREY OF MONMOUTH's *History of the Kings of Britain.*

Allegedly born in Bridlington, Yorkshire, around 1136, William attended the newly-founded Augustinian priory, where he spent his life as a canon. If this information is accurate, then it would be safe to assume that he traveled little or not at all, suggesting that his experiences and writing are vicariously founded. However, this is not meant to denigrate his work. E.A. Freeman, author of *William the Conqueror*, was impressed by Newburgh's historic integrity and bestowed upon him the title of "father of historical criticism." Various sources are quite complimentary, claiming that William's main purpose was to produce a philosophical commentary on the history of his own time; he produced not simply a chronicle, but real history with a proper sense of proportion and an intelligent, independent point of view.

Because William could not have had in-depth contact with public events in his era, he was evidently adept in making excellent judgment and relying upon information at his disposal. He venerated BEDE—which is perhaps why the eighth-century historian became known as the Venerable Bede—and drew from manuscripts such as GILDAS (BADONICUS), HENRY OF HUNTINGDON, and WILLIAM OF MALMESBURY.

According to informed historians, he wrote *Historia Rerum Anglicarum* (*History of English Affairs*) within a short period prior to his death, suggesting that he most likely had been collecting all the material during his lifetime. His account covers the period from William the Conqueror in 1066 to one year prior to his death, 1107. All of his material is unrelated to King Arthur, except he devotes the entire Preface of his chronicle to a castigation of GEOFFREY OF MONMOUTH's sections about King Arthur and Merlin. Those who supported William's viewpoint "vehemently denounced Geoffrey's motives," "severely criticized his fabrications," and labeled the pseudo-historian as "an impudent and shameless liar."

K.G. Madison, in Lacy's *Arthurian Encyclopedia*, softens the tirade: "William subjected Geoffrey of Monmouth's history of Arthur and Merlin to harsh but careful criticism. He pointed out that Bede had never mentioned Arthur, and that Geoffrey told of activities that should have made Arthur famous and known to other writers — who in fact know nothing of him."

William concluded,

> Now, since it is evident that these facts are established with historical authenticity by the venerable Bede, it appears that whatever Geoffrey has written, subsequent to Vortigern, either of Arthur, or his successors, or predecessors, is a fiction invented either by himself or by others, and promulgated either through an unchecked propensity to falsehood, or a desire to please the Britons, of whom vast numbers are said to be so stupid as to assert that Arthur is yet to come, and who cannot bear to hear of his death.
>
> Since, therefore, the ancient historians make not the slightest mention of these matters, it is plain that whatever this man published of Arthur and of Merlin are mendacious fictions, invented to gratify the curiosity of the undiscerning.

Richard Barber, in *Arthur of Albion*, writes the following: "As an author, Geoffrey had an immediate success by medieval standards. Since the spread of written works depended on laborious hand-copying of manuscripts, reputations in the itinerary field were slow in the making, but the *Historia* was accepted and enthusiastically read by most historians of the time, and there was very little opposition to it. William of Newburgh is the first writer to object to it in strong terms, at the end of the twelfth century."

In Barber's more recent book, *King Arthur: Hero and Legend*, he includes an addendum about William of Newburgh: "William shrewdly sums up Geoffrey's method of working: 'taking the ancient fictions of the Britons and adding his own to them, by translating them into the Latin tongue he cloaked them in the honest name of history.'"

Sources: R. Barber (AA); R. Barber (KA: H&L); (CE); W.L. Jones (LC); N. Lacy (AE); Will Newburgh (HEA/HRA).

Williams, Edward. *see* IOLO MORGANWG.

Wledig. A Welsh title of importance and/or royalty.

See also GWLEDIG and EMRYS.

Wolfram Von Eschenbach (*floruit* 1195–1225 / *lifespan* 1180–1240). Wolfram's date of birth is speculative, and his lifespan can only be an approximation, some claiming that he lived from 1170 to 1200, others claiming that his death date was 1216, and still others supplying the date of 1230. The floruit and lifespan listed above have been calculated following the typical rules of thumb and places Wolfram as a contemporary or near-contemporary with GOTTFRIED VON STRASSBURG and HARTMANN VON AUE, possibly slightly postdating LAYAMON and ROBERT DE BORON.

Although this man has been recognized by some as the greatest German epic poet of the high Middle Ages, Wolfram himself, in *Parzival*, claims he was illiterate, having his work recorded from dictation. Sidney Johnson writes: "Scholars have continued to speculate on Wolfram's literacy and how he actually composed, but perhaps it is significant that Wolfram always says: 'as I heard tell' or 'the story says'; he never says: 'as I read' or 'as it is written.'" Johnson describes Wolfram's work as "anything but polished" and "obscure and complex." His style has "the immediacy of conversation," undoubtedly because that is precisely what it was — Wolfram dictating his material to an antiquarian stenographer.

Wolfram acquired a niche in Arthuriana through the work *Parzival*, which he probably wrote in the first decade of the thirteenth century. Although this work is based upon Chrétien's *Le Conte du Graal*, Wolfram — evidently unaware of the Continuations written for Chrétien's *Perceval*— adds explicit information to his story. In Books 1 and 2, Parzival's father, GAHMURET, leaves Anjou, travels through North Africa, and eventually ends up in Wales. The name "Utepandragun" has a familiar ring as does King Lot "of Norway" and Gawan and Morholt of Ireland. Gahmuret marries HERZELOYDE, and soon after he is slain, leaving behind a pregnant wife.

Because Wolfram's romance contains Arthurian figures — sometimes with widely varying names for the same character — the chart below simplifies the comparison.

There are times when Wolfram supplies names for those who are unnamed in Chrétien's work:

1. ANFORTAS is the Fisher King;
2. Cunneware is the unnamed maiden slapped by Kay when Perceval comes to Arthur's court;
3. Antanor is the unnamed dwarf who is also slapped by Kay because of the midget's praise of Perceval.
4. Ither is the name given to the Red Knight.

In Wolfram's tale, Kay slaps Cunneware because the maiden has made fun of Parzival, but in Chrétien, Kay slaps her because she professes that Perceval will be a superior knight. In contrast, Chrétien's dwarf is thrown into the fire by Kay, not simply slapped.

The remainder of Wolfram's *Parzival* follows the sequence of Chrétien to some extent, with two notable differences. One is that there is a distinctive split between the Arthurian world and the Grail world, with Gawan exemplifying the former and Parzival the latter.

The second is that Wolfram claims in Book (Chapter) 8, he relied upon the Grail segment from KYOT the Provencal. However, Sidney Johnson refutes the existence of such an individual. Kyot supposedly provided the true story of the Grail recorded in a tale written in Arabic allegedly, according to Johnston, by "an astronomer named Flegetanis, who was part Jewish and who had read about the Grail in the stars. Kyot, the Christian, had to learn Arabic in order to read what Flegetanis had written. Thereupon, he searched through Latin chronicles to find the story of the Grail family, which he finally located in Anjou."

Wolfram's "Grail" is a flat stone, the Grail knights are called "templars," and Parzival is the one chosen to seek the Grail and thus release Anfortas (the Fisher King) from his agony.

Despite criticism, accusations, and his illiteracy, Wolfram has created a monumental work of art about a segment of Arthuriana. His accomplishments have been ranked favorably by succeeding generations.

Sources: (CE); A. Hatto (WVE: P); N. Lacy (AE); N. Lacy/G. Ashe (AH); E.H. Zeydel (PWVE).

Yder, Ider, Edern, Isdermus. Yder is one of the many names that enigmatically appears in several stories, impossible to unreservedly identify as referring either to one individual or to several different characters.

Yder is the main character in a French romance of that name. There is only one extant manuscript, most likely written in the mid–thirteenth century.

Character	Wolfram's Parzival	Other Arthurian Versions
Arthur's father	Utepandragun	Utherpendragon
Arthur's mother	Arnive	IGERNA/Ygerna
Arthur's sister	Sangive	ANNA (GM), Morgana
		Morgan le Fay
Arthur's half-brother	Keie	Kay
Arthur's Queen	Ginover	GUINEVERE, Guinever
Sangive's husband	King Lot of Norway	King LOT of Orkney
Sangive's eldest son	Gawan	Gawain
Sangive's daughters	Itonje, Cundrie	
Gawan's sisters	Itonje, Cundrie	
sorceress	Cundrie (not Gawain's sister)	
Parzival's mentor	Gurnemanz	Gornemant
Parzival's concubine	Condwi ramurs	Blancheflor
Parzival's rival	Clamide	Clamadeu

As it is recorded by Alison Adams in *The Arthurian Encyclopedia*, the figure of Yder is different from the material appearing in de Troyes' work. This anonymous romance tells the tale of an illegitimate Yder who vies for Queen Guenloie in a tournament. After he is wounded by Sir KAY, he is healed by Queen Guenloie and joins Arthur's Round Table. A jealousy evolves between Yder and ARTHUR because of GUINEVERE, and Arthur attempts to kill his adversary. The conflict is resolved and Yder succeeds in legitimatizing his birth by perpetrating the marriage of his own mother and his father, Nut.

In the romance titled *Erec et Enide* by Chrétien, Yder is initially one of Erec's foes. Accompanying Guinevere, who trails King Arthur's hunting party, Erec encounters a rude knight, a maiden and the knight's dwarf. At Guinevere's request, Erec approaches the knight to invite him to join Guinevere, but the dwarf blocks Erec's passage by lashing him with a whip across the face and neck. Rebuffed and unarmed, Erec returns to Guinevere to explain what has transpired.

The knight departs with Erec following in hopes of borrowing arms and armor from someone so that he can confront the arrogant warrior and his vile dwarf. When an opportunity finally allows Erec to borrow arms and armor from a vavasour, the two knights face each other in combat. After a vicious battle, Erec triumphs and requires Yder to travel to Arthur's court to seek pardon from Guinevere for the insult to her.

When Yder arrives at court, he falls at Guinevere's feet and offers repentance. He identifies himself as Yder, son of NUT. The queen frees the errant knight from his obligations on the condition that Yder remain at court as Arthur's loyal servant.

The story of GEREINT and Enid is the Welsh version of the same tale. Jean Markale writes of the two versions that "Chrétien's *Erec* was adapted into German by Hartmann von Aue towards the end of the twelfth century. The Welsh *Gereint and Enid* dating from the same period also appears to be an adaptation, possibly even a translation of the same work, although there are significant differences in the details. It is more likely, in fact, that the Welsh author and Chrétien used some common but unknown source."

The confusion of the name Yder is compounded in the *Erec and Enide/Gereint and Enid* tales. When Yder is ordered to King Arthur's court, the knights in attendance for Arthur are Gawain, Kay, and Girflet; the kings are Yder, Cadiolan, and Amauguin. Fortunately, translator D.D.R. Owen resolves the problem by explaining in a footnote that "King Yder, an ally of Arthur, is not to be confused with Yder son of Nut, Erec's opponent in the sparrow-hawk contest."

See also EDERN and IDER.

Sources: C.W. Carroll (CT: AR); E. Chambers (AOB); N. Fairbairn (TGKOA); N. Lacy (AE); J. Markale (KA: KOK); D.D.R. Owens (CT: AR).

Ygerna. In Geoffrey of Monmouth's *History of the Kings of Britain*, Ygerna is the equivalent of the *Tysilio*'s EIGR and Thomas Malory's IGRAINE. The three possibilities are quite similar. Ygerna is wife of GORLOIS, Duke of Cornwall, and Utherpendragon (UTERPENDRAGON) lusts after her. Gorlois fortifies her at Tintagel, and enmity develops between the Duke and Utherpendragon. MERLIN transforms Utherpendragon into Gorlois's likeness, and unknown to Utherpendragon, Gorlois is killed by the King's men while Utherpendragon seduces Ygerna. In GEOFFREY OF MONMOUTH's words, "Utherpendragon mourned for the death of Gorlois, but he was happy, all the same, that Ygerna was freed from her marital obligations. He returned to Tintagel Castle, captured it and seized Ygerna at the same time, she being what he really wanted. From that day on they lived together as equals, united by their great love for each other, and they had a son and daughter. The boy was called Arthur and the girl Anna."

See also ARNIVE.

Source: L. Thorpe (GM: HKB).

APPENDIX A
A CHARACTER INDEX OF MALORY'S *LE MORTE D'ARTHUR*

Because page numbers would vary depending upon publishers, editors, or translators, this index is structured so that the reader can quickly find the location of major and minor characters by book and chapter as formatted according to Harrison House's publication of Caxton's 1485 edition and Janet Cowan's edition printed by Penguin Classics. Although some incidental characters have been omitted, the ones listed below are at times further identified by genealogical connections, titles, or name variants to avoid confusion.

Norris Lacy's *The Arthurian Encyclopedia* contains only a handful of characters extracted from Malory's *Le Morte*, and Ronan Coghlan, author of *The Encyclopedia of Arthurian Legends*, lists perhaps a hundred entries contained in Malory's work, approximately half of the number listed in the index below. For those names which are not listed by Lacy, Goghlan, or this present text, the reader has the resource below to more easily locate obscure characters of Arthur's millennium. Significant knights are indicated by an asterisk (*).

Accolon
B 2 Chapter 11
B 4 Chapters 4, 8, 9, 10, 11, 12, 14, 16

Aglovale
B 7 Chapter 27, 28
B 10 Chapters 23, 48
B 11 Chapters 10, 11, 12
B 12 Chapter 7
B 13 Chapter 16
B 19 Chapter 11
B 20 Chapter 8

*Agravain (Agravaine)
B 1 Chapter 19
B 2 Chapter 11
B 7 Chapters 13, 25, 27, 35
B 8 Chapter 9
B 10 Chapters 11, 13, 25, 46, 55, 56, 58, 68
B 18 Chapters 1, 3, 10, 19, 20, 23
B 19 Chapters 1, 2, 11, 13
B 20 Chapters 1–5, 7, 9, 15

*Agwisance/Angwyshaunce, King of Ireland
B 1 Chapters 12, 14, 15, 16, 18
B 7 Chapters 27, 28
B 8 Chapters 8, 9, 11, 20, 21, 22, 23, 24, 27 (Anguish)
B 9 Chapter 21 (Anguish)
B 18 Chapters 8, 10, 18, 21, 22 (Anguish)
B 19 Chapter 11 (Anguish)

Alice la Beale Pilgrim, daughter of Duke Ansirus, wife of Alisander
B 10 Chapters 38, 39, 40
B 20 Chapter 5 (Bellanger's mother)

*Alisander
B 10 Chapters 32–40

B 18 Chapter 11
B 19 Chapter 11
B 20 Chapter 17

Andred
B 8 Chapters 15, 32, 34, 35
B 9 Chapters 19, 21, 37, 38
B 10 Chapter 28
B 19 Chapter 11

Anglides, Boudwin's wife, Alisander's son
B 10 Chapters 32–35

Annecians, Bor's godson
B 1 Chapter 17

Archbishop (Bishop) of Canterbury
B 1 Chapters 5, 6, 7, 9, 10
B 3 Chapter 2
B 7 Chapter 35
B 21 Chapters 1, 6, 10, 11, 13

Arthur

B 1 Chapter 5 (virtually all)

Astlabor/Estlabor, father of Palomides

B 10 Chapters 83, 84

*Bagdemagus

B 2 Chapter 11
B 6 Chapters 4, 6, 7
B 7 Chapters 1, 27, 28
B 8 Chapter 9
B 9 Chapter 1
B 10 Chapters 41, 43, 44, 45, 49, 50
B 13 Chapters 9, 10
B 17 Chapters 17, 18
B 19 Chapter 1
B 20 Chapter 19

*Balan

B 1 Chapter 18
B 2 Chapters 6, 7, 8, 9, 10, 11, 18, 19
B 13 Chapter 5

*Balin, the Knight with Two Swords

B 1 Chapters 18, 27
B 2 Chapters 2, 3, 4, 5, 6, 7, 8, 9, 11, 12, 13, 14, 15, 16, 17, 18, 19
B 10 Chapters 5, 24
B 13 Chapter 5

*Ban, King of Benwick, father of Launcelot

B 1 Chapters 10, 11, 13, 14, 15, 16 17, 18, 19
B 4 Chapter 1
B 6 Chapters 3, 8
B 8 Chapter 21
B 9 Chapters 27, 30, 32
B 10 Chapter 39-f. of Launcelot
B 12 Chapter 8-f. of Launcelot
B 15 Chapter 4
B 18 Chapter 23
B 20 Chapter 19

*Baudwin, King Mark's brother, father of Alisander

B 1 Chapters 6, 7, 9
B 5 Chapter 3
B 7 Chapter 26
B 18 Chapters 12, 17

*Beaumains (See also Gareth)

B 7 Chapters 1–12, 13 (identifies Beaumains as Gareth), 14–21, 22 (Gareth), 24, 25, 29, 31
B 19 Chapter 11 Beaumains/ Gareth

*Bedivere

B 5 Chapters 5, 6
B 7 Chapters 27, 28
B 18 Chapter 23
B 21 Chapters 3–7, 10, 13

Belinus of Britain

B 5 Chapter 1

Bellangere, Alisander's and Alice's son

B 20 Chapter 5

Belleus

B 6 Chapters 5, 18

Belliance, Frollo's brother

B 8 Chapter 41
B 20 Chapter 8

Bernard of Astolat, father of Elaine

B 18 Chapters 9, 10, 13, 14, 18, 19

Berrant le Apres (See King with the Hundred Knights)

*Blamore de Ganis, Bleoberis' brother

B 7 Chapter 13
B 8 Chapters 15, 17, 20–23, 38
B 9 Chapters 5, 21, 30, 35, 42
B 10 Chapter 44
B 18 Chapters 3, 11
B 19 Chapter 11
B 20 Chapter 5, 13, 19
B 21 Chapters 10, 13

Bleise, Merlin's master

B 1 Chapter 17

*Bleoberis de Ganis, brother of Blamore

B 8 17, 18, 20–23
B 9 Chapters 3, 4, 13, 21–23, 29, 35, 36, 42

B 10, Chapters 44, 45, 48, 53, 54, 56, 69, 75, 80, 81
B 11 Chapter 7
B 18 Chapters 3, 11, 23
B 19 Chapter 11
B 20 Chapters 5, 13, 18
B 21 Chapters 10, 13

Bloias de La Flandres

B 1 Chapter 15

Borre, Arthur's son by Lionors

B 1 Chapter 17

*Bors, King of Gaul

B 1 Chapters 10, 11, 13, 14, 15, 16, 17, 18, 19
B 5 Chapters 6, 8,
B 7 Chapters 13, 17, 18
B 9 Chapters 22, 23, 30, 31, 35, 42
B 10 Chapter 75
B 11 Chapters 4, 5, 6, 9, 10
B 12 Chapter 9
B 13 Chapters 1, 2, 4
B 16 Chapters 1, 3, 6–17
B 17 Chapters 2, 3, 7, 8, 10, 11, 12, 17, 19, 20–23
B 18 Chapters 1–7, 11, 15–18, 21, 23, 24
B 19 Chapter 11
B 20 Chapters 2, 3, 5, 6, 11–13, 18–20
B 21 Chapters 8, 9, 10, 12, 13

Bragwaine, maid of La Beale Isoud

B 8 Chapters 24, 29, 30, 35,
B 9 Chapters 10, 16, 20, 26, 31, 35, 38, 39

Brandegoris, King of Stranggore

B 1 Chapters 12, 14, 15, 16
B 19 Chapter 11

*Brandiles

B 7 Chapters 27, 28
B 9 Chapters 9, 14, 15
B 10 Chapters 11–13, 20
B 18 Chapters 3, 10, 11, 20
B 19 Chapters 1–3, 11
B 20 Chapter 8

Brastias

B 1 Chapters 1, 2, 4, 6, 7, 9. 10, 11, 14, 15, 17

Brenius of Britain

B 5 Chapter 1

Breunor

B 8 Chapters 24, 25, 26

Breunor le Noire (See also La Cote Male Taile)

B 7 Chapter 2
B 9 Chapters 1, 9

Breuse Saunce Piteé

B 8 Chapter 21
B 9 Chapters 5, 7, 25, 35, 40
B 10 Chapters 1, 2, 6, 25, 35, 44, 53, 65, 86, 87
B 12 Chapter 2
B 19 Chapter 11

Brian of the Forest

B 3 Chapter 6

Brian of the Isles

B 3 Chapter 13
B 7 Chapter 26
B 7 Chapter 28
B 9 Chapters 6, 9

Brian de Listonois

B 6 Chapter 9
B 19 Chapter 11

Briant de la Forest Savage of North Wales

B 1 Chapter 17
B 9 Chapter 27

Brisen (Dame)

B 11 Chapters 2, 3, 7, 8, 9
B 12 Chapters 4, 5

Cador of Cornwall

B 5 Chapters 1–3, 6–8
B 19 Chapter 11
B 21 Chapter 13

Carados (King)

B 1, Chapters 8, 9, 12, 15, 16
B 4 Chapter 21
B 6 Chapter 8
B 7 Chapters 26, 27, 28, 29
B 8 Chapters 20, 22, 28
B 9 Chapters 8, 25, 30, 32
B 10 Chapter 36
B 19 Chapter 11
B 20 Chapters 1, 15

Cardol, father of Sir Griflet

B 1 Chapter 10

Clariance, King of Northumberland

B 1 Chapters 12, 14, 15, 16

Claudas (King)

B 1 Chapters 10, 11, 17, 18
B 4 Chapter 1
B 5 Chapter 2
B 11 Chapter 6
B 17 Chapter 21
B 20 Chapters 18, 19

Colgrevaunce de Gore

B 1 Chapter 17
B 9 Chapter 23
B 16 Chapters 15, 16
B 19 Chapter 11
B 20 Chapters 2, 4, 7

Constantine, son of Cador

B 5 Chapter 3
B 21 Chapter 8

Constantine, son of Carados

B 19, Chapter 11

Constantine, son of Heleine

B 5 Chapter 1

Corneus (Duke), father of Sir Lucas

B 1 Chapter 10

Cradelment, King of North Wales

B 1 Chapter 12, 14, 15, 16

Dagonet, King Arthur's fool

B 9 Chapters 3, 18
B 10 Chapters 12, 13, 20

Damas

B 4, 7, 8, 12
B 20 Chapter 8

Darras

B 9 Chapters 35, 26, 39
B 19 Chapter 11

Dinadan, Sir Breunor's brother

B 7 Chapter 2, 27, 28
B 9 21–24, 27–29, 31, 33, 34–37, 39, 40
B 10 Chapters 3, 8–14, 16–22, 25–27,
31, 40, 42, 44, 45, 47–49, 55, 58, 60, 64, 66, 68–81, 86
B 19 Chapter 11

Dinas, King Mark's seneschal

B 7 Chapters 26, 28
B 8 Chapters 8, 32
B 9 Chapters 16, 21, 37, 38, 39
B 10 Chapters 28, 29, 32, 35, 50, 51
B 10 Chapter 11
B 20 Chapters 5, 18

Dodinas le Savage

B 4 Chapter 25
B 7 Chapter 28
B 8 Chapters 9, 15–17
B 9 Chapter 34
B 10 Chapters 4, 66
B 18 Chapters 10, 11
B19 Chapters 1, 2, 11

Dornard, one of Pellinor's sons

B 10 Chapter 48

Driant

B 8 Chapter 33
B 9 Chapters 22, 23
B 19 Chapter 11
B 20 Chapter 8

Duke de la Rowse

B 7 Chapters 31, 32, 35

***Ector**

B 1 Chapters 3, 4, 10, 14, 15, 17, 20, 21

Ector de Maris

B 6 Chapters 2, 9, 13, 18
B 7 Chapters 13, 27, 28
B 8 Chapter 19
B 9 Chapters 15, 22, 23, 30, 31, 35, 42, 43, 48
B 10 Chapters 21, 41, 45, 53, 54, 69, 71, 75, 79–81, 83, 86
B 11 Chapters 9, 10, 13, 14
B 12 Chapters 1, 7–10

B 16 Chapters 1–5, 17
B 17 Chapters 1, 16, 17
B 18 Chapters 2, 3, 11, 23
B 19 Chapter 11
B 20 Chapters 5, 12, 13, 17, 18
B 21 Chapters 10, 12, 13

Edward of the Red Castle

B 4 26, 27
B 10 Chapters 68, 74
B 19 Chapter 11

Elaine, daughter of King Pelles

B 11 Chapters 2–4, 6–9
B 12, Chapters 3–10
B 18, Chapters 9, 13–19

Elaine, wife of King Ban

B 4 Chapter 1

Elaine, wife of King Nentres

B 1 Chapter 2

Elizabeth, Tristram's mother, King Mark's sister

B 8 Chapters 1, 12

Epinogrus

B 7 Chapter 26
B 10 Chapters 65, 68, 82–84
B 18 Chapters 10, 11
B 19 Chapter 11

Ettard, Pelleas' damosel

B 4 Chapters 20–23
B 19 Chapter 11

Eustace, Duke of Canbenet

B 1 Chapter 14, 15

Evelake (King)

B 13 Chapters 10, 11
B 14 Chapters 3, 4
B 15 Chapter 4

Excalibur

B 1 Chapters 9, 25
B 2 Chapters 3, 11
B 4 Chapters 8, 9, 10, 12, 14
B 5 Chapter 8
B 21 Chapter 5

Fergus the Earl

Book 4 Chapter 25

B 9, Chapters 17, 21, 26
B 10 Chapters 26, 32, 35
B19 Chapter 11

Florence, son of Gawain

B 5 Chapters 9, 10, 11
B 19 Chapter 11
B 20 Chapters 2, 7

Froll of the Out Isles

B 8 Chapters 40, 41

Gahalantine

B 6 Chapters 6, 7, 18
B 19 Chapter 11
B 20 Chapters 5, 18
B 21 Chapters 10, 13

*Gaheris

B 1 Chapter 19
B 2 Chapter 11
B 3 Chapters 4, 6, 7, 8
B 4 Chapter 16
B 6 Chapters 7, 9, 18
B 7 Chapters 13, 25, 27, 35
B 8 Chapter 9
B 9 Chapters 1, 18, 23, 29, 31, 33, 37, 38, 39, 42
B 10 Chapters 5, 8, 24, 44, 46, 48, 55, 56, 58, 63, 68
B 11 Chapter 10
B 18, Chapters 3, 11, 23
B 19 Chapter 11
B 20 Chapters 1, 2, 8–11, 15, 16
B 21 Chapter 8

Gainus

B 5 Chapter 6

*Galahad, son of Launcelot

B 2 Chapters 16, 19
B 4 Chapter 1
B 8 Chapter 28
B 11 Chapters 1–4, 7, 9
B 12 Chapters 3, 5, 9, 10, 14
B 13 Chapters 1, 3–17
B 14 Chapters 1, 2, 4
B 15 Chapter 4
B 16 Chapters 1, 3, 5, 17
B 17 Chapters 1–5, 7–14, 17–21, 22 (Galahad dies), 23 (he is mourned)
B 18 Chapter 1
B 21 Chapter 9

Galahaut, the Haut Prince, Breunor's son

B 8 Chapters 26, 27

B 18 Chapters 8, 10, 12, 13, 18 (of Surluse), 21, 22, 23
B 19 Chapter 11 (called Duke Galahaut)

Galatine, Gawain's sword

B 5 Chapters 6, 10

Galleron

B 12 Chapters 13, 14
B 18 Chapters 10, 11
B 19 Chapter 11
B 20 Chapter 2

Galihodin

B 7 Chapters 27, 28
B 10 Chapters 49, 65, 66, 67
B 18 Chapters 3, 11, 23
B 19 Chapter 11
B 20 Chapters 5, 18
B 21 Chapters 10, 13

*Gareth (See also Beaumains)

B 1 Chapter 19
B 2 Chapter 11
B 6 Chapter 18
B 7 Chapters 5, 13, 20, 21, 22, 23, 24, 25, 26, 27, 28, 29, 30, 31, 32, 33, 34, 35
B 10 Chapters 57, 58, 60, 63, 64, 66–71, 73–81
B 13 Chapters 15, 16
B 18 Chapters 3, 18, 23, 24
B 19 Chapter 11
B 20 Chapters 1, 2, 8–12, 16
B 21 Chapter 8

Gaunter

B 6 Chapter 12

*Gawain

B 1 Chapters 2, 19
B 2 Chapters 10, 11, 13, 19
B 3 Chapters 2, 4, 5, 6, 7, 8, 15
B 4 Chapters 1, 3, 4, 16, 17, 18, 19, 20, 21, 22, 24, 25, 27, 28
B 5 Chapters 6, 8, 9, 10, 11, 12
B 6 Chapters 7, 9, 13, 15, 18
B 7 Chapters 1, 2, 3, 4, 5, 13, 14, 17, 18, 23, 25, 26, 27, 29, 30, 33, 34
B 8 Chapters 9, 10, 17, 28, 41
B 9 Chapters 3, 17, 24, 25, 30, 35, 42
B 10 Chapters 3, 5, 8, 11, 21,

22, 24, 25, 46, 49, 54, 55, 57, 58, 63, 66, 67, 68
B 11 Chapters 1, 4, 7, 10
B 13 Chapters 3, 4, 6, 7, 8, 15, 16
B 15 Chapter 6
B 16 Chapters 1, 2, 3, 5, 17
B 17 Chapters 1, 16
B 18 Chapters1, 3, 8, 10–15, 17–19, 23, 24
B 19 Chapters 11, 13
B 20 Chapters 1, 2, 5, 7–17, 19 20, 21, 22
B 21 Chapters 2 (Gawain's death), 3–5 (Gawain's spirit), 8

Gilbert the Bastard

B 6 Chapters 14, 15

Gingalin, Gawain's son

B 9 Chapter 17
B 19 Chapter 11
B 20 Chapter 2

Gouvernail

B 8 Chapters 3, 4, 6, 8, 11, 15, 16, 21, 24, 31, 35, 36
B 9 Chapters 10, 16, 17, 26, 27, 29, 31
B 10 Chapters 4, 5

Gracian

B 1 Chapter 11

Gorlois (Duke of Cornwall)

Book 1, Chapters 1, 2

*Griflet ·

B 1 Chapters 10, 11, 14, 15, 17, 21, 22, 23
B 4 Chapters 3, 4
B 8 Chapter 9
B 10 Chapters 12, 13, 67
B 13 Chapter 16
B 18 Chapters 10, 11, 23
B 19 Chapter 11
B 20 Chapter 8

Gringamore

B 7 Chapter 19–23, 26, 27, 33–35

* Guenever (Queen)

B 1 Chapter 18
B 3 Chapters 1, 2, 5, 15,
B 4 Chapters 2, 3 14

B 5 Chapters 3, 5, 12
B 6 Chapters 1, 3, 10, 11, 12, 15, 17
B 7 Chapters 28, 34
B 8 Chapters 31, 34, 37
B 9 Chapters 1, 12, 13, 31, 40, 43
B 10 Chapters 3, 6, 16, 26, 27, 36, 40–45, 47–49, 52, 56, 73, 81
B 11 Chapters 1, 2, 6, 8, 9, 10
B 12 Chapters 6, 9, 10, 11, 14
B 13 Chapter 8
B 16 Chapter 11
B 18 Chapters 1–7 (identified only as "queen"), 8, 15, 19–21, 25
B 19 Chapters 1–9, 13
B 20 Chapters 1, 3, 5–8, 11, 13, 14, 15 (identified as "queen"), 17, 19
B 21 Chapters 1, 2, 7–10

Sir Gwinas

B 1 Chapter 14, 15, 17

Helin, son of Bors

B 12 Chapter 9

Hellawes the Sorceress

B 6 Chapter 15

*Howel, King of Brittany

B 8 Chapters 35, 36, 40
B 9 Chapter 16
B 18 Chapters 22, 23

Howell, Duke of Brittany

B 5 Chapter 5
B 8 Chapter 2

Hue of the Red Castle

B 4 Chapters 26, 27

Ider, son of Uwaine

B 5 Chapter 2

Idres, King of Cornwall

B 1 Chapters 12, 14, 15, 16, 18

*Igraine

B 1 Chapters 1, 2, 3, 8, 19, 20, 21
B 2 Chapter 1
B 6 Chapter 11

Invisible Knight (Garlon)

B 2 Chapters 12, 13, 14

Ironside — See Knights of Color: Red

*Isoud (La Beale Isoud)

B 8 Chapters 9, 10, 11, 12, 19, 21, 23–25, 27–34, 35, 36, 39
B 9 Chapters 5, 10, 11, 16–21, 26, 31, 37, 41
B 10 Chapters 7, 8, 14–16, 22, 25, 26 30, 32, 50–53, 56, 60, 64–68, 70, 71, 73, 75–78, 80–82, 86–88
B 12 Chapters 11, 12, 14
B 19 Chapter 11
B 20 Chapter 6

Isoud (la Blanche Mains)

B 8 Chapters 35, 36, 38, 39
B 9 Chapters 5, 10, 16, 43

Jordanus

Book 1 Chapters 2, 3

*Joseph of Arimathea (Armathie)

B 2 Chapter 16
B 11 Chapters 2, 5
B 12 Chapter 14
B 13 Chapters 3, 10 (Joseph's shield), 11 (shield's design)
B 14 Chapter 3
B 15 Chapter 4
B 17 Chapters 18, 19, 20, 22

*Kay

B 1 Chapters 5, 6, 7, 9, 10, 11, 14, 15, 17
B 2 Chapter 10
B 4 Chapters 3, 4
B 5 Chapters 5, 8
B 6 Chapters 9, 11, 12, 13, 18
B 7 Chapters 1, 2, 4, 5, 10, 14, 23, 25, 27, 28
B 8 Chapter 9
B 9 Chapters 1, 2, 3, 9, 14, 24, 25, 30, 37, 38, 39
B 10 Chapters 3, 6, 8, 68, 79
B 11 Chapters 12, 13
B 13 Chapters 2, 3
B 18 Chapters 3, 10, 11, 20, 23, 24
B 19 Chapters 1, 2, 11
B 20 Chapter 8

Kehydius, son of King Howel

B 8 Chapters 36, 38, 39, 40

B 9 Chapters 10, 12, 16, 18
B 10 Chapter 86

King of Northgalis

B 6 Chapters 4, 6, 7, 16, 18
B 9 Chapters 21, 24, 27, 29–33
B 10 Chapters 41, 44, 45, 49, 69, 75
B 18 Chapters 8, 10, 12, 13, 17, 18, 21–23

*King with the Hundred Knights (Berrant le Apres)

B 1 Chapters 9, 12, 13, 14, 15, 16
B 8 Chapters 10, 27
B 9 Chapters 21, 29, 30, 31, 32, 33
B 10 Chapters 8, 45, 48, 60, 67
B 18 Chapters 8, 10, 12, 13, 18, 21–23
B 19 Chapter 11

Knight with the Black Shield

B 8 Chapters 9, 10
B 9 Chapters 29, 31–33, 37

Knights of Color

Black Knight of the Black Launds (Percard)

B 7 Chapters 7–9, 12, 14, 24

Blue Knight (Persant)

B 7 Chapters 11–14, 23, 24, 26–29, 35
B 18 Chapter 3
B 19 Chapters 1, 2, 3

Brown Knight

B 7 Chapter 32

Green Knight (Pertolepe)

B 7 Chapters 8–10, 12, 14, 23, 24, 28, 25
B 10 Chapter 49
B 19 Chapter 11
B 20 Chapter 8

Red Knight of the Red Launds (aka Perimones and Ironsides)

B 7 Chapters 2, 10, 13–18, 20, 23, 24, 26–29, 35
B 14 Chapter 8
B 18 Chapter 3 (Ironside)
B 19 Chapters 1, 2, 3, 11
B 20 Chapter 8 (Perimones)

*La Cote Male Taile (See also Breunor le Noire)

B 7 Chapters 2, 27, 28
B 9 Chapters 1–10
B 10 Chapter 68
B 18 Chapter 3
B 19 Chapter 11

Ladinus de la Rouse

B 1 Chapters 11, 17
*Lady of the Lake
B 1 Chapter 25
B 1 Chapter 25
B 2 Chapters 3, 4, 6
B 4 Chapter 5
B 9 Chapter 15
B 11 Chapter 3
B 19 Chapter 11

Lambegus, Tristram's servant

B 8 Chapters 30, 31, 32, 35
B 19 Chapter 11
B 20 Chapter 8

*Lamorak, Lamorake of Wales

B 1 Chapter 24
B 7 Chapters 9, 13, 14, 27, 28, 29, 35
B 8 Chapter 33, 34, 37, 38, 39, 40, 41
B 9 Chapters 1, 11, 12, 13, 16, 21, 42
B 10 Chapters 8–10, 13, 14, 17–25, 36, 44–50, 54, 55, 58, 63
B 11 Chapter 10
B 12 Chapter 7
B 18 Chapters 3, 8, 18, 23
B 19 Chapter 11
B 20 Chapters 5, 11, 12, 15

Lanceor

B 2 Chapter 4, 5, 6, 7
B 10 Chapter 5

*Launcelot de Lake

B 2 Chapter 19
B 3 Chapter 1
B 4 Chapters 1, 18, 28
B 5 Chapters 2, 3, 6–8, 12
B 6 Chapters 1–18
B 7 Chapters 2–5, 9, 13, 14, 17, 18, 23, 25–29, 33–35
B 8 Chapters 4, 10, 15, 17, 20–23, 26–28, 31–34, 36, 37, 39, 40

B 9 Chapters 1, 4–9, 12–15, 22–28, 30, 31, 33–40, 42, 43
B 10 Chapters 1, 4, 6, 7, 12–17, 20, 21, 22, 24, 26, 27, 30, 31, 35, 36–50, 52–58, 62, 63, 69–83, 85, 86, 88
B 11 Chapters 1–4, 6–10, 12–14
B 12 Chapters 1–11, 14
B 13 Chapters 1–8, 17–20
B 14 Chapter 1
B 15 Chapters 1–6
B 16 Chapters 1, 2, 4, 5, 11
B 17 Chapters 1, 2, 13–18, 21–23
B 18 Chapters 1–5, 7–24
B 19 Chapters 1, 3, 4–9, 11–13
B 20 Chapters 1–22

Lavaine

B 18 Chapters 9–12, 14–24
B 19 Chapters 3, 5, 6, 7. 9, 13
B 20 Chapters 3, 5, 12, 13, 17, 18

*Leodegrance, King of Cameliard

B 1 Chapter 17, 18
B 3 Chapter 1

Lile of Avelion

B 2 Chapters 1, 4, 5

*Lionel (Sir)

B 5 Chapter 6
B 6 Chapters 1, 2, 6, 7, 9
B 7 Chapters 27, 28
B 9 Chapter 35
B 11 Chapters 9, 19
B 12 Chapter 9
B 13 Chapters 1, 2
B 16 Chapters 9, 10 (Lionel assumed dead), 11, 13, 14 (still alive), 15–17
B 18 Chapters 2, 3, 11, 23
B 19 Chapter 11
B 20 Chapters 5, 12, 13, 18–20
B 21 Chapter 19

Lionors, daughter of Sanam, mother of Arthur's son Borre

B 1 Chapter 17

Lionses of Payarne

B 1 Chapters 10, 15, 17

Longinus, who speared the Lord

B 2 Chapter 16

Lot, King of Orkney

B 1 Chapters 2, 8, 9, 12, 14, 15, 16, 18, 19, 22?, 26?
B 2 Chapters 10, 11, 13
B 3 Chapter 4
B 7 Chapter 13

Lovell, son of Gawain

B 19 Chapter 11
B 20 Chapters 2, 7

Lucan the Butler, son of Duke Corneus

B 1 Chapter 10, 11, 14, 15, 17
B 9 Chapters 35, 36
B 10 Chapter 74
B 18 Chapters 11, 23
B 19 Chapter 11
B 20 Chapters 19, 20
B 21 Chapters 3–6

Lucius, emperor/procurer

B 5 Chapters 1–8, 12

Lynet, Beaumains' damosel, and sister of Lyonesse

B 7 Chapter 13–20, 22, 23, 25, 26, 33–35

Lyonesse, sister of Lynet

B 7 Chapters 13, 15–17, 19–23, 26, 27, 30, 31, 33–35

Maddock de la Montaine

B 9 Chapter 27

Mador de la Porte

B 6 Chapters 6, 7, 18
B 10 Chapter 45
B 18 Chapters 3–8
B 19 Chapter 11
B 20 Chapter 2

Margawse (Morgawse, Morgan) le Fay

B 1 Chapter 2, 20
B 2 Chapter 11
B 4 Chapters 4, 6, 7, 8, 9. 10, 11, 12, 13, 14, 15
B 6 Chapter 3
B 7 Chapters 13, 33
B 8 Chapters 34, 38

B 9 Chapters 13, 22, 23, 25, 40, 41, 42, 43
B 10 Chapters 1, 8 (King Lot's wife), 17, 20, 24 (King Lot's wife), 27, 35–38
B11 Chapters 1, 4
B 21 Chapter 6

Marhaus

B 4 Chapters 17, 18, 19, 24, 25, 27, 28
B 5 Chapter 8
B 6 Chapter 9
B 8 Chapters 4–8, 11, 12, 17, 22, 34, 38
B 9 Chapter 21
B 10 Chapters 6, 7, 16, 46, 77

Mark King of Cornwall

B 2 Chapters 7, 8
B 5 Chapter 3
B 8 Chapters 1, 4, 5, 6, 8, 12, 13, 14, 15, 16, 17, 18, 19, 24, 27, 29, 32, 33, 34, 35, 38, 39
B 9 Chapters 11, 14, 16, 17, 18, 19, 20, 21, 26, 37, 38, 39
B 10 Chapters 7–15, 20, 22, 23, 25–34, 37, 40, 50–53, 56, 82
B 19 Chapter 11
B 20 Chapter 7

Meliagaunt (Meliagaunce), son of Bagdemagus

B 7 Chapter 27
B 9 Chapters 12, 13
B 10 Chapters 41, 42, 43
B 19 Chapters 1–9, 13

Meliodas/Melyodas, Tristram's father

B 8 chapters 1, 2, 3, 12, 13, 16, 17

Meliot of Logurs, cousin of Nimue

B 3 Chapter 13
B 6 Chapters 14, 15, 18
B 7 Chapter 27
B 18 Chapters 10, 11
B 19 Chapter 11
B 20 Chapter 2

Melot de la Roche

B 1 Chapters 14, 15 (Moris?), 16 (Mariet?)

Merlin

B 1 Chapters 1, 2, 3, 4, 5, 6, 8, 9, 10, 11, 13, 14, 15, 17, 18, 20, 21, 22, 23, 24, 25, 27
B 2 Chapters 4, 8, 9, 10, 11, 16, 19
B 3 Chapters 1, 2, 3, 4, 5, 8, 10, 14, 15
B 10 Chapters 2, 5, 16, 63
B 14 Chapter 2

Miles of the Launds

B 1 Chapter 21
B 3 Chapter 15

Mordred

B 1 Chapter 27
B 2 Chapters 10, 11
B 6 Chapters 6, 7, 18
B 9 Chapters 3, 4, 5, 35
B 10 Chapters 11–13, 25, 39, 46, 58, 63, 68
B 11 Chapters 12, 13
B 18 Chapters 1, 3, 10, 11, 19, 23
B 19 Chapter 11
B 20 Chapters 1–4, 7, 9, 15, 18, 19
B 21 Chapters 1–4, 6–8

Morganore

B 1 Chapter 14, 16
B 19 Chapter 11

Nabon le Noire, a giant killed by Tristram

B 8 Chapter 37–40

Nentres, King of Garlot

B 1 Chapters 2, 8, 12, 14, 15, 16, 18
B 19 Chapter 11

Nero

B 2 Chapter 10

Nerovens de Lile

B 9 Chapters 5, 6, 7, 9

Nimue (Damosel of the Lake) wedded to Pelleas

B 3 Chapter 13
B 4 Chapters 1, 9, 10, 16, 22, 23, 28
B 9 Chapter 15
B 18 Chapter 8

B 19 Chapter 11
B 21 Chapter 6

Ontzlake

B 4 Chapter 7, 8, 12, 14

Palomides, Palamides

B 1 Chapter 19
B 7 Chapters 13, 26, 27, 29
B 8 Chapters 9, 10, 17, 22, 30,
    31, 32, 38
B 10 Chapters 1–6, 13, 14, 16–
    21, 25, 26, 36, 41, 42–47,
    49, 53, 54, 57–88
B 12 Chapters 11–14
B 18 Chapters 3, 10, 18, 23
B 19 Chapter 11
B 20 5, 12, 13, 17, 18

Patrise

B 18 Chapters 3, 4, 6, 7, 8

Pedivere

B 6 Chapter 17
B 11 Chapter 5

Pellam (King)

B 2 Chapters 15, 16, 19

Pelleas

B 4 Chapters 18, 20–23, 28
B 6 Chapter 12
B 10 Chapter 68
B 18 Chapters 8, 23
B 19 Chapters 1, 2, 3, 11
B 21 Chapter 6

Pelles (King)

B 11 Chapters 1–4, 6, 7
B 12 Chapters 4–6, 9, 10
B 13 Chapters 1, 4, 5
B 15 Chapters 4, 6
B 17 Chapters 5, 16, 17, 19. 20

Pellinor, Pellinore

B 1 Chapter 19, 20, 23, 24, 25
B 2 Chapters 10, 11, 13
B 3 Chapters 3, 4, 5, 11, 12, 13,
    14, 15
B 4 Chapters 1, 2, 4, 5
B 8 Chapter 38
B 9 Chapter 24

Pellinor's offspring

B 10 Chapters 19, 21, 23, 24,
    54
B 11 Chapter 10
B 12 Chapter 7

B 17 Chapter 2
B 19 Chapter 11

Pellounes

B 9 Chapters 26, 27, 29

***Percival, Percivale of
    Wales***

B 1 Chapter 24
B 2 Chapter 13
B 4 Chapter 18
B 7 Chapters 13, 27, 28
B 10 Chapters 23, 51, 53, 54, 68
B 11 Chapters 10–14
B 12 Chapters 1, 7–10
B 13 Chapters 3, 6, 17, 20
B 14 Chapters 1–10
B 16 Chapters 1, 3, 17
B 17 Chapters 1–4, 7, 8, 9 (Per-
    civale's sister), 10, 11, 12, 13,
    17, 19, 20–23
B 18 Chapter 1
B 19 Chapter 11

**Perimones–See Knights of
    Color: Red**

**Persant–See Knights of
    Color: Blue**

Persides de Bloise

B 9 Chapter 26, 27, 29, 31, 33,
    34, 35
B 11 Chapters 12, 13

Petipase

B 3 Chapter 9
B 7 Chapters 27, 28
B 19 Chapter 11
B 20 Chapter 2

Phariance

B 1 Chapters 10, 15, 17

Phelot

B 6 Chapter 16

Pinel

B 1 Chapter 14
B 18 Chapters 3, 8

Placidas

B 1 Chapter 11

Plenorius

B 9 Chapters 7, 8, 9
B 19 Chapter 11
B 20 Chapters 5, 18

Prastias

B 1 Chapter 3

Priamus

B 5 Chapters 10, 11, 12
B 19 Chapter 11
B 20 Chapter 8

Questing Beast

B 1 Chapters 19, 20
B 9 Chapter 12
B 10 Chapters 20, 41, 53
B 12 Chapter 14

**Red Knight of the Red
    Launds (See Knights of
    Color) Rience (King)**

B 1 Chapters 17, 18, 26, 27
B 2 Chapters 1, 3

Sadok

B 7 Chapters 26, 28
B 10 Chapters 33, 35, 50, 51,
    68, 74
B 19 Chapter 11
B 20 Chapters 5, 18

Safer, Palomides' brother

B 7 Chapters 13, 26, 27
B 10 Chapters 16, 19, 36, 45,
    46, 82, 83, 84
B 12 Chapters 12, 13
B 18 Chapters 3, 10, 11, 23
B 20 Chapters 5, 12, 13, 17, 18

Sagramore le Desirous

B 4 Chapter 25
B 6 Chapters 13, 18
B 7 Chapters 27, 28, 30
B 8 Chapters 9, 15, 16, 17
B 9 Chapters 24, 25, 31
B 10 Chapters 4, 38, 65
B 11 Chapter 10
B 18 Chapters 10, 11
B 19 Chapters 1, 2, 11

**Sanam the Earl, father of
    damosel Lionors**

B 1 Chapter 17

scabbard

B 1 Chapter 25
B 2 Chapters 1, 11
B 4 Chapters 1, 8, 14

Segwarides

B 7 Chapters 26, 27

B 8 Chapters 13–16, 18, 38, 39
B 9 Chapter 21
B 10 Chapters 16, 60, 83, 84
B 20 Chapter 8

Sorlouse of the Forest

B 3 Chapter 6

Suppinabiles, messenger from Brittany to England

B 8 Chapters 36, 37

Tor, son of Pellinore

B 3 Chapters 3, 4, 5, 9–11, 15
B 4 Chapters 1, 5
B 7 Chapters 27, 28
B 9 Chapter 14
B 10 Chapters 9, 10, 11, 19, 23
B 19 Chapter 11
B 20 Chapter 8

Tristram

B 2 Chapter 8
B 4 Chapters 18, 25, 28
B 5 Chapter 3
B 6 Chapter 12
B 7 Chapters 9, 13, 14, 26, 28, 29, 35
B 8 Chapters 1–40
B 9 Chapters 10–12, 14–37, 39–43
B 10 Chapters 1–8, 12–17, 20–
32, 35, 36, 39, 40, 44, 50–60, 62–88
B 11 Chapters 1, 7
B 12 Chapters 9, 11–14
B 18 Chapters 18, 23
B 19 Chapter 11
B 20 Chapters 5, 6, 15

Turquine (Sir)

B 6 Chapters 2, 7, 8, 9 (Turquine slain), 10, 18
B 7 Chapters 26, 28, 29
B 20 Chapters 1, 15

Ulfius

B 1 Chapters 1, 2, 6, 7, 9, 10, 11, 14, 15, 17, 20, 21

Uriens, King of Gore

B 1 Chapters 2, 8, 12 (father of Uwaine), 15, 16, 18
B 2 Chapter 11
B 4 Chapters 4, 6, 8, 11, 13, 16
B 7 Chapters 27, 28
B 10 Chapters 11, 74
B 16 Chapter 2
B 18 Chapters 22, 23
B 19 Chapter 11

Uther Pendragon

B 1 Chapters 1, 2, 4, 6, 8, 20, 21, 23
B 2 Chapters 1, 11

B 3 Chapter 1
B 6 Chapter 11

Uwaine

B 1 Chapter 12
B 4 Chapters 13, 16–19, 25–28
B 5 Chapter 2
B 6 Chapter 13, 18,
B 7 Chapters 27, 28 (Uwaine les Avoutres)
B 9 Chapters 35, 36, 37 (Uwaine le Fise de Roy Ureine), 43
B 10 Chapters 1, 11–14, 46, 66, 74
B 11 Chapter 10
B 13 Chapters 9, 10, 15, 16
B 16 Chapters 2, 3
B 19 Chapter 11

Uwaine le Blanchemains (le Blanche Mains), son of Uriens

B 1 Chapter 2
B 7 Chapter 27
B 9 Chapters 37, 43

Uwaine le Fise de Roy Ureine (son of King Uriens, above)

B 9 Chapter 37

Yvain (See Uwaine)

APPENDIX B
HARLEIAN MS 3859

Folio	Section	Comments
174B	1–6	The Six Ages of the World.
174B–177A	7–18	British Originis. Sec. 14 (folio 176A) names CUNEDDA; Sec. 16 explains lunar cycles.
177A–179B	19–30	Roman conquest and occupation of Britain
179B–185B	31–49	The first independent section of Historia Brittonum. The Fifth Century, VORTIGERN, Germanus 1-2-3, Kentish Chronicles 1-2-3, EMRYŚ Ambrosius, Vortigern genealogy.
185B–187A	50–55	Patrick.
187A–B	56	Campaigns of ARTHUR.
187B–188B	57–62	Anglican Genealogies, Anglican-Mercian source in late eighth century, English to Welsh. Sec. 62 = MAELGWN. Maelgwn is more commonly known as Maglocunus son of CATGOLAUN LAUHIR, aka CADWALLON.
188B–189B	57, 62–65	Diverse sources. Northern Histories = preponderance of English, not British.
189B–190A	66	Vortigern's reign, recapitualtion of 31–49.
190A–193A		*Annales Cambriae* (Welsh Annales).
193A–195A		Welsh genealogies, Cunedda and sons, late fourth–early fifth century territories.
195A–195B	66	Cities of Britain.
195B–198A	67–76	The Wonders of Britain, Mona, and Ireland.

BIBLIOGRAPHY

Adam of Domerham *see* Chambers, E.K.; Hearne, Thomas.

Æthelweard *see* Campbell, Alistair.

Alcock, Leslie. *Arthur's Britain: History and Archaeology C.E. 367–634.* London: Penguin, 1989.

_____. *Was This Camelot? Excavations at Cadbury Castle, 1966–1970.* New York: Stein and Day, 1972.

Anderson, W.B., ed. and trans. Sidonius: *Poems and Letters, Vol. I.* Cambridge, Mass.: Harvard University Press, reprinted 1956, 1963.

_____. Sidonius: *Poems and Letters, Vol. II.* Cambridge, Mass.: Harvard University Press, reprinted 1956, 1963.

Anglo-Saxon Chronicle see Garmonsway, G.N.

Annales Cambriae see Morris, John, *Nennius: British History.*

Ashe, Geoffrey. *The Discovery of King Arthur.* London: Debrett's Peerage, 1985

_____. *King Arthur's Avalon: The Story of Glastonbury.* London and Glasgow: William Collins Sons, 1957.

_____. *Kings and Queens of Early Britain.* Chicago: Academy Chicago, 1990.

_____. *The Landscape of King Arthur.* New York: Henry Holt, 1987.

_____. *Mythology of the British Isles.* London: Methuen, 1992.

_____. "The Origins of the Arthurian Legend," *Arthuriana*, Vol. 5 No. 3 (Fall 1995): 3–24.

_____, ed. *The Quest for Arthur's Britain.* New York, Washington, London: Frederick Praeger, 1969.

_____. *The Traveller's Guide to Arthurian Britain.* Glastonbury, Somerset: Gothic Image, 1997.

Aubert, O.-L. *Celtic Legends of Brittany, Fourth Edition.* Brittany: Keltia Graphic, 1999.

Babbington, C., and J. Lumby, eds. *Polychronicon Ranulphi Higden*, 9 vol. London: Longman, 1865–86.

Barber, Chris, and David Pykitt. *Journey to Avalon.* Abergavenny, Gwent: Blorenge, 1993.

Barber, Richard W. *Arthur of Albion.* London: Boydell, 1961.

_____. *The Figure of Arthur.* London: Longman, 1972.

_____. *King Arthur: Hero and Legend.* R.B. Woodbridge, Suffolk: Boydell, 1986.

Bartlett, John. *Familiar Quotations.* Boston: Little, Brown, 1955.

Bartram, Peter C. *Welsh Genealogies AD 300–1400.* 8 volumes. Cardiff: University of Wales Press, 1974.

Blair, Peter Hunter. *Roman Britain and Early England, 55 B.C.–C.E. 871.* New York, London: W.W. Norton, by arrangement with Thomas Nelson and Sons, 1966.

Bede *see* Sherley-Price, Leo.

Blaisdell, Foster, and Marianne Kalinke, trans. *Erex Saga and Ivens Saga.* Lincoln: University of Nebraska Press, 1977.

Blake, Steve, and Scott Lloyd. *The Keys to Avalon.* Dorset, Boston, Australia: Element, 2000.

_____. *Pendragon: The Definitive Account of the Origins of Arthur.* Guilford, Conn.: Lyons Press, 2003.

Bradley, H. "Ptolemy's Geography of the British Isles," *Archaeologia* xlviii 379, 1928.

Brehaut, Ernest, trans. Gregory of Tours: *History of the Franks.* New York: Columbia University Press, 1916.

Bromwich, Rachel, ed. *The Beginnings of Welsh Poetry: Studies by Sir Ifor Williams.* Cardiff: University of Wales Press, 1972.

_____. "Celtic Elements in Arthurian Romance: A General Survey," *The Legend of Arthur in the Middle Ages*, edited by P.B. Grout, et al. Cambridge: D.S. Brewer, 1983.

_____, ed./trans. *Trioedd Ynys Prydein: Triads of the Island of Britain.* 3rd ed. Cardiff: University of Wales Press, 2006.

_____. "The Welsh Triads." *Arthurian Literature in the Middle Ages.* Edited by R.S. Loomis. Oxford: Clarendon Press, 1959.

Bromwich, Rachel, A.O.H. Jarman, and Brynley Roberts, eds. *The Arthur of the Welsh: The Arthurian Legend in Medieval Welsh Literature.* Cardiff: University of Wales Press, 1991.

Bruce, James Douglas. *The Evolution of Arthurian Romance from the Beginnings Down to the Year 1300.* 2nd ed. Baltimore: Johns Hopkins Press, 1928.

Bryant, Nigel, trans. *Merlin and the Grail: Joseph of Arimathea, Merlin, Perceval; The Trilogy of Arthurian Romances attributed to Robert de Boron*. Cambridge: D.S. Brewer, 2001.

Bury, J.B. "The Notitia Dignitatum," *Journal of Roman Studies* 10 (1920).

Butler, H.E., ed. *The Autobiography of Giraldus Cambrensis*. London: Jonathan Cape, 1937.

Cable, James, trans. *The Death of King Arthur*. Harmondsworth: Penguin Classics, 1971.

Camden, William *see* Gibson, Edmond.

Campbell, Alistair, ed. *The Chronicle of Æthelweard*. Edinburgh: Thomas Nelson and Sons, 1962.

Caradoc of Llancarven: *Life of Gildas see* Williams, Hugh, ed.

Carley, James P. *The Chronicle of Glastonbury Abbey: An Edition, Translation and Study of John of Glastonbury's* Cronica Sive Antiquitates Glastoniensis Ecclesie. Trans. by David Townsend. Woodbridge, Suffolk: Boydell, 1985.

_____. *Glastonbury Abbey: The Holy House at the Head of the Moors adventurous*. New York: St. Martin's Press, 1988.

Carroll, Carleton W., trans. Chrètien de Troyes: *Arthurian Romances*. London: Penguin, 1991.

Castleden, Rodney. *King Arthur: The Truth Behind the Legend*. London and New York: Routledge, 2000.

Catholic Encyclopedia (online). Updated 15 September 2003.

Cawley, A.C., ed. *Pearl and Sir Gawain and the Green Knight*. London and New York: Everyman's Library, 1962.

Chadwick, Nora. *Celtic Britain*. London: Readers Union Thames and Hudson, 1965.

Chambers, E.K. *Arthur of Britain*. Cambridge: Speculum Historiale, 1964.

Chandler, John. *John Leland's Travels in Tudor England*. Phoenix Mill, Stroud, Gloucester: Sutton, 1998.

Chrétien de Troyes *see* Carroll, Carleton W.; Cline, Ruth Harwood; Comfort, W.W.; Kibler, William; Owen, D.D.R.; Raffel, Burton.

"Church of St. Brynach, Nevern, Pembrokeshire." Distributed pamphlet under the guidance of the vicar, churchwardens and parishioners, 3rd ed. Wales: Cardigan, E.L. Jones and Son, 1994.

Clayton, Peter. *Guide to the Archaeological Sites of Britain*. London: B.T. Batsford, 1985.

Clinch, Rosemary, and Michael Williams. *King Arthur in Somerset*. Parkwood, Callington, Cornwall: Penwell, 1987.

Cline, Ruth Harwood, trans. Chrétien de Troyes: *Perceval or The Story of the Grail*. Athens: University of Georgia Press, 1985.

Codrington, Thomas. *Roman Roads in Britain*. New York: Macmillan, 1919.

Coghlan, Ronan. *The Encyclopedia of Arthurian Legends*. Shaftsbury, Dorset, Rockport, Mass.: Element Books, 1991.

Coles, J. M., and B.J. Orme. *Prehistory of the Somerset Levels*. Hertford: Stephen Austin and Sons, 1982.

Collingwood, R.G., and J.N.L. Myres. *Roman Britain and the English Settlements*. 2nd ed. Oxford: Clarendon, 1937.

Columbia Encyclopedia, Sixth Edition (online). Columbia University Press, 2003.

Comfort, W.W., trans. Chretien de Troyes: *Arthurian Romances*. London and New York: J.M. Dent and Sons, Everyman's Library, 1965.

Constantius of Lyons *see* of Stevenson, Josephus, "Preface," *Nennii*, pp. xxiii–xv.

Cornelius, Geoffrey. *The Starlore Handbook: The Starwatcher's Essential Guide to the 88 Constellations, Their Myths and Symbols*. United Kingdom: Duncan Baird, 2000.

Costain, Thomas B. *The Three Edwards*. Garden City, New York: Doubleday, 1962.

Cowen, Janet, ed. *Sir Thomas Malory: Le Morte D'Arthur, Vols. 1 and 2*. London: Penguin, 1986.

Cunliffe, Barry. *The City of Bath*. New Haven, Conn.: Yale University Press, 1986.

_____. *The Roman Baths: A View Over 2000 Years*. England: Barwell, 1993.

Curley, Michael J. *Geoffrey of Monmouth*. New York: Twayne, 1994.

Davies, John. *A History of Wales*. London: Allen Lane, Penguin, 1993.

Davison, M.E. "The Frequency Distribution of the Dates of Easter," *Irish Astronomical Journal*, Vol. 14 (5/6), 1980.

Delaney, Frank. *Legends of the Celts*. New York: Sterling, 1991.

Dewing, H.B., trans. Procopius: *History of the Wars*. Cambridge, Mass.: Harvard University Press, 1919.

Duckett, Eleanor Shipley. *Medieval Portraits from East and West*. Ann Arbor: University of Michigan Press, 1972.

Eisner, Sigmund. *The Tristan Legend: A Study in Sources*. Evanston, Ill.: Northwestern University Press, 1969.

Ekwall, Eilert. *The Concise Oxford Dictionary of English Place-names*. Oxford: Clarendon Press, 1991.

Ellis, Peter Berresford. *The Chronicles of the Celts: New Tellings of their Myths and Legends*. New York: Carrol and Graff, 1999.

_____. *Dictionary of Celtic Mythology*. London: Constable, 1992.

_____. *The Druids.* Grand Rapids, Mich.: William B. Eerdmans, 1994.

Evans, D.H. "Valley Crucis Abbey." *Valle Crucis Abbey.* Cadw: Welsh Historic Monuments, 1987.

Evans, J. Gwenogvryn, with Jun Rhys. *The Text of the Book of Llan Dav, Reproduced from the Gwynsaney Manuscript.* Oxford, 1893.

Evans, Sebastian, Trans. *Geoffrey of Monmouth.* London: J.M. Dent, Aldine House, 1904.

Fairbairn, Neil. *A Traveller's Guide to the Kingdoms of Arthur.* Harrisburg: Historical Times, 1983.

Fedrick, Alan S., trans. Béroul: *The Romance of Tristan.* Harmondsworth: Penguin, 1970.

Ferrill, Arther. *The Fall of the Roman Empire: The Military Explanation.* London: Thames and Hudson, 1986.

Field, P.J.C. *The Life and Times of Sir Thomas Malory.* Cambridge: D.S. Brewer, 1993.

Fisher, D.J.V. *The Anglo-Saxon Age: c. 400–1042.* New York: Marboro, 1973.

Fletcher, Robert H. *The Arthurian Material in the Chronicles.* New York: Burt Franklin, 1966.

Forester, Thomas, ed. and trans. *The Chronicle of Henry of Huntingdon, Comprising the History of England, from the Invasion of Julius Caesar to the Accession of Henry II.* London: Henry G. Bohn, 1853.

Fowler, D.C. *Transactions of the Bristol and Gloucester Archaeological Society.* John Trevisa, scholar and translator. No. 89, 99–108.

Galbraith, V.H. "An Autograph MS of Ranulph Higden," *Poychronicon, Huntington Library Quarterly,* Vol. xxiii(i), 1959.

Gantz, Jeffrey, trans. *The Mabinogion.* New York: Viking Penguin, 1987.

Garmonsway, G.N. *The Anglo-Saxon Chronicle.* London: Everyman's Library, 1990.

Geoffrey of Monmouth *see* Thorpe, Lewis.

Gerald of Wales *see* Butler, H.E.

Germanus (Saint) *see* Thompson, Edward Arthur.

Gibbon, Edward. *The Decline and Fall of the Roman Empire.* New York: Nelson Doubleday, 1963.

Gibson, Edmond, trans. *Camden's Britannia, Newly Translated into English with Large Additions and Improvements.* Printed by F. Collins, for A. Swale, at the Unicorn at the West-end of St. Paul's Church-yard, and A. and J. Churchill, at the Black Swan in Pater-noster-Row, 1695.

Gildas Albanius *see* Stevenson, Josephus.

Gildas Badonicus *see* Stevenson, Josephus; Winterbottom, Michael.

Giles, J.A., ed. *Six Old English Chronicles.* London: George Bell and Sons, 1885.

Giraldus Cambrensis *see* Butler, H.E.

Gottfried von Strassburg *see* Loomis, R.S., and Laura Hibbard Loomis; Owen, D.D.R.

Graham, Frank. *Dictionary of Roman Military Terms.* Northumberland: Butler and Butler, 1989.

Grant, Michael. *Tacitus: The Annales of Imperial Rome.* Middlesex, England: Penguin Books, 1986.

Gregory, Stewart, ed. *Thomas of Britain: Tristan.* New York: Garland, 1991.

Gregory of Tours, *History of the Franks see* Brehaut, Ernest; Thorpe, Lewis.

Griscom, Acton. *The Historia Regum Britanniae of Geoffrey of Monmouth.* London, New York, Toronto: Longmans, Green, 1929.

Grout, P.B., and R.A. Lodge, C.E. Pickford, E.K.C. Varty, eds. *The Legend of Arthur in the Middle Ages.* Woodbridge, Suffolk: D.D. Brewer, 1983.

Hadas, Moses. *A History of Rome from its Origins to 529 A.A. as Told by the Roman Historians.* Garden City, New York: Doubleday, 1956.

Hammer, Jacob. *Geoffrey of Monmouth: Historia Regum Britanniae: A Variant Version Edited from Manuscripts.* Cambridge, Mass.: Mediaeval Academy of America, 1951.

Harris, Bruce S., editor. *The Collected Drawings of Aubrey Beardsley.* New York: Bounty Books, 1967.

Hartmann von Auc *see* Keller, Thomas; McConeghy, Patrick; Thomas, J.W.

Hatto, Arthur Thomas, trans. Wolfram von Eschenbach: *Parzival.* New York: Penguin, 1980.

Hearne, Thomas, ed. *Adam of Domerham: Historia de rebus gestic Glastoniensibus, 2 Vols.* Oxford, 1726.

Henry of Huntingdon. *The Chronicle of Henry of Huntingdon (Historia Anglorum).* Trans. and ed., Thomas Forester. London: Henry G. Bohn, 1853.

Higden, Ranulph *see* Galbraith, V.H.

Holmes, Michael. *King Arthur: A Military History.* Strand, London: Blandford Books, 1996.

Hopkins, Andrea. *The Book of Guinevere: Legendary Queen of Camelot.* New York: Crescent Books, 1996.

Hubert, Henri. *The History of the Celtic People.* London: Bracken Books, 1993.

Jackson, Kenneth Hurlstone. "The Arthur of History," *Arthurian Literature in the Middle Ages.* Edited by R.S. Loomis. Oxford: Clarendon Press, 1959.

Jackson, Kenneth Hurlstone. *The Gododdin: The Oldest Scottish Poem.* Edinburgh: University Press, 1969.

Jarman, A.O.H. "The Arthurian Allusions in *The Black Book of Carmarthen.*" *The Legend of Arthur in the Middle Ages,* edited by P.B. Grout, et al. Cambridge: D.S. Brewer, 1983.

John of Glastonbury *see* Carley, James.

Jones, Gwyn, and Thomas Jones, trans. *The Mabinogion*. London: Everyman, J.M. Dent, 1993.

Jones, W. Lewis. *Latin Chroniclers from the Eleventh to the Thirteenth Centuries*. From *The Cambridge History of English and American Literature*, 1907–1921. www.bartleby.com.

Joseph of Arimathea *see* Carley, James P., *The Chronicle of Glastonbury Abbey*; *Magna Tabula*; Robinson, J. Armitage; Scott, John; Skeat, W.W.

Jung, Emma, and Marie-Louise von Franz. *The Grail Legend*, trans. by Andrea Dykes. Boston: Sigo Press, 1980.

Keller, Thomas L., trans. Hartmann von Aue: *Erec*. New York: Garland, 1987.

Kibler, William. *Chrétien de Troyes: Arthurian Romances*. London: Penguin Books, 1991.

Knight, Jeremy. *Valle Crucis Abbey/Pillar of Eliseg*. Cardiff, Wales: Cadw Welsh Historic Monuments, 1987.

Korrel, Peter. *An Arthurian Triangle: A Study of the Origin, Development, and Characterization of Arthur, Guinevere, and Modred*. Leiden: E.J. Brill, 1984.

Lacy, Norris, ed. *The Arthurian Encyclopedia*. New York and London: Garland, 1986.

Lacy, Norris, ed., trans. Béroul: *The Romance of Tristan*. New York: Garland, 1989.

Lacy, Norris, and Geoffrey Ashe. *The Arthurian Handbook*. New York and London: Garland, 1988.

Latin Chroniclers see Jones, W. Lewis.

Layamon *see* Mason, Eugene.

Leeds, Edward Thurlow. *Archaeology of the Anglo-Saxon Settlements*. Oxford: Clarendon Press, 1914.

Leland, John *see* Alcock, Leslie, *Arthur's Britain* and *Was This Camelot?*; Chandler, John; *Columbia Encyclopedia*; Smith, L.T.

Lewis, Edwin C. *Welsh Dictionary*. London, Chicago: Teach Yourself Books, 2000.

Lhuyd, Edward *see* Knight, Jeremy; O'Sullivan, Anne, and William O'Sullivan.

Littleton, C. Scott, and Linda A. Malcor. *From Scythia to Camelot*. New York and London: Garland, 1994.

Loomis, Roger Sherman. *The Development of Arthurian Romance*. New York and Evanston: Harper Torchbooks, 1963.

_____, ed. *Arthurian Literature in the Middle Ages: A Collaborative History*. Oxford: Clarendon Press, 1959.

_____, trans. *The Romance of Tristram and Ysolt: Thomas of Britain*. New York: Octagon Books, 1982.

Loomis, R.S., and Laura Hibbard Loomis, eds. *Medieval Romances*. New York: Modern Library, 1957.

Loomis, R.S., and Rudolph Willard. *Medieval English Verse and Prose*. New York: Appleton-Century-Crofts, 1948.

Luttrell, Claude. *The Creation of the First Arthurian Romance: A Quest*. London: Edward Arnold, 1974.

Magna Tabula. Oxford. Bodleian Library, MS Lat. Hist. A. 2.

Malcor, Linda A. "Lucius Artorius Castus, Part 2: The Battles in Britain." *The Heroic Age*, Issue 2 (Autumn-Winter, 1999).

Malone, Kemp. "The Historicity of Arthur," *Journal of English and Germanic Philology*, 23, 463.

Malory, Thomas. *Le Morte D'Arthur*. New York: Harrison House, 1985. *See also* Whitehead, Frederick.

Markale, Jean. *King Arthur: King of Kings*. London and New York: Gordon and Cremonesi, 1976.

Mason, Eugene, trans. *Arthurian Chronicles: Wace and Layamon*. London: Dent and Sons, Everyman's Library, 1962.

Mathisen, Ralph W. *An Online Encyclopedia of Roman Emperors: Libius Severus (461–4654 C.E.)*, 1997.

Matthews, Caitlin, and John Matthews. *Ladies of the Lake*. London: Aquarian Press, 1992.

McConeghy, Patrick, ed., trans. Hartmann von Aue: *Iwein*. New York: Garland, 1984.

McManus, Damian. *A Guide to Ogam*. Maynooth: An Sagaart, 1997.

Mermier, Guy R., ed., trans. Béroul: *Roman de Tristan: English-French*. New York: P. Lang, 1987.

Mierow, Charles C. *Jordanes: The Origin and Deeds of the Goths*. Princeton, N.J.: Princeton University Press, 1908.

Morris, John. *The Age of Arthur: A History of the British Isles from 350 to 650*. London: Weidenfeld and Nicolson, 1989.

Morris, John, ed., trans. Nennius: *British History and the Welsh Annales*. London and Chichester: Phillimore, 1980.

Le Morte D'Arthur see Cowen, Janet.

Myers, Alec Reginald. "Edward IV," *Encyclopædia Britannica*, Vol. 8, pp. 6–8. Chicago: William Benton, 1967.

Myres, J.N.L., and R.G. Collingwood. *Roman Britain and the English Settlements*. 2nd ed. Oxford: Clarendon Press, 1937.

Oost, Stewart Irvin. *Galla Placidia Augusta: A Biographical Essay*. Chicago and London: University of Chicago Press, 1968.

Ordnance Survey. *Historical Map and Guide of Roman Britain*. 4th ed. 1994.

O'Sullivan, Anne, and William O'Sullivan. *Archaeologia Britannica, Vol. 1*. Shannon: Irish University Press, 1971.

O'Sullivan, Thomas. *The De Excidio of Gildas: Its Authenticity and Date.* Reprinted with permission of the Trustees of Columbia University Press, 1978.

Owen, D.D.R., trans. Chrétien de Troyes: *Arthurian Romances.* London: J.M. Dent, 1991.

_____, trans. Gottfried von Strassburg: *Tristran.* Harmondsworth: Penguin Classics, 1960.

Parry, John Jay, trans. Geoffrey of Monmouth: *Vita Merlini (The Life of Merlin).* sacred-texts.com/ neu/eng/vm/.

Petrie, W.M. Flinders. "Neglected British History," *Proceedings of the British Academy.* London: Humphrey Milford, Oxford University Press, November 7, 1917.

Phillips, Graham, and Martin Keatman. *King Arthur: The True Story.* London: Century Random House, 1992.

Piggott, Stuart. *The Druids.* London: Thames and Hudson, 1968.

Pitt-Rivers (Fox-Pitt-Rivers), Lieutenant-General. *Excavations in Cranbourne Chase Near Rushmore on the Borders of Dorset and Wilts, 1880–1888, with Observations on the Human Remains by J.G. Garson, M.D. Volume II.* Printed privately, 1892.

Plummer, Charles, ed. *Two of the Saxon Chronicles Parallel with Supplementary Extracts from the Others.* Oxford: Clarendon Press, 1899.

Pollard, Alfred, abridgment. *The Romance of King Arthur and his Knights of the Round Table.* New York: Weathervane Books, 1917.

Procopius *see* Dewing, H.B.

Ptolemy *see* Bradley, H.

Pugh, Thomas Brynmor. "Henry VI," *Encyclopædia Britannica*, Vol. 11, pp. 364–365. Chicago: William Benton, 1967.

Radford, C.A. Ralegh. "Glastonbury Abbey," *The Quest for Arthur's Britain*, ed. by Geoffrey Ashe. New York, Washington, London: Fredrick A. Praeger, 1969.

Raffel, Burton, trans. Chrétien de Troyes: *Perceval, or The Story of the Grail.* New Haven and London: Yale University Press, 1999.

Rees, W.J. *An Historical Atlas of Wales.* London, 1959.

_____. *Lives of the Cambro-British Saints*, from *Vita Iltuti*, printed from *Cotton MS Versp.* A, xiv.

Reno, Frank D. "Emending Fifth-Century British History," *The Heroic Age* (online).

_____. *Historic Figures of the Arthurian Era.* Jefferson, N.C., and London: McFarland, 2000.

_____. *The Historic King Arthur: Authenticating the Celtic Hero of Post-Roman Britain.* Jefferson, N.C., and London: McFarland, 1996.

_____. "O, Ambrosius, Ambrosius, Wherefore Art Thou Not Arthur?" *The Heroic Age* (online).

Rhys, John. *Celtic Britain.* London: Senate, 1996.

_____. *Celtic Folklore, Vol. 2.* London: Wildwood House, 1980.

_____. *Studies in the Arthurian Legend.* Oxford: Clarendon Press, 1901.

Richmond, I.A. *Roman Britain.* Maryland: Penguin Books, 1964.

Roach, William, ed. *The Didot-Perceval.* Philadelphia: University of Pennsylvania Press, 1941.

Robert de Boron *see* Bryant, Nigel.

Roberts, Brynley. "'Culhwch ac Olwen,' the Triads, Saints' Lives" in *The Arthur of the Welsh: The Arthurian Legend in Medieval Welsh Literature.* Edited by Rachel Bromwich, A.O.H. Jarman, and Brynley F. Roberts. Cardiff: University of Wales Press, 1991.

Roberts, Peter, trans. *The Chronicle of the Kings of Britain: From the Welsh Copy Attributed to Tysilio.* Llanerch Publishers, first published in 1811.

Robinson, J. Armitage. *Two Glastonbury Legends: King Arthur and St. Joseph of Arimathea.* Cambridge: University Press, 1926.

Ryan, Pamela. *A Dictionary of King Arthur's Knights.* Charleston, S.C.: Nautical and Aviation Publishing, 2001.

Salway, Peter. *The Oxford Illustrated History of Roman Britain.* Oxford: Oxford University Press, 1993.

Sawyer, Peter H. *Anglo-Saxon Charters: An Annotated List and Bibliography.* London: Offices of the Royal Historical Society, University College London, 1968.

Scott, John. *The Early History of Glastonbury: An Edition, Translation, and Study of William of Malmesbury's* De Antiquitate Glastonie Ecclesie. Woodbridge, Suffolk: Boydell Press, 1981.

Scullard, H.H. *Roman Britain: Outpost of the Empire.* London: Thames and Hudson, 1979.

Sherley-Price, Leo, trans. Bede: *A History of the English Church and People.* New York: Dorset Press, 1955.

Skeat, W.W. *The Alliterative Joseph of Arimathea.* Early English Text Society, OS 44 London, 1871.

Skeels, D. *Didot Perceval.* Seattle, Wash.: University of Washington Press, 1966.

Skene, William F. *The Four Ancient Books of Wales Containing the Cymric Poems Attributed to the Bards of the Sixth Century*, Vol. I. Edinburgh: Edmonston and Douglas, 1868.

Smith, L.T. *The Itinerary of John Leland In or About the years 1535–1543*, Vol. I. London, 1907.

Snyder, Christopher. *An Age of Tyrants: Britain and the Britons C.E. 400–600.* Philadelphia: University of Pennsylvania Press, 1998.

Spence, Lewis. *The Mysteries of Britain: Secret Rites and Traditions of Ancient Britain.* London: Senate, imprint of Studio Editions, 1994.

Squire, Charles. *Celtic Myths and Legends*. Originally published *Celtic Myth and Legend, Poetry and Romance*. New York: Gramercy Books, 1994.

Stephens, Thomas. *The Literature of the Kymry*, 2nd ed. London: Longmans, Green, 1876.

Stevenson, Josephus. *Gildas: De Excidio Britanniae*. Vaduz: Kraus Reprint Ltd., Reprinted from a copy in the collections of the New York Public Library, 1964.

_____. *Nennii: Historia Brittonum*. Londini: Kraus Reprint, 1964.

_____. *Ralph of Coggeshall: Chronicon Anglicanum*. From the Rolls Series (*Rerum Britannicarum medii aevi scriptores*, no. 66). London: Longman, 1875.

Tacitus *see* Grant, Michael.

Taylor, Ronald Jack. "Gottfried von Strassburg," *Encyclopædia Britannica*, Vol. 10, p. 610. Chicago: William Benton, 1967.

Thomas, Charles. *Britain and Ireland in Early Christian Times: C.E. 400–800*. New York: Mc-Graw-Hill, 1971.

_____. *Celtic Britain*. London: Thames and Hudson, 1997.

Thomas, J.W., trans. *Hartmann von Aue: Erec*. Lincoln: University of Nebraska Press, 1982.

Thompson, Edward Arthur. "Constantine: Roman and Byzantine Emperors;" "Constantine: Flavius Claudius Constantinus." *Encyclopædia Britannica*, Vol. 6, pp. 384–388, 1967.

_____. *Romans and Barbarians: The Decline of the Western Empire*. Madison: University of Wisconsin Press, 1980.

_____. *Saint Germanus of Auxerre and the End of Roman Britain*. St. Edmunds, Suffolk: St. Edmundsbury Press, 1984.

Thorpe, Lewis, trans. *Geoffrey of Monmouth: The History of the Kings of Britain*. Middlesex, England: Penguin Books, 1966.

_____. *Gerald of Wales: The Journey Through Wales and The Description of Wales*. London: Penguin Books, 1978.

_____. *Gregory of Tours: The History of the Franks*. London: Penguin, 1974,

Treharne, R.F. *The Glastonbury Legends: Joseph of Arimathea, the Holy Grail, and King Arthur*. London: Cresset Press, 1967.

Turlin, Heinrich von dem. *The Crown (Diu Crone)*. University of Nebraska Press, 1989.

Tysilio see Roberts, Peter.

Wace *see* Mason, Eugene.

Wade-Evans, Arthur W. *The Emergence of England and Wales*. Cambridge: W. Heffer and Sons, 1959.

Webster, Graham. *The Cornovii*. Stroud, Gloucester: Alan Sutton, 1991.

_____, and Phillip Barker. *Wroxeter: Roman City*. London: English Heritage, 1993.

Weston, Jessie. *Chief Middle English Poets*. Boston: Houghton Mifflin, 1914.

Whitehead, Frederick. "Sir Thomas Malory," *Encyclopædia Britannica*, Vol. 14, pp. 706–707. Chicago: William Benton, 1967.

Whitelock, Dorothy, David Douglas, and Susie Tucker, eds. *The Anglo-Saxon Chronicle*. Piscataway, N.J.: Rutgers University Press, 1961.

Wildman, S.G. *The Black Horsemen: English Inns and King Arthur*. London: John Baker, 1971.

Wilhelm, James J., ed. *The Romance of Arthur*. Prose Merlin XIV. New York: Garland Publications, 1994.

William of Newburgh. Trans. P.G. Walsh and M.J. Kennedy. *The History of English Affairs/Historia Rerum Anglicanum*. Warminster, Wiltshire: 1988. *See also* Jones, W. Lewis, *Latin Chroniclers*.

Williams, Gwyn A. *Excalibur: The Search for Arthur*. Woodlands, London: BBC Books, 1994.

Williams, Hugh. *Caradoc of Llancarvan: Life of Gildas*, 2 Vols., London: 1899–1901.

Williams, Sir Ifor. *Lectures on Early Welsh Poetry*. Dublin: Dublin Institute for advanced Studies, 1944.

Winterbottom, Michael, ed., trans. Gildas: *The Ruin of Britain and Other Works*. Chichester, England: Phillimore, 1978.

Wolfram von Eschenbach *see* Hatto, Arthur Thomas; Zeydel, Edwin.

Wright, R.P., and Kenneth Hurlstone Jackson. "A Late Inscription from Wroxeter." *Antiquarian Journal*, 48 (1968): 296–300.

Wyld, Henry Cecil. "Layamon as an English Poet," *The Review of English Studies* 6 (January 1930).

Zeydel, Edwin H., in collaboration with Baynard Quincy Morgan, trans. *The Parzival of Wolfram von Eschenbach*. Chapel Hill: University of North Carolina Press, 1951.

INDEX

Abloyc 9, 65
Accolon 9, 196
Adam of Domerham 9–10, 32, 95, 127, 154, 155, 158, 159, 239
Addaon 10; *see also* Avaon
adventi of the Saxons 49, 54, 84, 95, 125, 208, 219, 232
Ægidius 10–11, 19, 177, 213, 222
Ælle 11, 53, 54, 64, 89
Æsc 11–13, 198; *see also* Octha; Osla Big Knife
Æternus 13, 55, 65, 66, 84, 85, 88, 100, 101, 105, 118, 140, 205, 223, 230
Æthelweard 13–14, 83, 195
Aëtius 14–16, 48, 89, 105, 106, 108, 110, 169
Agitio 15, 89
Agitium 14, 15, 16; *see also* Aëtius
Agloval 16
agnomen 16, 174; *see also cognomen*; *nomen*; *praenomen*
Agravain 16, 74, 75, 106, 110, 172, 173, 193, 204
Agricius 14, 16
Agricola Longhand 16–17
Agwisance 17, 54
Alaric 15, 45, 79, 108, 147, 169, 170
Aldhelm of Almsbury 17, 117
Aldor 17, 18, 19, 89, 207
Aldroneus 15, 17–18, 78, 81, 89, 112, 137
Alfred the Great 18, 81, 54, 112
amanuensis 68, 81, 143, 189
Ambrosius 18–19, 20, 132
Ambrosius Aurelianus 17, 18, 19–21, 25, 28, 29, 31, 45, 48, 66, 75, 78, 81, 101, 106, 120, 122, 139, 157, 174, 179, 185, 188, 189, 192, 195, 198, 202, 205, 206, 208, 213, 214, 215, 228, 232
amerauder 21, 225
Amfortas/Anfortas 21, 23, 104, 241
Amhar 21
Amlaud 21
Amren 21
Anator *see* Wolfram Von Eschenbach
Andredescester 11

Aneirin 21–22, 23, 30, 44, 88, 138, 140, 189, 202, 223
Angles 23–24, 48, 49, 140, 143
Anglians 24–25, 30, 120, 126, 148, 201, 218–221
The Anglo-Saxon Chronicle 11, 12, 13, 14, 19, 23, 24, 25, 27, 28, 29, 55, 62, 64, 65, 68, 69, 70, 81, 82, 83, 84, 85, 86, 89, 90, 100, 101, 117, 118, 141, 142, 143, 145, 148, 149, 157, 160, 195, 198, 206, 208, 218, 219, 235
Anguish 25; *see also* Agwisance
Anna 25, 29, 46, 48, 56, 111, 132, 147, 172, 190, 242
Annales Cambriae 71, 76, 83, 85, 93, 100, 109, 139, 145, 169, 177, 178, 179, 181, 184, 188, 190, 195, 202, 206, 227, 228
anonym 25
Antanor 25
Anthemius 19, 25–26, 102, 106, 107, 131, 158, 169, 176, 177, 212, 213, 215, 220, 222
Antonine Wall 22, 63, 66, 96, 126, 219
apocrapha 154
apologue 207, 211
Aquae Sulis 43, 122, 123; *see also* Bath (City of)
Arcturus 19, 26–27, 72
Armorica *see* Brittany
Arnive 27
Arthur (historic) 12, 17, 18, 21, 25, 27–30, 28, 29, 30, 31, 32, 33, 34, 44, 47, 62, 64, 82, 106, 109, 112, 120, 122, 146, 212, 214; battle of Badon (*id est*, Ambrosius Aurelianus' battle) *see* Baddon battle; burial sites (quoits) 10, 34, 35, 36, 41, 44, 59, 60, 94, 127, 128, 155, 167; eleven battles 28; profile 187
Arthur (legendary) 9, 10, 22, 16, 30–44, 46, 48, 50, 57, 58, 61, 63, 73, 83, 96, 104, 105, 111, 119, 120, 127, 131, 132, 133, 141, 144, 145, 147, 164, 149, 150, 151, 152, 155, 156, 161, 163, 167, 168, 172, 173, 175, 190, 196, 199, 203, 204, 210, 216, 226, 236, 242

Arthur (legendary: possessions) 44, 57
Arthur of Dalriada 44
Arthuriana 11, 12, 13, 17, 22, 26, 42, 44–47, 51, 55, 73, 76, 84, 86, 87, 91, 93, 95, 101, 102, 107–109, 111, 117, 130, 133, 140, 147, 149, 157, 158, 162, 172, 174, 180, 181, 191, 192, 194, 214, 219, 225, 234, 235, 240, 241
Arthursus the Bear 44, 71, 72
Arviragus 44–45
Ataulphus 15, 45, 79, 81, 108
Aurelius Ambrosius 18, 20, 21, 25, 45–46, 48, 56, 78, 81, 111, 112, 137, 142, 147, 157, 172, 188, 190, 198, 199, 207, 226
Aurelius Caninus 46, 78, 124
Avalon, Avallon (Isle) 32, 50, 61, 62, 91, 128, 155, 174, 196, 210, 212, 238
Avaon 46–47, 88, 211

Badon battle 12, 13, 14, 20, 24, 30, 41, 46, 48, 66, 68, 73, 83, 92, 120, 122, 124, 125, 127, 149, 151, 157, 174, 202, 203, 227
Badon Hill 20, 30, 31, 43, 77, 117, 122, 125, 126
Bath, City of 42, 43, 57, 65, 67, 73, 120, 122, 127
Beaumains 47, 109
Bede 12, 15, 16, 17, 19, 20, 22, 24, 30, 47–49, 70, 74, 79, 95, 105, 112, 120, 123, 127, 141, 148, 169, 181, 195, 199, 206, 214, 220, 221, 226, 227, 229, 239
Bedivere 21, 50, 111, 133, 163, 175
Bedwyr 50–51, 161
Béroul 51, 133
Blanchefleur 51–52, 208, 215; *see also* Blanchefor; Elizabeth
Blanchefor 52, 75, 132
Black Book of Carmarthen 50, 114, 161, 189, 233
Black Ravens 22, 30, 31, 138, 203
Bleise 52
Boötes 71
Bragwaine 52–53, 54, 204
Brangoene 53; *see also* Bragwaine
bretwalda 11, 53–54, 64, 65

Breunor 54–55; *see also* Breunor le Noire; La Cote Male Taile
Breunor le Noire 55; *see also* Breunor; La Cote Male Taile
Britanniae Flavia 125, 126
Britanniae Maxima 126
Britanniae Prima 124, 125, 126
Britanniae Secunda 125, 126
Britanniae Valentia 126
British Historical Miscellany 28, 84, 108, 225, 227, 235
Britons 10, 12, 15, 16, 19, 20, 25, 26, 30, 49, 55, 56, 78, 87, 89, 90, 95, 125, 131, 137, 142, 143, 148, 153, 155, 157, 158, 198, 204, 207, 209, 212, 213, 222, 236, 240
Brittany/Breton/Little Britain/ Armorica 15, 17, 19, 22, 25, 26, 32, 49, 53, 55, 56, 57, 58, 72, 76, 78, 89, 93, 102, 103, 105, 111, 112, 113, 115, 117, 131, 138, 181, 184, 207
Brude 55–56
Brydw 55, 56, 100, 139, 181
Brython 56
Bryttwealas 236
Budic *see* Budicius
Budicius 25, 56–57, 111, 172
Burgundians 102, 158, 212, 222

Cabal, Cavall (Arthur's dog) 44, 57, 115, 172
Cador 32, 57–58, 73, 77, 211, 226
Cadwallon (Cadwalla) 58, 118, 136; *see also* Catgolaun Lauhir
Cadwr 57, 58; *see also* Cador
Caerleon 44, 47, 58, 151, 152
Cai 58; *see also* Kay
Caledonii 173
Calogrenant 58–59, 75
Camden, William 59–61, 95, 171
Camelot 32, 37, 44, 64, 74, 97, 100, 107, 108, 168, 178; *see also* South Cadbury
Camlann battle (Camblam) 14, 50, 66, 69, 73, 128, 151, 155, 190, 192, 203
Canterbury Abbey 9
Caradoc of Llancarfan 61–62, 63, 119, 120, 134, 136, 149, 183
Carnwennen (Arthur's knife) 44
Castrum Corrigie 143
Cat Coit Celidon 173
Categern 62, 71, 117, 171
Cateyrn (Categern) 29, 56, 62, 116
Catgolaun Lauhir 62–63
Catigern/Catiger (Categern) 20, 21, 29, 205
Cattigirn (Categern) 56, 63
Caw 32, 63, 119, 149, 184
Caxton, William 63–64, 146, 181, 196
Ceaulin 53, 64–65, 90

Ceawlin 11, 54, 82, 91
Ceol 82
Cerdic 11, 13, 14, 19, 62, 64, 65–71, 73, 81, 82, 83, 84, 90, 91, 99, 100, 101, 118, 145, 147, 150, 157, 211, 214, 236
Cerdicesforda 14, 83, 90, 236
Cerdicesora 13, 14, 83, 236
Ceredig 19
Ceredig of Elmet 71
Cerne Abbas 71–72
Chalice Well 36, 104
Cheldric 67, 73, 145, 147, 222
Chelric 67, 73, 145, 147; *see also* Cerdic
Cherdic 67, 73, 96, 145, 147; *see also* Cerdic
Childeric 11, 63, 133
Chrétien de Troyes 25, 32, 51, 73–75, 83, 91, 92, 101, 103, 104, 140, 156, 166, 182, 184, 195, 198, 207, 209, 214, 216, 217
chronological calibration 92, 103, 124, 169, 190, 227
Cinglas 75, 84; *see also* Cuneglasus
Cissa 11
City of Legions 28, 173, 226, 229
Clamadeu 75
Clamide 75; *see also* Wolfram Von Eschenbach
Cledric (Cerdic) 57, 67
cognomen 75, 174, 206; *see also agnomen; nomen; praenomen*
Colgrevance (Calogrenant) 59, 75
Combrogi 75; *see also* cymry
Comes Britanniae 21
Comes Britanniarum 48, 75–76, 81, 95, 103 105, 108, 109, 112, 148
Comes Litoris Saxonici 75
Commodus 72
"compacting" 144
Condwiramurs 76; *see also* Wolfram Von Eschenbach
Constans 18, 76, 45, 46, 78, 79, 112, 137, 207
Constantine 78–79, 137, 232
Constantine (son of Cador, successor to Arthur) 58, 78
Constantine (III) 76–78, 123, 192
Constantine of Brittany 18, 45, 46
Constantine the Usurper 29, 47, 48, 79, 112, 148; *see also* Constantinus, Flavius
Constantinus, Flavius 79, 208
Constantius I 81
Constantius III 15, 16, 20, 29, 45, 47, 48, 75, 79–81, 103, 104, 105, 108, 109, 110, 112, 148, 206, 207, 208, 226
Constantius Hericus 116

consulibus 20, 75, 81, 103, 108, 112
Cornovii 24, 43, 48, 56, 62, 117, 121, 122, 123, 153, 182
Cornwall 30, 31, 35, 43, 44, 46, 54, 55, 57, 58, 61, 73, 77, 78, 84, 91, 93, 97, 109, 114, 115, 117; 121, 122, 135, 155, 161, 183, 193, 203, 211, 215, 224, 226; *see also* Dumnonia
La Cote Male Taile 54, 55, 162
Council of the Provinces 46, 93, 141, 143, 183, 186, 211
Creoda 14, 18, 62, 64, 66, 69, 81–83, 90, 91
Creuddyn 83
Culhwch 50, 83–84, 149, 161, 211
Cundrie 84; *see also* Wolfram Von Eschenbach
Cunedag 84; *see also* Cunedda
Cunedda 9, 55, 62, 65, 66, 67, 70, 71, 73, 75, 78, 84–86, 87, 88, 90, 92, 97, 99, 100, 101, 104, 105, 118, 139, 140, 162, 172, 179, 184, 202, 205, 206, 223, 225, 230 (migration); fifth son 86; *see also* Cerdic
Cuneglasus 62, 71, 75, 78, 86, 87, 88, 124, 202; *see also* Cinglas
Cunneware 86; *see also* Wolfram Von Eschenbach
Cunorix 86–88
Cyfarwyddiaid 88, 135
Cyhelin 88–89, 138, 207
Cymen 11, 89
Cymry 56, 89–90, 236
Cyndeyrn (Categern) 62
Cynfarch 171
Cyngen 56, 100, 171
Cynric 13, 14, 62, 64, 66, 82, 90–91, 157
Cynyr Farfog 91

Dagonet 91, 204
De Antiquitate 31, 127, 144, 146, 152, 154, 157, 158, 159, 160, 236, 237, 238
De Excidio 14, 16, 17, 19, 27, 30, 46, 55, 63, 66, 69, 78, 86, 87, 93, 117, 119, 120, 123, 124, 125, 132, 140, 143, 149, 157, 178, 184, 189, 192, 195, 201, 202, 217, 219, 226, 229, 233
Death of Arthur 191
Death of Mordred 191
Didot-Perceval 91
Dinabutius 91–92
Dinas Emyrs 29, 93
Dionysius Exiguus 92, 122, 190, 228
discordium 228
Docmail 92
Dodinel 92–93
dragon banner 173

"Dream of Rhonabwy" 13, 30, 46, 58, 63, 65, 67, 96, 119, 151, 190, 201, 203, 211
Druids 88, 93, 153, 187, 189
Drustan, Drust 93; *see also* Tristram
Dubglas River 173
Dumnonia 31, 76, 114, 116, 117, 121, 124, 126, 192
Dunaut 93
Dunstan (Saint) 60, 93–95, 128, 237
dux bellorum 19, 20, 30, 95, 127, 173, 199, 219, 225
Dux Britanniarum 66, 75
Dyfed 85, 87, 88, 127

East Anglia 11, 24, 29, 30, 48, 49, 68, 70, 100, 105, 122, 141, 201, 217, 218; *see also* Gildas Badonicus
Easter Annals 103, 227
Ebissa 73, 95–96, 143, 199, 234
Ector 96, 152, 161, 193
Edern 96–97, 115
Edyrn 97; *see also* Etern
Eigr 21, 97, 242; *see also* Ygerna
Eigyr (Eigr, Ygerna) 57
Elaine 97–99, 108
Eldol (Eidiol) 99, 143, 183, 235
Elesa 70, 71, 99, 118; *see also* Eliseg
Eliseg 70, 71, 100
Eliseg's Pillar 56, 71, 171; *see also* Eliseg
Elizabeth 100; *see also* Blanchefleur; Rivalin
emereto 229
Emrys 19, 18, 20, 93, 101, 185
Emyr Llydaw 57, 101; *see also* Budicius
English Saxons 24, 54, 70, 116, 217, 218
Enniaun Girt 62, 75, 84
Eobba 24
epithet 10, 13, 17, 18, 21, 25, 29, 43, 44, 46, 56, 57, 65, 68, 70, 71, 72, 76, 78, 85, 88, 101, 102, 104, 105, 107, 109, 113, 123, 139, 162, 163, 167, 169, 184, 189, 195, 203, 205, 206, 207, 214, 221, 223, 225, 226, 229, 231, 232, 233
Erec 74, 127, 140, 242
Esla 70, 100, 101, 118; *see also* Eliseg
Eslit 101
Etern 101
Ethelbert 53
Ethelwerd 101; *see also* Æthelweard
Eugein Dantguin 62, 101; *see also* Owein Dantguin
Euric 11, 26, 101–102, 158, 212, 213, 222
Excalibur/Caliburn (Arthur's

sword) 9, 44, 106, 163, 164, 234
Exuperantius 102–103, 113, 148

fantasy 154
Faustus 56
Felix 103, 228, 224
fiction 154
Fisher King 74, 91, 103–104, 182, 208, 210, 217
Five Britains 126
Fleuriot, Leon 213, 214
foederati 49, 56, 66, 70, 79, 104–105, 120, 123, 202, 221, 227
Forest of Brocéliande 184
Four Ancient Books of Wales 160, 194, 223
Franks 10, 11, 26, 222
Frollo 50, 105–107

Gaheris 16, 106, 110, 172, 173, 182, 193
Gahmuret 106, 146; *see also* Wolfram Von Eschenbach
Gaiseric 106, 169, 170
Galahad 97, 104, 106–108, 156, 216
Galla Placidia 15, 16, 45, 79, 81, 103, 106, 108–109, 110, 113, 123, 147, 169, 208, 226
Gallic Sea 29, 70
Gandin 109
Ganhumara 109, 135
Ganieda 109, 134, 188; *see also* Merlin
Gareth 16, 47, 109–110, 172, 173, 193
Gaudentius 15, 110, 170
Gawain 16, 25, 32, 64, 106, 110–111, 140, 147, 156, 172, 173, 175, 182, 193, 204, 205, 209, 210, 242
"Genealogical Preface" 13, 14, 19, 24, 64, 65, 69, 70, 82, 83, 100
Geoffrey of Monmouth 9, 10, 13, 15, 16, 18, 24, 25, 27, 29, 30, 31, 111–114, 45, 48, 50, 56, 62, 64, 73, 74, 77, 79, 88, 91, 93, 109, 127, 130, 131, 132, 134, 135, 137, 138, 141, 145, 146, 154, 167, 172, 174, 175, 176, 181, 185, 189, 190, 194, 211, 212, 225, 239; *see also* Chrétien de Troyes; Layamon; Wace
Geraint 114–115; *see also* Gereint; Gerontius
Gerald of Wales 115, 127; *see also* Giraldus Cambrensis
Gerbert de Montreuil (Continuator) 115
Gereint 115–116, 140, 242
"Gereint and Enid" 21, 67, 115
German Saxons 24, 25, 54, 70, 73, 91, 116, 125, 217, 218
Germanus of Auxerre 17, 48, 56,

95, 100, 116–117, 139, 171, 195, 235; *see also* Mark the Hermit
Gerontius/Geraint 47, 79, 117–118
Gewis 70, 118; *see also* Eliseg
Gewissae (confederates) 48, 118, 150, 151, 218
Gildas Albanius 32, 61, 63, 115, 118–120, 136, 144, 149, 157, 183, 184, 238
Gildas Badonicus 12, 14, 15, 16, 17, 18, 19, 20, 22, 24, 27, 30, 31, 45, 46, 47, 49, 61, 62, 63, 66, 67, 70, 71, 76, 78, 86, 87, 88, 89, 92, 105, 112, 120–122, 124, 140, 144, 149, 153, 178, 181, 183, 184, 192, 195, 198, 203, 206, 208, 214, 217, 218, 219, 221, 226, 227, 229, 231, 234, 239
Ginover 127
Giraldus Cambrensis 9, 32, 34, 51, 61, 93, 95, 9, 10, 32, 44, 93, 94, 95, 97, 136, 149, 168, 210, 216, 239
Glastonbury Abbey 9, 10, 44, 93, 97, 127, 128, 130, 136, 144, 154, 155, 156, 158, 168, 210, 236, 237, 238
Glastonbury Cross (Leaden Cross) 59, 61, 95, 128, 168
Glastonbury Isle/Isle of Glass 61, 62, 128, 129; *see also* Yneswitrin
The Glastonbury Legends 144
Gloius 130
Gloui (son of Vitalinus/Guithelinus) 130, 228
Goeznovius 130–132, 213
Gogyrfan/Gogfran/Leodegrance (Guinever's father) 132, 136; *see also* Leodegrance
Gorlois 25, 34, 46, 57, 58, 97, 132, 152, 187, 226, 242
Gornemant of Gohort 132
Gottfried Von Strassburg 51, 93, 132–133, 140, 161, 182, 193, 204, 215, 224, 240
Great Easter Cycle 92, 227
Gregory of Tours 133, 212, 213, 220, 222
Griflet 17, 50, 74, 133–134, 204
Guaul (Wall) 96, 142, 199, 200
Guendoloena 134
Guinevere/Guennuvar/Gwenwyvar 10, 16, 32, 55, 58, 61, 73, 74, 75, 97, 98, 109, 110, 111, 115, 134–137, 139, 145, 155, 165, 166, 170, 175, 183, 184, 204, 210, 216, 242
Guinevere (false) 137, 170
Guithelinus 15, 17, 18, 20, 45, 78, 112, 113, 137–138, 207, 228
Gurnemanz/Goarnemant 23, 138; *see also* Gwawrddur
Guttyn Owain 138, 235
Gwawrddur 22, 30, 138
Gwenhwyfach 136, 138–139

gwledig/gwledic 9, 19, 53, 66, 89, 101, 139, 161, 215
Gwrhyr, Interpreter of Languages (evocative name for Cerdic the Interpreter) 67, 84, 139, 161, 211
Gwrleis (Gorlis) 57
Gwrtheyrn 139
Gwtheyrn/Guitheryn 56, 65, 71, 171; see also Vortigern
gwyddbwyll 203, 211
Gwyr 139
Gwyr y Gogledd 21, 56, 139–140, 198, 203

Hadrian's Wall 22, 30, 66, 97, 126, 127, 142, 174, 201, 220
Hartman von Aue 51, 99, 118, 127, 133, 140, 240
Heinrich Von Freiberg 140, 160, 224
Hengist 12, 20, 21, 24, 25, 27, 28, 29, 30, 46, 48, 49, 62, 66, 67, 68, 70, 73, 84, 87, 91, 95, 96, 127, 140–144, 148, 149, 150, 160, 185, 186, 195, 196, 198, 199, 210, 219, 233, 234
Henry VIII 167
Henry de Blois 144–145, 237
Henry of Huntingdon 20, 32, 64, 90, 112, 145–146, 195, 218, 233, 239
Herzeloyde 146, 240
Higden, Ranulf 64, 146–147, 239
Historia Brittonum 54, 56, 57, 65–67, 69, 71, 72, 73, 75, 76, 78, 81–88, 94, 96, 100, 101, 111, 113, 116, 117, 122, 126, 127, 130, 132, 137, 139, 141, 145, 148, 157, 158, 162, 172, 173, 174, 181, 183, 185, 186, 189, 194, 195, 196, 198, 199, 202, 205, 210, 211, 215, 221, 223, 225, 226, 228, 230, 231, 233, 234, 240
Hoel I/Howel 25, 56, 115, 147, 175, 190, 211
Honorius (Emperor) 15, 20, 47, 75, 79, 81, 103, 105, 108, 110, 147–148, 137
Horsa 20, 21, 24, 25, 27, 29, 49, 62, 84, 141, 148–149 (death of), 150, 160, 195, 198, 199, 233
"How Culhwch Won Olwen" 21, 31, 50, 57, 63, 65, 67, 83, 96, 121, 135, 136, 138, 149, 172, 190
Howell 32
Hueil 63, 120, 149–150, 157
Hwicca 48, 118, 150, 151, 218
Hyrpe 150–151, 203

Iazyges 22
Iddawg 46, 151–152
Ider/Yder 96, 152, 156, 198
Igraine 152–153
imperator 21
impious easterners 30, 50, 120, 140, 153, 201

Incarnation of Christ 45, 92, 103, 108, 122, 155, 228; see also chronological calibration; Dionysius
inscribed stones 29, 65 70, 87, 88, 95, 171
interpolation 10, 22, 31, 89, 118, 127, 144, 145, 159, 162, 184, 185, 194, 195, 200, 225, 226, 228, 236, 237, 238, 239
Iolo Morganwg 90, 153–154, 223
Isoud La Beale/Iseult the Blonde (Irish) 51, 54, 74, 133, 140, 154, 160, 162, 193, 224
Isoud La Blanche Mains/Iseult of the White Hands (Brittany) 133, 140, 154, 160, 161, 162, 204, 224, 225
Ither 154

John of Glastonbury 32, 44, 61, 95, 119, 136, 147, 151, 152, 154–157, 158, 198, 216
Jordanes 131, 133, 157–158, 177, 212, 213, 220, 222
Joseph of Arimathea 9, 10, 36, 44, 104, 106, 144, 154, 155, 156, 157, 158–160, 182, 209, 216, 237
Jutes 24, 140, 141, 160, 218, 227

Kahedîn 154, 160, 224
Katigern 62; see also Categern
Kay 25, 47, 50, 51, 54, 58, 67, 74, 96, 111, 160–161, 165, 175, 204, 208, 242
Kehydius 53, 161–162
Kent 12, 24, 30, 48, 49, 64, 65, 70, 118, 120, 127, 141, 142, 143, 148, 150, 160, 218
Kindred of Eight 162
kontus 173
Kyot 162

Lady of the Lake 133, 162–163, 164, 193, 196, 229
Lailoken 185
Lamorak 16, 106, 163, 182
Lancelot 16, 47, 54, 73, 97, 98, 105, 108, 110, 134, 137, 156, 165–166, 204, 205
"lateral thinking" 213
Lawman 166
Layamon 32, 51, 74, 166–167, 195, 214
legionary fortresses 43, 55, 87, 105, 122, 126, 199
Leland, John 33, 95, 167–169, 210
Leo I (Emperor) 25, 106, 169, 172, 212
Leo I (Pope) 169–170, 213, 227
Leodegrance 170; see also Gogyr-fan
Lhuyd, Edward 100, 170–172

Liathan 66, 78, 84, 162, 172
liber vetustissimus 30, 93, 112, 135, 185, 190, 207, 235
Libius Severus 172
Little Solsbury Hill 43, 122, 123, 127
Llamrei (Arthur's horse) 44, 63, 172
Lleu 172
Lot (Loth) 25, 56, 106, 110, 111, 139, 147, 172–173
Lucius Artorius Castus 22, 26, 30, 44, 122, 127, 173–174, 199, 219
Lucius Domitius Aurelianus 174–175, 198
Lucius (Hiberius) 50, 58, 91, 105, 111, 161, 175–177
lunar cycle 92, 190, 228

The Mabinogion 18, 21, 30, 31, 46, 50, 57, 58, 63, 67, 83, 88, 91, 96, 97, 104, 114, 115, 119, 135, 138, 154, 161, 172, 181, 189, 198, 201, 203, 208, 211, 214
Mabon 67, 84, 177
Maelgwn 55, 84, 139, 177–178, 181, 223
Maglocunus map Catgolaun Lauhir 62, 78, 87, 124 178–179, 202, 203, 233; see also Appendix B
Maglocunus map Clutor 168, 179–181, 233
Magnus 17, 87, 100, 181
Malory, Sir Thomas 9, 32, 64, 75, 134, 176, 181–182, 193, 194, 198, 204, 205, 217, 224, 225, 229
Manau Gododdin 21, 66, 78, 84, 85, 86, 140, 179, 181
Manessier 182, 217
Marcian 15, 26, 102, 169
Margawse 16, 172, 182, 193
Marhaus 182, 194
Mark of Cornwall 52, 53, 54, 74, 109, 140, 182, 183, 194, 224, 225; see also Tristram
Mark the Hermit 183
Maugantius 183, 186
Maximus 47, 221, 223
Melkin 167
Melwas/Melegant 15, 61, 62, 74, 136, 165, 183–184
Mercia 24, 49, 126, 141, 218
Meriaun 184
Merlin 9, 10, 20, 46, 92, 93, 96, 99, 101, 109, 134, 152, 153, 163, 164, 170, 173, 184–188, 190, 196, 197, 198, 216, 234, 242
Merlin (Vita Merlini) 188
Merlinus Ambrosius 19, 92, 109, 186, 189–190
Merovingian Cross 60
Meton of Athens 92, 122, 190
Middle Anglia 49, 151, 218

migrations 10, 18, 48, 49, 55, 66, 84–87, 96, 104, 117, 118, 121, 131, 140, 141, 143, 160, 162, 182, 185, 218, 234

Modron 190; *see also* Morgan le Fay

Mommsen, Theodor 69, 70, 158, 172, 184, 185, 188, 199, 215, 231

Mordred 16, 25, 33, 73, 75, 91, 110, 111, 133, 135, 139, 145, 190–192, 147, 151, 155, 172, 173, 175, 182, 183, 216

Morgan le Fay 9, 16, 74, 106, 110, 111, 128, 140, 173, 192–193, 182, 196

Morgana 25, 193

Morolt 182, 193–194

Mount Ambris 185

Mount Areynes 152

Mount Killarus 185

Mount of Frogs 152

Nennius 12, 19, 20, 24, 27, 48, 72, 87, 112, 122, 127, 141, 148, 183, 194–196, 206, 226

Nimuë 163, 196–198, 229

nomen 174, 198, 206; *see also* agnomen; cognomen; praenomen

Northumbria 11, 24, 53, 54, 64, 140, 141, 148, 198, 202, 218

Nut/Nudd 96, 97, 101, 115, 151, 198, 242

Octha 11, 13, 24, 25, 27, 28, 29, 66, 68, 73, 95, 96, 141, 143, 145, 150, 198–199, 210, 233

Odovacer 222

Oeric 48

Offa 199–201

Offa's Dyke 100, 125

Ogham 87, 88, 100, 179, 180, 181, 186

Oisc 141

Old Oswestry 132, 136

Old Saxons 23, 24, 48, 49, 141, 218

"oldest Briton manuscript" 167

orientali sacrilegorum (impious easterners) 24, 30, 49, 105, 120, 123, 140, 153, 20, 217, 233

Osla Big Knife 13, 32, 46, 63, 84, 151, 201–202, 203, 204, 211

Osmail 202

Outigern 202

Owein Dantguin 30, 31, 151, 202–204, 211

Palomides/Palamides 91, 109, 204–205

Parzival, Parsival 23, 27, 138, 146, 224

Passion of Christ 44, 92, 103, 108, 122, 227, 228; *see also* chronological calibration; Victorius Aquitaine

Pascent/Paschent 56, 62, 132, 205

Paternus Pesrut 13, 65, 70, 84, 85, 105, 118, 140, 205–206, 222, 230

"patterned thinking" 214

Pelleas 196

Pellinor 16, 173, 196, 205

Pendragon 75, 103, 137, 173, 206–207

Peniarth 2 223

Peniarth 6 135

Peniarth 16 135

Perceval 16, 25, 74, 75, 91, 103, 104, 132, 156, 196, 207–209, 216, 217

Perceval de Gales 16

Peredur 32, 188, 207, 208, 209–210

Picts 18, 57, 126, 215, 218–220, 224

Pomparles Bridge 167

praefectus 102, 103, 113, 148, 208, 210, 226

praenomen 174, 210; *see also* agnomen; cognomen; nomen

Prydwyn (Arthur's ship) 44

pseudo history 30, 67, 68, 90, 146, 153, 154, 181, 196, 240

Questing Beast 205

Ralph of Coggeshall 51, 95, 146, 168, 210

"reasonable age" 12, 83

Red Book of Hergest 30, 83, 114, 189, 233

Renwein 25, 143, 210–211, 233

Rhieinwyldd 21, 211

Rhongomyniad (Arthur's shield) 44

Ribble River 173

Ribchester 173

Richard of Cirencester 211–212

Ricimer 26, 172, 176, 177, 212, 213

Riothamus 10, 19, 25, 26, 102, 105, 131, 133, 157, 158, 169, 212–215, 220, 222, 225

Rivalin 51, 52, 215

Robert de Boron 104, 156, 185, 215–217

Round House 200

Round Table 34, 35, 36, 40, 42, 44, 50, 55, 58, 64, 74, 91, 108, 110, 137, 156, 167, 170, 196, 216, 234

Rumaun 217

sacrilegious easterners 217; *see also orientali sacrilegorum*

Sagremor 58, 74, 93, 182, 217

St. Brynach's Church, Nevern, Wales 45, 179, 203, 229

St Davids 9, 44, 172

Sarmatian 22, 149, 151, 173, 174; *see also* Lucius Artorius Castus

Sawley Glosses 226

Saxones 28, 48, 49, 118, 125, 140, 218, 227

Saxons 10, 20, 48, 77, 120, 148, 218, 219

Scotti (Irish) 18, 57, 96, 126, 215, 218, 220

scribal dates and errors 122, 149, 227

Septimius Severus 48, 125, 174, 195, 199, 219–220

Severa 56, 100, 139, 171, 181

Severn River (Hafren) 30, 43, 46, 86, 114, 117, 123, 203, 228

Sidonius Apollinaris 177, 212, 213, 220

Siege Perilous 108, 216

Sigebert of Gembloux 175, 221, 225

Skene, William 194

Slaughter Bridge 44

South Cadbury 32, 33, 37; *see also* Camelot

Stilicho 79, 81

Stonehenge 41, 42, 185

superbus tyrannus 105, 123, 150, 195, 208–214, 221, 227, 229, 230

Syagrius 19, 133, 213, 222

Tacitus 13, 65, 100, 205, 223, 230

Taliesin 10, 46, 88, 178, 188, 189, 202, 223

Taurus 224, 228

Thanceastre 143

Thanet/Tanet Isle 73, 127, 144, 233

Thomas D'Angleterre 51, 133, 224

Tintagel 25, 33, 34, 38, 44, 93, 152, 187

Trécesson Castle 165

Trevisa, John 146

Trevrizent 23, 224

Tristan 51, 52, 74, 109, 133, 140, 154, 193, 194, 204, 215, 224

Tristram 51, 52, 53, 54, 55, 93, 100, 105, 162, 196, 204, 217, 224–225

Two Glastonbury Legends: King Arthur and St. Joseph of Arimathea 144

Twrch Trwyth 63, 67, 201

Typiaun 225

Tysilio 15, 17, 18, 50, 57, 62, 78, 89, 93, 96, 97, 99, 105, 112, 132, 138, 143, 175, 195, 199, 205, 207, 235

Tywyssawc 225

Uriens 9, 173, 193

Uriscampum 131, 225

ursus 44, 72

ursus horribilis 26

uter- 225

uterine 226

Uterpendragon 57, 111, 112, 132, 138, 145, 187, 207, 225–226
Utherpendragon 18, 19, 25, 29, 46, 48, 56, 57, 76, 152, 72, 185, 199, 206, 214, 216, 242; burial site (Stonehenge) 42

Vad Velen 178, 223
Valentinian III 16, 101, 103, 108, 123, 148, 169, 206, 221, 226–227
Victorius of Aquitaine 92, 122, 190, 227–228
Visigoths 26
Vitalinus 15, 137, 179, 228–229
Vitalis 228
Viviane/Vivien 163, 196, 229
Vortigern 10, 12, 13, 17, 18, 19, 20, 24, 29, 46, 48, 55, 56, 62, 65, 67, 70, 73, 85, 87, 88, 91, 92, 93, 95, 96, 99, 100, 103, 104, 105, 120, 123, 127, 131, 132, 138, 139, 148, 167–171, 181, 183, 185, 186, 195, 196, 199, 208, 210, 214, 215, 219, 221, 227, 228, 229–237
Vortimer 19, 20, 29, 55, 56, 62, 65, 85, 88, 105, 141, 150, 171, 181, 195, 205, 211, 214, 223, 233
Vortipor 17, 78, 124, 233–234
Vulgate Cycle 216

Wace 34, 36, 39, 58, 74, 90, 156, 167, 195, 214, 234–235
Wales 55, 66, 69, 84, 85, 91, 120, 122, 124, 125, 126, 140, 199
Wall of Severus 199, 200, 219
Walter Archdeacon 235
Welsh 11, 12, 13, 14, 22, 23, 24, 30, 31, 64, 65, 66, 69, 74, 75, 83, 89, 120, 121, 125, 127, 142, 195, 209, 235–236
Welsh Triads 23, 30, 47, 88, 135, 138, 206, 233
Wessex 13, 14, 54, 64, 65, 68, 69, 70, 83, 84, 114, 117, 147, 157, 236
West Saxon 11, 13, 14, 19, 24, 48, 49, 64, 71, 73, 81, 82, 83, 86, 90, 100, 101, 114, 118, 218
White Book of Rhydderch 30, 83, 114 30, 83, 114, 233
William of Malmesbury 9, 32, 61, 112, 127, 144, 146, 152, 154, 155, 156, 158, 159, 160, 195, 236–239
William of Newburgh 10, 51, 195, 239–240
William of 1019 131, 213
Winchester 35, 44, 64, 76, 77, 91, 112, 192, 234
wledig 18, 21, 240; *see also* gwledig
Wolfram Von Eschenbach 23, 27, 32, 51, 104, 106, 133, 138, 146, 241, 224, 240–241
The Wrekin 43, 120
Wroxeter 43, 87, 105, 117, 120, 122, 123, 126, 127

Y Gododdin 21, 22, 30, 44, 93, 138, 140, 223
Yder 241
Ygerna (Igraine) 18, 21, 25, 27, 34, 46, 57, 97, 187, 172, 208, 226, 242
Ygraine 211
Yniswitrin/Ynis Witrin/Ynestrin 31, 32, 45, 61, 144, 156, 157, 159, 238
Ysbaddaden 50
Yvain 74